SwiftUI

by Tutorials

By Antonio Bello, Bill Morefield, Audrey Tam & Sarah Reichelt

SwiftUI by Tutorials

By Antonio Bello, Bill Morefield, Audrey Tam & Sarah Reichelt

Notice of Rights

Notice of Liability

Trademarks

ISBN: 978-1-950325-88-7

Table of Contents

Book License

Before You Begin

This section tells you a few things you need to know before you get started, such as what you'll need for hardware and software, where to find the project files for this book, and more.

What You Need

To follow along with this book, you'll need the following:

- A Mac running **macOS Ventura** (13.2) or later.
- **Xcode 14.2 or later.** Xcode is the main development tool for iOS. You'll need Xcode 14.2 or later to make use of SwiftUI and the latest features explained throughout the book. You can download the latest version of Xcode from Apple's developer site here: apple.co/2asi58y — If you have an Apple Developer account, you can also download any Xcode version here: apple.co/3GWcz96.

> **Note**: The code covered in this book was developed and tested with Swift 5.5, macOS Monterey and Xcode 13.1 — so even though you can work with slightly earlier versions of them, we encourage you to update to those versions to follow along the book without unexpected errors.

Book Source Code & Forums

Where to Download the Materials for This Book

The materials for this book can be cloned or downloaded from the GitHub book materials repository:

- https://github.com/kodecocodes/sui-materials/tree/editions/5.0

Forums

We've also set up an official forum for the book at https://forums.kodeco.com/c/books/swiftui-by-tutorials. This is a great place to ask questions about the book or to submit any errors you may find.

"To Magdalena, Andrea and Alex. Thanks for your patience, and for supporting me all the time, watching me tapping on the keyboard all day long."

— Antonio Bello

"To my parents for buying me that first computer when it was a lot weirder idea than it is now. To them and rest of my family for putting up with all those questions as a child."

— Bill Morefield

"To the Kodeco (kodeco.com) community, who help create my happy place."

— Audrey Tam

"To Tim who has agreed to all my crazy computer purchases for ever and who patiently listens to me complain about all my bugs."

— Sarah Reichelt

About the Authors

Antonio Bello is an author of this book. Antonio has spent most of his life writing code, and he's gained a lot of experience in several languages and technologies. A decade ago he fell in love with iOS development, and that's what he mostly works on since then, although he's always open for challenges and for playing with new toys. When he's not working, he's probably playing drums or making songs in his small, but well fitted, home production studio.

Bill Morefield is an author of this book. Bill has spent most of his professional life writing code. At some point he has worked in almost every language other than COBOL. He bought his first Apple computer to learn to program for the iPhone and got hooked on the platform. He manages the web and mobile development team for a college in Tennessee, where he still gets to write code. When not attached to a keyboard he enjoys hiking and photography.

Audrey Tam is an author of this book. As a retired computer science academic, she's a technology generalist with expertise in translating new knowledge into learning materials. Audrey now teaches short courses in iOS app development to non-programmers, and attends nearly all Melbourne Cocoaheads monthly meetings. She also enjoys long train journeys, knitting, and trekking in the Aussie wilderness.

Sarah Reichelt is an author of this book. She got hooked onto trying to make computers do what she told them a very long time ago and has never stopped loving it. She was inspired by Swift and now by SwiftUI to learn a new approach to this, and is a keen evangelist for developing Mac apps. When not at her computer, Sarah loves coffee, puzzles, reading and cooking - the day hasn't started until the first cup of coffee is drunk and the crossword is done!

About the Editors

Pablo Mateo is the final pass editor for this book. He is Head of Customer Engagement at at one of the biggest Banks in the world, and was also founder and CTO of a Technology Development company in Madrid. His expertise is focused on web and mobile app development, although he first started as a Creative Art Director. He has been for many years the Main Professor of the iOS and Android Mobile Development Masters Degree at a well-known technology school in Madrid (CICE). He has a masters degree in Artificial Intelligence & Machine-Learning and is currently learning Quantum Computing at MIT.

Gustavo Graña is a Tech Editor for this book. He started coding coding 20 years ago to solve daily problems he faced in the early 2000 to communicate, first with mIRC scripting language, but it quickly evolved into a broader interest in other areas of technology. He works with mobile since 2010 and with Swift since 2014. He is motivated by making an impact on the day-to-day with technology, trying to make life easier for others. Outside the area of technology, Gustavo is always eager to know how to have a healthier life.

Jeremy Greenwood is a Tech Editor for this book. He brings over 20 years of experience in tech, building, testing, and innovating digital products. His natural curiosity to understand the ins and outs of his craft have given him expertise in all layers of the stack, from hardware circuitry and embedded protocols to visual experiences. Jeremy is passionate about taking product ideas from the drawing board to digital screens and finds joy in the opportunity to impact users through software. He is keen on the details which elevate a project from ordinary to extraordinary. When not working on software, Jeremy can most likely be found in the woods on a trail, dreaming about creative solutions to everyday problems.

Leanna Guzzi is the editor of this book. She has recently moved to America with her husband and cat. She loves winter, cheese and all things literature. When she isn't empowering young minds and convincing everyone to read, she is planning her next snowboarding or adventure holiday.

Section I: Diving Into SwiftUI

Start your SwiftUI journey with the foundations you need.

Chapter 1: Introduction

> *"SwiftUI is an innovative, exceptionally simple way to build user interfaces across all Apple platforms with the power of Swift."*
>
> — Apple

SwiftUI is a new paradigm in Apple-related development. In 2014, after years of programming apps with Objective-C, Apple surprised the world with a new open-source language: **Swift**. Since its release, Swift has updated and evolved. And it is becoming one of the most beloved and powerful programming languages today.

SwiftUI's introduction in 2019 created another opportunity for a paradigm shift in the industry. After years of using UIKit and AppKit to create user interfaces, SwiftUI presented a fresh, new way to create UI for your apps. In many ways, SwiftUI is much simpler and powerful than its predecessors, and even more, it is cross-platform over the Apple ecosystem.

One of the most important things, though, is SwiftUI's declarative nature. For years, developers have worked with imperative programming models, dealing with state-management problems and complex code. But now, you have in your hands a declarative, straightforward way to build amazing user interfaces. And don't worry; if you loved working with UIKit or AppKit, rest assured that you can integrate those frameworks with your SwiftUI code.

SwiftUI has been continuously improving throughout these years. Swift has become one of the industry standards for progressive, modern programming languages. Now that we are in the 5th edition of this book, we can confirm that SwiftUI is following the same path.

Come embark upon the exciting voyage waiting for you inside this book. You'll learn all the tips and tricks we have to share in this new way of creating user interfaces. You´ll discover what SwiftUI has to offer, how powerful it is, and how quickly and easy it is to start working with it.

Book Structure

The book is divided into six sections and twenty-two chapters in which you will learn how to build great and engaging declarative user interfaces for your apps.

- **Section I: Diving Into SwiftUI**: The first four chapters will introduce SwiftUI. You will work with a SwiftUI adapted version of our famous color-matching tutorials game: *BullsEye*. You will start by learning the terminology, how to preview your user interface in the canvas and how to use the power of reusable modifiers. In this first section, you will even get started with testing and debugging to create powerful tested apps.
- **Section II: Building Blocks of SwiftUI**: User interfaces require controls for users to interact with them. Learn all you need to know about most of the available user controls and input interfaces such as TextFields, Buttons, Toggles, Sliders, and many more. Get to know the capabilities of vertical and horizontal stacks, container views and dive deeper into modifiers and how to implement them. To do so, you will work this time with *Kuchi* an impressive language flashcard app.
- **Section III: State & Data Flow**: Your app will probably not stick to a single view. You must learn how to bind data to the UI, how reactive updates work and how to manage state changes. You will keep improving the *Kuchi* app by adding more advanced controls like calendar or color pickers. You´ll learn how to trigger updates to the user interface, how to test it and how to implement gestures. And to make it even better, you´ll learn how to navigate your app with VoiceOver and how you can improve it with accessibility for people with certain disabilities.
- **Section IV: Navigation & Data Display**: To learn about navigation and how to provide data to your users, you will build a flight-information app. Set a navigation hierarchy to navigate through the different views. Create tabs and learn how to display information in grids or lists. And become an expert on all of them. Alert your users and pop up messages with Sheet and Alert Views. Many more advanced concepts are waiting for you in these chapters!

- **Section V: UI Extensions**: The airport app needs a more visual approach to display all its information. So learn about graphics, gradients, and how to display information with drawings and custom graphics. Make it more appealing by using animations and adding transitions. And finally, get out of your comfort zone with complex interfaces and learn more advanced concepts. After this, you will be able to build almost any interface you can imagine.
- **Section VI: SwiftUI for macOS**: As you might know, SwiftUI is cross-platform, so you can use it to develop apps for different Apple devices. Prepare a document-based markdown app for macOS and check by yourself how easily you can transfer all the knowledge you've been acquiring throughout the book to building macOS apps with SwiftUI. And even better, learn how you can start with an existing iOS app and how you can reuse the code, views, and assets and how easily you can adapt it for the mac.

About This Book

We wrote this book with beginner-to-advanced developers in mind. The only requirements for reading this book are a basic understanding of Swift and iOS development. SwiftUI is a recent and new paradigm, so developers of all backgrounds are welcome to discover this great technology with us. As you work through this book, you'll progress from beginner topics to more advanced concepts in a paced, familiar fashion.

A great starting point before this book is our *SwiftUI Apprentice* book https://www.kodeco.com/books/swiftui-apprentice. But if you've worked through our classic beginner books — the *Swift Apprentice: Fundamentals* swift-apprentice-fundamentals (swift-apprentice-fundamentals), _Swift Apprentice: Beyond the Basics https://www.kodeco.com/books/swift-apprentice-beyond-the-basics and the *UIKit Apprentice* https://www.kodeco.com/books/uikit-apprentice — or have similar development experience, you're also ready to read this book. You'll additionally benefit from a working knowledge of design patterns — such as working through *Design Patterns by Tutorials* https://www.kodeco.com/books/design-patterns-by-tutorials — but this isn't strictly required.

Chapter 2: Getting Started

By Audrey Tam

SwiftUI is some of the most exciting news since Apple first announced Swift in 2014. It's an enormous step towards Apple's goal of getting everyone coding; it simplifies the basics so that you can spend more time on custom features that delight your users.

If you're reading this book, you're just as excited as I am about developing apps with this new framework. This chapter will get you comfortable with the basics of creating a SwiftUI app and live-previewing it in Xcode.

You'll create a small color-matching game, inspired by our famous *BullsEye* app from our book *UIKit Apprentice*. The goal of the app is to try and match a randomly generated color by selecting colors from the RGB color space:

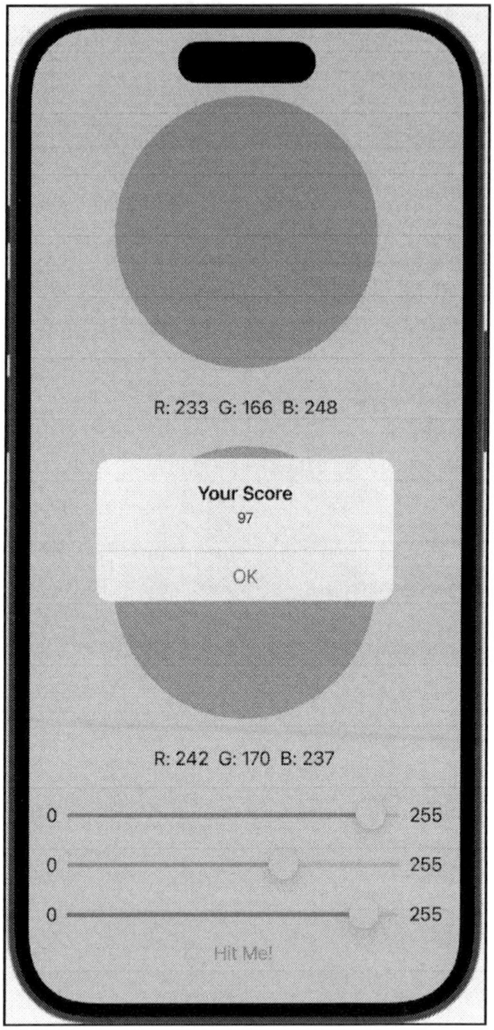

Playing the game

In this chapter, you will:

- Learn how to use the Xcode canvas to create your UI side-by-side with its code, and see how they stay in sync. A change to one side always updates the other side.
- Create a reusable view for the sliders seen in the image.

- Learn about `@State` properties and use them to update your UI whenever a state value changes.
- Present an alert to show the user's score.

Time to get started!

Getting Started

Open the **UIKit/RGBullsEye** starter project from the chapter materials, and build and run:

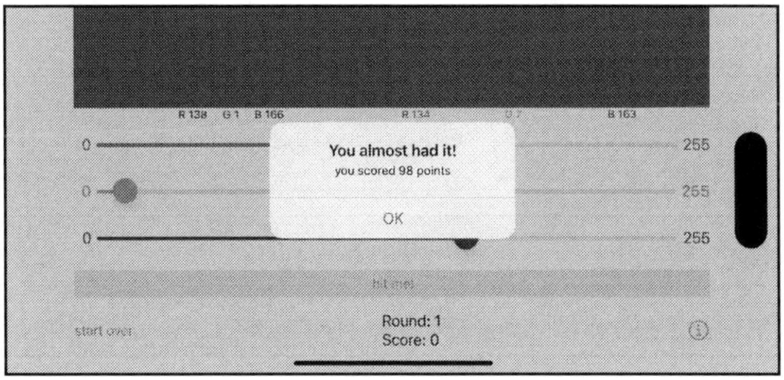

UIKit RGBullsEye starter app

This app displays a target color with randomly generated red, green and blue values. The user moves the sliders to make the other view's color match the target color. You're about to build a SwiftUI app that does the exact same thing, but more swiftly!

Exploring the SwiftUI Starter Project

Open the **SwiftUI/RGBullsEye** starter project from the chapter materials.

In the project navigator, open the **RGBullsEye** group to see what's here: the **AppDelegate.swift**, which you may be used to seeing, is now **RGBullsEyeApp**. This creates the app's `WindowGroup` from `ContentView()`:

```
@main
struct RGBullsEyeApp: App {
  var body: some Scene {
    WindowGroup {
      ContentView()
    }
  }
}
```

The `@main` attribute means this structure contains the entry point for the app. The `App` protocol takes care of generating the static `main` function that actually runs. When the app starts, it displays this instance of `ContentView`, which is defined in the **ContentView** file. It's a `struct` that conforms to the `View` protocol:

```
struct ContentView: View {
  var body: some View {
    Text("Hello, world!")
      .padding()
  }
}
```

This is SwiftUI declaring that the `body` of `ContentView` contains a `Text` view that displays **Hello World**. The `padding()` modifier adds 10 points padding around the text.

There's a **Model** group containing files that define a `Game` structure with properties and methods and an `RGB` structure to wrap the red, green and blue color values. The `Color` extension provides a custom initializer to create a `Color` view from an `RGB` structure.

Previewing Your ContentView

In the **ContentView** file, below the `ContentView` structure, `ContentView_Previews` contains a view that contains an instance of `ContentView`:

```
struct ContentView_Previews : PreviewProvider {
  static var previews: some View {
    ContentView()
  }
}
```

This is where you can specify sample data for the preview, and you can compare different screen and font sizes. But where *is* the preview?

There's a big blank space — the canvas — next to or below the code, with this at the top:

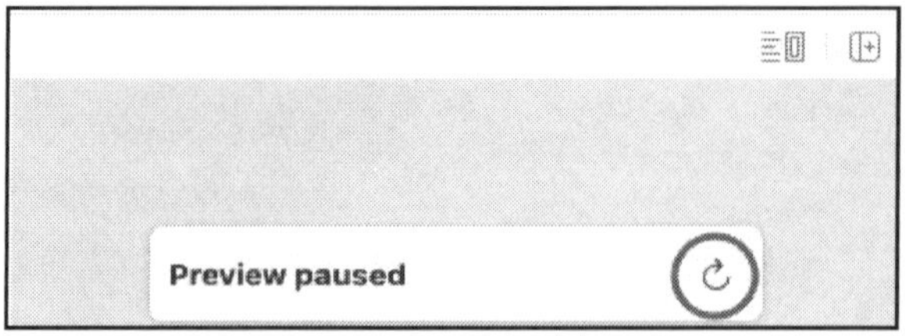

Preview Resume button

> **Note**: If your Xcode window's width is less than its height, and the canvas Layout setting is *Automatic*, the canvas appears *below* the code editor.

By default, the preview uses the currently active scheme's run destination.

Click the refresh button and wait a while to see the preview:

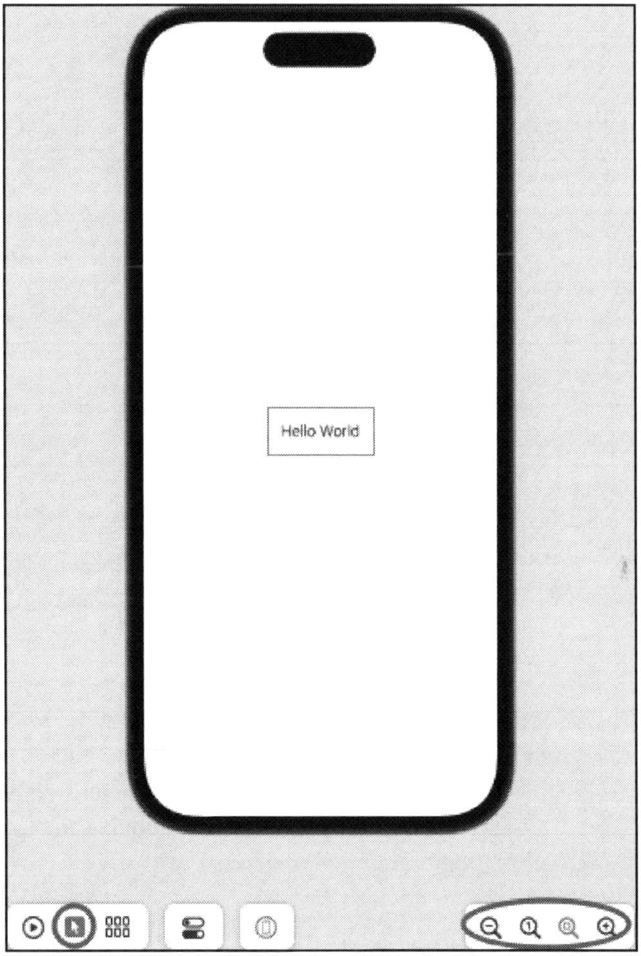

Hello World preview

Explore the zoom buttons: **Zoom Out**, **Zoom to 100%**, **Zoom to Fit** and **Zoom In**. Click the **Selectable** button below the preview, then click the `Text` view in the canvas to see the padding box.

> **Note**: If you don't see the canvas or the refresh button, click the **Editor Options** button and select **Canvas**:

Editor options

> **Note**: Instead of clicking the refresh button, you can use the very useful keyboard shortcut **Option-Command-P**. It works even if the refresh button isn't displayed immediately after you change something in the view.

Creating Your UI

Your SwiftUI app doesn't have a storyboard or a view controller. The **ContentView** file takes over their jobs. You can use any combination of code and drag-from-object-library to create your UI, and you can perform storyboard-like actions directly in your code! Best of all, everything stays in sync all the time!

SwiftUI is **declarative**: You declare how you want the UI to look, and SwiftUI converts your declarations into efficient code that gets the job done. Apple encourages you to create as many views as you need to keep your code easy to read. Reusable parameterized views are especially recommended. It's just like extracting code into a function, and you'll create one later in this chapter.

For this chapter, you'll mostly use the canvas, similar to how you'd layout your UI in Interface Builder (IB).

Some SwiftUI Vocabulary

Before you dive into creating your views, you need to know some vocabulary.

- **Canvas and Minimap**: To get the full SwiftUI experience, you need at least **Xcode 11** and **macOS 10.15**. Then you'll be able to preview your app's views in the **canvas**, alongside the code editor. Also available is a **minimap** of your code: It doesn't appear in my screenshots because I unchecked it in **Editor Options**.
- **Modifiers:** Instead of setting attributes or properties of UIKit objects, you can call **modifier methods** for foreground color, font, padding and a lot more.
- **Container views**: If you've previously used stack views, you'll find it pretty easy to create this app's UI in SwiftUI, using `HStack` and `VStack` **container views**. There are other container views, including `ZStack` and `Group`. You'll learn about them in depth in **Chapter 7: "Introducing Stacks & Containers"**.

In addition to container views, there are SwiftUI views for many of the UIKit objects you know and love, like `Text`, `Button` and `Slider`. The **+** button in the toolbar displays the **Library** of SwiftUI views and modifiers, as well as code snippets, media, color and symbols.

Creating the Target Color View

In RGBullsEye, the target color view, which is the color your user is trying to match, is a `Color` view above a `Text` view. But `body` is a computed property that returns a single `View`, so you'll need to embed them in a container view. In this scenario, you'll use a `VStack` (vertical stack).

This is your workflow:

1. **Embed** the `Text` view in a `VStack` and edit the text.
2. Add a `Color` view to the stack.

Step 1: Make sure you're in **Selectable** mode. **Command-click** the **Hello World** `Text` view in the canvas — notice Xcode highlights the code line — and select **Embed in VStack**:

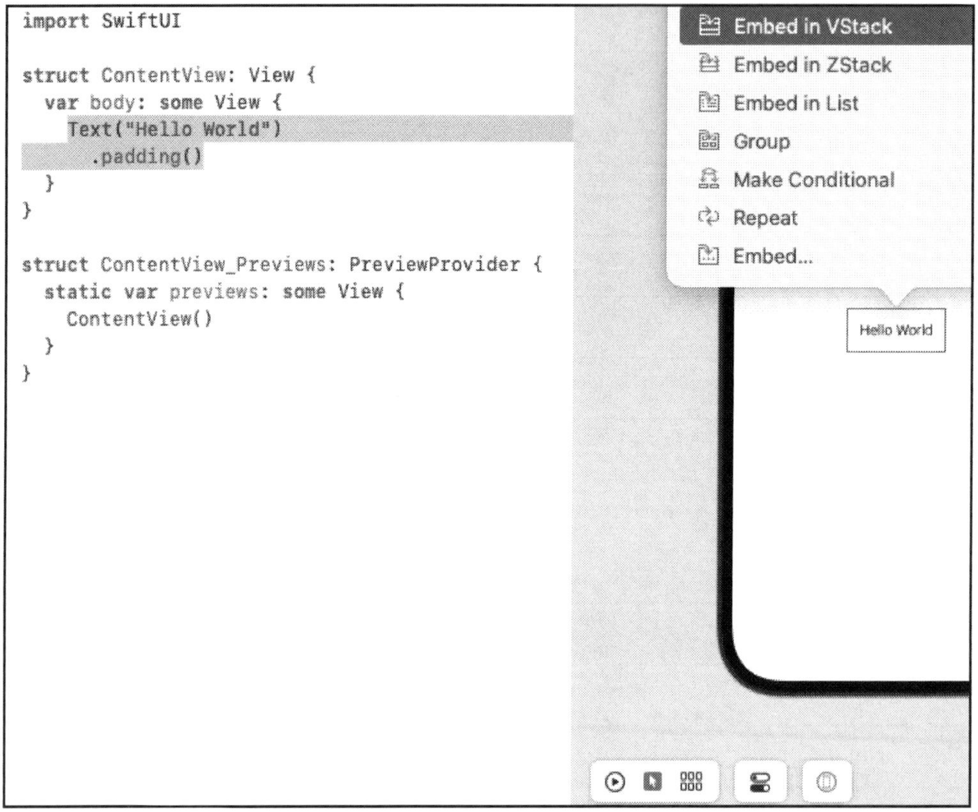

Embed Text view in VStack

> **Note**: If **Command-click** only shows the *definition* of `Text`, use **Control-Command-click** instead. You just have a different setting in Xcode navigation preferences.

The canvas looks the same, but there's now a `VStack` in your code.

Change "Hello World" to "R: ??? G: ??? B: ???": You could do this directly in the code, but, just so you know you can do this, open the **Attributes** inspector then click the `Text` view in the canvas and edit the text in the inspector:

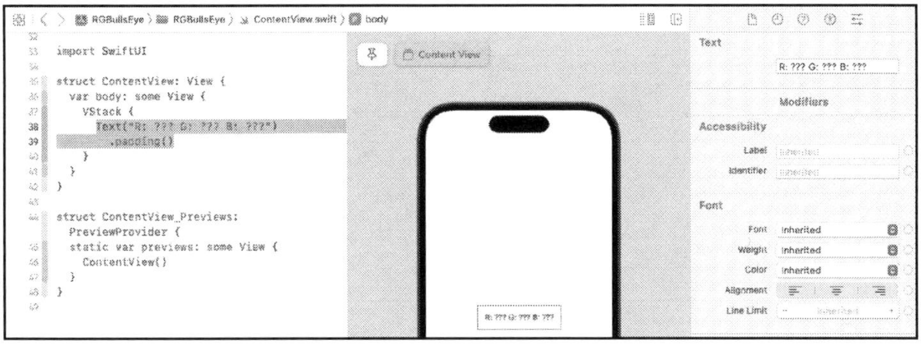

Edit text in the Attributes inspector.

Your code updates to match! Just for fun, change the text in your code and watch it change in the canvas. Then change it back. Efficient, right?

> **Note**: You can also **Control-Option-click** the `Text` view in the code editor to open the SwiftUI inspector in-place. This *should* also work in the canvas, but doesn't (at time of writing). If you **Command-click** a view in the canvas, you can select **Show SwiftUI Inspector...** from the menu.

Step 2: Click the + button in the toolbar to open the **Library**. Make sure the selected library is **Views**, then search for **color**. Drag this object onto the `Text` view in the canvas. While dragging, move the cursor down until you see the hint **Insert Color in Vertical Stack** — *not* **Add Color to a new Vertical Stack...** — but keep the cursor near the *top* of the `Text` view because you want to insert it *above* the text. Then release the `Color` object.

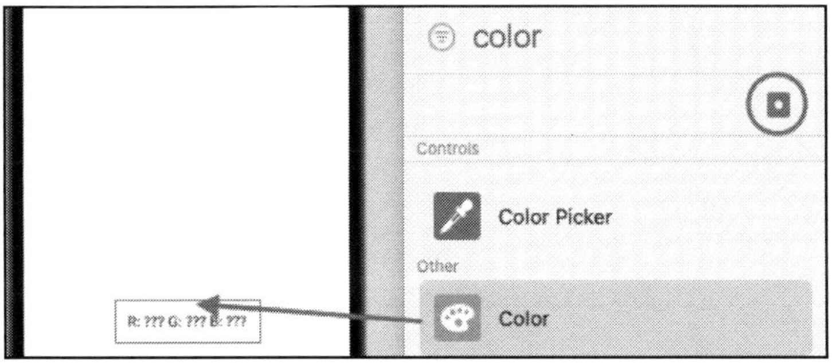

Insert Color into VStack

And there's your `Color` view inside the `VStack`, in both the canvas and your code!

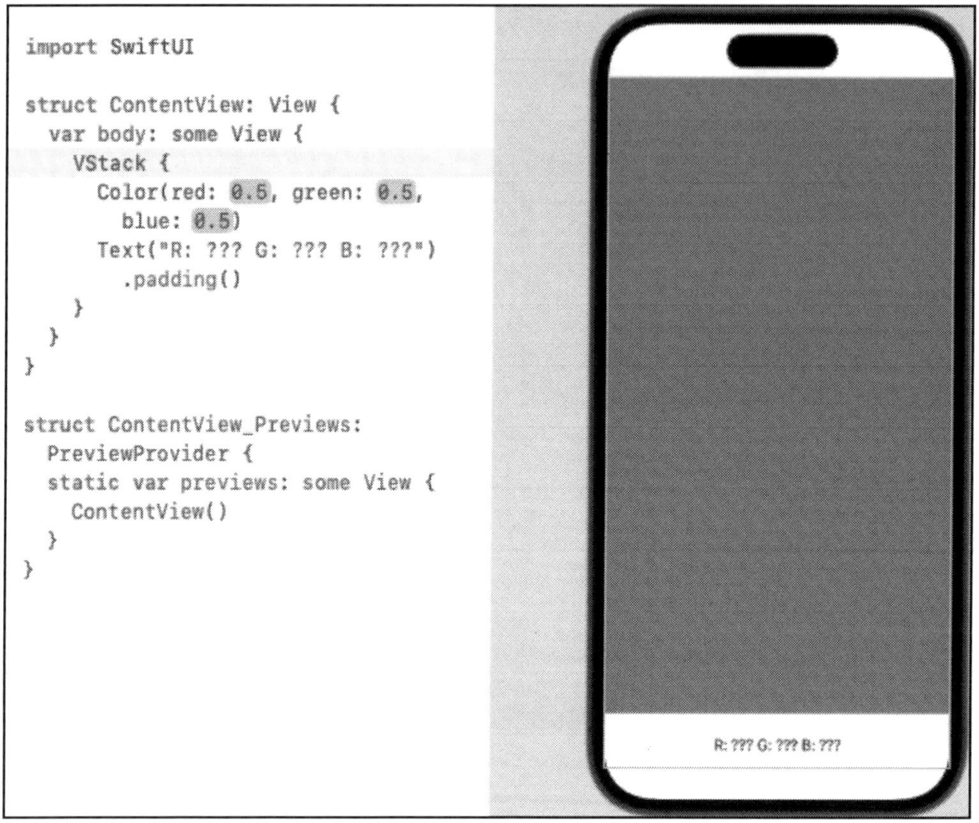

Color view in VStack

The **0.5** values are highlighted because they're just placeholders. For now, just accept them by selecting each, then pressing **Enter**.

> **Note**: In IB, you could drag several objects onto the view, then select them all and embed them in a stack view. But the SwiftUI **Embed** command only works on a *single* object.

Creating the Guess Color View

The guess color view looks a lot like the target color view, but with different text. It goes *below* the target color view, so you'll just add it to the `VStack`.

In the code editor, copy the `Color` and `Text` code, including the `padding()`, and paste them below the `padding()` line. Or select the code and press **Command-D** to duplicate it.

Change the string in the *second* `Text` view to `"R: 204 G: 76 B: 178"`. These sample values will create a bright fuchsia color :].

Your `VStack` now looks like this:

```
VStack {
  Color(red: 0.5, green: 0.5, blue: 0.5)
  Text("R: ??? G: ??? B: ???")
    .padding()
  Color(red: 0.5, green: 0.5, blue: 0.5)
  Text("R: 204 G: 76 B: 178")
    .padding()
}
```

Creating the Button and Slider

The color sliders and **Hit me!** button go *below* the color blocks so again, you'll just add them to your `VStack`.

Earlier, you dragged a `Color` view onto the canvas. This time, you'll drag `Slider` and `Button` views into your code.

> **Note**: To keep the **Library** open, **Option-click** the + button.

Open the library and drag a `Button` into the code editor. Hover *slightly below* the second `padding` line until a new line opens for you to drop the object.

If the button doesn't appear right away, press **Option-Command-P** or click **Resume**:

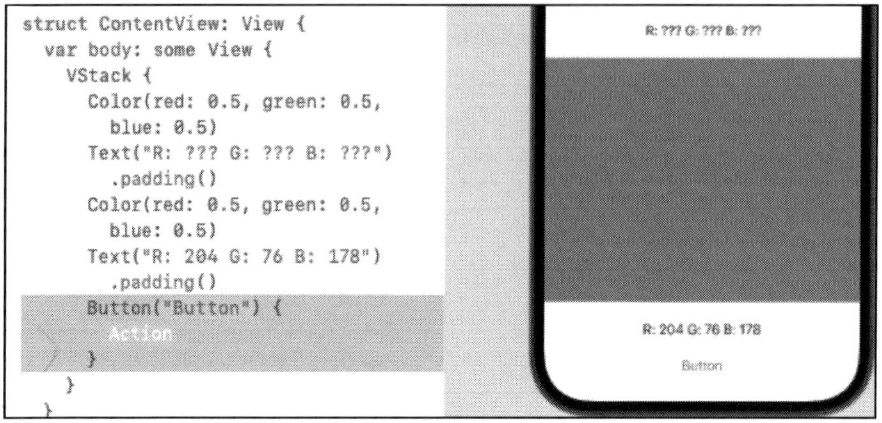

Add Button to code

Change the button label to `"Hit Me!"` and delete the `Action` placeholder, leaving the closure empty.

Now that the button makes it clear where the `VStack` bottom edge is, drag a **Slider** from the **Library** onto your canvas, just *above* the `Button`:

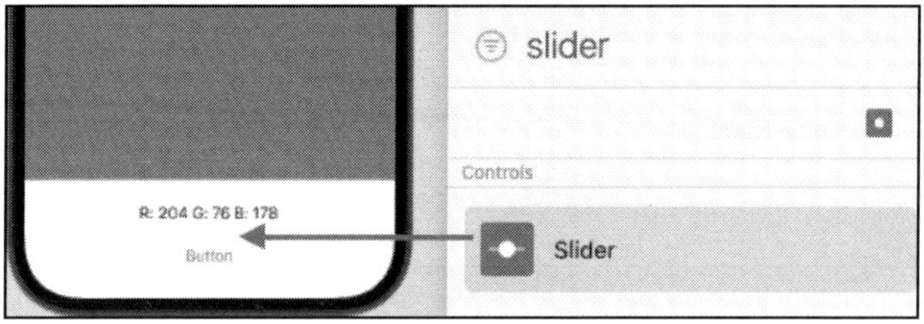

Insert Slider in Vertical Stack

Make sure the prompt says **Insert Slider in Vertical Stack**.

In the code editor, set the `Slider value` to **.constant(0.5)**. You'll learn why it's not just 0.5 in the section on **Bindings**.

Here's what it looks like:

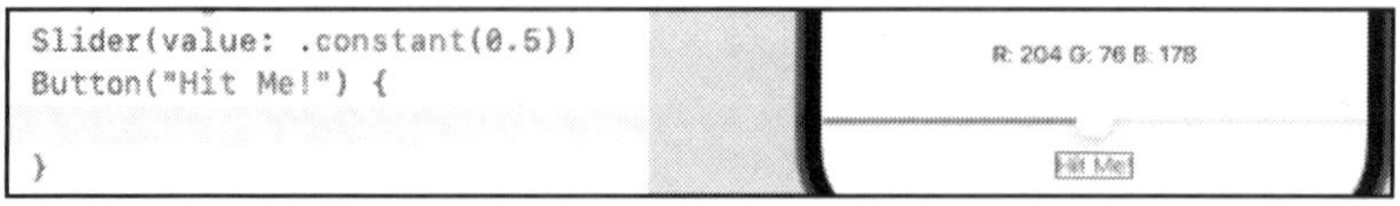

Button & Slider in VStack

> **Note:** If your slider thumb isn't centered, refresh the preview (**Option-Command-P**) until it is.

Well, yes, you do need *three* sliders, but the slider values will update the UI, and this is the topic of the next section. So you'll get the red slider working, then extract it to a reusable subview with parameters to create all three sliders.

Updating the UI

If the UI should update when a SwiftUI view property's value changes, you designate it as a `@State` property. In SwiftUI, when a `@State` property's value changes, the view invalidates its appearance and recomputes the `body`. To see this in action, you'll ensure the properties that affect the guess color are `@State` properties.

Using @State Properties

Add these properties at the top of `struct ContentView`, above the `body` property:

```
@State var game = Game()
@State var guess: RGB
```

You create a `Game` object to access the properties and methods required to display and run the RGBullsEye game. Look at **Model/Game** to see one of these properties is the `target` `RGB` object:

```
var target = RGB.random()
```

Creating `game` initializes the red, green and blue values of `target` to random values between 0 and 1.

You also need a local RGB object `guess` to store the slider values.

You *could* initialize `guess` to `RGB()`, which initializes `red`, `green` and `blue` to 0.5 (the color gray). I've left it uninitialized to show you what you must do if you don't initialize it.

Back in **ContentView**, scroll down to the `ContentView_Previews` struct, which instantiates a `ContentView` to display in the preview. The initializer now needs a parameter value for `guess`. Change `ContentView()` to this:

```
ContentView(guess: RGB(red: 0.8, green: 0.3, blue: 0.7))
```

These values will display the fuchsia color in the preview.

You must also replace the `ContentView()` initializer in the **RGBullsEyeApp** file. This time, use the default initializer:

```
ContentView(guess: RGB())
```

When the app loads its initial scene, the slider thumbs will be centered. The guess color starts out gray.

Updating the Color Views

Back in **ContentView**, edit the `Color` view *above* `Text("R: ??? G: ??? B: ???")` to use the `target` property of the game object:

```
Color(rgbStruct: game.target)
```

You're using the `RGB` struct initializer defined in **Model/ColorExtension** to create a `Color` view with the `target` color values.

Press **Option-Command-P** to see a random target color in the preview.

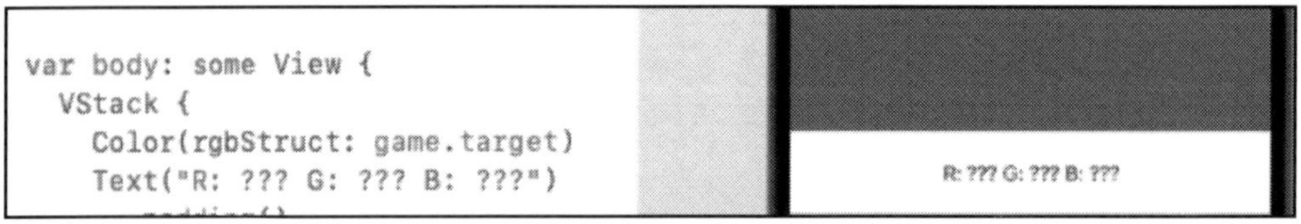

Random target color

> **Note**: The preview refreshes itself periodically, as well as when you click the refresh button, so don't be surprised to see the target color change, all by itself, every so often.

Similarly, modify the **guess** `Color` to use the `guess` color values:

```
Color(rgbStruct: guess)
```

Refresh the preview to see the fuchsia color you set up in the preview `ContentView`:

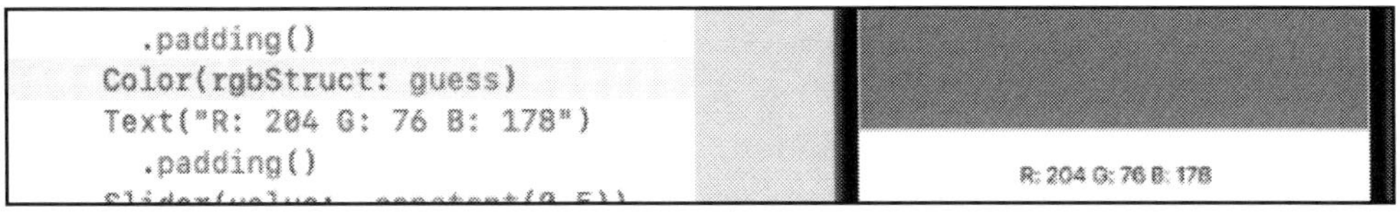

Guess color set in preview

The R, G and B values in the guess `Text` view match the color, but you'll soon make them respond to slider values set by the user.

Making Reusable Views

Because the sliders are basically identical, you'll define *one* slider view, then *reuse* it for the other two sliders. This is exactly as Apple recommends.

Making the Red Slider

First, pretend you're not thinking about reuse, and just create the red slider. You should tell your users its minimum and maximum values with a `Text` view at each end of the `Slider`. To achieve this *horizontal* layout, you'll need an `HStack`.

Make sure the preview canvas is open, then **Command-click** the `Slider` view (in code or canvas) and select **Embed in HStack**. Now, insert `Text` views above and below (in code) or to the left and right (in canvas). Change the `Placeholder` text to `0` and 255, then update the preview to see how it looks:

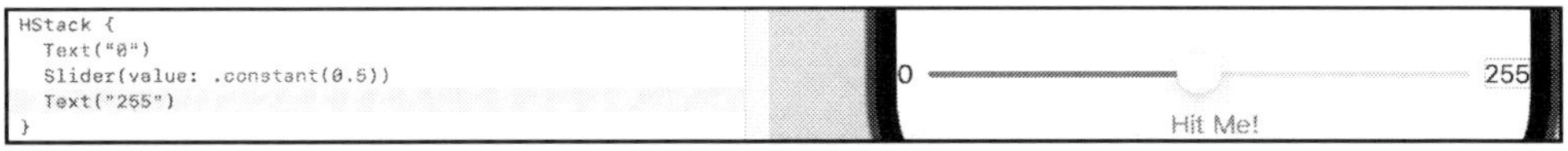

Slider from 0 to 255

> **Note**: You and I know the slider goes from 0 to 1, but the **255** end label and 0-to-255 RGB values are for your users, who might feel more comfortable thinking of RGB values between 0 and 255, as in the hexadecimal representation of colors.

The numbers look cramped, so you'll fix that and also make this look and behave like a *red* slider.

First, in the code editor, **Control-Option-click** the `HStack` to open its attributes inspector. In the **Padding** section, click the left and right checkboxes.

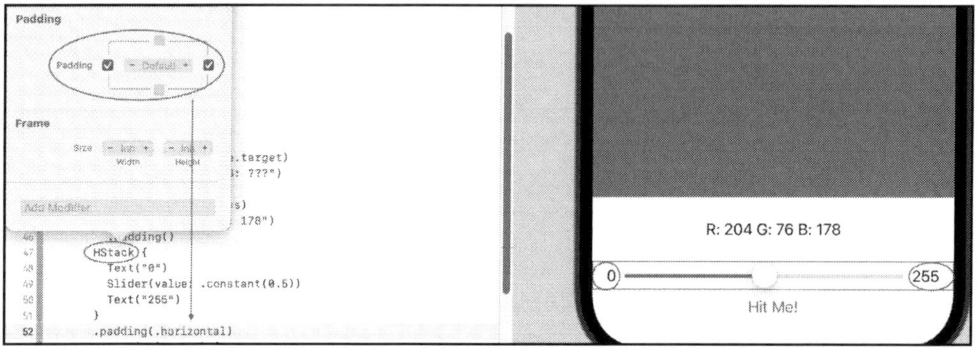

Add horizontal padding

Clicking the left or right checkbox adds the modifier `padding(.leading)` or `padding(.trailing)` to `HStack`. Then, when you click the *other* (right or left) checkbox, the `padding` value changes to `.horizontal`. And now there's space between the screen edges and the slider labels.

> **Note**: The quickest way to add padding *all around a view* is to type `.padding()` in the code editor. The attributes inspector is useful when you want to set padding on only some edges.

Next, edit the `Slider` value and add a modifier:

```
Slider(value: $guess.red)
  .accentColor(.red)
```

The modifier sets the slider's `minimumTrackTintColor` to red.

But what's with the `$guess`? You'll find out real soon, but first, check that it's working.

Down in the preview code, change the `red` value to something different from 0.8, like **0.3**, then press **Option-Command-P**:

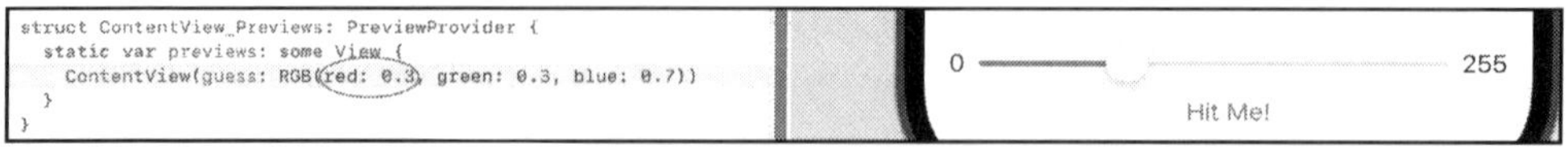

Red slider value 0.3

Awesome, `guess.red` is **0.3**, and the slider thumb is right where you'd expect it to be! The leading track is red, and the number labels aren't squashed up against the edges.

Bindings

So back to that `$`. It's actually pretty cool and ultra-powerful for such a little symbol. By itself, `guess.red` is just the value. It's read-only. But `$guess.red` is a *read-write* **binding**. You need it here to update the guess color while the user is changing the slider's value.

To see the difference, set the values in the `Text` view below the guess `Color` view: Change `Text("R: 204 G: 76 B: 178")` to the following:

```
Text(
  "R: \(Int(guess.red * 255.0))"
    + "  G: \(Int(guess.green * 255.0))"
    + "  B: \(Int(guess.blue * 255.0))")
```

Here, you're only *using* (read-only) the guess values, not changing them, so you don't need the `$` prefix.

This string displays the color values of an `RGB` object as integers between 0 and 255. The `RGB` struct includes a method for this. Replace the multi-line `Text` code with this:

```
Text(guess.intString())
```

Press **Option-Command-P**:

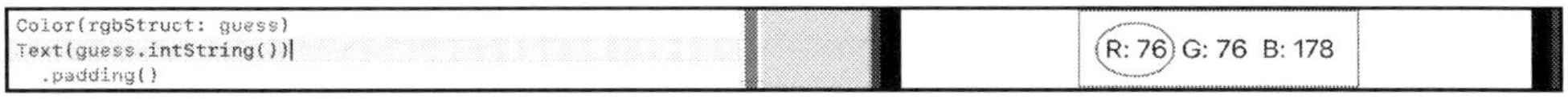

*R value 76 = 255 * 0.3*

And now the **R** value is **76**. That's `255 * 0.3`, as it should be!

Extracting Subviews

Next, the purpose of this section is to create a reusable view from the red slider `HStack`. To be reusable, the view needs some parameters. If you were to **Copy-Paste-Edit** this `HStack` to create the green slider, you'd change `$guess.red` to `$guess.green` and `.red` to `.green`. So these are your parameters.

Make sure the preview canvas is open, then **Command-click** the `HStack` and select **Extract Subview**:

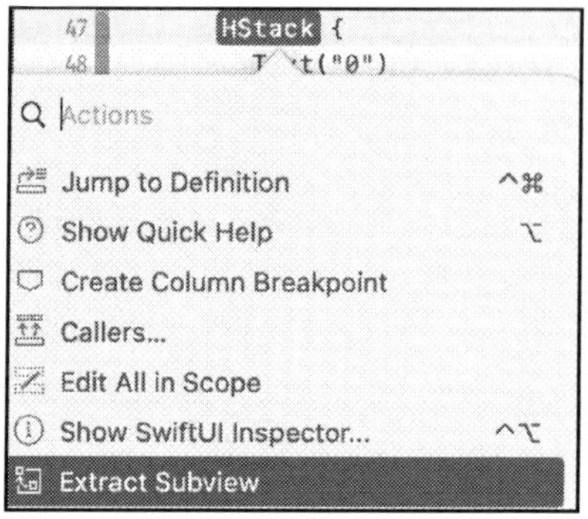

Extract HStack to subview

This works the same as **Refactor ▸ Extract to Function**, but for SwiftUI views.

Name the extracted view **ColorSlider**.

> **Note**: Right after you select **Extract Subview** from the menu, `ExtractedView` is highlighted. If you rename it while it's highlighted, the new name appears in two places: where you extracted it from and also in the extracted subview, down at the bottom of the file. If you don't rename it in time, then you have to manually change the name of the extracted subview in these two places.

Don't worry about all the error messages that appear. They'll go away when you've finished editing your new subview.

Now add these properties at the top of `struct ColorSlider`, before the `body` property:

```
@Binding var value: Double
var trackColor: Color
```

For the `value` property, you use `@Binding` instead of `@State`, because the `ColorSlider` view doesn't *own* this data. It receives an initial value from its parent view and mutates it.

Now, replace `value: $guess.red` with `$value` and `.accentColor(.red)` with `.accentColor(trackColor)`:

```
Slider(value: $value)
  .accentColor(trackColor)
```

Then go back up to the call to `ColorSlider()` in the `VStack`. Click the **Missing arguments** error icon to open it, then click the **Fix** button to add the missing arguments. Fill in these parameter values:

```
ColorSlider(value: $guess.red, trackColor: .red)
```

Check that the preview still shows the red slider correctly, then **Command-D** this line to create the other two sliders:

```
ColorSlider(value: $guess.green, trackColor: .green)
ColorSlider(value: $guess.blue, trackColor: .blue)
```

Refresh the preview to see all three sliders:

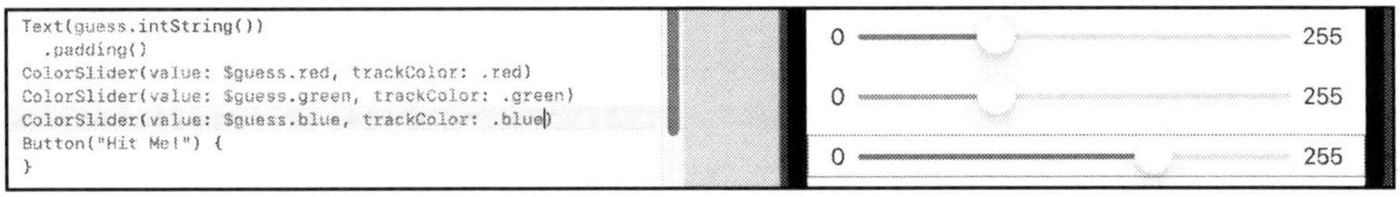

Three sliders

Everything's working! You can't wait to play the game? Coming right up!

First, set the `guess` parameter in `previews` to `RGB()`:

```
ContentView(guess: RGB())
```

Live Preview

You don't have to fire up Simulator to play the game: In the **Preview** toolbar, click the **Live Preview** button:

Live preview button

Wait for the **Preview spinner** to stop; if necessary, click **Try Again**.

Now move those sliders to match the color!

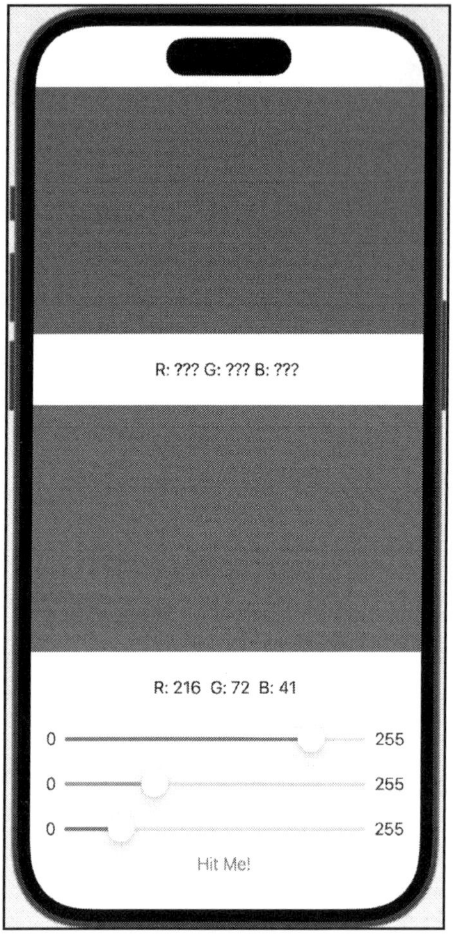

Playing the game

Stop and think about what's happening here. Compared with how the UIKit app works, the SwiftUI views *update themselves* whenever the slider values change! The UIKit app puts all that code into the slider action. Every `@State` property is a **source of truth**, and views depend on **state**, not on a sequence of events.

How amazing is that! Go ahead and do a victory lap to the kitchen, get your favorite drink and snacks, then come back for the final step! You want to know your score, don't you?

Presenting an Alert

After using the sliders to get a good color match, your user taps the **Hit Me!** button, just like in the original UIKit game. And just like in the original, an `Alert` should appear, displaying the score.

The `RGB` structure has a method `difference(target:)` to compute the difference between the `guess` and `target` `RGB` objects, and the `Game` structure has a method `check(guess:)` that uses `difference(target:)` to compute the score.

You'll call `check(guess:)` in the `action` of your `Button` view:

```
Button("Hit Me!") {
  // action
}
```

A `Button` has an action and a label, just like a `UIButton`. The action you want to happen is the presentation of an `Alert` view. But if you just create an `Alert` in the `Button` action, it won't do anything.

Instead, you create the `Alert` as a subview of `ContentView`, and add a `@State` property of type `Bool`. Then you set the value of this property to `true` when you want the `Alert` view to appear. In this case, you do this in the `Button` action. When the user dismisses the alert, the value changes to `false`, and the alert disappears.

So add this `@State` property to `ContentView`, initialized to `false`:

```
@State var showScore = false
```

Then add the `action` code in your `Button` closure:

```
showScore = true
game.check(guess: guess)
```

There's more than one way to configure a `Button`. The label can be either a single object or a closure, usually containing an `Image` view and a `Text` view. The action can be either a function call or a closure. If either the label or the action is a single statement, you can put it in the parentheses. The other parameter can be a trailing closure.

In this case, the label is just a `String`, so you put that in the parentheses and put the action in the trailing closure. This is actually the default configuration when you add a `Button` from the Library.

Finally, add this `alert` modifier to the `Button` (after its closing curly brace):

```
.alert(isPresented: $showScore) {
  Alert(
    title: Text("Your Score"),
    message: Text(String(game.scoreRound)),
    dismissButton: .default(Text("OK")) {
      game.startNewRound()
      guess = RGB()
    })
}
```

You pass the `$showScore` **binding** because its value will change when the user dismisses the alert, and this changed value will update the UI: It will stop presenting the alert.

When the `Button` action calls `game.check(guess:)`, this method computes the score for this round. You create a `String` from this number, to display in the alert's `message`.

The simplest `Alert` initializer has a default dismiss button with label "OK", so you only need to include the `dismissButton` parameter when you want to configure an action. In this case, you start a new round, which sets a new `target` color. Then you reset the `guess` color to gray.

Displaying the Target Values

There's one last bit of functionality you need to implement. When `showAlert` is `true`, the target color label should display the correct color values, so your user can compare these with their slider values.

Make sure the preview canvas is open, then **Command-click** `Text` in this line:

```
Text("R: ??? G: ??? B: ???")
```

Select **Make Conditional**:

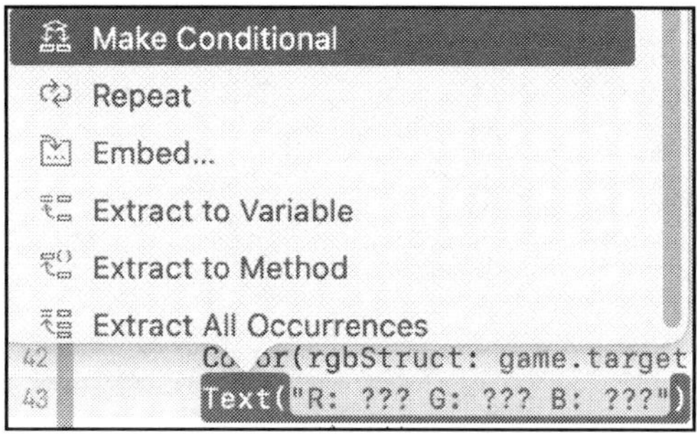

Embed Text view in an if-else

Note: SwiftUI has a lot of nested closures, so Xcode helps you keep your braces in order. If you need to enclose more than one line of code in a closure, select the other lines and press **Option-Command-[** or **Option-Command-]** to move them up or down. These keyboard shortcuts are tremendously useful in SwiftUI. If you need to look them up, they're listed in the Xcode menu under **Editor▸Structure**.

Now edit the `if-else` to look like this:

```
if !showScore {
  Text("R: ??? G: ??? B: ???")
    .padding()
} else {
  Text(game.target.intString())
    .padding()
}
```

When the user taps the button to show the alert, the target color label shows the actual color values.

Refresh the **live preview**. You might have to turn off **live preview**, click **Resume**, then turn on **live preview**. See how high you can score:

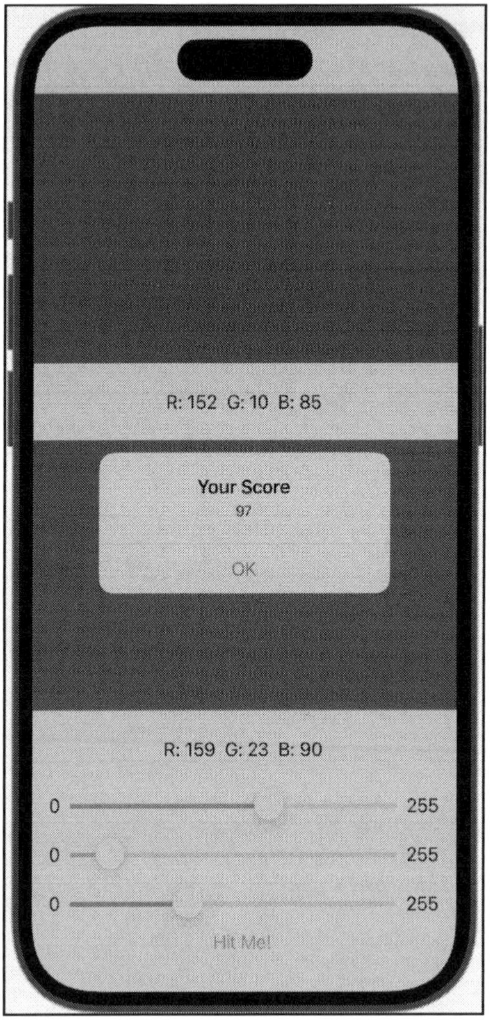

Score!

Hey, when you've got a live preview, who needs Simulator?

> **Note**: As you develop your own apps, you might find the preview doesn't always work as well as this. If it looks odd, or crashes, try running in a simulator. If *that* doesn't work, run it on a device.

Making it Prettier

Your app has all its functionality, so now's a good time to start improving how it looks. Instead of colored rectangles, how about circles?

Replace the target `Color` view with this colored `Circle`:

```
Circle()
  .fill(Color(rgbStruct: game.target))
```

And similarly for the guess `Color` view:

```
Circle()
  .fill(Color(rgbStruct: guess))
```

Refresh the preview to admire your circles:

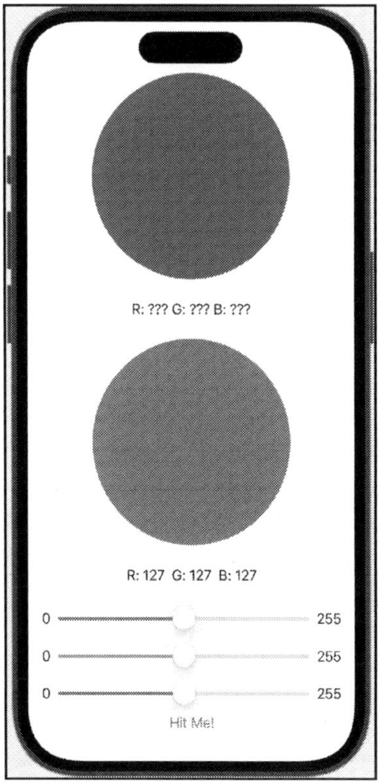

Color circles

In the next chapter, you'll customize these circles a lot more, so it's a good idea to extract another subview.

Challenge

Challenge: Create a ColorCircle Subview

Create a `ColorCircle` subview so that you can replace the `Circle().fill...` lines with these:

```
ColorCircle(rgb: game.target)
ColorCircle(rgb: guess)
```

The `ColorCircle` struct doesn't need any bindings.

The solution is in the **challenge/final** folder for this chapter.

Key Points

- The Xcode canvas lets you create your UI side-by-side with its code, and they stay in sync: A change to one side always updates the other side.
- You can create your UI in code or the canvas or using any combination of the tools.
- You organize your view objects with horizontal and vertical stacks, just like using stack views in storyboards.
- **Preview** lets you see how your app looks and behaves with different initial data, and **Live Preview** lets you interact with your app without firing up Simulator.
- You should aim to create reusable views. Xcode's **Extract Subview** tool makes this easy.
- SwiftUI updates your UI whenever a `@State` property's value changes. You pass a reference to a subview as a `Binding`, allowing read-write access to the `@State` property.

Chapter 3: Diving Deeper Into SwiftUI

By Audrey Tam

SwiftUI's declarative style makes it easy to implement eye-catching designs. In this chapter, you'll use SwiftUI modifiers to give RGBullsEye a design makeover with *neumorphism*, the latest design trend.

Neumorphism

Neumorphism gained popularity in 2020 as the new skeuomorphism, a pushback against super-flat minimal UI. It can cause accessibility issues and is best used for non-functional elements like your app's color circles or in designs with obvious UI elements.

A neumorphic UI element appears to push up from below its background, producing a flat 3D effect. Imagine the element protrudes a little from the screen, and the sun is setting northwest of the element. This produces a highlight on the upper-left edge and a shadow at the lower-right edge. Or the sun rises southeast of the element, so the highlight is on the lower-right edge and the shadow is at the upper left edge:

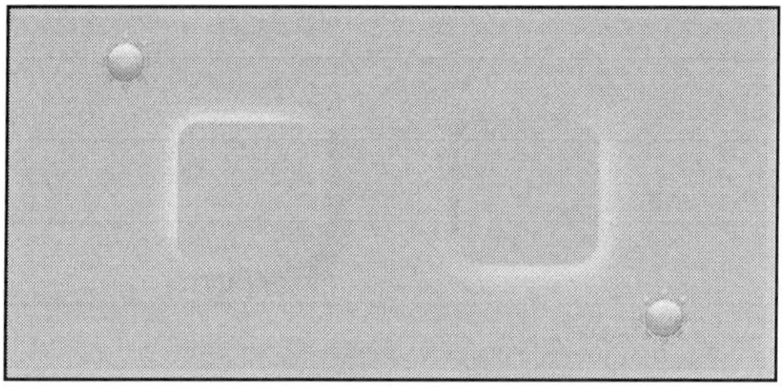

Northwest and southeast highlights and shadows

You need three colors to create these highlights and shadows:

- A neutral color for the background and element surface.
- A lighter color for the highlight.
- A darker color for the shadow.

This example uses colors that create high contrast, just to make it really visible. In your project, you'll use colors that create a more subtle effect.

You'll add highlights and shadows to the color circles, labels and button in RGBullsEye to implement this Figma design:

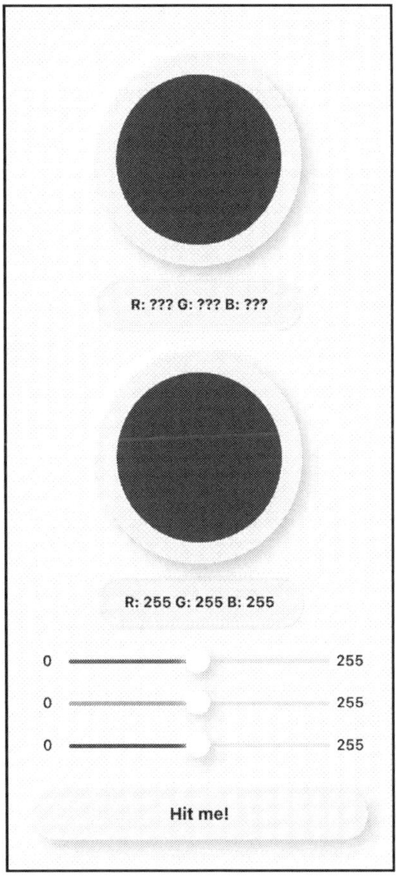

Figma design

This design was laid out for a 375x812-point screen (iPhone 11 Pro or 13 mini), although most of the screenshots use an iPhone 14 Pro (393 x 852). You'll set up your design with the size values from the Figma design, then change these to screen-size-dependent values.

> **Note**: Many developers skip the Figma/Sketch design step and just design directly in SwiftUI — it's that easy!

Views and Modifiers

Open the project in this chapter's **starter** folder. It's the same as the final challenge project from the previous chapter, but `ColorCircle` is in its own file with a `size` parameter, and **Assets.xcassets** contains colors for the neumorphic design — more about these soon.

In the **ContentView** file, with the canvas open, click the **+** button or press **Command-Shift-L** to open the **Library**:

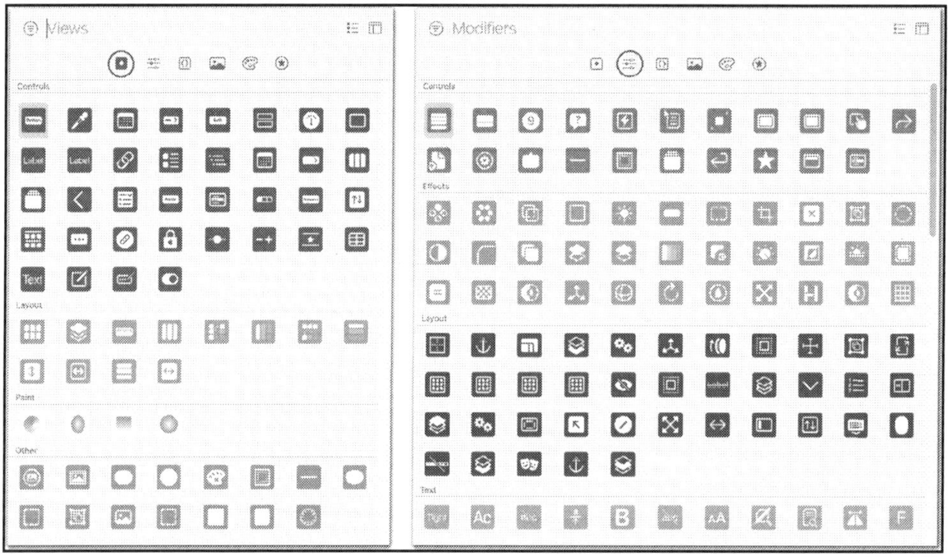

Library of primitive views and modifiers

> **Note**: To save space, I switched to icon view and hid the details.

A SwiftUI view is a piece of your UI: You combine small views to build larger views. There are lots of primitive views like `Text` and `Color`, which you can use as basic building blocks for your custom views.

The first tab lists **primitive views**, grouped as controls, layout, paint and other views. Many of these, especially the controls, are familiar to you as UIKit elements, but some are unique to SwiftUI. You'll learn how to use them in upcoming chapters.

The second tab lists **modifiers** for controls, effects, layout, text, image and more. A modifier is a method that creates a new view from the existing view. You can chain modifiers like a pipeline to customize any view.

SwiftUI encourages you to create small reusable views, then customize them with modifiers for the specific context where you use them. And don't worry, SwiftUI collapses the modified view into an efficient data structure, so you get all this convenience with no visible performance hit.

You can apply many of these modifiers to any type of view. And sometimes the order matters, as you'll soon see.

Implementing Neumorphism

Assets.xcassets contains Element, Highlight and Shadow colors for both light and dark mode:

- Element: #F1F3F7; Dark: #292A2D
- Highlight: #FFFFFF (20% opacity); Dark: #3D3E42
- Shadow: #BDCDE1; Dark: #1A1A1A

The **Model/ColorExtension** file includes static properties for these:

```
static let element = Color("Element")
static let highlight = Color("Highlight")
static let shadow = Color("Shadow")
```

Shadows for Neumorphism

First, you'll create custom modifiers for northwest and southeast shadows.

Create a new **Swift file** named **ViewExtension** and replace its `import Foundation` statement with the following code:

```
import SwiftUI

extension View {
  func northWestShadow(
    radius: CGFloat = 16,
    offset: CGFloat = 6
  ) -> some View {
    return self
      .shadow(
        color: .highlight, radius: radius, x: -offset,
          y: -offset)
      .shadow(
        color: .shadow, radius: radius, x: offset, y: offset)
```

```
  }

  func southEastShadow(
    radius: CGFloat = 16,
    offset: CGFloat = 6
  ) -> some View {
    return self
      .shadow(
        color: .shadow, radius: radius, x: -offset, y: -offset)
      .shadow(
        color: .highlight, radius: radius, x: offset, y: offset)
  }
}
```

The `shadow(color:radius:x:y:)` modifier adds a shadow of the specified `color` and `radius` (size) to the view, offset by (x, y). The default `Color` is black with opacity 0.33 and the default offset is (0, 0).

For your northwest and southeast shadow modifiers, you apply a shadow at the view's upper-left corner (negative offset values) and a different color shadow at its lower-right corner (positive offset values). For a northwest shadow, the upper-left color is `highlight` and the lower-right color is `shadow`. You switch these colors for a southeast shadow.

The colored circles and button use the same radius and offset values, so you set these as default values. Later on, the text labels need smaller values, which you'll pass as arguments.

It doesn't matter which order you apply the `shadow` modifiers. I've ordered them with the upper-left corner first, so it's easy to visualize the direction of the neumorphic shadow.

Setting the Background Color

For these shadows to work, the view background must be the same color as the UI elements. Head back to **ContentView** to set this up.

You'll use a `ZStack` to set the entire screen's background color to `element`. The Z-direction is *perpendicular* to the screen surface, so it's a good way to *layer* views on the screen. Items *lower* in a `ZStack` closure appear *higher* in the stack view. Think of it as placing the first view down on the screen surface, then layering the next view on top of that, and so on.

So here's what you do: Embed the `VStack` in a `ZStack` then add `Color.element` before the `VStack`.

```
ZStack {
  Color.element
  VStack {...}
}
```

Refresh the preview. You layered the `Color` below the `VStack`, but the color doesn't extend into the safe area. To fix this, add this modifier to `Color.element`:

```
.ignoresSafeArea()
```

> **Note**: You *could* add this modifier to `ZStack` instead of to `Color`, but then the `ZStack` would feel free to spread its content views into the safe area, which probably isn't what you want.

Now your app looks the same as before, except the background is not quite white. Next, you'll give the color circles a border, then apply a highlight and shadow to that border.

Creating a Neumorphic Border

The easiest way to create a border is to layer the RGB-colored circle on top of an `element`-colored circle using — you guessed it — a `ZStack`.

In **ColorCircle**, replace the contents of `body` with the following:

```
ZStack {
  Circle()
    .fill(Color.element)
    .northWestShadow()
  Circle()
    .fill(Color(red: rgb.red, green: rgb.green, blue: rgb.blue))
    .padding(20)
}
.frame(width: size, height: size)
```

You embed `Circle()` in a `ZStack`, add an `element`-colored `Circle` before it, then add padding to make the RGB circle smaller. To get the shadow effect, you apply `northWestShadow()` to the border circle.

> **Note**: The modifier `fill(_:style:)` can only be applied to shapes, so changing the order of modifiers flags an error:

```
Circle()
  .padding(20)
  .fill(Color(red: rgb.red, green: rgb.green, blue: rgb.blue))
```

Finally, you set both `width` and `height` to `size`.

If necessary, refresh the preview to see how this looks:

Neumorphic color circle on white background

Yes, there's a shadow, but the `ColorCircle` preview has a white background, so you don't see the full effect of the shadow.

Scroll down to `previews` and change its contents to the following:

```
ZStack {
  Color.element
  ColorCircle(rgb: RGB(), size: 200)
}
.frame(width: 300, height: 300)
.previewLayout(.sizeThatFits)
```

You set the background color to `element` the same way as in `ContentView`. There's no safe area to worry about because the preview frame is already set big enough to show off the shadow.

Neumorphic color circle on element-colored background

Against the not-quite-white background, the highlight on the upper left edge stands out more and the shadow of the lower-right edge appears less dark. Comment out and uncomment `Color.element` in `previews` to confirm this for yourself.

Now go back to **ContentView** and refresh its preview:

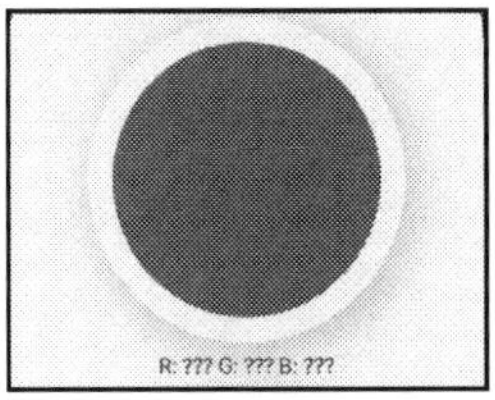

Neumorphic target color circle

Congratulations, your circles are now neumorphic!

Order of Modifiers

When you apply more than one modifier to a view, sometimes the order matters.

Modifiers like `padding` and `frame` change the view's layout or position. Modifiers like `background` or `border` fill or wrap a view. Normally, you want to set up a view's layout and position *before* you fill or wrap it.

For example, in **ContentView**, add a `border` modifier after the `padding` modifier of `Text(guess.intString)`:

```
.padding()
.border(Color.purple)
```

Border around padded text

The default amount of `padding` surrounds the `Text` view's text, then you put a purple `border` around the *padded* text.

Now change the order:

```
.border(Color.purple)
.padding()
```

Padding around bordered text

If you apply the `border` first, it goes around the *intrinsic area* of the text. If you select `padding()` in the code editor, you can see where it is, but all it does is keep the neighboring elements at a distance.

Delete `.border(Color.purple)`.

Some modifiers can only be applied to certain kinds of views. For example, these modifiers can only be applied to `Text` views:

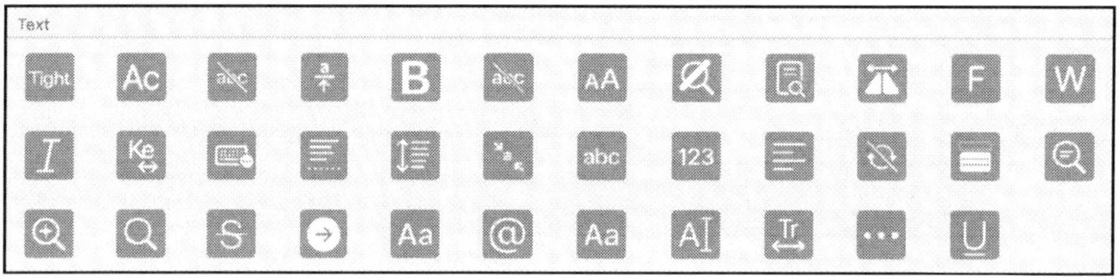

Text modifiers

Some, but not all, of these modifiers return a `Text` view. For example, `font`, `fontWeight`, `bold` and `italic` modify a `Text` view to produce another `Text` view. So you can apply these modifiers in any order.

But `lineLimit` returns `some View`, so this flags an error:

```
Text(guess.intString)
  .lineLimit(0)
  .bold()
```

And this order is OK:

```
Text(guess.intString)
  .bold()
  .lineLimit(0)
```

You'll learn more about using modifiers in **Chapter 5: "Intro to Controls: Text & Image"**.

Creating a Neumorphic Button

Next, still in **ContentView**, let's make your **Hit Me!** button pop!

To cast a shadow, the button needs a more substantial shape. Add these modifiers below the action, before the `alert`:

```
.frame(width: 327, height: 48)
.background(Capsule())
```

You set the background to a capsule shape. `Capsule` is a `RoundedRectangle` with the corner radius value set to half the length of its shorter side. It fills the frame you specified.

The fill color defaults to `primary` which, in light mode, is black.

This is a neumorphic button, so add these modifiers to `Capsule()`, to set its fill color to `element` and apply a northwest shadow:

```
.fill(Color.element)
.northWestShadow()
```

And here's your neumorphic button:

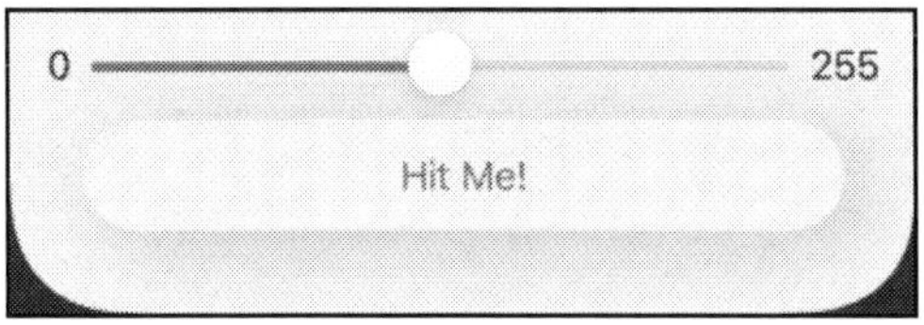

Neumorphic button

Creating a Custom Button Style

When you start customizing a button, it's a good idea to create a custom button style. Even if you're not planning to reuse it in this app, your code will be less cluttered. Especially if you decide to add more options to this button style.

So create a new **Swift file** named **NeuButtonStyle** and replace `import Foundation` with the following code:

```
import SwiftUI

struct NeuButtonStyle: ButtonStyle {
  let width: CGFloat
  let height: CGFloat
```

```
  func makeBody(configuration: Self.Configuration)
  -> some View {
    configuration.label
      // Move frame and background modifiers here
  }
}
```

ButtonStyle is a protocol that provides a ButtonStyleConfiguration with two properties: the button's label and a Boolean that's true when the user is pressing the button.

You'll implement makeBody(configuration:) to modify label.

You already figured out how you want to modify the Button, so **cut** the frame and background modifiers from the Button in **ContentView** and paste them below configuration.label in NeuButtonStyle.

Then replace the frame's width and height values with the corresponding properties of NeuButtonStyle.

Your button style code now looks like this:

```
struct NeuButtonStyle: ButtonStyle {
  let width: CGFloat
  let height: CGFloat

  func makeBody(configuration: Self.Configuration)
  -> some View {
    configuration.label
      .frame(width: width, height: height)
      .background(
        Capsule()
          .fill(Color.element)
          .northWestShadow()
      )
  }
}
```

Back in **ContentView**, modify the Button with this line of code:

```
.buttonStyle(NeuButtonStyle(width: 327, height: 48))
```

This width value works for iPhones like the iPhone 14. To support smaller or larger iPhones, you'll learn how to pass values that fit later on.

Now refresh the preview. It should look the same as before:

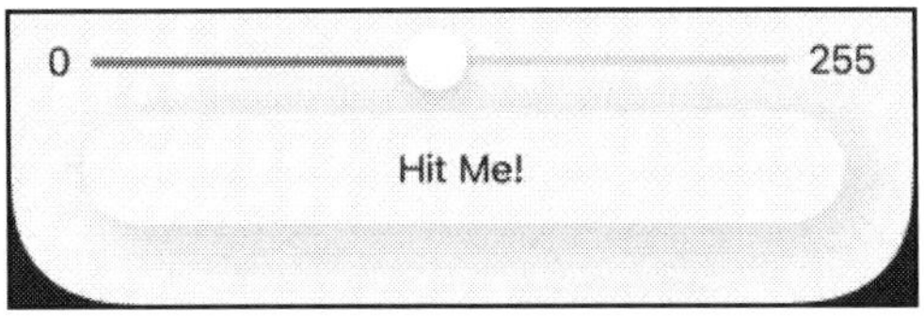

Neumorphic button using NeuButtonStyle

But... it's *not* the same. The button label is now black, not blue!

Fixing Button Style Issues

When you create a custom button style, you lose the default label color and the default visual feedback when the user taps the button.

Label color isn't a problem if you're already using a custom color. If not, you would just add this modifier to `configuration.label` in the `NeuButtonStyle` structure:

```
.foregroundColor(Color(UIColor.systemBlue))
```

However, the Figma design's button text *is* black, so this *isn't* a problem.

Now to tackle the visual feedback issue.

Creating a button style actually makes *you* responsible for defining what happens when the user taps the button. In fact, the configuration label's description is "a view that describes the effect of pressing the button".

Live-preview `ContentView` and tap the button: The button's appearance doesn't change at all when you tap it. This isn't a good user experience. Fortunately, it's easy to recover the default behavior.

Before you leave the **ContentView** file, click the **pin button** in the upper-left corner of the canvas:

Pin the ContentView preview

You're going to be working in the **NeuButtonStyle** file, making changes that affect **ContentView**. *Pinning* its preview means you'll be able to see the effect of your changes without having to bounce back and forth between the two files.

Now, in **NeuButtonStyle**, add this line above the `frame` modifier:

```
.opacity(configuration.isPressed ? 0.2 : 1)
```

When the user taps the button, you reduce the label's opacity, producing the standard dimming effect.

Check this in the live preview of `ContentView`.

If you want to take advantage of your neumorphic button, you can turn off or switch the direction of the shadow when the user taps the button.

In `NeuButtonStyle`, replace the contents of `background` with this:

```
Group {
  if configuration.isPressed {
    Capsule()
      .fill(Color.element)
  } else {
    Capsule()
      .fill(Color.element)
      .northWestShadow()
  }
}
```

`Group` is another SwiftUI container. It doesn't do any layout. It's just useful when you need to wrap code that's more complicated than a single view.

If the user is pressing the button, you show a flat button. Otherwise, you show the shadowed button.

Tap the button in the live preview. Hold down the button to see the shadow disappears.

A variation on this is to apply `southEastShadow()` when `isPressed` is `true`:

```
Group {
  if configuration.isPressed {
    Capsule()
      .fill(Color.element)
      .southEastShadow()   // Add this line
  } else {
    Capsule()
      .fill(Color.element)
```

```
        .northWestShadow()
    }
  }
```

Creating a Beveled Edge

Next, you'll create a new look for the color circles' labels. You'll use `Capsule` again, to unify the design. But you'll create a bevel edge effect, to differentiate it from the button.

Create a new **SwiftUI View** file and name it **BevelText**.

Replace the contents of the `BevelText` structure with the following:

```
let text: String
let width: CGFloat
let height: CGFloat

var body: some View {
  Text(text)
}
```

Back in **ContentView**, replace the `Text` views **and their** `padding` with `BevelText` views:

```
if !showScore {
  BevelText(
    text: "R: ??? G: ??? B: ???", width: 200, height: 48)
} else {
  BevelText(
    text: game.target.intString(), width: 200, height: 48)
}
ColorCircle(rgb: guess, size: 200)
BevelText(text: guess.intString(), width: 200, height: 48)
```

`BevelText` views don't need `padding` because their frame height is 48 points.

Now, in the **BevelText** canvas, select the **Bevel Text** preview so you can focus on it. Replace the contents of `previews` with the following:

```
ZStack {
  Color.element
  BevelText(
    text: "R: ??? G: ??? B: ???", width: 200, height: 48)
}
.frame(width: 300, height: 100)
```

```
.previewLayout(.sizeThatFits)
```

You layer `BevelText` on top of the `element`-color background. This is your starting point for creating a capsule with a bevel edge.

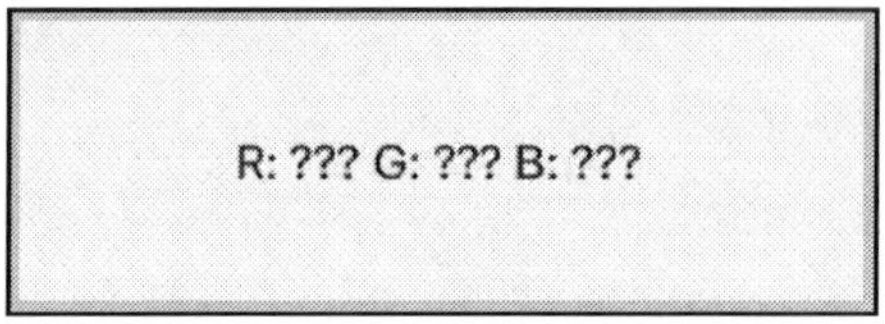

BevelText: Getting started

In the `body` of `BevelText`, add these two modifiers to `Text`:

```
.frame(width: width, height: height)
.background(
  Capsule()
    .fill(Color.element)
    .northWestShadow(radius: 3, offset: 1)
)
```

Refresh the preview. This is the outer capsule shape. It's just a smaller version of `NeuButtonStyle`:

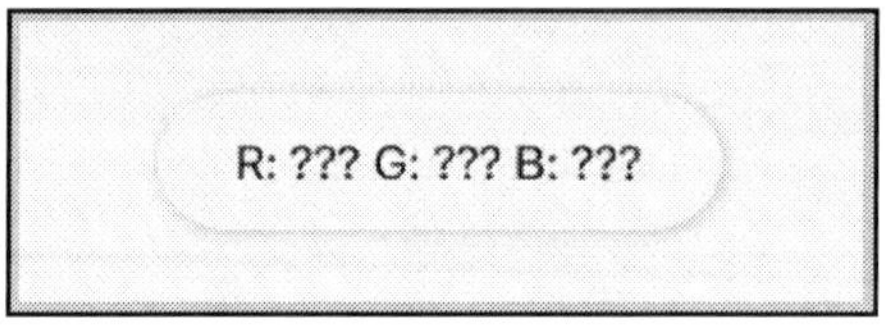

Outer Capsule with northwest shadow

Now embed this in a `ZStack` so you can layer another `Capsule` onto it, inset by 3 points:

```
ZStack {
  Capsule()
    .fill(Color.element)
    .northWestShadow(radius: 3, offset: 1)
  Capsule()
    .inset(by: 3)
    .fill(Color.element)
    .southEastShadow(radius: 1, offset: 1)
}
```

Imagine the sun is setting in the northwest: It *highlights* the outer upper-left edge and the inner lower-right edge and casts *shadows* from the inner upper-left edge and the outer lower-right edge.

To get this effect, you apply the *southeast* shadow to the inner `Capsule`.

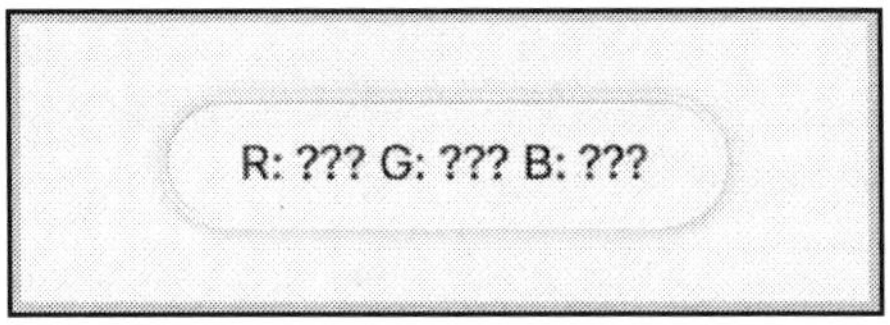

BevelText: Finished

> **Note**: Thanks to *Caroline Begbie* for this elegantly simple implementation.

And now, select the **ContentView** preview to enjoy the results:

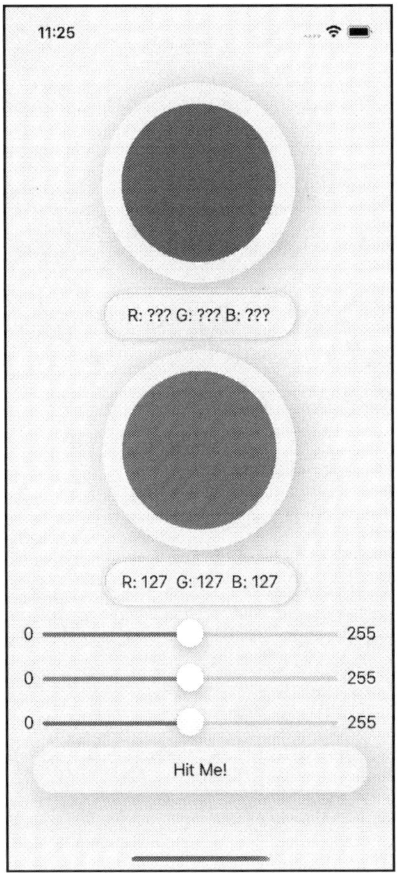

Neumorphism accomplished!

"Debugging" Dark Mode

Remember that the color sets in **Assets** have dark mode values. What does this design look like in dark mode?

It's easy to preview in dark mode. Click the **Device Settings** button and switch on **Color Scheme**: It defaults to **Dark appearance**:

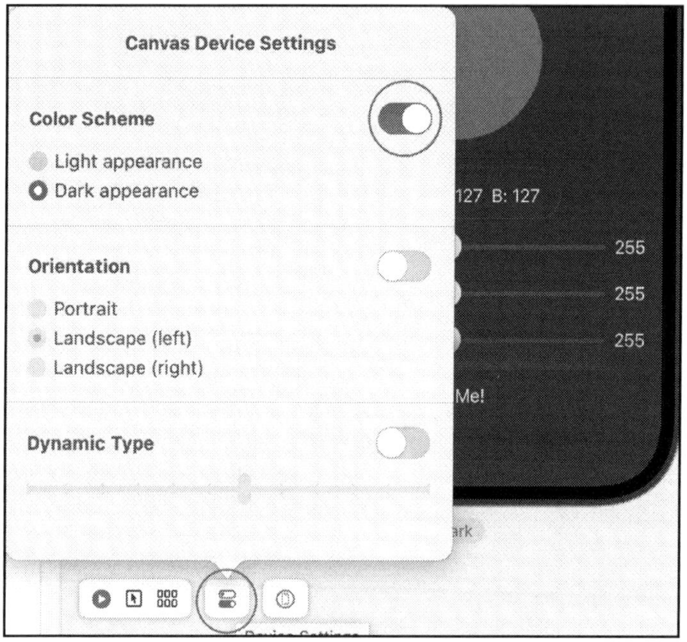

Set preview's color scheme to Dark appearance.

Thanks to the magic of color sets, you get dark mode shadows for free!

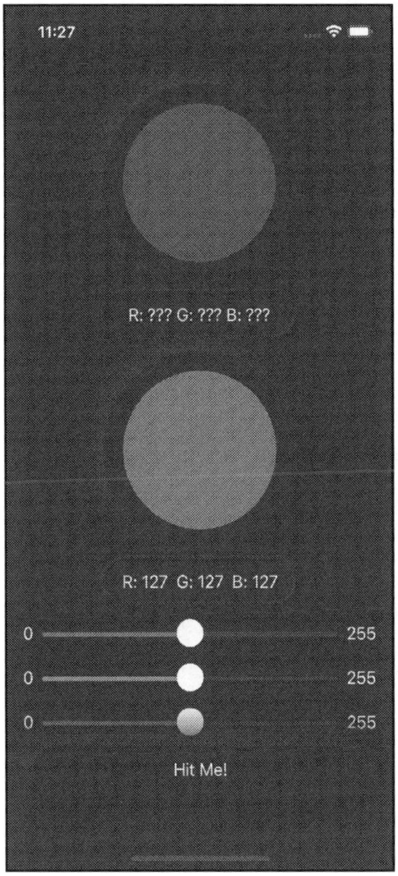

Neumorphism: Dark mode

There seems to be a problem, however. In live preview, tap **Hit Me!**. The alert's color scheme isn't dark?!

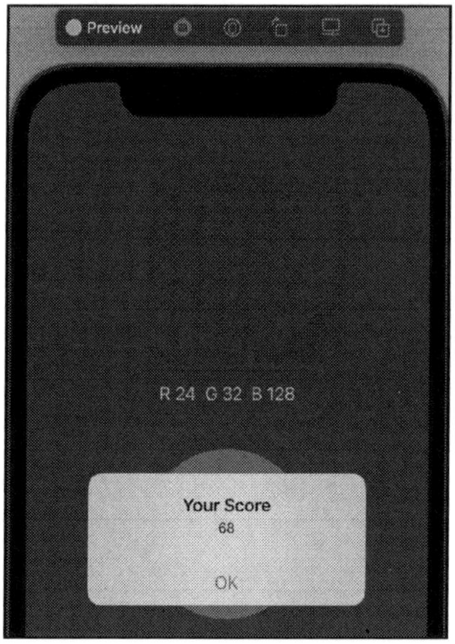

Alert's color scheme isn't dark?!

I spent a lot of time trying to figure out a way around this. But this is a fine example of why you shouldn't rely entirely on the preview.

Build and run the app on the **iPhone 14 Pro simulator**. The first thing you notice is the preview's dark color scheme doesn't affect the simulator.

Not a problem: Click the **Environment Overrides** button in the debug toolbar and enable **Appearance ▸ Dark**:

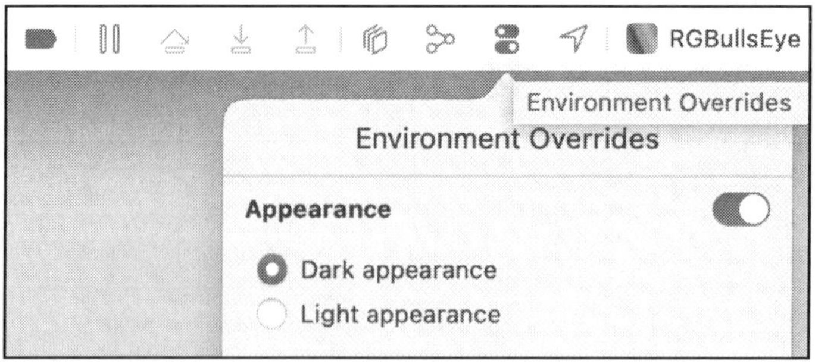

Override color scheme while running in a simulator.

> **Note**: Apple has a list of `EnvironmentValues`built-in (https://apple.co/2yJJk7T). Many of these correspond to device user settings like accessibility, locale, calendar and color scheme.

Now the simulator displays the app in dark mode. Tap **Hit Me!**:

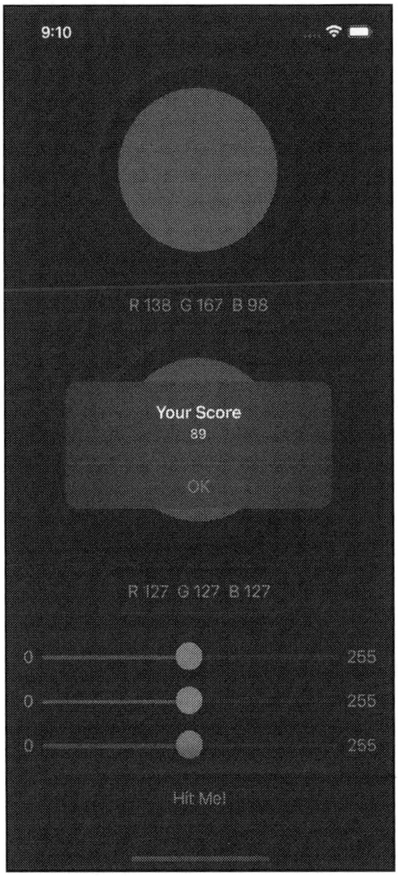

Simulator: Alert's color scheme is dark.

Dark mode, dark alert, just as it should be!

So if the preview doesn't show what you expect to see, try running it on a simulated or real device before you waste any time trying to fix a phantom problem.

Modifying Font

You need *one more thing* to put the finishing touch on the Figma design: All the text needs to be a little bigger and a little bolder.

In **ContentView**, add this modifier to the `VStack` that contains all the UI elements:

```
.font(.headline)
```

You set a *view-level environment value* for the `VStack` that affects all of its child views. So now *all* the text uses headline font size:

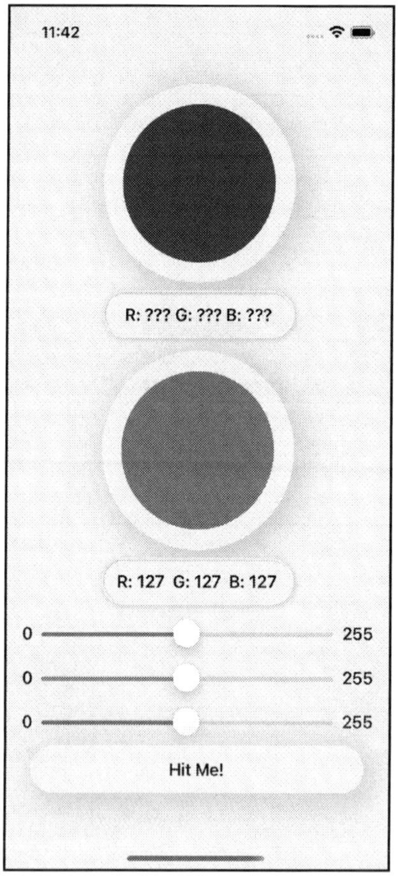

Headline font size applies to all the text.

You can override this overall `Text` modifier: Add this modifier to the `HStack` in the `ColorSlider` structure:

```
.font(.subheadline)
```

Now the slider labels use the smaller, not-bold font:

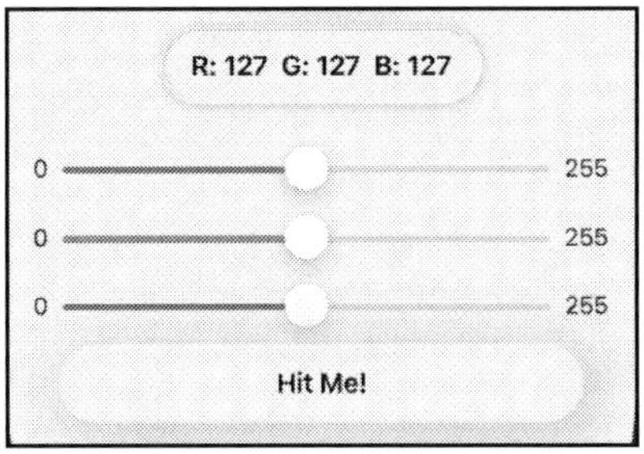

Slider labels use subheadline font size.

Adapting to the Device Screen Size

OK, time to see how this design looks on a smaller screen. By default, the preview uses the currently active scheme's run destination. To check how your design fits in a different screen, you can select a different run destination, or you can specify a `previewDevice` for `previews`.

Changing the Run Destination

Change the run destination to **iPhone 14 Pro Max**. Xcode takes a while to start up this simulator in the background, and eventually the preview updates to use this simulator:

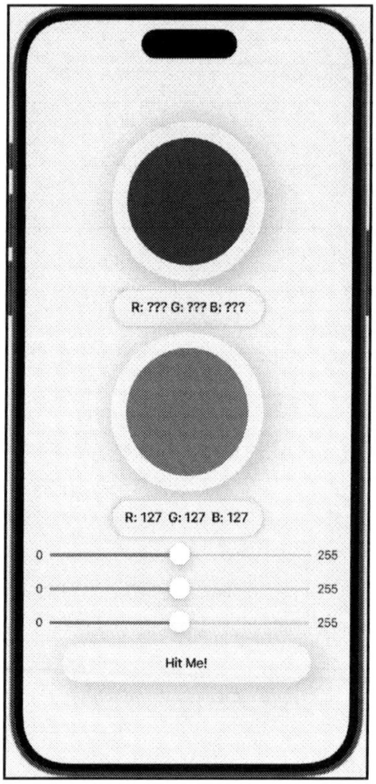

Run destination: iPhone 14 Pro Max

The height of this screen is 932 points, so there's more blank space. You could make the circles larger. But by how much?

Specifying a previewDevice

When you install Xcode 14, there might be only a few iPhone simulators in the destination run menu — mine lists only the iPhone 14 sizes and the SE 3rd generation. But Apple's support page lists all the iPhone models compatible with iOS 16 (https://apple.co/3l94uYm).

Check your destination run menu: Is **iPhone 8** listed? If not, select **Add Additional Simulators...**, type in *iPhone 8*, then click **Create**.

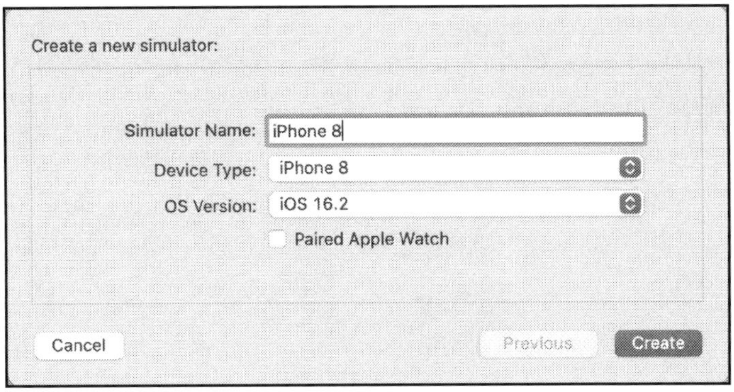

Add additional simulator: iPhone 8

Now, add this modifier to `ContentView(guess: RGB())`:

```
.previewDevice(
  PreviewDevice(
    rawValue: "iPhone 8"))
```

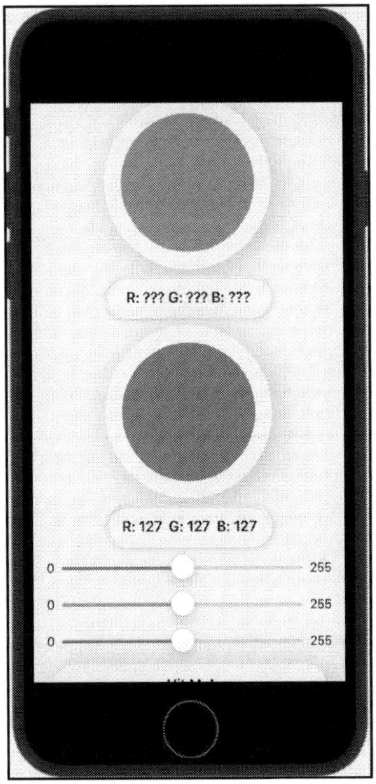

Preview device: iPhone 8

The height of an iPhone 8 screen is only 667 points, so the top circle is clipped, and only part of the button is visible. You can fix this problem by making the color circles smaller. But by how much?

Calculating Size Proportions

In **ContentView**, add these properties below the `@State` properties:

```
let circleSize: CGFloat = 0.275
let labelHeight: CGFloat = 0.06
let labelWidth: CGFloat = 0.53
let buttonWidth: CGFloat = 0.87
```

I worked out these proportions from the original 375x812 Figma design, after checking that the safe area height of an iPhone 13 mini is 728 points. These fractions yield close to the values you hard-wired into your code: `circleSize` * 728 = 200.2, `labelHeight` * 728 = 43.68, `labelWidth` * 375 = 198.75, `buttonWidth` * 375 = 326.25.

The button height is also `labelHeight`.

Now, if your code can detect the height and width of the screen size, it can calculate the right sizes for these elements.

Getting Screen Size From GeometryReader

This is what you'll do: Embed the `ZStack` in a `GeometryReader` to access its `size` and `frame` values.

> **Note**: Learn more about `GeometryReader` in **Chapter 18: "Drawing & Custom Graphics"**.

The **Command-click** menu has a handy catch-all item **Embed...**:

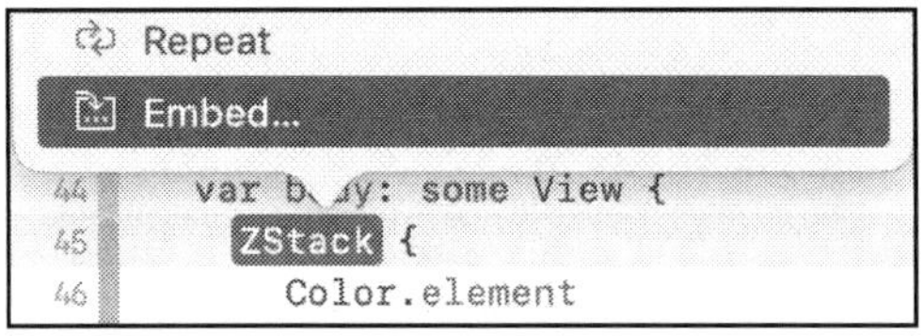

Embed ZStack in ... some container.

In **ContentView**, embed the top-level `ZStack` in this generic `Container`, then change `Container` to `GeometryReader`:

```
GeometryReader { proxy in
  ZStack {
```

`GeometryReader` provides you with a `GeometryProxy` object that has a `frame` method and `size` and `safeAreaInset` properties. You name this object `proxy`.

In the two `ColorCircle` initializers, replace `size: 200` with

```
size: proxy.size.height * circleSize
```

In the three `BevelText` initializers, replace `width: 200, height: 48` with

```
width: proxy.size.width * labelWidth,
height: proxy.size.height * labelHeight
```

Replace `(NeuButtonStyle(...))` with

```
(NeuButtonStyle(
  width: proxy.size.width * buttonWidth,
  height: proxy.size.height * labelHeight))
```

Next, you'll preview all three sizes — iPhone 8, iPhone 14 Pro and iPhone 14 Pro Max — to check everything now fits.

Previewing Different Devices

To see all three screen sizes at once, you *could* build and run the app on two simulators. Instead, you'll add previews to `ContentView_Previews`.

In `previews`, **Command-click** `ContentView` and select **Group**:

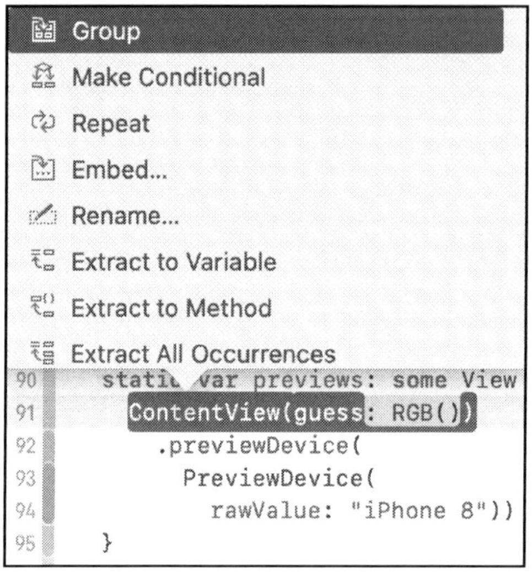

Embed ContentView in Group.

You've embedded `ContentView` in a `Group`.

Now, click anywhere in the `ContentView` line, then press **Command-D** to duplicate just this one line.

Next, *select* the second `ContentView` line and its `previewDevice` modifier, then press **Command-D** to duplicate these **two lines**. Add a line break to move the duplicate to its own line.

You now have three `ContentView` items in a `Group`:

```
Group {
  ContentView(guess: RGB())
  ContentView(guess: RGB())
    .previewDevice(
      PreviewDevice(
        rawValue: "iPhone 8"))
  ContentView(guess: RGB())
    .previewDevice(
      PreviewDevice(
        rawValue: "iPhone 8"))
}
```

And the canvas shows three preview buttons:

Three preview buttons

The **first preview button** shows the first `ContentView` in the `Group`: This is the currently selected run destination, which is still iPhone 14 Pro Max — the largest screen size.

Change the first `.previewDevice` modifier to display **iPhone 14 Pro**:

```
ContentView(guess: RGB())
  .previewDevice(
    PreviewDevice(
      rawValue: "iPhone 14 Pro"))
```

Click the **second preview button** to see the **iPhone 14 Pro** preview, then click the **third preview button** to view the **iPhone 8** preview:

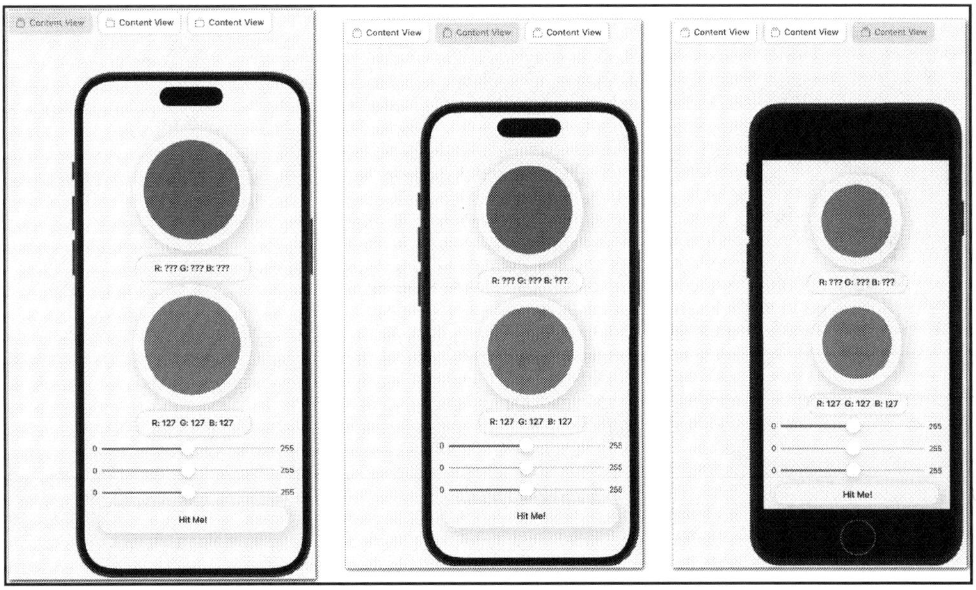

Previews of 14 Pro Max, 14 Pro and 8

It's a tighter fit on the smallest iPhone, but everything's visible, and the design elements have resized to fit.

Key Points

- SwiftUI views and modifiers help you quickly implement your design ideas.
- The **Library** contains a list of primitive views and a list of modifier methods. You can easily create custom views, button styles and modifiers.
- Neumorphism is the new skeumorphism. It's easy to implement with color sets and the SwiftUI `shadow` modifier.
- You can use `ZStack` to layer your UI elements. For example, lay down a background color and extend it into the safe area, then layer the rest of your UI onto this.
- Usually, you want to apply a modifier that changes the view's layout or position *before* you fill it or wrap a border around it.
- Some modifiers can be applied to all view types, while others can be applied only to specific view types, like `Text` or shapes. Not all `Text` modifiers return a `Text` view.
- Create a custom `ButtonStyle` by implementing its `makeBody(configuration:)` method. You'll lose some default behavior like label color and dimming when tapped.
- If the preview doesn't show what you expect to see, try running it on a simulated or real device before you waste any time trying to fix a phantom problem.
- Use `GeometryReader` to access the device's frame and size properties.

Chapter 4: Testing & Debugging

By Bill Morefield

Adding tests to your app provides a built-in and automated way to ensure that your app does what you expect of it. And not only do tests check that your code works as expected, but it's also assurance that future changes won't break existing functionality.

In this chapter, you'll learn how to implement UI tests in your SwiftUI app, and what to watch out for when testing your UI under this new paradigm.

Different Types of Tests

There are three types of tests that you'll use in your apps. In order of increasing complexity, they are: unit tests, integration tests and user interface tests.

The base of all testing, and the foundation of all other tests, is the **unit test**. Each unit test ensures that you get the expected output when a function processes a given input. Multiple unit tests may test the same piece of code, but each unit test itself should only focus on a single unit of code. A unit test should take milliseconds to execute. You'll run them often, so you want them to run fast.

The next test up the testing hierarchy is the **integration test**. Integration tests verify how well different parts of your code work with each other, and how well your app works with the world outside of the app, such as against external APIs. Integration tests are more complex than unit tests; they usually take longer to run, and as a result, you'll run them less often.

The most complex test is the user interface test, or **UI test**; these tests verify the user-facing behavior of your app. They simulate user interaction with the app and verify the user interface behaves as expected after responding to the interaction.

As you move up the testing hierarchy, each level of test checks a broader scope of action in the app. For example, a unit test would verify that the `calculateTotal()` method in your app returns the correct amount for an order. An integration test would verify that your app correctly determines that the items in the order are in stock. A UI test would verify that after adding an item to an order, the amount displayed to the user displays the correct value.

This chapter focuses on how to write UI tests for SwiftUI apps. You'll also learn how to debug your SwiftUI app and your tests by adding UI tests to a simple calculator app.

Debugging SwiftUI Apps

Begin by opening the starter project for this chapter, and build and run the app; it's a simple calculator. The app also supports Catalyst, so it works on iOS, iPadOS and the Mac. Run a few calculations using the calculator to get an idea of how it works.

Debugging SwiftUI takes a bit more forethought and planning than most tests because the user interface and code mix together under the SwiftUI paradigm. Since SwiftUI views are nothing but code, they execute just like any other code would.

Open **SwiftCalcView** and look for the following lines of code. They should be near line 138:

```
Button {
  if let val = Double(display) {
    memory += val
    display = ""
    pendingOperation = .none
  } else {
    // Add Bug Fix Here
    display = "Error"
  }
} label: {
  Text("M+")
}
.buttonStyle(CalcButtonStyle())
```

This code defines a button for the user interface. The first block defines the action to perform when the user taps the button. The next block defines what the button looks like in the view. Even though the two pieces of code are adjacent, they won't execute at the same time.

Setting Breakpoints

To stop code during the execution of an app, you set a breakpoint to tell the debugger to halt code execution when it reaches a particular line of code. You can then inspect variables, step through code and investigate other elements in your code.

To set a breakpoint, you put your cursor on the line in question and then press **Command** + \ or select **Debug ▸ Breakpoints ▸ Create Breakpoint at Current Line** from the menu. You can also click on the margin at the line where you want the breakpoint.

Use one of these methods to set two breakpoints; one on the button, and then one on the first line of code in the `action:` for the **M+** button as shown below:

```
Button {
  if let val = Double(display) {
    memory += val
    display = ""
    pendingOperation = .none
  } else {
    // Add Bug Fix Here
    display = "Error"
  }
} label: {
  Text("M+")
}
.buttonStyle(CalcButtonStyle())
```

App breakpoints

> **Note**: Prior to Xcode 13, you could run the preview in debug mode. Apple removed this feature in Xcode 13 and you must run the app in the simulator or a device to debug your app's views. Breakpoints will be ignored by the preview.

Run your app. After a moment, the app reaches the breakpoint at the `Text` control for the button. When it reaches the breakpoint for the `Text()`, execution pauses just as it would with any other code.

When execution reaches a breakpoint, the app pauses and Xcode returns control to you. At the bottom of the Xcode window, you'll see the **Debug Area** consisting of two windows below the code editor. If you don't see the Debug Area, go to **View ▸ Debug Area ▸ Show Debug Area** or press **Shift + Command + Y** to toggle the Debug Area.

The left pane of the Debug Area contains the **Variables View**. It shows you the current status and value of active variables in your app. The right pane contains an interactive Console, the most complex and powerful tool for debugging in Xcode.

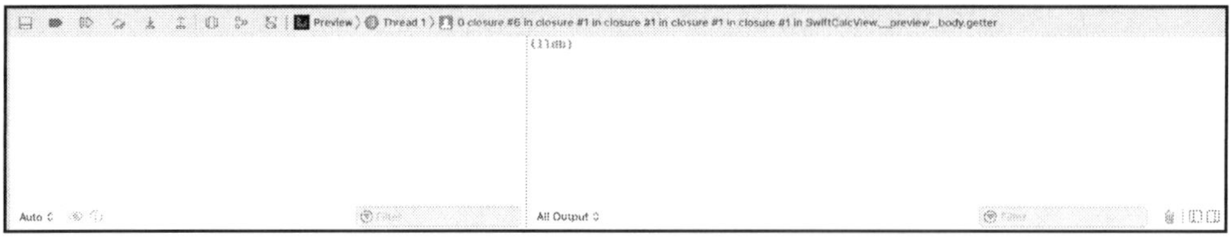

Variables Console

Using breakpoints does more than halt code; it can also tell you whether or not the execution of the app actually reached this piece of code. If a breakpoint doesn't trigger, then you know something caused the app to skip the code.

The mixing of code and UI elements in SwiftUI can be confusing, but breakpoints can help you make sense of what is executing and when. If you add a breakpoint and it never breaks, then you know that the execution never reached the declaration and the interface will not contain the element. If your breakpoint does get hit, you can investigate the state of the app at that point.

Exploring Breakpoint Control

When stopped at a breakpoint, you'll see a toolbar between the code editor and debug area. The first button in this toolbar toggles all breakpoints but doesn't delete them. The second button continues the execution of the app. You can also select **Debug ▸ Continue** in the menu to continue app execution.

The next three buttons allow you to step through your code. Clicking the first executes the current line of code, including any method or function calls. The second button also executes the current line of code, but if there is a method call, it pauses at the first line of code inside that method or function. The final button executes code through to the end of the current method or function.

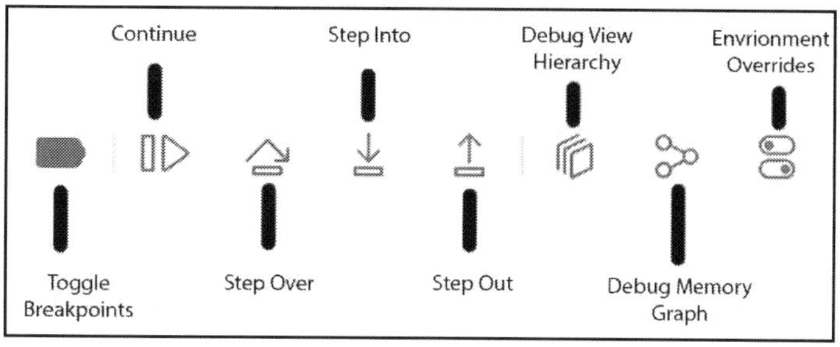

Debug bar

The next three buttons provide more insight into your app. The first, **Debug View Hierarchy**, shows a 3d rendering of your app views you can manipulate. The second button debugs the memory graph. This will show you the memory regions your app is using and the size of each region. The final button allows you to override environment settings such as dynamic type and apply accessibility options.

Continue execution of the app by using either the toolbar button or the menu. After another short pause, you'll see the view appear.

Tap the **M+** button on the preview to see your breakpoint trigger. When it does, the code pauses at the breakpoint on the first line of the `Button`'s action block.

At the **(lldb)** prompt in the console, execute the following:

```
po _memory
```

The **po** command in the console lets you examine the state of an object. Note the underscore at the start of the variable name. For now, just know that within a SwiftUI view you will need to prefix the name of the variable with an underscore. You'll see the result shows the contents of the `memory` state variable:

```
(lldb) po _memory
▿ State<Double>
  - _value : 0.0
  ▿ _location : Optional<AnyLocation<Double>>
    ▿ some : <StoredLocation<Double>: 0x600002fbf1e0>
```

Debugger output

Adding UI Tests

There's a bug in this code that you'll notice when you **Continue**. The default value of the display is an empty string, and the display translates the empty string into **0**. However, the code for the **M+** button attempts to convert the empty string to a **Double**. When that conversion fails, the value **Error** appears to the user.

Even if you don't write a test for every case in your app, it's a beneficial practice to create tests when you find bugs. Creating a test ensures that you have, in fact, fixed the bug. It also provides early notice if this bug were to reappear in the future. In the next section, you're going to write a UI test for this bug.

> **Note**: Delete the breakpoints you just created. You can do so by right-clicking on the breakpoint and choosing **Delete Breakpoint**. You can disable the breakpoints by clicking on them. They should turn light blue. Press them again whenever you want to reactivate them.

In the starter project, go to **File ▸ New ▸ Target...**. Select **iOS** and scroll down to find the **Test** section. Click **UI Testing Bundle** and click **Next**.

Xcode suggests a name for the test bundle that combines the name of the project and the type of test. Accept the suggestion of **SwiftCalcUITests**. Select **SwiftCalc** as the **Project** and **Target to be Tested**. Finally, click **Finish**.

In the Project navigator, you'll see a new group named **SwiftCalcUITests**. This new target contains the framework where you build your UI tests; expand the group and open **SwiftCalcUITests**.

You'll see the file starts by importing `XCTest`. The `XCTest` framework contains Apple's default testing libraries. You'll also see the test class inherits from `XCTestCase`, from which all test classes inherit their behavior.

You'll also see four default methods provided in the Xcode template. The first two methods are an important part of your test process. The test process calls `setUpWithError()` before each test method in the class, and then calls `tearDownWithError()` after each test method completes.

Remember: a test should verify that a known set of inputs results in an expected set of outputs. You use `setUpWithError()` to ensure your app is in this known state before each test method begins. You use `tearDownWithError()` to clean up after each test so that you're back to a known starting condition for the next test.

Note the following line in `setUpWithError()`:

```
continueAfterFailure = false
```

This line stops testing if a failure occurs. Setting this value to `false` stops the test process after the first failure. Given the nature of UI testing, you will almost always end up in an unknown state when a test fails. Rather than continue what are often long-running tests for very little and potentially incorrect information, you should stop and fix the problem now.

In this chapter, you won't have any other setup or cleanup work to perform for your tests.

The third method in the template is `testExample()`, which contains a sample test. You'll also see the method has a small gray diamond next to its name in place of the line number; this means that Xcode recognizes it as a test, but the test hasn't been run yet. Once the test runs, the diamond will change to a green checkmark, if the test passes, or to a white **X** on a red background after completion, if the test fails.

Test names *must* begin with **test**. If not, the testing framework ignores the method and will not execute it when testing. For example, the framework ignores a method named `myCoolTest()`, but it will execute `testMyCoolCode()`.

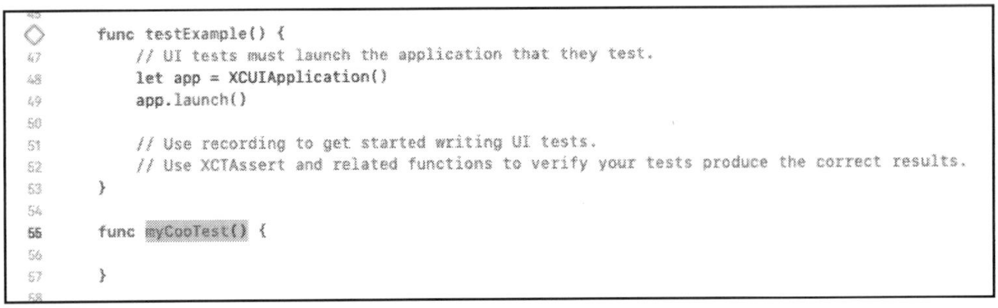

Test names must start with 'test'. Note the lack of a diamond next to myCooltest()

Creating a UI Test

Proper test names should be precise and clear about what the test validates since an app can end up with a large number of tests. Clear names make it easy to understand what failed. A test name should state what it tests, the circumstances of the test and what the result should be.

Rename `testExample()` to `testPressMemoryPlusAtAppStartShowZeroInDisplay()`. Does that feel really long? Test names are not the place or time for brevity; the name should clearly provide all three elements at a glance.

A UI test begins with the app in the "just started" state, so you can write each test as though the app has just started. Note that this doesn't mean the app state is reset each run. You use the `setUpWithError()` and `tearDownWithError()` methods to ensure your app is in a particular known state before each test and to clean up any changes made during the test. If you expect settings, data, configuration, location or other information to be present at the time the test is run, then you must set those up.

Clear the comments after the `app.launch()` command, and add a breakpoint at `app.launch()` line in the test.

There are several ways to start UI tests. First, you can go to the **Test Navigator** by pressing **Command + 6** in Xcode. You'll see your test along with the default `testLaunchPerformance()` test. Hover your mouse over the gray diamond to the left of the function name, and you'll see a Play button.

If you hover over the name of the class or the testing framework either in the Test Navigator or the source code, a similar Play button appears that will start a group of tests to run in sequence.

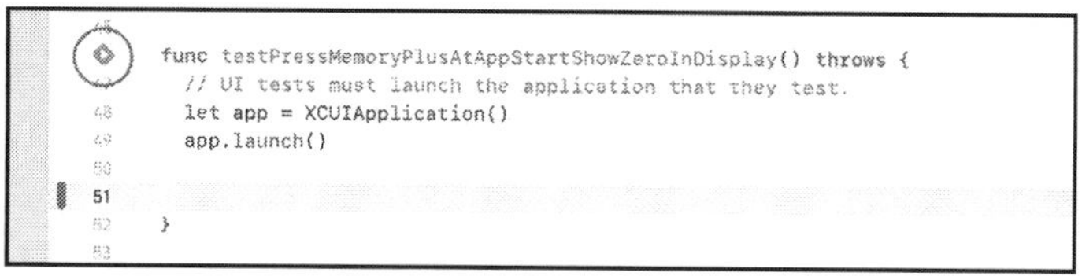

Run test icon

This test isn't complete, as it doesn't test anything. This is a good time to run it and learn a bit about how a test runs. For now, use either method to start your `testPressMemoryPlusAtAppStartShowZeroInDisplay()` test.

Tests are Swift code, so you can debug tests just like you debug your app! You'll sometimes need to determine why a test doesn't behave as expected. When the test reaches the breakpoint, you'll see execution stop, just as your breakpoint would behave in any other code.

The main element you'll want to explore is the `app` element where you placed the breakpoint. Step over the command to launch the app using the toolbar button, pressing **F6** or selecting **Debug ▸ Step Over** in the menu. In the simulator, you'll see the app launch. Once you have the **(lldb)** prompt in the console, enter `po app`.

You'll see output similar to the following:

```
Attributes: Application, pid: 99972, label: 'SwiftCalc'
Element subtree:
 →Application, 0x6000038c96c0, pid: 99972, label: 'SwiftCalc'
    Window (Main), 0x6000038c9500, {{0.0, 0.0}, {414.0, 896.0}}
      Other, 0x6000038cc0e0, {{0.0, 0.0}, {414.0, 896.0}}
        Other, 0x6000038cc1c0, {{0.0, 0.0}, {414.0, 896.0}}
          Other, 0x6000038cc2a0, {{0.0, 0.0}, {414.0, 896.0}}
            Other, 0x6000038f0000, {{0.0, 48.0}, {414.0, 347.0}}
              StaticText, 0x6000038f0d20, {{368.5, 64.0}, {17.5, 33.5}}, label: '0'
              Other, 0x6000038f0e00, {{0.0, 121.5}, {414.0, 265.0}}
                Button, 0x6000038f0ee0, {{74.5, 121.5}, {45.0, 45.0}}, label: 'MC'
                Button, 0x6000038f0fc0, {{129.5, 121.5}, {45.0, 45.0}}, label: 'MR'
                Button, 0x6000038f10a0, {{184.5, 121.5}, {45.0, 45.0}}, label: 'M+'
                Button, 0x6000038f1180, {{239.5, 121.5}, {45.0, 45.0}}, label: 'C'
                Button, 0x6000038c9340, {{294.5, 121.5}, {45.0, 45.0}}, label: 'AC'
                Button, 0x6000038c9420, {{74.5, 176.5}, {45.0, 45.0}}, label: '√'
                Button, 0x6000038c9260, {{129.5, 176.5}, {45.0, 45.0}}, label: '7'
                Button, 0x6000038c9180, {{184.5, 176.5}, {45.0, 45.0}}, label: '8'
                Button, 0x6000038c90a0, {{239.5, 176.5}, {45.0, 45.0}}, label: '9'
                Button, 0x6000038c8fc0, {{294.5, 176.5}, {45.0, 45.0}}, label: '÷'
                Button, 0x6000038c97a0, {{74.5, 231.5}, {45.0, 45.0}}, label: 'π'
                Button, 0x6000038c9880, {{129.5, 231.5}, {45.0, 45.0}}, label: '4'
```

po app command

You're examining the app object, which you declared as an `XCUIApplication`, a subclass of `XCUIElement`. You'll be working with this object in all of your UI tests.

The app object contains a tree that begins with the application and continues through all of the UI elements in your app. Each of these elements is also of type `XCUIElement`. You'll access the UI elements in your app by running filter queries against the app object to select items in the tree that you see.

Next, you'll see how to run a query to find buttons in the app.

Accessing UI Elements

Add the following code to the end of the test method:

```
let memoryButton = app.buttons["M+"]
memoryButton.tap()
```

`XCUIApplication` contains a set of elements for each type of user interface object. This query first filters for only `.buttons` in the app. It then filters to the element which has a label of **M+**.

SwiftUI apps render to the native elements of the platform; they're not new components. Even though SwiftUI provides a new way to define an interface, it still uses the existing elements of the platform. A SwiftUI `Button` becomes a `UIButton` on iOS and a `NSButton` on macOS. In this app, the filter matches the label you saw in the output from **`po app`**.

```
Button, 0x600002498540, {{184.5, 102.5}, {45.0, 45.0}}, label:
'M+'
```

Once you have the button object, you call `tap()` on the button. This method simulates someone tapping on the button. Delete the breakpoint on the app launch, and re-run the test.

```
func testPressMemoryPlusAtAppStartShowZeroInDisplay() {
    // UI tests must launch the application that they test.
    let app = XCUIApplication()
    app.launch()

    let memoryButton = app.buttons["M+"]
    memoryButton.tap()
}
```

First test run

You'll see the app start and run in the simulator as the test runs. If you watch the simulator, you'll see the display of the calculator show **Error** just as it did when you ran it manually. Once the tests are done, the app will stop. You'll see the gray diamond changes into a green checkmark both next to the function and in the Test Navigator.

The green check signifies a passed test. In this case, the test didn't check anything. The framework treats a test that doesn't fail as a passing test.

In a UI test, the known set of inputs to your test is the set of interactions with the app. Here you performed an interaction by tapping the **M+** button, so now you need to check the result. In the next section, you'll see how to get the value from a control.

Reading the User Interface

You found the **M+** button by matching the label of the button. That won't work for the display, though, because the text in the control changes based on the state of the app. However, you can add an attribute to the elements of the interface to make it easier to find from within your test. Open **DisplayView**. In the view, look for the **two** comments `// Add display identifier` and replace both with the following line:

```
.accessibilityIdentifier("display")
```

This method sets the `accessibilityIdentifer` for the resulting UI element. Despite the name, **VoiceOver** doesn't read the `accessibilityIdentifer` attribute; this simply provides a way to give a UI element a constant identifier for testing. If you don't provide this identifier for an element, it will generally be the same as the `label` for the control as it was with the **M+** button.

Go back to **SwiftCalcUITests**. Add the following code at the end of `testPressMemoryPlusAtAppStartShowZeroInDisplay()`:

```
// 1
let display = app.staticTexts["display"]
// 2
let displayText = display.label
// 3
XCTAssert(displayText == "0")
```

You've written your first real test! Here's what each step does:

1. You use the `accessibility(identifier:)` you added to find the display element in your app.
2. The result of step 1 is an `XCUIElement`, as are most UI elements in a UI test. You want to investigate the `label` property of the element which contains the text of the label.
3. You use an assertion to verify the label matches the expected result. All testing assertions begin with the prefix `XCT` — a holdover from Objective-C naming conventions. In each test, you perform one or more assertions that determine if the test passes or fails.

In this case, you are checking that the text for display is the string "0". You already know the result will be a failing test, but still, run the completed test to see what happens. You'll get the expected failure and see a white **X** on red.

```
func testPressMemoryPlusAtAppStartShowZeroInDisplay() {
    // UI tests must launch the application that they test.
    let app = XCUIApplication()
    app.launch()

    let memoryButton = app.buttons["M+"]
    memoryButton.tap()
    // 1
    let display = app.staticTexts["display"]
    // 2
    let displayText = display.label
    // 3
    XCTAssert(displayText == "0")
}
```

Failed first test

Now that you have a test in place, you can fix the bug!

Fixing the Bug

Open **SwiftCalcView**, find the comment in the action for the **M+** button that reads `// Add Bug Fix Here`, and change the next line to read:

```
display = ""
```

Re-run the test. You'll see that it passes.

```
func testPressMemoryPlusAtAppStartShowZeroInDisplay() {
    // UI tests must launch the application that they test.
    let app = XCUIApplication()
    app.launch()

    let memoryButton = app.buttons["M+"]
    memoryButton.tap()
    // 1
    let display = app.staticTexts["display"]
    // 2
    let displayText = display.label
    // 3
    XCTAssert(displayText == "0")
}
```

First passing test

You may be wondering why you went through the extra effort: You changed one line of code to fix the bug, but you added another framework to your app and had to write five lines of code to create the test.

Although this may feel like a lot of work to prove that you've fixed a tiny issue, you'll find this pattern of writing a failing test, fixing the bug and then verifying that the test passes, to be a useful pattern. Taking an existing app without tests, and adding a test each time you fix a bug, quickly builds a useful set of tests for now, and more importantly, for the future.

Adding More Complex Tests

Ideally, you would be building out your UI tests at the same time as you built out your UI. This way, as your UI becomes more fleshed out, your test suite will expand along with it. However, with the realities of modern development, you'll usually be adding tests after the application already exists.

Add a more complex test that verifies adding two single-digit numbers gives the correct sum. Open **SwiftCalcUITests** and add the following test at the end of the class:

```
func testAddingTwoDigits() {
  let app = XCUIApplication()
  app.launch()

  let threeButton = app.buttons["3"]
  threeButton.tap()

  let addButton = app.buttons["+"]
  addButton.tap()

  let fiveButton = app.buttons["5"]
  fiveButton.tap()

  let equalButton = app.buttons["="]
  equalButton.tap()

  let display = app.staticTexts["display"]
  let displayText = display.label
  XCTAssert(displayText == "8")
}
```

When you run the test, you might not expect it to fail. Three plus five does equal eight, right? Take a moment to see if you can figure out why before continuing.

Your test compares the label of the display to the string **8**. Place a breakpoint at `XCTAssert` statement and rerun the test. Wait until execution stops at the breakpoint. At the console prompt enter **`po displayText`**.

You'll see the text of the display reads **8.0**, not **8**. A UI test focuses on the user interface and not on the behind-the-scenes elements. A unit test, in contrast, would check that the code properly calculated **3 + 5 = 8**. The UI test should verify what the user sees when performing this calculation.

Change the final line of the test to:

```
XCTAssert(displayText == "8.0")
```

Re-run the test, and you'll see it passes now.

```
func testAddingTwoDigits() {
  let app = XCUIApplication()
  app.launch()

  let threeButton = app.buttons["3"]
  threeButton.tap()

  let addButton = app.buttons["+"]
  addButton.tap()

  let fiveButton = app.buttons["5"]
  fiveButton.tap()

  let equalButton = app.buttons["="]
  equalButton.tap()

  let display = app.staticTexts["display"]
  let displayText = display.label
  XCTAssert(displayText == "8.0")
}
```

Passing test

`XCTAssert()` evaluates a condition and fails if it's not true. If you had used the more specific `XCTAssertEqual(displayText, "8")` for the initial assertion, it would have provided the information you discovered using the debugger in the failure message. You used `XCTAssert()` to explore debugging a failed test. Change your test to `XCTAssertEqual(displayText, "8.0")` and verify it still passes.

Next, you'll make a change to the user interface, and, because you want to form good testing habits, you'll add a test to verify the change.

Simulating User Interaction

You'll first add a gesture so that swiping the memory display to the left clears it. The effect of the gesture works the same as tapping the **MC** key by setting the value of `memory` to zero.

Open **MemoryView**. At the top of the `body` definition, right before `HStack`, add a gesture:

```
let memorySwipe = DragGesture(minimumDistance: 20)
  .onEnded { _ in
```

```
    memory = 0.0
  }
```

You can add this gesture to the memory display. Find the text `// Add gesture here` and replace it with:

```
.gesture(memorySwipe)
```

Like with main display, you will also add an identifier to the memory display. Add the following line below `Text("\(memory)")`:

```
.accessibilityIdentifier("memoryDisplay")
```

Build and run the app; type in a few digits and tap **M+** to store the value in memory. The memory display appears and shows the stored digits. Swipe the memory display to the left, and verify the display clears.

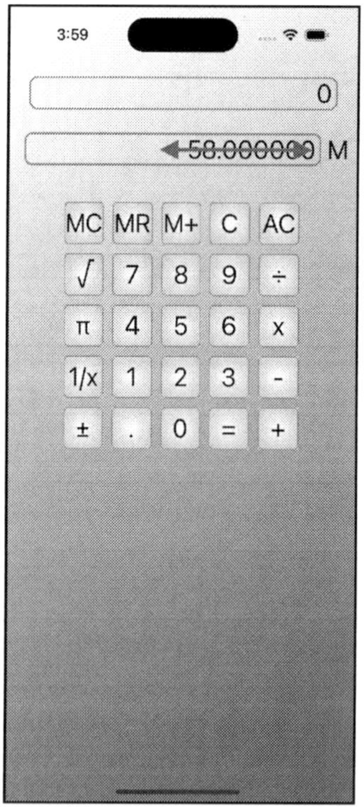

Swipe app

Now, because you're practicing good development and testing habits, you'll add a UI test to verify this behavior. The steps of the test replicate the actions you just performed manually.

Open **SwiftCalcUITests** and add the following code after the existing tests:

```
func testSwipeToClearMemory() {
  let app = XCUIApplication()
  app.launch()

  let threeButton = app.buttons["3"]
  threeButton.tap()
  let fiveButton = app.buttons["5"]
  fiveButton.tap()

  let memoryButton = app.buttons["M+"]
  memoryButton.tap()

  let memoryDisplay = app.staticTexts["memoryDisplay"]
  // 1
  XCTAssert(memoryDisplay.exists)
  // 2
  memoryDisplay.swipeLeft()
  // 3
  XCTAssertFalse(memoryDisplay.exists)
}
```

You've seen most of this code before. Here's what the new code does:

1. The `exists` property on an `XCUIElement` is `true` when the element exists. If the memory display were not visible, then this assert would fail.

2. The `swipeLeft()` method produces a swipe action to the left on the calling element. There are additional methods for `swipeRight()`, `swipeUp()` and `swipeDown()`.

3. The `XCTAssertFalse()` test acts as an opposite for `XCTAssert`. It succeeds when the checked value is `false` instead of `true`. The swipe should set `memory` to zero after the gesture, and the action should hide the memory display, wiping it out of existence.

Run the test, and you'll see it confirms that your UI works as expected.

There are many testing elements beyond those discussed in this chapter. Some of the common attributes and methods that you haven't had a chance to use in this chapter are:

- **.isHittable**: An element is hittable if the element exists and the user can click, tap or press it at its current location. An offscreen element exists but is not hittable.

- **.typeText()**: This method acts as though the user types the text into the calling control.

- **.press(forDuration:)**: This allows you to perform a one-finger touch for a specified amount of time.
- **.press(forDuration:thenDragTo:)**: The `swipe` methods provide no guarantee of the velocity of the gesture. You can use this method to perform a more precise drag action.
- **.waitForExistence()**: Useful to pause when an element may not appear on the screen immediately.

You'll find a complete list of methods and properties in Apple's documentation at https://developer.apple.com/documentation/xctest/xcuielement.

Testing Multiple Platforms

Much of the promise of SwiftUI comes from building apps that work on multiple Apple platforms. Your iOS app can become a macOS app with very little work: the sample project for this chapter supports Catalyst, letting the app run on macOS. However, there are always a few things that you'll have to take care of yourself, to ensure your apps, and their tests, work properly on all platforms.

In Xcode, change the target device for the app to **My Mac (Mac Catalyst)**. In the project settings, select the **SwiftCalc** target. Choose **Signing and Capabilities**, set **Team** and verify that **Signing Certificate** is set to **Sign to Run Locally**. Now build and run the app to see it run for macOS.

You will learn about using SwiftUI with different operating systems in **Chapter 22: "Building a Mac App"**. Since, as you expect, running on different platforms may require tweaks to the user interface, testing the UI on various operating systems will require different tests. Some UI actions translate directly; for instance, tapping a button on an iOS device works just like clicking your mouse on a button would on macOS.

With the target device still set to **My Mac (Mac Catalyst)**, build and run your tests. You'll see `XCTAssertFalse(memoryDisplay.exists)` now fails. That's because there's no equivalent to a `.swipeLeft()` action in macOS. Earlier versions of Xcode would give you a compilation error: "Value of type 'XCUIElement' has no member 'swipeLeft'" that made this clear.

The solution lies in Xcode's conditional compilation blocks. These blocks tell Xcode to only compile the wrapped code when one or more of the conditions are true at compile time. A block begins with `#if` followed by a test. You can optionally use `#elseif` and `#else` as with traditional `if` statements, and you end the block with `#endif`.

You want to exclude the failing test when testing the app under Catalyst. Wrap the `testSwipeToClearMemory()` test inside a `targetEnvironment` check to exclude tests from Catalyst:

```
#if !targetEnvironment(macCatalyst)
  // Test to exclude
#endif
```

You can also specify the operating system as a condition. The operating system can be any one of `macOS`, `iOS`, `watchOS`, `tvOS` or `Linux`. For example, to exclude tests from watchOS, wrap the tests with a similar check that excludes watchOS:

```
#if !os(watchOS)
  // Your XCTest code
#endif
```

A best practice when designing UI tests for cross-platform apps is to keep tests for specific operating systems together in a single test class. Use conditional compilation wrappers to isolate the code to compile only under the target platform and operating system.

Change your target device back to an iOS device before continuing to the next section.

Debugging Views and State Changes

When debugging a SwiftUI app, you'll often run into situations where performance suffers because a view redraws more often than expected. Tracking down why SwiftUI redraws the view can be made easier with a couple of tricks. You can use a technique from Peter Steinberger (https://gist.github.com/steipete/579edd8bd8b25dc8a89b546b54d9222f) to identify when a view redraws that assigns a random background color to the view. Open **DisplayView** and add the following code after the import statement:

```
extension Color {
  // Return a random color
```

```
  static var random: Color {
    return Color(
      red: .random(in: 0...1),
      green: .random(in: 0...1),
      blue: .random(in: 0...1)
    )
  }
}
```

This code creates an extension for the `Color` type named `random`. Each time called, it will present a new random color. When you apply it to a view, each time the view redraws, it will receive a new background color making it easy to identify redrawn views visually.

To use the extension, apply to a view as you would with any other color. At the end of the `HStack` for the view, add the following code:

```
.background(Color.random)
```

Run the app and tap a few numbers buttons to change the display. You'll see the background color of the `DisplayView` change to a random color each time you tap a button.

Random background color when view changes

While this can show you what view changes, it doesn't tell you why. SwiftUI 3.0 introduced a new method to help solve that problem. You can use the new `Self._printChanges()` method to determine what caused the view to redraw. Open **DisplayView** and add the following code after the `var body: some View {` declaring the `body` property for the view:

```
let _ = Self._printChanges()
```

This odd-looking code tells SwiftUI to identify the change that led to SwiftUI deciding to redraw the view. SwiftUI will display the name of the view and the properties that changed each time it draws the view. Notice that the method begins with an underscore hinting that you should only use this when debugging and remove it from a finished app. You must place it inside the `body` property of the view you want to monitor.

Run the app and again type a few buttons. You'll still see the background color of the display change with each tap. In the interactive console, you'll see a message stating the view that changed along with the property or properties that caused the view to redraw with each tap.

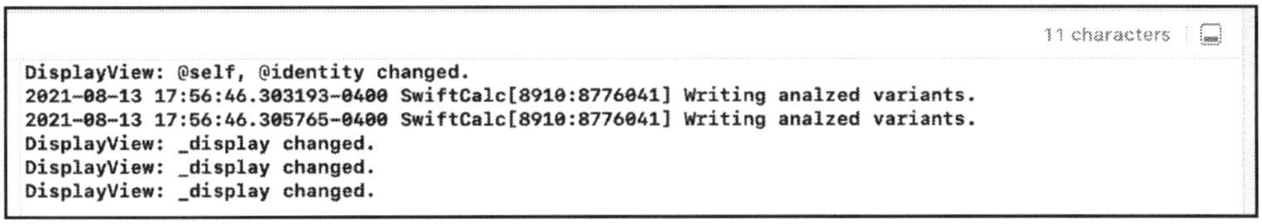

Displaying properties that cause view to redraw

Don't forget to take these out before you ship your app.

Challenge

Challenge: Add Swipe Gesture

As noted earlier, the swipe gesture to clear the memory doesn't work under Catalyst. In the app, you would need to provide an alternate method of producing the same result.

For the Catalyst version of this app, add a double-tap gesture to the memory display to accomplish the same result as the swipe gesture. Update `testSwipeToClearMemory()` to check the functionality appropriately on each environment.

Challenge Solution

You should begin by adding the new double-tap gesture. Change the current gesture definition of `memorySwipe` in **MemoryView** to:

```
#if targetEnvironment(macCatalyst)
let doubleTap = TapGesture(count: 2)
  .onEnded { _ in
    self.memory = 0.0
  }
#else
let memorySwipe = DragGesture(minimumDistance: 20)
  .onEnded { _ in
    self.memory = 0.0
  }
#endif
```

This keeps the current swipe gesture on phones and tablets but creates a tap gesture that expects two taps on Catalyst.

Now update the memory display to similarly use the correct gesture for each environment:

```
#if targetEnvironment(macCatalyst)
Text("\(memory)")
  .accessibility(identifier: "memoryDisplay")
  .padding(.horizontal, 5)
  .frame(
    width: geometry.size.width * 0.85,
    alignment: .trailing
  )
  .overlay(
```

```
    RoundedRectangle(cornerRadius: 8)
      .stroke(lineWidth: 2)
      .foregroundColor(Color.gray)
  )
  // Add gesture here
  .gesture(doubleTap)
#else
Text("\(memory)")
  .accessibility(identifier: "memoryDisplay")
  .padding(.horizontal, 5)
  .frame(
    width: geometry.size.width * 0.85,
    alignment: .trailing
  )
  .overlay(
    RoundedRectangle(cornerRadius: 8)
      .stroke(lineWidth: 2)
      .foregroundColor(Color.gray)
  )
  // Add gesture here
  .gesture(memorySwipe)
#endif
```

SwiftUI doesn't support putting a `targetEnvironment()` condition within the modifiers to a view. That means you have to place the view twice, changing the desired gesture in each. Normally, you would extract the view into a subview to reduce the amount of code.

Lastly, remove any current target restrictions on the `testSwipeToClearMemory()` test and replace `memoryDisplay.swipeLeft()` in the method with:

```
#if targetEnvironment(macCatalyst)
memoryDisplay.doubleTap()
#else
memoryDisplay.swipeLeft()
#endif
```

This will call the appropriate UI gesture on each environment. Run your test on both **My Mac** and the **iOS Simulator** to validate your changes.

Key Points

- Building and debugging tests require a bit more attention due to the combination of code and user interface elements in SwiftUI.
- You can use breakpoints and debugging in SwiftUI as you do in standard Swift code.
- Tests automate checking the behavior of your code. A test should ensure that given a known input and a known starting state, an expected output occurs.
- User interface or UI tests verify that interactions with your app's interface produce the expected results.
- Add an `accessibilityIdentifer` to elements that do not have static text for their label to improve location for testing.
- You find all user interface elements from the `XCUIApplication` element used to launch the app in the test.
- Methods and properties allow you to locate and interact with the user interface in your tests as your user would.
- Different platforms often need different user interface tests. Use conditional compilation to match tests to the platform and operating system.
- You can use `Self._printChanges()` to view the state change that causes the view to redraw.

Where to Go From Here?

- This chapter provided an introduction to testing and debugging your SwiftUI projects. Your starting point to go more in-depth should be Apple's documentation on XCTest at https://developer.apple.com/documentation/xctest.
- Our book *iOS Test-Driven Development by Tutorials* provides a more in-depth look at testing iOS apps and test-driven development. You can find that book here: https://www.kodeco.com/books/ios-test-driven-development-by-tutorials.
- You'll also find more about testing in the WWDC 2019 video **Testing in Xcode** at https://developer.apple.com/videos/play/wwdc2019/413/.
- You'll find a lot more information about the Xcode debugger and using it in our deep-dive book *Advanced Apple Debugging & Reverse Engineering*, available here: https://www.kodeco.com/books/advanced-apple-debugging-reverse-engineering.
- Apple often releases new videos on the changes related to debugging each year at WWDC. For 2019, there's a video dedicated to Debugging in Xcode 11 at https://developer.apple.com/videos/play/wwdc2019/412/.
- For 2021, there's a video on breakpoint improvements at https://developer.apple.com/videos/play/wwdc2021/10209/.
- Once you're ready to go deeper into debugging, you'll also want to watch **LLDB: Beyond "po"** at https://developer.apple.com/videos/play/wwdc2019/429/.
- For more debugging memory use see: https://developer.apple.com/documentation/xcode/gathering-information-about-memory-use.

Section II: Building Blocks of SwiftUI

Build on what you have learned in Section I to begin using SwiftUI in more complex and advanced apps.

Chapter 5: Intro to Controls: Text & Image

By Antonio Bello

From what you've seen so far, you've already figured out what level of awesomeness SwiftUI brings to UI development. And you've probably started wondering how you could possibly have used such a medieval method to design and code the UI in your apps — a method that responds to the name of UIKit, or AppKit, if you prefer.

Armored Knights

In the previous chapters, you've only scratched the surface of SwiftUI and learned how to create some basic UI. Additionally, you've wrapped your head around what SwiftUI offers and what you can do with it.

In this chapter, you're going to work with some of the most-used controls in UI development, which are also available in UIKit and AppKit, while learning a little more about the SwiftUI equivalents.

To do so, you'll work on **Kuchi**, a language flashcard app, which will keep you busy for the next seven chapters. Enjoy!

Getting Started

First, open the starter project for this chapter, and you'll see that it's quite empty. There's almost no user interface; only some resources and support files. If you build and run, all you'll get is a blank view.

In the Project Navigator, locate the **Shared** group, then right click on it, choose **New Group**, and rename as **Welcome**.

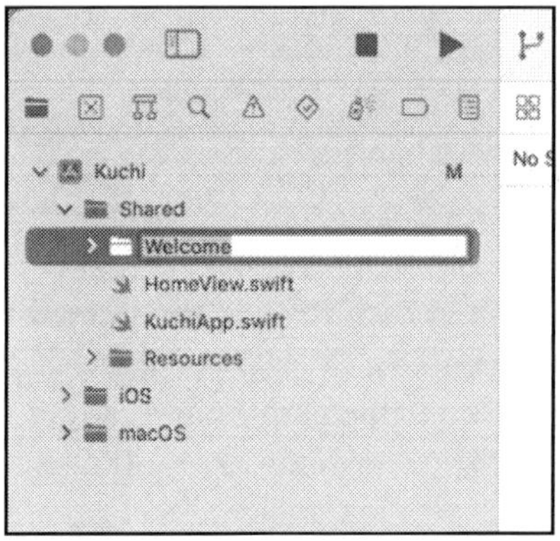

Create the Welcome group

Next right-click on it, and choose **New File**.

In the popup that comes next, choose **SwiftUI View**, then click **Next**.

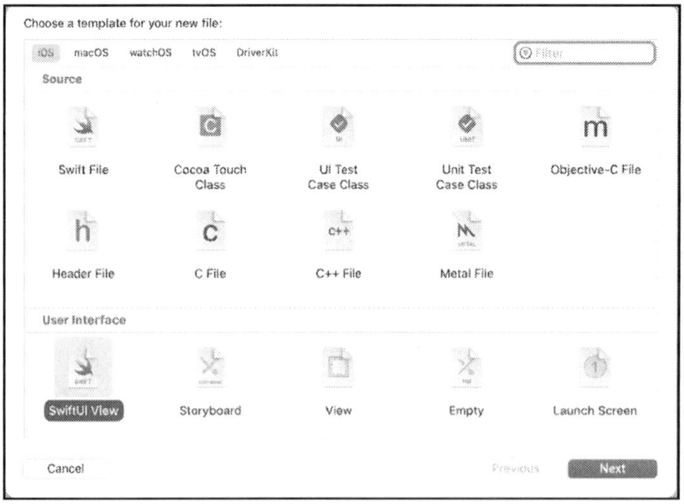

Select SwiftUI View

Then type **WelcomeView** in the **Save As** field, ensure that both *iOS and macOS* targets are selected, and click on **Create**. You now have a blank new view to start with.

Changing the Root View

Before doing anything, you need to configure the app to use the new `WelcomeView` as the starting view. Open **KuchiApp.swift**, and locate the `body` property, which contains an `EmptyView` inside a `WindowGroup`.

```
var body: some Scene {
  WindowGroup {
    EmptyView()
  }
}
```

This code determines the view that's created and displayed when the app is launched. The view currently created is `EmptyView`, which is... well, an empty view: the simplest possible view you could possibly use. Replace it with an instance of the new view you've just created, `WelcomeView`:

```
WindowGroup {
  WelcomeView()
}
```

Now, if you compile and run, when the app starts, `WelcomeView` will be your first view:

Hello World

While you're on it, also replace `EmptyView` in the preview, which looks like:

```
struct KuchiApp_Previews: PreviewProvider {
  static var previews: some View {
    EmptyView()
  }
}
```

And, after the replacement, must look like:

```
struct KuchiApp_Previews: PreviewProvider {
  static var previews: some View {
    WelcomeView()
  }
}
```

WelcomeView!

Now, take a look at the newly created view. Open **WelcomeView**, and you will notice there isn't much in it:

- The `WelcomeView` struct, containing the `body` property, and a `Text` component.
- A preview provider named `WelcomeView_Previews`.

But that's all you need to get started. `body` is the only thing a view requires — well, besides implementing a great and stylish UI, but that's your job!

In Xcode, make sure that you have the canvas visible in the **assistant** panel, and click the resume button if necessary, to activate or reactivate the preview. You should see a welcome message like this:

Hello World image

Text

Input requires context. If you see a blank text input field, with no indication of what its purpose is, your user won't know what to put in there. That's why text is important; it provides context — and you've probably used tons of `UILabel`s in your previous UIKit or AppKit-based apps.

As you've already seen, the component to display text is called, simply, `Text`. In its simplest and most commonly used initializer, `Text` takes a single parameter: the text to display. Change the string to **"Welcome to Kuchi"**:

```
Text("Welcome to Kuchi")
```

Xcode will automatically update the text shown in the preview. Nice! Simple stuff so far, but every long journey always starts with a single step.

Welcome to Kuchi

Modifiers

Now that you've displayed some text on your screen, the next natural step is to change its appearance. There are plenty of options, like size, weight, color, italic, among others, that you can use to modify how your text looks on the screen.

> **Note**: In the previous chapters, you've already learned how to use a modifier to change the look or behavior of a view. A **modifier** is a `View` instance method that creates a copy of the view, does something to the view copy (such as changing the font size or the color), and returns the modified view.

Kuchi Package

To change the look of a `Text` instance, you use modifiers. But beyond that, more generally, *any* view can be altered using modifiers.

If you want to make the text larger, say, 60 points, add the following `font` modifier:

```
Text("Welcome to Kuchi")
  .font(.system(size: 60))
```

Then bold the text by adding the next line:

```
Text("Welcome to Kuchi")
  .font(.system(size: 60))
  .bold()
```

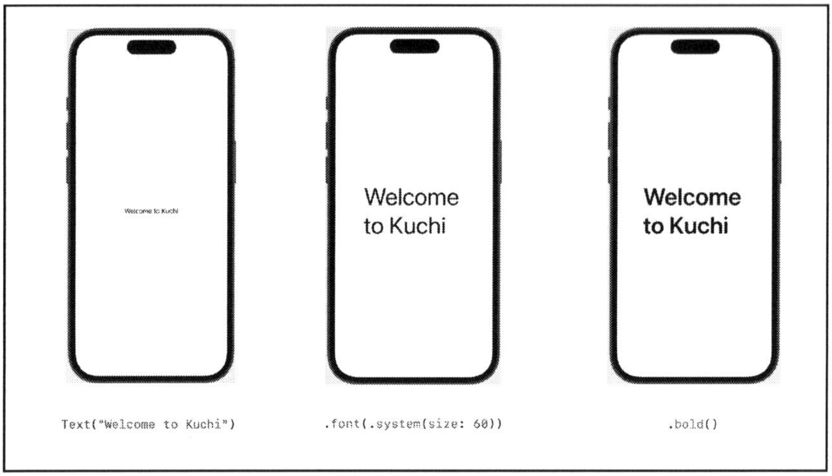

Kuchi Steps

Then you can make it a nice red color:

```
Text("Welcome to Kuchi")
  .font(.system(size: 60))
  .bold()
  .foregroundColor(.red)
```

Next, you can center-align the text:

```
Text("Welcome to Kuchi")
  .font(.system(size: 60))
  .bold()
  .foregroundColor(.red)
  .multilineTextAlignment(.center)
```

And, finally, you can force it to be rendered in one line:

```
Text("Welcome to Kuchi")
  .font(.system(size: 60))
  .bold()
  .foregroundColor(.red)
  .multilineTextAlignment(.center)
  .lineLimit(1)
```

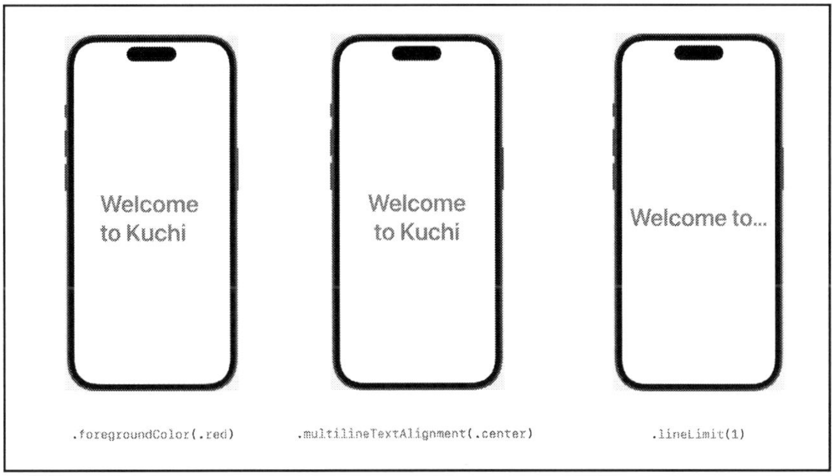

Kuchi Steps 2

Which doesn't look nice... but it's good to know that you can limit the number of lines, considering that by default `lineLimit` is nil, meaning that the text will take as many lines as needed.

So it would definitely look better if you limit the number of lines to two:

```
Text("Welcome to Kuchi")
  .font(.system(size: 60))
  .bold()
  .foregroundColor(.red)
  .multilineTextAlignment(.center)
  .lineLimit(2)
```

Kuchi Steps 3

Although it's safe to assume that default values for this UI component won't change, they might change in the future. For example, in SwiftUI 1.0 the default value for `lineLimit` was `1`, but it's been changed to `nil` in 2.0. Likewise, the text alignment was `.center` in SwiftUI 1.0, but it became `.leading` in 2.0.

That is to say *it's good practice to not rely too much on default values, because they can change in future versions.*

So far you've exclusively used code to add and configure modifiers, but SwiftUI, in tandem with Xcode, offers two alternatives for the lazy, er, I mean *efficient* coders out there.

First of all, make sure the preview is in **Selectable** mode — new to Xcode 14, by default the preview is displayed in **Live** (i.e. interactive) mode:

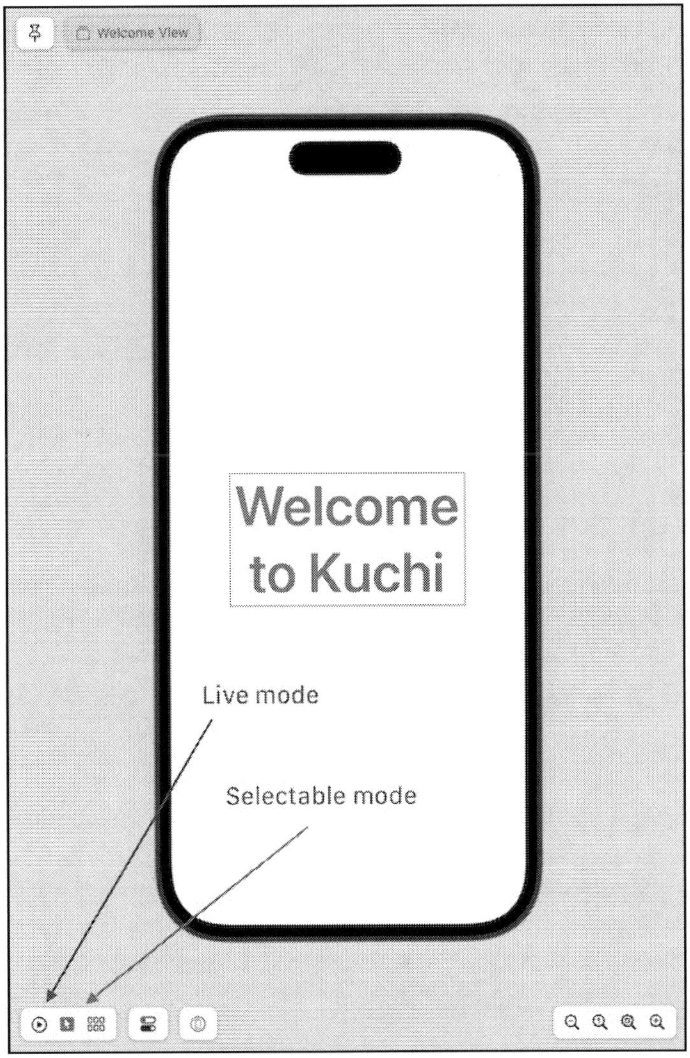

Canvas Selectable mode

Now you can inspect the the view in two different ways:

- With the canvas inspector popup, which appears when you **Command-click** on a view component onto the canvas:

Canvas modifiers

- With the attributes inspector, which appears by pressing **Option-Command-4**, and displays the modifiers for the view currently selected in the canvas:

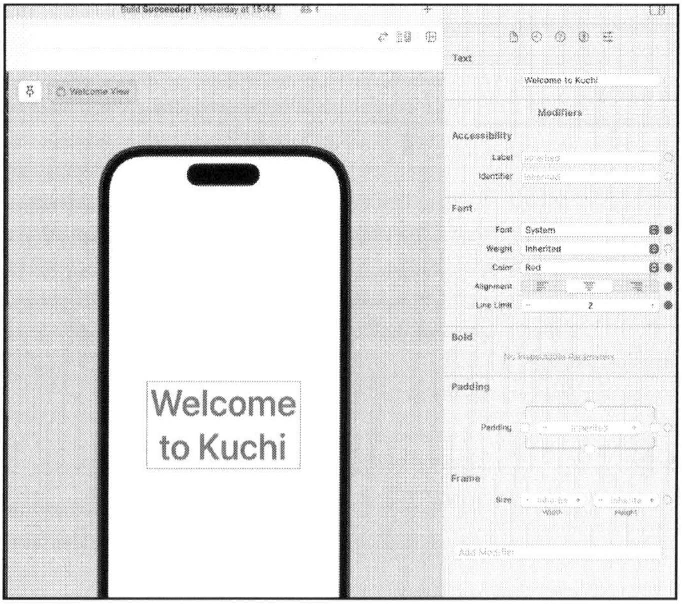

Inspector modifiers

`Text` is such a simple component, but it has *so* many modifiers. And that's just the beginning! There are two categories of modifiers that SwiftUI offers:

- Modifiers bundled with the `View` protocol, available to any view.
- Modifiers specific to a type, available only to instances of that type.

`View` has lots of pre-made and ready-to-use modifiers that are implemented in protocol extensions. For a full list, you can browse the documentation; in Xcode, **Option-click** `View` in the source editor, and then click **Open in Developer Documentation**.

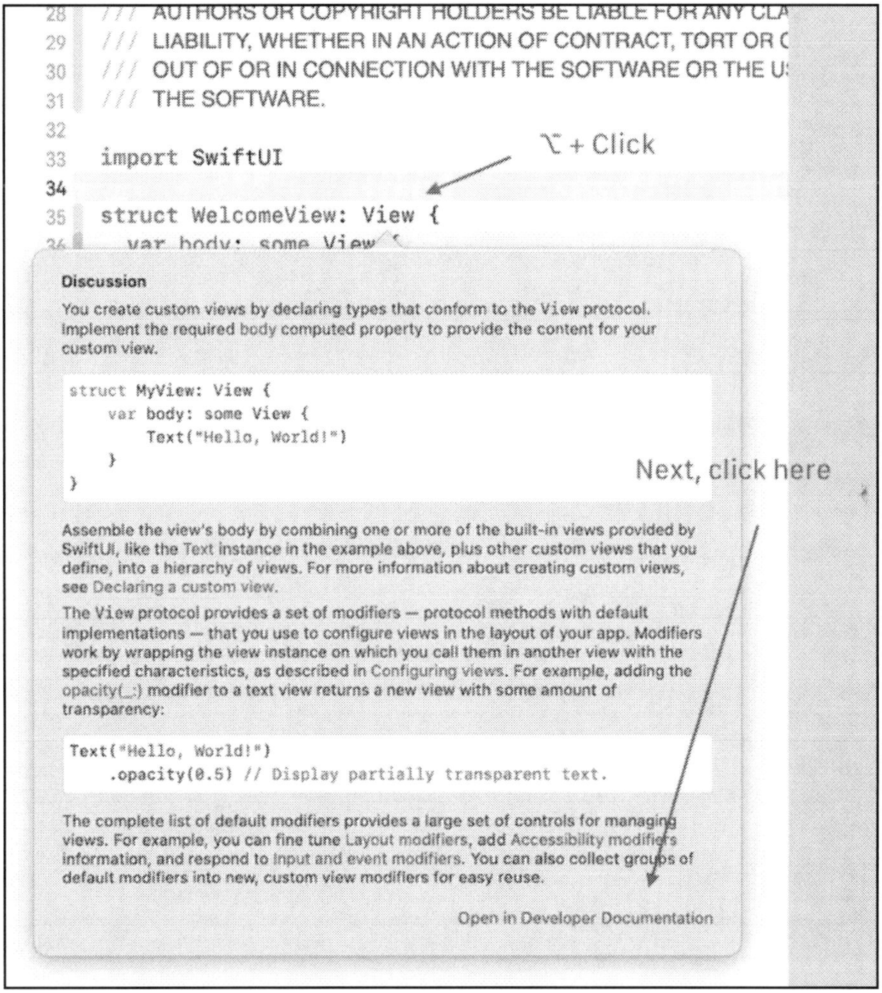

XCode documentation

Browsing the documentation is always helpful when learning, but sometimes you need a faster way to search for a modifier. Maybe you don't remember the modifier's name, or maybe you are simply wondering if such a modifier exists.

Again, Xcode and SwiftUI can help with that! As you might remember from **Chapter 3: Diving Deeper Into SwiftUI**, Xcode now has a **Modifiers Library**, similar to the **Object Library** available in older versions of Xcode.

To access the library, click the leftmost + button, located at the top-right corner of your Xcode window. The library allows you to browse and search by name, and, most importantly, groups all modifiers by category, so chances are that you'll quickly find what you're looking for, if it actually exists.

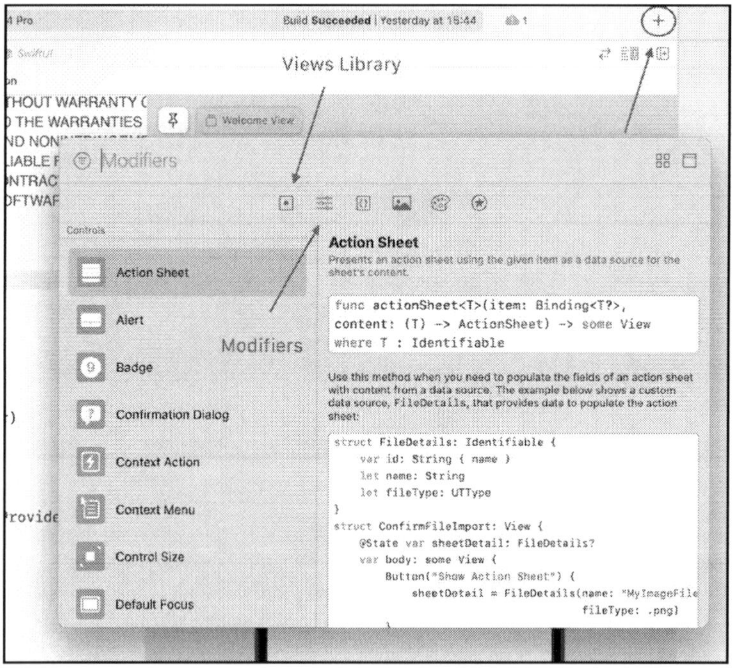

Views and modifiers libraries

Note that the library also contains the **Views Library**, which you can use to browse and select views, and drag them onto the canvas, for two-way user interface development.

Are Modifiers Efficient?

Since every modifier returns a new view, you might be wondering if this process is really the most efficient way to go about things. SwiftUI embeds a view into a new view every time you invoke a modifier. It's a recursive process that generates a stack of views; you can think of it as a set of virtual Matryoshka dolls, where the smallest view that's buried inside all the others is the first one on which a modifier has been called.

Russian Dolls

Intuitively, this looks like a waste of resources. The truth is that SwiftUI flattens this stack into an efficient data structure that is used for the actual rendering of the view.

You should feel free to use as many modifiers as you need, without reserve and without fear of impacting the efficiency of your view.

Order of Modifiers

Is the order in which you invoke modifiers important? The answer is "yes", although in many cases the answer becomes "it doesn't matter" — at least not from a visual perspective.

For example, if you apply a bold modifier, and then make it red:

```
Text("Welcome to Kuchi")
  .bold()
  .foregroundColor(.red)
```

...or first make it red, and then bold:

```
Text("Welcome to Kuchi")
  .foregroundColor(.red)
  .bold()
```

...you won't notice any difference.

Modifiers

However, if you apply a background color and then apply padding, you *will* get a different result. `.padding` is a modifier that adds spacing between the view the modifier is applied to and the view's parent. Without parameters, SwiftUI adds a default padding in all four directions, but you can configure that padding yourself.

Consider the following configuration below:

```
Text("Welcome to Kuchi")
  .background(Color.red)
  .padding()
```

You add a red background color to the text, and then apply padding. But if you invert that order:

```
Text("Welcome to Kuchi")
  .padding()
  .background(Color.red)
```

You apply the padding first, resulting in a larger view, and then apply the red background. You'll immediately notice that the result is different:

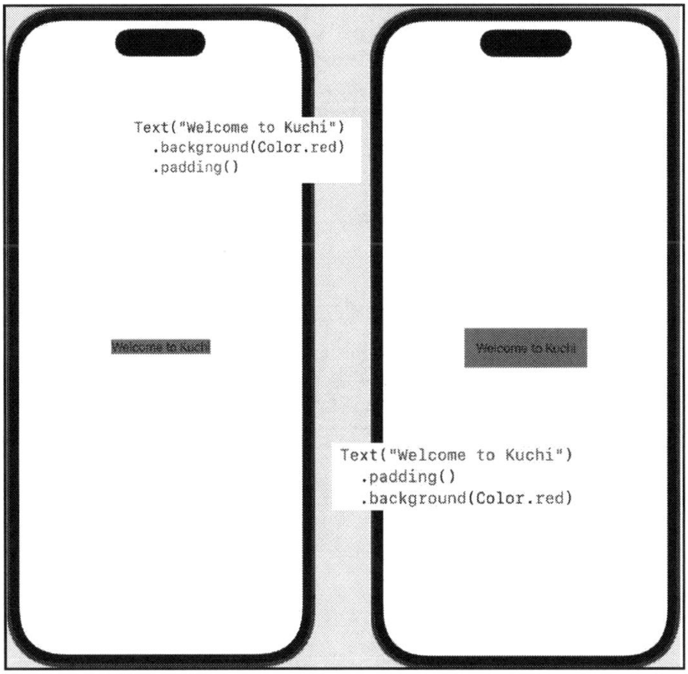

Modifiers background

This is because the *view* where you apply the *background* color is different in each case. Another way to look at it is that the *view* to which you apply the *padding* is different.

This is clearly visible if you set different background colors before and after applying the padding:

```
Text("Welcome to Kuchi")
  .background(Color.yellow)
  .padding()
  .background(Color.red)
```

Modifiers color padding

The padding adds some space between the text and the edges of the view. When you apply the background color before the padding, that modification is applied to the view that contains the text, which is a view large enough to contain just the displayed text and nothing more. The `padding` modifier adds a *new* view, to which the *second* background color is applied to.

Image

An image is worth a thousand words. That may be a cliché, but it's absolutely true when it comes to your UI. This section shows you how to add an image to your UI.

First, remove the welcome `Text` from `body` and replace it with an `Image` component as shown below:

```
var body: some View {
  Image(systemName: "table")
}
```

This is what you'll see on screen:

Raw image

Changing the Image Size

When you create an image without providing any modifiers, SwiftUI will render the image at its native resolution and maintain the image's aspect ratio. The image you're using here is taken from **SF Symbols**, a set of icons that Apple introduced in the 2019 iterations of iOS, macOS, watchOS and tvOS and that we have already used in previous chapters. For more information, check out the links at the end.

If you want to resize an image, you have to apply the `resizable` modifier, which takes two parameters: an inset and a resizing mode. The resizing mode can be either `.tile` or `.stretch`.

If you don't provide any parameters, SwiftUI assumes no inset for all four directions (top, bottom, leading and trailing) and `.stretch` resizing mode.

> **Note**: If you *don't* apply the `resizable` modifier, the image will keep its native size. When you apply a modifier that either directly or indirectly changes the image's size, that change is applied to the *actual* view the modifier is applied to, but *not* to the image itself, which will retain its original size.

So if images are worth a thousand words, then code examples must be worth a thousand images! To embed an image in a square frame, 30 points wide and high, you simply add the `frame` modifier to the image:

```
var body: some View {
  Image(systemName: "table")
    .frame(width: 30, height: 30)
}
```

The preview won't show any difference; you'll still see the image at its original size. However, if you click the image to select it, Xcode will show the selection highlight as a blue border:

Non-resizable image

The outermost view has the correct size, but, as you may have expected, the image didn't scale to match.

Now, prepend `frame` with the `resizable` modifier:

```
var body: some View {
  Image(systemName: "table")
    .resizable()
    .frame(width: 30, height: 30)
}
```

The output should be a lot closer to what you expected:

Resizable image

> **Note**: You've given the image an absolute size, measured in points. However, for accessibility reasons, and to help your app adapt to different resolutions, orientations, devices and platforms, it's always a good idea to let SwiftUI decide how to scale images, and more generally, most of your UI content. You'll cover that briefly in this chapter, but you'll go into scaling more in-depth in the next chapter.

If you want to transform and manipulate that image to make it look like a *bordered* and *circular red-colored* grid with a *light gray background*, add the following code after `.frame`:

```
// 1
.cornerRadius(30 / 2)
// 2
.overlay(Circle().stroke(Color.gray, lineWidth: 1))
// 3
.background(Color(white: 0.9))
// 4
.clipShape(Circle())
// 5
.foregroundColor(.red)
```

Here's what you're doing:

1. You set the corner radius to half the size of the image.
2. Next, you add a thin gray border.
3. You then add a light gray background color.
4. Next, you clip the resulting image using a circle shape, which removes the excess colored background.
5. Finally, you set the foreground color to red.

Here's how the sequence of modifiers affects the resulting image at each step:

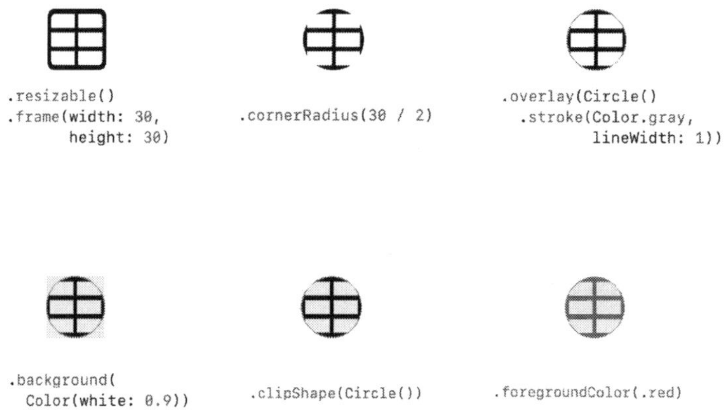

Image modifiers stack

It turns out one of the modifiers in the previous code is redundant. If you remove that modifier, the resulting image is the same. Can you tell which modifier is redundant?

It might not be obvious at first glance, but the corner radius, which makes the image circular, actually clips the image. But isn't that what the shape clipping at the 4th line is doing? Try it out! Delete or comment out the corner radius modifier, and you'll see that the resulting image doesn't change.

You can safely remove that line of code - But it's good to know how to apply a corner radius to a view.

Last thought for this section: have you considered how easy it was to manipulate and transform an image with just a few lines of code? How many lines of code would you have written in UIKit or AppKit to achieve the same result? Quite a lot more, I believe.

Brief Overview of Stack Views

Before moving to the next topic, you'll need to recover the code you removed while working on the `Image` in the previous section.

To add the `Text` view again, alter the implementation of `body` so it looks as follows — here the `Text` font size has been reduced to from 60 to 30, otherwise it would look too big compared to the image:

```
Image(systemName: "table")
  .resizable()
  .frame(width: 30, height: 30)
  .overlay(Circle().stroke(Color.gray, lineWidth: 1))
  .background(Color(white: 0.9))
  .clipShape(Circle())
  .foregroundColor(.red)

Text("Welcome to Kuchi")
  .font(.system(size: 30))
  .bold()
  .foregroundColor(.red)
  .lineLimit(2)
  .multilineTextAlignment(.center)
```

Note that this is **not** the correct way to add multiple subviews to a view. With a few exceptions, the `View`'s `body` property expects one and only one subview.

In SwiftUI 1.0, the code above would have caused a compilation error, now it compiles and even works in the simulator: all subviews will be stacked vertically. However if you preview it in Xcode, it will show one preview per subview.

If you want to embed more than one subview in a view, you have to rely on a container view. The simplest and most commonly used container views is the **stack**, the SwiftUI counterpart of UIKit's `UIStackView`.

Stacks come in 3 different flavors: **horizontal**, **vertical** and, for the lack of a better term, **on top of one another**. For now we'll use the horizontal version, which is the SwiftUI counterpart of UIKit's `UIStackView` in horizontal layout mode.

Embed the two views into an `HStack`:

```
HStack {
  Image(systemName: "table")
    ...
  Text("Welcome to Kuchi")
    ...
}
```

> **Note**: You'll learn about `HStack` in **Chapter 7: "Introducing Stacks & Containers"**. All you need to know right now is that `HStack` is a *container view*, which allows you to group multiple views in a horizontal layout.

This is how the view looks like in the Xcode preview:

First hstack

More on Image

Two sections ago, you played with the `Image` view, creating an icon at the end of the process. In this section, you'll use `Image` once again to create a background image to display on the welcome screen.

To do that, you need to know about another container view, `ZStack`, which stacks views one on top of the other, like sheets of papers in a stack — that's why it's been described with the *on top of one another* term.

This is different from `HStack` (and `VStack`, which you'll meet later in this chapter) which arranges views next to one another instead.

Since you need to add a background image, `ZStack` seems to fit the purpose. Embed the `HStack` of the previous section inside a `ZStack`:

```
ZStack {
  HStack {
    ...
  }
}
```

Nothing changes in the canvas preview. Now, add this `Image` view before `HStack`, still inside of the `ZStack`:

```
Image("welcome-background", bundle: nil)
```

Welcome

The image looks okay, but it has too much presence and color.

`View` and `Image` have a comprehensive list of modifiers that let you manipulate the appearance of an image. These include **opacity**, **blur**, **contrast**, **brightness**, **hue**, **clipping**, **interpolation**, and **aliasing**. Many of these modifiers are defined in the `View` protocol, so they're not limited to just images; you could, theoretically, use them on any view.

Use this image as a reference to see what each modifier does. I encourage you to add modifiers one at a time in Xcode, to see the live result build up in the canvas preview:

Background image modifiers

The final code for the image should look as follows:

```
// 1
Image("welcome-background", bundle: nil)
  // 2
  .resizable()
```

```
    // 3
    .scaledToFit()
    // 4
    .aspectRatio(1 / 1, contentMode: .fill)
    // 5
    .edgesIgnoringSafeArea(.all)
    // 6
    .saturation(0.5)
    // 7
    .blur(radius: 5)
    // 8
    .opacity(0.08)
```

Going over this code, here is what you just did:

1. This is the `Image` you've just added.
2. `.resizable`: Make it resizeable. By default, SwiftUI tries to use all of the space at its disposal, without worrying about the aspect ratio.
3. `.scaledToFit`: Maximize the image so that it's fully visible within the parent, with respect to the original ratio.
4. `.aspectRatio`: Set the aspect ratio, which is `1:1` by default. Setting `contentMode` to `.fill` makes the image fill the entire parent view, so a portion of the image will extend beyond the view's boundaries.
5. `.edgesIgnoringSafeArea`: Ignore the safe area insets, extending the view outside the safe area, so that it occupies the entire parent space.

   Here, you're ignoring all edges, but it can also be configured on a per-edge basis. To do that, you pass an array of the edges to ignore: `.top`, `.bottom`, `.leading`, `.trailing`, but also `.vertical` and `.horizontal`, which combine the two vertical and the two horizontal edges respectively.
6. `.saturation`: Reduce the color saturation so that the image appears less vibrant.
7. `.blur`: Add some blur. Who doesn't love blur?
8. `.opacity`: Make the image more transparent, which has the side effect of dimming to make it a little less prominent.

Once again, there's a redundant modifier in that view. Can you figure out which one it was?

Yes, it's the third line: the `.scaledToFit` modifier. You already made the image fit the parent with `.resizable`, and then `.aspectRatio` makes the image fill the parent instead. Comment the `.scaledToFit` modifier, and you'll see that the final result doesn't change.

Can you guess what happens if you switch `scaledToFit` and `aspectRatio`? Would you expect the final result to change?

You've probably figured it out already: `scaledToFit` overrides the fill mode set in the previous line — so now *that* becomes the redundant modifier. However, if you change the aspect ratio, to something like 2:

```
.aspectRatio(2 / 1, contentMode: .fill)
```

The result is quite different in this case, because you're making the width twice as wide, while keeping the height unaltered:

Custom ratio

That said, you can revert that aspect radio change, and safely delete the redundant `.scaledToFit`. The code for the background would then look like the following:

```
Image("welcome-background", bundle: nil)
  .resizable()
  .aspectRatio(1 / 1, contentMode: .fill)
  .edgesIgnoringSafeArea(.all)
  .saturation(0.5)
  .blur(radius: 5)
  .opacity(0.08)
```

Splitting Text

Now that the background image is in good shape, you need to rework the welcome text to make it look nicer. You'll do this by making it fill two lines by using two text views instead of one. Since the text should be split vertically, all you have to do is add a `VStack` around the welcome text, like so:

```
VStack {
  Text("Welcome to Kuchi")
    .font(.system(size: 30))
    .bold()
    .foregroundColor(.red)
    .multilineTextAlignment(.center)
    .lineLimit(2)
}
```

Next, you can split the text into two separate views:

```
VStack {
  Text("Welcome to")
    .font(.system(size: 30))
    .bold()
    .foregroundColor(.red)
    .multilineTextAlignment(.center)
    .lineLimit(2)
  Text("Kuchi")
    .font(.system(size: 30))
    .bold()
    .foregroundColor(.red)
    .multilineTextAlignment(.center)
    .lineLimit(2)
}
```

You may notice that the last three modifiers in each `Text` are the same. Since they are modifiers implemented in `View`, you can refactor the code by applying them to the parent stack view, instead of to each individual view:

```
VStack {
  Text("Welcome to")
    .font(.system(size: 30))
    .bold()
  Text("Kuchi")
    .font(.system(size: 30))
    .bold()
}
.foregroundColor(.red)
.multilineTextAlignment(.center)
.lineLimit(2)
```

This is a very powerful feature: when you have a container view, and you want one or more modifiers to be applied to all subviews, simply apply those modifiers to the container.

> **Note**: You might be wondering why you didn't do the same thing for the first two modifiers of each contained view. Look at the documentation for `.font` and `.bold`, and you'll see that these are modifiers on the `Text` type. Therefore they aren't available on `View` and `VStack`.

To make the text appear nicer in respect to the image at its left, it's better to make the two text views left aligned instead of centered. Because of the refactoring you've just done, you need to change that in one place only, instead of two:

```
.multilineTextAlignment(.leading)
```

But you may notice that it doesn't work. That's because you've split the text to two different `Text`, and each one is sized accordingly to its content, so changing the text alignment won't have any visual effect.

In order to align the two `Text` views to the left, you have to change the alignment of the views contained in the `VStack`, which, by default, are centered - unfortunately there's no modifier to change that, the only way is to specify the alignment in the initializer.

Remove the `.multilineTextAlignment(.leading)` modifier, and pass the `alignment` parameter to `VStack` as follows:

```
VStack(alignment: .leading) {
```

The line limit is also no longer needed. You could just remove it, but that would make the text free to span over multiple lines - unlikely to happen in this case, but just in case you can just ask each `Text` view to stay in one line only, by changing `2` to `1`:

```
.lineLimit(1)
```

The `VStack` code should now look like:

```
VStack(alignment: .leading) {
  Text("Welcome to")
    .font(.system(size: 30))
    .bold()
  Text("Kuchi")
    .font(.system(size: 30))
    .bold()
}
.foregroundColor(.red)
.lineLimit(1)
```

Wouldn't it be nice if the two lines of text had different font sizes? To achieve this, use the `.headline` style on the welcome text, replacing `.font(.system(size: 30))` with the following:

```
.font(.headline)
```

For the Kuchi text, use a `.largeTitle` instead, replacing `.font(.system(size: 30))` with the following:

```
.font(.largeTitle)
```

Finally, you'll style the container slightly to make it a little less cramped. You'll need some padding between the image and the text; you can use the `.padding` modifier and pass `.horizontal`, which adds padding horizontally on both sides. You could alternately pass other edges, such as top or leading, either standalone or as an array of edges. Also, you can specify an optional length for the padding. If you don't specify this, SwiftUI will apply a default.

The code for the entire text stack should look like this:

```
VStack(alignment: .leading) {
  Text("Welcome to")
    .font(.headline)
    .bold()
  Text("Kuchi")
    .font(.largeTitle)
    .bold()
}
.foregroundColor(.red)
.lineLimit(1)
.padding(.horizontal)
```

The resulting view should appear as follows:

Welcome to Kuchi

Markdown

New to SwiftUI 3.0, `Text` now supports a subset of **markdown**, which is a markup language for creating formatted text. If you don't know what it is, check out the links at the end of this chapter.

Usage of markdown is possible because of the additions made to the new `AttributedString` type introduced in iOS 15 and macOS 12, which is the Swift "native" counterpart of the `NSAttributedString` type that you've probably used in the past. To make it clear, `AttributedString` is to `NSAttributedString` as `String` is to `NSString`.

The two `Text` components you've used above use the `.bold()` modifier to make the text bold. You can also get rid of it and use markdown to achieve the same result:

```
Text("**Welcome to**")
  .font(.headline)
Text("**Kuchi**")
  .font(.largeTitle)
```

Feel free to experiment with it and try other formatters, such as italic (`*Kuchi*` or `_Kuchi_`) and strikethrough (`~~Kuchi~~`). But keep in mind that only the following ones are currently supported:

- Bold
- Italic
- Strikethrough
- Inline code
- Link

Sorry, no ordered or unordered lists work as of now. :-[

Although in this simple example no method has a distinctive advantage over the other, the real power of markdown becomes perceivable when you need to apply formatting to substrings of a text.

For instance, if you want to print a text like "I am an *awesome* **SwiftUI Software Engineer**", using "native" SwiftUI you'd have to use three different `Text` components (one for the unformatted text, one for the italic and one for the bold), whereas using markdown you'd use one `Text`, with its text set to `I am an _awesome_ **SwiftUI Software Engineer**`.

Note that `Text` interprets markdown only when used with string literals — if you have your text stored in a variable or property, it won't work. But fear not, there's a known workaround for that, which is to wrap the variable in an initializer, such as `Text(.init(myTextInAVariable))`.

Accessibility With Fonts

Initially, all of your views that display text used a `font(.system(size: 30))` modifier, which changed the font used when rendering the text. Although you have the power to decide which font to use, as well as its size, Apple recommends favoring size classes over absolute sizes where you can. This is why, in the previous section, you used styles such as `.headline` and `.largeTitle` in place of `.system(size: 30)`

All sizes are defined in `Font` as pseudo-enum cases: They're actually static properties. UIKit and AppKit have corresponding class sizes, so you probably already know a little bit about `title`, `headline`, `body`, or other properties like that.

Using size classes gives the user the freedom to increase or decrease all fonts used in your app relative to a reference size: if the reference size is increased, all fonts become larger in proportion, and if decreased, then the fonts become smaller. This is a huge help to people with eyesight issues or visual impairments.

That was a long journey! The concepts here are pretty simple but necessary to get you started in your SwiftUI development.

Before moving on, undo the changes to the `Text` components so they use `.bold()` instead of markdown - This was a brief introduction markdown, but you won't use it in the Kuchi app.

Label: Combining Image and Text

`Image` and `Text` are frequently used one next to the other. Combining them is pretty easy — you just need to embed them into an `HStack`. However, to simplify your work, Apple has given you a component specifically for that purpose: `Label`.

Given the work you've done so far, resulting in a view with text and image, it's time to test this new component.

`Label` has a few initializers, taking a raw string, and either a resource identifier or a system image identifier. For example, to display welcome text along with a waving hand icon, you'd write code like this:

```
Label("Welcome", systemImage: "hand.wave")
```

This displays a label as follows:

Label Example

It also allows you to provide your custom view for the text and image. Since you've already put quite a lot of effort to customize your text and image, it's the most appropriate choice to follow.

This initializer takes two parameters: a `title` and an `icon`, and it looks like this:

```
init(title: () -> Title, icon: () -> Icon)
```

To see it in action, you need to refactor this code:

```
HStack {
  Image(systemName: "table")
    .resizable()
    .frame(width: 30, height: 30)
    .overlay(Circle().stroke(Color.gray, lineWidth: 1))
    .background(Color(white: 0.9))
    .clipShape(Circle())
    .foregroundColor(.red)

  VStack(alignment: .leading) {
    Text("Welcome to")
      .font(.headline)
      .bold()
    Text("Kuchi")
      .font(.largeTitle)
      .bold()
  }
  .foregroundColor(.red)
  .lineLimit(1)
  .padding(.horizontal)
}
```

So the `Image` goes to the `Label`'s `icon` parameter, and the `VStack` (along with its modifiers) to the `title` parameter.

Change the above code (`HStack` included) to:

```
Label {
  // 1
  VStack(alignment: .leading) {
    Text("Welcome to")
      .font(.headline)
      .bold()
    Text("Kuchi")
      .font(.largeTitle)
      .bold()
  }
  .foregroundColor(.red)
  .lineLimit(2)
  .multilineTextAlignment(.leading)
  .padding(.horizontal)
// 2
} icon: {
  // 3
  Image(systemName: "table")
    .resizable()
    .frame(width: 30, height: 30)
    .overlay(Circle().stroke(Color.gray, lineWidth: 1))
    .background(Color(white: 0.9))
    .clipShape(Circle())
    .foregroundColor(.red)
}
```

Here's what's happening above:

1. This is the text component, consisting of two `Texts` embedded in a vertical stack.
2. Note how the Swift multiple closures syntax is used here.
3. This is the image component.

After applying this change, you notice, however, that it doesn't look very good: The icon and the text are not vertically aligned.

Refactored with label

To fix this, you need to override the way the label arranges its components. You can apply a style to a `Label`; the problem is that none of the available seems to fit with your needs:

- `DefaultLabelStyle`: This is the default value, which corresponds to specifying no style at all. It displays both the title and the icon.
- `IconOnlyLabelStyle`: This displays the icon only, ignoring the title.
- `TitleOnlyLabelStyle`: This displays the title only, hiding the icon.

The good news is that if none fits, you can build your own. To create a custom style, you need to create a struct that conforms to the `LabelStyle` protocol, which has one requirement only:

```
func makeBody(configuration: Self.Configuration) -> Self.Body
```

Add a new file to the **Welcome** group using the **Swift File** template, and name it **HorizontallyAlignedLabelStyle.swift**. Be sure to select both iOS and macOS targets.

Next, create an empty skeleton for the style:

```
import SwiftUI

struct HorizontallyAlignedLabelStyle: LabelStyle {
  func makeBody(configuration: Configuration) -> some View {
    return EmptyView()
  }
}
```

The `configuration` parameter contains both the `text` and the `icon` parameters passed to the `Label` initializer — all you have to do is embed them into an `HStack`:

```
func makeBody(configuration: Configuration) -> some View {
  HStack {
    configuration.icon
    configuration.title
  }
}
```

This solves the alignment issue, because `HStack` by default vertically aligns all its children at the center.

And that's all! You've created a custom style. To apply it, you need to add, you guessed it, a modifier to the `Label` that you added earlier in **WelcomeView.swift**.

In `WelcomeView`, at the bottom of `Label` (after the last closing curly brace) add the following modifier:

```
.labelStyle(HorizontallyAlignedLabelStyle())
```

As you can see, the modifier is named `labelStyle()`, and it takes an instance of a label style, which, as mentioned earlier, is a type that conforms to the `LabelStyle` protocol.

This is how it looks:

Label with Custom Style

And yes, you don't, and shouldn't, see any difference to what you got in the version without the `Label`.

Key Points

- You use the `Text` and `Image` views to display and configure text and images respectively.
- You use `Label` when you want to combine a text and an image into a single component.
- `Text` natively "understands" markdown.
- You use modifiers to change the appearance of your views. Modifiers can be quite powerful when used in combination, but remember to be aware of the order of the modifiers, because in some cases it does matter.
- Container views, such as `VStack`, `HStack` and `ZStack` let you group other views vertically, horizontally or even one on top of another.

Where to Go From Here?

SwiftUI is still fairly new and evolving as a technology. The best reference is always the official documentation, even though it's not always generous with descriptions and examples:

- SwiftUI documentation: apple.co/2MlBqJJ
- The `View` reference documentation: apple.co/2LEh5Qs

If you want to take a look and browse through the SF Symbols image library:

- SF Symbols: apple.co/2YPtrIx
- SF Symbols App (download): bit.ly/3HjgBL0

To know more about **Markdown**, check out:

- Markdown on Wikipedia: bit.ly/2VBwiIt
- AttributedString: apple.co/3htf3B0

In the next chapter, you'll learn about other UI components that are commonly used, with particular attention to text fields and buttons.

Chapter 6: Controls & User Input

By Antonio Bello

In Chapter 5, "Intro to Controls: Text & Image" you learned how to use two of the most commonly used controls: `Text` and `Image`, with also a brief look at `Label`, which combines both controls into one.

In this chapter, you'll learn more about other commonly-used controls for user input, such as `TextField`, `Button` and `Stepper` and more, as well as the power of refactoring.

A Simple Registration Form

The **Welcome to Kuchi** screen you implemented in Chapter 5 was good to get you started with `Text` and `Image`, and to get your feet wet with modifiers. Now, you're going to add some interactivity to the app by implementing a simple form to ask the user to enter her name.

The starter project for this chapter is nearly identical to the final one from Chapter 5 — that's right, you'll start from where you left off. The only difference is that you'll find some new files included needed to get your work done for this chapter.

If you *don't* want to keep working on your own copy, and prefer to use this chapter's starter project, you can skip to the **A bit of refactoring** below right away.

If you, on the other hand, prefer to keep working on your own copy of the project borrowed from the previous chapter, you need to manually add to both iOS and macOS targets the additional files needed in this chapter from the starter project:

- **Shared/Profile/Profile.swift**
- **Shared/Profile/Settings.swift**
- **Shared/Profile/UserManager.swift**

To do so, it's better if you just add the **Shared/Profile** folder, so that Xcode can create the **Profile** group, and automatically add all files in it contained without any extra step. To do so:

- In the Project navigator right click on the **Shared** group.
- Choose **Add files to "Kuchi"** in the dropdown menu.
- Make sure that both iOS and macOS targets are selected.

- Make sure that the **Copy items if needed** is enabled.
- Select the **Profile** folder from this chapter's starter project, and then click **Add**.

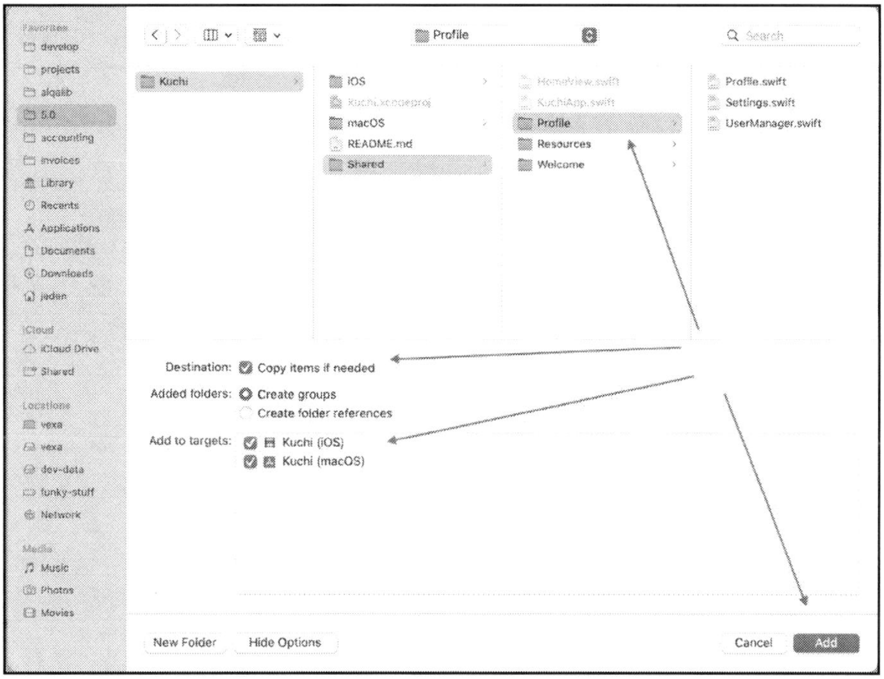

Adding the Profile group

You will use these new files later in this chapter — but feel free to take a look.

A Bit of Refactoring

Often, you'll need to refactor your work to make it more reusable and to minimize the amount of code you write for each view. This is a pattern that's used frequently and often recommended by Apple.

The new registration view you will be building will have the same background image as the welcome view you created in Chapter 5. Here's the first case where refactoring will come in handy. You could simply copy code from the welcome view and paste it, but that's not very reusable and maintainable, is it?

First of all, create a **Components** group in the Project navigator by right-clicking on the **Shared/Welcome** group and choosing **New Group**.

Then, create a new component view by right-clicking the **Components** group, and creating a new **SwiftUI View** named **WelcomeBackgroundImage** — again, be sure to add to both targets, iOS and macOS.

Next, open **WelcomeView**, select the following lines of code, which define the background image, and copy them:

```
Image("welcome-background")
  .resizable()
  .aspectRatio(1 / 1, contentMode: .fill)
  .edgesIgnoringSafeArea(.all)
  .saturation(0.5)
  .blur(radius: 5)
  .opacity(0.08)
```

Then, paste in the `body` implementation of `WelcomeBackgroundImage` the code you've copied above (replacing the default `Text` it contains). The `body` should now look as follows:

```
var body: some View {
  Image("welcome-background")
    .resizable()
    .aspectRatio(1 / 1, contentMode: .fill)
    .edgesIgnoringSafeArea(.all)
    .saturation(0.5)
    .blur(radius: 5)
    .opacity(0.08)
}
```

Now, go back to **WelcomeView** and replace the lines of code you previously copied with the newly created view, so that it looks like this:

```
var body: some View {
  ZStack {
    WelcomeBackgroundImage()

    Label {
      ...
```

Make sure that you've enabled automatic preview (resume it if necessary), and you'll notice that nothing has changed, which is what you'd expect — because you refactored your code without making any functional changes.

Refactored welcome view

Since the topic of this section is refactoring, you'll go a step further and refactor:

- The icon image that's displayed in the welcome view.
- The entire Welcome view, composed by the icon and the "Welcome to Kuchi" text.

Exercise: Now that you've unlocked the *SwiftUI refactoring ninja* achievement, why don't you try to do the two refactoring on your own, and then compare your work with how it's been done below? You can name the two new views `LogoImage` and `WelcomeMessageView`.

Refactoring the Logo Image

In **WelcomeView.swift** select the code for the `Image`:

```
Image(systemName: "table")
  .resizable()
  .frame(width: 30, height: 30)
  .overlay(Circle().stroke(Color.gray, lineWidth: 1))
  .background(Color(white: 0.9))
  .clipShape(Circle())
  .foregroundColor(.red)
```

Then:

- Copy the code to your clipboard.
- Replace the code with `LogoImage()`.
- Create a new **LogoImage.swift** file in the **Components** group, using the **SwiftUI** template.
- Replace the `body` implementation of **LogoImage** with the code you've copied from the welcome view.

If you open **WelcomeView** and resume the preview, once again you won't notice any differences — which means the refactoring worked.

Refactoring the Welcome Message

In **WelcomeView**, you'll do this a bit differently:

- Command-Click on `Label`. A popup menu will appear:

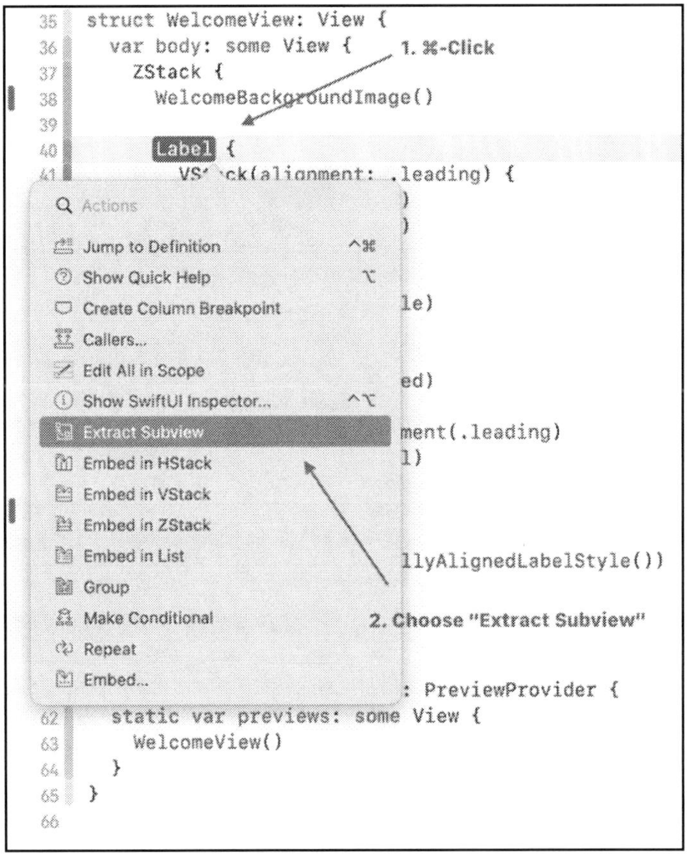

Refactored subview

- Choose **Extract Subview**. Xcode will replace the selected component with `ExtractedView()`, and will move its implementation at the end of the file, in a new `ExtractedView` struct.

```
struct WelcomeView: View {
  var body: some View {
    ZStack {
      WelcomeBackgroundImage()

      ExtractedView()
    }
  }
}

struct WelcomeView_Previews: PreviewProvider {
  static var previews: some View {
    WelcomeView()
  }
}

struct ExtractedView: View {
  var body: some View {
    Label {
      VStack(alignment: .leading) {
        Text("Welcome to")
          .font(.headline)
          .bold()
        Text("Kuchi")
          .font(.largeTitle)
          .bold()
      }
      .foregroundColor(.red)
      .lineLimit(2)
      .multilineTextAlignment(.leading)
      .padding(.horizontal)
    } icon: {
      LogoImage()
    }
    .labelStyle(HorizontallyAlignedLabelStyle())
  }
}
```

Refactored extracted subview

- If Xcode is not so kind to put the new view name in edit mode, right click on `ExtractedView` and choose **Refactor** and then **Rename**.
- Type a new name in — Call it `WelcomeMessageView` and press Enter.
- Now you're going to move it to a new file. Select the entire `WelcomeMessageView` struct and cut it.
- Next, create a new **WelcomeMessageView** file in the **Components** group, using the **SwiftUI** template.
- Replace the implementation of `WelcomeMessageView` with the code you've cut from the welcome view.

Once again, if you open **WelcomeView** and resume the preview, you won't notice any difference.

Good job! You've just refactored the welcome view making it, and the components it consists of, much more reusable.

Creating the Registration View

The new registration view is... well, new, so you'll have to create a file for it. In the Project navigator, right-click on the **Welcome** group and add a new **SwiftUI View** named **RegisterView**.

Next, replace its `body` implementation with:

```
VStack {
  WelcomeMessageView()
}
```

And with a single line of code, you've just proved how easy and powerful a reusable small components can be.

Initial Register View

You can also add a background view, which, thanks to the previous refactoring, is as simple as adding a couple lines of code. Replace the `body` implementation with this code:

```
ZStack {
  WelcomeBackgroundImage()
  VStack {
    WelcomeMessageView()
  }
}
```

Voilà, lunch is served. Faster than a microwave!

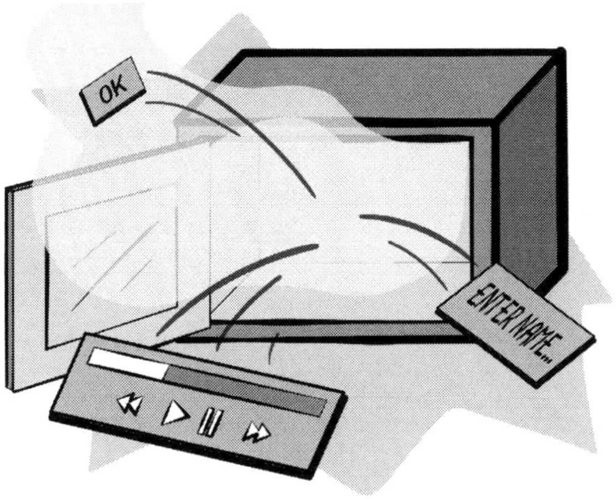

Microwave

If you try to *run* the app, you'll notice it still displays the welcome view. Well, probably you won't notice that easily, because the two views look exactly the same. But that's not the point. :]

Anyway, the app is still configured to display the welcome view on launch. To change that, open **KuchiApp** and replace `WelcomeView` with `RegisterView`:

```
var body: some Scene {
  WindowGroup {
    RegisterView()
  }
}
```

And do the same to the preview, so that it looks like:

```
struct KuchiApp_Previews: PreviewProvider {
  static var previews: some View {
    RegisterView()
  }
}
```

Power to the User: The TextField

With the refactoring done, you can now focus on giving the user a way to enter her name into the app.

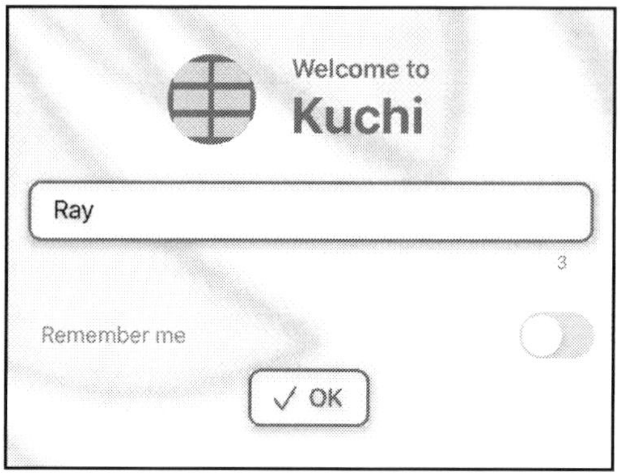

Registration form

In the previous section, you added a `VStack` container to `RegisterView`, and that wasn't a random decision, because you need it now to stack content vertically.

`TextField` is the control you use to let the user enter data, usually by way of the keyboard. If you've built an iOS or macOS app before, you've probably met its older cousins, `UITextField` and `NSTextField`.

In its simplest form, you can add the control using the initializer that takes a title and a text binding.

The `title` is the *placeholder* text that appears inside the text field when it is empty, whereas the `binding` is the managed property that takes care of the 2-way connection between the text field's text and the property itself.

You will learn more about binding in **Chapter 8: "State & Data Flow — Part I"**. For now you just need to know that to create and use a binding you have to:

- Add the `@State` attribute to a property.
- Prefix the property with `$` to pass the binding instead of the property value.

So, add this property to `RegisterView`:

```
@State var name: String = ""
```

And then add the text field after `WelcomeMessageView()`:

```
TextField("Type your name...", text: $name)
```

You'd expect a text field to appear in the preview, but nothing happens — it looks the same as before. What gives?

A closer inspection reveals the problem: if you click `TextField` in the code editor, you'll notice that the text field gets selected in the preview — it's just that it's too wide, as you can see from the blue rectangle:

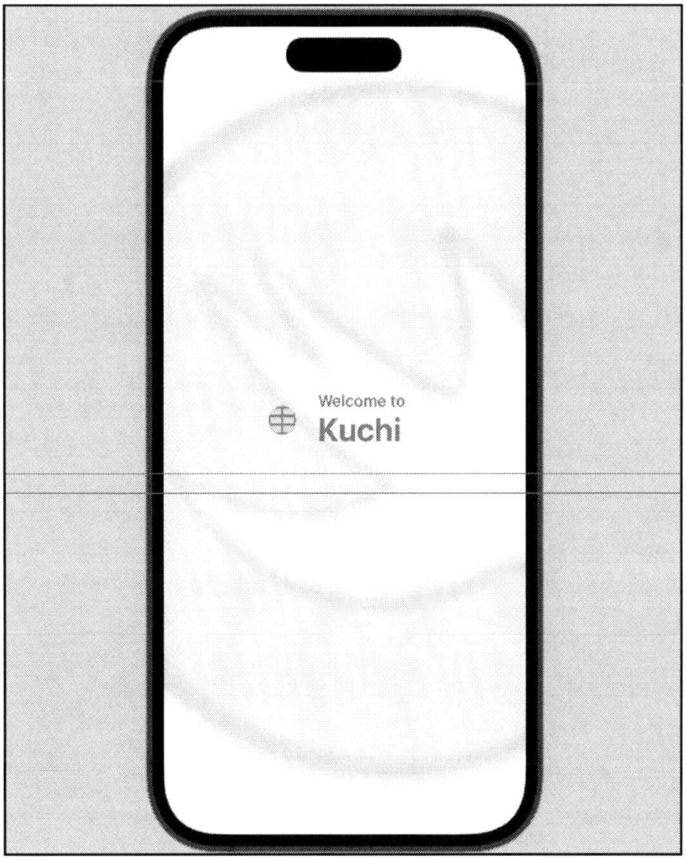

Wide text field

> **Challenge**: Can you figure out why is this happening? Hint: it's caused by the background image.

The reason is that the background image is configured with `.fill` content mode, which means that the image expands to occupy as much of the parent view space as possible. Because the image is a square, it fits the parent vertically, but that means that, horizontally, it goes way beyond the screen boundaries.

The way to fix this is to avoid using a `ZStack` and to position the background view behind the actual content using the `.background` modifier on the `VStack` instead.

Remove the `ZStack` from the register view, and then add `WelcomeBackgroundImage()` as a `.background` modifier to the `VStack`:

```
var body: some View {
  VStack {
    WelcomeMessageView()
    TextField("Type your name...", text: $name)
  }
  .background(WelcomeBackgroundImage())
}
```

> **Note**: In UIKit, views have a `backgroundColor` property, which you can use to specify a uniform background color. The SwiftUI counterpart is more polymorphic; the `.background` modifier accepts any type that conforms to `View`, which includes `Color`, `Image`, `Shape`, among others.

With this change, the text field is now visible, but the background looks too small.

Background too small

The reason is that `VStack` is not using the entire screen, but only what it needs to render its content. In the picture above you can see its actual size, highlighted in blue.

To fix this problem, add two `Spacer`s, one at the beginning and the other at the end of `VStack`, as follows:

```
VStack {
  Spacer() // <-- 1st spacer to add

  WelcomeMessageView()
  TextField("Type your name...", text: $name)

  Spacer() // <-- 2nd spacer to add
} .background(WelcomeBackgroundImage())
```

You'll know more about `Spacer` in the next chapter, what you need to know for now is that it expands in a way to use all space at its disposal. With this change, now the background images expand as expected.

Text field visible

Styling the TextField

Unless you're going for a very minimalistic look, you might not be satisfied with the text field's styling.

To make it look better, you need to add some padding and a border. For the border, you can take advantage of the `.textFieldStyle` modifier, which applies a style to the text field.

Currently, SwiftUI provides four different styles, which are compared in the image below:

Text field styles

The "no style" case is explicitly mentioned, but it corresponds to `DefaultTextFieldStyle`. You can see that there's no noticeable difference between `DefaultTextFieldStyle` and `PlainTextFieldStyle`. However, `RoundedBorderTextFieldStyle` presents a border with slightly rounded corners. Note that there's also a fifth style, `SquareBorderTextFieldStyle`, but it's available on macOS only.

For Kuchi, you're going to provide a different, custom style. There are three options for doing this:

- Apply modifiers to the `TextField` as needed.
- Create your own text field style, by defining a concrete type conforming to the `TextFieldStyle` protocol.
- Create a custom modifier, by defining a concrete type conforming to the `ViewModifier` protocol.

Whichever solution you choose, it consists of directly or indirectly applying a list of modifiers in sequence, one after the other, so the most logical way to start is with the first method.

Apply the following modifiers to the text field:

```
.padding(
  EdgeInsets(
    top: 8, leading: 16, bottom: 8, trailing: 16))
.background(Color.white)
.overlay(
  RoundedRectangle(cornerRadius: 8)
    .stroke(lineWidth: 2)
    .foregroundColor(.blue)
)
.shadow(
  color: Color.gray.opacity(0.4),
  radius: 3, x: 1, y: 2)
```

The figure below shows the effect of each modifier:

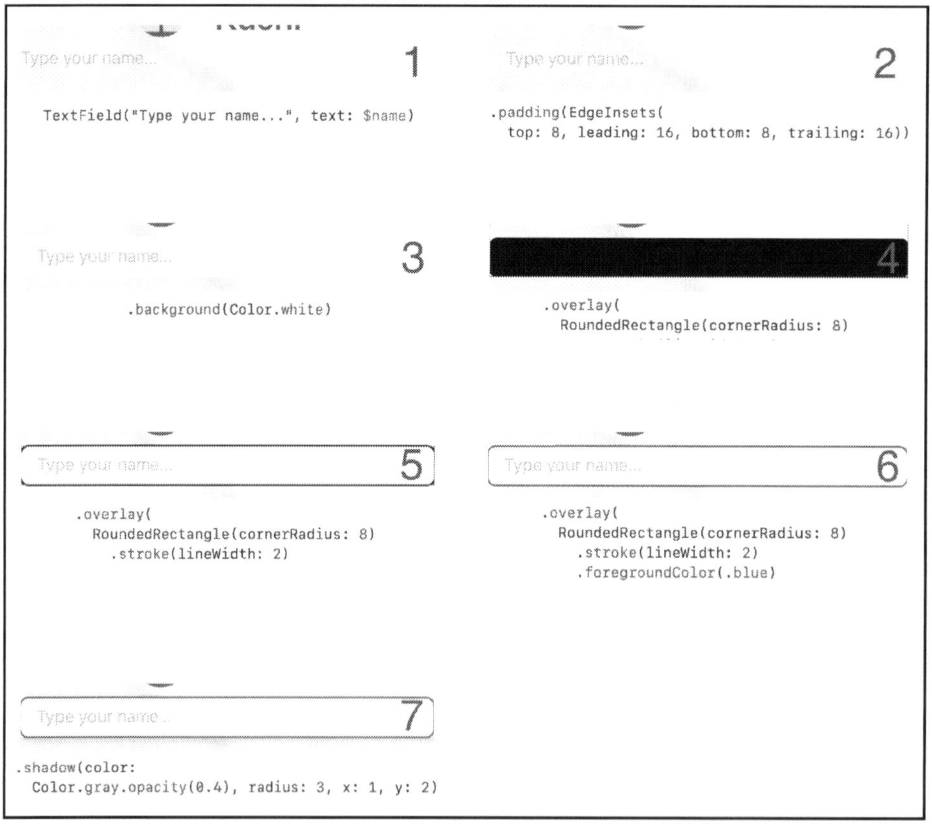

Text field border style

This is what each does:

1. Creates an unmodified text field.
2. Adds padding of 16 points vertically, and 8 points horizontally.
3. Adds a non-transparent white background.
4. Creates an overlay for the border, using a rounded rectangle with a corner radius of 8.
5. Adds a stroke effect to keep the border only, leaving the content behind visible.
6. Makes the border blue.
7. Adds a shadow.

You'll notice that the text field has no spacing from the left and right edges; the padding you added in Step 2 adds padding between the text field and the views it contains. To add padding between the text field and its parent view, you'll need to add a padding modifier to the view that contains the text field, the `VStack`.

In the containing VStack, right before .background(WelcomeBackgroundImage()), but after the stack's closing bracket, add the following:

```
.padding()
```

Form with padding

Creating a Custom Text Style

Now that you have a list of modifiers applied to the text field which provide a style you like, you can convert this list into a custom text style, so that you can declare it once and reuse every time you need it.

A custom text field style must adopt the TextFieldStyle, which declares one method only:

```
public func _body(
  configuration: TextField<Self._Label>) -> some View
```

It receives the text field in the `configuration` parameters, to which you can apply as many modifiers as you want, returning the resulting view.

In **RegisterView**, before the `RegisterView` struct, create a new custom text style:

```
struct KuchiTextStyle: TextFieldStyle {
  public func _body(
    configuration: TextField<Self._Label>) -> some View {
      return configuration
  }
}
```

Left as is, this text style doesn't do anything, because it returns the same text field it receives. To customize it, you need to add modifiers.

So, move the four modifiers you applied earlier to the text field to this method. In `RegisterView` select and cut these lines:

```
.padding(
  EdgeInsets(
    top: 8, leading: 16, bottom: 8, trailing: 16))
.background(Color.white)
.overlay(
  RoundedRectangle(cornerRadius: 8)
    .stroke(lineWidth: 2)
    .foregroundColor(.blue)
)
.shadow(
  color: Color.gray.opacity(0.4),
  radius: 3, x: 1, y: 2)
```

and paste them into the `KuchiTextStyle`'s `body` implementation, after the `return configuration` statement, so that it looks like:

```
public func _body(
  configuration: TextField<Self._Label>) -> some View {

  return configuration
    .padding(
      EdgeInsets(
        top: 8, leading: 16, bottom: 8, trailing: 16))
    .background(Color.white)
    .overlay(
      RoundedRectangle(cornerRadius: 8)
        .stroke(lineWidth: 2)
        .foregroundColor(.blue)
    )
    .shadow(color: Color.gray.opacity(0.4),
            radius: 3, x: 1, y: 2)
}
```

What you are returning is the resulting text field after applying the four modifiers.

Now you can use this new style. Head back to `RegisterView`, and add it to the text field, using the `textFieldStyle` modifier, so that it looks like:

```
TextField("Type your name...", text: $name)
  .textFieldStyle(KuchiTextStyle())
```

Here you create a new instance of `KuchiTextStyle`, and pass it to the `textFieldStyle`. Simple!

If you look at the preview, you'll see the same as before refactoring — nothing has changed from a functional standpoint — which is expected.

Form with custom text style

Now, you don't need this custom style anymore, because in the next section you'll go for the custom modifier path. Undo all the changes (pressing **Control + Z** repeatedly) until you see the 4 modifiers applied again to the text field, and the newly created `KuchiTextStyle` gone — verify that the `RegisterView`'s `body` implementation is:

```
var body: some View {
  VStack {
    Spacer()

    WelcomeMessageView()
    TextField("Type your name...", text: $name)
      .padding(
        EdgeInsets(top: 8, leading: 16, bottom: 8, trailing:
16))
      .background(Color.white)
      .overlay(
        RoundedRectangle(cornerRadius: 8)
          .stroke(lineWidth: 2)
          .foregroundColor(.blue)
      )
      .shadow(color: Color.gray.opacity(0.4),
              radius: 3, x: 1, y: 2)

    Spacer()
  }
  .padding()
  .background(WelcomeBackgroundImage())
}
```

Creating a Custom Modifier

The reason for preferring the custom modifier over the custom text field style is that you can apply the same modifier to any view, including buttons — which, spoiler alert, is what you're going to do soon.

Add a new file to the **Components** group using the **SwiftUI View** template, and name it **BorderedViewModifier**.

First, delete the autogenerated `BorderedViewModifier_Previews` struct, as you don't need it for a custom modifier. Next, change the protocol that `BorderedViewModifier` conforms to, from `View` to `ViewModifier`:

```
struct BorderedViewModifier: ViewModifier {
```

A `ViewModifier` defines a `body` member, but instead of being a property, it's a function that takes content — the view the modifier is applied to — and returns another view resulting from the modifier being applied to the content. You see a recurring pattern because it's conceptually similar to the custom text field style.

Replace the `body` property with the following function:

```
func body(content: Content) -> some View {
  content
}
```

The code, as is, returns the same view the modifier is applied to. Don't worry, you're not done yet! :]

Go back to **RegisterView**, then *select and cut* again all modifiers applied to the text field:

```
.padding(
  EdgeInsets(top: 8, leading: 16, bottom: 8, trailing: 16))
.background(Color.white)
.overlay(
  RoundedRectangle(cornerRadius: 8)
    .stroke(lineWidth: 2)
    .foregroundColor(.blue)
)
.shadow(
  color: Color.gray.opacity(0.4),
  radius: 3, x: 1, y: 2)
```

Next, switch back to **BorderedViewModifier** and paste these modifiers after `content`:

```
func body(content: Content) -> some View {
  content
    .padding(
      EdgeInsets(top: 8, leading: 16, bottom: 8, trailing: 16))
    .background(Color.white)
    .overlay(
      RoundedRectangle(cornerRadius: 8)
        .stroke(lineWidth: 2)
        .foregroundColor(.blue)
    )
    .shadow(
      color: Color.gray.opacity(0.4),
      radius: 3, x: 1, y: 2)
}
```

That's it. Now you have a new custom modifier. To apply it, you need to create an instance of `ModifiedContent`, a struct that comes with SwiftUI. Its initializer takes two parameters:

- The content view
- The modifier

Reopen `RegisterView`, and embed the `TextField` in a `ModifiedContent` instance, as follows:

```
ModifiedContent(
  content: TextField("Type your name...", text: $name),
  modifier: BorderedViewModifier()
)
```

After the preview updates, you see that the blue border is correctly applied. But hey, let's be honest, that code doesn't look fantastic. Wouldn't it be better if you could replace it with a simpler modifier call, like any regular modifier call?

Turns out all you need to do is create a convenience method in a view extension. Open `BorderedViewModifier`, and add the following extension at the end of the file:

```
extension View {
  func bordered() -> some View {
    ModifiedContent(
      content: self,
      modifier: BorderedViewModifier()
    )
  }
}
```

Now, you can go back to `RegisterView` and replace the `ModifiedContent` component with the following:

```
TextField("Type your name...", text: $name)
  .bordered()
```

The preview will confirm that the modifier is correctly applied — and, you've already guessed, what you see is the same as before, because, again, you haven't applied any functional change, just code refactoring.

Form custom modifier

Keyboard and Layout

If you run the app (making sure that the soft keyboard is enabled if you're using the simulator) you notice that when you tap the text field the keyboard is automatically displayed, and the layout automatically adjusted to make sure that the text field is visible and not covered by the keyboard itself.

However at a closer inspection you can notice that the background image slides to the right when the keyboard appears, and moves back to its original position when it disappears.

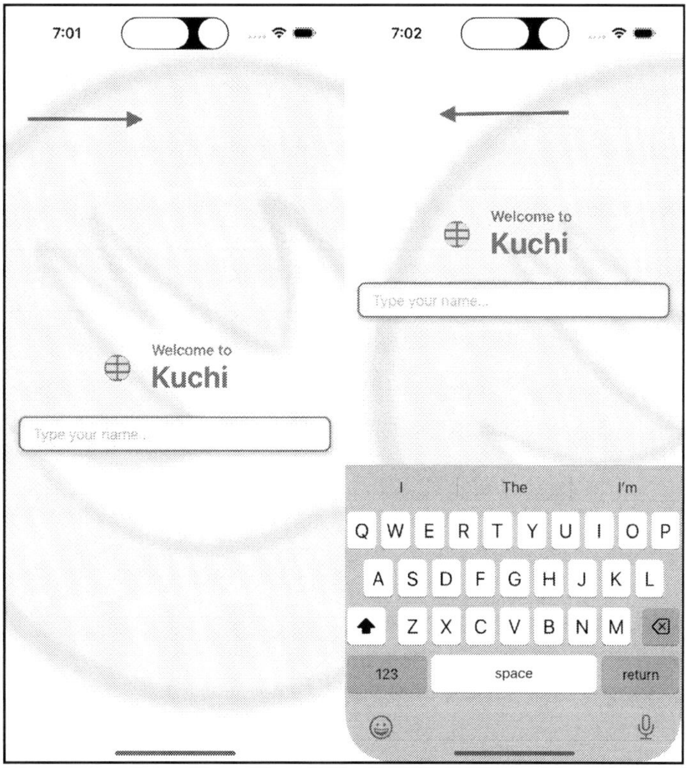

Background image sliding to the right

The reason behind that behavior is that the height of the view changes when the keyboard is displayed, as you can see by inspecting the view hierarchy using Xcode's **Debug View Hierarchy** tool:

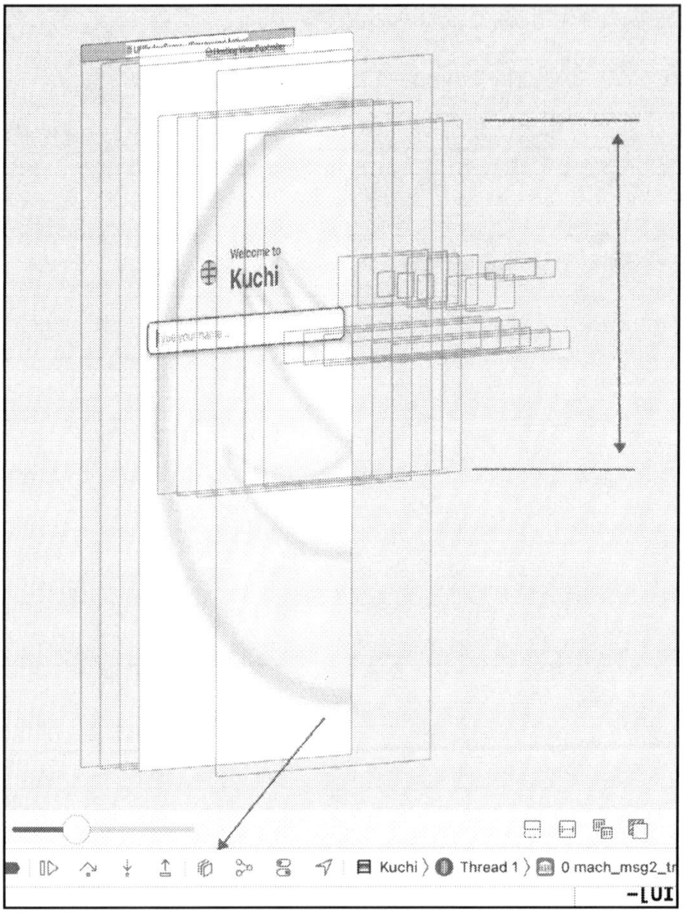

View height reduction when the keyboard is visible

One way to fix this is to embed the background image in a `GeometryReader` and constraint its width. Open **WelcomeBackgroundImage** and replace the content of the `body` property with the following code:

```
// 1
GeometryReader { geometry in
  Image("welcome-background")
    .resizable()
    .aspectRatio(1 / 1, contentMode: .fill)
    // 2
    .frame(width: geometry.size.width, alignment: .center)
    .edgesIgnoringSafeArea(.all)
    .saturation(0.5)
    .blur(radius: 5)
    .opacity(0.08)
}
```

The `GeometryReader` is a powerful (but not to be abused) tool that allows to use the size and coordinates of its parent to constraint children views. You will learn more about how SwiftUI layouts views in **Chapter 7: "Introducing Stacks and Containers"**.

Here's what you achieve with these two additions:

1. You wrap the image into a geometry reader.
2. You constraint the image to have the same width as the geometry reader's parent.

This gives the image the ability to expand its height to the maximum available to it, corresponding to the height proposed by the geometry reader's parent, making it independent from the view that contains the keyboard, and its height in particular.

Keyboard and Form Tuning

Now that the background is fixed, this is how the simple form built so far should look like when running the app in the simulator, and with the soft keyboard enabled:

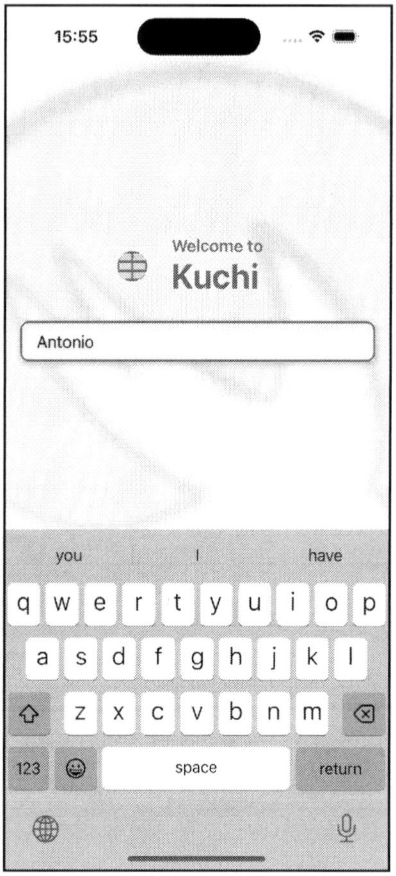

Wide text field

The action key on the keyboard is labelled **return**, but in some cases you want to change it, so that it displays **next** if you have more fields you want to move the focus to, or **done** when the field is the last of the form.

You can change the label of the action button in a very easy way, thanks to, you guessed, a `TextField`'s modifier. Open **RegisterView.swift** and right after the text field, but before the `.bordered()` modifier, add this line:

```
.submitLabel(.done)
```

This instructs the keyboard to show the text associated to the **done** action. You can't specify a custom label though: you are limited to the enum cases of the `SubmitLabel` type: `done`, `go`, `send`, `join`, `route`, `search`, `return`, `next` and `continue`.

Note that changing the label won't alter the key's behavior — when you press the done button, the keyboard will be dismissed as it did before the change. However you can associate an action — more on that in the next section: "Taps and buttons".

Another feature that SwiftUI offers is the ability to specify and determine at any time which control has the focus. To achieve that, you need to add a property to the view - it can be of any type, as long as it conforms to the `Hashable` protocol.

> **Spoiler alert**: You will undo the changes you're doing now, to implement at the end of this same section an alternative version achieving the same result.

The most natural way to handle focus is by using an enum, with a case for each control that can obtain the focus — in the case of this `RegisterView` there's one field only to enter the user's name. So define an enum inside the `RegisterView` struct:

```
struct RegisterView: View {
  // Add this enum
  enum Field: Hashable {
    case name
  }
  ...
}
```

Next, add a property to the view, using the `@FocusState` attribute after `name`:

```
@FocusState var focusedField: Field?
```

Last, you need to create an association between the enum case and the text field — this needs to be a two way binding, so that:

- When an enum case is assigned to `focusedField`, the associated component will get the focus.
- When a component obtains the focus (in response to a user's action), the `focusedField` property will be set to its corresponding enum case.

The binding is done using, you guessed again, a modifier, which takes a focus state property binding, plus a value which determines the value associated to the component.

Add the `.focused` modifier to the text field as follows:

```
TextField("Type your name...", text: $userManager.profile.name)
  // Add this modifier
  .focused($focusedField, equals: .name)
  .submitLabel(.done)
  .bordered()
```

With this modifier you're telling SwiftUI:

- When `focusField` is `.name`, give this text field focus.
- When this field gets focus, set `focusField` to `.name`.

Now, if you run the app, you won't notice any difference — that's because you've created the binding, but you're not using yet. You could think of initializing the field with a default value, so that a field has focus when the view is displayed, but that's considered an anti-pattern, and it won't have any effect — feel free to try it.

What you can do in this simple form is to remove the focus from the text field when the OK button is tapped. You'll do that later in this chapter.

However, in this form you have one field only, so using an enum is a bit overkill, don't you agree? The Apple Engineers have thought about that, and implemented an alternative way that relies on booleans rather than enums.

The idea is to bind a component to a boolean property. If you have multiple components, you need a dedicated property for each component.

Since this solution is a better fit in the current scenario, let's change the implementation to use it:

- First of all, delete the `Field` enum altogether.
- Next, replace the `focusField` property with this new implementation:

  ```
  @FocusState var nameFieldFocused: Bool
  ```

  The new property is a boolean, so it can be either `true` or `false`, reflecting the current focus state of the bound component, which can be with focus or without focus.

As anticipated a few lines above, you'll use the focus later in this chapter, when discussing about submitting the form — be patient to see it in action.

A Peek at TextField's Initializer

`TextField` has several initializers, many available in pairs, with each pair having a localized and non-localized version for the `title` parameter.

The version used in this chapter is the non-localized version that takes a title and a binding for the editable text:

```
public init<S>(
  _ title: S,
  text: Binding<String>
) where S : StringProtocol
```

There are several other initializer overloads — one of which is the one taking an additional closures that can be used to perform more processing before and after the user input:

- `onEditingChanged`: Called when the edit obtains focus (when the Boolean parameter is `true`) or loses focus (when the parameter is `false`).

Another pair of initializers take an additional formatter. The non localized version has this signature:

```
public init<S, T>(
  _ title: S,
  value: Binding<T>,
  formatter: Formatter
) where S : StringProtocol
```

The differences from the other pair are such:

1. The `formatter` parameter, which is an instance of a class inherited from `Foundation`'s abstract class `Formatter`. It's usable when the edited value is of a different type than String — for instance, a number or a date — but you can also create custom formatters.

2. The `T` generic parameter determines the actual underlying type handled by the `TextField`.

For more information about formatters, take a look at Data Formatting (https://apple.co/2MNqO7q).

Another interesting overload takes a new pair of parameters that you can pass to the initializer:

- `prompt` lets you pass a `Text` instance that will be used for the placeholder text — The difference compared to the `title` parameter is that you can apply custom formatting, such as changing font.
- `label` lets you pass a `View` which describes the purpose of the text field.

These two parameters are used in different ways depending on the platform where the app runs:

- On macOS the label is displayed next to the leading edge of the text field, and the prompt as the placeholder text.
- On iOS the label will be used as placeholder, if provided, otherwise the prompt will be used.

Taps and Buttons

Now that you've got a form, the most natural thing you'd want your user to do is to submit the form. And the most natural way of doing *that* is using a dear old submit button.

The SwiftUI button is far more flexible than its UIKit/AppKit counterpart. You aren't limited to using a text label alone or in combination with an image for its content.

Instead, you can use anything for your button that's a `View`. You can see this from its declaration, which makes use of a generic type:

```
struct Button<Label> where Label : View
```

The generic type is the button's visual content, which must conform to `View`.

That means a button can contain not only a base component, such as a `Text` or an `Image`, but also any composite component, such as a pair of `Text` and `Image` controls, enclosed in a vertical or horizontal stack, or even anything more complex that you can dream up.

Adding a button is as easy as declaring it: you simply specify a label and attach a handler. Its signature is:

```
init(
  action: @escaping () -> Void,
  @ViewBuilder label: () -> Label
)
```

The initializer takes two parameters, which are actually two closures:

- **action**: The trigger handler.
- **label**: The button content.

> **Note**: The tap handler parameter is referred to as **action** instead of **tap** or **tapAction** — and if you read the documentation, it's called a **trigger handler**, not **tap handler**.
>
> That's because in iOS it's a tap, but in macOS it can be a mouse click, in watchOS a digital crown press, and so forth.

> **Note**: The button initializer takes the trigger handler as the first parameter, instead of the last, breaking the common practice in Swift of giving action closures the last position.
>
> This means that you can't use the *single trailing closure syntax*. The reason is very likely because that pattern changes in SwiftUI, where the last parameter is always the view declaration — which, by the way, can use the same trailing closure syntax. However you can always use the *multiple trailing closure syntax*, new to Swift 5.3.

Submitting the Form

Although you can add an inline closure, it's better to avoid cluttering the view declaration with code. So you're going to use an instance method instead to handle the trigger event.

In RegisterView add the button after the TextField:

```
Button(action: registerUser) {
  Text("OK")
}
```

Then, after the RegisterView struct, add this extension, containing the registerUser() event handler:

```
// MARK: - Event Handlers
extension RegisterView {
  func registerUser() {
    print("Button triggered")
  }
}
```

Now run the app in the Simulator and when you press **OK** a message will be printed to the Xcode console.

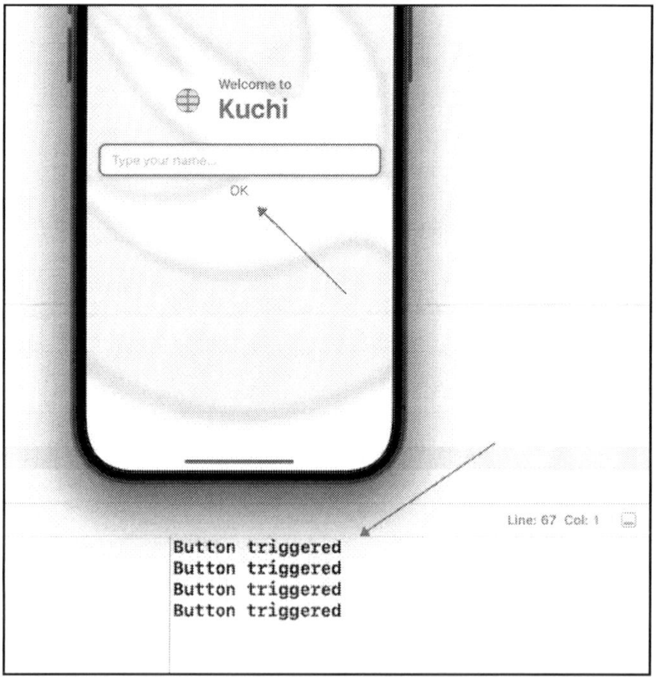

Button tap

Now that the trigger handler is wired up, you should do something more useful than printing a message to the console. The project comes with a UserManager class that takes care of saving and restoring a user and the user settings respectively to and from the user defaults.

UserManager conforms to ObservableObject, a protocol that enables the class to be used in views. It triggers a view update when the instance state changes. This class exposes two properties — profile and settings – marked with the @Published attribute, which identifies the state that triggers view reloads.

That said, you can delete the name property in RegisterView, and replace with an instance of UserManager:

```
@EnvironmentObject var userManager: UserManager
```

It's marked with the @EnvironmentObject attribute because you're going to inject an instance of it once for the whole app, and retrieve it from the environment anywhere it is needed. You will learn more about ObservableObject and @EnvironmentObject in **Chapter 9: "State & Data Flow — Part II"**.

Next, in the TextField, you have to change the $name reference to $userManager.profile.name, so that it looks like the following:

```
TextField("Type your name...", text: $userManager.profile.name)
  .focused($nameFieldFocused)
  .submitLabel(.done)
  .bordered()
```

Lastly, in registerUser() replace the print statement with this more useful implementation:

```
func registerUser() {
  userManager.persistProfile()
}
```

Now, if you try to preview this view, it will fail. That's because, as mentioned above, an instance of UserManager should be injected. You do this in the RegisterView_Previews struct, by passing a user manager to the view via a .environmentObject modifier. Update the RegisterView_Previews implementation so that it looks like this:

```
struct RegisterView_Previews: PreviewProvider {
  static let user = UserManager(name: "Ray")

  static var previews: some View {
    RegisterView()
      .environmentObject(user)
  }
}
```

Likewise, if you run the app in the Simulator, it will crash. The change you've just made is only for the preview, and it doesn't affect the running app. You need to make changes in **KuchiApp.swift** as well. Open it and add this property and initializer to `KuchiApp`:

```
let userManager = UserManager()

init() {
  userManager.load()
}
```

This creates an instance of `UserManager`, and makes sure the stored user, if available, is loaded. Next, use the `environmentObject` modifier on the `RegisterView` instance to inject it:

```
var body: some Scene {
  WindowGroup {
    RegisterView()
        // Add this line
      .environmentObject(userManager)
  }
}
```

Last, you also need to update the app preview, which will crash if you don't provide the user manager like you did for `RegisterView_Previews`. Scroll down to the end of the file and replace the whole `KuchiApp_Previews` with:

```
struct KuchiApp_Previews: PreviewProvider {
  static let userManager = UserManager(name: "Ray")
  static var previews: some View {
    RegisterView()
      .environmentObject(userManager)
  }
}
```

Styling the Button

The button is fully operative now; it looks good, but not *great*. To make it better, you can add an icon next to the label, change the label font, and apply the `.bordered()` modifier you created for the `TextField` earlier.

In **RegisterView.swift**, locate the button, and replace it with this code:

```
Button(action: self.registerUser) {
  // 1
  HStack {
    // 2
    Image(systemName: "checkmark")
      // 3
      .resizable()
      .frame(width: 16, height: 16, alignment: .center)
    Text("OK")
      // 4
      .font(.body)
      .bold()
  }
}
// 5
.bordered()
```

You should already be able to discern what this code does, but here's a breakdown:

1. As previously stated, the `label` parameter can return multiple child views, but here you're using a horizontal stack to group views horizontally. If you omit this, the two components will be laid out vertically instead.
2. You add a checkmark icon.
3. You make the icon resizable, centered, and with fixed 16×16 size. You need to use `.resizable()` because otherwise the image would keep its original size, and ignore the size of the view it is contained in.
4. You change the label font, specifying a `.body` type and a bold weight.
5. You apply the `.bordered` modifier that you've created earlier, to add a blue border with rounded corners.

If you did everything correctly, this is what your preview should look like:

Styled button

New to SwiftUI 3.0, you can also use a style thanks to the new `.buttonStyle(_:)` modifier, which accepts an instance of a type conforming to the `PrimitiveButtonStyle` protocol.

There's a list of predefined styles with which you can immediately use, such as `bordered`, `borderedProminent`, `borderless`, `card`, `link` and `plain` (note that each platform uses a subset of them, so for example `link` and `card` are not available in iOS). There's also an `automatic` style, which you can use to let SwiftUI decide what's the most appropriate style to use, depending on which platform the app is running.

And, in case you're wondering, you can also create your own style — in fact that modifier just needs an object that conforms to `PrimitiveButtonStyle`, so it works in a similar way to how custom styles are created for text fields, as you briefly saw in the previous chapter.

Reacting to Input: Validation

Now that you've added a button to submit the form, the next step in a reactive user interface is to react to the user input *while* the user is entering it.

It might be quite useful for different reasons, such as:

- Validating the data while it is entered
- Showing a counter of the number of characters typed in

But the list doesn't end there. The old way of monitoring the input entered by the user in UIKit was either by way of a delegate or subscribing to a Notification Center event. You're likely tempted to look for a similar way to react to input changes, such as a modifier that takes a handler closure, which is called every time the user presses a key.

However, the SwiftUI way to monitor for input changes is different.

Say you want to validate the user input, and keep the OK button disabled until the input is valid. In the old days, you'd subscribe for a value changed event, perform a logical expression to determine whether to enable or disable the button, and then update the button state.

The difference in SwiftUI is that you pass the logical expression to a button's modifier, and... there is no "and". That's all. When a status change occurs, the view is rerendered, the logical expression is re-evaluated, and the button's `disabled` status is updated.

In **RegisterView**, add this modifier to the OK button:

```
.disabled(!userManager.isUserNameValid())
```

This modifier changes the `disabled` state. It belongs to the `View` protocol, so it applies to any view. It takes one parameter only: a Boolean stating whether the view is interactable or not.

When the user types in the `TextField`, the `userManager.profile.name` property changes, and that triggers a view update. So, when the button is rerendered, the expression in `.disabled()` is re-evaluated, and therefore the button state is automatically updated when the input changes.

In this app, the requirement for a name is that it has to be at least three characters long — and this is what `isUserNameValid()` checks. Now you can run the app and edit the name: you'll notice that if the name length is less than 3, the button gets disabled, and it's enabled again as soon as you type the 3rd character in.

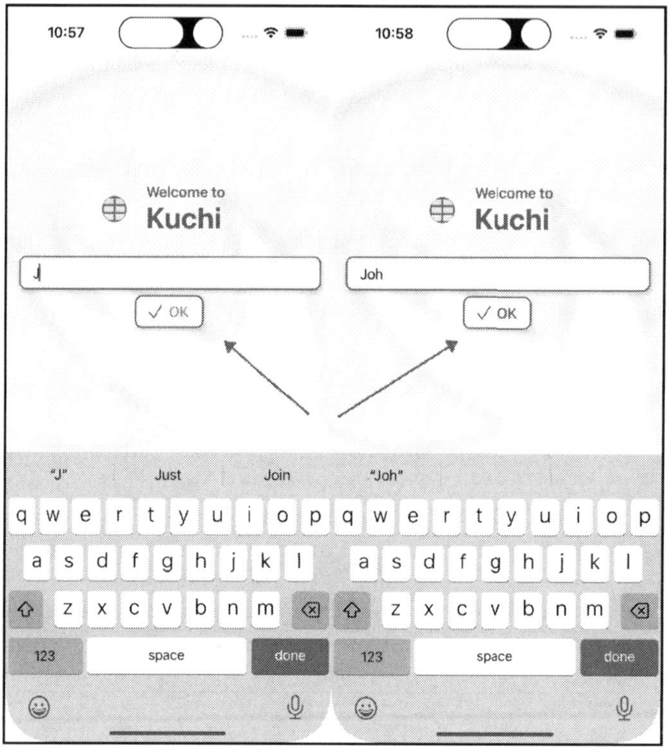

Button enabled or not

Reacting to Input: Counting Characters

If you'd want to add a label showing the number of characters entered by the user, the process is very similar. After the `TextField`, add this code:

```
HStack {
  // 1
  Spacer()
  // 2
  Text("\(userManager.profile.name.count)")
    .font(.caption)
    // 3
    .foregroundColor(
      userManager.isUserNameValid() ? .green : .red)
    .padding(.trailing)
```

```
}
// 4
.padding(.bottom)
```

Going over this line-by-line:

1. You use a spacer to push the Text to the right, in a pseudo-right-alignment way.
2. This is a simple `Text` control, whose text is the count of characters of the `name` property.
3. You use a green text color if the input passes validation, red otherwise.
4. This adds some spacing from the OK button.

You can now run the app, or enable live preview in Xcode, to see the counter in action. As you type, it will display the number of entered characters, using a green number, unless the count is less than 3, in which case it will turn red.

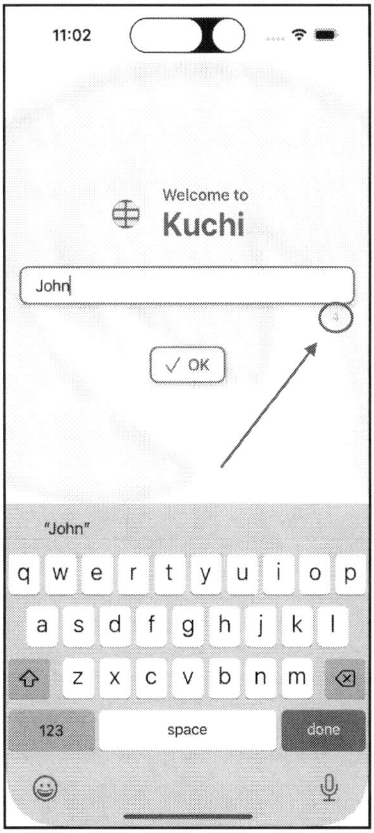

Name counter

Toggle Control

Next up: a new component. The toggle is a Boolean control that can have an on or off state. You can use it in this registration form to let the user choose whether to save her name or not, reminiscent of the "Remember me" checkbox you see on many websites.

The `Toggle` initializer is similar to the one used for the `TextField`. One of its initializers takes a binding and a label view:

```
public init(
  isOn: Binding<Bool>,
  @ViewBuilder label: () -> Label
)
```

For the binding, although you *could* use a state property owned by `RegisterView`, it's better to store it in a place that can be accessed from other views. The `UserManager` class already defines a `settings` property dedicated to that purpose.

After the `HStack` you added earlier for the name counter, and before the `Button`, add the following code:

```
HStack {
  // 1
  Spacer()

  // 2
  Toggle(isOn: $userManager.settings.rememberUser) {
    // 3
    Text("Remember me")
      // 4
      .font(.subheadline)
      .foregroundColor(.gray)
  }
    // 5
    .fixedSize()
}
```

Form toggle

The code is very simple and straightforward:

1. You need the spacer to add flexible spacing to the left, to push the toggle toward the right, and make it right-aligned.
2. You create the `Toggle` component, binding to `$userManager.settings.rememberUser`.
3. This is the label displayed before the component itself.
4. You alter the default style of the label to make it smaller and gray.
5. You ask the toggle to choose its ideal size. Without it, the toggle will try to expand horizontally, taking all the available space.

This change alone won't actually add anything functional to the app, besides storing the toggle state as a property. Replace the implementation of `registerUser()` with:

```
func registerUser() {
  // 1
  if userManager.settings.rememberUser {
    // 2
    userManager.persistProfile()
  } else {
    // 3
    userManager.clear()
  }

  // 4
  userManager.persistSettings()
  userManager.setRegistered()
}
```

In this updated version:

1. You check if the user chose whether to remember herself or not.
2. If yes, then make the profile persistent.
3. Otherwise, clear the user defaults.
4. Finally, store the settings and mark the user as registered.

To see this in effect, you need to run the app. The first time you run it, no user profile will be stored. Enter a name, enable the "Remember me" toggle, and press OK; the next time you launch the app, it will prefill the `TextField` with the name you entered.

Handling the Focus and the Keyboard

Now that everything is wired up, and the buttons correctly handles the tap, let's get back to the focus. The form implemented in this registration view is very simple, so there's no advanced use of focus management, but there's one thing you can do to improve the user experience.

If you run the app in the simulator, and you tap the text field to edit the user's name, the text field obtains the focus, and the soft keyboard is displayed. When you tap the OK button you notice that the text field still retains the focus, and the keyboard is still on screen.

Wouldn't it be better, in terms of user experience, if the text field releases the focus, and, consequently, the keyboard is automatically hidden?

Given the code you added earlier, the boolean property:

```
@FocusState var nameFieldFocused: Bool
```

And the `.focused()` modifier applied to the text field:

```
TextField("Type your name...", text: $userManager.profile.name)
  .focused($nameFieldFocused)
  .submitLabel(.done)
  .bordered()
```

If you want to release the focus, and automatically hide the keyboard, all you have to do is to set that property to `false`. The proper place to do that is in the button's trigger handler (remember? It's no longer called the tap handler :-)), which is the `registerUser` method.

So set that property to `false` at the beginning of `registerUser()`:

```
func registerUser() {
  // Add this line
  nameFieldFocused = false

  if userManager.settings.rememberUser {
    userManager.persistProfile()
  } else {
    userManager.clear()
  }

  userManager.persistSettings()
  userManager.setRegistered()
}
```

If you now run the app and tap the text field, when you tap the **OK** button the keyboard is automatically dismissed and the text field loses the focus. Mission accomplished!

One additional improvement is to make the keyboard's **Done** button to replicate the tap on OK. You can easily do it by using, could you guess? That's right, a modifier. Add this modifier to the text field:

```
TextField("Type your name...", text: $userManager.profile.name)
  .focused($nameFieldFocused)
  .submitLabel(.done)
  // Add this modifier
  .onSubmit(registerUser)
```

```
.bordered()
```

With the `.onSubmit()` modifier you're asking the text field to execute `registerMethod()` when the submit button on the keyboard has been actioned.

Note that it also works if you press the **Enter** key on a physical keyboard (this is useful when running on macOS), but also in iOS — in case you don't have a keyboard to connect to your phone, you can simply try in the simulator after connecting your mac keyboard (**I/O -> Keyboard -> Connect Hardware Keyboard** from the menu, or **⌘+⇧+K**, to toggle on and off).

Note that `.onSubmit()` is not a modifier that works on and with the keyboard only. It comes into play when a control is submitted, whatever has been used for submitting it — tapping the Done button of the soft keyboard does cause a submit, and so does pressing the Enter key on a hardware keyboard, and similar equivalents for other platforms.

And, not least important, `.onSubmit()` is part of the `View` protocol — that means it is available to any view, although it has not much sense in some of them (think of a label, for example).

Other Controls

If you've developed for iOS or macOS before you encountered SwiftUI, you know that there are several other controls besides the ones discussed so far. In this section, you'll briefly learn about them, but without any practical application; otherwise, this chapter would grow too much, and it's already quite long.

Slider

A slider is used to let the user select a numeric value using a cursor that can be freely moved within a specified range, by specific increments.

There are several initializers you can choose from, but probably the most used is:

```
public init<V>(
  value: Binding<V>,
  in bounds: ClosedRange<V>,
  step: V.Stride = 1,
  onEditingChanged: @escaping (Bool) -> Void = { _ in }
) where V : BinaryFloatingPoint, V.Stride : BinaryFloatingPoint
```

Which takes:

1. `value`: A value binding
2. `bounds`: A range
3. `step`: The interval of each step
4. `onEditingChanged`: An optional closure called when editing starts or ends

Below is an example of this in action:

```
@State var amount: Double = 0
...

VStack {
  HStack {
    Text("0")
    Slider(
      value: $amount,
      in: 0.0 ... 10.0,
      step: 0.5
    )
    Text("10")
  }
  Text("\(amount)")
}
```

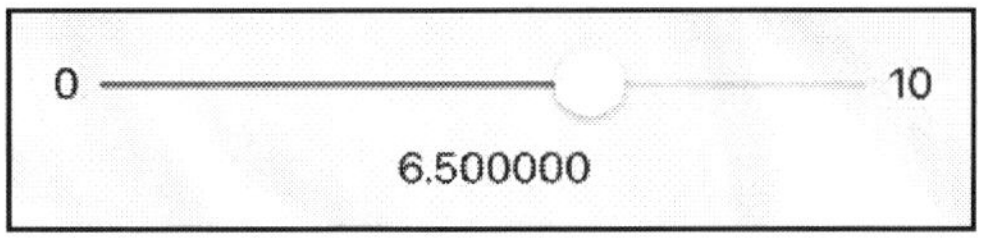

Slider

In this example, the slider is bound to the `amount` state property and is configured with an interval ranging from 0 to 10, and increments and decrements in steps of 0.5.

The `HStack` is used to add two labels at the left and right of the slider, specifying respectively the minimum and maximum values. The `VStack` is used to position a centered `Text` control below the slider, displaying the currently selected value.

Stepper

`Stepper` is conceptually similar to `Slider`, but instead of a sliding cursor, it provides two buttons: one to increase and another to decrease the value bound to the control.

There are several initializers, with one of the most common ones being this:

```
public init<S, V>(
  _ title: S,
  value: Binding<V>,
  in bounds: ClosedRange<V>,
  step: V.Stride = 1,
  onEditingChanged: @escaping (Bool) -> Void = { _ in }
) where S : StringProtocol, V : Strideable
```

This takes the following arguments:

1. `title`: A title, usually containing the current bound value
2. `value`: A value binding
3. `bounds`: A range
4. `step`: The interval of each step
5. `onEditingChanged`: An optional closure called when editing starts or ends

An example of its usage is:

```
@State var quantity = 0.0
...

Stepper(
  "Quantity: \(quantity)",
  value: $quantity,
  in: 0 ... 10,
  step: 0.5
)
```

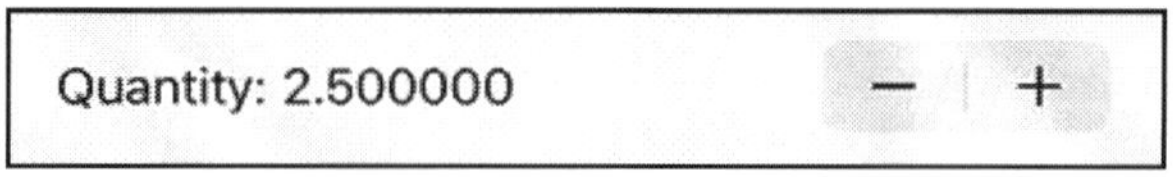

Stepper

SecureField

`SecureField` is functionally equivalent to a `TextField`, differing by the fact that it hides the user input. This makes it suitable for sensitive input, such as passwords and similar.

It offers a few initializers, one of which is the following:

```
public init<S>(
  _ title: S,
  text: Binding<String>
) where S : StringProtocol
```

Similar to the controls described earlier, it takes the following arguments:

1. `title`: A title, which is the placeholder text displayed inside the control when no input has been entered
2. `text`: A text binding

To use it for entering a password, you'd write something like:

```
@State var password = ""
...

SecureField.init("Password", text: $password)
  .textFieldStyle(RoundedBorderTextFieldStyle())
```

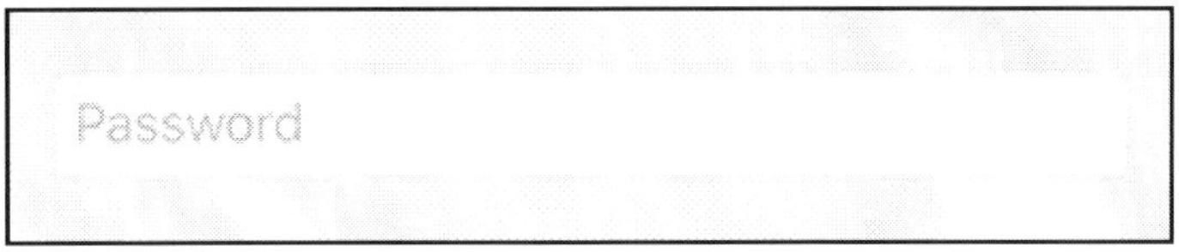

Password empty

Password entered

Key Points

Phew — what a long chapter. Congratulations for staying tuned and focused for so long! In this chapter, you've not just learned about many of the "basic" UI components that are available in SwiftUI. You've also learned the following facts:

- Refactoring and reusing views are two important aspects that should never be neglected or forgotten.
- You can create your own modifiers using `ViewModifier`.
- To handle user input, you use a `TextField` component or a `SecureField` if the input is sensitive.
- Buttons are more flexible than their UIKit/AppKit counterparts and enable you to make any collection of views into a button.
- Validating input is much easier in SwiftUI, because you simply set the rules, and SwiftUI takes care of applying those rules when the state changes.
- SwiftUI has other controls to handle user input, like toggles, sliders, and steppers.

Where to Go From Here?

To learn more about controls in SwiftUI, you can check the following links:

- Official Documentation: Views and Controls apple.co/2MQgZG1
- WWDC 2019 - SwiftUI Essentials apple.co/2Le3qy6
- More on the `GeometryReader`: bit.ly/3Rid2bn

In the next chapter, you'll learn more about view containers. See you there!

Chapter 7: Introducing Stacks & Containers

By Antonio Bello

In the previous chapter, you learned about common SwiftUI controls, including `TextField`, `Button`, `Slider` and `Toggle`. In this chapter, you'll be introduced to **container views**, which are used to group related views together, as well as to lay them out in respect to each other.

Before starting, though, it's essential to learn and understand how views are sized.

Preparing the Project

Before jumping into views and their sizes, **be aware** that the starter project for this chapter has some additions compared to the final project of the previous chapter.

If you want to keep working on your own copy, worry not! Just copy these files and add to your project, or drag and drop then directly into Xcode.

- **Practice/ChallengeView.swift**
- **Practice/ChallengesViewModel.swift**
- **Practice/ChoicesRow.swift**
- **Practice/ChoicesView.swift**
- **Practice/CongratulationsView.swift**
- **Practice/PracticeView.swift**
- **Practice/QuestionView.swift**
- **StarterView.swift**
- **HistoryView.swift**

Layout and Priorities

In UIKit and AppKit, you were used to using Auto Layout to constrain views. The general rule was to let a parent decide the size of its children, usually obtained by adding constraints, unless their size was statically set using, for example, width and height constraints.

To make a comparison with a family model, Auto Layout is a conservative model, or patriarchal to both parents, if you prefer.

SwiftUI works oppositely instead: The children choose their size, in response to a size proposed by the parent. It's more of a modern family model — if you have kids, you know what I mean!

Size expectation

If you have a `Text`, and you put it in a `View`, the `Text` is given a proposed size when the view is rendered, corresponding to the parent's frame size. However, the `Text` will calculate the size of the text to display and will choose the size necessary to fit that text, plus additional padding, if any.

Layout for Views With a Single Child

Open the starter project and go to **Practice/ChallengeView.swift**, which is a new view created out of the SwiftUI View template. You can see that it contains a single `Text`:

```
struct ChallengeView: View {
  var body: some View {
    Text("Hello World!")
  }
}
```

If you reactivate the preview in Xcode, you'll see the text displayed at the center of the screen.

> **Note**: Every view is positioned, by default, at the center of its parent.

Blank Hello World

This screenshot doesn't give any indication about the Text's frame size. Try adding a red background:

```
Text("Hello World!")
  .background(Color.red)
```

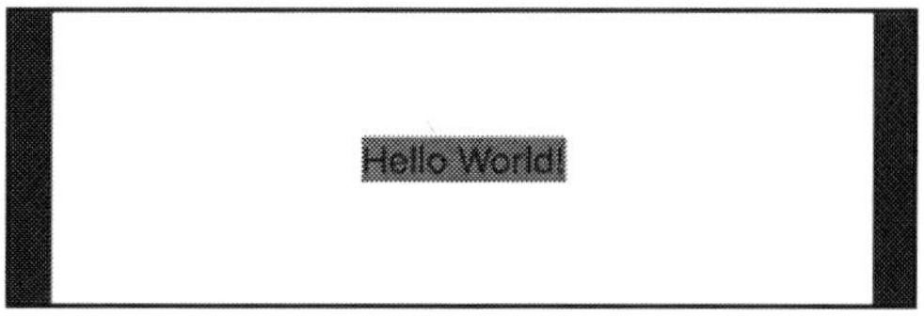

Hello World 1

Now you can see that the Text sizes itself with the bare minimum to contain the text it renders. Change the text to "A great and warm welcome to Kuchi":

```
Text("A great and warm welcome to Kuchi")
  .background(Color.red)
```

You'll see that the Text resizes its frame to accommodate the new content.

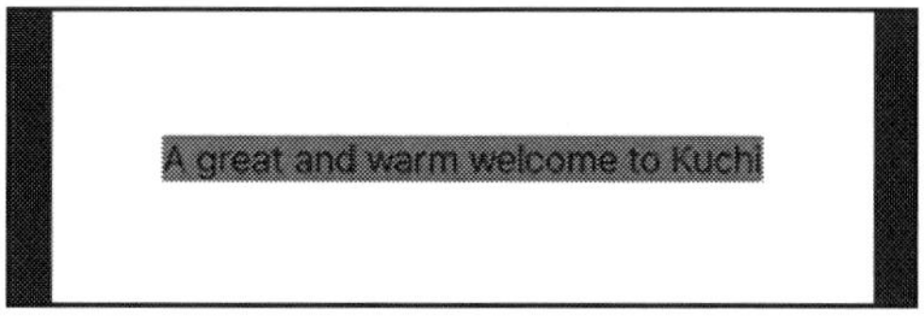

Hello World 2

The rules that SwiftUI applies to determine the size of a parent view and a child view are:

1. The parent view determines the available frame at its disposal.
2. The parent view proposes that frame size to the child view.
3. Based on the proposal from the parent, the child view chooses its size.
4. The parent view sizes itself such that it contains its child view.

This process is recursive, starting at the root view, down to the last leaf view in the view hierarchy.

> **Note**: Each modifier applied to a view creates a new view that embeds the original view. The set of rules described above applies to all the views, regardless of whether they are individual components, or views generated by modifiers.

To see this in action, try specifying a fixed frame for `Text`, plus a new background color:

```
Text("A great and warm welcome to Kuchi")
  .background(Color.red)
  // fixed frame size
  .frame(width: 150, height: 50, alignment: .center)
  .background(Color.yellow)
```

Hello World 3

Interestingly, you can see that the `Text` has a size that differs from the size of the view created by the `.frame` modifier. This shouldn't surprise you, because the four rules described above are applied here:

1. The frame view has a fixed size of 150×50 points.
2. The frame view proposes that size to the `Text`.
3. The `Text` finds a way to display the text within that size, but using the minimum without having to truncate (when possible).

Rule 4 is skipped, because the frame view already has a defined size. The `Text` automatically arranges the text to display in two lines, because it realizes that it doesn't fit in a single line of maximum 150 points without truncation.

If you expand the frame size, you have an additional proof of how views determine their size. Try, for example, a larger 300×100 size:

```
.frame(width: 300, height: 100, alignment: .center)
```

Hello World 4

Now `Text` has enough width at its disposal to render the text in a single line. However, it still occupies the exact space needed to render the text (in red background), whereas the frame view uses the fixed frame size (in yellow background).

Can you guess what happens if the size of the parent view is not enough to contain the child view? In the case of a `Text`, it will just truncate the text. Try reducing its frame size to 100x50:

```
.frame(width: 100, height: 50, alignment: .center)
```

Hello World 5

This happens in absence of other conditions, such as using the `.minimumScaleFactor` modifier, which, if needed, causes the text to shrink up to the scale factor passed as parameter, which is a value between 0 and 1:

```
Text("A great and warm welcome to Kuchi")
  .background(Color.red)
  .frame(width: 100, height: 50, alignment: .center)
  // Add this scale factor
  .minimumScaleFactor(0.5)
  .background(Color.yellow)
```

Hello World 6

Generally speaking, the component will always try to fit the content within the size proposed by its parent. If the component can't do that because it needs more space, it will apply rules appropriate to, and strictly dependent from, the component type.

This reinforces the concept that, in SwiftUI, each view chooses its own size. It *considers* proposals made by its parent, and it tries to adapt to that suggestion to the best of its ability, but that's always dependent on what type of component the view is.

Take an image, for instance. In the absence of other constraints, it will be rendered at its original resolution, as you can see if you replace the `Text` component with an `Image`:

```
Image("welcome-background")
  .background(Color.red)
  .frame(width: 100, height: 50, alignment: .center)
  .background(Color.yellow)
```

This is the same image you used in **Chapter 5: "Intro to Controls: Text & Image"**.

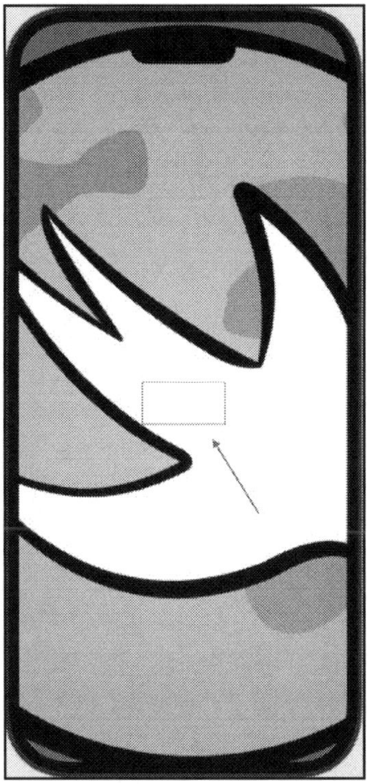

Hello World 7

The red arrow highlights the 100×50 static frame, but you can see that the image has been rendered at its native resolution, completely ignoring the proposed size — at least in the absence of any other constraints, such as the `.resizable` modifier, which would enable the image to automatically scale up or down in order to occupy all the available space offered by its parent:

```
Image("welcome-background")
  .resizable()
```

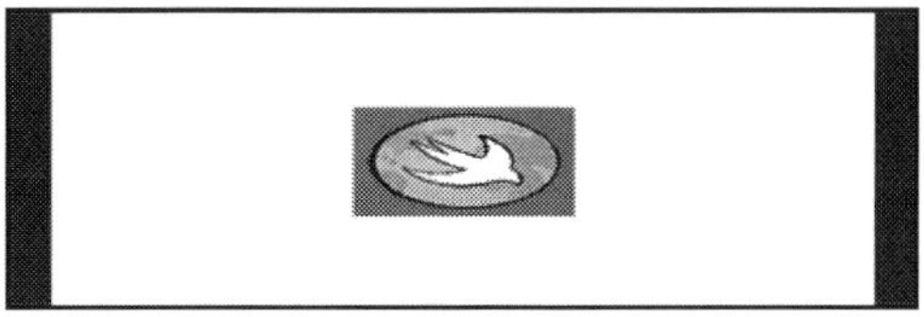

Hello World 8

So, in the end, you realize that there's no way for a parent to enforce a size on a child. What a parent *can* do is propose a size, and eventually constrain the child inside a frame of its choice, but that doesn't affect the ability of the child to choose a size that's smaller or larger.

Some components, like `Text`, try to be *adaptive* by choosing a size that best fits with the size proposed by the parent, but still with an eye to the size of the text to render. Other components, like `Image`, instead simply disregard the proposed size.

In the middle, there are views which are more or less adaptive, but also neutral, meaning that they don't have any reason to choose a size. They will just pass that decision to their own children, and size themselves to merely wrap their children.

An example is the `.padding` modifier, which does not have an intrinsic size — it simply takes the child's size, adds the specified padding to each of the four edges (top, left, right, bottom), and uses that to create the view that embeds the child.

Stack Views

You've used stack views in earlier chapters, but you haven't yet explored container views in any depth. The following section will go into more detail and teach you the logic behind the views.

Layout for Container Views

In the case of a container view, i.e., a view that contains two or more child views, the rules that determine children's sizes are:

1. The container view determines the available frame at its disposal, which usually is the size proposed by the parent.
2. **The container view selects the child view with the most restrictive constraints or, in case of equivalent constraints, with the smallest size.**
3. The container view proposes a size to the child view. **The proposed size is the available size divided equally by the number of** (the remaining) **children views.**
4. The child view, based on the proposal from the parent, chooses its size.
5. **The container view subtracts from the available frame the size chosen by the child view, and goes back to step no. 2, until all children views have been processed.**

The differences between this and the case of views with a single child that you've seen in the previous section are highlighted in bold text.

Back to the code! Restore the `Text` as it was before you replaced with the image, and duplicate it inside an `HStack`:

```
HStack {
  Text("A great and warm welcome to Kuchi")
    .background(Color.red)
  Text("A great and warm welcome to Kuchi")
    .background(Color.red)
}
.background(Color.yellow)
```

You've already encountered `HStack` in the previous chapters, so you should know that it lays out its children views horizontally. Since the two children are equal, you might expect that they have the same size. But this is what you get instead (make sure to *not* use a Pro Max iPhone to preview this content):

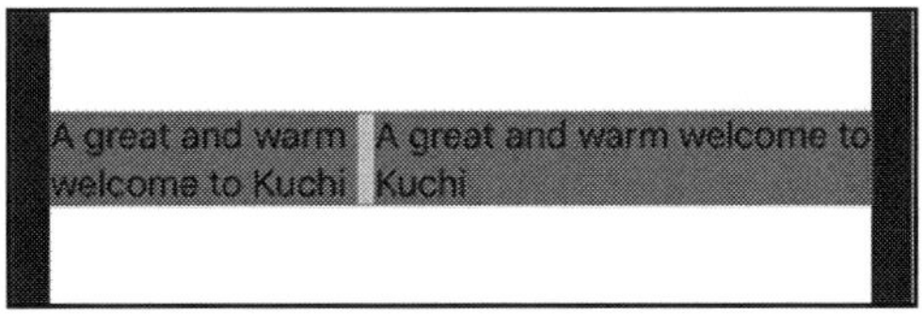

Hello World 9

Why is that? A step-by-step breakdown is necessary here:

1. The stack receives a proposed size from its parent, and divides it in two equal parts.
2. The stack proposes the first size to one of the children. They are equal, so it sends the proposal to the first child, the one to the left.
3. The `Text` finds that it needs less than the proposed size, because it must display the text in two lines, and can format it such that the two lines have similar lengths.
4. The stack subtracts the size taken by the first `Text` and proposes the resulting size to the second `Text`.
5. The `Text` decides to use all the proposed size.

Now try making the second `Text` slightly smaller, by replacing an `m` with an `n`, for example, in the word `warm`:

```
Text("A great and warm welcome to Kuchi")
  .background(Color.red)
Text("A great and warn welcome to Kuchi") // <- Replace `m` with
                                          //    `n` in `warm`
  .background(Color.red)
```

Being smaller now, the second `Text` takes precedence; in fact, it's the first one to be proposed a size. The resulting layout is this:

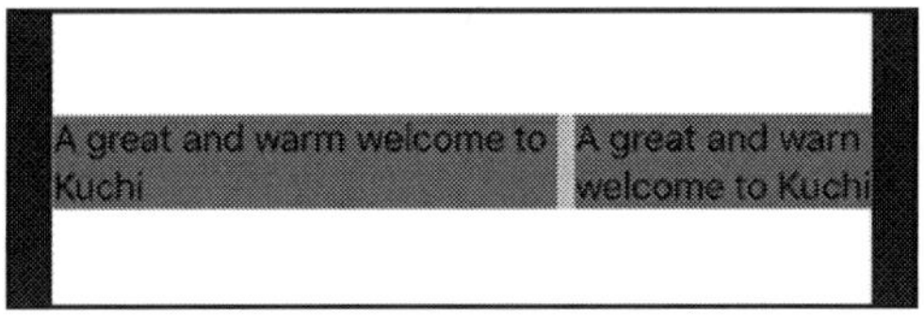

Hello World 10

You can experiment with the difference between longer and stronger texts in the two `Text` controls if you like.

Layout Priority

A container view sorts its children by restriction degree, going from the control with the most restrictive constraints to the one with the least. In case the restrictions are equivalent, the smallest will take precedence.

However, there are cases when you will want to alter this order. This can be achieved in two different ways, usually for different goals:

- Alter the view behavior via a **modifier**.
- Alter the view's layout **priority**.

Modifier

You can use a modifier to make the view more or less adaptive. Examples include:

- `Image` is one of the least adaptive components, because it ignores the size proposed by its parent. But its behavior drastically changes after applying the `resizable` modifier, which enables it to blindly accept any size proposed by the parent.

- `Text` is very adaptive, as it tries to format and wrap the text in order to best fit with the proposed size. But it becomes less adaptive when it's forced to use a maximum number of lines, via the `lineLimit` modifier.

Changes of the adaptivity degree directly affect a control's weight in the sort order.

Priority

You also have the option of changing the layout priority using the `.layoutPriority` modifier. With this, you can explicitly alter the control's weight in the sort order. It takes a `Double` value, which can be either positive or negative. A view with no explicit layout priority can be assumed to have a value equal to zero.

Go back to the **ChallengeView** file, and replace the view content with a stack of three `Text` copies. Make sure to use the *iPhone 14 Pro* for previewing, as other screen sizes would probably show different results:

```
HStack(spacing: 2) {
  Text("A great welcome to Kuchi")
    .background(Color.red)

  Text("A great welcome to Kuchi")
    .background(Color.red)

  Text("A great welcome to Kuchi")
    .background(Color.red)
}
.background(Color.yellow)
```

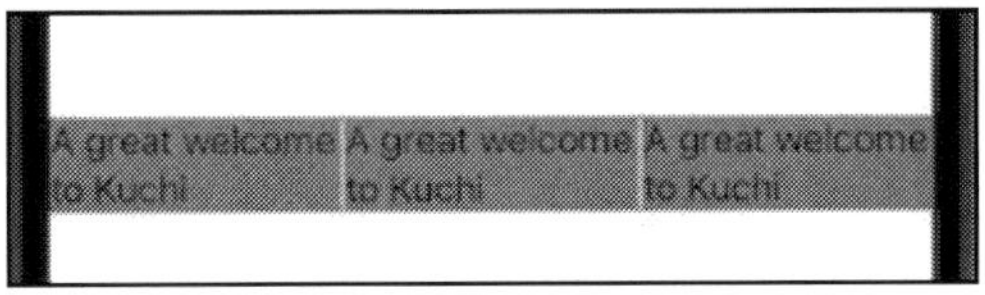

Hello World 11

Now try some explicit priorities. You can use any scale when setting priorities; for example, limit to values in the [0, 1] or [-1, +1] range, or go for integer values only, and so forth.

What's important is that **`Stack` processes views starting from the absolute highest down to the absolute lowest**. If the absolute lowest is below zero, views without an explicitly priority are processed *before* all the ones with negative value.

Add a layout priority of `1` to the second `Text`:

```
HStack {
  Text("A great and warm welcome to Kuchi")
    .background(Color.red)

  Text("A great and warm welcome to Kuchi")
    .layoutPriority(1)
    .background(Color.red)

  Text("A great and warm welcome to Kuchi")
    .background(Color.red)
}
```

You can see that it is given the opportunity to use as much space as needed.

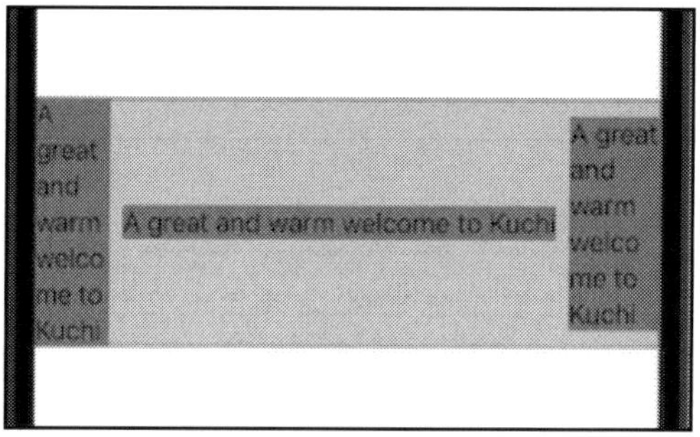

Hello World 12

Now try adding a negative priority to the first `Text`:

```
HStack {
  Text("A great and warm welcome to Kuchi")
    .layoutPriority(-1)
    .background(Color.red)

  Text("A great and warm welcome to Kuchi")
    .layoutPriority(1)
    .background(Color.red)

  Text("A great and warm welcome to Kuchi")
    .background(Color.red)
}
```

With this, you can expect it to be the last element to be processed.

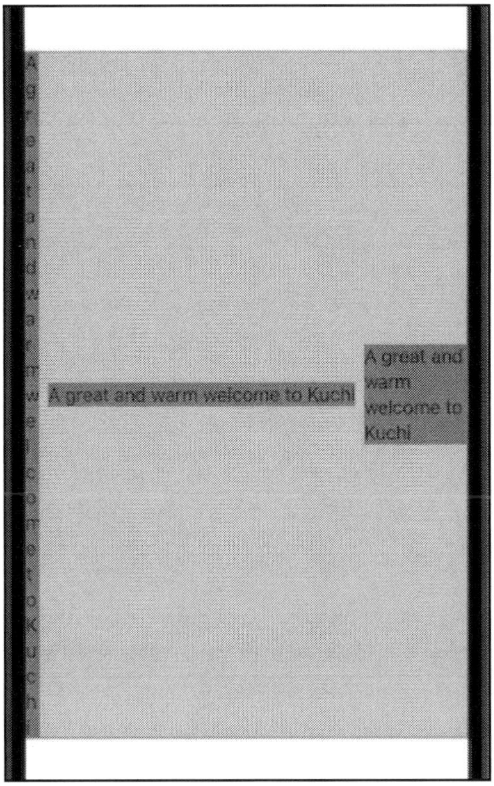

Hello World 13

And in fact, it is given a very small width. To counterbalance that, the control expands vertically.

There's an important distinction between the two ways of altering the adaptive degree: **manually setting the layout priority doesn't just alter the sort order, but also the size that is proposed**.

For views with the same priority, the parent view proposes a size that's evenly proportional to the number of children. In the case of different priorities, the parent view uses a different algorithm: **it subtracts the bare minimum size of all children with lower priorities, and proposes that resulting size to the child (or children, if more than one) having the highest layout priority**.

Look again at the result of the previous example. `HStack` lays out controls horizontally, so width is the most constraining size, because children views compete for width, whereas they have virtually no constraints vertically.

So, let's focus on width:

1. `HStack` calculates the minimum width required by the child view with lower priority. This happens to be the `Text` at the left, which has priority `-1`, and whose width is determined by the text displayed vertically in full. It therefore occupies the minimum possible width, highlighted in blue in the following zoomed-in image:

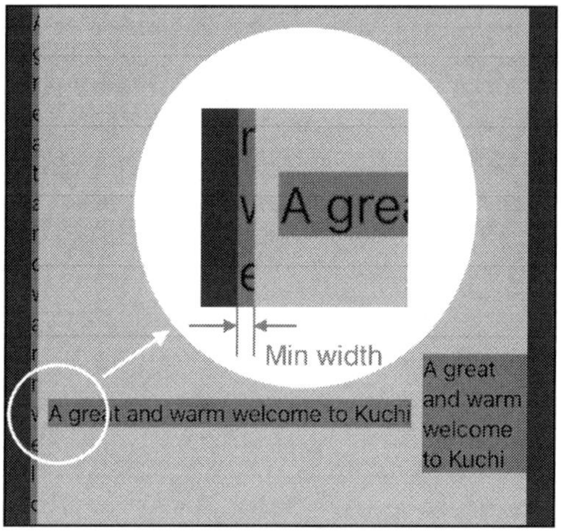

Hello World 14

2. `HStack` finds the child view with highest priority, which is the middle `Text`, having priority `1`, the highest among its children.

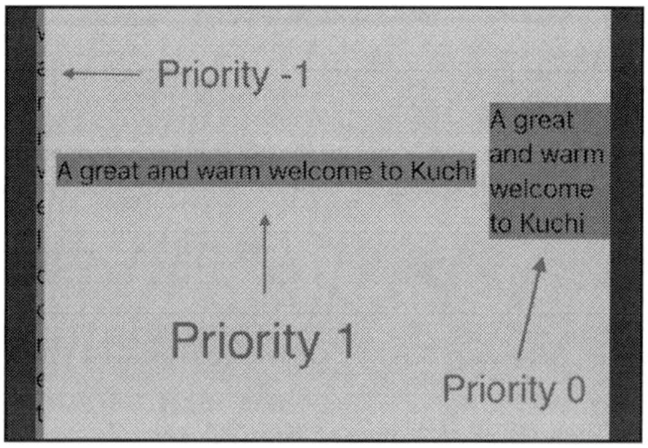

Hello World 15

3. `HStack` assigns a virtual minimum width to all children views having a priority lower than the maximum. The minimum width is the one calculated at step 1, and the number of children views having lower priority is two:

- The `Text` at left with priority `-1`
- The `Text` at right with no priority set (which, by default, it means priority `0`).

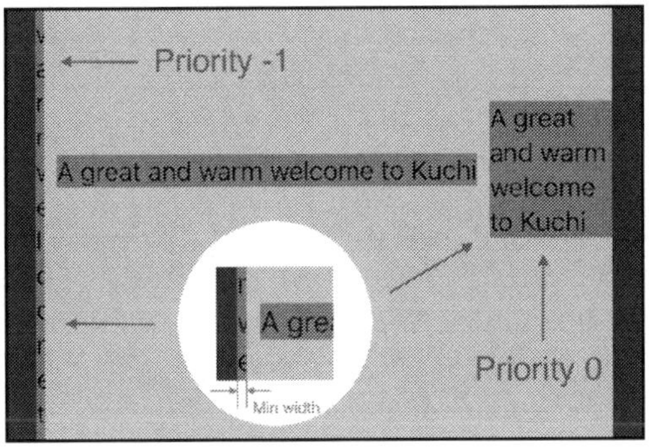

Hello World 16

4. Given the width at its disposal, for each child view with lower priority, `HStack` subtracts its minimum width, which in this case is two times the minimum width calculated at step 1. The resulting width is proposed to the child view with the highest priority, the `Text` at center.

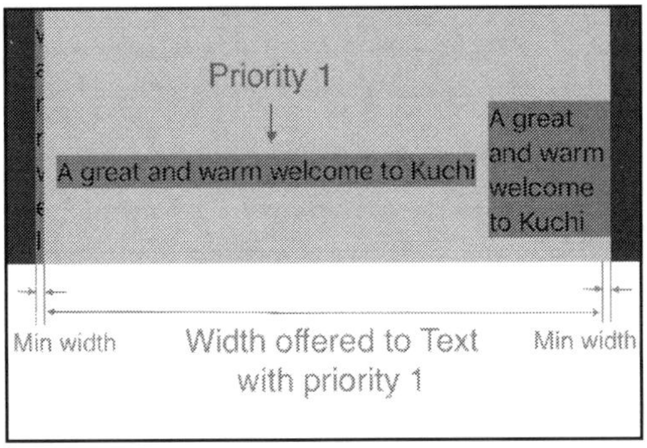

Hello World 17

5. The `Text` at center decides to take the width necessary to display the text in one line.

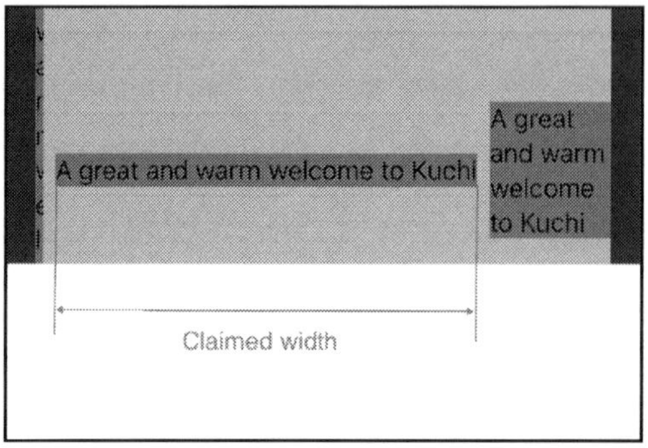

Hello World 18

At this point, the stack can process the next view, which is the `Text` with priority `0`, at the right side. The algorithm is the same; what's different is that the remaining width is now:

1. The width at `HStack`'s disposal.
2. Minus the size already taken by the `Text` with priority `1`.
3. Minus the minimum size required by the `Text` with priority `-1`.

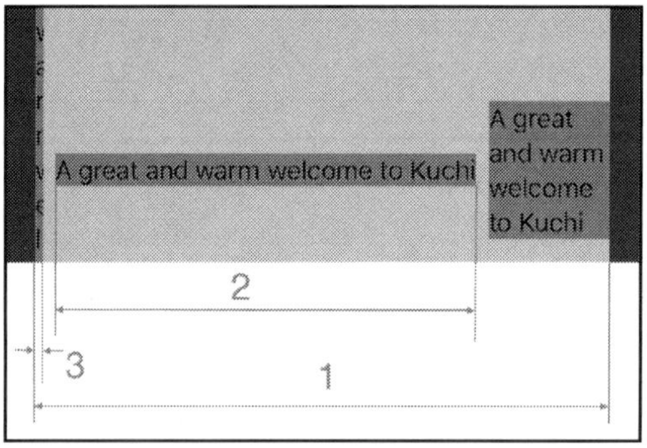

Hello World 19

You see that the `Text` with priority 0 makes best use of the size at its disposal, by wrapping its text across 4 lines. This leaves no size other components can compete for, besides the bare minimum computed at step 1 of the previous list. That's a guaranteed size; it's like having a guaranteed minimum salary, maybe extremely low, but still guaranteed regardless of how greedy your superiors are!

The HStack and the VStack

`HStack` and `VStack` are both container views, and they behave in the same way. The only difference is the orientation:

- `HStack` lays subviews out **horizontally**.
- `VStack` lays subviews out **vertically**.

AppKit and UIKit have a similar component, `UIStackView`, which works in dual mode, having an `axis` property which determines in which direction its subviews are laid out.

You've already seen `HStack` and `VStack` in this and in previous chapters. In many cases, using the initializer that takes the content view only. In reality, it takes two additional parameters, which come with default values:

```
// HStack
init(
  alignment: VerticalAlignment = .center,
  spacing: CGFloat? = nil,
  @ViewBuilder content: () -> Content
)

// VStack
init(
  alignment: HorizontalAlignment = .center,
  spacing: CGFloat? = nil,
  @ViewBuilder content: () -> Content
)
```

- **alignment** is the vertical and horizontal alignment respectively for HStack and VStack, it determines how subviews are aligned, defaulted to `.center` in both cases.
- **spacing** is the distance between children. When `nil`, a default, platform-dependent distance is used. So if you want zero, you have to set it explicitly.

The `content` parameter is the usual closure that produces a child view. But containers can usually return more than one child, as you've seen in the example of this section where the `HStack` contains three `Text` components.

The `@ViewBuilder` attribute is what makes that possible: It enables a closure that returns a child view to provide multiple children views instead.

A Note on Alignment

While the `VStack` alignment can have three possible values — `.center`, `.leading` and `.trailing` — the `HStack` counterpart is a bit richer. Apart from center, bottom and top, it also has two very useful cases:

- **firstTextBaseline**: Aligns views based on the topmost text baseline view.
- **lastTextBaseline**: Aligns views based on the bottom-most text baseline view.

These come in handy when you have texts of different sizes and/or fonts, and you want them to be aligned in a visually appealing fashion.

An example is worth a thousands words so, still in `ChallengeView`, replace its `body` property with:

```
var body: some View {
  HStack() {
    Text("Welcome to Kuchi").font(.caption)
    Text("Welcome to Kuchi").font(.title)
    Button(action: {}, label: { Text("OK").font(.body) })
  }
}
```

This renders as a simple `HStack` with two `Text`s and a `Button`, each having a different font size. If you preview it as-is, you see that the three children are centered vertically:

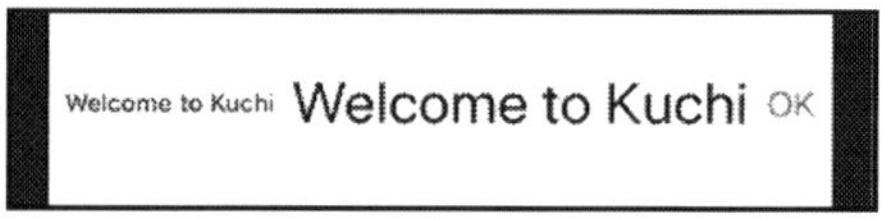

HStack center

But that doesn't look very good, does it? To make it look nicer, it would be better to have the text aligned at bottom, which you can do by specifying the `HStack` alignment in its initializer:

```
HStack(alignment: .bottom) {
```

But again, this isn't very pleasing to the eye:

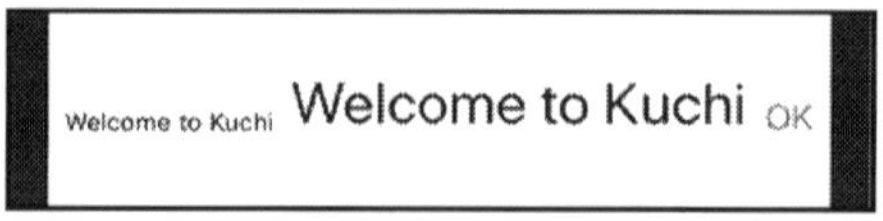

HStack bottom

And this is where the two baseline cases can come to the rescue. Try using `.firstTextBaseline`:

```
HStack(alignment: .firstTextBaseline) {
```

The smaller text and the button are now moved up slightly to match the larger text's baseline. That looks much better, right?

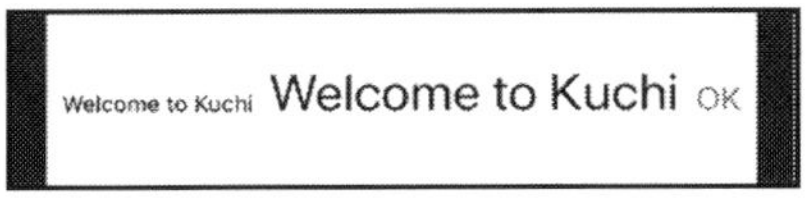

HStack base

The ZStack

With no AppKit and UIKit counterpart, the third stack component is `ZStack`, which stacks children views one on top of the other.

In `ZStack`, children are sorted by the position in which they are declared, which means that the first subview is rendered at the bottom of the stack, and the last one is at the top.

Interestingly, `.layoutPriority` applied to children views doesn't affect their Z-order, so it's not possible to alter the order in which they are defined in the `ZStack`'s body.

As with the other container views, `ZStack` positions its children views at its center by default.

Speaking of size, if the `HStack` has its height determined by its tallest subview, and the `VStack` has its width determined by its widest subview, both the width and height of a `ZStack` are determined respectively by its widest and the tallest subviews.

You'll use `ZStack` in a moment to build a portion of the congratulations view in the Kuchi app.

Other Container Views

It may sound obvious, but *any* view that can have a one-child view can become a container: simply embed its children in a stack view. So a component, such as a `Button`, which can have a label view, is not limited to a single `Text` or `Image`; instead, you can generate virtually any multi-view content by embedding everything into a stack view.

Stack views can also be nested one inside another, and this is very useful for composing complex user interfaces. Remember, however, that if a view becomes too complex, it could (and should!) be split into smaller pieces.

> **Note**: Stack views are limited to only containing 10 children. This is because stack views, amoung other `View` types, are initialed with a `@ViewBuilder`, which itself can be initialized with up to 10 views. At the time of this writing, this is easily verifiable by creating a stack with 11 children. The compiler will issue one of those cryptic error messages to tell you you've strayed too far.

Back to Kuchi

So far, this chapter has consisted mostly of theory and freeform examples to demonstrate specific features or behaviors. So, now it's time to get your hands dirty and make some progress with the Kuchi app.

The Congratulations View

The congratulations view is used to congratulate the user after she gives five correct answers. Open **CongratulationsView** and take a look at its content.

```
struct CongratulationsView: View {
  let avatarSize: CGFloat = 120
  let userName: String

  init(userName: String) {
    self.userName = userName
  }

  var body: some View {
    EmptyView()
  }
}
```

If this is the first time you encounter `EmptyView`, it's just... an empty view. You can use it as a placeholder everywhere a view is expected, but you don't yet have any view for it, either by design, or because you haven't built it yet.

Content in this view will be laid out vertically — so a good kick-off is adding a `VStack`, replacing the empty view:

```
var body: some View {
  VStack {
  }
}
```

Next, add a static congratulations `Text` inside, using a large font size of gray color:

```
VStack {
  Text("Congratulations!")
    .font(.title)
    .foregroundColor(.gray)
}
```

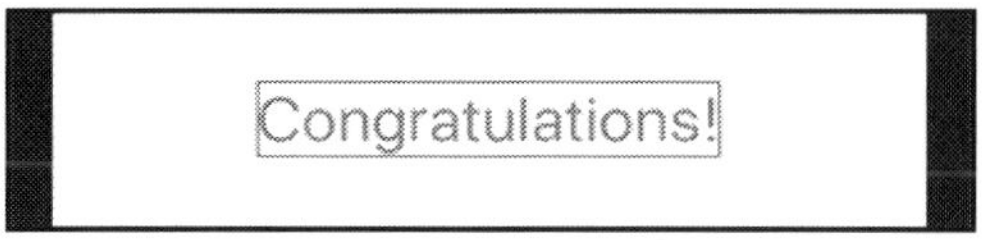

Congratulations view

Right after that congratulations `Text`, add another smaller `Text`:

```
Text("You're awesome!")
  .fontWeight(.bold)
  .foregroundColor(.gray)
```

Congrats View 2

The bottom of this view should contain a button to close the view and go back. Add the following to the bottom of the stack:

```
Button(action: {
  challengesViewModel.restart()
}, label: {
  Text("Play Again")
})
.padding(.top)
```

The button label shows a simple "Play Again" message, and the action is to reset the status of the challenge in the `challengesViewModel` property. But there's a problem: This property doesn't yet exist in the view. So, you'll need to add it.

For now, you can add the property and initialize it inline, directly in `CongratulationsView`.

```
struct CongratulationsView: View {
  // Add this property
  @ObservedObject
  var challengesViewModel = ChallengesViewModel()
  ...
```

In the next chapter, **Chapter 8: "State & Data Flow — Part I"**, you'll see how you can make this property an environment object, similarly to how you did with `UserManager` in the previous chapter, **Chapter 6: "Controls & User Input"**.

This is how the congratulations view looks:

Congrats View 3

User Avatar

But let's not stop there — surely you can make this look even better! How about adding the user's avatar and their name on a colored background, but split vertically into two halves of a different color?

Something like this:

Congrats View 4

Vstack

It might look complicated at first glance, but it only consists of three layers:

1. The background, split in two halves of different colors
2. The user avatar
3. The name of the user

You might already have figured out that you need a `ZStack` to implement it.

Between the two `Texts` in the `VStack`, add the following code:

```
// 1
ZStack {
  // 2
  VStack(spacing: 0) {
    Rectangle()
      // 3
      .frame(height: 90)
      .foregroundColor(
        Color(red: 0.5, green: 0, blue: 0).opacity(0.2))
    Rectangle()
      // 3
      .frame(height: 90)
      .foregroundColor(
        Color(red: 0.6, green: 0.1, blue: 0.1).opacity(0.4))
  }

  // 4
  Image(systemName: "person.fill")
    .resizable()
    .padding()
    .frame(width: avatarSize, height: avatarSize)
    .background(Color.white.opacity(0.5))
    .cornerRadius(avatarSize / 2, antialiased: true)
    .shadow(radius: 4)

  // 5
  VStack() {
    Spacer()
```

```
        Text(userName)
          .font(.largeTitle)
          .foregroundColor(.white)
          .fontWeight(.bold)
          .shadow(radius: 7)
      }
      .padding()
    }
    // 6
    .frame(height: 180)
```

Phew — that's a lot of code! But don't be intimidated — it's mostly familiar code that you've already used in the previous chapter. Here's what's happening:

1. You use a `ZStack` to layer content on top of one another
2. The bottom layer (the one added first) is the background, which is split into two halves.
3. Each of the two halves has a fixed height of 90 points and different background colors. This tells the `VStack` how tall it should be.
4. This is the user avatar, configured with a predefined size, and with a semi-transparent background color, rounded corners and some shadow. Notice how easy it is to customize an image!
5. The final `VStack` contains the name of the user, aligned to the bottom. The `Spacer` is used to make sure that the `Text` is pushed to the bottom. More on `Spacer` in a moment.
6. This entire `ZStack` is set to a fixed height.

The resulting view should look like this:

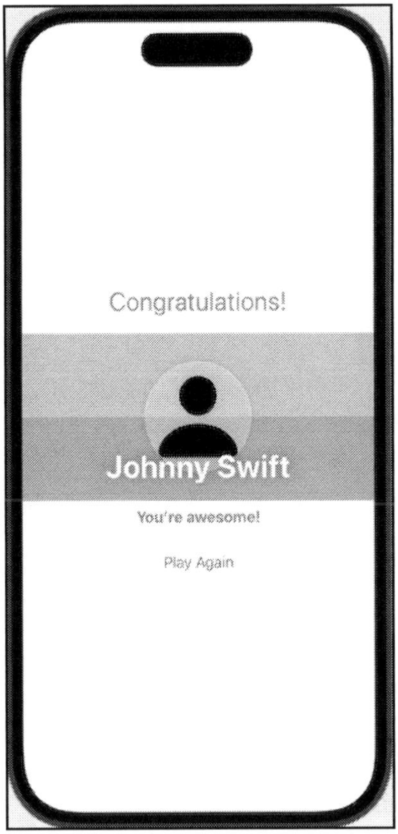

Congrats View

Much nicer, right?

The Spacer View

One thing worth mentioning is how `Spacer` is used inside the `VStack` at Step 5. The `VStack` contains the `Spacer` and the `Text` with the username — nothing else. So you might wonder why it's even necessary?

If you remove both the `Spacer` and the `VStack`, the user name would still be displayed, but it would be centered vertically:

Congrats View 2

In order to push it down, you use a `VStack`, containing a `Spacer` at top and the `Text` at bottom. The `Spacer` expands along the major axis of its containing stack (or in both directions, if not in a stack) — so, as a side effect, it pushes the `Text` down.

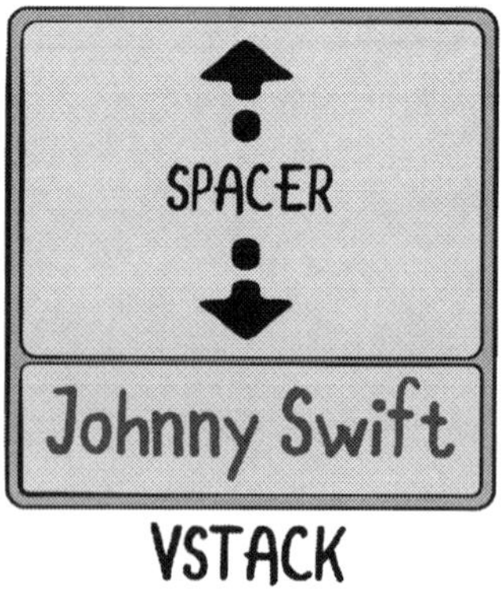

Spacer

Following the layout rules described at the beginning of this chapter, this is how it works:

1. The `VStack` is proposed a size by its parent, the `ZStack`.
2. `VStack` finds that the child view with less layout flexibility is the `Text`, so it proposes a size. In the absence of layout priority, as in this case, the proposed size is half the size at its disposal.
3. The `Text` computes the size it needs and sends the ticket back to the `VStack`.
4. The `VStack` subtracts the size claimed by the `Text` from the size at its disposal, and proposes that to the `Spacer`.
5. The `Spacer`, being flexible and unpretentious, accepts the proposal.

Challenge: The view would look much better if the button were aligned to the bottom of the screen. How could you do that?

There are probably several ways of achieving that result, but it can be done with `Spacers` alone.

In order to push the button down, you need to add a `Spacer` between the button and the text above it:

```
Text("You're awesome!")
  .fontWeight(.bold)
  .foregroundColor(.gray)

Spacer() // <== The spacer goes here

Button(action: {
  self.challengesViewModel.restart()
}, label: {
  Text("Play Again")
})
```

However, although you've achieved the desired result, something's not quite right:

Congrats View 3

The button is now anchored to the bottom, but everything else has been pushed toward the top. To fix that, all you have to do is add another `Spacer` before the first `Text` in the `VStack`:

```
VStack {
  Spacer() // <== The spacer goes here

  Text("Congratulations!")
  ...
```

Mission accomplished!

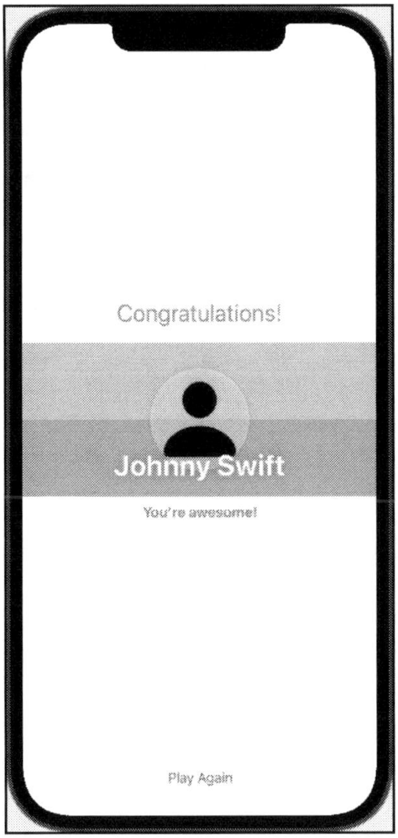

Congrats View 4

You're done with the congratulations view for now. It delivers the message nicely, now you can take care of another view.

Completing the Challenge View

Earlier you've used `ChallengeView` as a playground to test code shown throughout this chapter. Now you need to fill it with more useful code. The challenge view is designed to show a question and a list of answers.

Both use views defined in **QuestionView** and **ChoicesView**. The answers view, however, is hidden the first time the challenge view is shown, and it appears when the user taps anywhere on the screen.

First up, you need to add some properties that the view will need later. Open **ChallengeView** and add the following two properties:

```
let challengeTest: ChallengeTest

@State var showAnswers = false
```

As with previous examples, the preview is complaining about something. In `ChallengeView_Previews`, replace its entire implementation, including `previews`, with:

```
// 1
static let challengeTest = ChallengeTest(
  challenge: Challenge(
    question: "おねがい します",
    pronunciation: "Onegai shimasu",
    answer: "Please"
  ),
  answers: ["Thank you", "Hello", "Goodbye"]
)

static var previews: some View {
  // 2
  return ChallengeView(challengeTest: challengeTest)
}
```

Straightforward stuff here:

1. You create a challenge test to use in preview mode.
2. You pass that test to the view initializer.

`ChallengeView` is used inside `PracticeView`, and again, `ChallengeView` expects a parameter that you need to pass in. Open **PracticeView**, and replace the `ChallengeView()` line with:

```
ChallengeView(challengeTest: challengeTest!)
```

Force unwrapping is fine in this instance, as you're checking for `nil` on the line above.

With all that setup out of the way, you're ready to build the actual challenge view. As previously mentioned, the view is designed to show a question and a list of answers. To achieve this, replace the body of **ChallengeView** with:

```
var body: some View {
  // 1
  VStack {
    // 2
    Button(action: {
      showAnswers.toggle()
    }) {
      // 3
      QuestionView(question: challengeTest.challenge.question)
        .frame(height: 300)
    }

    // 4
    if showAnswers {
      Divider()
      // 5
      ChoicesView(challengeTest: challengeTest)
        .frame(height: 300)
        .padding()
    }
  }
}
```

Here's what's going on:

1. The two views are stacked vertically, so you use a `VStack`.
2. This button wraps the `QuestionView`, and on tap, it toggles the visibility of the `ChoicesView`.
3. This is `QuestionView` which, as mentioned, is implemented in its own file.
4. There's some conditional logic here to display `ChoicesView` only when `showAnswers` is `true`.
5. This is `ChoicesView`, implemented in its own file too. It receives a challenge test as a parameter, which you provide via an instance property.

You can now enable the live preview mode in Xcode, and test what you've just implemented. When you click on the previewed device screen, it will toggle the visibility of the answers view.

Challenge View preview

Reworking the App Launch

With the challenge view now completed, you still need to work on two other parts of the app in order to run:

1. Change the initial view when the app starts.
2. Amend `WelcomeView`.

The first part is very simple, as you've already done it in the previous chapters. Open **KuchiApp**, and replace `RegisterView()` with `StarterView()`, leaving everything else unaltered. This is what `KuchiApp` should look like:

```
@main
struct KuchiApp: App {
  let userManager = UserManager()

  init() {
    userManager.load()
  }

  var body: some Scene {
    WindowGroup {
      StarterView()
        .environmentObject(userManager)
    }
  }
}
```

Likewise, apply the same replacement to `KuchiApp_Previews`, so that it looks like:

```
struct KuchiApp_Previews: PreviewProvider {
  static let userManager = UserManager(name: "Ray")
  static var previews: some View {
    StarterView()
      .environmentObject(userManager)
  }
}
```

If you open **StarterView**, you see that it works as a proxy view, choosing which view to display depending on a flag in the user manager:

```
var body: some View {
  if self.userViewModel.isRegistered {
    WelcomeView()
  } else {
    RegisterView()
  }
}
```

If `isRegistered` is true, it shows `WelcomeView`, otherwise `RegisterView`, which was the view displayed at launch time, before you replaced it just a few moments ago.

Now, time to take care of `WelcomeView`. You need to change it so that it shows a welcome message the first time it is displayed, and it goes to the practice view after.

Open **WelcomeView**, and add these three properties:

```
@EnvironmentObject var userManager: UserManager
@ObservedObject var challengesViewModel = ChallengesViewModel()
@State var showPractice = false
```

You've already used `userManager` and `challengesViewModel` elsewhere, there's nothing more to say here. `showPractice` is a state flag that you can use to determine which view to show.

Because you introduced an uninitialized property (`userManager`) to the view, you need to update `WelcomeView_Previews` to include this. In `WelcomeView_Previews`, do this by adding the `.environmentObject(UserManager())` modifier where `WelcomeView` is instantiated. This is how it should look like:

```
struct WelcomeView_Previews: PreviewProvider {
  static var previews: some View {
    WelcomeView()
      .environmentObject(UserManager())
  }
}
```

Next, replace the `body` of `WelcomeView` with this:

```
var body: some View {
  if showPractice {
    // 1
    PracticeView(
      challengeTest: $challengesViewModel.currentChallenge,
      userName: $userManager.profile.name
    )
  } else {
    // 2
    ZStack {
      WelcomeBackgroundImage()

      VStack {
        Text(verbatim: "Hi, \(userManager.profile.name)")

        WelcomeMessageView()

        // 3
        Button(action: {
          self.showPractice = true
        }, label: {
          HStack {
            Image(systemName: "play")
            Text(verbatim: "Start")
          }
        })
      }
    }
  }
}
```

The new logic is:

1. If the `showPractice` flag is true, you show `PracticeView`
2. Otherwise, go to the other path, showing a welcome message
3. This button is used to acknowledge the welcome message and start practicing, by setting the `showPractice` flag when it is tapped.

With all this done, you can run the app.

Congratulations on the achievement! Here are a few screenshots of how the app looks.

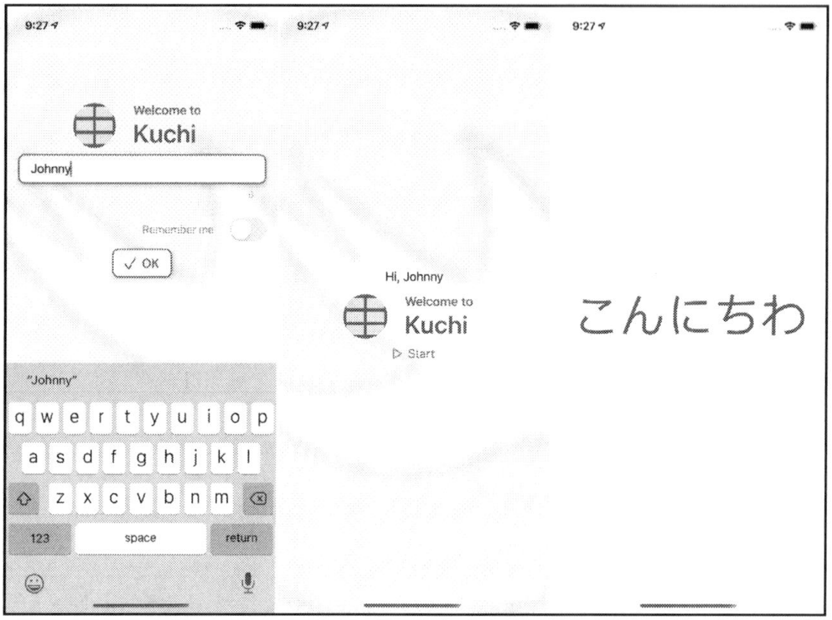

Kuchi

Kuchi 2

The Lazy Stacks

Stacks are very useful to lay out views in one direction or another. In most cases, they are all you need for that purpose. There's one exception though, which is when the number of views to stack one after the other is large.

If you have used either `UITableView` or `NSTableView`, you have probably figured out where the problem is. A large number of views means a lot of processing to create the views themselves, and a lot of memory to keep them all — if the user never scrolls down or right to the last element, it would be a huge waste of CPU cycles and memory.

So it's better to load cells on demand, as needed, starting with the bare minimum to keep the screen crowded, and keep loading other views as the user demands for more.

This is what lazy stacks do. And unlike their energetic counterparts, the lazy ones come in two flavors only, horizontal and vertical, respectively `LazyHStack` and `LazyVStack` — if you think for a moment you realize that only a fool would stack tens or hundreds of views one on top of another in the Z axis. :-]

Although you can add views to stack up manually, lazy stacks really shine when you iterate over a data source, making the lazy stack an efficient data driven stack component.

Practice History

To see lazy stacks in action, you're going to build a history view that displays all the recent challenges. Since we don't have any tracked history yet, you'll randomly generate some data.

Open **HistoryView** and take a look at its content. It defines:

- `History`: A data structure for the history, consisting of a date and a challenge.
- `random()` and `random(count:)`: A couple methods to generate some random history.

All this content is stuff you should already be familiar with, so there's no need for a step by step guide to get there from an empty file.

All that said, you can focus on the body property, which contains an EmptyView for now. Replace that with an empty lazy vertical stack:

```
var body: some View {
  LazyVStack {
  }
}
```

Now you need to iterate over all elements of the history property, which for now is randomly generated with a size of 2000 elements. To iterate, you might be tempted to use a for-in statement, but you can't - free to try, but all you'll get is a compilation error.

Instead you'll use ForEach, which looks like a statement, but in reality it's just a view that can generate content dynamically. Its initializer takes three parameters:

```
init(
  _ data: Data,
  id: KeyPath<Data.Element, ID>,
  content: @escaping (Data.Element) -> Content
)
```

- data is the collection to iterate over.
- id is a key path of the element type, History in your case, pointing to a property that can let each element of the collection to be uniquely identified - such property must conform to Hashable
- content is the view for each element - defined in the form of a closure that takes the element to display as parameter.

Inside the body of LazyVStack add the following:

```
ForEach(history, id: \.self) { element in
}
```

This loops through all elements of history, using the element itself as id - if you look at the declaration of History, you see that it implements the Hashable protocol.

To display the element, you can use the getElement(_:) method, which creates and returns a simple cell:

```
ForEach(history, id: \.self) { element in
  getElement(element)
}
```

If you resume the preview, you'll see this. Not bad at all!

Lazy Stack

If you enable the live preview, you notice that you cannot scroll — the content is fixed. No worries, all you have to do is embed the stack into a scroll view:

```
ScrollView {
  LazyVStack {
    ForEach(history, id: \.self) { element in
      getElement(element)
    }
  }
}
```

Now the content is scrollable vertically. It would be nice to add a header — and that's dead easy to achieve, simply embed `ForEach` into a `Section`:

```
Section(header: header) {
  ForEach(history, id: \.self) { element in
    getElement(element)
  }
}
```

You pass the `header` property to `Section`, which defines a text view with a gray background.

Lazy Stack with header

If you run it through live preview, you notice that the header scrolls with the rest of the view — but it would be better if it would stay anchored to the top. For this you can use the `pinnedViews` parameter of `LazyVStack`'s initializer to specify that section headers must be pinned.

Add the `pinnedViews` parameter as follows:

```
LazyVStack(spacing: 0, pinnedViews: [.sectionHeaders]) {
  Section(header: header) {
    ForEach(history, id: \.self) { element in
      getElement(element)
    }
  }
}
```

Note that you can also define a footer in sections, and pin them as well.

Key Points

Another long chapter — but you did a great job of getting through it! A lot of concepts have been covered here, the most important ones being:

- SwiftUI handles layout differently and more easily (at least, from the developer's point of view) than Auto Layout.
- Views choose their own size; their parents cannot impose size but only propose instead.
- Some views are more adaptive than others. For instance, `Text` tries to adapt to the size suggested by its parent, while `Image` simply ignores that and displays the image at its native resolution.
- There are three types of stack views; `VStack` for vertical layouts, `HStack` for horizontal layouts, and `ZStack` for stacking content on top of another.
- Stack views propose sizes to their children starting from the least adaptive to the most adaptive.
- **Horizontal** and **Vertical** stack views also have **lazy** counterparts, which load content on demand, as opposed to rendering everything upfront.
- The order in which children are processed by stack views can be altered by using the `layoutPriority` modifier.

Where to Go From Here?

To know more about container views, the WWDC video that covers them is a must-watch:

- WWDC 2019: Session 237 "Building Custom Views with SwiftUI" (https://apple.co/2lVpSSc)

Also recommended is the official documentation, which currently is a bit lacking in the verbosity department, but hopefully, that will improve soon.

- Stack Views: Official documentation (https://apple.co/2lXlbr1)

There are a few other container views that have not been covered in this chapter:

- `Form`
- `Group`
- `GroupBox`

You can check out the documentation for more information on these. Good luck in your adventures with SwiftUI stack and container views!

Section III: State & Data Flow

Learn how your user interface reacts to data flow and state changes.

Chapter 8: State & Data Flow — Part I

By Antonio Bello

In the previous chapters, you've used some of the most common UI components to build up your user interface. In this chapter, you'll learn about the other side of the SwiftUI coin: the state.

MVC: The Mammoth View Controller

If you've worked with UIKit or AppKit, you should be familiar with the concept of **MVC**, which, despite this section's title, stands for **Model View Controller**. It's vulgarly known as *Massive View Controller*.

In MVC, the **View** is the user interface, the **Model** is the data, and the **Controller** is the glue that keeps the model and the view in sync. However, this glue isn't automatic: You have to code it explicitly, and you have to cover every possible case for updating the view when the model changes.

Consider a view controller with a `name` and a `UITextField` (or `NSTextField`, in the macOS world):

```
class ViewController: UIViewController {
  var name: String?
  @IBOutlet var nameTextField: UITextField!
}
```

If you want `name` to be displayed in the text field, you have to manually copy it using a statement like:

```
nameTextField.text = name
```

Likewise, if you want to copy the contents of the text field into the `name` property, you have to manually do it with a statement like:

```
name = nameTextField.text
```

If you change the value in either of the two, the other doesn't update automatically — you have to do it manually, with code.

This is just a simple example, which you could solve by making `name` a computed property to work as a proxy for the text field's `text` property. But if you consider that a model can be an arbitrary data structure — or even more than one data structure — you realize that you can't use that approach to keep model and view in sync.

Besides the model, the UI also depends on a state. Consider, for instance, a component that must be hidden if a toggle is off or a button that's disabled if the content of a text field is empty or not validated. Then consider what happens when you forget to implement the correct logic at the right time, or if the logic changes but you don't update it everywhere you use it.

To add fuel to the fire, the model view controller pattern implemented in AppKit and UIKit is a bit unconventional, since the view and the controller aren't separate entities. Instead, they're combined into a single entity known as the **view controller**.

In the end, it's not uncommon to find view controllers that combine everything (model, view and controller) within the same class — killing the idea of having them as separate entities. That's what caused the "Model" term in *Model View Controller* to be replaced with "Massive", making it a brand new fat pattern known as *Massive View Controller*.

To sum up, this is how things worked before SwiftUI:

- The *massive view controller* problem is real.
- Keeping the model and UI in sync is a manual process.
- The state is not always in sync with the UI.
- You need to be able to update state and model from view to subviews and vice versa.
- All this is error-prone and open to bugs.

A Functional User Interface

The beauty of SwiftUI is that the user interface becomes **functional**. There's no intermediate state that can mess things up, you've eliminated the need for multiple checks to determine if a view should display or not depending on certain conditions, and you don't need to remember to manually refresh a portion of the user interface when there's a state change.

You're also freed from the burden of having to remember to avoid circular references in closures by using `[weak self]`. Since views are value types, captures happen using copies rather than references.

Being functional, rendering now always produces the same result given the same input, and changing the input automatically triggers an update. Connecting the right wires pushes data to the user interface, rather than the user interface having to pull data.

That doesn't mean that you can now look for a new job and change careers. :] You still control how you implement the user interface and how to link data to the UI. It's just that it's much simpler now, and much less error-prone. Not to mention that it's more elegant.

SwiftUI has many positive aspects — among them is that it's primarily:

- **Declarative**: You don't implement the user interface — you declare it.
- **Functional**: Given the same state, the rendered UI is always the same. In other words, the UI is a function of the state.
- **Reactive**: When the state changes, SwiftUI automatically updates the UI — but also the other way around, when the UI changes (typically in response to user input), the state is automatically updated.

This chapter focuses mostly on the last aspect: Managing the relationship between state and UI, and how to propagate state from a view to its subviews.

Now, open the starter project and build and run. You can use either the starter project that comes with this chapter or the copy of the project you developed in the previous chapter.

Proceed until you reach the challenge view, the first view in the picture below, which displays a Japanese word. Tap it and it will display a list of three options for your answer, as in the second view. If you tap the wrong option, it will display an error message. Otherwise, you'll see an alert that you've chosen the correct answer, shown in the third view.

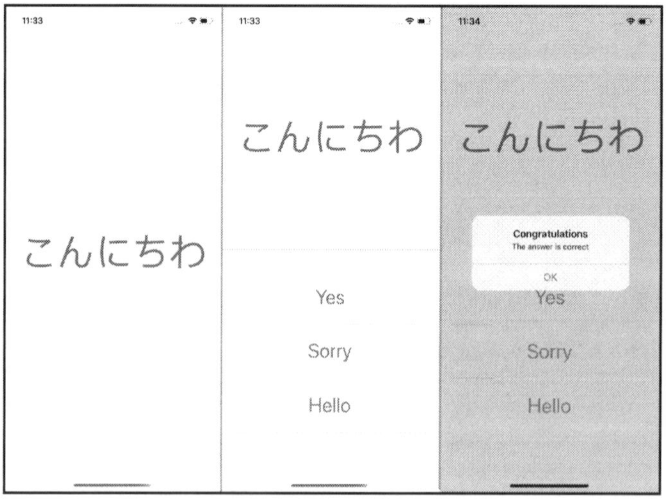

Initial Challenge View

And that's it — there's no option to move forward and try another challenge. You need to fix that... and guess what, you're going to use `@State` to do it.

State

If you've read along in this book so far, you've already encountered the `@State` attribute and you've developed an idea of what it's for and how to use it. But it's been an acquaintance — it's time to let it become a friend.

> **Spoiler Alert:** Now, you'll try a few things to understand some of the concepts of this chapter. Bear with it, the reason will be clear at the end.

The first thing you'll do is add a couple of counters to keep track of:

- The number of answered questions.
- The total number of challenges.

Create a new SwiftUI View in the **Practice** group and name it **ScoreView**.

Next, add two properties to keep track of the number of answers and questions:

```
var numberOfAnswered = 0
var numberOfQuestions = 5
```

Then replace the auto-generated `body` with this:

```
var body: some View {
  HStack {
    Text("\(numberOfAnswered)/\(numberOfQuestions)")
      .font(.caption)
      .padding(4)
    Spacer()
  }
}
```

In Xcode, resume the preview. This is what you should see:

Score View

Now, embed this new view into `ChallengeView` by adding it after the button:

```
Button(action: {
  self.showAnswers.toggle()
}) {
  QuestionView(question: challengeTest.challenge.question)
    .frame(height: 300)
}
// -Insert this-
ScoreView()
```

The preview looks like this:

Challenge Score View

Go back to `ScoreView`, which will display the current progress calculated as the number of challenges compared to the total number of challenges. For now, you only want to simulate progress. To do this, you'll add a button that increments the number of challenges when you tap it.

To achieve that, replace the body implementation with (and for now ignore the compilation error):

```
var body: some View {
  // 1
  Button(action: {
    // 2
    self.numberOfAnswered += 1
  }) {
    // 3
    HStack {
      Text("\(numberOfAnswered)/\(numberOfQuestions)")
        .font(.caption)
        .padding(4)
      Spacer()
    }
  }
}
```

Here you've:

1. Added a button.
2. Incremented `numberOfAnswered` in its action handler.
3. Embedded the previous content in the button's body.

Don't waste time trying to resume the preview, because it won't work; it doesn't even compile.

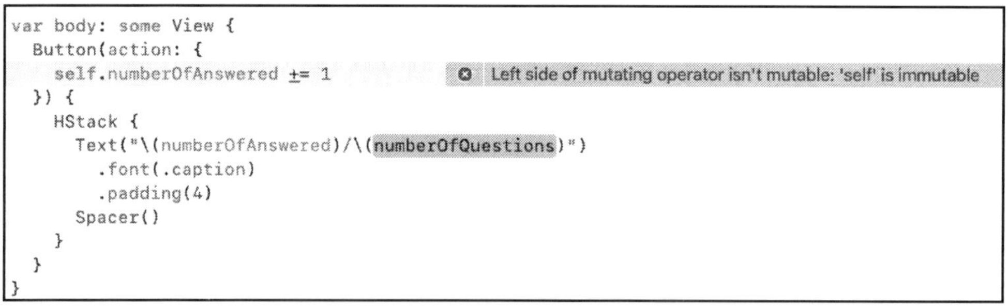

Score View error

Why is that? Simply, you can't mutate the state of the view by modifying its properties from inside the `body`.

Embedding the State Into a Struct

What if you try moving the properties to a separate structure? Move `numberOfAnswered` to an internal `State` struct and make it a property of the view:

```
struct ScoreView: View {
  var numberOfQuestions = 5

  // 1
  struct State {
    var numberOfAnswered = 0
  }

  // 2
  var state = State()

  var body: some View {
    ...
  }
}
```

As mentioned, here you:

1. Encapsulate `numberOfAnswered` into a struct.
2. Add a new property, an instance of that struct.

Next, update the text inside the `HStack` to reflect the property's new location:

```
Text("\(state.numberOfAnswered)/\(numberOfQuestions)")
```

and the button's action:

```
self.state.numberOfAnswered += 1
```

But when you try to compile, you get the same error. Unfortunately, this didn't work, either. That's not surprising, because the struct is a value type and you're still trying to mutate the internal state of the view.

Embedding the State Into a Class

By replacing a value type with a reference type, however, things change considerably. Try making `State` a class:

```
class State {
  var numberOfAnswered = 0
}
```

The error disappears and you can restore the preview, if Xcode has disabled. Try enabling live preview:

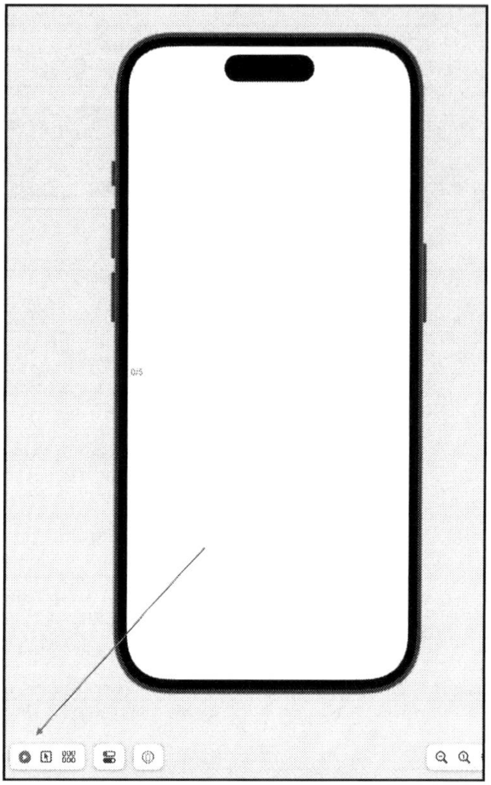

Score view live preview

Now, you can tap the view and it reacts visually, by flashing, but the displayed text doesn't change. It's anchored to `0/5`.

Add a print statement to the button's action handler, after you increment `numberOfAnswered`:

```
self.state.numberOfAnswered += 1
print("Answered: \(self.state.numberOfAnswered)")
```

Run the app and tap the text and you'll see the console displays a new value at every tap. This means the state updates, but the view doesn't.

> **Note**: For this step, you'll need to run in the simulator to see the output of the `print` statement.

This is actually the expected behavior if you're using UIKit. If the model changes, it's your responsibility to update the relevant part of the user interface.

Wrap to Class, Embed to Struct

Now that you've seen it still doesn't work, here's a challenge: What if you want to get rid of the class and use a struct, *again*?

If you're wondering why you'd want to do that, it will become clear as you read through this unconventional section of the chapter.

If you remember, the reason why the struct didn't work earlier is because a struct is a value type. Modifying a value type requires mutability, but the `body` cannot mutate the struct that contains it.

To update without mutating, you simply have to wrap the mutating property into a reference type — in other words, a class. So add this before `ScoreView`:

```
class Box<T> {
  var wrappedValue: T
  init(initialValue value: T) { self.wrappedValue = value }
}
```

This lets you wrap a value type (actually any type) inside a class. Now make `State` a struct again and make its property an instance of `Box<Int>`:

```
struct State {
  var numberOfAnswered = Box<Int>(initialValue: 0)
}
```

Now, this will work because you can mutate the `value` contained in `Box` without modifying `numberOfAnswered`. You'd mutate it only if you make it point to another instance, but instead, you're just going to update the instance that the property points to.

Xcode is still showing you two compilation errors because you have to use the `wrappedValue` property of `Box` rather than the `Box` instance itself. You'll fix those next. In the `Button`'s action closure, update the increment statement as follows:

```
self.state.numberOfAnswered.wrappedValue += 1
```

Here, you increment the `wrappedValue` of `numberOfAnswered`. Similarly, update the print statement that comes next:

```
print("Answered: \(self.state.numberOfAnswered.wrappedValue)")
```

And, finally, the `Text` inside `HStack`:

```
Text("\(state.numberOfAnswered.wrappedValue)/\
(numberOfQuestions)")
```

If you run the app, you notice that the counter still doesn't update when tapped, but the incremented value is printed to the console.

The Real State

At this point, you can officially ask: What's the point of all this discussion?

It's time to replace `State` with a similar struct from SwiftUI. Delete the `Box` class you added earlier, delete the `State` struct, and, finally, replace the `state` property with the following property:

```
var _numberOfAnswered = State<Int>(initialValue: 0)
```

Note that you renamed the property by prefixing it with an underscore. The reason why will be revealed soon.

Fix the compilation errors by renaming `numberOfAnswered` as `_numberOfAnswered`, and removing `state`. This is how `ScoreView` should look now:

```
struct ScoreView: View {
  var numberOfQuestions = 5
  var _numberOfAnswered = State<Int>(initialValue: 0)

  var body: some View {
    Button(action: {
      self._numberOfAnswered.wrappedValue += 1
      print("Answered: \(self._numberOfAnswered)")
    }) {
      HStack {
        Text("\(_numberOfAnswered.wrappedValue)/\
(numberOfQuestions)")
          .font(.caption)
          .padding(4)
        Spacer()
      }
    }
  }
}
```

Build and run, then navigate to `ChallengeView`. If you tap the score view... magic! The counter updates every time you tap it.

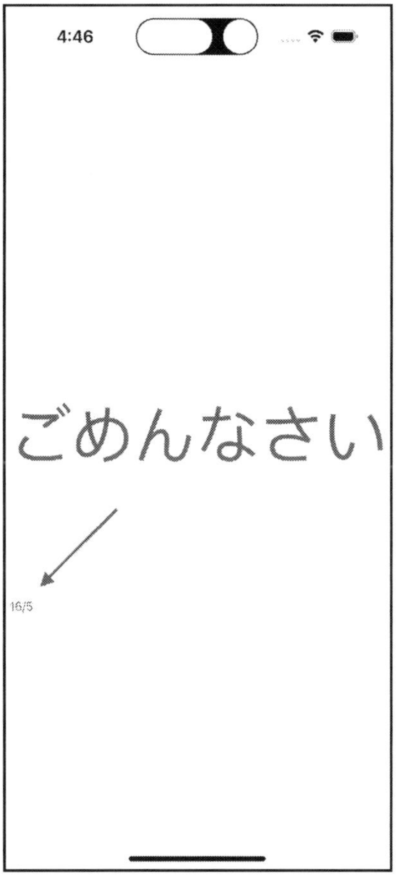

Score view updating

So, what's `State`? From the official SwiftUI documentation at apple.co/2WrfKzk:

> A property wrapper type that can read and write a value managed by SwiftUI.

It's like the Box inside the State struct you created earlier, but with the additional capability that the view containing it can monitor it.

> SwiftUI manages the storage of any property you declare as a state. When the state value changes, the view invalidates its appearance and recomputes the body. Use the state as the *single source of truth* for a given view.

Remember the term, **single source of truth** — you'll meet it again soon, and frequently.

When the wrapped value changes, SwiftUI re-renders the portion of the view that uses that value.

You've used state variables in earlier chapters. Now, you might wonder: What's the relationship between State<Value>, the @State attribute and the $ operator?

Replace _numberOfAnswered with the following:

```
@State var numberOfAnswered = 0
```

This looks more familiar. You can now compile and run, and you'll see that it still works.

So what's happening? The property declared with the @State attribute is a property wrapper, and the compiler generates an actual implementation of State<Int> type, prefixing the name by an underscore, _numberOfAnswered.

You can prove this by noting that you're still referencing this property in body:

```
var body: some View {
  Button(action: {
    // 1
    self._numberOfAnswered.wrappedValue += 1
    // 2
    print("Answered: \(self._numberOfAnswered.wrappedValue)")
  }) {
    HStack {
      // 3
      Text("\(_numberOfAnswered.wrappedValue)/\
(numberOfQuestions)")
        .font(.caption)
        .padding(4)
      Spacer()
    }
  }
}
```

There are three places where you use `_numberOfAnswered`:

1. In the button's action handler, to increment the counter of answers.
2. Still in the button's action handler, to print that counter.
3. In the button's embedded view, to display the number of answers against the total number of questions.

You can now replace each of them with the actual property that you've declared, `numberOfAnswered`. Just reference the property as-is. In the first two cases, replace it with:

```
self.numberOfAnswered += 1
print("Answered: \(self.numberOfAnswered)")
```

The compiler will translate these into the actual statements, which increase and read the `wrappedValue` of `numberOfAnswered`.

In the third case you do the same, replacing it with:

```
Text("\(numberOfAnswered)/\(numberOfQuestions)")
```

Compile and run the app. Once you navigate to `ChallengeView`, you won't notice any visual or behavioral change — which means that the replacement worked.

Now, you need to roll back the changes you added for testing purposes. Remove the button and leave only its body, which consists of the `HStack`:

```
var body: some View {
  HStack {
    Text("\(numberOfAnswered)/\(numberOfQuestions)")
      .font(.caption)
      .padding(4)
    Spacer()
  }
}
```

What have you learned? If you have a property in your view, and you use that property in the view's body, when the property value changes, **the view is unaffected**.

If you make the property a state property by applying the `@State` attribute, thanks to some magic that SwiftUI and the compiler do under the hood, **the view reacts to property changes**, refreshing the relevant portion of the view hierarchy that references that property.

Not Everything is Reactive

The score view defines two properties. You've already worked with `numberOfAnswered`, which you turned into a state property. What about the other one, `numberOfQuestions`? Why isn't it a state property as well?

`numberOfAnswered` is dynamic, meaning that its value changes over the life of the view. In fact, it increments every time the user provides a correct answer. On the other hand, `numberOfQuestions` is *not* dynamic: It represents the total number of questions.

Since its value never changes, you don't need to make it a state variable. Moreover, you don't even need it to be a `var` — you can turn it into an immutable and initialize it via an initializer.

Replace its declaration with:

```
let numberOfQuestions: Int
```

Next, you need to update the preview view by providing the new parameter, as follows:

```
ScoreView(numberOfQuestions: 5)
```

Also apply the same change to the other place where you reference the view, in `ChallengeView`. The compiler will help you find the exact line, just compile and follow all the compilation errors.

Using Binding for Two-Way Reactions

A state variable is not only useful to trigger a UI update when its value changes; it also works the other way around.

How Binding is (not) Handled in UIKit

Think for a moment about a text field or text view in UIKit/AppKit: They both expose a `text` property, which you can use to set the value the text field/view displays and to read the text the user enters.

You can say that the UI component owns the data that it displays, or that the user enters, in its `text` property.

To get a notification when that value changes, you have to use either a delegate (text view) or subscribe to be notified when an editing changed event occurs (text field).

If you want to implement validation as the user enters text, you have to provide a method that is called every time the text changes. Then you have to manually update the UI. For example, you might enable or disable a button, or you could show a validation error.

Owning the Reference, not the Data

SwiftUI makes this process simpler. It uses a declarative approach and leverages the reactive nature of state properties to automatically update the user interface when the state property changes.

In SwiftUI, components don't own the data — instead, they hold a reference to data that's stored elsewhere. This enables SwiftUI to automatically update the user interface when the model changes. Since it knows which views reference the model, it can figure out which portion of the user interface to update when the model changes.

To achieve this, it uses **binding**, which is a sophisticated way to handle references.

In **Chapter 6: Controls & User Input**, you played with a `TextField` in the Kuchi app. You used a state property to hold the user's name, which you later replaced with an environment object.

Now, you'll rework that form again, this time focusing exclusively on the text field.

Open **RegisterView** in the **Welcome** folder and comment out `RegisterView`, including its extension, and `RegisterView_Previews`, so that you can resume them later. Then, add this simplified code:

```
struct RegisterView: View {
  var name: String = ""

  var body: some View {
    VStack {
      TextField("Type your name...", text: name)
        .bordered()

    }
    .padding()
    .background(WelcomeBackgroundImage())
  }
}

struct RegisterView_Previews: PreviewProvider {
  static var previews: some View {
    RegisterView()
  }
}
```

As soon as you do that, the compiler will complain about `name` not being a `Binding<String>`. So, what's a binding? According to the official documentation:

> A **binding** is a two-way connection between a property that stores data, and a view that displays and changes the data. A binding connects a property to a *source of truth* stored elsewhere, instead of storing data directly.

You heard about this earlier, when you read that the component doesn't own the data, it holds a reference to the data that's stored elsewhere. You'll find out what *source of truth* means soon.

So, a state property contains a binding in its `projectedValue` property. To fix that here, change the type of the `name` property to `State<String>`:

```
var name: State<String> = State(initialValue: "")
```

Next, reference this property in the text field:

```
TextField("Type your name...", text: name.projectedValue)
```

Great, the compilation error disappears now. Enable the live preview and you can interact with the text field and input some text.

Editing in a Text Field

However, you don't have any proof that it actually works, so you'll add a `Text` component that displays the name after `TextField`:

```
Text(name.wrappedValue)
```

You don't need the binding here because you only need to display the text without modifying it, so you use the `wrappedValue` property.

Resume live preview. Now, when you type any text, it replicates in the `Text` component below `TextField`:

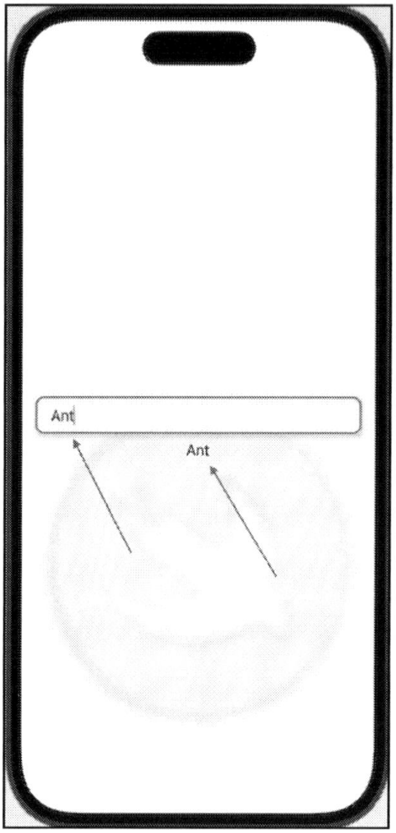

State and binding

This means that:

1. When the user modifies the text, `TextField` updates the underlying data using the binding of the `name` state property.
2. When the data changes, the `name` state property triggers an update to all UI components that reference the data.
3. The `Text` view receives the update request and updates its content by re-rendering the value that the `name`'s `wrappedValue` contains.

Now that you've seen what a binding is and where it belongs, it's better to get rid of the `State` property declaration and use the more fascinating counterpart defined by the corresponding attribute.

Replace the `name` property declaration once again, this time with:

```
@State var name: String = ""
```

You access a binding by using the `$` operator, so you can simply replace `name.projectedValue` in the text field with `$name`:

```
TextField("Type your name...", text: $name)
```

To reference the value only, use the raw property name instead as if it were the value instead of a wrapper.

```
Text(name)
```

Since you haven't made any functional changes, just used a different sugar syntax, you won't notice any difference when you test the view in the live preview.

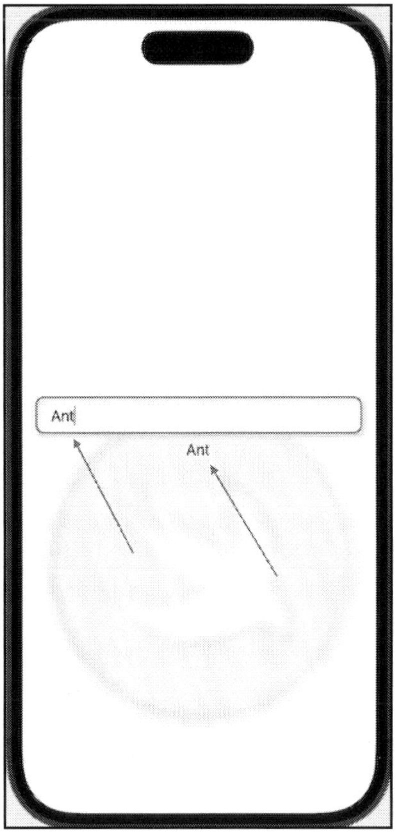

State and binding

The beauty of SwiftUI doesn't end there. You can use a state property to declaratively change the behavior or aspect of the user interface.

If you wanted, for example, to hide the text if the name length is less than three characters, you can just surround it with an `if` statement:

```
if name.count >= 3 {
  Text(name)
}
```

That expression re-evaluates automatically when `name` changes. Besides declaring it, you don't have to do anything else — no subscription to a changed event, no logic to manually execute. You simply declare it, and SwiftUI will take care of it for you.

Cleaning up

Before moving on to the next topic, delete the code that you added in **RegisterView** and restore the code you commented out at the beginning of this section.

Defining the Single Source of Truth

You hear this term everywhere people discuss SwiftUI, including, of course, in this book. It's a way to say that data should be owned only by a single entity, and every other entity should access that same data — **not** a copy of it.

It's natural to find similarities between value and reference types. When you pass a value type, you actually pass a copy of it, so any change made to it is limited to the lifetime of the copy. It doesn't affect the original. Likewise, changes made to the original data don't propagate and don't affect the copy.

This is how you do **not** want to handle UI state because when you change the state, you want that change to automatically apply to the user interface. If the data is a reference type, every time you move data around, you're actually passing a reference to the data. Any change made to the data is visible from anywhere you access the data, regardless of who made the actual change.

In SwiftUI, you can think of the single source of truth as a reference type with attached behavior.

Earlier, you created `ScoreView`, where you ended up using a state property named `numberOfAnswered`. The number of answered questions isn't determined nor changed in this view. Those actions take place in its parent view, `ChallengeView`, even if indirectly.

Consider `ScoreView` as an independent component of its own, unaware of why it's used and without a state. Here, you use it merely to display the number of completed answers versus the total number of answers.

Open **ChallengeView** and add a new state property right after `showAnswers`:

```
@State var numberOfAnswered = 0
```

You might think that all you need to do now is to pass this property to `ScoreView`. You actually *do* need to do that, but that's not the only thing.

Test what happens if you only pass the property. In **ScoreView**, remove the inline initialization of `numberOfAnswered` so that you're forced to use an initializer:

```
@State var numberOfAnswered: Int
```

At the same time, you need to update the preview to provide that new parameter. Replace its implementation with:

```
struct ScoreView_Previews: PreviewProvider {
  // 1
  @State static var numberOfAnswered: Int = 0

  static var previews: some View {
    // 2
    ScoreView(
      numberOfQuestions: 5,
      numberOfAnswered: numberOfAnswered
    )
  }
}
```

Here you're:

1. Creating a new state property.
2. Passing the new property to the `ScoreView`'s initializer.

Now, you need to update `ChallengeView` to pass the additional parameter as well. Replace the line that uses `ScoreView` with:

```
ScoreView(
  numberOfQuestions: 5,
  numberOfAnswered: numberOfAnswered
)
```

So far, you don't have a way to test if this works — and it shouldn't. `ChallengeView` has a button and an action handler in it. Add this line to temporarily increment the property to the button's action section:

```
self.numberOfAnswered += 1
```

Next, after `ScoreView`, add a text view showing the counter value:

```
Text("ChallengeView Counter: \(numberOfAnswered)")
```

Do the same in **ScoreView**, right before the spacer:

```
Text("ScoreView Counter: \(numberOfAnswered)")
```

Now, go back to `ChallengeView` and ensure that the live preview is active. Tap the upper half of the screen repeatedly and you'll notice that the `ChallengeView` counter increments, but not the `ScoreView` counter.

Why is that? A property marked as `@State` has, in reality, a `State<Value>` type, which is a value type. When you pass it to a method, it actually passes a copy.

Since a state property owns the data, you're also passing a copy of the data, so the original and the copy have different lives.

In SwiftUI terms, by copying a `@State` property, you end up having multiple sources of truth — or, if it helps you better understand the concept, multiple sources of **untruth**. Every state property has its relative truth, which, at some point, won't match the other sources' truth.

Here's an example to clarify the concept. If you want to share the phone number of your favorite pizza delivery with the rest of your family, you can write it on some sticker notes and give one to each family member.

Here, you're creating multiple sources of truth: If the phone number changes, not everyone will know.

Instead of writing the phone number down, you can write on the note: "The phone number is hanging on the fridge." Now, the note on the fridge is a single source of truth because everyone can update it and everyone is sure that the number is up to date.

Back to your code. Instead of passing the data, you have to pass a reference to it. The **binding** is the reference that you need. So go to `ScoreView` and update the state property to be a binding instead:

```
@Binding var numberOfAnswered: Int
```

Both `ChallengeView` and the preview now report errors because `ScoreView` expects a binding in its second parameter. You'll handle `ChallengeView` first.

Just as you did in the previous example with the text field, you obtain a binding by prefixing the property name with the `$` operator. So replace the statement with:

```
ScoreView(
  numberOfQuestions: 5,
  numberOfAnswered: $numberOfAnswered
)
```

You need to repeat that same change in `ScoreView`'s preview. Once that's done, try `ChallengeView` using live preview. When you tap now, both counters update:

State and Binding 2

So what have you achieved?

1. You used a state variable to store the counter that tracks the number of answered questions.
2. You passed a binding to `ScoreView` so it can access the same underlying data.
3. When you change the data, either through the state property or the binding property, you made that change available to everyone who references that data.

Cleaning up Again

In the section above, you added some temporary code that you can now remove.

In `ChallengeView`:

1. Remove `numberOfAnswered`, which you'll rework soon:

```
@State var numberOfAnswered = 0
```

2. Remove the increment statement in the button's action handler:

```
self.numberOfAnswered += 1
```

3. Use again the single parameter initializer for `ScoreView`:

```
ScoreView(numberOfQuestions: 5)
```

4. Remove the text control that prints the value of `numberOfAnswered`:

```
Text("ChallengeView Counter: \(numberOfAnswered)")
```

In `ScoreView`:

1. Make `numberOfAnswered` a state property again, instead of a binding:

```
@State var numberOfAnswered: Int = 0
```

2. Remove the other text control, which prints `numberOfAnswered`:

```
Text("ScoreView Counter: \(numberOfAnswered)")
```

3. In the preview struct, remove the second parameter passed to `ScoreView`'s initializer:

```
ScoreView(numberOfQuestions: 5)
```

And that's all. You used this temporary code to better understand the differences between `@State` and `@Binding`, and how they relate with the concept of *single source of truth*.

Key Points

This was an intense and theoretical chapter. But in the end, the concepts are simple, once you understand how they work. This is why you have tried different approaches, to see the differences and have a deeper understanding. Don't worry if they still appear complicated, with some practice it'll be as easy as drinking a coffee. :]

To summarize what you've learned:

- You use `@State` to create a property with data owned by the view where you declare it. When the property value changes, the UI that uses this property automatically re-renders.
- With `@Binding`, you create a property similar to a state property, but with the data stored and owned elsewhere: in a state property or an observable object of an ancestor view.

This is just half of what concerns state and data flow. In the next chapter you'll look at making your own reference types observable, and how to use the environment.

Where to Go From Here?

You've only covered a few of the basics of state so far. In the next chapter you'll dive deeper into state and data management in SwiftUI.

To get the most out of state with SwiftUI, there's a wealth of material that continues to grow and evolve. These include:

- SwiftUI documentation: apple.co/2MlBqJJ
- State and data flow reference documentation: apple.co/2YzOdyp

To become a power SwiftUI developer, you'd do well to check out the **Combine** documentation: apple.co/2L7kWTy.

Last, the **SwiftUI Attributes Cheat Sheet**: bit.ly/35Xt7eU is a helpful reference.

Chapter 9: State & Data Flow – Part II

By Antonio Bello

In the previous chapter you learned how to use `@State` and `@Binding`, and the power that they brought to you in a transparent and easy to use way.

In this chapter you'll learn about other tools that allows you to make your own types efficiently reactive, or reactively efficient. :]

Before diving into it, while you're still dry, a word about the project. You can use the starter project that comes with this chapter, but since it is an exact copy of the final project from the previous chapter, you can also reuse what you've worked on, if you prefer — no change needed.

The Art of Observation

So, you use a binding to pass data that a source of truth owns, and a state to additionally own the data itself. You have everything you need to create an awesome user interface, right? Wrong!

Consider that you have a model made up of several properties and you want to use it as a state variable. If you implement the model as a value type, like a struct, it works properly, but it's not efficient.

In fact, if you have an instance of a struct and you modify one of its properties, you actually replace the entire instance by a copy of it with the updated property. In other words, the entire instance mutates.

When you change a property of your model, you'd expect that only the UI that references that property should refresh. In reality, you've modified the whole struct instance, so the update will trigger a refresh in all places that reference the struct.

Depending on the use case, this could have a low impact or it could affect performance considerably.

That doesn't mean you shouldn't use structs, just that you should avoid putting unrelated properties in the same model. This prevents cases where updating a property value triggers a UI update that doesn't use that property.

If you implement your model as a reference type instead — that is, a class — it won't actually work. If a property is a reference type, it mutates only if you assign a new reference. Any change made to the actual instance doesn't change the property itself, which means it won't trigger any UI refresh.

Making an Object Observable

The good news is that you have four new types that come to your rescue. Given the considerations expressed above, your custom model could:

- Be a reference type.
- Be able to specify which properties must trigger — or not trigger — UI updates.

You need the four new types to:

- Declare a **class** observable. This enables it to be used similarly to state properties.
- Declare a **class property** observable.

- Declare a **property that's an instance of an observable class type**, observed. That is, you have an *observable class type*, you have a *property instance of that class*, and you want to make that *property observed*. This is what lets you use an observable class as an observed property in a view.

There are already two classes in the Kuchi project that you can use as observable objects: `UserManager` and `ChallengesViewModel`.

To make a class observable, make it conform to `ObservableObject`. The class becomes a **publisher**. The protocol defines one `objectWillChange` property only, which synthesizes automatically. That means you aren't required to implement it — the compiler will do it for you.

Open **Profile/UserManager** and look at the class declaration:

```
// 1
final class UserManager: ObservableObject {
  // 2
  @Published
  var profile: Profile = Profile()

  @Published
  var settings: Settings = Settings()

  @Published
  var isRegistered: Bool
  ...
}
```

Here you can see that:

1. The class conforms to `ObservableObject`, which makes it a publisher.
2. You define three properties and decorate them with the `@Published` attribute. These properties work in a similar way as a state property does in a view.

The same considerations you made for state properties apply to published properties as well:

- They should be value types, either basic data types or structures.
- With structures, it's better to limit the number of properties they contain to the minimum required, avoiding one-struct-for-all scenarios.

Once you have an observable class, using it is pretty simple — it's just like using a state variable.

Observing an Object

As mentioned earlier, there's another observable class in the project, in **Practice/ChallengesViewModel**. Its purpose is to define and serve challenges, which consist of a Japanese word, its English translation and a list of potential answers. Only one answer is correct.

There's a property that contains the currently-active challenge:

```
@Published var currentChallenge: ChallengeTest?
```

As you see, it's a published property (which, as stated above, is like a state property):

- It defines a single source of truth.
- It has a binding.
- Whenever it's updated, it triggers a UI refresh that references it.

The most natural place to use this property is in the challenge view. Later, you'll realize that is not entirely true — in fact the view already contains a challenge property. But for now, just pretend it is.

Open **ChallengeView** and add this property after the existing `challengeTest`:

```
@ObservedObject var challengesViewModel = ChallengesViewModel()
```

Next, replace the two occurrences of `challengeTest` with `challengesViewModel.currentChallenge!`. The first is where you use `QuestionView`:

```
QuestionView(question:
  challengesViewModel.currentChallenge!.challenge.question)
```

The second is a few lines below, where you use `ChoicesView`:

```
ChoicesView(
  challengeTest: challengesViewModel.currentChallenge!)
```

Run the app now and navigate to the challenge view. You won't notice any difference. Tapping the upper half of the view will toggle the choices view, as before.

You can, however, temporarily apply a change to the published property to verify that changes are reflected to the UI. In the button's action handler, call the view model's method to advance to the next challenge:

```
Button(action: {
  showAnswers.toggle()
  // 1
  challengesViewModel.generateRandomChallenge()
}) {
  QuestionView(question:
    challengesViewModel.currentChallenge!.challenge.question
  )
    .frame(height: 300)
}
```

`generateRandomChallenge()` picks a new random challenge and puts it in `currentChallenge`. Since the property changes, it triggers a UI refresh. Now, when you run the app and tap the upper half of the view, it will switch to a new challenge.

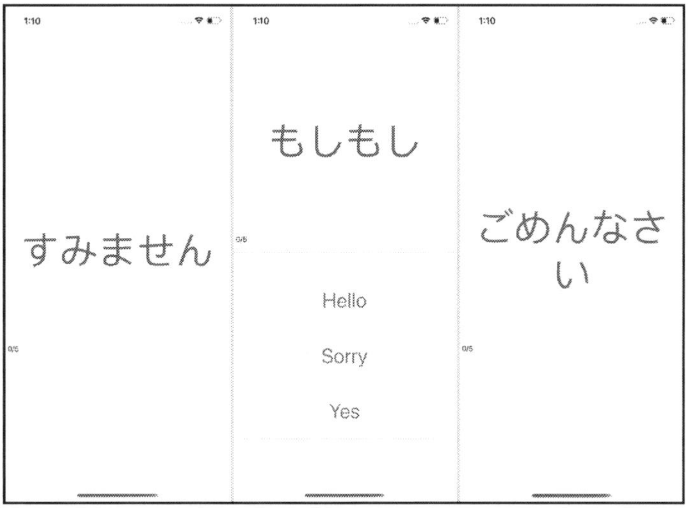

Current selection

You obtained this by adding the `@ObservedObject` attribute to the `challengesViewModel` property, instance of `ChallengesViewModel`. As mentioned earlier, this class defines a `@Published` property named `currentChallenge`, which you reference in the code (by passing it to `QuestionView` and `ChoicesView`).

When in the button tap handler you call `generateRandomChallenge()`, that property is mutated, and that causes the places where it is referenced to redraw, so both `QuestionView` and `ChoicesView` are refreshed, and that is what makes the new challenge to be displayed.

However, `ChallengeView` is not the right place for `ChallengesViewModel` to reside, so you better move it to a more appropriate place. Undo the changes made above by:

1. Deleting `challengesViewModel`.
2. Replacing the two occurrences of `challengesViewModel.currentChallenge!` with `challengeTest`.
3. Deleting `self.challengesViewModel.generateRandomChallenge()` from the button's action handler.

Alternately, press **Command-Z** repeatedly until you undo all the changes.

> **Note**: You have made this to see the differences between one approach and the other. Sorry for making you go back, but this way it clarifies the next explanation.

So, where should `challengesViewModel` go? `PracticeView` references `ChallengeView`. It already contains two properties that are both bindings, so they reference data stored elsewhere.

The purpose of this view is to display a challenge if the user hasn't completed them all. Otherwise, it will show a congratulations view.

`WelcomeView`, in turn, references `PracticeView`. You can see that it already contains a `challengesViewModel` property, an instance of `ChallengesViewModel`. It's also declared as `@ObservedObject`, which enables its published properties to behave like state properties.

So this is the right place where `challengesViewModel` should be, and it's not a coincidence that it is already declared and initialized there.

Sharing in the Environment

You've already played with the app in this chapter, so you've probably noticed that the game lacks progress.

When you select the correct answer in a challenge, not much happens other than getting a confirmation alert. The app should advance to the next challenge. You'll fix that next.

Open **ChallengesViewModel** and you'll find two methods to log correct and incorrect answers:

```
func saveCorrectAnswer(for challenge: Challenge) {
  correctAnswers.append(challenge)
}

func saveWrongAnswer(for challenge: Challenge) {
  wrongAnswers.append(challenge)
}
```

After saving a correct answer, you want to advance to the next challenge. There's another method in the class, `generateRandomChallenge()`, which is perfect for this goal.

Now, you need to use these methods. It turns out, `ChoicesView`, the view where the user selects one of the options, already uses them.

Look at the view implementation, and you'll notice that:

- It has a `challengesViewModel` property, declared as `@ObservedObject`.
- It invokes `generateRandomChallenge()` in the Alert dismiss button's handler.
- It invokes both `saveCorrectAnswer()` and `saveWrongAnswer()` in `checkAnswer(at:)`.

However, the app doesn't work as expected; when you've completed one challenge, it doesn't advance to the next.

The reason is simple: You're creating an instance of `ChallengesViewModel` here, but also in `WelcomeView`. So they're two different instances, and any change made to one doesn't propagate to the other.

This is about the *source of truth* discussed in the previous chapter — here you have two different sources of truth, but there should be only one.

A possible solution is to pass `challengesViewModel` from `WelcomeView` down to `ChoicesView`, via initializers — but that's not elegant. Fortunately, there's a better way.

This might be a typical case where a singleton could do the job pretty well. But, confidentially speaking, the singleton pattern is not the best pattern to use — it creates unnecessary dependencies that you can easily avoid using other patterns, such as **dependency injection**.

Environment and Objects

SwiftUI provides a way to achieve that. It's not a dependency injection, just a way to put an object into something like a bag and retrieve it whenever you need it. The bag is called the **environment**, and the object an **environment object**.

This pattern uses two of the most popular SwiftUI ways to do things: a modifier and an attribute.

- Using `environmentObject(_:)`, you inject an object into the environment.
- Using `@EnvironmentObject`, you pull an object (actually a reference to an object) out of the environment and store it in a property.

Once you inject an object into the environment, *it's accessible to the view and its subviews, but it's not accessible from the view's parent and above.*

Just to be sure, inject it into the root view for now. Open **KuchiApp** and, in `body`, locate where `StarterView` instantiates. You'll find that another object is injected into the environment: an instance of `UserManager`. You're going to use the same pattern.

Add this line right after the `userManager` property declaration, at line 37:

```
let userManager = UserManager()
// Add this line
let challengesViewModel = ChallengesViewModel()
```

This creates a new instance of the challenges view model class. Now you can inject it into the environment using the `environmentObject(:_)` modifier:

```
var body: some Scene {
  WindowGroup {
    StarterView()
      .environmentObject(userManager)
      // Add this line
      .environmentObject(challengesViewModel)
  }
}
```

Now all the views in the `StarterView`'s hierarchy have access to that instance.

> **Note**: You're injecting an unnamed instance into the environment. When you pull it using the `@EnvironmentObject`, you just specify the instance type. This is important to remember because it means that you can only inject one instance per type into the environment. If you inject another instance, it will replace the previous one.

Now, you have to make a change in all the places that use `ChallengesViewModel`. So in `WelcomeView`, replace this property:

```
@ObservedObject var challengesViewModel = ChallengesViewModel()
```

with:

```
@EnvironmentObject var challengesViewModel: ChallengesViewModel
```

- You're using the `@EnvironmentObject` attribute, specifying that this property must be initialized with an instance of `ChallengesViewModel` taken from the view's environment.
- You no longer need to instantiate it because the property is initialized with an existing instance — more precisely, the instance you created earlier in **KuchiApp**

Do the same property replacement in `ChoicesView`.

Now, build and run and test the app. When you provide a correct answer, it advances to the next challenge.

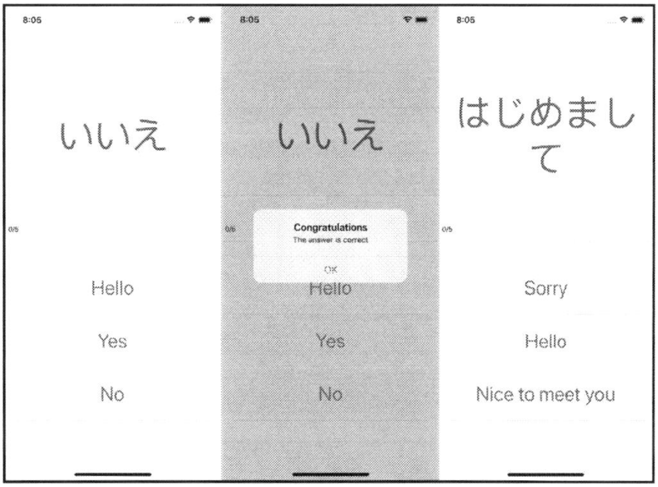

Challenge sequence

However, there are two issues:

1. The answered challenges counter doesn't update.
2. After five correct answers, it shows the congratulations view, but you can't get away from it. the **Play Again** button does nothing:

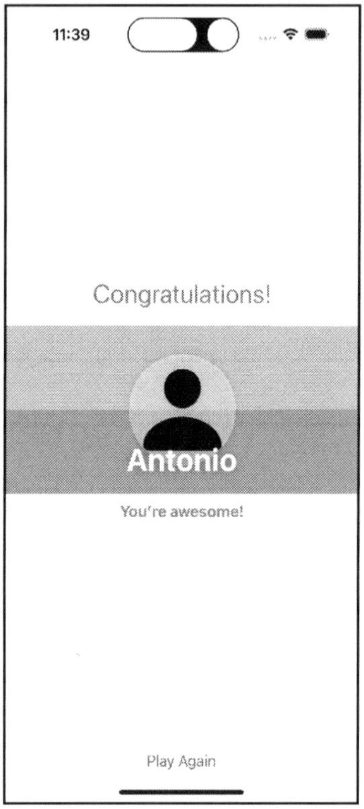

Congrats view

Environment and Duplicates (to Avoid)

So earlier you left the app with two issues that you're going to get rid of now.

The latter (getting away from the congratulations view) is a simple fix. Open **Practice/CongratulationsView** and locate the button at the bottom of the file. Its action handler calls `challengesViewModel.restart()`, which seems the correct way to exit the congratulations view and start over with a new challenge session.

If you look at `challengesViewModel`, you see that it's an observed object instantiated inline, whereas it should be taken from the environment, so that there's one single source of truth.

Replace it, as you did with the other cases, with:

```
@EnvironmentObject var challengesViewModel: ChallengesViewModel
```

Now, build and run and go to the end of the challenge session. When the congratulations view displays, you can now tap the button to restart the session.

As for the other issue (the answered challenges counter not updating) open **Practice/ScoreView**. You may notice that `numberOfAnswered`, which holds the number of correct answers, is a state property, whereas, in order to function properly, it should be passed as a binding from its superview — again, to comply with the *single source of truth* rule.

You could be tempted to get the challenge view model from the environment, but that would add an unnecessary dependency. This is a simple view that's supposed to display a pair of numbers, so it's better to make it as dumb as possible.

To let the parent pass the parameter, you need to change it to a binding. In `numberOfAnswered`, replace `@State` with `@Binding` and remove the initialization, so it looks like:

```
@Binding var numberOfAnswered: Int
```

Now that the property is a binding, you must provide it in the initializer. In fact, the preview now gives an error because of the missing argument. Just add it, passed as binding:

```
ScoreView(
  numberOfQuestions: 5,
  numberOfAnswered: $numberOfAnswered
)
```

Likewise, `ChallengeView`, where you use `ScoreView`, gives a similar error, but you don't have any state or binding property to pass. So add a `numberOfAnswered` to `ChallengeView`, as you did before:

```
@Binding var numberOfAnswered: Int
```

And pass it to `ScoreView`:

```
ScoreView(
  numberOfQuestions: 5,
  numberOfAnswered: $numberOfAnswered
)
```

The preview, again, isn't happy about these changes, so you have to add some code to make it compile. You need to pass a `numberOfAnswered` binding. You can add a state property to `ChallengeView_Previews`

```
@State static var numberOfAnswered: Int = 0
```

Next, update the line where you use `ChallengeView` by passing the expected parameter:

```
return ChallengeView(
  challengeTest: challengeTest,
  numberOfAnswered: $numberOfAnswered
)
```

Almost done. You use `ChallengeView` in `PracticeView`, so now the compilation error affects this view. Repeat these familiar steps for the last time — promise!

Add a binding property to `PracticeView`:

```
@Binding var numberOfAnswered: Int
```

Pass the binding to the `ChallengeView` initializer:

```
ChallengeView(
  challengeTest: challengeTest!,
  numberOfAnswered: $numberOfAnswered
)
```

`PracticeView_Previews` already has a `numberOfAnswered` state property, so all you need to do is to pass this new property as a binding to `ChallengeView`:

```
return PracticeView(
  challengeTest: .constant(challengeTest),
  userName: .constant("Johnny Swift"),
  numberOfAnswered: $numberOfAnswered
)
```

Now, `WelcomeView` is the last step of this recursive journey. In it, you already have the challenges view model, taken straight from the environment — you just need to add the property that needs to be passed down to `ScoreView`.

In `ChallengesViewModel`, you can see that there's already a `numberOfAnswered` computed property:

```
var numberOfAnswered: Int { return correctAnswers.count }
```

As you can see, it's read-only (it implements a getter, but not a setter) — will it work as a binding? Not so well. Go back to WelcomeView and pass this new property as a binding to PracticeView:

```
PracticeView(
  challengeTest: $challengesViewModel.currentChallenge,
  userName: $userManager.profile.name,
  // Add this
  numberOfAnswered: $challengesViewModel.numberOfAnswered
)
```

The compiler will inform you that it's a read-only property so it can't be assigned. How can you fix this?

Binding has a static method called constant() that creates a binding from an immutable value. This looks like a solution! Replace that line with:

```
numberOfAnswered: .constant(challengesViewModel.numberOfAnswered
)
```

And voila, now it works!

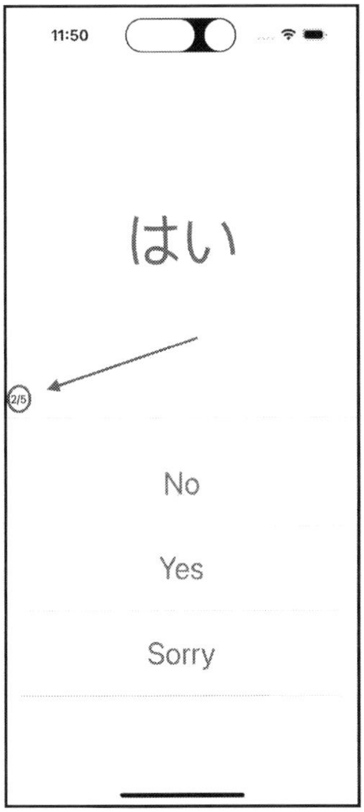

Score Working

Object Ownership

In the previous sections you've seen that there are three different ways a view can obtain an observable object:

- By receiving it in the initializer (usually a binding)
- By extracting it from the environment
- By creating an instance of itself (usually a state property)

In the first two cases, the object is owned by another entity, which can be a parent view or the app (`KuchiApp` in our case), a dependency container, or the environment.

In the latter case, the instance is owned by the view, but you must not forget that a view is a value type, and that a value type doesn't really mutate: a new instance incorporating the mutation is created. As a direct consequence, if a view has ownership of a reference type, chances are that when the view mutates, the referenced object is recycled, and a new instance is created.

This happens if the view instantiates a reference type itself, but it can also happen if the reference type is passed via the initializer.

Compare this code:

```
struct SomeView: View {
  @ObservedObject var userManager = UserManager()
  ...
}
```

With:

```
struct SomeView: View {
  @ObservedObject var userManager: UserManager

  init(userManager: UserManager) {
    self.userManager = userManager
  }
}
```

- In the former case, `userManager` is instantiated every time an instance of `SomeView` is created. This also includes cases where the view is re-rendered — since it is a value type, re-rendering implies creating a new instance.
- In the latter case, whether `userManager` is created every time `SomeView` is instantiated depends on where it is created.

Let's look into that case — Now compare:

```
struct SomeOtherView: View {
  var body: some View {
    SomeView(userManager: UserManager())
  }
}
```

With:

```
struct SomeOtherView: View {
  let userManager = UserManager()

  var body: some View {
    SomeView(userManager: userManager)
  }
}
```

- In the former case, an instance of `UserManager` is created every time `SomeView` is instantiated.
- In the latter case, `UserManager` is instantiated once, and that same instance is always passed to every new instance of `SomeView`

So when passing an instance of a reference type to a view's initializer, it's good practice to keep a reference by instantiating and assigning to a property (latter case), rather than creating it in place, right where it is passed to the view (former case)

Generally speaking, passing an observable object via the initializer is not elegant, unless really needed. If a view requires ownership of an observable object, then any parent that uses that view should create the instance, keep a reference (as seen in the previous code snippet, using the `userManager` property), and pass it down to the initializer.

Since SwiftUI 2.0 you have a new way to solve issues of this type, where a view is the owner of an observable object, but the observable object should not follow the view lifecycle — which means, it should be instantiated once, regardless of how many times the view that owns it is mutated.

The new way is called `@StateObject`, and you can think of it as a `@State` for reference types. SwiftUI will make sure that when a view is mutated all its state object properties are retained. It's like having a static property bound to a mutating value type — since mutation means new instance, SwiftUI takes case of transferring instances of state objects from the mutating to the mutated instance of the value type.

Using a state object, you solve the problem described above with just this code:

```
struct SomeView: View {
  @StateObject var userManager = UserManager()
  ...
}
```

Here the view creates and owns the instance of a reference type, and that instance is carried over when the view is re-instantiated as a consequence to a state mutation (i.e. at least one of its properties is updated). No more need of creating the reference type instance elsewhere and pass it to the initializer.

Note that `@StateObject` is a brand new tool, not meant to be a replacement for other tools. Use the proper tool for each problem:

- When you want a view to own an observable object, because it conceptually belongs to it, your tool is `@StateObject`.
- When an observable object is owned elsewhere, either `@ObservedObject` or `@EnvironmentObject` are your tools — choosing one or the other depends from each specific case.

Understanding Environment Properties

SwiftUI provides another interesting and useful way to put the environment to work. Earlier in this chapter, you used it to inject environmental objects that can be pulled from any view down through the view hierarchy.

SwiftUI automatically populates the same environment with system-managed environment values. The list is pretty long, and it's available at apple.co/2yJO5C1.

For example, you'll find a property that specifies which color scheme you're using, dark or light. This isn't just informative — it's reactive, meaning that if the property value changes, it triggers a UI update wherever the property is used.

In Kuchi, you're going to fix an issue in the challenge view: It doesn't look good if the device is in landscape mode:

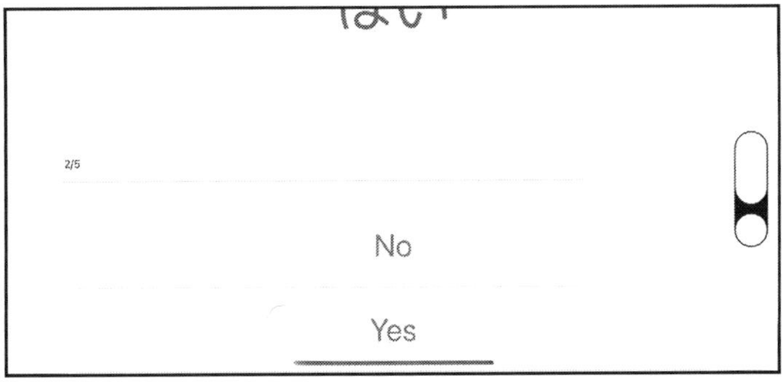

Challenge view in landscape

To make it look better, you want to detect when the device orientation changes and react to that change accordingly. Unfortunately, there's no such property, at least not an explicit one.

In fact, you can use `verticalSizeClass`, whose type is an `enum`. It states whether the vertical size class of the device and orientation is `.compact` or `.regular`.

To read the property value and subscribe to changes, you have a new `@Environment` attribute at your disposal so you can pass the property key path to it. So go ahead and add this property to `ChallengeView`:

```
@Environment(\.verticalSizeClass) var verticalSizeClass
```

Although you can give the property any arbitrary name, it's better to stick with the original name specified in the key path, to avoid confusion. You don't need to specify the type; you already know it, since it's an existing property.

Once you've done this, you can differentiate the layout depending on the value of that property. Replace the entire `body` implementation with:

```
var body: some View {
  // 1
  if verticalSizeClass == .compact {
    // 2
    VStack {
      // 3
      HStack {
        Button(action: {
          showAnswers = !showAnswers
        }) {
          QuestionView(
```

```
            question: challengeTest.challenge.question)
        }
        if showAnswers {
          Divider()
          ChoicesView(challengeTest: challengeTest)
        }
      }
      ScoreView(
        numberOfQuestions: 5,
        numberOfAnswered: $numberOfAnswered
      )
    }
  } else {
    // 4
    VStack {
      Button(action: {
        showAnswers = !showAnswers
      }) {
        QuestionView(
          question: challengeTest.challenge.question)
          .frame(height: 300)
      }
      ScoreView(
        numberOfQuestions: 5,
        numberOfAnswered: $numberOfAnswered
      )
      if showAnswers {
        Divider()
        ChoicesView(challengeTest: challengeTest)
          .frame(height: 300)
          .padding()
      }
    }
  }
}
```

It seems there are a lot of changes, but really, it's mostly duplicated code with some adjustments:

1. Here, you check if the vertical class is compact. If it is, it means the device is in landscape mode.
2. This is the view implementation for the landscape mode. You use the vertical stack to display `ScoreView` at the bottom.

3. The horizontal stack just shows `QuestionView` and `ChoicesView` next to one another.
4. This is the previous implementation, which is still good for portrait layout.

Now, build and run and go to the challenge view. When you change the device's orientation, the layout adapts automatically. Neat!

Challenge view in landscape

One thing that's worth mentioning is that at any level in the hierarchy, you can manually assign a different value to any environment property by using a view modifier: `.environment(_:_:)`.

You can test that by setting the vertical size class in one of `ChallengeView`'s parents. Open `WelcomeView` and add this modifier to `PracticeView`:

```
PracticeView(
  challengeTest: $challengesViewModel.currentChallenge,
  userName: $userManager.profile.name,
  numberOfAnswered:
    .constant(challengesViewModel.numberOfAnswered)
)
// Add this modifier
.environment(\.verticalSizeClass, .compact)
```

You're now forcing the vertical size class to be compact for `PracticeView` and all its subviews down in the hierarchy. It takes the key path of the property to modify and the new value — pretty intuitive. :]

Now, just build and run and you'll have the proof: However you rotate the device, `ChallengeView` always shows its landscape layout!

Fixed orientation

Remove that modifier once you're done testing, since it's not a "feature" you'd want to leave in the app. :]

Creating Custom Environment Properties

Environment properties are so useful and versatile that it would be great if you could create your own. Well, as it turns out, you can!

Creating a custom environment property is a two-step process:

1. You have to create a struct type that you'll use as the property key, conforming to `EnvironmentKey`.
2. You add the newly-computed property in an `EnvironmentValues` extension, using the subscript operator to read and set values.

Some code is worth more than words. `ScoreView` has an immutable `numberOfQuestions` property, which defines the number of challenges per session.

If you look at `ChallengeView`, you can see that it passes a constant instead of the actual number defined in `ChallengesViewModel`. This is a good candidate to demonstrate how to create and use a custom environment property.

Go to `ChallengesViewModel` and, at the beginning of the file, add this struct:

```
struct QuestionsPerSessionKey: EnvironmentKey {
  static var defaultValue: Int = 5
}
```

This defines:

- The key to use with the subscript operator.
- The default value assigned to the property, if it's not explicitly initialized elsewhere.

Next, you define the actual property. Add this code after the struct:

```
// 1
extension EnvironmentValues {
  // 2
  var questionsPerSession: Int {
    // 3
    get { self[QuestionsPerSessionKey.self] }
    set { self[QuestionsPerSessionKey.self] = newValue }
  }
}
```

So, to create the new property, you have to:

1. Create an `EnvironmentValues` extension.
2. Add a `questionsPerSession` computed property.
3. Use the `QuestionsPerSessionKey` type to access the property for both reading and writing.

Now, add a property to `ChallengesViewModel` that defines the number of questions. It's better to make it read-only, so it can't be changed from outside the class:

```
private(set) var numberOfQuestions = 6
```

In generateRandomChallenge(), it's also better to replace the 5 constant with the value of this property:

```
func generateRandomChallenge() {
  if correctAnswers.count < numberOfQuestions {
    currentChallenge = getRandomChallenge()
  } else {
    currentChallenge = nil
  }
}
```

This method generates a new challenge if the number of correct answers is less than the number of questions. Otherwise, it sets currentChallenge to nil, indicating the session is over.

In WelcomeView, add this new environment property to the PracticeView's environment so it will be available to PracticeView and all its subviews:

```
PracticeView(
  challengeTest: $challengesViewModel.currentChallenge,
  userName: $userManager.profile.name,
  numberOfAnswered:
    .constant(challengesViewModel.numberOfAnswered)
)
// Add this
.environment(
  \.questionsPerSession,
  challengesViewModel.numberOfQuestions
)
```

Now, you're ready to use the new property. Go to ChallengeView and add this property:

```
@Environment(\.questionsPerSession) var questionsPerSession
```

This pulls questionsPerSession from the environment. Compare it with the other environment variable declared in the same file, verticalSizeClass. The only difference is the name. Note how you don't need to specify the type, since it's inferred from the questionsPerSession computed property you added earlier to the EnvironmentValues extension.

Finally, in the **two places** that reference `ScoreView`, replace `5` with the new variable, `questionsPerSession`:

```
ScoreView(
  numberOfQuestions: questionsPerSession,
  numberOfAnswered: $numberOfAnswered
)
```

Build and run; now, `ScoreView` reports the new number of questions (6 instead of the previously hardcoded 5).

Custom environment property

Key Points

This was another intense chapter. But in the end, as with the previous one, concepts are simple, once you understand how they work.

To summarize what you've learned:

- Using `@ObservedObject`, you can create a property, an instance of a class conforming to `ObservableObject`. The class can define one or more `@Published` properties. These work like state variables, except you implement them in a class rather than within the view.
- With `@StateObject` you have the `@State` equivalent, but for reference types.
- You use `@EnvironmentObject` as a bag where you can inject observable objects. You can then pull them from the view you injected them into *and* all its descendants.
- `@Environment` lets you access a system environment value, such as `colorScheme` or `locale`. You can create an environment property, which has all the advantages of a binding, including reactivity.
- You can also use `@Environment` to create your own custom environment properties.

Where to Go From Here?

This chapter completes the state and data flow topic — whereas in the previous chapter you learned how to use observable properties in your views, and how to pass them around, in this chapter you looked at defining and using your own observable types, as well as getting your hands on environment properties.

Suggestions for what to read next are the same as the previous chapter, since, as just said, they both are about the same macro-topic.

- SwiftUI documentation: apple.co/2MlBqJJ
- State and data flow reference documentation: apple.co/2YzOdyp

Being familiar with **Combine** can also be beneficial, so check out the documentation at apple.co/2L7kWTy. You probably already know, but in case you don't, this book has a brother, **Combine: Asynchronous Programming with Swift**, which you can find at https://bit.ly/3qTFPnG.

Chapter 10: More User Input & App Storage

By Antonio Bello

In the last two chapters, you learned how to use **state** and how easy it is to make the UI react to state changes; you also implemented **reactivity** to your custom reference types.

In this chapter, you'll meet a few other input controls: lists with sections, steppers, toggles and pickers. To do so, you'll work on a new Kuchi app section dedicated to its settings.

Since you'll implement this new feature as a separate new view, you might think you need to add some navigation to the app — and you'd be right. In fact, you'll add tab-based navigation later on.

For now, you'll create a new setup view and make it the default view displayed when you launch the app.

You'll find the starter project, along with the final project, in the materials for this chapter. It's almost the same final project you left in the previous chapter, so feel free to use your own copy that you've worked on so far. However, in this case, you need to manually add the content of the **Shared/Utils** folder to the project, which contains these three files:

- **Color+Extension**: contains some `UIColor` extension methods.
- **LocalNotifications**: helper class to create local notifications.
- **Appearance**: defines an enumeration used to describe the app's appearance.

Creating the Settings View

Before doing anything else, you must create the new settings view and make it the default view displayed at launch.

Open the starter project or your project from the previous chapter. In the **Shared** folder, create a new group, call it **Settings**, then create a new file inside it using the **SwiftUI** template, and name it **SettingsView**.

New setting group

Now, to make `Settings` the initial view, open **KuchiApp** and, in `body`, replace the code that instantiates `StarterView`, along with its modifiers, with:

```
SettingsView()
```

If you now run the app, it'll show the classic, but never outdated, `Hello, World!` message that every developer has met at least a hundred times in their developer life.

Empty settings view

Now that everything is set up, you can focus on building the settings view. Your goal is to create something that looks like this:

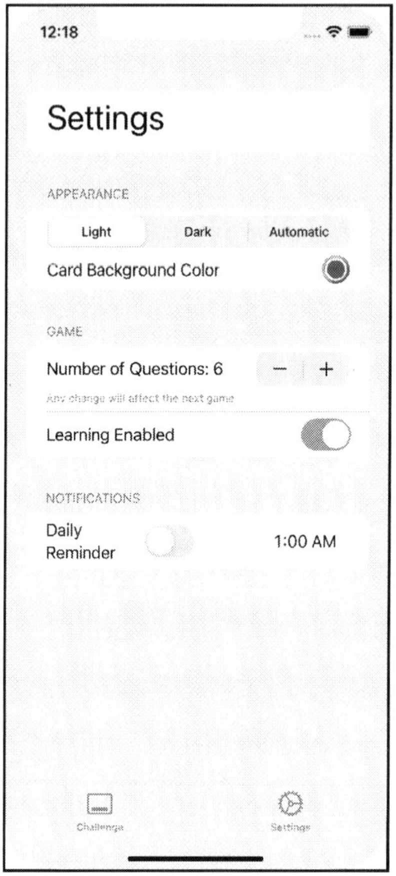

Final settings view

You can see that the view has:

- A **Settings** title.
- Three sections: **Appearance**, **Game** and **Notifications**.
- One or more items (settings) per section.

To implement this structure in UIKit, you would probably opt for a `UITableView` with static content or a vertical `UIStackView`. In AppKit, you'd use a slightly similar way.

In SwiftUI, you'll use a `List`, a container view that arranges rows of data in a single column. Additionally, you'll use a `Section` for each of the three sections listed above. This is just an implementation-oriented peek, and you'll learn more about lists in **Chapter 14: "Lists"**.

The Skeleton List

Adding a list is as easy as declaring it in the usual way you've already done several times in SwiftUI. Before starting, resume the preview so you have visual feedback of what you're doing in real-time, step by step.

In the `SettingsView`'s `body`, replace the welcome text with:

```
List {
}
```

Next, add the title inside the `List`:

```
Text("Settings")
  .font(.largeTitle)
  .padding(.bottom, 8)
```

You're using two modifiers to:

- Select the `largeTitle` text style.
- Add a bottom padding.

Last, for now, add three sections after the `Text`, respectively, for appearance, game and notifications:

```
Section(header: Text("Appearance")) {
}

Section(header: Text("Game")) {
}

Section(header: Text("Notifications")) {
}
```

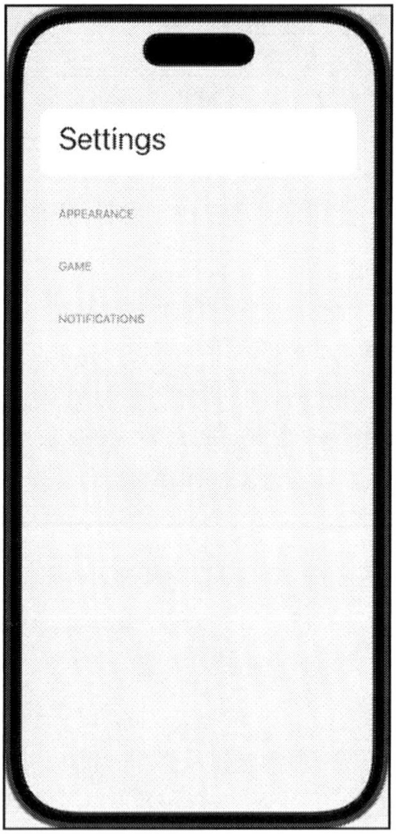

Sections

The Stepper Component

It's good practice to start from the beginning; in fact, you'll start populating the ... erm ... second section. :]

The **Game** section contains two settings, the first of which is the number of questions. You remember from the previous chapters that a session is a sequence of challenges, the number of which is set to six in `ChallengesViewModel`.

Because you like to win easily or because you like to put your name in the Guinness World Records, you might want to model the number of questions per session accordingly to your taste.

So the first setting you'll add to the Kuchi app is to let you choose how many questions you wish per session.

You could use a text field where you have to input a number manually. Still, you'd need to add validation to ensure that the input is convertible to a positive integer — there's a better and more elegant control that fits.

As you might have already guessed by reading the title of this section, this control is the stepper, aka a pair of buttons that allow you to increase or decrease an integer value and an associated label. You've already briefly met the stepper in **Chapter 6: "Controls & User Input"**.

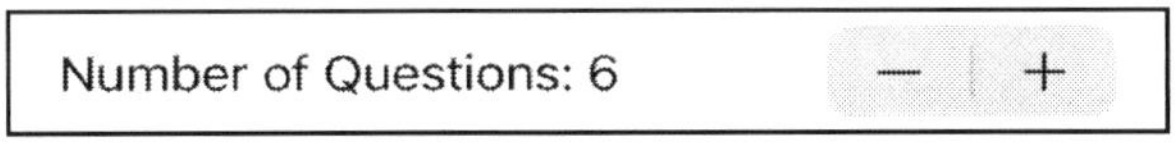

Stepper

First, at the top of `SettingsView`, add a state variable to hold the number of questions:

```
@State var numberOfQuestions = 6
```

Then, in the second section, **Game**, add this code:

```
// 1
VStack(alignment: .leading) {
  // 2
  Stepper(
    "Number of Questions: \(numberOfQuestions)",
    value: $numberOfQuestions,
    // 3
    in: 3 ... 20
  )
  // 4
  Text("Any change will affect the next game")
    .font(.caption2)
    .foregroundColor(.secondary)
}
```

Here's what's going on:

1. Along with the stepper, you're showing an informative label beneath it, so you're using a vertical stack to stack the stepper and the label, both aligned to the left.
2. This is the stepper, which has a label showing the currently selected number of questions and a binding.
3. Look how cool this is! You're forcing the stepper to stay in the 3-20 range, you don't need to validate it; you just prevent the user from choosing values outside that range.
4. This is the informative label, properly stylized, below the stepper.

If you resume the preview, this is what you'll see:

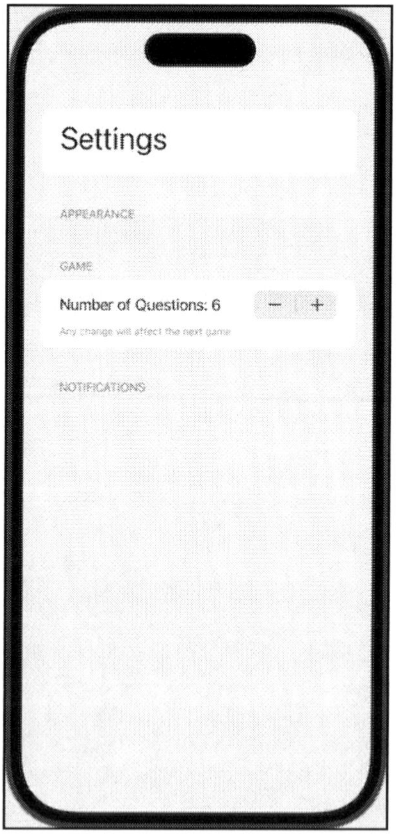

Number of questions

If you activate the live preview, you can play with the control to amend the property value, and you can easily find that you can't go beyond the limits defined by the 3-20 range you specified in the control declaration.

> **Note**: Spoiler alert! You've added a state property, and it's not the only one you'll add in this chapter. Although, for now, it works fine, it's not the best way to handle a state that must ideally survive app restarts. You'll look into that later in this chapter when discussing `AppStorage`.

The Toggle Component

The second setting you'll add is a switch that enables or disables the **Learning** section of the Kuchi app. Before you go and browse all the previous chapters to search for something you might have forgotten, you should be aware that there's no such section yet, you'll add it in the next chapter.

You've already used the toggle component in **Chapter 6: "Controls & User Input" **to enable the "Remember Me" feature that allows the app to remember the user's name. So you should already know how to use it.

At the top of `SettingsView`, add a new piece of state:

```
@State var learningEnabled: Bool = true
```

Then, in the **Game** section, after the vertical stack, add this code:

```
Toggle("Learning Enabled", isOn: $learningEnabled)
```

You're simply creating a toggle with a label and a binding.

Now, if you resume the preview, you'll see this:

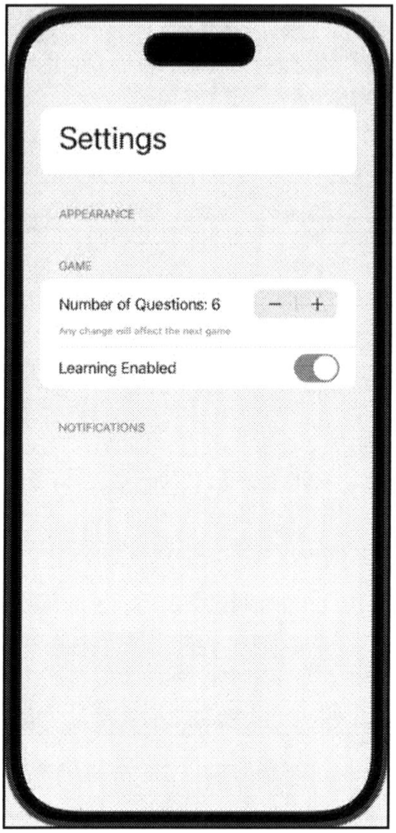

Learning enabled

The settings view is taking shape!

The Date Picker Component

The following section you'll take care of is **Notifications**. You might be wondering what notifications have to do with Kuchi.

When you're learning something new, and it requires constant effort, you must dedicate time regularly. You can't afford to skip practicing, and that mustn't happen just because you forget it!

So, ask the app to remind you.

To implement it, you only need two controls:

- A toggle to enable or disable the notification.
- A time picker to select the time of the day you want the reminder to show up.

> **Note**: What we're calling **time picker** is, in reality, a `DatePicker` configured to handle the time component only. There's no standalone time picker component in SwiftUI.

Since both relate to the same settings, you'll lay them out horizontally, so, you guessed right, you'll embed them in an `HStack`

First, in `SettingsView` add the following state property below the ones previously added:

```
@State var dailyReminderEnabled = false
```

Then, in the **Notifications** section, add the following:

```
HStack {
  Toggle("Daily Reminder", isOn: $dailyReminderEnabled)
}
```

Here you're using a toggle component to turn the daily reminder on and off.

Now you can resume the preview and see the new toggle in place.

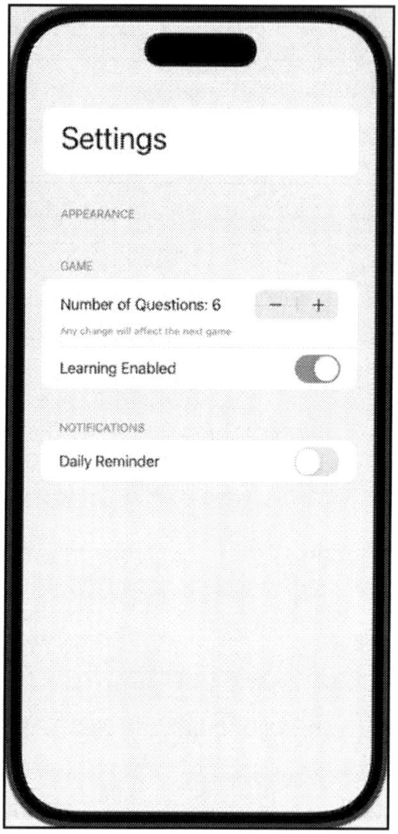

Notifications toggle

Currently, it does nothing, which is unsurprising, as you still need to add behavior to its state change. More on that soon.

Now, you can add a time picker. Add this code after the reminder toggle:

```
DatePicker(
  // 1
  "",
  // 2
  selection: $dailyReminderTime
)
```

`DatePicker` has a few initializers, differing by whether they use a `Text` or a custom `View` for the label and by the inclusion of a validity range or not.

In the version you've used above:

1. You're using the `Text` label, but since you already have a `Text` for the label, you added it as part of the daily reminder switch, and you're passing an empty string.
2. This is the binding to a state property you must add.

To get it to compile, add the new state property after `dailyReminderEnabled`:

```
@State var dailyReminderTime = Date(timeIntervalSince1970: 0)
```

Resume the preview, and enable live preview. Or, if you prefer, launch the app in the simulator. Notice the two fields after the switch, one for the date and one for the time.

Now, if you tap the date part of the component, it will display a pop-up to let you choose a date. Likewise, tapping the time part will show a pop-up to select a time. And needless to say, if you select a date or a time, it will automatically store to `dailyReminderTime`.

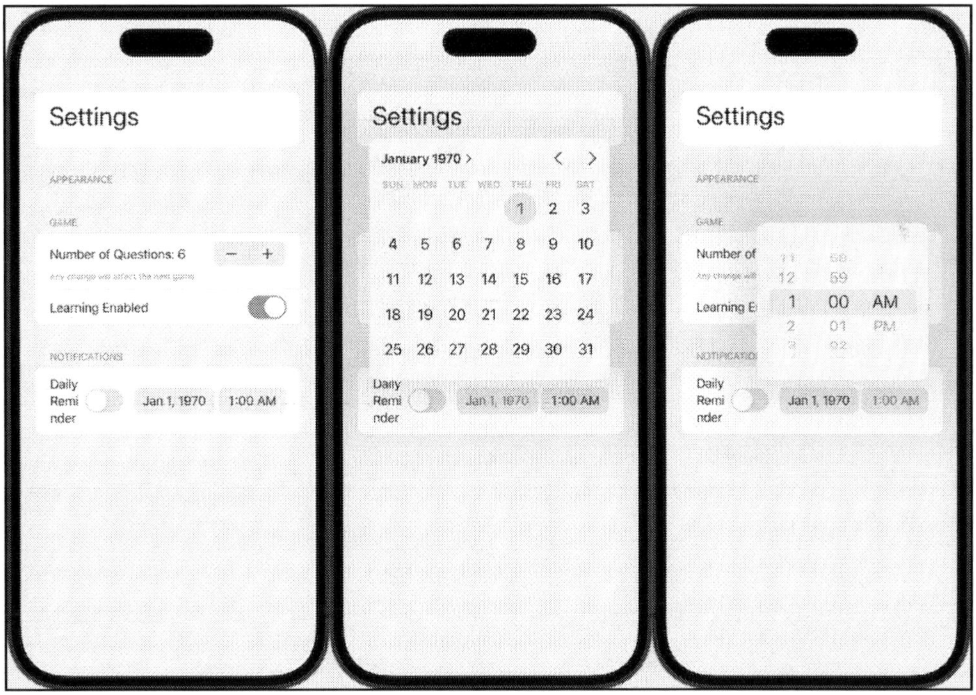

Date picker

Date Picker Styles

In iOS, the date picker comes in three different styles, which you can configure using the `.datePickerStyle()` modifier, similarly to how it works for `TextField`, which you encountered in **Chapter 6: "Controls & User Input"**. The three styles are:

- `CompactDatePickerStyle`: This is what you'll use in Kuchi. It consists of two compact fields showing the selected date and time. When you tap one, it will display a pop-up to edit the relevant part.

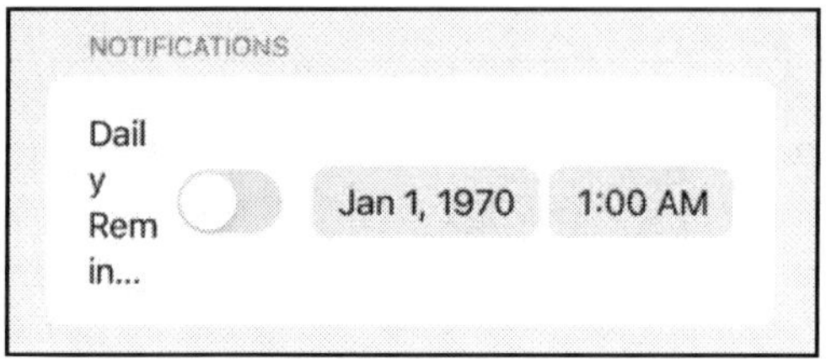

Compact date picker

- `WheelDatePickerStyle`: It's the classic wheel where you can swipe up and down to compose the date and time, field by field. If you've ever developed in UIKit, you should know what it is. :]

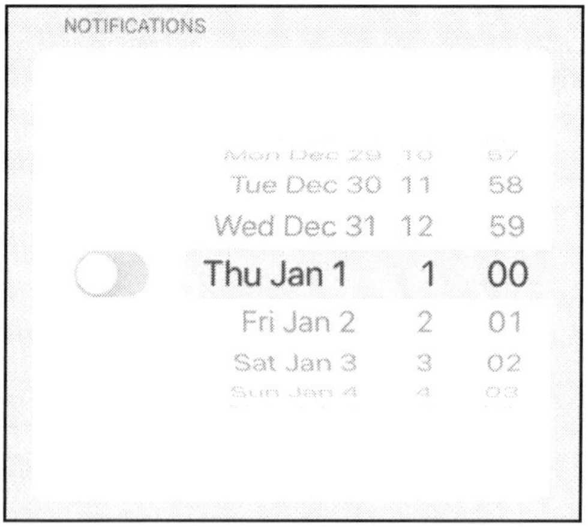

Wheel date picker

- `GraphicalDatePickerStyle`: An embedded calendar component.

Graphical date picker

In macOS, there are three styles too:

- `GraphicalDatePickerStyle`: This is the macOS counterpart of the iOS style seen above.

Graphical date picker macos

- `FieldDatePickerStyle`: This is a text field where you can type your date and/or time.

Field date picker

- `StepperFieldDatePickerStyle`: This is similar to the previous one, but with a stepper that lets you use your mouse to select values.

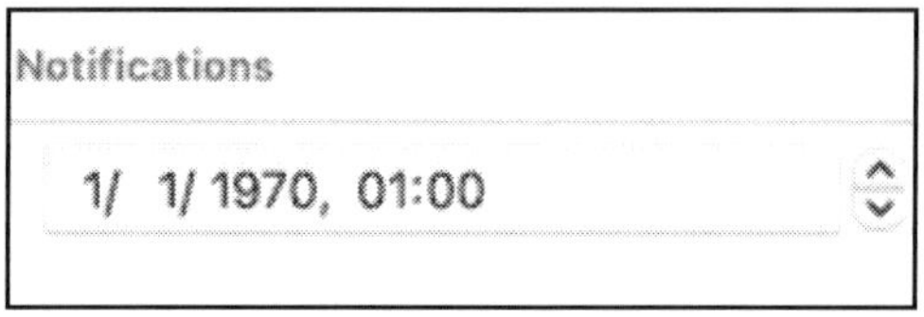

Stepper date picker

For both platforms, there's an additional `DefaultDatePickerStyle`, which is an alias for a style, but different per platform:

- In iOS, the default style is `CompactDatePickerStyle`.
- In macOS, it's `StepperFieldDatePickerStyle`.

Configuring the Daily Reminder Time Picker

After some theory, it's time to get back to Kuchi. The date picker with compact style looks great, but there's one issue: you don't need the date. This picker is to select a time of the day, but there's no date component because you want it to remind you *every* day.

This is very easy to achieve. The initializer takes an additional `displayedComponents` parameter, which can be either `.hourAndMinute`, `.date`, or both. In your case, you want it to be just `hourAndMinute`, so add it after `selection`:

```
DatePicker(
  "",
  selection: $dailyReminderTime,
  // Add this, but don't forget the trailing
  // comma in the previous line
  displayedComponents: .hourAndMinute
)
```

Now you can resume the live preview, or run the app if you prefer, and play with the time picker.

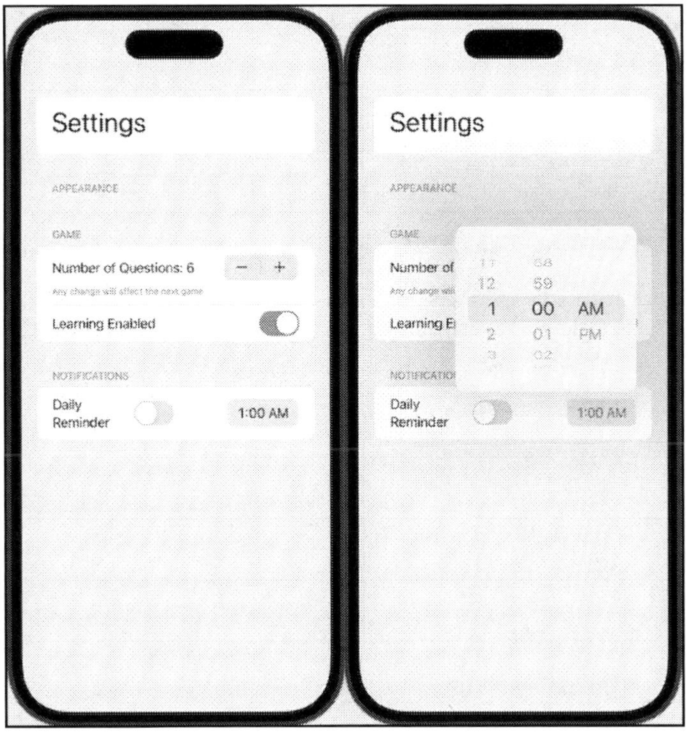

Time picker

You probably noticed another problem while testing the app: if the switch is off, the time picker should disable, but it always stays enabled instead. Thanks to SwiftUI's reactivity, this is very simple to achieve. Declare that the date picker's enabled property must follow the value of the switch's value.

Add the following modifier to `DatePicker`:

```
.disabled(dailyReminderEnabled == false)
```

With it, you're binding `dailyReminderEnabled` to the time picker's `disabled` property. Try it now; when you turn the switch off, the time picker will automatically disable.

Activating Notifications

Now that the user interface part of the time picker is complete, you need to make it functional. The requirements are pretty simple:

1. If the daily notification switch turns on, create the daily notification.
2. If the time changes, cancel the previous notification and create a new one with the updated time by selecting with the time picker.
3. If the daily notification switch turns off, cancel the current notification.

In UIKit and AppKit Jurassic worlds, you would probably hook to a value-changed event and do the processing in there. You should already know that the SwiftUI way of doing things is different and that, often, you can achieve the same goal in different ways.

Both the switch and the time picker have an associated state variable each, which holds the current selection. When the user changes the switch state, either turning on or off, the component automatically updates the binding, which is the `dailyReminderEnabled` property.

Adding a Custom Handler to the Toggle

It would be nice if you could intercept when the binding updates and inject a call to a method that creates or removes a local notification. This is exactly what you're going to do now.

The toggle button is declared as:

```
Toggle("Daily Reminder", isOn: $dailyReminderEnabled)
```

Replace the `$dailyReminderEnabled` binding with an explicit binding, as follows:

```
Toggle("Daily Reminder", isOn:
  // 1
  Binding(
    // 2
    get: { dailyReminderEnabled },
    // 3
    set: { newValue in
      // 4
      dailyReminderEnabled = newValue
    }
  )
)
```

If you remember when you met bindings a couple of chapters ago, a **binding** is a property wrapper type that can read and write a value owned by a source of truth. Here, the source of truth is `dailyReminderEnabled`, and you achieve the read and write via two closures that you pass to the binding initializer:

1. This is the binding that you're creating.
2. This is the `get` implementation, a closure that returns the source of truth's value.
3. This is the `set` counterpart, where you set the value into the source of truth's wrapped value.
4. Here's where you set the value.

Now if you enable live preview or run the app, you won't notice any difference. This implementation, left as is, doesn't add anything new from a functional standpoint.

As mentioned earlier, you only want to inject a method call when a new value is set. In the binding's `set` closure, after setting the new value into `dailyReminderEnabled`, add this method call:

```
configureNotification()
```

This method doesn't exist yet, it will be responsible of creating or removing a notification. Add it after `body`:

```
func configureNotification() {
  if dailyReminderEnabled {
    // 1
    LocalNotifications.shared.createReminder(
      time: dailyReminderTime)
  } else {
    // 2
    LocalNotifications.shared.deleteReminder()
  }
}
```

Depending on the value of `dailyReminderEnabled`:

1. Create a new reminder with the currently selected time.
2. Delete the reminder.

Shared/Utils/LocalNotifications contains the details of how to schedule and cancel a notification. However, the way a custom handler injects into a binding is a little verbose. You could create a `Binding` extension method that automatically does what you did with the custom getter and setter above. Still, there's actually another way that SwiftUI already provides: the `onChange(of:perform:)` modifier.

Restore the previous implementation of the Daily Reminder toggle so you use the state variable and not the custom binding:

```
Toggle("Daily Reminder", isOn: $dailyReminderEnabled)
```

Now add to it a call to the modifier mentioned above, passing `dailyReminderEnabled` as value and a call to `configureNotification()` as closure:

```
.onChange(
  of: dailyReminderEnabled,
  perform: { _ in configureNotification() }
)
```

This tells SwiftUI: *Hey, when* dailyReminderEnabled *changes, please execute this closure*. The value can be any type conforming to `Equatable`, so it's not restricted to state or binding only, and the closure takes the new value, of the same type, as a parameter.

Adding a Custom Handler to the Time Picker

Now you need to replicate what you did to the toggle. Still in `SettingsView`, add the same modifier to the `DatePicker`:

```
.onChange(
  of: dailyReminderTime,
  perform: { _ in configureNotification() }
)
```

The only difference is that you're now monitoring dailyReminderTime instead of dailyReminderEnabled.

Note that .onChange(of:perform:) is part of the View protocol so you can use it on any view. You could, for example, move the two uses you've done above from their respective components to HStack, Section or List. For example, in case you opt for the section, the code would look like this:

```
Section(header: Text("Notifications")) {
  HStack {
    Toggle("Daily Reminder", isOn: $dailyReminderEnabled)
    DatePicker(
      "",
      selection: $dailyReminderTime,
      displayedComponents: .hourAndMinute
    )
  }
}
.onChange(
  of: dailyReminderEnabled,
  perform: { _ in configureNotification() }
)
.onChange(
  of: dailyReminderTime,
  perform: { _ in configureNotification() }
)
```

Testing the Notifications

After all these changes, notifications are fully working. Every time the state of the toggle or the time picker changes, you invoke configureNotification(), which either cancels a schedule or schedules a new notification.

After so much effort, you can see what you've achieved! You need to run the app on a simulator or a device, notifications won't work in live preview. Follow these steps:

1. Enable **Daily Reminder**.
2. Take note of your current time, and add one minute.
3. Tap on the time picker, and select that time.
4. Set the app to the background by going to the home screen.
5. Wait for the notification to appear.

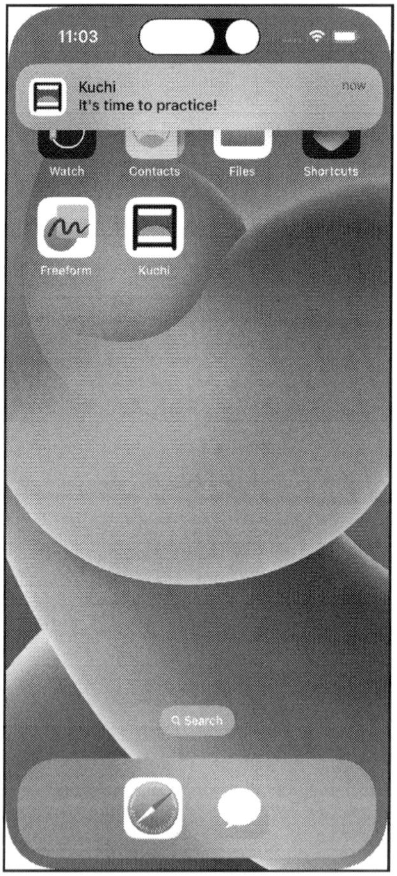

Local notification

The Color Picker Component

Now swift ... ehm, shift your focus on the app's appearance. :]

In the next chapter, you'll add a learning screen to the app where you can play with swipeable cards. They have a solid background color, which was statically set to red in previous iterations of this book.

Why not prepare a setting that allows the user to select a background color of their choice, instead of defaulting to red?

To achieve that, you'll use a `ColorPicker`. To store the selected color, you're going to need a state variable. Add the following to the top of `SettingsView`, right after `dailyReminderTime`:

```
@State var cardBackgroundColor: Color = .red
```

Next, in the `body` under the **Appearance** section, add the color picker:

```
ColorPicker(
  "Card Background Color",
  selection: $cardBackgroundColor
)
```

And that's it, very simple. The initializer takes three parameters:

- A label.
- A binding.
- An optional flag stating if opacity is supported, which, by default, is `true`.

There are several overloads with minor differences from each other. One that's worth mentioning allows you to specify a label as a view rather than a string, this is quite common in SwiftUI's components.

You can run it in a simulator, a device, or live preview. When you tap the small colored circle at the right, a pop-up displays, offering you several ways to choose a color.

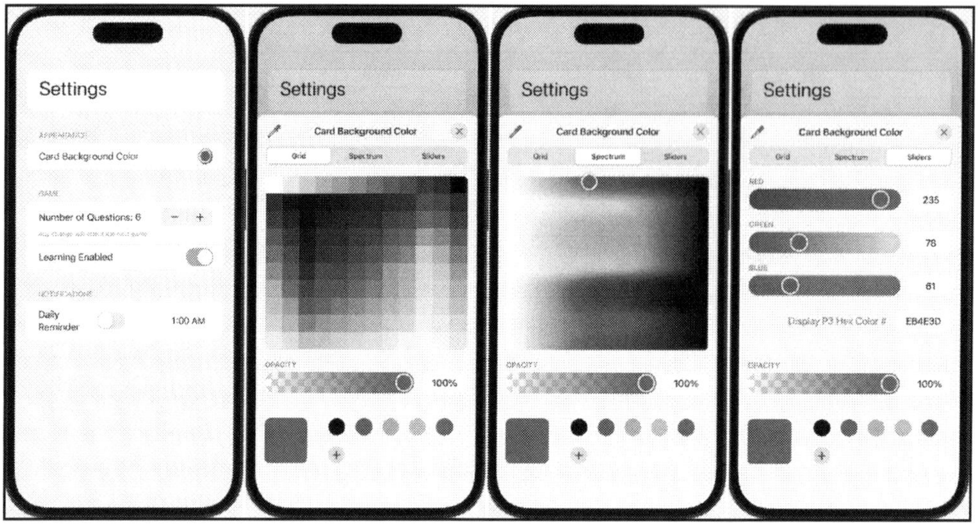

Color picker

It would be superfluous to say that when you select a new color, it's automatically set in the `cardBackgroundColor` state property.

The Picker Component

The last setting you're offering to your users is the ability to select the app appearance, either light or dark, a popular setting among modern apps.

You'll give the user a set of three options to choose from:

- Light
- Dark
- Automatic

The last option is basically a way to say, "use the same appearance as configured in the Settings app".

To implement this setting you'll be using the **picker** component, which is formally described as a control for selecting a set of mutually exclusive values.

Using it is very simple: you provide a binding that determines the currently selected value and declare a set of mutually exclusive options.

A good way to start is by declaring the state variable. Add it after `numberOfQuestions`:

```
@State var appearance: Appearance = .automatic
```

`Appearance` is an enum defined in **Utils/Appearance**, with three cases matching the options mentioned earlier: `.light`, `.dark` and `.automatic`.

Since you'll add a new component to the Appearance section, which already contains the color picker, you must add a stack view to lay the two components out vertically. So enclose the color picker in a `VStack`:

```
VStack(alignment: .leading) {
  ColorPicker(
    "Card Background Color",
    selection: $cardBackgroundColor
  )
}
```

Now, before the color picker, add the new picker component:

```
// 1
Picker("", selection: $appearance) {
  // 2
  Text(Appearance.light.name)
  Text(Appearance.dark.name)
  Text(Appearance.automatic.name)
}
```

1. The first parameter passed to the picker initializer is a label, which you don't need here. There's an initializer overload that accepts a custom view instead of a text, so you're free to customize the label as much as you like.

   You have already figured out that the second parameter is the binding.

2. The content of the picker lists all possible options.

This is how it looks:

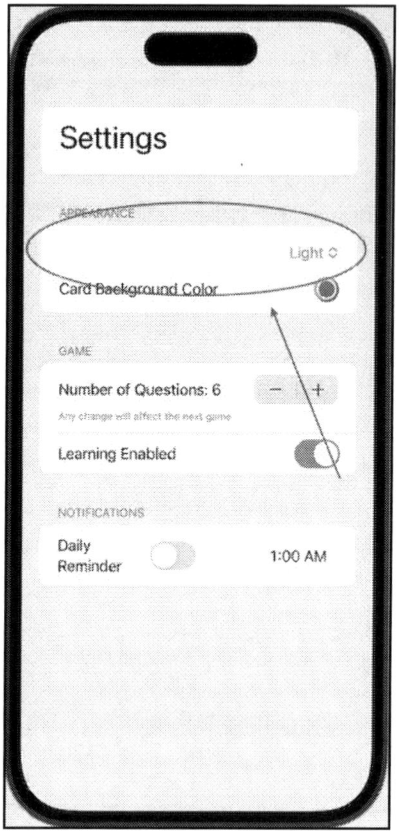

Default picker

Be honest: it doesn't look good, just a blank line with a disclosure icon. But there are other problems: it needs to be actionable. If you run the app in the simulator, you'll notice you can't select a new value.

Styling the Picker

In order to change the style, you have a modifier at your disposal. It's an established pattern in SwiftUI and should already look familiar to you. In this case, it's called `.pickerStyle(_:)`.

You can browse the documentation to know all available styles at apple.co/3nyViIG.

If you look at the screenshot at the beginning of this chapter, you'll see that the desired look for the appearance control is like a segmented control. To achieve that, you can use `SegmentedPickerStyle`, which displays all options in a segmented control.

Add this modifier to the picker:

```
.pickerStyle(SegmentedPickerStyle())
```

This changes the look of the picker to:

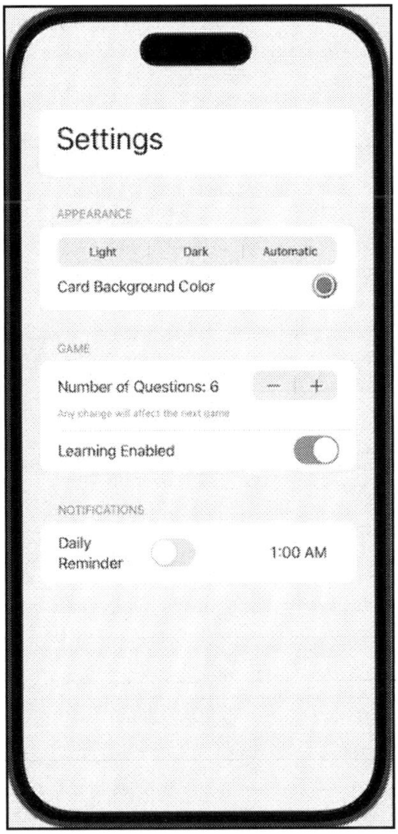

Picker segmented

Much better. However, if you run the app, you'll notice that the following:

- It doesn't highlight its default value, set in the `appearance` property initialization.
- It's not actionable: It does nothing if you try to interact with it.

Binding Options to the Picker State

If you look at the picker declaration, you can notice that:

- The currently selected item is bound to the appearance property.
- The list of items is just a list of strings (Appearance.light.name resolves to a string).

```
Picker("Pick", selection: $appearance) {
  Text(Appearance.light.name)
  Text(Appearance.dark.name)
  Text(Appearance.automatic.name)
}
```

When you select an option, how would the picker know what to put into appearance? Likewise, how does the picker know which corresponding item to select if the code changes the appearance.So, you need to bind each picker option to a specific value of its selection binding. In the case of this appearance picker, that means binding each option to a case of the Appearance enum.

You can create that binding with the tag(:_) modifier, which differentiates and identifies views in lists and pickers.

The tag modifier takes a value, which can be any type conforming to the Hashable protocol. Enumerations automatically implement it so that you can use enum cases out of the box.

For each of the three cases, add the tag modifier, passing the corresponding enum case:

```
Text(Appearance.light.name).tag(Appearance.light)
Text(Appearance.dark.name).tag(Appearance.dark)
Text(Appearance.automatic.name).tag(Appearance.automatic)
```

Now when you run or live preview the app:

- You immediately see that `.automatic` is the preselected option. That's because you initialize `appearance` with that value.
- Whenever you tap a non-selected option, the selection changes and you have a visual clue.

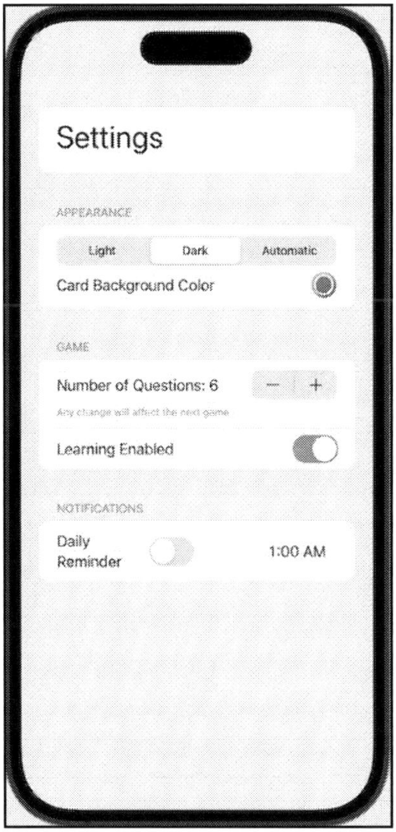

Settings view

Iterating Options Programmatically

A keen eye like yours has probably realized that:

- The picker options have the same format: A `Text` with a `.tag` modifier, fed with data from enum cases.
- Enumerations in Swift are enumerable and iterable.

Even if you haven't noticed, don't worry, it's not that obvious. Why, rather than listing all options explicitly, you can't iterate over them in a loop or similar?

Of course, the answer is *yes, you can*. You can leverage the `CaseIterable` protocol and use the `ForEach` struct. `Appearance` already adopts `CaseIterable`, but if you use this technique in your enumerations, remember to make them conform to that protocol.

Replace the three options in the picker with the following:

```
ForEach(Appearance.allCases) { appearance in
  Text(appearance.name).tag(appearance)
}
```

It's now more compact, easier to read and less error-prone. Not to mention that if you decide to add 10 more enum cases, you won't need to update this view: it's automatically populated, whichever the number of cases `Appearance` has.

The Tab Bar

Well done, now you've got a working settings view! But, currently, it's the only view that your app provides access to. At the beginning of this chapter, you replaced `StarterView` with `SettingsView` as the only view. Of course, this doesn't make sense even in the least meaningless apps.

So, you need some navigation, and the tab bar fits perfectly with what you need — also taking into account that, as mentioned earlier, you'll add a new **Learn** section in the next chapter.

For what matters in this chapter, your new tab bar needs to handle two views:

- `StarterView`
- `SettingsView`

You need a new view to host the tab bar, which acts as a master view that selects the embedded view to display. There's already a view in the project called `HomeView`, located in the **Shared** folder, which contains an empty view.

Replace its `body` content with:

```
// 1
TabView {
  EmptyView()
}
// 2
.accentColor(.orange)
```

This is very simple, you are:

1. Creating a tab view; it only has an empty view for now.
2. Using the `accentColor` modifier, make the icon and text orange when the user selects a tab.

Now you need to add the two tabs. The first is for the new settings view, so inside `TabView`, replace `EmptyView()` with:

```
// 1
SettingsView()
  // 2
  .tabItem({
    // 3
    VStack {
      Image(systemName: "gear")
      Text("Settings")
    }
  })
  // 4
  .tag(2)
```

Adding a tab is pretty straightforward:

1. This is the view displayed when the tab is active.
2. You use the `tabItem` modifier to configure the tab.
3. You're displaying an icon and a label below it, using a `VStack` to keep them together.
4. This is the index of the settings tab. You're assigning a value of 2 because it will be the rightmost, i.e., the last. Afterward, you'll add the next two tabs and the other in the next chapter.

If you resume the preview, this is what you'll see:

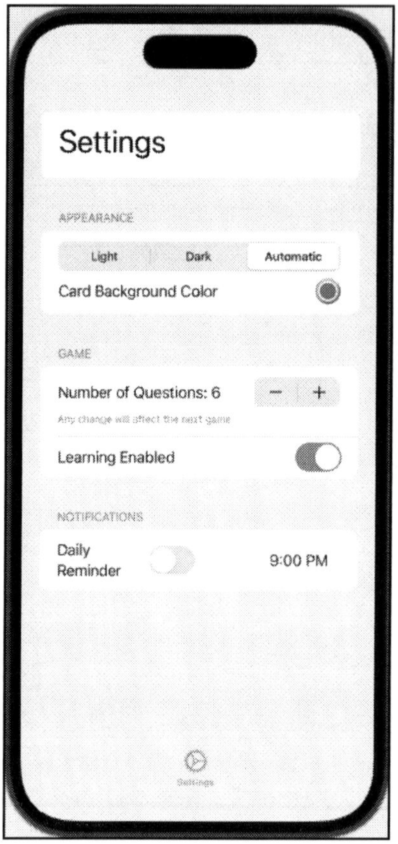

Settings tab

To add the second tab, you first need to do some refactoring: In `WelcomeView`, you have to replace the instance of `PracticeView` with the new `HomeView`.

To do so, first, open up **WelcomeView**. You see that in `body` the `if` branch shows `PracticeView` — *cut* the following code:

```
PracticeView(
  challengeTest: $challengesViewModel.currentChallenge,
  userName: $userManager.profile.name,
  numberOfAnswered:
    .constant(challengesViewModel.numberOfAnswered)
)
  .environment(
    \.questionsPerSession,
    challengesViewModel.numberOfQuestions
  )
```

And replace it with:

```
HomeView()
```

Next, go back to `HomeView`, and right before the `SettingsView` tab, paste the code you cut above:

```
PracticeView(
  challengeTest: $challengesViewModel.currentChallenge,
  userName: $userManager.profile.name,
  numberOfAnswered:
    .constant(challengesViewModel.numberOfAnswered)
)
  .environment(
    \.questionsPerSession,
    challengesViewModel.numberOfQuestions
  )
```

Because of missing properties, this creates a few things that you need to correct. You'll fix these soon. But first, you'll finish the body of `HomeView`.

Before the `environment` modifier of `PracticeView`, add this code to configure the tab:

```
.tabItem({
  VStack {
    Image(systemName: "rectangle.dock")
    Text("Challenge")
  }
})
.tag(1)
```

As done previously for the settings tab, this adds a new tab to the tab bar and assigns a tag of 1. Since you order tabs by tag, the practice tab will appear before the settings bar, for which you assigned a value of 2, which is the expected behavior.

To avoid any ambiguity, be sure that `body` looks like this:

```
TabView {
  PracticeView(
    challengeTest: $challengesViewModel.currentChallenge,
    userName: $userManager.profile.name,

numberOfAnswered: .constant(challengesViewModel.numberOfAnswered
)
  )
  .tabItem({
    VStack {
      Image(systemName: "rectangle.dock")
```

```
        Text("Challenge")
      }
    })
    .tag(1)
    .environment(
      \.questionsPerSession,
      challengesViewModel.numberOfQuestions
    )

    SettingsView()
      .tabItem({
        VStack {
          Image(systemName: "gear")
          Text("Settings")
        }
      })
      .tag(2)
  }
  .accentColor(.orange)
```

Next, you'll fix those errors. `HomeView` requires two properties that you left in `WelcomeView`. Go back to it, and copy them:

```
@EnvironmentObject var userManager: UserManager
@EnvironmentObject var challengesViewModel: ChallengesViewModel
```

Then paste them at the top of `HomeView`, before `body`. Since they are environment objects, if you want to take a peek at how the view looks like using the preview, you need to add them to the `HomeView()` initializer in `HomeView_Previews`.

Do so by replacing the contents of `previews` with:

```
HomeView()
  .environmentObject(UserManager())
  .environmentObject(ChallengesViewModel())
```

You can now resume the preview and see the new **Challenge** tab added at the left of **Settings**.

Challenge settings tab

If you want to make things right, in `WelcomeView`, you notice that `challengeViewModel` is no longer used so that you can delete the property.

There's one last thing left, which you can see if you run the app: The settings view displays instead of the `HomeView` you created earlier. At the beginning of this chapter, you replaced the starter view with the settings view as the default view displayed at launch — it's time to restore that view.

Open **KuchiApp** and replace the content of `WindowGroup` with:

```
StarterView()
  .environmentObject(userManager)
  .environmentObject(challengesViewModel)
```

Now when you run the app, after the welcome view, you'll see the `HomeView` with the two tabs you added in this section.

One last adjustment to ensure everything works smoothly, you need to wire the tab view to something so that it can remember what tab is currently active. If you look at the tab view in the code, you'll notice it has defined tabs. But no place stores the currently selected tab or its index .

You need this because if `TabView` is re-rendered (or the entire `HomeView`), it would forget the previously selected tab and just make the first one selected.

To keep track of the currently selected tab index, in `HomeView` add a state property before `userManager`:

```
@State var selectedTab = 0
```

Next, pass a binding of it to the `TabView`'s initializer:

```
TabView(selection: $selectedTab) {
```

And that's all. Amazingly simple!

App Storage

The settings view you've created in this chapter looks great, but it misses two important points:

1. Changes are not persistent. If you change, for example, the number of questions to 4, then you restart the app, the app will forget your change and will reinitialize that value to 6.
2. Changes are not functional. If you change the number of questions to 4, then switch to the Challenge tab, it will still display "0/6", meaning it still uses 6 for the number of questions to ask per session.

You would probably use `UserDefaults` to store user settings, and that's what you'll do, just in a different way.

In fact, SwiftUI has introduced a new property wrapper that works like `@State` but with the value read from and written to `UserDefaults`.

The attribute to use is `@AppStorage`, and you use it just like `@State` and `@Binding`, except that you must provide a key representing the name under which you store the value in the `UserDefaults`.

Storing Settings to UserDefaults

Open **SettingView** and replace the line that declares where the state variable `numberOfQuestions` with:

```
@AppStorage("numberOfQuestions")
var numberOfQuestions = 6
```

You pass the key as the first unnamed parameter, `"numberOfQuestions"` — it's common practice to avoid confusion with the same name for the key and the property name.

You must also provide an initial value, which is stored in `UserDefaults` if the key doesn't exist yet, and you're using the same value as before, which is 6.

You can also optionally pass an instance of `UserDefaults`, in which case it will be used to read from and store to the handled value.

To verify that it works:

1. Launch the app.
2. Go to settings and change the number of questions to 4.
3. Wait a couple of seconds, writing to user defaults is not synchronous and happens in the background.
4. Relaunch the app.
5. Go to settings: The number of questions is 4, meaning it remembered the change.

However, this change alone doesn't fix the second issue. If you switch to the Challenge tab, it still displays `0/6`, meaning the number of questions hasn't changed.

To fix that, open **Practice/ChallengesViewModel**, locate the `numberOfQuestions` property, and apply the same changes you did in `SettingsView`, by turning the state property into an app storage property and initializing it:

```
@AppStorage("numberOfQuestions")
private(set) var numberOfQuestions = 6
```

Now you have the same property, but in two different places: **ChallengesViewModel** and **SettingsView**. Under the hood, the application stores this property in the user defaults, ensuring that the single source of truth rule is not violated. To make a comparison, `@AppStorage` looks more like a binding than a state attribute.

However, there are better approaches than this for several reasons, the first of which is that you must provide an initial value in all cases. If you want to change it in the future but forget to update in one place, you'll have a different initial value depending on which property you reference first.

So it's better to keep one *copy* only and always reference that from elsewhere. Since you already declared it there, the most suitable candidate is **ChallengesViewModel**. So go ahead and remove the numberOfQuestions property from SettingsView.

The compiler will immediately inform you that something is wrong — you need to change where you reference this property in order to point to the updated location. The only control using it is the stepper, replace its code with:

```
Stepper(
  "Number of Questions: \
(challengesViewModel.numberOfQuestions)",
  value: $challengesViewModel.numberOfQuestions,
  in: 3 ... 200
)
```

The changes you've applied consist of replacing the two occurrences of numberOfQuestions with challengesViewModel.numberOfQuestions.

But you also need to add a reference to challengesViewModel to SettingsView. Add this property before learningEnabled:

```
@EnvironmentObject
var challengesViewModel: ChallengesViewModel
```

Lastly, for now, you also need to supply to the preview, which would otherwise make previewing to crash. Go to the bottom of the **SettingsView** file and replace the content of the previews property with:

```
SettingsView()
  .environmentObject(ChallengesViewModel())
```

You may notice that the compiler is still complaining about numberOfQuestions having no access to the setter — that's because you declare the property as private(set). Just remove this access modifier so that it looks like this:

```
@AppStorage("numberOfQuestions")
var numberOfQuestions = 6
```

It might sound like everything is complete, but you need more. You need to do a few other updates for the app storage variable to work correctly.

If you open **Shared/Practice/ScoreView**, you'll notice that it has a numberOfQuestions property, which is immutable, and initialized when the view is instantiated. If you want it to follow the value you can change in the settings view, you need to turn it into a binding.

Replace:

```
let numberOfQuestions: Int
```

With:

```
@Binding var numberOfQuestions: Int
```

You also need to make the preview view compliant with this change. Add a state property to it:

```
@State static var numberOfQuestions: Int = 6
```

Next, still, in the preview, update the value passed to the numberOfQuestions parameter with the state property you've just created. previews should now look like this:

```
ScoreView(
  numberOfQuestions: $numberOfQuestions,
  numberOfAnswered: $numberOfAnswered
)
```

You use ScoreView in ChallengeView, so you need to do some work on it too. It has a questionsPerSession property, which is an environment variable:

```
@Environment(\.questionsPerSession) var questionsPerSession
```

As done for the settings view above, you need to delete it.

ChallengeView does not have a reference to ChallengesViewModel, so you inject it from the environment. Add the property after verticalSizeClasses:

```
@EnvironmentObject
var challengesViewModel: ChallengesViewModel
```

Next, locate the two places where ScoreView is instantiated in the body implementation, and update the reference to questionsPerSession to point to the challenges view model:

```
ScoreView(
```

```
    // Update this parameter
    numberOfQuestions: $challengesViewModel.numberOfQuestions,
    numberOfAnswered: $numberOfAnswered
  )
```

Almost done. In `ChallengeView`, before replacing with an app storage property, you had an environment variable, and that environment variable must have been injected from elsewhere. That elsewhere is **HomeView**, open it and delete these lines under `PracticeView`:

```
  .environment(
    \.questionsPerSession,
    challengesViewModel.numberOfQuestions
  )
```

Now everything is set up. If available, this change will retrieve' numberOfQuestion' from the `UserDefaults`. Otherwise, it will initialize with the provided initial value. Since in the previous run, you assigned a new value from the settings view, this is what you'll see in the challenge view if you run the app in the simulator:

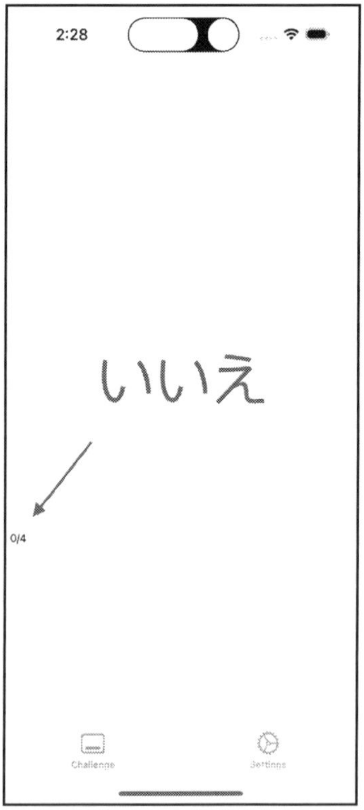

Number of questions updated

Try changing its value again from settings, when you switch back to challenge, you'll find the new value updated.

Storable Types

If you have ever used `UserDefaults`, you know you can't store any arbitrary type. You're restricted to:

- Basic data types: `Int`, `Double`, `String` and `Bool`.
- Composite types: `Data` and `URL`.
- Any type adopting `RawRepresentable`.

To store types that are not explicitly handled by `AppStorage`, you have two choices:

- Make the type `RawRepresentable`
- Use a shadow property

Using RawRepresentable

A real example of the former case is `appearance`, which is of the `Appearance` enum type, hence not storable by default. However, if you open **Shared/Utils/Appearance**, you'll notice that the enumeration implicitly conforms to `RawRepresentable`, having it as a raw value of `Int` Type. Remember, if you specify a raw value type for an enum, it will automatically conform to `RawRepresentable`.

So in `SettingsView` make `appearance` an `AppStorage` property by replacing its declaration line with:

```
@AppStorage("appearance") var appearance: Appearance
= .automatic
```

Note that even if the setting is permanently stored and remembered across app relaunches, it won't affect the actual app appearance, you'll fix that later. Feel free to verify that when you change its value and relaunch the app, it remembers the value you selected and appears as selected in the settings view.

Using a Shadow Property

In cases where a supported type is not an option and so is conforming to RawRepresentable, you can declare a shadow property that is AppStorage friendly.

A real use case in Kuchi is for the dailyReminderTime property. You have already declared it as state property and verified that it works with the date picker, but it's of Date type, which is not handled by AppStorage.

Without touching it, you add a new property using a type that's handled by AppStorage. You can convert a date into a double, and vice-versa, so you can use the Double type.

In SettingsView, add this property after dailyReminderTime:

```
@AppStorage("dailyReminderTime")
var dailyReminderTimeShadow: Double = 0
```

This property will go to the UserDefaults, whereas dailyReminderTime is what's bound to the date picker. Now you need to link the two properties so that:

1. When you select a new time using the date picker, the new Date value is copied into the shadow property, hence saved to UserDefaults.
2. When the value is read from UserDefaults and stored in the shadow property, the dailyReminderTime is reinitialized properly.

For the first, DatePicker already has an explicit binding defined via the onChange(of:perform:) modifier, which you needed in order to be able to update the local notification every time you choose a new time.

All you need to do is to convert the new Date value to Double and store it in the shadow property. Do it in the second onChange modifier, the one monitoring dailyReminderTime, so that it looks like this:

```
.onChange(
  of: dailyReminderTime,
  perform: { newValue in
    dailyReminderTimeShadow = newValue.timeIntervalSince1970
    configureNotification()
  }
)
```

This copies the number of seconds since the midnight of Jan 1, 1970, as a double value, into the shadow property.

For the second, you can take advantage of the `.onAppear()` modifier, taking a closure that is executed every time the view displays. Add it after the `onChange` modifiers:

```
.onAppear {
  dailyReminderTime = Date(timeIntervalSince1970:
dailyReminderTimeShadow)
}
```

With it, every time the `Section` displays, the value stored in the shadow property converts to a date and stored into `dailyReminderTime`.

You need to turn the `dailyReminderEnabled` from state to app storage property, and replace it with this line:

```
@AppStorage("dailyReminderEnabled")
var dailyReminderEnabled = false
```

Now you can verify that it works. Follow these steps:

1. Run the app, either in the simulator or device.
2. Go to the settings tab.
3. Enable daily reminders.
4. If it asks you to allow notifications, allow it.
5. Choose a time.
6. Relaunch the app.
7. Go to the settings view again.

You can now see that the daily reminders setting is still enabled, and the date picker shows the time you selected.

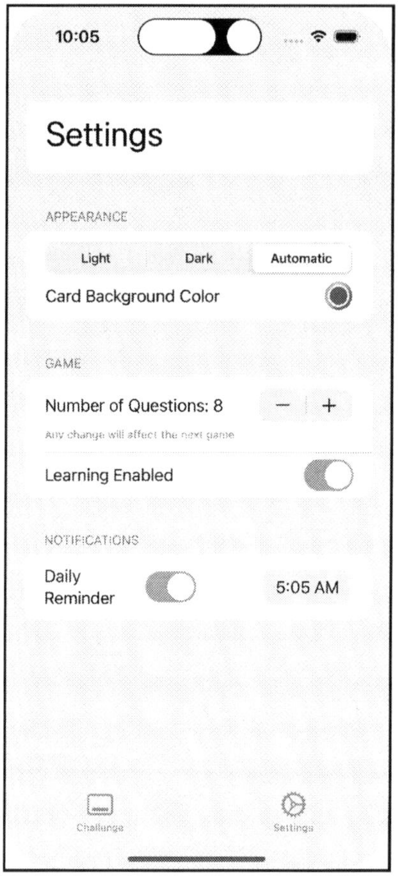

Testing daily reminder

Enabling Appearance

The last thing left for this chapter is that you need to make the picker you added at the beginning of this chapter change the app's appearance. Right now, if you change it, it won't have any effect.

Earlier, you turned the `appearance` property into an `AppStorage` property. That's just one aspect of it, you also need to react to its changes.

Since this is an app-wide setting, you need to work on the `KuchiApp`. Open `KuchiApp` and add this property below `userManager`:

```
@AppStorage("appearance")
```

```
var appearance: Appearance = .automatic
```

To apply the appearance, there's a modifier called `.preferredColorScheme(_:)`. You can apply it to any view, so you're not limited to applying it to the entire app. But in the case of Kuchi, that's actually what you want to achieve.

The `.preferredColorScheme(:_)` modifier accepts a `ColorScheme` parameter, which is an enum with two cases: `.dark` and `.light` — the `Appearance` modifier defined in Kuchi, which adds a third `.automatic` case, exposes a `getColorScheme()` method that converts from `Appearance` to `ColorScheme`.

Add this modifier to `StarterView()`, after the two environment objects:

```
.preferredColorScheme(appearance.getColorScheme())
```

Now you can run the app, go to the settings view, and change from light to dark appearance, and vice-versa. Magically, but not surprisingly, the app will immediately turn from light to dark back and forth, as expected.

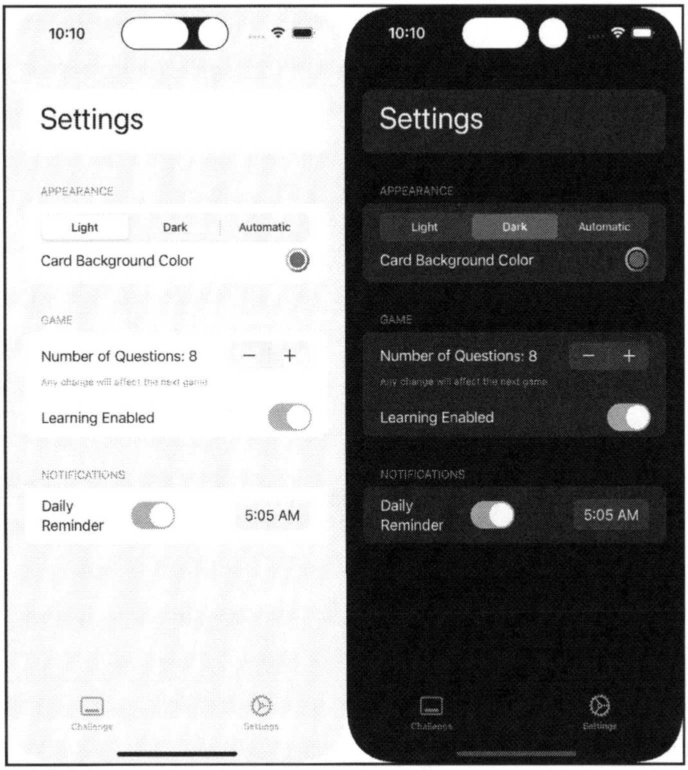

Testing appearance

> **Note**: If you set the appearance to automatic, you might need to relaunch the app for the setting to take effect.

You can change the system appearance on your iPhone from the Settings app in the **Display & Brightness** section.

If you're using the simulator, instead, still in the Settings app, you need to look into the **Developer** section. Alternatively, you can reach out the **Feature → Toggle Appearance** menu item or its handy **⇧+⌘+E** shortcut.

SceneStorage

Alongside `AppStorage`, SwiftUI also offers a `@SceneStorage` attribute that works like `@AppStorage`, except that the persisted storage is limited to a scene instead of being app-wide. This is very useful if you have a multi-scene app. Unfortunately, Kuchi isn't so you won't cover it here. But it's definitely beneficial for you to know! In the **Where to Go From Here** sections, there's a resource on learning more about both `AppStorage` and `SceneStorage`.

Key Points

- In this chapter, you've played with some of the UI components SwiftUI offers by using them to build a settings view in the Kuchi app. There are a few more, and you can use the ones you've used here differently. Take, for example, the date picker, which you can use to pick a date, a time, or both.
- You've looked at the three different styles of components; the stepper component, the toggle component and the date picker.
- You've also witnessed how easy creating a tabbed UI is.
- Lastly, you used `AppStorage` to persist settings to the user defaults.

Where to Go From Here?

This is just a short list of documentation you can browse to know more about the components you've seen here and what you haven't.

- `List`: apple.co/2IhW0KW
- `Section`: apple.co/2JNAKOa
- SwiftUI Components: apple.co/39vBy50
- Picker and Picker Styles: apple.co/3nyViIG
- `SceneStorage` and `AppStorage`: apple.co/37lgyeG

Chapter 11: Gestures

By Antonio Bello

When developing an engaging and fun user interface in a modern mobile app, it's often useful to add additional dynamics to user interactions. Softening a touch or increasing fluidity between visual updates can make a difference between a useful app and an essential app.

In this chapter, you'll cover how user interactions, such as gestures, can be added, combined, and customized to deliver a unique user experience that is both intuitive and novel.

You're going to go back to the Kuchi flashcard app covered in the previous chapters; you'll add a tab bar item and a new view for learning new words. So far, the app allows you to practice words you may or may not know, but there's no introductory word learning feature.

There's quite some work to be done in order to get the project ready to take gestures. Exceptionally for this chapter only, you'll find two starter projects under the **starter** folder, contained in these folders:

- **starter-chapter**
- **starter-gestures**

If you want to do all the preparatory work, either reuse the project you completed in the previous chapter, or use the one contained in **starter-chapter** and keep reading.

If you want to **skip the preparatory work** and jump to **gestures** right away, then skip the next **Adding the Learn Feature** section (but it's recommended to at least taking a quick look anyway) and start reading **Your first gesture**.

If you decided to take the blue pill, start by **opening the starter project** from the **starter/starter-chapter** folder — or your own project brought from the previous project if you prefer.

Adding the Learn Feature

In the previous chapter you added a tab bar to the app, with two tabs only: **Challenge** and **Settings**. Now you're going to add a 3rd tab, occupying the first position in the tabs list, which will take care of the **Learn** section.

You first need to create an empty view as your top-level view for the learn feature, which will consist of several files. You will place them in a new group called **Learn**. This will sit at the same level as the existing *Practice* folder.

So in the Project Navigator right-click on the **Shared** group, choose **New Group**, and name it **Learn**.

The view you'll be building will be used for learning new words; therefore, it can intuitively be called `LearnView`. So, go ahead and create a new SwiftUI view file named **LearnView** inside the Learn group.

Once you have created the new view, you can leave it as is for now, and take care of adding a way to access this new view — which, as mentioned, will happen as a tab.

Open **HomeView** and before the `PracticeView` tab add this new tab:

```
LearnView()
  .tabItem({
    VStack {
      Image(systemName: "bookmark")
      Text("Learn")
    }
  })
  .tag(0)
```

If you resume the preview, this is what you'll see:

The newly created learn tab

Creating a Flashcard

With the new **Learn** tab in place, the first component of the Learn feature you'll be working on is the flash card. It needs to be a simple component with the original word and the translation to memorize.

When talking about the card, two distinct understandings within the app are useful to recognize: the visual card (a UI component) and the card data (the state).

Both are integral to the card feature, and the card itself is a composite of both elements. However, the visual card cannot exist without state; to start with, you need a data structure that can represent the state.

Using the **Swift** file template, create a new file in your **Learn** folder named **FlashCard**. It's going to be an empty struct for now — add it:

```
struct FlashCard {
}
```

Within the struct, you'll need the data the user is trying to learn. In this case, it's the word. Add a property of type `Challenge` with the name `card` to your struct:

```
var card: Challenge
```

This is the basic data structure for your flashcard, but to make it useful for your SwiftUI views, you'll need a few more properties.

First, an `id` may be useful for iterating through multiple flashcards in a view. This is best achieved by making a structure conform to the `Identifiable` protocol, as the `ForEach` SwiftUI block will look for an `id` unless an explicit identifier has been specified.

As there are no `id` generators within the app, you can simply rely on `Foundation`'s `UUID` constructor to provide a unique identifier each time a `FlashCard` is created. Add the following property to `FlashCard`:

```
let id = UUID()
```

As you can see, there's no explicit use of the `Identifiable` protocol yet. This will be covered shortly. The final step needed within your basic `FlashCard` state structure is to add a flag called `isActive`. Add the following property:

```
var isActive = true
```

This is a simple property for filtering cards that are intended to be part of the learning session.

The user may not want to go through a whole deck of cards that they already know every time so this allows you to selectively filter cards whether through user curation or internal logic. To ensure compliance with the `Identifiable` protocol, add it to the struct declaration:

```
struct FlashCard: Identifiable {
  ...
}
```

You don't need to do anything extra to make FlashCard identifiable, but you will want to make sure it's Equatable. This will enable you to provide comparisons quickly and easily in code, to ensure the same card is not duplicated, or that one card matches another when relevant.

Add this extension after FlashCard:

```
extension FlashCard: Equatable {
  static func == (lhs: FlashCard, rhs: FlashCard) -> Bool {
    return lhs.card.question == rhs.card.question
        && lhs.card.answer == rhs.card.answer
  }
}
```

With this property, you'll be able to use the == operator to compare two flash cards.

There you go; that's your FlashCard state object defined and ready for use! The user is not going to be learning one card at a time though, so you'll need to build on this object with the concept of a deck. There is a deck for the Practice feature of the app as a simple array of cards, but the Learn feature has different needs so you're going to be more explicit with how the deck works this time.

Building a Flash Deck

Although the deck is not a new concept, the *Learn* feature is going to be more explicit than *Practice* with the deck of cards by creating a whole new state structure for use in the UI. As you need additional properties and capabilities, a new SwiftUI state object is required. Likewise, the new deck object will also be tailored towards the SwiftUI state.

Start by creating a new Swift file called **FlashDeck** inside the **Learn** group, using the **Swift File** template. FlashDeck needs just a single property: an array of FlashCard objects — Add the following class:

```
class FlashDeck {
  var cards: [FlashCard]
}
```

What makes the FlashDeck a powerful SwiftUI state object comes from two modifications. The first will be from a constructor.

Add the following:

```
init(from words: [Challenge]) {
  cards = words.map {
    FlashCard(card: $0)
  }
}
```

This constructor simply maps the words (`Challenges`) passed in into `FlashCards`.

The second power-up for the `FlashDeck` model comes from `Combine`. To make the UI responsive to changes in the deck, the `cards` property will be prefixed with the `@Published` attribute to allow subscribers of the model to receive notifications of updates.

Change the `cards` property from:

```
var cards: [FlashCard]
```

Into:

```
@Published var cards: [FlashCard]
```

And finally, you need to extend the class to be an `ObservableObject` (as per **Chapter 9: "State & Data Flow - Part II"**):

```
class FlashDeck: ObservableObject {
  ...
}
```

You now have your `FlashCard` and `FlashDeck` built and ready to go.

Final State

Your final state work for the Learn feature will be your top-level store, which will hold your deck (and cards) and provide the user control to manage your deck and receive updates within your UI. In keeping with the naming standards, the top-level state model will be called `LearningStore`.

Create a new file name **LearningStore** in the **Learn** group, using the **Swift File** template.

Next, populate the file with the following:

```
class LearningStore {
  // 1
  @Published var deck: FlashDeck

  // 2
  @Published var card: FlashCard?

  // 3
  @Published var score = 0

  // 4
  init(deck: [Challenge]) {
    self.deck = FlashDeck(from: deck)
    self.card = getNextCard()
  }

  // 5
  func getNextCard() -> FlashCard? {
    guard let card = deck.cards.last else {
      return nil
    }

    self.card = card
    deck.cards.removeLast()

    return self.card
  }
}
```

Going over this step-by-step:

1. Like in `FlashDeck`, you'll use `Combine` to provide `@Published` attributes to your properties. The store will maintain the complete deck (`deck`),
2. ... the current card (`card`),
3. ... and the current score (`score`).
4. You add an initializer that sets up the deck.
5. You also add a convenience method, which will get the next card in the deck. It does this by removing the last card of the deck and returning it.

The final step of setting up this store is to make it conform to `ObservableObject`:

```
class LearningStore: ObservableObject {
  ...
}
```

Phew — that's a lot of setup without any UI code, right? But you've now made a nice foundation for building the view for the Learn feature.

Building the User Interface

The UI for the Learn feature will be formed around a 3-tier view. The first is your currently empty `LearnView`. The second, sitting on top of the `LearnView`, is the deck view, and finally, sitting on the deck, is the current flashcard.

You'll start by adding the missing views: `DeckView` and `CardView`.

First up, still in the **Learn** group, create a SwiftUI view file named **CardView** using the **SwiftUI View** template, and replace the contents of `body` with:

```
ZStack {
  Rectangle()
    .fill(Color.red)
    .frame(width: 320, height: 210)
    .cornerRadius(12)
  VStack {
    Spacer()
    Text("Apple")
      .font(.largeTitle)
      .foregroundColor(.white)
    Text("Omena")
      .font(.caption)
      .foregroundColor(.white)
    Spacer()
  }
}
.shadow(radius: 8)
.frame(width: 320, height: 210)
.animation(.spring(), value: 0)
```

This creates a simple red card view with rounded corners and a couple of text labels centered on the card. You'll be expanding on this view later in the tutorial.

If you preview this in the Canvas you should see the following:

The deck card

Next up, the deck view. Create a SwiftUI file named (you guessed it) **DeckView** and replace the contents of `body` with:

```
ZStack {
  CardView()
  CardView()
}
```

This is a simple view containing two cards, but you'll flesh this view out shortly by using the state objects you created earlier to support the loading of dynamically generated cards into the learning flow.

As the cards are stacked on top of each other, previewing the deck view in the Canvas will give you the same result as before.

Next, you need to add `DeckView` to `LearnView`.

Go back to **LearnView** and replace the contents of `body` with the following:

```
VStack {
  Spacer()
  Text("Swipe left if you remembered"
    + "\nSwipe right if you didn't")
    .font(.headline)
  DeckView()
  Spacer()
  Text("Remembered 0/0")
}
```

This is fairly simple: you have a `Text` label providing instructions, a score at the bottom, and the `DeckView` in the center of the screen.

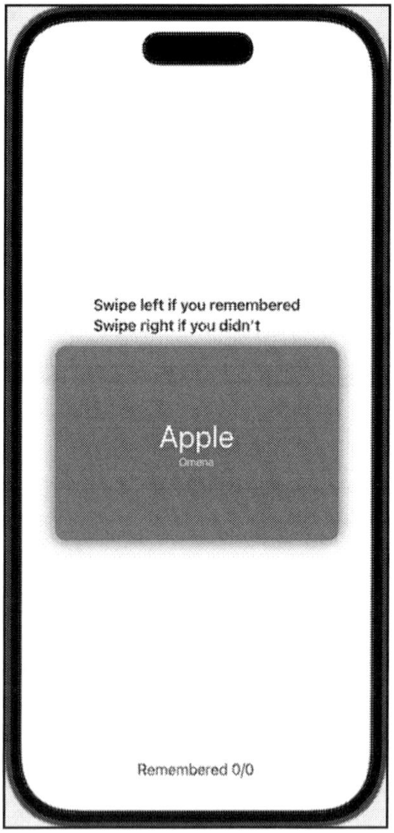

The learn view

Adding LearningStore to the Views

Staying inside `LearnView`, you can add the store you previously created as a property to the view:

```
@StateObject var learningStore =
  LearningStore(deck: ChallengesViewModel.challenges)
```

As `LearningStore` is a `StateObject`, it can be used within the `LearnView` to ensure the view is rebuilt when any of the published properties change. With this setup, you can even update the score `Text` at the bottom of the view.

Replace:

```
Text("Remembered 0/0")
```

With:

```
Text("Remembered \(learningStore.score)"
  + "/\(learningStore.deck.cards.count)")
```

That's good for now. You'll come back to `LearnView` later, but now `DeckView` needs to be able to receive some of the data from within the `LearningStore` to pipe card data through to the individual `CardView` components.

To enable this, open up **DeckView** and add the following at the top of the struct, before `body`:

```
@ObservedObject var deck: FlashDeck

let onMemorized: () -> Void

init(deck: FlashDeck, onMemorized: @escaping () -> Void) {
  self.onMemorized = onMemorized
  self.deck = deck
}
```

You're adding a `FlashDeck` property for getting the items the view will be subscribing to, as well as a callback `onMemorized`, for when the user memorizes a card. Both are passed in through a custom initializer.

For the preview to still work, you need to update `DeckView_Previews`'s `previews` to the following:

```
DeckView(
  deck: FlashDeck(from: ChallengesViewModel.challenges),
  onMemorized: {}
)
```

And finally, inside **LearnView** find `DeckView()` in the `body` and replace it with:

```
DeckView(
  deck: learningStore.deck,
  onMemorized: { learningStore.score += 1 }
)
```

Notice how you increase the score when the user memorizes the card. There's not yet a way to trigger the `onMemorized`, but you'll be adding this later in the chapter.

Next up, getting the data from the learning store into the individual cards. To do so, open up **CardView** and add the following to the top, before `body`:

```
let flashCard: FlashCard

init(_ card: FlashCard) {
  self.flashCard = card
}
```

Here you add a `FlashCard` property to the view and pass it in through the initializer. The property isn't a state object because you're not planning on changing the value of the `FlashCard` at any time; the card data is fixed for the lifetime of the object.

With an actual card model, you can also update the `body` of the view to use it. Replace the contents of the view's `VStack` content with:

```
Spacer()
Text(flashCard.card.question)
  .font(.largeTitle)
  .foregroundColor(.white)
Text(flashCard.card.answer)
  .font(.caption)
  .foregroundColor(.white)
Spacer()
```

Here you simply use the question and answer from the flashcard instead of hardcoded values.

With the new initializer, you need to make an update to the places where `CardView` is used, namely: `CardView_Previews` and `DeckView`.

Inside **CardView** update `CardView_Previews`'s `previews` to:

```
let card = FlashCard(
  card: Challenge(
    question: "こんにちわ",
    pronunciation: "Konnichiwa",
    answer: "Hello"
  )
)
return CardView(card)
```

Next, inside **DeckView**, you'll need to modify the `body` to dynamically support multiple `CardView`s. To add support for multiple `CardView`s, first add the following helper methods at the bottom of the view:

```
func getCardView(for card: FlashCard) -> CardView {
  let activeCards = deck.cards.filter { $0.isActive == true }
  if let lastCard = activeCards.last {
    if lastCard == card {
      return createCardView(for: card)
    }
  }

  let view = createCardView(for: card)

  return view
}

func createCardView(for card: FlashCard) -> CardView {
  let view = CardView(card)

  return view
}
```

These methods help with creating a `CardView` using a `FlashCard`.

Then, replace the contents of `body` of the view with the following:

```
ZStack {
  ForEach(deck.cards.filter { $0.isActive }) { card in
    getCardView(for: card)
  }
}
```

Here the `ForEach` takes all active cards from the deck and creates a `CardView` for each using the helper methods just created.

Looking at the Canvas for either `LearnView` or `DeckView`, you should now see a card like this:

Completed deck card

Applying Settings

In the previous chapter you added two settings that affect the Learning section:

- **Learning Enabled**, in the game category, used to enable or disable the learning screen.
- **Card Background Color** in the appearance category, used to personalize the card background.

Now it's time to put them to use. The first thing to do is to expose both parameters via the UserDefaults, turning them from `@State` into `@AppStorage` properties.

The first is very simple: In **SettingsView** replace the line where `learningEnabled` is declared with:

```
@AppStorage("learningEnabled")
var learningEnabled: Bool = true
```

As for the other property, it's of `Color` type, which is not a type that UserDefaults can handle, so you have to either make it `RawRepresentable`, or use a shadow property - see the previous chapter to know more about their differences.

You'll use the latter method, by adding a shadow property of `Int` type. Add this property before `cardBackgroundColor`:

```
@AppStorage("cardBackgroundColor")
var cardBackgroundColorInt: Int = 0xFF0000FF
```

Next, in body add a new onChange(of:perform) modifier to List, right after the other two that take care of daily reminder enabled and daily reminder time:

```
.onChange(of: cardBackgroundColor, perform: { newValue in
  cardBackgroundColorInt = newValue.asRgba
})
```

Last, in the .onAppear modifier, initialize the card background color from the shadow property - add this after setting dailyReminderTime:

```
cardBackgroundColor = Color(rgba: cardBackgroundColorInt)
```

With these settings adjustment accomplished, you need to use them appropriately.

You use learningEnabled to enable or disable the learning section, and the easiest way to achieve that is by showing or hiding the respective tab.

Open **HomeView** and add the same AppStorage property as defined in SettingsView:

```
@AppStorage("learningEnabled")
var learningEnabled: Bool = true
```

Next, surround the first tab with an if statement, so that the tab is included only if learningEnabled is true:

```
if learningEnabled {
  LearnView()
    .tabItem({
      VStack {
        Image(systemName: "bookmark")
        Text("Learn")
      }
    })
    .tag(0)
}
```

Note: For simplicity, you're using an anti-pattern that has been *discouraged* in the previous chapter — You are declaring the same learningEnabled app storage property in two different places, and you're going to do the same with the other property, cardBackgroundColor. The solution is to move these property to a dedicated data structure, as you did in the previous chapter by using ChallengesViewModel to host them.

Now run the app, go to the settings view, when you disable Learning Enabled you see the Learning tab disappearing, whereas if you enable it, it will reappear.

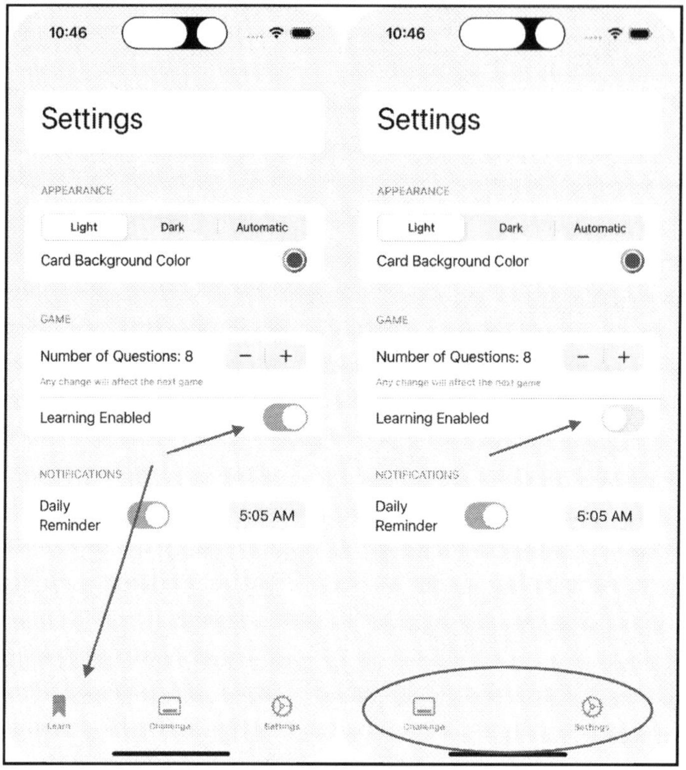

Settings with learning disabled

Now to change the card background color, add a corresponding property to `CardView`, in **CardView**:

```
@Binding var cardColor: Color
```

You declare it as a binding because you will pass it, so that the source of truth is defined elsewhere — namely, in `DeckView`.

You might be tempted to do it directly in `CardView`, but that would be inefficient, because you would read the same property from UserDefaults for each card, whereas passing it from `DeckView` you'd read it once, and pass the same binding to all cards via their respective initializers.

Replace the CardView's initializer to account for the new property:

```
init(
  _ card: FlashCard,
  cardColor: Binding<Color>
) {
  flashCard = card
  _cardColor = cardColor
}
```

Next, replace the statically-set red background color with the value of the newly added property. In body, the Rectangle view has a .fill(Color.red) modifier — replace it with:

```
.fill(cardColor)
```

Last for CardView, you need to amend the preview to handle the additional parameter. Replace CardView_Previews content with:

```
@State static var cardColor = Color.red

static var previews: some View {
  let card = FlashCard(
    card: Challenge(
      question: "こんにちわ",
      pronunciation: "Konnichiwa",
      answer: "Hello"
    )
  )
  return CardView(card, cardColor: $cardColor)
}
```

Now open up **DeckView** and add this property:

```
@AppStorage("cardBackgroundColor")
var cardBackgroundColorInt: Int = 0xFF0000FF
```

You will use just the shadow property instead of adding a second property — you'll convert it to Color when passing to CardView.

Next, replace the createCardView(for:) implementation with:

```
func createCardView(for card: FlashCard) -> CardView {
  // 1
  let view = CardView(card, cardColor: Binding(
      get: { Color(rgba: cardBackgroundColorInt) },
      set: { newValue in cardBackgroundColorInt =
newValue.asRgba }
```

```
    )
  )

  return view
}
```

Here you've passed the new `cardColor` parameter to the `CardView` initializer, using an explicit binding.

You can now run the app, re-enable learning if it was still disabled, and pick a card color of your choice — if you activate the **Learning** tab, you'll see that cards are now shown with the shiny newly selected background color.

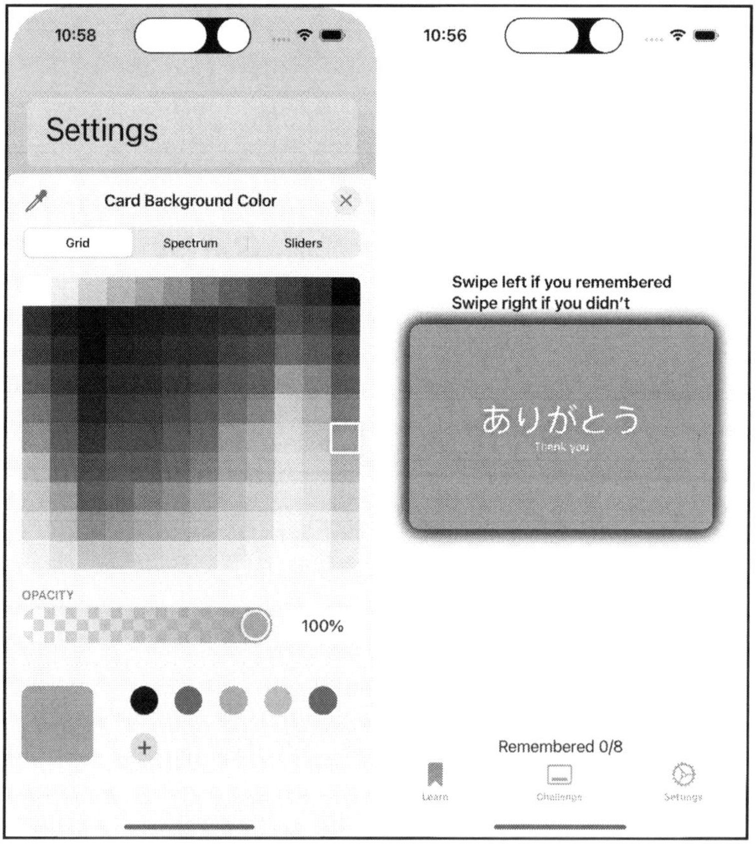

Choosing the card background color

Your First Gesture

> **Note**: If you skipped the previous section and jumped straight into this, open the updated starter project that you'll find in the **starter/starter-gestures** folder.

Gestures in SwiftUI are not that dissimilar from their cousins in AppKit and UIKit, but they are simpler and somewhat more elegant, giving a perception amongst some developers of being more powerful.

Although they're not any better than their predecessors in terms of capability, their SwiftUI approach makes for easier and more compelling uses for gestures where before they were often nice-to-haves.

Starting with a basic gesture, it's time to revisit `CardView`. Previously, you added both the original word and the translated word to `CardView`, which is somewhat useful. But what if the user wanted to test their knowledge without being given the answer immediately?

It would be nice if the card had the original word, and then the translated word could be displayed if needed.

To achieve this, you can add a simple tap gesture (literally a `TapGesture`) for this interaction to happen. Taps are ubiquitous and necessary, so it's a great place to start with gestures.

Start by opening **CardView**, then add the following property stating whether the answer has been revealed or not to the top of the view:

```
@State var revealed = false
```

Next, in the body add the following `.gesture` modifer at the bottom, after `.animation(_:)`:

```
.gesture(TapGesture()
  .onEnded {
    withAnimation(.easeIn, {
      revealed.toggle()
    })
})
```

Here you're using a pre-built gesture from Apple that adds a lot of convenience by dealing with human tap gestures consistently across all apps. The `onEnded` block enables you to provide additional code for what happens once the tap gesture has ended. In this case, you've provided an animation that eases in (`.easeIn`) with the `revealed` property being inverted.

Currently, inverting `revealed` does nothing, but what you want to do is have the `Text` displaying the translation render only when `revealed` is `true`.

To achieve this, inside `body`, replace the following:

```
Text(flashCard.card.answer)
  .font(.caption)
  .foregroundColor(.white)
```

With:

```
if revealed {
  Text(flashCard.card.answer)
    .font(.caption)
    .foregroundColor(.white)
}
```

Try previewing the app in the Canvas with Live Preview and tapping the card. You should see a rather fluid and pleasant ease-in animation for the translated word. This is as simple as gestures get, and with the animation blocks, it provides a level of fluidity and sophistication users will appreciate.

Tap gesture flow

Also notice how tapping the card multiple times in rapid succession will still give a seamless animation experience.

Easy, right?

Custom Gestures

Although the tap gesture, and other simple gestures, provide a lot of mileage for interactions, there are often cases when more sophisticated gestures are worthwhile additions, providing a greater sense of sophistication amongst the deluge of apps available in the App Store.

For this app, you still need to provide an interaction for the user to declare whether they've memorized a card or not. You can do this by adding a custom drag gesture and evaluating the result based on the direction of the drag. That's much more complicated than a simple tap gesture but, thanks to the elegance of SwiftUI, it's still quite painless compared to previous methods of achieving the same thing.

The first step is adding an enum that denotes the direction a card is discarded in. In **DeckView** add the following code before `DeckView`:

```
enum DiscardedDirection {
  case left
  case right
}
```

You could identify more complicated metrics for this interaction (up, down, ...), but this view only needs to understand two potential options.

Next, time to make cards draggable! In **CardView** add a new `typealias` and property to the top of the view, just below the `revealed` property:

```
typealias CardDrag = (
  _ card: FlashCard,
  _ direction: DiscardedDirection
) -> Void

let dragged: CardDrag
```

Called `dragged`, this property accepts the card to be dragged and the enum result for which direction the card was dragged in.

Next, update `init` to accept the dragged closure as a parameter:

```
init(
  _ card: FlashCard,
  cardColor: Binding<Color>,
  onDrag dragged: @escaping CardDrag = {_,_  in }
) {
  flashCard = card
  _cardColor = cardColor
```

```
    self.dragged = dragged
  }
```

Next up, you need to modify `DeckView` so it supports the new card functionality. Open up **DeckView** and replace the implementation `createCardView(for:)` with the following:

```
func createCardView(for card: FlashCard) -> CardView {
  let view = CardView(
    card,
    cardColor: Binding(
      get: { Color(rgba: cardBackgroundColorInt) },
      set: { newValue in cardBackgroundColorInt =
newValue.asRgba }
    ),
    onDrag: { card, direction in
      if direction == .left {
        onMemorized()
      }
    }
  )

  return view
}
```

Here you add the `onDrag` callback to the `CardView` instance.

If the drag direction is `.left`, you trigger `onMemorized()`, and the counter in `LearningStore` will be incremented by one — That's because when instantiating `DeckView` from `LearView` you passed a closure for the `onMemorized` parameter that does that:

```
DeckView(
  deck: learningStore.deck,
  onMemorized: { learningStore.score += 1 }
)
```

The final step is to add the actual drag gesture. Go back to **CardView**, then add the following property after `revealed`:

```
@State var offset: CGSize = .zero
```

You'll use this offset to move the card to a new position.

Next up, creating the drag gesture. At the top of the `body` change the line:

```
ZStack {
```

Into:

```
return ZStack {
```

You need to `return` the `ZStack` as you'll be adding the drag gesture setup above it. Right above this code line, and still inside the body, add the following:

```
let drag = DragGesture()
  // 1
  .onChanged { offset = $0.translation }
  // 2
  .onEnded {
    if $0.translation.width < -100 {
      offset = .init(width: -1000, height: 0)
      dragged(flashCard, .left)
    } else if $0.translation.width > 100 {
      offset = .init(width: 1000, height: 0)
      dragged(flashCard, .right)
    } else {
      offset = .zero
    }
  }
```

This `DragGesture` does most of the work for you, but there are a few things worth noting:

1. With each movement recorded during the drag, the `onChanged` event will occur. You're modifying the `offset` property (which is an x and y coordinate object) to match the drag motion of the user.

   For example, if the user started dragging at (0, 0) in the coordinate space, and the `onChanged` triggered when the user was still dragging at (200, -100) then the offset x-axis would be increased by 200 and the offset y-axis would be decreased by 100. Essentially this means the component would move right and up on the screen to match the motion of the user's finger.

2. The `onEnded` event occurs when the user stops dragging, typically when their finger is removed from the screen. At this point, you want to determine which direction the user dragged the card and whether they dragged it far enough to be considered a decision (at which point you record the decision and discard the card) or whether you consider it still undecided (at which point you reset the card to the original coordinates).

   You're using -100 and 100 as the decision markers for whether the user selected left or right during the drag, and that decision is being passed into the `dragged` closure.

That's all you need for the drag gesture. Now you simply need to add it to the `body` as a modifier along with the previously defined `offset`. Right above `.gesture(TapGesture(),` add:

```
.offset(offset)
.gesture(drag)
```

The drag gesture can be passed into the gesture method as a parameter, and you should see that the tap gesture is simply another gesture added to the object: there is no conflict with including multiple gestures and stacking them up in an object if needed.

There's a spring animation also included to make the card spring back to position smoothly — but it requires a small adjustment to work properly. It's currently specified as:

```
.animation(.spring(), value: 0)
```

But the `value` parameter should be a value that's monitored for changes, so that the animation is performed only when that value changes. Since you're using `offset` to calculate the position of the card, that's the value to use. Change as follows:

```
.animation(.spring(), value: offset)
```

Now you can **build and run** to check your progress. You can now drag the card around and swipe left and right.

You can also try previewing `LearnView` using Live Preview and see the drag gesture in action.

Card's drag gesture

But, what if you wanted to *combine* gestures?

Combining Gestures for More Complex Interactions

Perhaps you want to provide an elegant visual indicator to the user if they select the card long enough so that they understand there's further interaction available. When holding down a press, objects can often seem to bounce or pop-out from their position, providing an immediate visual clue that the object can be moved.

SwiftUI provides the ability to add such a change by combining two gestures. When combining gestures, SwiftUI provides a few options about how they interact:

- **Sequenced**: a gesture that follows another gesture.
- **Simultaneous**: gestures that are active at the same time.
- **Exclusive**: gestures that can be both added, but only one can be active at a time.

You're going to add a simultaneous gesture in this case because you want to provide a simple clue to the potential of the possible drag gesture, without preventing the drag gesture being invoked at the same time.

This may sound complicated, but it's incredibly simple, as you'll see.

First, add a new property to store the state of the drag gesture to `CardView`:

```
@GestureState var isLongPressed = false
```

You'll notice a new state attribute called `@GestureState`. This attribute enables the state of a gesture to be stored and read during a gesture to influence the effects that gesture may have on the drawing of the view.

This property will be used to record whether the card has been pressed for a long time or not, and will automatically be reset when the gesture is completed. If you use a `@State` property instead, the property won't be reset when the gesture has ended.

Next, at the top of the `body`, right below the setup of `drag`, add a new gesture for the long press:

```
let longPress = LongPressGesture()
  .updating($isLongPressed) { value, state, transition in
    state = value
  }
  .simultaneously(with: drag)
```

Note how you're creating a new gesture and combining it in *simultaneous* way with another gesture, `drag`.

This gesture is a `LongPressGesture`: another consistent gesture provided by Apple. In it, you're using the `updating` body to bind a value to the state, and then adding the previous drag gesture as a potential simultaneous gesture.

To see it in action, at the bottom of body replace the previously created drag gesture:

```
.gesture(drag)
```

With:

```
.gesture(longPress)
.scaleEffect(isLongPressed ? 1.1 : 1)
```

Note that you've also added a `scaleEffect` modifier to increase the scale of the view 10% if the `isLongPressed` property is `true`.

Try it out, either by previewing `LearnView` or running the app in the Simulator. You should now be able to press the card and see it scale, whilst still being able to drag it left or right.

You may notice that no animation is applied to this pulse effect — but that's easy to fix. Just add an animation for it, linked to the `isLongPressed` property after `.scaleEffect(:_)`:

```
.animation(
  .easeInOut(duration: 0.3),
  value: isLongPressed
)
```

Now if you run or preview again, you'll see that animation applied!

This is a simple, but effective simultaneous combined gesture written with just a handful of code and a simple gesture modifier. Great job!

However you can see that the tap gesture to reveal the translation that you added earlier no longer works: if you tap on the card, nothing happens — This happens because the long press gesture hides it.

A quick way to fix this is to use the `.simultaneousGesture()`. Replace:

```
.gesture(TapGesture()
  ...
)
```

With:

```
.simultaneousGesture(TapGesture()
  ...
)
```

And the *tap to reveal the translation* gesture will work again!

Key Points

And that's it: gestures are a wonderful way of turning a basic app into a pleasurable and intuitive user experience, and SwiftUI has added powerful modifiers to make it simple and effective in any and every app you write. In this chapter you've learned:

- How to create simple gestures from Apple's built-in library. Simply use the `gesture` modifier along with the gesture to use.
- How to create custom gestures for more unique interactions.
- How to combine animations and gestures for more fluid experiences.

Where to Go From Here?

You've done a lot with gestures but there's a lot more that's possible. Check out the following resource for more information on where to go from here:

SwiftUI gesture documentation: apple.co/3cBuVgd

Chapter 12: Accessibility

By Audrey Tam

Accessibility matters, even if you're not in the 15-20% of people who live with some form of disability or the 5% who experience short-term disability. Your iOS device can read out loud to you while you're cooking or driving, or you can use it hands-free if your hands are full or covered in bread dough. Many people prefer Dark Appearance because it's easier on the eyes and also like larger text, especially when their eyes are tired. And there are growing concerns about smartphone addiction. A popular tip is to set your iPhone to grayscale (https://bit.ly/3hoVUPm)!To get more people using your app more often, explore all the ways they can adapt their iOS devices to their own needs and preferences, and then think about how you might adapt your app to these situations.

Most app UIs are very visual experiences, so most accessibility work focuses on **VoiceOver** — a screen reader that lets people with low to no vision use Apple devices without needing to see their screens. VoiceOver reads out information to users about your app's UI elements. It's up to you to make sure this information helps users interact efficiently with your app.

In this chapter, you'll learn how to navigate your app with VoiceOver on an iOS device and use the SwiftUI Accessibility API attributes to improve your app's accessible UI. You'll add labels that provide context for UI elements and improve VoiceOver information by reordering, combining or ignoring child elements.

Apple's investing a lot of effort in helping you improve the accessibility of your apps. With SwiftUI, it's easier than ever before. The future is accessible (https://bit.ly/3htnuLe), and you can help make it happen!

Using VoiceOver on a Device

Xcode has an **Accessibility Inspector** app you can open with **Xcode ▸ Open Developer Tool ▸ Accessibility Inspector**. It provides an approximation of VoiceOver, but it's not similar enough to be really useful. Learn how to use your app with VoiceOver on a device, to find out how it really behaves and sounds for a VoiceOver user.

Setting up VoiceOver Shortcut

On your device, open **Settings ▸ Accessibility ▸ Accessibility Shortcut**, and select **VoiceOver**. This enables you to switch VoiceOver on and off by triple-clicking the device's side button.

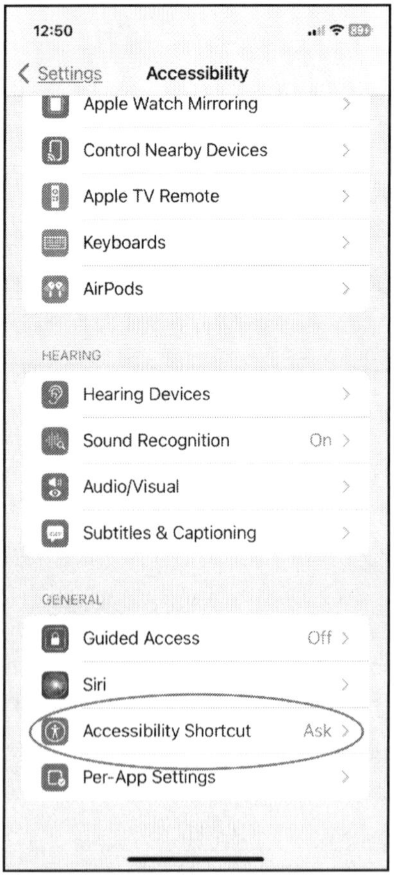

iPhone Settings: Accessibility shortcut includes VoiceOver.

Note: I check more than one shortcut option to avoid accidentally turning on VoiceOver when I'm trying to use Apple Pay. You could turn on **Settings ▸ Accessibility ▸ Touch ▸ Back Tap** and set Double-tap or Triple Tap to VoiceOver. Or just ask Siri to turn VoiceOver on or off.

Using VoiceOver

After setting up your shortcut(s), go back to **Settings ▸ Accessibility**, scroll down, then use a shortcut to start VoiceOver. VoiceOver says it's on, then says "Settings". **Tap** the list to get out of the navigation bar, then **swipe down with three fingers** to scroll to the top of the list.

Note: If your screen locks on an iPhone with Face ID: Wake iPhone and glance at it, then drag up from the bottom edge of the screen until you feel a vibration or hear two rising tones.

Now practice some basic navigation in VoiceOver.

First, **Swipe right** until you reach **VoiceOver**. Double-tap anywhere to *activate* this item.

A **split-tap** gesture is another way to activate an item: Touch and hold **Speech** with one finger, then tap the screen with another.

VoiceOver ▸ Speech

Make sure the **Detect Languages** option is on. You'll soon hear it in action.

Next, with two fingers, do a **Z** gesture. This takes you back to the previous screen.

Now, activate **Verbosity**: VoiceOver users can customize what VoiceOver reads out. These are my settings:

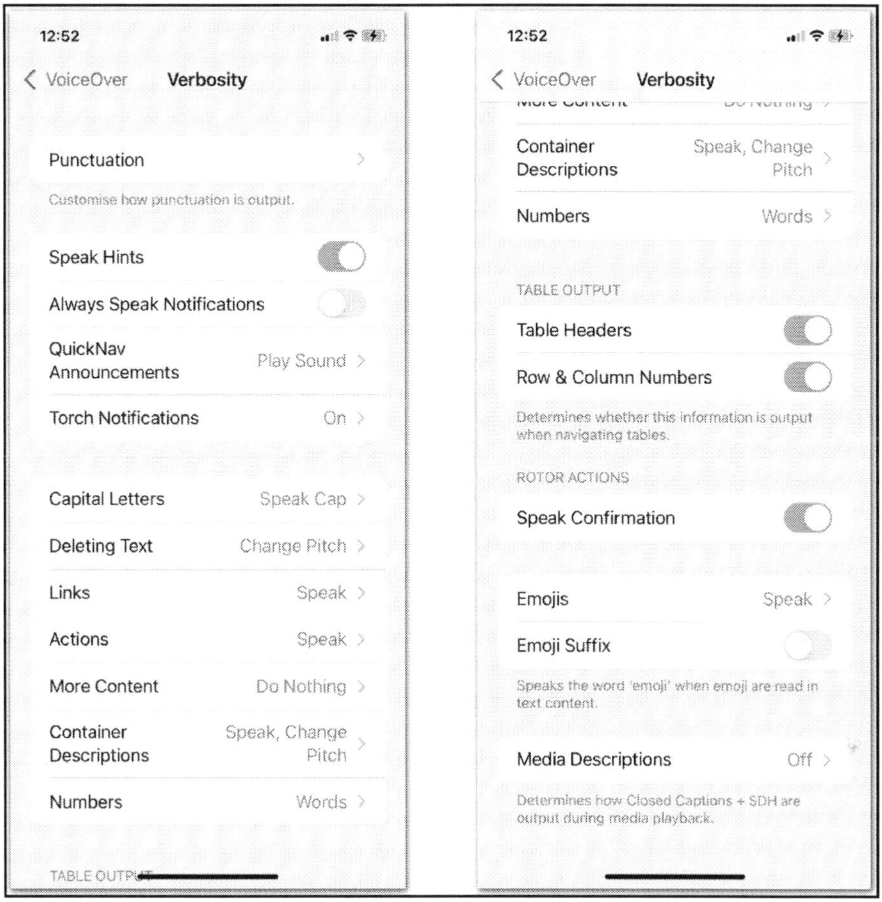

VoiceOver verbosity settings used for this chapter

If your device's settings are different, your VoiceOver might say slightly different things.

> **Note**: It's OK to turn off VoiceOver while you select your Verbosity settings. ;]

To get back to the home screen, drag up from the bottom edge of the screen until you feel a vibration or hear two rising tones. If you hear three rising tones, you'll get the app switcher.

There are many more gestures, and links to more information about VoiceOver, at Learn VoiceOver Gestures on iPhone (https://apple.co/38PipsI).

Accessibility in SwiftUI

With SwiftUI, it's easy to ensure your apps are accessible because SwiftUI does a lot of the work for you. SwiftUI elements support **Dynamic Type** and are accessible by default. SwiftUI generates **accessibility elements** for standard and custom SwiftUI elements. Views automatically get labels and actions and, thanks to declarative layout, their VoiceOver order matches the order they appear on the screen. SwiftUI tracks changes to views and sends notifications to keep VoiceOver up to date on visual changes in your app.

When the accessibility built into SwiftUI doesn't provide the right information in the right order, you'll use the SwiftUI Accessibility API to make your accessible elements understandable, interactable and navigable:

- **Understandable**: In this chapter, you'll learn what SwiftUI generates for VoiceOver from SwiftUI element initializers. Then, to clarify or add context to accessible elements, you'll override the generated default labels. You'll customize the accessibility labels and values, hiding elements that provide unnecessary or redundant information, and moving some information to hints that the user hears only if they seem unsure.

- **Interactable**: Aim to give your accessible elements appropriate default actions and create custom actions to simplify interaction for users of assistive technology. When your app has custom actions like context menus, double-tap-hold can display them. For example, in **Maps** with VoiceOver on, **double-tap-hold** an annotation to see the usual context menu.

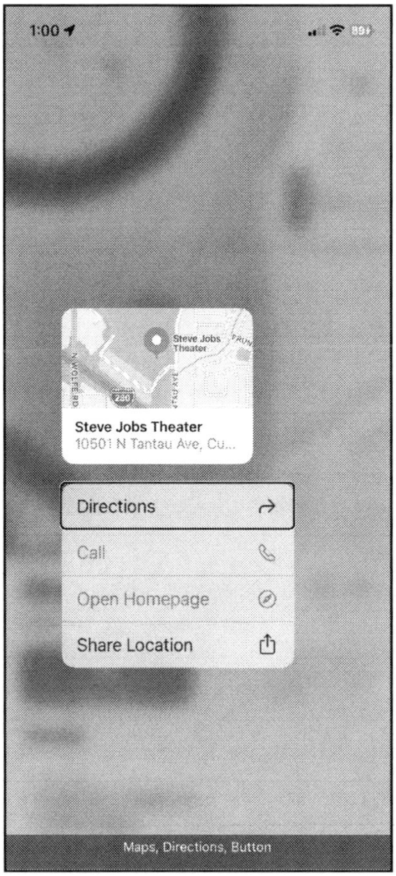

In VoiceOver, double-tap-hold annotation to show context menu.

- **Navigable**: You'll change the order that VoiceOver visits elements, and you'll group elements to reduce the number of steps and speed up navigation for VoiceOver users.

The amount of work for each accessible element could be as little as a few words or lines of code. Or you might need to refactor or add code, or even change a navigation link or alert into a modal sheet.

Most of the time, you'll add accessibility to your app without changing its appearance and behavior for users who aren't using VoiceOver. But sometimes, something you do for VoiceOver will inspire an improvement to your visual UI.

Accessibility API

Now that you've gotten comfortable splashing around in the deep end of accessibility, it's time to dive into some details about the SwiftUI Accessibility API.

When a user of your app turns on an iOS assistive technology like VoiceOver, they're actually interacting with an **accessible user interface** that iOS creates for your app. This accessible UI tells a VoiceOver user about the accessible elements of your UI — what they are and how to use them.

Every accessible UI element has these two **attributes**:

- **Frame**: The element's location and size in its `CGRect` structure.
- **Label**: The default value of an element's label — the label, name or text used to create the element. Apple's programming guide (https://apple.co/2WWrKtq) provides guidelines for creating labels and hints.

Depending on its nature, a UI element might have one or more of these three attributes:

- **Traits**: An element can have one or more traits, describing its type or state. The list of traits (https://apple.co/34VNb1X) includes `isButton`, `isModal`, `isSelected` and `updatesFrequently`. SwiftUI views have default traits. For example, a **Trait** of `Toggle` is **Button**. You can add traits with `accessibility(addTraits:)` or remove them with `accessibility(removeTraits:)`. VoiceOver reads out an element's traits, so never include them in its label.
- **Value**: A UI element has a value if its content can change. If the default value isn't meaningful to VoiceOver users, use `accessibilityValue(_:)` to create a more useful value. For example, `Slider` values often need context to convey any meaning to your users.
- **Hint**: This attribute is optional. If the user doesn't do anything after VoiceOver reads a label, VoiceOver reads the hint. Use `accessibilityHint(_:)` to describe what happens if the user interacts with the element.

The accessible UI doesn't change anything in your app's visible UI, so you can add more information, in a different order, than what your other users *see*.

> **Note**: There is one more accessibility attribute: `identifier`. This is only used in UITests. You would set an identifier for an element that doesn't have an accessibility label, or if an element's accessibility label is too long or ambiguous.

SwiftUI: Accessibility by Default

Open your **Kuchi** app or open the project in the starter folder, then open **Shared/Welcome/RegisterView** and locate the "Remember me" `Toggle`:

```
Toggle(isOn: $userManager.settings.rememberUser) {
  Text("Remember me")
    .font(.subheadline)
    .foregroundColor(.gray)
}
```

There's no explicit accessibility code here, just the type of element — **Toggle** — and its `Text` label. Yet, VoiceOver reads this as *Remember me, switch button, off, double-tap to toggle setting* because SwiftUI generates an **accessibility element**.

Xcode has an **Accessibility inspector**, to the left of the **Attributes inspector**. Under the right conditions, it shows you an element's accessibility settings, including what VoiceOver will say.

The conditions are:

- A preview of the view appears in the canvas.
- The canvas is in **Selectable** mode.
- The element is a standard SwiftUI view.
- You're holding your breath and have crossed all your fingers and toes ;]. Sometimes, it helps to click another inspector then re-select the Accessibility inspector.

To try this out in **RegisterView**, refresh the preview and switch to **Selectable** mode. Select the toggle (not just its label) in the preview or click `Toggle` in the code editor, then show the **Accessibility inspector**:

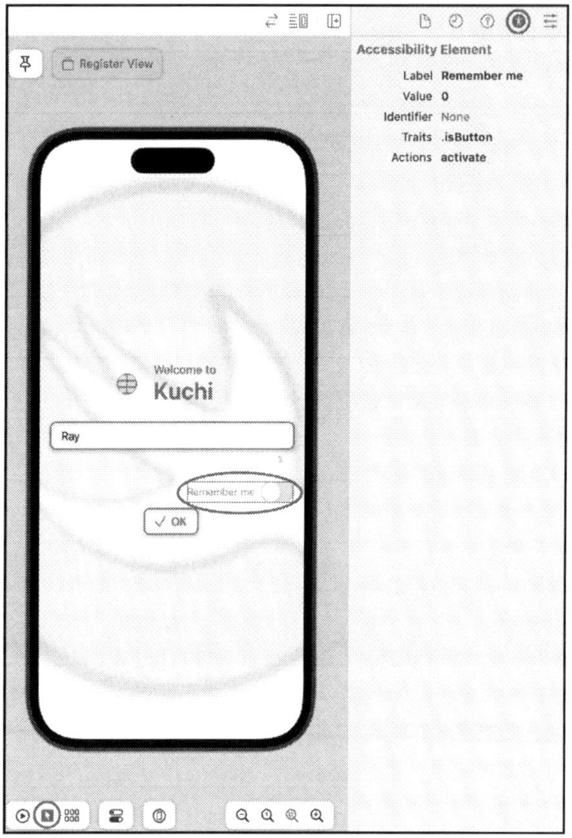

Toggle: Accessibility inspector

- **Label** defaults to the element's label **Remember me**.
- **Value** defaults to match the element's value: **0**, because the initial value of `Remember me` is `false`.
- **Traits** default to **.isButton** because this element is a `Toggle`.
- **Actions** default to **activate** — again, because this is a `Toggle`.

So VoiceOver reads out the label, the trait (with more detail than "button"), the value and activation instructions. You'll soon see how this information changes instantly when you make changes to the element.

You can close Kuchi for now. You'll be working with RGBullsEye for a while.

RGBullsEye

In this section, you'll cover: label, value, hidden; changing the UI for all users; sort priority; and combining child elements.

Reducing Jargon

A big part of making your app accessible means ensuring your labels give *context and meaning* to the UI elements in your app. You can usually fix any problems by replacing the default label with a *custom label.*

Open your **RGBullsEye** project or open the project in the starter folder. If necessary, customize it to run on your device: In the project window, select the **iOS target**. Then, in the **Signing & Capabilities** tab, select a team and customize the bundle ID. If necessary, adjust the project's **iOS Deployment Target** and the target's **Minimum Deployment**.

> **Note**: If you want to continue using your own RGBullsEye, copy these files from the starter project: **SuccessView.swift**, **ColorExtension.swift** (replace the one in your project), and **grayText.colorset** and **wand.imageset** from **Assets.xcassets**.

Now, connect your iOS device to your Mac, select it as the run destination, then build and run.

Start **VoiceOver**, then swipe up with two fingers to hear something like this:

R 3 question marks G 3 question marks B 3 question marks

R 127 grams 127 B 127 ...

And quite a lot more that sounds pretty meaningless. Your first task is obvious.

The color value `Text` views need accessibility labels.

In **ContentView**, add a meaningful accessibility label to the target `Text` view:

```
// BevelText(text: "R ??? G ??? B ???", ...)
.accessibilityLabel("Target red, green, blue, values you must
guess")
```

> **Note**: I've included commented-out lines in code blocks to show you **exactly** where you need to add code. You can copy and paste the whole code block into your code without breaking anything. **Don't** comment out the corresponding lines in your project.

You translate "???" to something that makes sense. The comma after "blue" isn't grammatically correct, but it makes VoiceOver pause before saying "values".

In the **Accessibility inspector**, your change appears immediately:

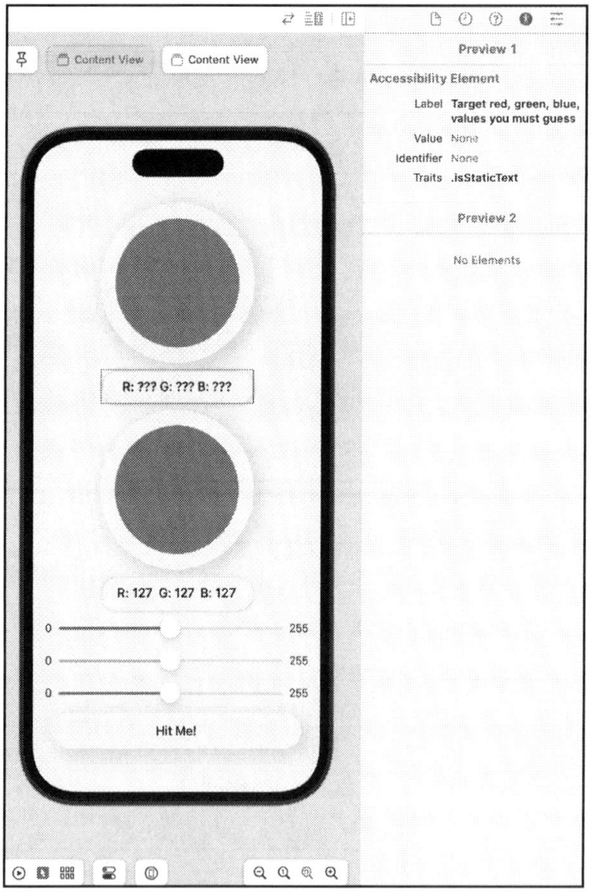

Target label changes immediately.

> **Note**: Xcode might have difficulty showing your phone in preview — switch your run destination back to what you had before.

For the guess color, you'll need a few computed variables to enable VoiceOver to say "Red", "Green" and "Blue" instead of "R", "G" (or "grams") and "B".

Now, in **Model/RGB**, replace `intString()` with the following code:

```
var rInt: Int {
  Int(red * 255.0)
}
var gInt: Int {
  Int(green * 255.0)
}
var bInt: Int {
  Int(blue * 255.0)
}

/// A String representing the integer values of an RGB instance.
func intString() -> String {
  "R \(rInt) G \(gInt) B \(bInt)"
}

func accString() -> String {
  "Red \(rInt), Green \(gInt), Blue \(bInt)."
}
```

You create computed variables for the red, green and blue integer values, then use these in the strings you display on screen (`intString()`) and read out in the accessibility label (`accString()`).

Now go back to **ContentView** and add this label to the guess `Text` view:

```
//BevelText(text: guess.intString(), ...)
.accessibilityLabel("Your guess: " + guess.accString())
```

Again, the **Accessibility inspector** shows your new label immediately:

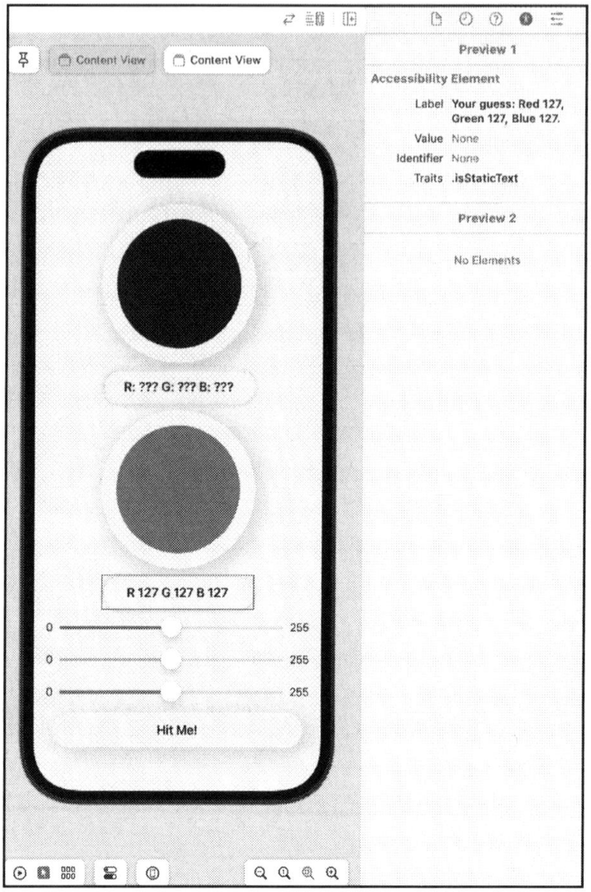

Guess label changes immediately.

Build and run on your device to hear VoiceOver say exactly what you told it to say.

Next, listen to VoiceOver read out a slider. You must swipe right twice to hear all three components:

0. 50 per cent, adjustable, swipe up or down with one finger to adjust the value. 255

> **Note**: The swipe up/down slider increments are too large to get a high score. To control the slider more accurately, tap a slider to select it, then double-tap and hold the slider thumb until you hear three rising tones. Now you can drag the slider in the usual way.

The issues here are:

1. Users don't need to hear "0" and "255".
2. The slider value is between 0 and 1, but the interface displays values between 0 and 255.

To solve these issues:

1. Don't read out "0" and "255".
2. Translate the slider value into an integer.

In **ContentView**, scroll down to `struct ColorSlider` and replace the contents of the `HStack` with the following code:

```
Text("0")
  .accessibilityHidden(true)
Slider(value: $value)
  .accentColor(trackColor)
  .accessibilityValue(
      String(describing: trackColor) + " " +
      String(Int(value * 255)))
Text("255")
  .accessibilityHidden(true)
```

You hide the "0" and "255" `Text` views from VoiceOver and tell VoiceOver to read the slider color and integer slider value.

> **Note**: `Color` conforms to the `CustomStringConvertible` protocol, so `String(describing: trackColor)` is "red", "green" or "blue".

In ContentView, select the red slider to see “0” and “255” are hidden, and the slider’s value is “red 127”:

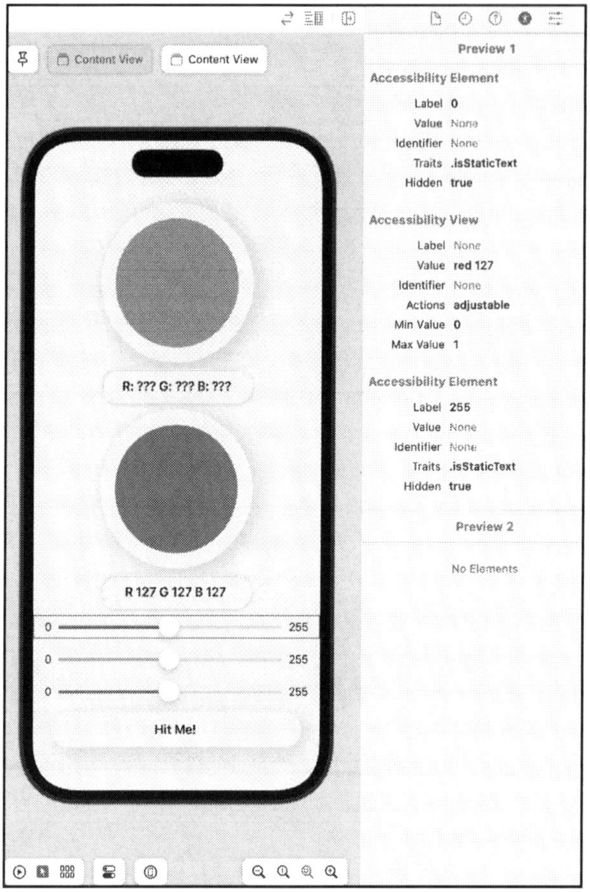

Improved Slider description

Build and run to hear your improved Slider descriptions.

Now that each element makes more sense, you’ll organize them so VoiceOver reads out the more useful ones first.

Reordering Navigation

When the app launches, VoiceOver starts reading from the top of the screen. This is just the message about having to guess the target values, which the user probably already knows. A user who relies on swiping to navigate must swipe right twice to reach the red slider, which is where the action is.

For someone playing this game, a more useful navigation order is to *start* with the sliders, then move to the guess string, and then to the button.

Here's how you do this. In **ContentView**, replace the guess `BevelText`, sliders and button with the following:

```
BevelText(
  text: guess.intString(),
  width: proxy.size.width * labelWidth,
  height: proxy.size.height * labelHeight)
  .accessibilityLabel("Your guess: " + guess.accString())
  .accessibilitySortPriority(2)  // add this line
  ColorSlider(value: $guess.red, trackColor: .red)
    .accessibilitySortPriority(5)  // add this line
  ColorSlider(value: $guess.green, trackColor: .green)
    .accessibilitySortPriority(4)  // add this line
  ColorSlider(value: $guess.blue, trackColor: .blue)
    .accessibilitySortPriority(3)  // add this line
Button("Hit Me!") {
  self.showScore = true
  self.game.check(guess: guess)
}
.accessibilitySortPriority(1)  // add this line
```

You change the sort priority of these five elements. VoiceOver starts reading from the element with the highest sort value (5). The color `Text` views have the default sort priority 0.

This sort order lets the user immediately start moving the sliders. Then they listen to the full RGB values of their guess. And then they activate **Hit Me!**.

Build and run on your device. VoiceOver reads "Red 127". Swiping right moves to "Green 127" then "Blue 127" then "Your guess: ..." then "Hit me, button".

Now, what happens after the user activates **Hit me**?

Organizing Information

Activate the **Hit Me!** button to show the alert. Swipe right twice to hear all three parts:

Alert, Your Score. 92. OK, Button.

There are two problems:

1. You must swipe right to hear your score, which is the most important information, then again to select the OK button.
2. The target `Text` view now shows the target's color values, but there's no way to get VoiceOver to read them.

It would be nice if you could combine the three parts of the alert into a single accessibility label, then add the target color values as an accessibility value or hint. Unfortunately, you can't use accessibility modifiers with the SwiftUI `Alert` view.

> **Note**: `UIAlertController` can set its `view.accessibilityLabel` and `view.accessibilityValue`, so one solution would be to use this instead of `Alert`. You'll learn about integrating UIKit in "Complex Interfaces".

Here's a situation where you can change the UI to benefit *all* your users.

Modify the Alert for All Users

In **ContentView**, in the body of `ContentView`, replace the first two arguments of `Alert` with these:

```
title: Text("You scored \(game.scoreRound)"),
message: Text("Target values: " + game.target.accString()),
```

You include the score in `title` and present the target color values in `message`. You must use the accessible string so VoiceOver can read "Red", "Green" and "Blue" instead of "R", "G" and "B".

OK, here's a confession: The Figma design for RGBullsEye actually has a full-screen `SuccessView` modal sheet instead of the `Alert`. I didn't implement it, back in "Diving Deeper into SwiftUI", because it would have covered the guess and target color values, and the design didn't include this information in the modal. But now that you're including the target color values in the alert, you might as well do the same in `SuccessView`. And you can also show the user's guess color values.

SuccessView is already in the starter project. It displays the target and guess color values on the backgrounds of those colors.

> **Note**: Thanks to the nifty computed variable `accessibleFontColor` from an older version of Apple's Scrumdinger app (https://apple.co/3mXdqeL), the text colors are black or white, depending on the background colors. You'll find this code in **Model/ColorExtension**.

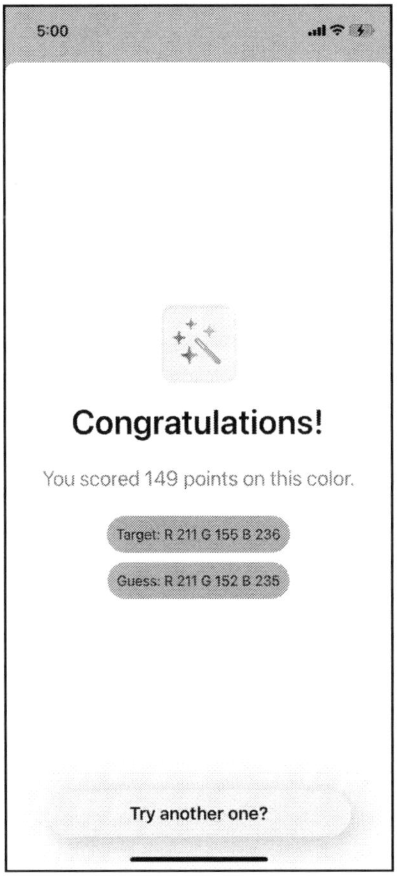

Success view modal sheet

So your next task is to replace the `alert` with `SuccessView`.

Refactor to Use SuccessView Modal Sheet

In **ContentView**, replace `.alert(...) { ... }` with the following:

```
.sheet(isPresented: $showScore) {
  SuccessView(
    game: $game,
    score: game.scoreRound,
    target: game.target,
    guess: $guess)
}
```

Build and run on your device, then activate the **Hit Me!** button. Swipe right enough times to hear VoiceOver read something like this:

wand, Image. Congratulations! You scored 77 points on this color. Target: R 157 G 219 B 163. Guess: R 127 G127 B127. Try another one, Button.

The advantage of using a modal sheet instead of an `Alert` is you can now *combine* the `Text` views into a single readout. You can also attach accessibility modifiers to each component.

To make VoiceOver read the text elements as a single unit, the easiest solution is to *combine* them into a single accessibility element.

In **SuccessView**, refresh the preview, switch to **Selectable** mode, show the **Accessibility inspector**, then select the first `VStack`:

SuccessView elements

Now, add this modifier to the first `VStack` in **SuccessView**:

```
.accessibilityElement(children: .combine)
```

All of the text elements are useful, so you just combine them to make VoiceOver read them without stopping after each one.

See what's happened in the **Accessibility inspector**:

Improved SuccessView description

Magical!

Exercise: In **SuccessView**, fix the remaining accessibility issues.

First, hide the "wand" image from VoiceOver. Do this *after* the `resizable()` modifier because `resizable()` is an `Image` modifier and `accessibilityHidden(_:)` doesn't return an `Image`.

Next, tell VoiceOver to read out the accessible strings for the target and guess colors.

The solution is in the **challenge** folder.

Note: Using Xcode 14, combining the `VStack` elements already omits the `Image` from VoiceOver. This might be a bug, so it's safer to explicitly hide any elements you don't want VoiceOver to read out.

Keep RGBullsEye open in Xcode. There are still a couple of things for you to see.

Adapting to User Settings

Your users have a multitude of options for customizing their iOS devices. Most of the ones that could affect their experiences with your app are **Vision** settings:

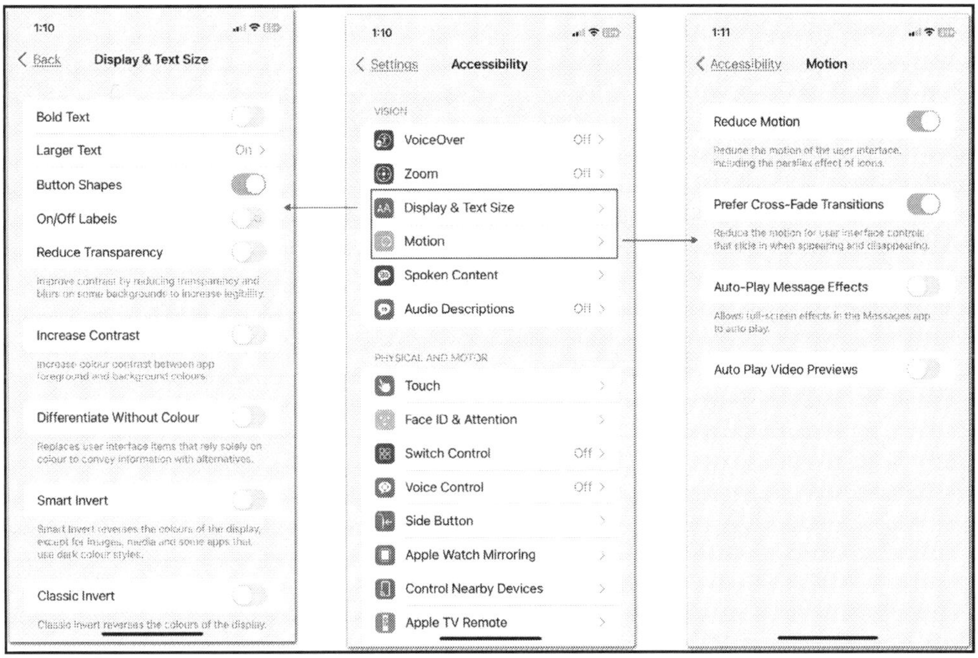

Vision accessibility settings

For some of these options, your app can check if it's enabled, then adapt itself. But for some options, there isn't (yet?) an `@Environment` or `UIAccessibility` variable, so you might have to tweak your design to work for *all* your users.

Trying Out Device Settings in Xcode

To see how these accessibility settings affect your app, you *could* turn them on or off, in different combinations, directly in your device's **Settings**. Oh, joy. Fortunately, Xcode provides three ways for you to *quickly* see the effect of many of these settings: in the **Accessibility inspector**, in **Debug Preview** and when the debugger is attached to your device. It's much quicker and easier than going through the **Settings** app on your device, so you're more likely to check, and therefore more likely to fix any problems sooner.

Build and run on your device. When it's running, open **Environment Overrides** in the debug toolbar:

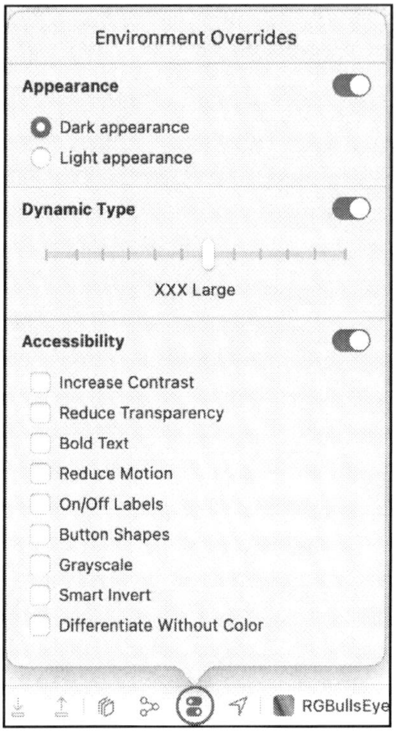

Debug toolbar: Environment Overrides

You can use this tool to check Dark/Light Appearance, Dynamic Type text size, Increase Contrast, Bold Text, On/Off Labels and Button Shapes. You must change the actual settings on your device to check Reduce Motion and Grayscale. The Smart Invert environment override inverts most colors, but it's safer to use the actual setting on your device, just to be sure.

Dark screens are really popular and play an important role in eye health as well as with accessibility, so you definitely must ensure your apps look good in **Dark Appearance**. You've already seen in "Diving Deeper Into SwiftUI" how to automatically adapt to dark appearance by setting a **Dark Appearance** for your custom colors. You can also set light appearance and high-contrast versions. `UIColor` has system colors like `systemBlue`, but also *semantic* colors like `label`, `systemFill`, `systemBackground` and `placeholderText` that automatically adapt to Dark Appearance.

You can also check Dark/Light Appearance and Dynamic Type text size with the preview canvas **Device Settings** or **Variants**.

In "Intro to Controls: Text & Image", you switched from using a specific font size like `font(.system(size: 30))` to using standard text styles like `font(.headline)` and `font(.largeTitle)`. These respond to a user's accessibility setting for **Display & Text Size ▸ Larger Text**, so your app automatically supports **Dynamic Type**.

Apple's Typography documentation (https://apple.co/37SCpvt) shows size and weight for standard text styles at different Dynamic Type sizes, and the preview **Variants** option makes it easy to check:

Use preview Variants mode to check your app supports dynamic type.

The largest two sizes need some tweaking.

Now close RGBullsEye.

Checking Environment Variables

What can you do in your app to adapt to larger text sizes? New in iOS 16 is `AnyLayout`, which makes it easy to switch between layout containers — from `HStack` to `VStack` — depending on the **Dynamic Type** setting:

```
struct ContentView: View {
  @Environment(\.dynamicTypeSize) var dynamicTypeSize

  var body: some View {
    let layout = dynamicTypeSize <= .medium ?
      AnyLayout(HStackLayout()) : AnyLayout(VStackLayout())

    layout {
      Text("First label")
      Text("Second label")
    }
  }
}
```

The environment value `dynamicTypeSize` is the font size users can set in their device's **Settings ▸ Accessibility ▸ Display & Text Size ▸ Larger Text**. Some other environment values are:

- **Invert colors** `accessibilityInvertColors`: The **Smart Invert** accessibility option reverses colors of the display and *shouldn't* invert colors of images, media and some apps that use dark color styles. But it's currently behaving more like **Classic Invert**, which reverses *all* colors. For elements you don't want inverted, use `accessibilityIgnoresInvertColors(true)`.

- **Increase contrast** `colorSchemeContrast`: This accessibility option alters color and text styling, and adjusts dynamic type to the user's preferred text size. In RGBullsEye, it darkens the slider track colors. If your app detects this option is enabled, it should ensure color contrast ratios are 7:1 or higher. Or consider designing your UI so color contrast ratios are 7:1 or higher for **all** users. You can check the contrast ratio of specific foreground and background colors at contrastchecker.com.

- **Reduce transparency** `accessibilityReduceTransparency`: This accessibility option reduces the transparency and blurs on some backgrounds. If your app detects this option is enabled, it should ensure all alpha values are set to 1.0.

- **Reduce motion** `accessibilityReduceMotion`: This accessibility option slows down, reduces or removes some animations, like the spinning **Activity** app awards. Check it on your device with **Settings ▸ Accessibility ▸ Motion**. Your app should run animations only if this option isn't enabled:

```
@Environment(\.accessibilityReduceMotion) var reduceMotion
...
  if animated && !reduceMotion { /* animate at will! */ }
```

You'll get to use this soon!

- **Bold Text** `legibilityWeight`: This accessibility option displays all text in boldface characters, so large font text uses even more space.

- **On/Off Labels** `UIAccessibility.isOnOffSwitchLabelsEnabled`: This accessibility option shows **1 or 0** in a toggle that is **on or off**. If this messes up your custom toggle, consider redesigning it. Or replace it with a standard toggle if this option is enabled.

- **Button Shapes** `UIAccessibility.buttonShapesEnabled`: This accessibility option re-creates the outline around tappable elements from earlier iOS versions, before label-only buttons became the default. If this messes up your custom button, consider redesigning it for all users.

- **Grayscale** `UIAccessibility.isGrayscaleEnabled`: This accessibility option turns on a color filter that shows only the relative luminance of colors. Check it on your device with **Settings ▸ Accessibility ▸ Display & Text Size ▸ Color Filters ▸ Grayscale**. Consider using higher contrast colors for elements so they're still distinct in grayscale. You can check how specific foreground and background colors look in grayscale at contrastchecker.com.

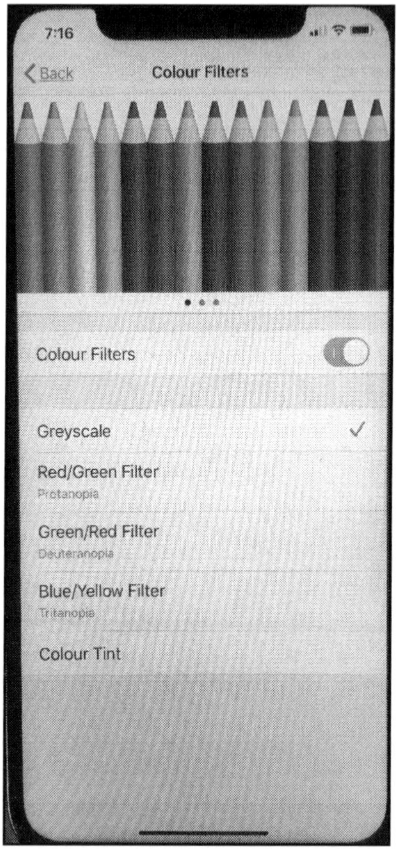

Display & Text Size▸Color Filters▸Grayscale

> **Note**: Color filters don't show up in screenshots. I had to use another phone's camera to take this photo of my phone.

- **Differentiate Without Color** `accessibilityDifferentiateWithoutColor`: This accessibility option replaces UI items that rely on color to convey information with alternatives. You should always try to use shapes or additional text in addition to color.

There is also `accessibilityEnabled`: This is `true` if VoiceOver, Voice Control or Switch Control is enabled. Check `UIAccessibility.isVoiceOverRunning` or `UIAccessibility.isSwitchControlRunning`. There's no way to check for Voice Control, unless the user has **not** enabled VoiceOver or Switch Control:

```
accessibilityEnabled == true
  && !UIAccessibility.isVoiceOverRunning
  && !UIAccessibility.isSwitchControlRunning
```

> **Note**: This seems to be a reasonable test for VoiceControl, as VoiceOver and VoiceControl don't work well together, and Switch Control users like Ian Mackay in this Tecla article (https://bit.ly/3mcc42s) might prefer to use Voice Control in quiet environments.

There are many other `UIAccessibility` properties in Apple's documentation (https://apple.co/3Kok5fB), listed under **Capabilities**. Check these values whenever you need them, to ensure you're getting their current status.

You'll see a few of these in action in the next two apps.

Kuchi

In this section, you'll cover keyboard input and fixing dark appearance.

Open the starter **Kuchi** project and customize the bundle ID and team. Then connect your iOS device to your Mac and select the **Kuchi (iOS)** run target and your device. If necessary, adjust the **iOS Deployment target** in the target window, then build and run.

RegisterView

The first time Kuchi launches, it displays `RegisterView`.

Register view

Start VoiceOver, then swipe up with two fingers to hear something like this:

Welcome to, Kuchi. Type your name, ellipsis, Text field. 0. Remember me, Switch button, off. Selected, OK, dimmed; Button. welcome-background, Logo Other, Outdoor (or Night Sky), Screenshot, Tachometer.

Hiding Unnecessary Elements

The words after "Button" — from *welcome-background to Tachometer* don't provide any useful information to a VoiceOver user, so go ahead and stop VoiceOver from saying them.

In **Shared/Welcome/Components/WelcomeBackgroundImage**, *hide* the `Image` from VoiceOver:

```
//Image("welcome-background")
//  .resizable()
  .accessibilityHidden(true)
```

> **Reminder**: I include commented-out lines in code blocks to show you **exactly** where you need to add code. You can copy and paste the whole code block into your code without breaking anything. **Don't** comment out the corresponding lines in your project.

You add `accessibilityHidden(_:)` *after* `resizable()` because `resizable()` is an `Image` modifier, and `accessibilityHidden(_:)` doesn't return an `Image`.

Another unnecessary element is in the **Welcome to Kuchi** label: Sometimes VoiceOver reads the icon as "Logo other".

Welcome to Kuchi label

So go to **LogoImage** to hide this image:

```
//Image(systemName: "table")
//  .resizable()
  .accessibilityHidden(true)
```

What's next? In **Shared/Welcome/RegisterView**, in the text field's placeholder text, VoiceOver reads "..." as "ellipsis".

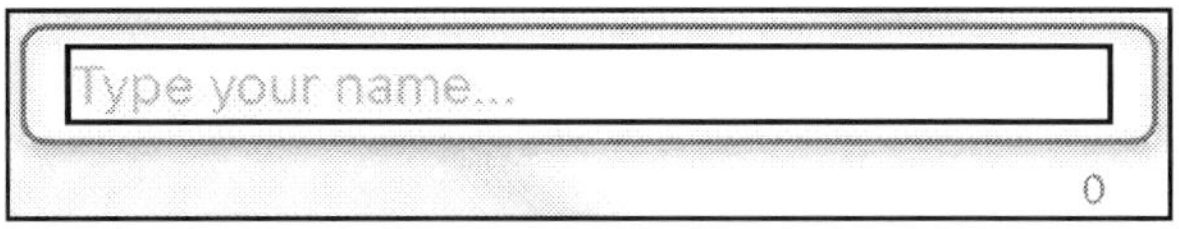

Text field and character counter

This provides no useful information to anyone, so just delete it *for all users*.

```
TextField("Type your name", text: $userManager.profile.name)
```

Adding Descriptions

Next, you'll add some descriptions.

VoiceOver reads out the number "0", with no context. This `Text` view keeps count of the number of characters the user types in the `TextField`. The **OK** button is disabled while this number is less than 3. This isn't obvious to non-VoiceOver users, but they can see, while they're typing, when the **OK** button becomes enabled.

If a VoiceOver user can't get past your registration page, you've lost a user! Help them out...

In the first `HStack`, add these accessibility modifiers to the `Text` view:

```
//Text("\(userManager.profile.name.count)")
  .accessibilityLabel("name has \
(userManager.profile.name.count) letters")
  .accessibilityHint("name needs 3 or more letters to enable OK
button")
```

You provide a more descriptive label for VoiceOver to read. If the user doesn't immediately move on to another interface element, VoiceOver reads the hint.

The accessibility of the **Remember me** toggle is fine.

Remember-me toggle and OK button

By default, VoiceOver reads its on/off state and tells the user what to do with it. Its label is a standard login option, so doesn't need more explanation.

But the **OK** button needs work. VoiceOver should tell users what happens when they tap it. Tapping a button is a command for the app to act, and its accessibility label should tell the user what this command is. In this case, tapping **OK** "registers user". So add an accessibility label to the **OK** `Button`:

```
//Button(action: registerUser) {
//...
//}
.accessibilityLabel("OK registers user")
//.bordered()
```

Adding an accessibility label means VoiceOver won't read the `Text` string, so you include "OK" in the accessibility label.

Just in case the user skipped listening to the character counter hint, also add it to the **OK** `Button`:

```
.accessibilityHint("name needs 3 or more letters to enable this
button")
```

Finally, VoiceOver says the **OK** button is "dimmed", but "disabled" would be more informative.

➤ Add an accessibility *value* to the **OK** `Button`:

```
.accessibilityValue(
  userManager.isUserNameValid() ? "enabled" : "disabled")
```

You've added a total of three accessibility modifiers to the **OK** `Button`.

Build and run the app on your device, then swipe up with two fingers to listen to VoiceOver read something like this:

Welcome to Kuchi. Type your name, Text field. Name has 0 letters. Remember me, Switch button, off. Selected. OK registers user, disabled, dimmed; Button. Name needs 3 or more letters to enable OK button.

That's better, although VoiceOver might not read the hint unless you do nothing for quite a while. What's next?

Tap the text field. VoiceOver says something like this:

Type your name, Text field. Double-tap to edit

That's clear enough. Go ahead and double-tap, ~~to~~ hear this:

Text field, is editing. Type your name, Character mode, insertion point at start. Use the rotor to access misspelled words

The keyboard appears:

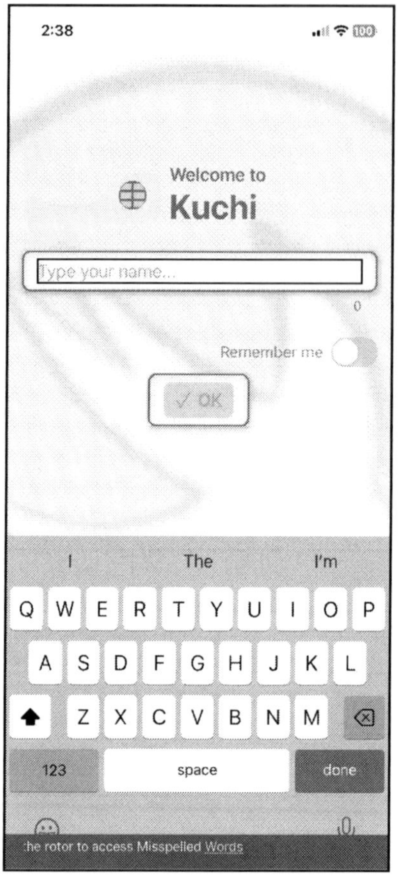

Keyboard for text field input

To type your name, activate each key to enter it in the text field.

When you tap a key, VoiceOver reads it and, if you pause, uses the NATO phonetic alphabet (Alpha, Bravo, Charlie, Delta, Echo, etc.) to made sure you know which letter you tapped. When you activate a key, VoiceOver repeats it.

> **Note**: Blind users would use Braille Screen Input.

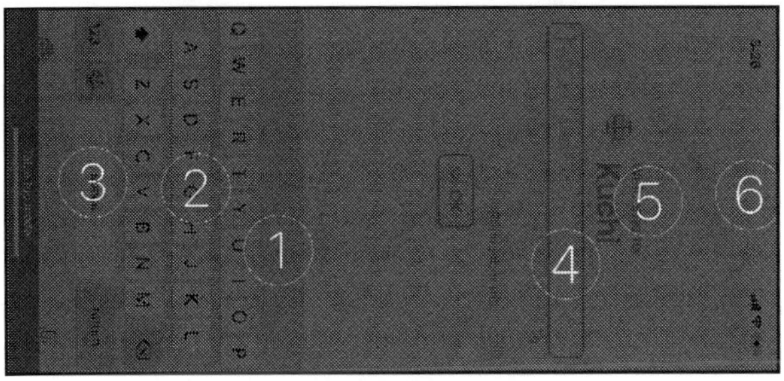

Braille Screen Input

Activate the keyboard's **done** key to dismiss it, then tap **OK** to hear VoiceOver say:

OK registers user, enabled, Button, name needs 3 or more letters to enable this button.

Fixing Dark Appearance

If your phone is set to dark appearance, you've noticed a big problem: The name field is white, and you can't see what you're typing. There's actually an easy fix.

`TextField` has a modifier `.bordered()`. Jump to its definition in **BorderedViewModifier**. `BorderedViewModifier` specifies the background color:

```
.background(Color.white)
```

Change this to the semantic color `.background`:

```
.background(.background)
```

Go back to **RegisterView** and use the canvas **Device Settings** to see how it now looks in **Dark Appearance**:

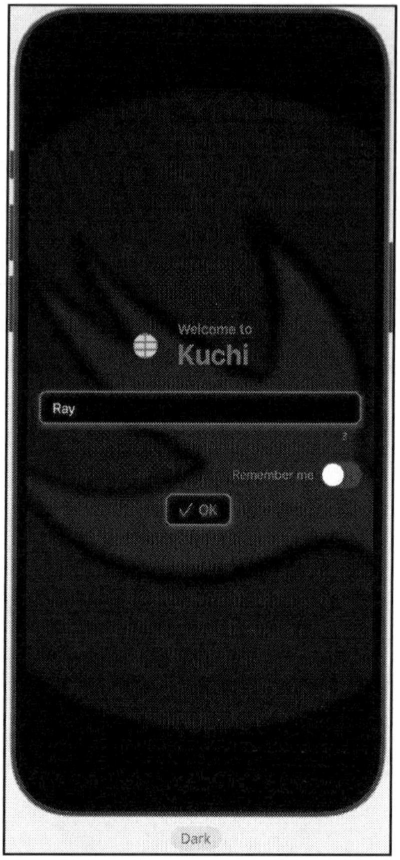

Dark appearance fixed

> **Note**: Sometimes, you have to run the app in a simulator or on your device, then use **Environment Overrides** to see the real dark appearance.

Fun Fact

If you continue on to the Japanese phrases, you'll get a delightful surprise: The **Settings/Accessibility/VoiceOver/Speech/Detect Languages** option means VoiceOver reads out the text in Japanese. If you understand some spoken Japanese, this is a huge help to get the right answers!

Close Kuchi.

MountainAirport

In this section, you'll cover: Motion, cross-fade; hidden; and increase button's tappable area and visibility.

The third starter project is a peek into the future. MountainAirport is the sample app for the next two sections of this book, where you'll learn to draw and animate custom graphics in SwiftUI.

Open, build and run **MountainAirport** on your device with VoiceOver on. Swipe up with two fingers to hear:

Mountain Airport, Heading. Aeroplane Mode, Image. Flight Status. Departure and arrival information, link-pattern, image. Aeroplane, Gift Card, Logo Other. Search, Image. Search. Search Flights. Search Upcoming Flights, link-pattern, image. Logo Other, Underwater. Your Awards, Favorite, Image, Star. Earn rewards for your airport interactions, link-pattern, image. Logo Other, Sign.

Not Animating

Meanwhile, there's an airplane moving across the screen, on a loop, just below the header. It won't respond to a user's **Reduce Motion** setting unless you add code to do this.

In **WelcomeView**, add this environment variable to `WelcomeView`:

```
@Environment(\.accessibilityReduceMotion) var reduceMotion
```

Now, scroll down to body and replace `WelcomeAnimation()` and its modifiers with this conditional:

```
if !reduceMotion {
  WelcomeAnimation()
    .frame(height: 40)
    .padding()
} else {
  Image(systemName: "airplane")
    .resizable()
    .accessibilityHidden(true)
    .aspectRatio(1.0, contentMode: .fit)
    .frame(height: 40)
    .padding()
}
```

If the user's device has **Reduce Motion** turned on, you show a still image of the airplane symbol — using the same modifiers as in `WelcomeAnimation` — but hide its label from VoiceOver.

On your device, go to **Settings ▸ Accessibility ▸ Motion** and turn on **Reduce Motion**:

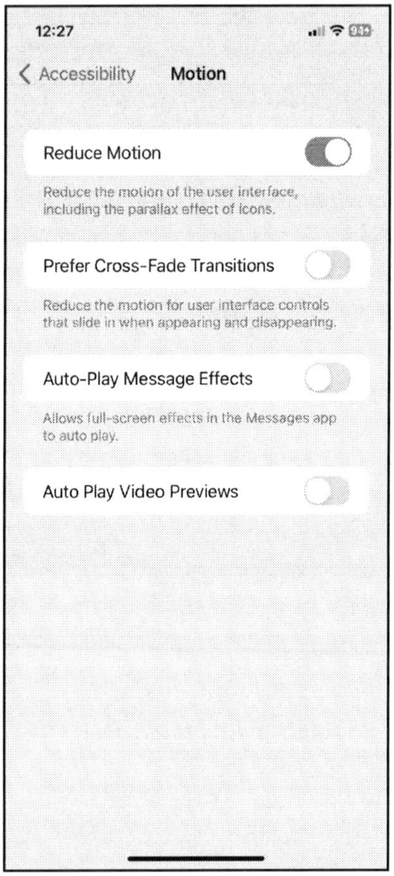

Reduce Motion options

Now, build and run on your device to see an unanimated airplane:

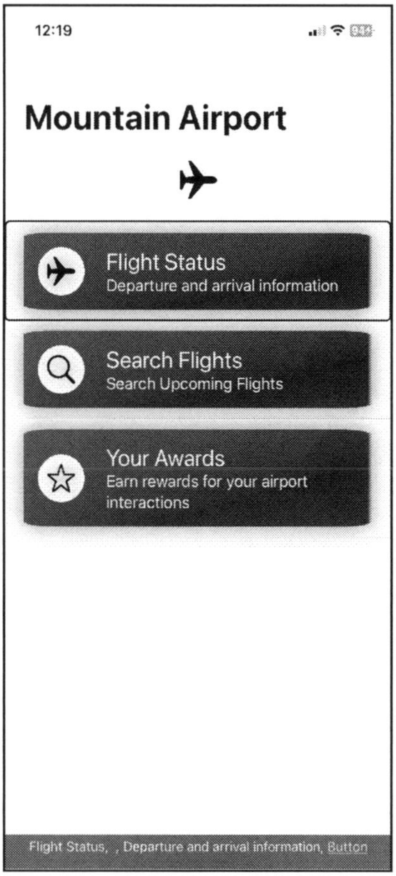

Unanimated airplane

That was easy! Now to streamline what VoiceOver says...

Hiding & Combining Labels

By now, you know you should hide the background image — "link-pattern, image" — from VoiceOver.

In **WelcomeButtonView**, add this accessibility modifier to the `Image`:

```
// .background(
  // Image("link-pattern")
    // .resizable()
    .accessibilityHidden(true)
```

Remember to put it *after* `resizable()`.

Also hide the label images by adding the same accessibility modifier to the first item in the `HStack`:

```
// Image(systemName: imageName)
  // .resizable()
  .accessibilityHidden(true)
```

Further improve your VoiceOver experience by adding these modifiers to the `title` and `subTitle` stack:

```
// VStack(alignment: .leading) {
  // Text(title)
    // .font(.title2)
  // Text(subTitle)
    // .font(.subheadline)
// }
.accessibilityElement(children: .combine)
.accessibilityAddTraits(.isButton)
```

You combine the `title` and `subTitle` texts into a single label and ensure the user knows this is a button.

Build and run on your device again. You can navigate the three buttons much faster now, and it's crystal clear that they're buttons.

Next, activate **Flight Status**.

Flight Status: A Tweak for All Users

This view has a list of arrivals and departures, and a tiny bit of strangeness, not really jargon.

To start, tap a flight to listen to VoiceOver.

VoiceOver reads out all three lines at once, and it doesn't read out the icons. Great! Just two small issues: It reads out the relative time interval as something like "open bracket, 3 hours ago, right paren", and also reads out the "middle dot" punctuation between the airport and the gate number.

Fix both issues in **FlightStatusBoard/FlightRow**

In the `VStack`, change the first `HStack` to remove the parentheses:

```
HStack {
  Text(flight.flightStatus)
  Text(flight.localTime, formatter: timeFormatter)
  // Text("(") +
  Text(flight.localTime, formatter: relativeTimeFormatter)
  //+ Text(")")
}.foregroundColor(flight.statusColor)
```

> **Note**: I moved the + after `relativeTimeFormatter)` to the next line.

Fix the second issue in the last `HStack`: Replace the middle dot with a hyphen:

```
Text("-")
```

A hyphen is more commonly used than middle-dot, so VoiceOver doesn't read it out. It just treats it like a comma.

One more issue: There's a tab bar at the bottom. If you didn't know about it and just kept swiping right, VoiceOver wouldn't read it until you'd gone through every item in the list!

You might think sort priority will help you here, but there's nowhere to attach it.

About all you can do is provide a hint on the **Hide Past** `Toggle` in **FlightStatusBoard**, in `navigationBarItems`, down at the bottom of `body`:

```
//Toggle(...)
.accessibilityHint("Use the tab bar to list only arrivals or
departures.")
```

Build and run again and check how this sounds now. Much cleaner!

FlightDetails: Animations

MountainAirport is the sample app for the drawing and animation chapters so, of course, it has more animations than the airplane moving across the welcome view. Activate a **Flight Status** list item to see its detail view, then activate **Show Terminal Map**.

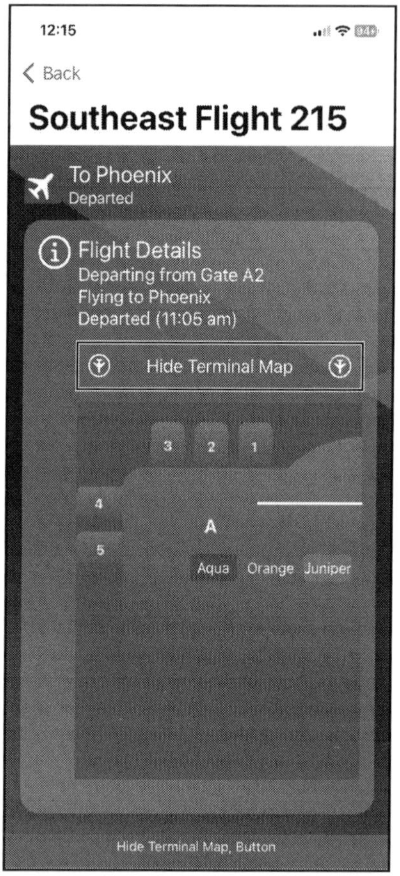

Terminal map animation

When you create this animation in "Animations", consider checking the environment value `accessibilityReduceMotion`. If the user's device has this setting, your app should replace the map animation with a drawing and stop the airplane icons from swinging around.

Now, return to the welcome view: Activate the **Back** button or do a Z gesture with two fingers.

FlightSearch: View Transitions

There's no accessibility setting to stop an app's animations, but users *can* control view transitions.

To see the view transitions in MountainAirport, go to **Settings ▸ Accessibility ▸ Motion** on your device and check that **Prefer Cross-Fade Transitions** is **off**.

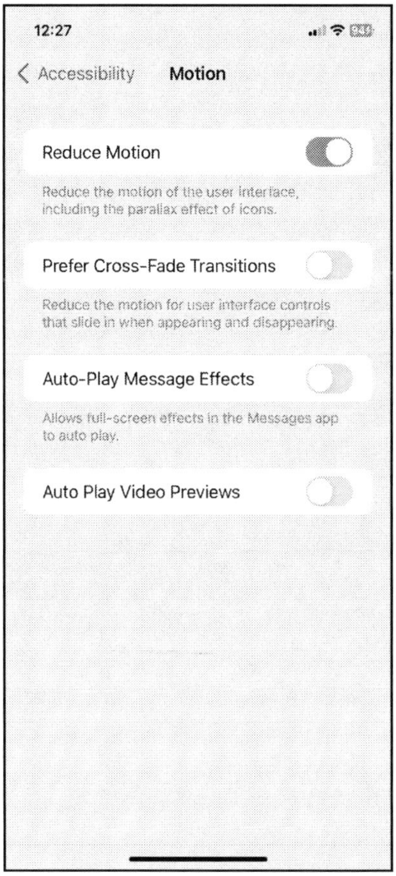

Prefer cross-fade transitions is off.

Build and run on your device, then activate the **Search Flights** button. Select the **Departures** filter, then navigate down the list to a **canceled** flight and activate it.

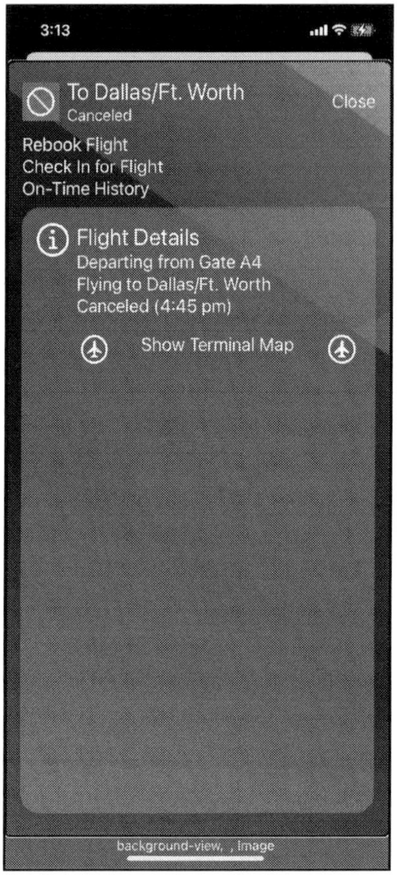

Flight Details of canceled flight

This view has several view transitions, starting with the detail view itself, which is a modal view.

Activate each button to see its transition:

- **Rebook Flight** displays an alert.
- **Check In for Flight** displays a small action sheet.
- **On-Time History** displays a popover.

Close the **On-Time History** popover with a two-finger Z gesture, then **Close** the detail view.

Now, open **Settings ▸ Accessibility ▸ Motion** and turn on **Reduce Motion** *and* **Prefer Cross-Fade Transitions**:

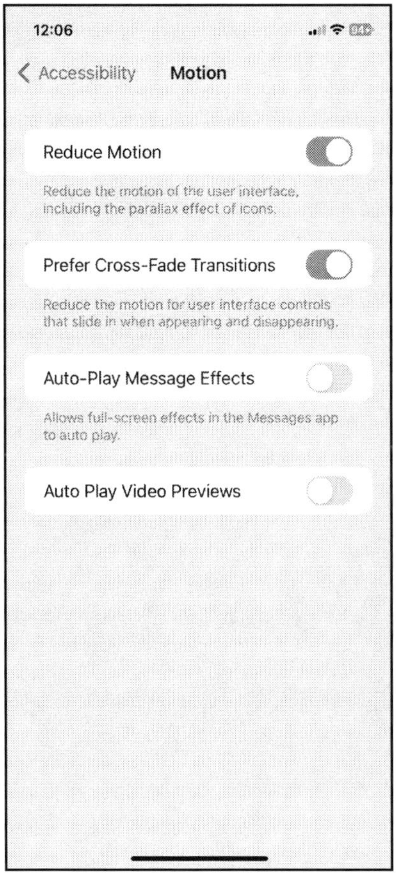

Prefer cross-fade transitions is on.

Return to **MountainAirport**. Select the canceled flight again and activate each button in turn.

The `FlightSearchDetails` modal sheet and **On-Time History** popover now *cross-fade* instead of sliding up. So you don't have to do anything special to your app, as long as you use standard SwiftUI elements.

The **Rebook Flight** alert and **Check in for Flight** action sheet transitions don't change, but hopefully don't disturb much, as they're much smaller views.

Making Buttons Larger

There's one last issue with this view: The buttons are too small.

Here are two options:

- Increase each button's frame height: In **SearchFlights/FlightSearchDetails**, modify each button with `.frame(height: 44.0)`.
- Rewrite each button so its label is a trailing closure, then add padding to the `Text` view.

Also, it's not obvious they're buttons, but that's an easy one. Just open **Settings ▸ Accessibility ▸ Display & Text Size** and turn on **Button Shapes**. Then return to **MountainAirport** and reopen the flight details view.

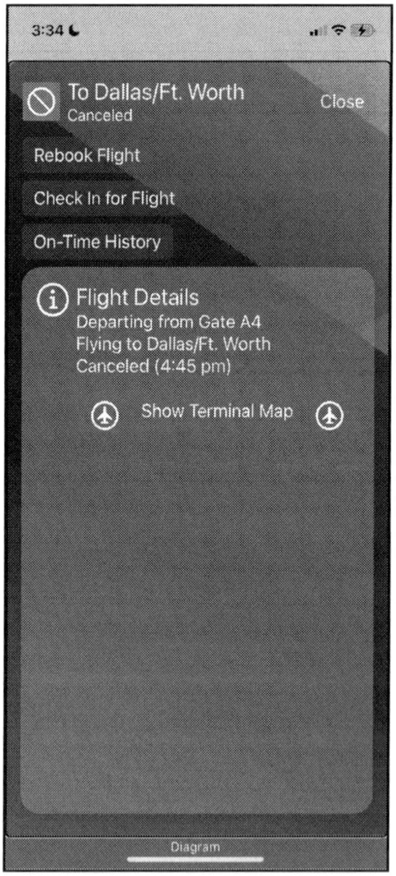

Button Shapes in action

This setting re-creates the outline around tappable elements from earlier iOS versions, before label-only buttons became the default. Although against this background, the outline is barely visible, at least the outlines push the buttons further apart.

That's enough fixing. Now for the final test.

Truly Testing Your App's Accessibility

Once again, return to the welcome view of **MountainAirport**.

To truly test whether a VoiceOver user can use your app, turn on the **screen curtain**: **Triple-tap** with three fingers.

> **Note**: If you have the zoom accessibility feature enabled, you'll need to **quadruple-tap** with three fingers.

This turns off the display while keeping the screen contents active. VoiceOver users can use this for privacy.

Now, navigate to the **Flight Status** list, turn on **Hide Past**, list only departures, then find the next (not canceled) departure that's more than one hour away.

> **Note**: Sometimes swipe-right/left doesn't work. Swipe up with two fingers to get VoiceOver to read continuously from the top.

Did you succeed? Good for you!

Lastly, **Triple-tap** with three fingers to show the display, then **triple-click** the side button to turn off VoiceOver.

Congratulations, you're well on your way to becoming an accessibility ninja!

Key Points

- Use VoiceOver on a device to hear how your app really sounds.
- Accessibility is built into SwiftUI. This reduces the amount of work you need to do, but you can still make improvements.
- Use semantic font sizes to support Dynamic Type. Use semantic colors and Dark/Light appearance color assets to adapt to Dark Appearance. Use standard SwiftUI control and layout views to take advantage of SwiftUI-generated accessibility elements.
- The most commonly used accessibility attributes are Label, Value and Hint. Use Hidden to hide UI elements from VoiceOver. Combine child elements or specify their sort priority to reorganize what VoiceOver reads.
- Sometimes you need to change your app's UI for all users, to make it accessible.
- Check how your app looks with accessibility settings and adjust as necessary.
- Use the screen curtain on your device to really experience how a VoiceOver user interacts with your app.

Where to Go From Here?

There are lots of resources to help you make your apps accessible. Here are just a few:

- Apple HIG for accessibility (https://apple.co/34ZS76a)
- WWDC 2022 Accessibility sessions (https://apple.co/3AHdRDd)
- WWDC 2021 Accessibility sessions (https://apple.co/3kK6zY6)
- WWDC 2020 Accessibility sessions (https://apple.co/3rQNQMa)
- WWDC 2019 Accessibility sessions (https://apple.co/2KFu5Xe)
- iOS Accessibility in SwiftUI Tutorials: This three-part tutorial includes accessibility inspector, color contrast ratio, headings for faster navigation and AVSpeechSynthesizer. Part 1 (https://bit.ly/418z3xH). [This is the Kodeco link.]

Section IV: Navigation & Data Display

Move through your app screens with SwiftUI and discover how to display data in them.

Chapter 13: Navigation

By Bill Morefield

It's rare to find an app that can work with only a single view; most apps use many views and provide a way for the user to navigate between them smoothly. The navigation you design has to balance many needs:

- You need to display data logically to the user.
- You need to provide a consistent way to move between views.
- You need to make it easy for the user to figure out how to perform a particular task.

SwiftUI provides a unified interface to manage navigation while also displaying data. SwiftUI 4.0 introduced significant changes to navigation for SwiftUI apps. In this chapter, you'll explore building a navigation structure for an app using these new views.

Getting Started

Open the starter project for this chapter; you'll find a very early version of a flight-data app for an airport. You'll build out the navigation for this app. You would likely get the flight information from an external API in a real-world app. For this app, you'll be using mock data.

To start, expand the **Models** folder in the app. Open **FlightData.swift**, and you'll find the implementation of the mock data for this app. The `FlightData` class generates a schedule for fifteen days of flights with thirty flights per day starting with today's date using the `generateSchedule()` method. The class uses a seeded random number generator to produce consistent flight data every time, with only the start date changing.

Now, open and examine **FlightInformation.swift**, which encapsulates information about flights. You'll use this mock data throughout the following chapters.

Open **WelcomeView.swift**. The view includes a `@StateObject` named `flightInfo` that holds this mock data for the app.

Creating Navigation Views

Build and run the starter app. There's a bare-bones implementation with a graphic and a single option to view the day's flight status board.

Initial app

Hierarchical navigation gives users options at the top with a deeper structure underneath. Before SwiftUI 4.0, you would use a `NavigationView` to build hierarchical navigation. The new types use a `NavigationStack` to produce single-column navigation and `NavigationSplitView` to produce multiple-column navigation. In this chapter, you'll create this view to use hierarchical navigation compatible with multiple platforms.

The `NavigationSplitView` supports a split-view interface on larger devices, separating the app's views into separate panes. One view generally remains static, while the second changes as the user navigates through the view stack. On smaller screens, like the iPhone, it falls back and works in a single column as a `NavigationStack`. Using a `NavigationSplitView` in a cross-platform app will make it easier for you to adapt to both small and large screens.

Open **WelcomeView.swift** and replace the view body with the following:

```
NavigationSplitView {
  Text("Sidebar")
} detail: {
  Text("Detail")
}
```

You use the `init(sidebar:detail:)` initializer of `NavigationSplitView` to create a view with two columns. You could create a third column using the `init(sidebar:content:detail:)` initializer, but two columns work better for this app. The view inside the view closure fills the entire screen for an iPhone.

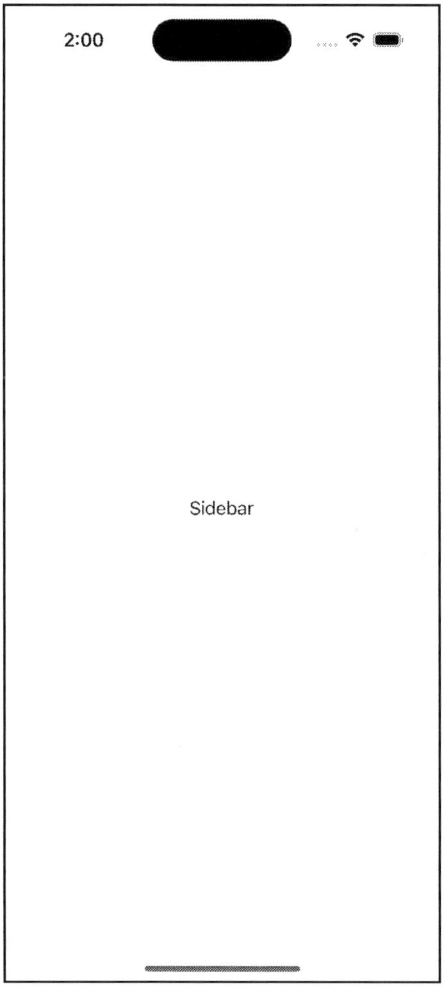

Split Navigation on an iPhone

You'll see both columns on a larger device like an iPad. The sidebar will be initially hidden and can be shown by tapping the **Show Sidebar** button or making a sliding gesture from the left side of the screen.

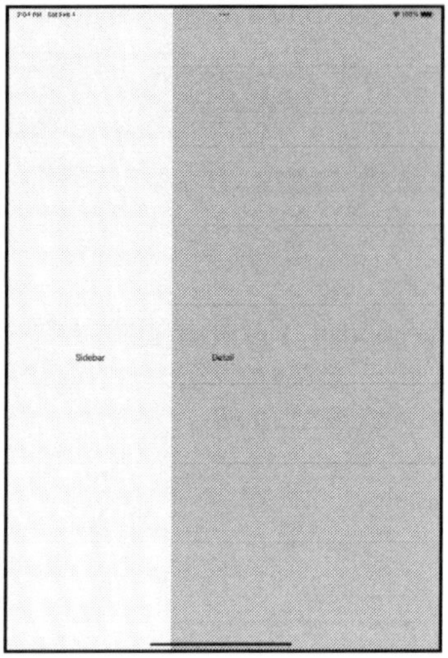

Split Navigation on an iPad

With this structure in place, you can fill in the two columns. First, create the sidebar view to drive the navigation. Above the `WelcomeView` implementation, add the following code:

```
enum FlightViewId: CaseIterable {
  case showFlightStatus
}

struct ViewButton: Identifiable {
  var id: FlightViewId
  var title: String
  var subtitle: String
}
```

This code defines a new `FlightViewId` enumerable, which implements the `CaseIterable` protocol. Initially, it will have only a single case, `showFlightStatus`. You then define the `ViewButton` struct. This struct contains three properties: an `id`, `title` and `subtitle`. You'll use these properties to define the buttons in the sidebar. The struct also implements the `Identifiable` protocol, which you learn more about in **Chapter 14: "Lists"**. For now, know that the `id` property fulfills the protocol.

Now, add the following code before the body of the view:

```
var sidebarButtons: [ViewButton] {
```

```
  var buttons: [ViewButton] = []

  buttons.append(
    ViewButton(
      id: .showFlightStatus,
      title: "Flight Status",
      subtitle: "Departure and arrival information"
    )
  )

  return buttons
}
```

This computed property will provide an array of `ViewButton` structs that define the options for the sidebar. You'll add more buttons in this and the following chapters as you expand the **Mountain Airport** app.

There's one more step before you build the sidebar. Add the following property after `flightInfo`:

```
@State private var selectedView: FlightViewId?
```

This property will store the `FlightViewId` when the user taps an item in the `List`. You use a nullable type to handle the case before the user taps a button.

Now you can create the list for the sidebar. Replace the `Text("Sidebar")` view with:

```
// 1
List(sidebarButtons, selection: $selectedView) { button in
  // 2
  VStack {
    Text(button.title)
    Text(button.subtitle)
  }
}
// 3
.listStyle(.plain)
.navigationTitle("Mountain Airport")
```

Here's how this sets up the sidebar:

1. You'll find SwiftUI expects the sidebar to provide a list. You use the `selection` parameter to pass in the `selectedView` property. When the user taps a button from the list, SwiftUI will store the `id` property of the current `ViewButton` objects into the `selectedView` property. SwiftUI knows a change to the property passed to the `selection` parameter should cause state changes. If you change the property elsewhere, it'll still trigger navigation.

2. You display the button's title and subtitle in a `VStack`.

3. First, you specify the `plain` list style since you'll add some polish to it in a moment. You then use the `navigationTitle(_:)` modifier to provide a title for the `NavigationSplitView`. It might seem odd to call `navigationTitle(_:)` on the `List` and not the `NavigationSplitView`. But remember, you're defining a hierarchy of views. A view's title typically changes when migrating through the view stack. The `navigationTitle(_:)` modifier locates the navigation view for the attached control and adjusts the title accordingly.

Build and run the app. On a small screen, the title appears above the list, while the list shows your single navigation item.

Sidebar with First Navigation Link

On a larger screen, you'll see that the sidebar matches the small screen display while the details show the static `Text` view. In the next section, you'll apply some styling to the list.

Polishing the Links

Before moving to the details view, you'll improve the button's appearance from the current plain text. Create a new SwiftUI View named **WelcomeButtonView.swift**. Replace the default view with the following:

```
struct WelcomeButtonView: View {
  var title: String
  var subTitle: String

  var body: some View {
    VStack(alignment: .leading) {
      Text(title)
        .font(.title)
        .foregroundColor(.white)
      Text(subTitle)
        .font(.subheadline)
        .foregroundColor(.white)
    }.padding()
    // 1
    .frame(maxWidth: .infinity, alignment: .leading)
    // 2
    .background(
      Image("link-pattern")
        .resizable()
        .clipped()
    )
  }
}
```

Here are a couple of things to note:

1. Using `maxWidth: .infinity` sets the view to fill the available horizontal space.
2. You also use the `background(_:)` modifier to provide an image background. You'll learn more about this in **Chapter 18: "Drawing & Custom Graphics"**.

This change provides a more visually appealing view to replace the simple text link. It also provides a short description to accompany each menu option.

Change the contents of the preview to provide default data:

```
WelcomeButtonView(
  title: "Flight Status",
  subTitle: "Departure and Arrival Information"
)
```

Go back to **WelcomeView.swift**. Replace the current `VStack` view under `// 2` with:

```
WelcomeButtonView(
  title: button.title,
  subTitle: button.subtitle
)
```

Run the app to see your new sidebar link.

Styled Sidebar Links

Having improved the look of your sidebar, you'll now put this list to work and implement the child view.

Building the Details View

Your details view will show the user a list of today's flights. Open **FlightStatusBoard.swift**. At the top of the `FlightStatusBoard` struct, add a variable that you'll use to pass in the list of flights for the day:

```
var flights: [FlightInformation]
```

Change the view body to:

```
List(flights, id: \.id) { flight in
  Text(flight.statusBoardName)
}
.navigationTitle("Today's Flight Status")
```

This code will loop through the array of flights showing a row for each. You've also set the title for the navigation view to reflect the view's purpose.

You'll learn more about lists in **Chapter 14: "Lists"**.

You also need to provide sample data for the preview. The mock data class provides a method `.generateTestFlights(_)` for this purpose. Change the preview to provide this sample data:

```
FlightStatusBoard(
  flights: FlightData.generateTestFlights(date: Date())
)
```

Now you'll implement the details view for your `NavigationSplitView`. Go to **WelcomeView.swift** and replace the `Text("Details")` in the `details` closure with:

```
// 1
if let view = selectedView {
  // 2
  switch view {
  case .showFlightStatus:
    // 3
    FlightStatusBoard(flights:
flightInfo.getDaysFlights(Date()))
  }
} else {
  // 4
  Text("Select an option in the sidebar.")
}
```

Here's how this handles the implementation view:

1. You attempt to unwrap `selectedView` into `view`. Once the user chooses an item from the `List`, `view` now contains the `id` for the selected item. Until then, the unwrap fails, and you'll show the view under comment four.
2. As `view` contains the `FlightViewId` for the selected item in the sidebar, you create a `switch` statement to handle this and future options.
3. For the `showFlightStatus` case, you display the `FlightStatusBoard` view and pass in the flights for today.
4. If the unwrap attempt in step one failed, you display a `Text` view asking the user to select an option.

Run the app. On the Welcome view, tap the **Flight Status** button. You'll see your new view listing the day's flights:

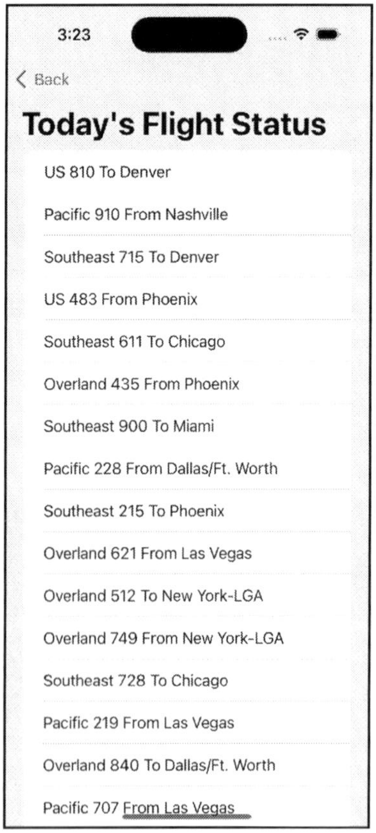

Flight list

Next, you'll extend the `FlightStatusBoard` view to support its own navigation structure.

Building a NavigationStack

With the two-column navigation you've created, you can implement the details views separately from the initial view. Your **Flight Status** option displays a list of today's flights. Next, you'll show information on a flight when the user taps it on the list. To do so, you'll wrap this list inside a new `NavigationStack` implemented inside the overall `NavigationSplitView` details view.

The project already includes a file in the **FlightDetails** group named **FlightDetails.swift** that will show the details for a flight. To allow the user to see this view when tapping on a flight on the status board, go to **FlightStatusBoard.swift** and change the view to the following:

```
// 1
NavigationStack {
  List(flights, id: \.id) { flight in
    // 2
    NavigationLink(flight.statusBoardName, value: flight)
  }
  // 3
  .navigationDestination(
    // 4
    for: FlightInformation.self,
    // 5
    destination: { flight in
      FlightDetails(flight: flight)
    }
  )
  .navigationTitle("Today's Flight Status")
}
```

There's a lot here, and if you're familiar with the earlier navigation types in SwiftUI, it'll look odd. Here's how this implements the navigation to the flight details.

1. First, you create a new `NavigationStack`. This shows a root view and presents subsequent views over the current view.

2. Before SwiftUI 4.0, the `NavigationLink` expected a view to display to the user and a destination to present when the user tapped the displayed view. Now, instead of a view to show, you provide a `value` to the `NavigationLink` view. This line passes the `FlightInformation` object for this row of the `List`. You use a convenience initializer that takes a string and produces a `Text` view showing that string.

3. You still need to let SwiftUI know to display a view. You use the `navigationDestination(for:destination:)` modifier to tell SwiftUI how to handle a value of a given type. Notice that you apply it to the `List` inside the `NavigationStack`. You should also not place it inside a looping container such as `List`, `ScrollView`, etc.

4. The `for` parameter specifies the type of `value` this modifier will handle. In step two, you pass an instance of `FlightInformation` as the `value` property. Passing `FlightInformation.self` to `for` tells SwiftUI to use this method for values of the `FlightInformation` type.

5. The `destination` parameter tells SwiftUI what to do when it's passed the matching type. The closure receives a `FlightInformation` instance called `flight`, which is then used to initialize `FlightDetails`.

The preview will show you the new list. On iOS, you'll get the small right-pointing disclosure arrow at the end of each row. This visual indicator shows the user that tapping the row will lead to more information and comes automatically when combining a `List` and `NavigationStack`:

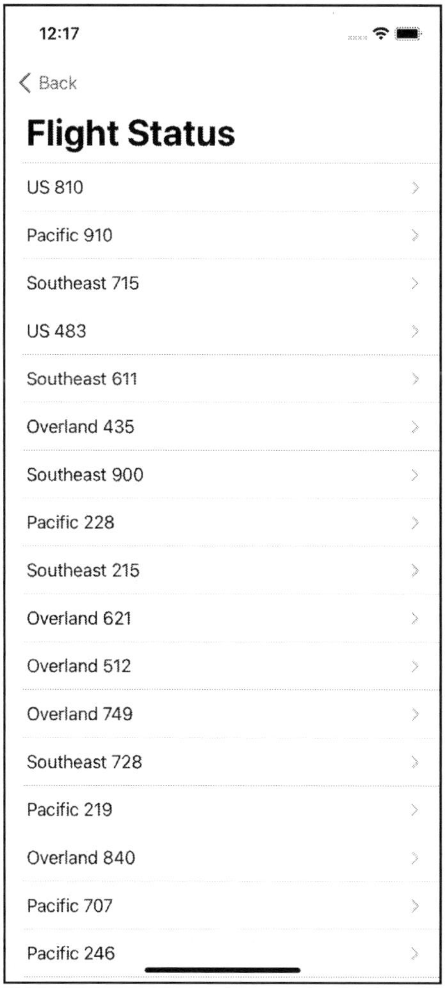

Flight list with arrow

Run the app and tap on **Flight Status**. Now tap on any flight, and you'll see the details for that flight.

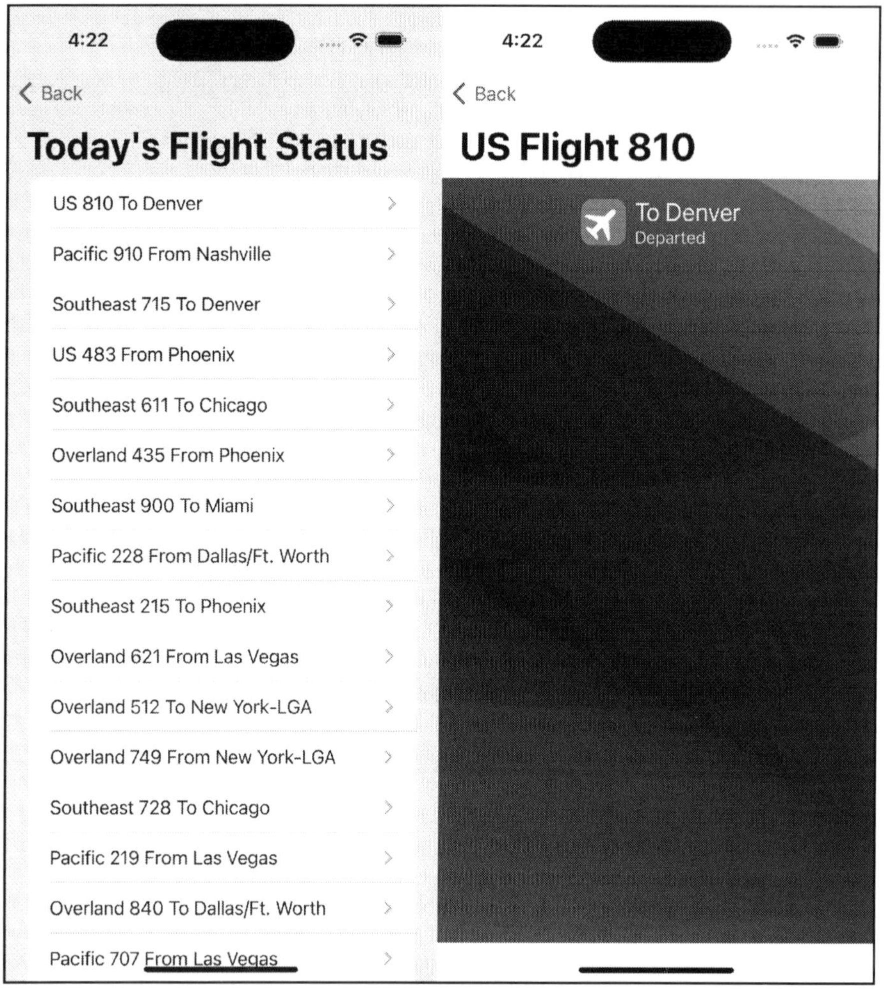

Flight details view

Now that you've implemented a stacked hierarchy, you'll see how to customize the navigation bar in the next section.

Adding Items to the Navigation Bar

Creating a navigation view stack adds a navigation bar to each view. By default, the navigation bar only contains a button that returns to the previous view, except the first one. Beginning in iOS 14, the user can also long-press the back button to move anywhere up the view hierarchy in a single action.

Navigation Stack

> **Note**: If you do not provide the title for a view, it'll show as blank in the displayed list.

You can add additional items to the navigation bar, but you want to avoid overcrowding it with too many controls. Now, you'll add a toggle to this app to hide flights that have landed or departed.

Still in **FlightStatusBoard.swift**, add the following code after the declaration of `flights`:

```
@State private var hidePast = false
```

You'll set this state variable to hide past flights. Now, add a computed property after the new state variable to filter flights based on this variable:

```
var shownFlights: [FlightInformation] {
  hidePast ?
    flights.filter { $0.localTime >= Date() } :
    flights
}
```

Change the variable passed to `List` to use the computed property instead of `flights`:

```
List(shownFlights, id: \.id) { flight in
```

With those changes, you can filter the list of flights by changing the `hidePast` state variable using a toggle on the navigation bar. Add the following code after the `navigationTitle(_:)` modifier to add such a toggle:

```
.navigationBarItems(
  trailing: Toggle("Hide Past", isOn: $hidePast)
)
```

The `navigationBarItems(trailing:)` modifier adds views to the trailing edge of the navigation bar. You'll find a corresponding modifier, `navigationBarItems(leading:)`, to add views to the leading edge, should you ever need that.

You provide the views inside the closure. Here you add a toggle that'll change the `hidePast` property. As `hidePast` is a state variable, SwiftUI will refresh and update the list when the value changes. Also, you use the **Button** style toggle to conserve space.

Looking at the live preview will not show the new toggle because the preview has no idea the view will be inside a NavigationStack derived from another view. To see the live preview as it should appear, change the body of the preview to:

```
NavigationStack {
  FlightStatusBoard(
    flights: FlightData.generateTestFlights(date: Date())
  )
}
```

Since you wrapped the preview inside a NavigationStack, you'll see the toggle appear in the preview. Run the app, navigate to one of the flight boards, and try the toggle to see it in action.

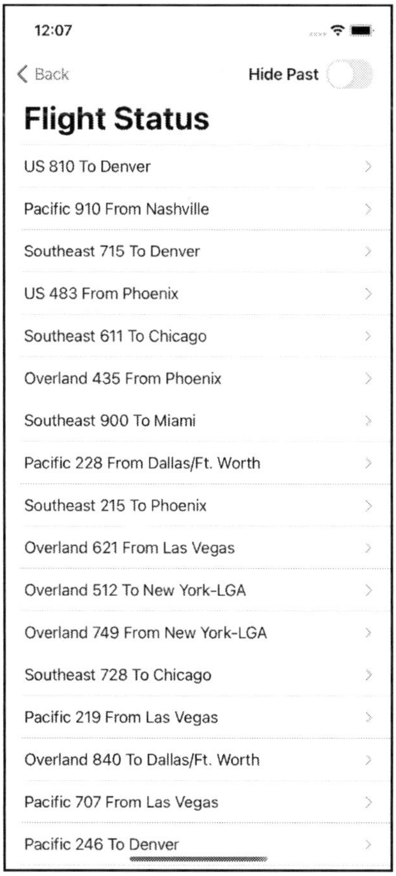

Toggle

Great job!

Navigating With Code

As you saw earlier, passing data down the navigation stack is simple. You can send the data as a read-only variable or pass a binding to allow the child view to make changes that are reflected in the parent view. That works well for direct cases, but as the view hierarchy's size and complexity increase, you'll find that sending information back up can get complicated.

The navigation hierarchy also supports multiple paths to the same view. In these cases, you could end up having to pass parameters solely to pass data between other views:

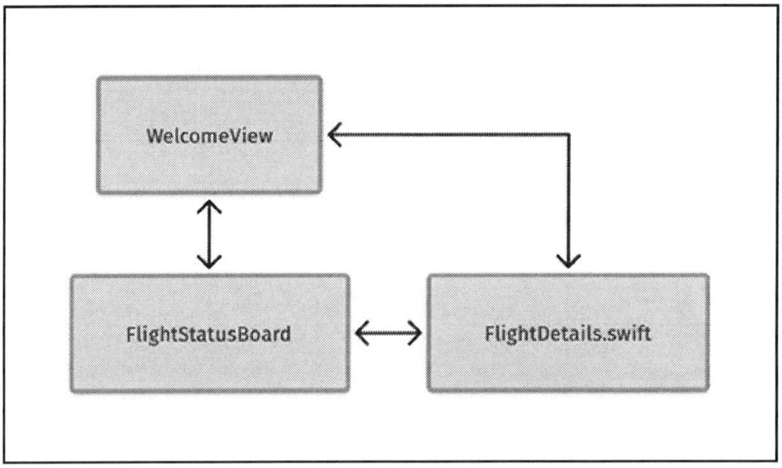

Navigation diagram

Fortunately, there's a better way. A SwiftUI view automatically shares its environment with any view below it in the view hierarchy. This feature allows you to put anything into the environment, then view or modify it within any other view in the hierarchy. You'll now update the app to use this ability to save the most recent flight a user viewed and show that in place of the first flight from the previous section.

First, you'll create a class to add to the environment. Under the Models group, create a new file named **FlightNavigationInfo.swift**. Change the file to read:

```
import SwiftUI

class FlightNavigationInfo: ObservableObject {
  @Published var lastFlightId: Int?
}
```

The single property will store the id of the last flight the user views. Now, you'll add this to the parent navigation view. Open **WelcomeView.swift** and, at the end of the variables at the top of the struct, add the following code:

```
@StateObject var lastFlightInfo = FlightNavigationInfo()
```

This line creates a `StateObject` you can now attach to the environment for the `NavigationView`. At the closing brace of the details closure, add the following code:

```
.environmentObject(lastFlightInfo)
```

This modifier adds the `FlightNavigationInfo` object to the environment for your navigation. You must add it to the `NavigationSplitView` and not to a view within it for the environment to flow through your view hierarchy.

Next, add a new case for the `FlightViewId` enum by adding the following to the end of it:

```
case showLastFlight
```

Now, add the following code to the `sidebarButtons` computed property just before the `return` statement:

```
if
  let flightId = lastFlightInfo.lastFlightId,
  let flight = flightInfo.getFlightById(flightId) {
  buttons.append(
    ViewButton(
      id: .showLastFlight,
      title: "\(flight.flightName)",
      subtitle: "The Last Flight You Viewed"
    )
  )
}
```

This code attempts to unwrap `lastFlightInfo.lastFlightId`. If successful, it then uses the `getFlightById(_:)` method to get the flight for the flight id and attempts to unwrap that. If both succeed, you have the last flight the user viewed in the `flight` variable. You then add a button to the sidebar navigation using the new `showLastFlight` type and with the name of the flight as the title.

You now need to implement the details for this new navigation option. Inside the details closure, find the `switch view` statement and add the following as the last case:

```
case .showLastFlight:
```

```
if
  let flightId = lastFlightInfo.lastFlightId,
  let flight = flightInfo.getFlightById(flightId) {
  FlightDetails(flight: flight)
}
```

Much as you did inside the `sidebarButtons` computed property, you attempt to unwrap the `lastFlightInfo. lastFlightId` property and use it to get the last flight corresponding to that id. If those succeed, you show the `FlightDetails` view showing that flight.

The last step is to set the value through the environment when the user views a flight's details. Open **FlightDetails.swift** and add a reference to the environment object to the view after the `flight` property:

```
@EnvironmentObject var lastFlightInfo: FlightNavigationInfo
```

With this reference to the view's environment, add the following code after the closing brace for the `ZStack`:

```
.onAppear {
  lastFlightInfo.lastFlightId = flight.id
}
```

Any code in the `onAppear(_)` closure runs when the view appears. In this case, when SwiftUI renders the `ZStack`, it'll execute the code and store the `id` for this flight in the environment. When the user returns to the root welcome view, that view will read the value and show the button.

This also causes the live view to crash because it doesn't know about the new environment object. To fix this, you must provide an environment object for the preview. Adding the following modifier after preview's `NavigationStack`:

```
.environmentObject(FlightNavigationInfo())
```

You also need to make the same change to `FlightStatusBoard`. Open **FlightStatusBoard.swift** and add the following modifier to the preview's `FlightStatusBoard`:

```
.environmentObject(FlightNavigationInfo())
```

Run the app. The second button does not show since the identifier is initially `nil`. Tap **Flight Status** and then tap any flight. Return to the Welcome view, where the new button appears and shows the flight you selected. Tapping it takes you to the flight's details.

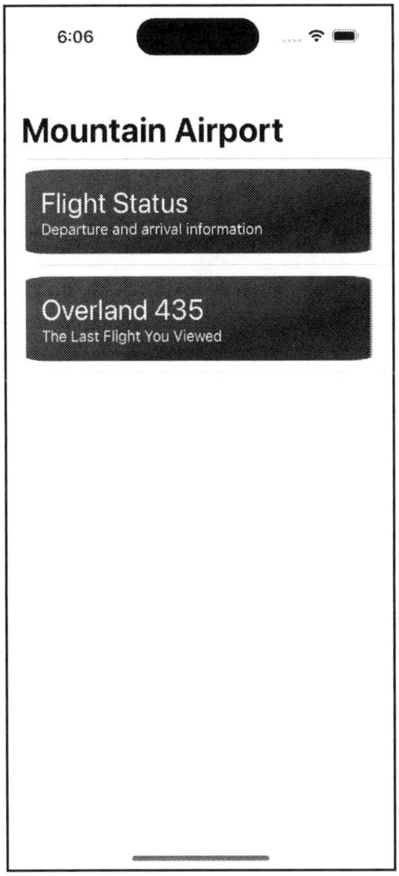

Selected flight in Welcome view

In the next section, you'll learn about programmatic navigation and the `NavigationPath`.

Navigating Using Code

The last flight option you added to the sidebar in the previous section brings up the details for the flight. While it works, it's a good idea to let the user go back from these details to the same list of flights like when they select the **Flight Status** option. Until now, your navigation changes have come from user interaction. You'll find times like this when you want to trigger navigation through your code. In this section, you'll see how to interact with the navigation stack through code and use this to make this change.

First, you'll need a way to provide a flight to the **FlightStatusBoard** view. Open **FlightStatusBoard.swift** and add the following property after `flights`.

```
var flightToShow: FlightInformation?
```

This code creates an optional property. You'll change this view so if set; it will automatically navigate to the detail for that flight. If `nil`, then the view acts as it currently does.

Next, add the following state property after `hidePast`:

```
@State private var path: [FlightInformation] = []
```

This property contains an array of `FlightInformation` objects that you initialize to an empty array. Now update the declaration of the `NavigationStack` to:

```
NavigationStack(path: $path) {
```

By default, a `NavigationStack` manages the state of the navigation stack itself. You can pass an object through the `path` parameter to `NavigationStack`, and SwiftUI will share control of the stack through this object. In this case, you know all the values will be `FlightInformation` objects, so use an array of that type for the navigation path. Initializing it to an empty array starts as a stack with no views. In more complex cases where you can have multiple object types, you use a `NavigationPath` to store any value conforming to the `Hashable` protocol.

You can use the `path` property to modify the navigation stack programmatically. Add the following code after the closing brace of the `NavigationStack`:

```
.onAppear {
  if let flight = flightToShow {
    path.append(flight)
  }
}
```

The `onAppear(perform:)` modifier executes its closure before the attached view appears. In this case, the code block will run before the `NavigationStack` appears to the user. If you successfully unwrap the `flightToShow` property, you append the unwrapped object to the `path` property. Doing so has the same result as if the user tapped an item in the list for the flight and navigates to the details for this flight.

This action also shows the power of the new separation between navigation actions (through `NavigationLink`) and results (through `navigationDestination(for:destination:)`). You don't need to add code telling SwiftUI how to handle appending a `FlightInformation` object since it already knows how to do so through your `navigationDestination(for:destination:)` for `FlightInformation.self`.

To finish the change, open **WelcomeView.swift** and find the code for the `.showLastFlight:` case of the switch statement. Replace the call to `FlightDetails(flight: flight)` with:

```
FlightStatusBoard(
  flights: flightInfo.getDaysFlights(Date()),
  flightToShow: flight
)
```

You now show the `FlightStatusBoard` and pass the flight in through the `flightToShow` parameter instead of showing the flight details directly.

Run the app. Tap **Flight Status** and then tap a flight. Return to the Welcome view, where the new button appears and shows the flight you selected. Tapping it navigates to the status board. After a brief pause, you'll see the details for the flight appear. Tap and hold the **Back** button to confirm that the status board appears in the navigation.

Flight Details Showing Program Controlled Navigation

Now that you've explored the navigation view, you'll explore tabbed navigation and see how to integrate the two within the same app.

Using Tabbed Navigation

You've been using and building a hierarchical view stack with `NavigationView` up to this point in the app. Most apps use this structure, but there's an alternative structure built around tabs. Tabs work well for content where the user wants to flip between options. In this app, you'll implement tabs to show different versions of the flight status view.

Open **FlightStatusBoard.swift**. First, you'll extract the portion of the view that creates the list into a separate view. This change will make it easier to use across the tabs. Add the following new view above the `FlightStatusBoard` struct:

```
struct FlightList: View {
  var flights: [FlightInformation]
  var flightToShow: FlightInformation?
  @State private var path: [FlightInformation] = []

  var body: some View {
    NavigationStack(path: $path) {
      List(flights, id: \.id) { flight in
        NavigationLink(flight.statusBoardName, value: flight)
      }
      .navigationDestination(
        for: FlightInformation.self,
        destination: { flight in
          FlightDetails(flight: flight)
        }
      )
    }
    .onAppear {
      if let flight = flightToShow {
        path.append(flight)
      }
    }
  }
}
```

Next, delete the `path` property from the `FlightStatusBoard` view since you've moved the `NavigationStack` to the extracted view. Change the body of `FlightStatusBoard` to:

```
// 1
TabView {
  // 2
  FlightList(
    flights: shownFlights.filter { $0.direction == .arrival }
  )
  // 3
```

```
    .tabItem {
      // 4
      Image("descending-airplane")
        .resizable()
      Text("Arrivals")
    }
    // 5
    FlightList(
      flights: shownFlights,
      flightToShow: flightToShow
    )
    .tabItem {
      Image(systemName: "airplane")
        .resizable()
      Text("All")
    }
    FlightList(
      flights: shownFlights.filter { $0.direction == .departure }
    )
    .tabItem {
      Image("ascending-airplane")
      Text("Departures")
    }
  }
  .navigationTitle("Today's Flight Status")
  .navigationBarItems(
    trailing: Toggle("Hide Past", isOn: $hidePast)
  )
```

Here's how the tab view code works:

1. You declare that you're creating a tab view with the `TabView` control. The first tab will show arriving flights, the second all flights and the third departing flights.
2. You provide a view for each tab to the enclosure of `TabView` showing the extracted `FlightList` view. Note that you do not pass the `flightToShow` to the view since the flight may not appear in the departure or arriving lists.
3. You apply the `tabItem(_:)` modifier to the tab to set an image, text, or combination of the two.
4. Each tab displays an image and a text label. You can only use `Text`, `Image`, or an `Image` followed by `Text` as the tab label. If you use anything else, the tab will appear visible but empty. You don't need to create a `VStack` even when using multiple items.
5. You pass the `flightToShow` property only to the complete list of flights since there's no guarantee it will appear in the other tabs. You'll ensure this tab shows when the view needs to navigate to the chosen flight in a moment.

> **Note**: You may wonder why the view uses a custom image for the descending and ascending aircraft instead of modifying the SF Symbol font used for the central tab. Most modifiers to `Image` within the tab toolbar won't process, including a rotation.

Run the app. Tap on the **Flight Status** option, and you'll see that your view now has three tabs allowing you to view all flights or only flights departing or arriving at the airport. Note that the toggle in the navigation still works. Also, the two navigation structures don't conflict. You can select any flight as before and see more details about it.

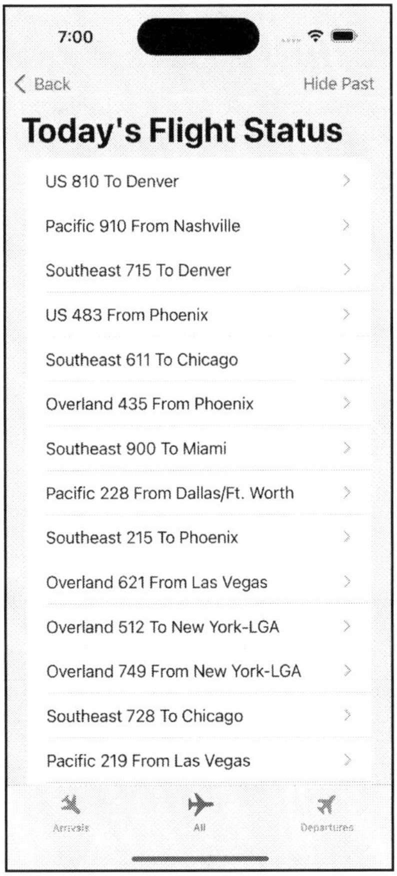

Flight status with tabs

Setting Tabs

Remembering the last tab selected when the user returns to the view would be a nice addition. To do that, in **FlightStatusBoard.swift**, below the `hidePast` state variable, add the following line:

```
@AppStorage("FlightStatusCurrentTab") var selectedTab = 1
```

You use the new `@AppStorage` feature to persist an integer to **UserDefaults**. You also specify a default to use the first time the view displays on a device. You now need to add a unique identifier to each tab. First, change the definition of the `TabView` to:

```
TabView(selection: $selectedTab) {
```

You now pass a binding to the `selectedTab` to the `selection` parameter of `TabView`. Using `AppStorage` persists the value to **UserDefaults** so that the app will remember the change for future access. You now need to attach an identifier to each tab. After the `tabItem` closure for the **Arrivals** tab, add the following modifier:

```
.tag(0)
```

You use the `tag(_:)` modifier to give each tab a unique identifier, in this case, an integer. You often use an enumerable here, but that complicates storing the value in this example. For the tab showing all flights, add the following code after the `tabItem` closure:

```
.tag(1)
```

Finally, after the `tabItem` closure for the **Departures** tab, add the following code:

```
.tag(2)
```

Both of these add identifiers to the remaining tabs; the binding works both ways. If you set `selectedTab` to a value, SwiftUI will activate the tab with the corresponding identifier. If the user changes the active tab, then `selectedTab` will receive the identifier of the chosen tab.

To ensure when you pass a value in the `flightToShow` property, the user sees the tab with all flights, add the following modifier at the end of the `TabView` closure before the `navigationTitle(_:)` modifier:

```
.onAppear {
  if flightToShow != nil {
```

```
        selectedTab = 1
    }
}
```

This code sets the `selectedTab` to one when you pass a value through the `flightToShow` property to ensure that the complete list of flights shows in the view since `hidePast` defaults to false. This way, the user will always see the flight in the list when they return from the details page.

Run the app. and then tap **Flight Status**. You'll see the view defaults to the **All** tab since the tag for it matches the default value you provided of **1**. Select another tab and then tap the **Back** button to return to the Welcome View. Now tap **Flight Status** again, and confirm that that view starts with the tab you selected in the previous step.

> **Note**: If your app design works better with pages, you can change the tabs into pages with the `tabViewStyle(_:)` modifier on the `TabView`.

Setting Tab Badges

SwiftUI 3.0 introduced controls that let you set a badge for each tab. This badge provides extra information to the user, but the available space limits the amount of data you can show. You'll add a badge item to indicate the number of incoming and outgoing flights to the Flight Status and a short text badge showing the date.

First, open **FlightStatusBoard.swift** and add the following code to the first `tabItem` just before the `.tag(0)` line:

```
.badge(shownFlights.filter { $0.direction == .arrival }.count)
```

The simplest badge displays a number on the tab icon. Here, you use the same filter to limit the `FlightList` view and the `count` property to get the number of flights. Add a similar line to the last `tabItem` before the `.tag(2)` line:

```
.badge(shownFlights.filter { $0.direction == .departure }.count)
```

Again, you use the same filter and get a count with the `count` property of the collection. In most cases, you'll add a number indicator to a tab, but you can also add a short text filter.

Add the following code to the top of the body after the `shownFlights` property:

```
var shortDateString: String {
  let dateF = DateFormatter()
  dateF.timeStyle = .none
  dateF.dateFormat = "MMM d"
  return dateF.string(from: Date())
}
```

This property returns a string with the month and date. You can then use this property as a badge. Add the following line after the second `tabItem` before the `.tag(1)` modifier:

```
.badge(shortDateString)
```

Now run the app, and tap on the **Flight Status** option. You'll see the new badges on each tab at the bottom of the view:

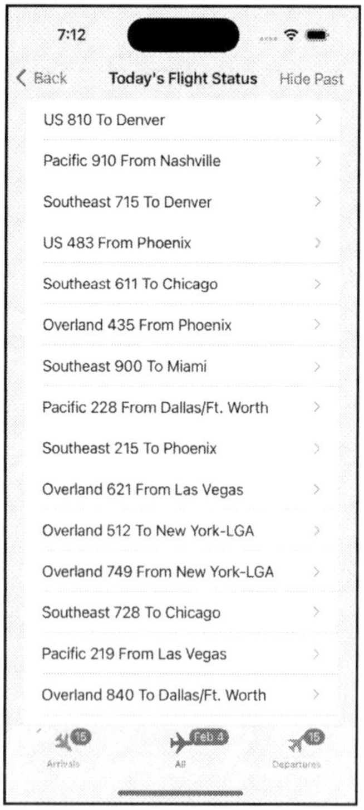

Badges

Well done! You've now built a navigation structure for the app. In the next chapter, you'll learn more about showing data in a view, including the `List` you used in this chapter.

Key Points

- Starting in SwiftUI 4.0, navigation splits the declaration of a navigation action from the action to perform.
- Split navigation can create a navigation structure with two or three columns. The framework will collapse the columns on small screen devices to appear identical to stack navigation.
- Navigation stack creates a hierarchy of views. The user can move further into the stack and can back up from within the stack.
- A `NavigationLink` shows a view that provides a value associated with the view. The `navigationDestination` modifier informs SwiftUI how to act when provided a value of a given type.
- You apply changes to navigation views to controls in the stack and not to the navigation type itself.
- You can access the view stack in your code by passing a binding to a mutable collection through the `path` parameter. In simple cases, this can be a collection of the type being used for navigation. If you need multiple types, you can use a `NavigationPath`.
- Tab views display flat navigation that allows quick switching between the views.

Where to Go From Here?

To learn about migrating the older navigation types to the new ones introduced with SwiftUI 4.0, see **Migrating to new navigation types** at https://developer.apple.com/documentation/swiftui/migrating-to-new-navigation-types.

The first stop when looking for information on user interfaces on Apple platforms should be the Human Interface Guidelines on Navigation for iOS, watchOS and tvOS:

- iOS: https://developer.apple.com/design/human-interface-guidelines/ios/app-architecture/navigation/
- watchOS: https://developer.apple.com/design/human-interface-guidelines/watchos/app-architecture/navigation/
- tvOS: https://developer.apple.com/design/human-interface-guidelines/tvos/app-architecture/navigation/

Navigation in macOS provides more options and creates a more complex topic. SwiftUI imposes some limitations that make it more like iOS development, and the above link provides a good starting point.

Chapter 14: Lists

By Bill Morefield

Most apps focus on displaying some type of data to the user. Whether upcoming appointments, past orders or new products, you must clearly show the user the information they come to your app for.

In the previous chapter, you saw a preview of iterating through data when displaying the flights for a day and allowing the user to interact with this data. In this chapter, you'll dive deeper into the ways SwiftUI provides you to show a list of items to the user of your app.

Iterating Through Data

Open the starter project for this chapter and go to **FlightList.swift** in the **FlightStatusBoard** group. You'll see a slightly different view than the one you created in the previous chapter. In place of `List`, which you'll work with later in this chapter, you'll start by examining `ForEach`.

SwiftUI uses `ForEach` as a fundamental element to loop over data. When you pass it a collection of data, it then creates multiple sub-views using a provided closure, one for each data item. `ForEach` works with any type of collected data. You can think of `ForEach` as the SwiftUI version of the `for-in` loop in traditional Swift code.

Run the app, tap **Flight Status** — and you'll notice a mess.

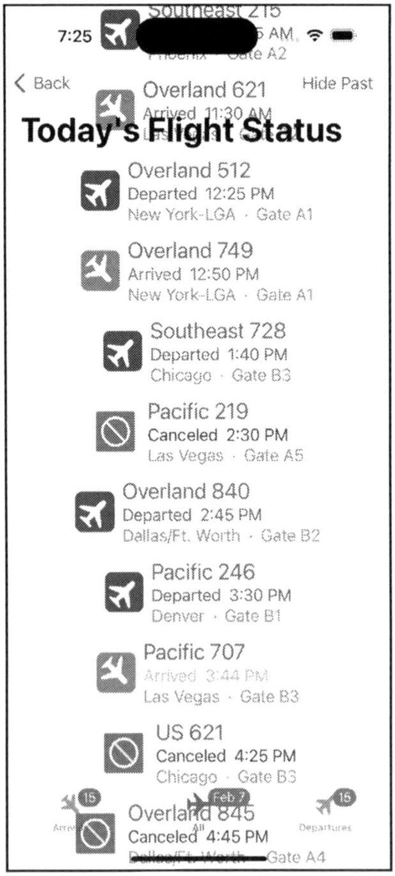

Bad schedule

Remember that ForEach operates as an iterator. It doesn't provide any structure. As a result, you've created many views but not provided a layout for them. They're all at the top level, not contained in anything else. SwiftUI tries to fit everything together, but the result is a mess. To fix both issues, add some structure around the loop:

```
ScrollView {
  VStack {
    ForEach(flights, id: \.id) { flight in
      NavigationLink(value: flight) {
        FlightRow(flight: flight)
      }
    }
    .navigationDestination(
      for: FlightInformation.self,
      destination: { flight in
        FlightDetails(flight: flight)
      }
    )
  }
}
```

You wrapped the `ForEach` loop inside a `VStack` — giving you a vertical stack of rows — and a `ScrollView` — that allows scrolling the rows since there's more content than will fit onto the view. SwiftUI picks up that you've wrapped a `VStack` and applies vertical scrolling to match. If a line of text within the view became longer than the view's width, SwiftUI wouldn't automatically add horizontal scrolling.

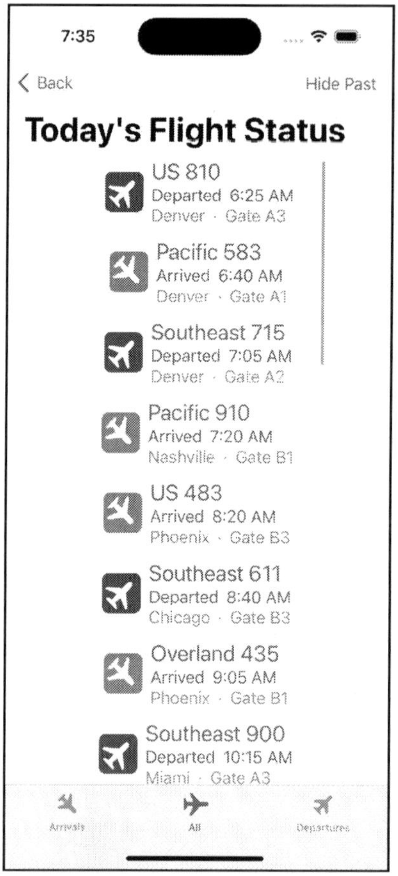

Scrolled list

You can override this default scrolling direction by passing in the desired scroll axes to `ScrollView`. To scroll the view in both directions, you would change the call to:

```
ScrollView([.horizontal, .vertical]) {
```

`ScrollView` provides a useful, general way to let a user browse through data that won't fit onto a single screen.

Also note the `id:` parameter is passed a keypath to a property of the type in the array. This parameter hints that SwiftUI has expectations for the data sent to an iteration. In the next section, you'll explore these expectations and make your data work more smoothly with SwiftUI.

Making Your Data Work Better With Iteration

The data passed into `ForEach` must provide a way to identify each element of the array as unique. In this loop, you use the `id:` parameter to tell SwiftUI to use the `\.id` property of **FlightInformation** as the unique identifier for each element in the array.

The only requirement for the unique identifier, other than being unique, is implementing the `Hashable` protocol. The native Swift `String` and `Int` types do. You can also use the Foundation `UUID` and `URL` types if that better fits your data. Since the `.id` property of **FlightInformation** object is an `Int`, it works perfectly as the unique identifier.

If your data object implements `Hashable`, you can also tell SwiftUI to use the entire object as the unique identifier. To do so, you would pass `\.self` to the `id:` parameter. Use this technique to iterate over a set of integers or other native objects that implement the `Hashable` protocol.

You can also remove the need to specify the unique identifier altogether by making your type conform to the `Identifiable` protocol. This protocol, new in Swift 5.1, provides a defined mechanism telling SwiftUI the unique identifier for a piece of data. This protocol's only requirement is to have an `id` property that conforms to the `Hashable` protocol. Since **FlightInformation** already has such a property, you simply have to let SwiftUI know this.

Open **FlightInformation.swift** in the **Models** group. At the end of the file, add the following code:

```
extension FlightInformation: Identifiable {
}
```

The extension tells SwiftUI that `FlightInformation` implements `Identifiable`. Since `FlightInformation` already meets the protocol requirements with an `id` parameter, you don't need to make any other changes to it.

Since you no longer need to specify the identifier to SwiftUI, open **FlightList.swift** and change the `ForEach` declaration for the `FlightList` view to:

```
ForEach(flights) { flight in
```

Run the app, tap **Flight Status** and you'll see the list works as before:

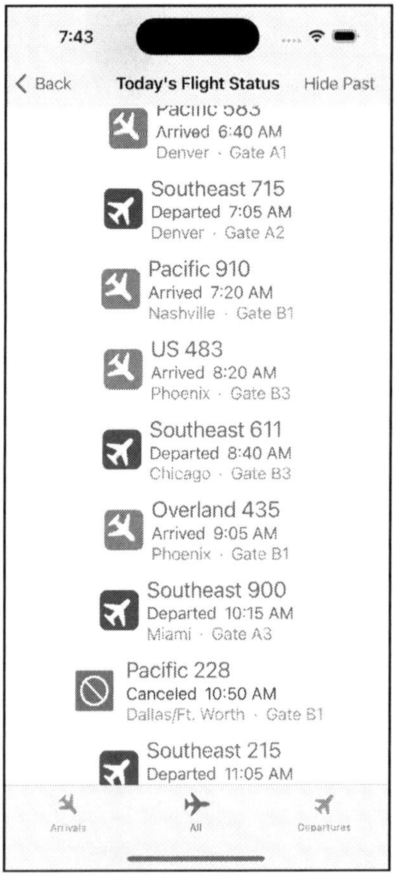

List Functions as Before with Identifiable

Improving Performance

When a `VStack` or `HStack` renders, SwiftUI creates all the cells at once. For a view such as this with only thirty rows, that probably doesn't matter. For rows with hundreds of potential rows, that's a waste of resources since most are not visible to the user. Using the **Lazy** versions of these stacks introduced in SwiftUI 2.0 (iOS 14, macOS 11, etc.) provides a quick performance improvement when iterating over large data sets.

You will see moving to the **Lazy** stack can introduce side-effects you should know. In the previous loop, change the `VStack` inside the `ScrollView` to `LazyVStack`. Run the app and go to the Flight Status view again.

Even with this small amount of data, you might notice an improvement in the initial rendering speed and performance when scrolling the view. Now each row renders only when it first appears on the screen. This change mainly saves resources when you have a lot of data, most of which the user will never see. Those unwanted flights will never be rendered or take up resources on the device. Once created, the view remains and SwiftUI will not remove it when it scrolls out of sight.

You will also see the view subtly changed. A `VStack` fills only the space needed for the contents. A `LazyVStack` uses a flexible width that will take up all available space. This change means the row in the `LazyVStack` will expand to take up the view's entire width.

You can see this comparing the two views before and after the change. As a `VStack` the scrolling list only occupies the middle of the view, and you must be within that area to scroll. In the `LazyVStack`, the row takes up the entire space of the view, and you can scroll anywhere in it. Also, notice the different positions of the scroll bars between the views.

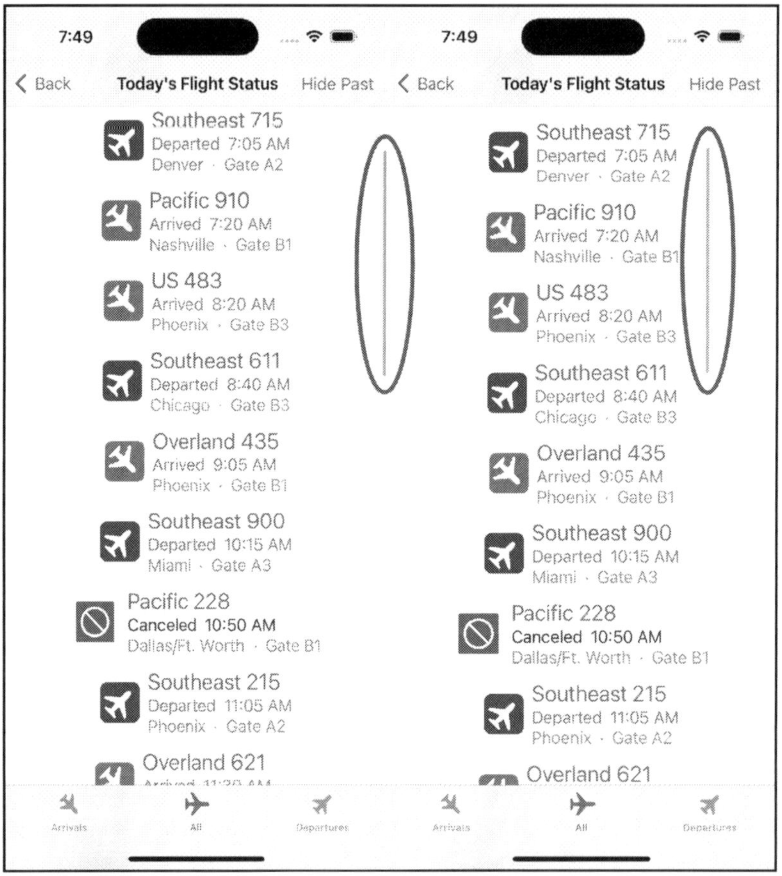

Lazy vs not

Setting the Scroll Position in Code

A major weakness of the first version of SwiftUI was the lack of a way to set the scrolling position programmatically. SwiftUI 2.0, introduced with iOS 14 and macOS Big Sur, added `ScrollViewReader` that allows setting the current position from code. You'll use it to scroll the flight status list to the next flight automatically. Replace the current `ScrollView` with the following code:

```
ScrollViewReader { scrollProxy in
  ScrollView {
    LazyVStack {
      ForEach(flights) { flight in
        NavigationLink(value: flight) {
          FlightRow(flight: flight)
        }
      }
      .navigationDestination(
        for: FlightInformation.self,
        destination: { flight in
          FlightDetails(flight: flight)
        }
      )
    }
  }
  // onAppear()
}
```

You've wrapped the `ScrollView` inside a `ScrollViewReader`. You'll use the `ScrollViewProxy` passed to the closure as `scrollProxy` to set the position. Since you've made your data conform to `Identifiable`, each row already has a unique identifier you can use to identify it later. You could also use the `id(_:)` modifier on `NavigationLink` to tag each row in the list with a unique identifier.

Now, add a property to get the `id` for the next flight that occurs. Add the following code after the `path` state property:

```
var nextFlightId: Int {
  guard let flight = flights.first(
    where: {
      $0.localTime >= Date()
    }
  ) else {
    return flights.last?.id ?? 0
  }
  return flight.id
}
```

This property looks for the first flight whose local time is at or after the current time. If one doesn't exist, it returns the `id` property of the day's last flight. If there is a later flight, the method returns its `id` property.

Now, you can move the scroll position to the row with this `id` when the view appears. You must do this inside the `ScrollViewReader` structure to have access to the proxy. The `ScrollView` is the perfect place for this. Replace the `// onAppear()` comment with the following code:

```
.onAppear {
  scrollProxy.scrollTo(nextFlightId)
}
```

The `onAppear(perform:)` modifier executes before the `ScrollView` appears. You call `scrollTo(_:)` on `ScrollViewProxy` to scroll to the next flight's id.

Run the app. You'll see the view moves so the next flight shows at the bottom of the view.

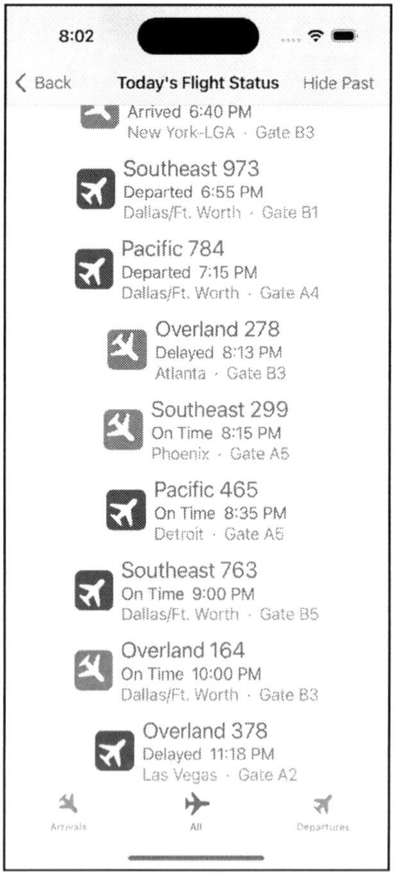

Positioning List to the Next Flight

You can specify the `anchor` parameter to change this location. In this case, it makes sense to place the flight in the middle of the view so change the `scrollTo(_:anchor:)` call to:

```
scrollProxy.scrollTo(nextFlightId, anchor: .center)
```

In cases in which there is not enough data to place the requested row at the requested position, the view will scroll to either the first or last element as close to the desired position as it can. Note that the scrolling works even combined with a `LazyVStack`, meaning you can scroll to a view that SwiftUI hasn't rendered yet.

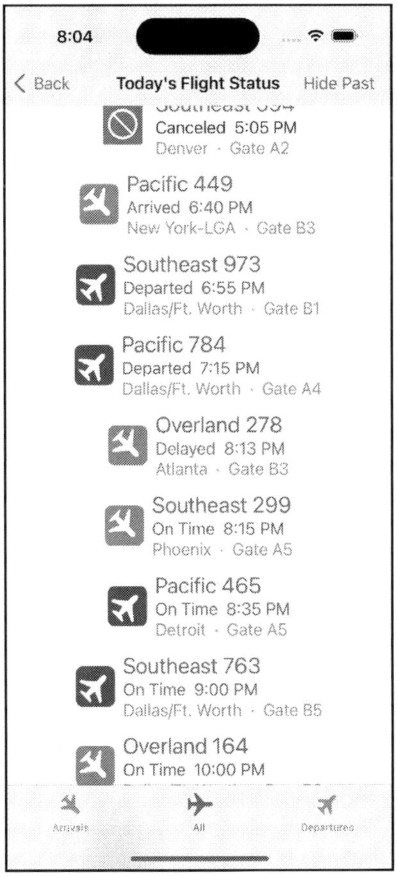

Late view

`ForEach` provides a flexible way to iterate through data. Since iterating through data and displaying it to the user is such a common task, all platforms have a built-in control to accomplish it. SwiftUI allows you to use this platform-specific control using a `List`.

Creating Lists

SwiftUI provides the `List` struct that does the heavy lifting for you and uses the platform-specific control to display the data. A `List` is a container much like a `VStack` or `HStack` that you can populate with static views, dynamic data or other iterative views.

A `List` provides some of the features you did manually when using `ForEach`. Go to **FlightList.swift** in the **FlightStatusBoard** group and remove the `ScrollView` and `LazyVStack`. Replace the `ForEach` with a `List`. Your view should now look like:

```
ScrollViewReader { scrollProxy in
  List(flights) { flight in
    NavigationLink(value: flight) {
      FlightRow(flight: flight)
    }
  }
  .navigationDestination(
    for: FlightInformation.self,
    destination: { flight in
      FlightDetails(flight: flight)
    }
  )
  .onAppear {
    scrollProxy.scrollTo(nextFlightId, anchor: .center)
  }
}
```

`List` iterates over the passed data as `ForEach` did, calling the closure for each element and passing the current element to that closure. Inside the closure, you define the view that will display for each row in the list.

In this view, you show a `NavigationLink` showing information about the flight, which links to more details.

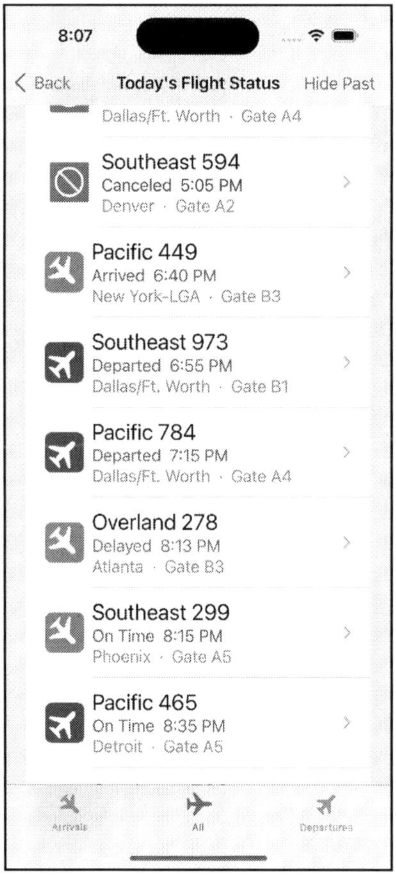

Flight list

Notice the similarity in the code with `ForEach`. `ForEach` allows you to iterate over almost any collection of data and create a view for each element. `List` acts much as a more specific case of `ForEach` to display rows of one-column data. Almost every framework and platform provides a version of this control, as it's a pretty standard user interface element.

A `List` automatically provides a vertical stack of the rows and handles scrolling. The `ScrollViewReader` works as before. On iOS related platforms, you also get the small right-pointing disclosure arrow automatically when a row of the list contains a `NavigationLink`. The row for the closure also takes up the entire width of the view.

Now that you've explored `List` and `ForEach`, you'll work with them to build an interface allowing the user to search flights.

Building Search Results

To start building the search view, open **SearchFlights.swift** under the **SearchFlights** group. You'll see view to allow the user to search for flights. However, the search functionality isn't in place yet. In this section, you're going to fix that.

Prior to SwiftUI 3.0 you needed to manually handle search functionality. Now SwiftUI provides a framework to help you with this common task. For now, you'll keep things simple and explore search in more depth in **Chapter 15: Advanced Lists**. First, at the top of the body add a new `@State` property after the existing ones:

```
@State private var city = ""
```

This property will hold the current search term. Next go the end of the `VStack` and add the following code before the `.navigationTitle(_:)` modifier:

```
.searchable(text: $city)
```

That's it. Even though this is a simple case, that's all you need for SwiftUI to set up a search box. Run the app, tap **Search Flights** and you'll see a new text box for search.

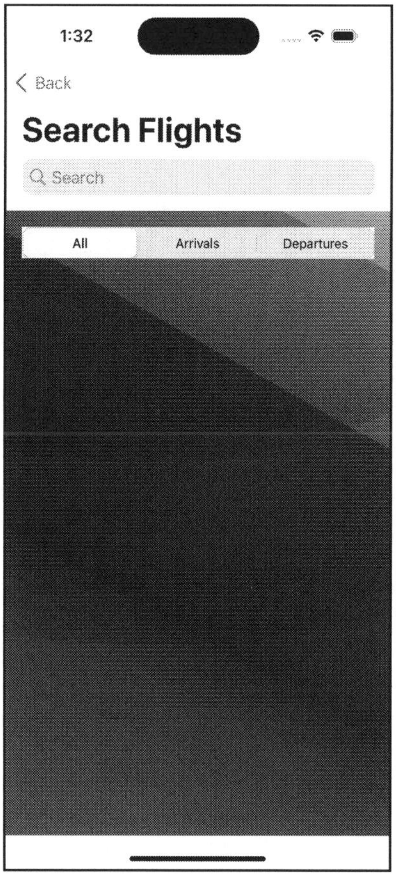

New Search Field

Now you have a place for the user to search, but nothing happens when you enter part of a city name in the field. To add filtering to the app, you'll need to update the `matchingFlights` parameter to take into account the `city` property. Inside `matchingFlights` add the following code just before the `return` statement:

```
if !city.isEmpty {
  matchingFlights = matchingFlights.filter {
    $0.otherAirport.lowercased().contains(city.lowercased())
  }
}
```

This code will check if `city` is anything other than an empty string. If so, then it filters to only the flights where the name of the other airport contains the text in the `city` property. You convert both to lowercase text before the comparison to match regardless of the case of the fields. This lets **phoenix** match **Phoenix**. You use `contains` so that you can match using only part of the name of the city. This lets **pho** match **Phoenix** as the letters are contained within the city name.

Look for the `// Insert Results` comment and replace it with the following:

```
List(matchingFlights) { flight in
  SearchResultRow(flight: flight)
}
```

That's all you need to display the search results. You pass the `matchingFlights` parameter that filters for only the passed flights that match the search parameters. Since you already made **FlightInformation** implement the `Identifiable` protocol, `List` knows how to manage it. As for performance, SwiftUI always renders a `List` lazily, requiring no special effort on your part.

Run the app and try a few search parameters such as part of a city name. You'll see the search quickly update to match your query.

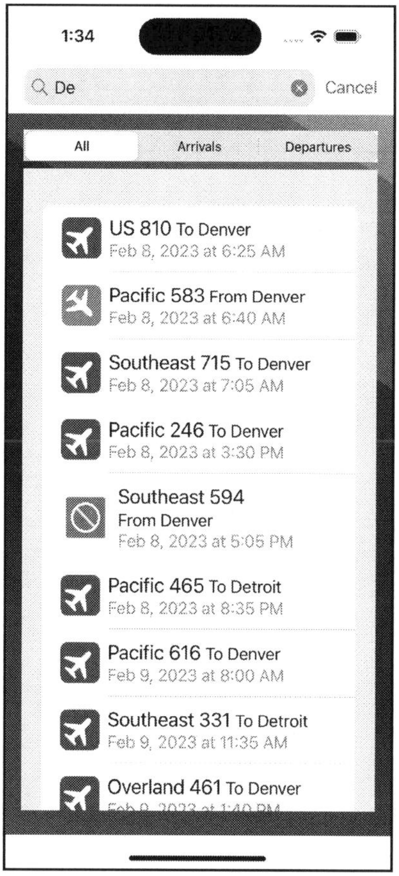

Searching flights

Building a Hierarchical List

SwiftUI added support for displaying hierarchical data in version 2.0. Much as the `NavigationLink` gives you a structure to organize views from general to more specific, a hierarchical list gives you an excellent way to display data that moves from general to more specific. In this section, you will update the search results into a hierarchical list that displays dates and then displays the flights for that date under it.

The data for a hierarchical list requires a specific format in addition to the standard requirements. For each element in the list, you need to create an optional property that contains a list of children in the hierarchy for the current row. Those children must be of the same type as the current element.

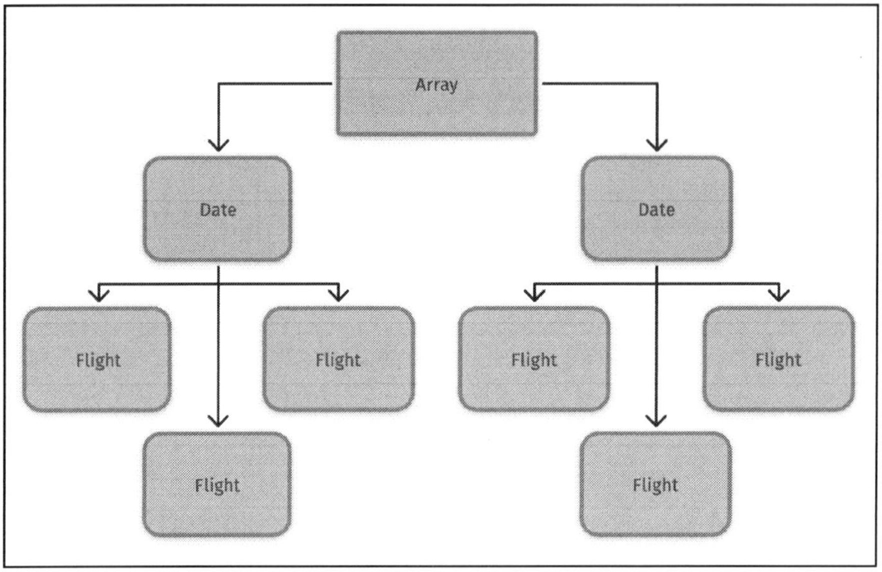

Hierarchical list

First you'll create this data structure. Open **SearchFlights.swift** and add the following code to the view after the `matchingFlights` property:

```
struct HierarchicalFlightRow: Identifiable {
  var label: String
  var flight: FlightInformation?
  var children: [HierarchicalFlightRow]?

  var id = UUID()
}
```

This struct contains a string for a label for the top-level rows showing the date. It also stores two optional properties: information about a flight and a list of child rows for this row. You will set the flight at the bottom node and the children for other rows.

The struct also provides the id property needed to fulfill the Identifiable protocol's requirements by giving each record a new **UUID** when created. A UUID, by definition, will be a unique value. For this more complex structure, it's a quick way to avoid duplicate values that could cause rows not to appear. Now add the following code below the new struct:

```
func hierarchicalFlightRowFromFlight(_ flight:
FlightInformation)
  -> HierarchicalFlightRow {
  return HierarchicalFlightRow(
    label: longDateFormatter.string(from: flight.localTime),
    flight: flight,
    children: nil
  )
}
```

This method creates a HierarchicalFlightRow object from an existing FlightInformation object. You'll use this to generate the leaf nodes of the hierarchy structure with flight information.

Another element that you'll need is a list of dates that contain a flight. Add the following code after the hierarchicalFlightRowFromFlight(_:) method:

```
var flightDates: [Date] {
  let allDates = matchingFlights.map { $0.localTime.dateOnly }
  let uniqueDates = Array(Set(allDates))
  return uniqueDates.sorted()
}
```

This computed property builds an array with the dates from all flights matching the current search parameters using a map. It gets only the date component of the time using the dateOnly extension defined in DateExtensions.swift. You convert the array to a set and back to remove duplicate values from the array. You return the sorted results.

You'll also need to filter for flights that take place on a specified day. Add the following code after the flightDates property:

```
func flightsForDay(date: Date) -> [FlightInformation] {
  matchingFlights.filter {
    Calendar.current.isDate($0.localTime, inSameDayAs: date)
  }
}
```

This function uses `Calendar.isDate(_:inSameDayAs:)` method to choose only flights matching the search parameters that occur on the passed date. You're combining multiple filtering operations, the first filtering on the search parameters to get `matchingFlights` and then using it as a source to get the matching flights for the selected day. You could do these in either order, but since the search criteria will typically remove more elements, doing it first improves performance.

With those properties and methods created, you can build the hierarchical data structure you need to display a hierarchical list. Add the following property to the view.

```
var hierarchicalFlights: [HierarchicalFlightRow] {
  // 1
  var rows: [HierarchicalFlightRow] = []

  // 2
  for date in flightDates {
    // 3
    let newRow = HierarchicalFlightRow(
      label: longDateFormatter.string(from: date),
      // 4
      children: flightsForDay(date: date).map {
        hierarchicalFlightRowFromFlight($0)
      }
    )
    rows.append(newRow)
  }
  return rows
}
```

Here's how this builds the hierarchical data structure.

1. You create an empty array that will be at the top level of the hierarchy.
2. You next loop through each of the dates found in the `flightDates` property.

3. Next, create a new `HierarchicalFlightRow` object for the date. The label for the row will be the long name for the date. You can find the date formatter in **DateFormatters.swift**.

4. The `children` property takes a bit more work. First, you use `flightsForDay(date:)` to get the flights that match the search parameters for this date. You then `map` each flight into a `HierarchicalFlightRow` containing information on the flight using the previously defined method.

With the hierarchy of data set up, you can now set the list to use it. Change the list in the view to:

```
// 1
List(hierarchicalFlights, children: \.children) { row in
  // 2
  if let flight = row.flight {
    SearchResultRow(flight: flight)
  } else {
    Text(row.label)
  }
}
```

While that was a lot of setup work, the result makes the hierarchical list easy to implement:

1. The list uses the `hierarchicalFlights` computed property to get the hierarchical structure. You use the `children` parameter on the `List` to pass a keypath to the property of the `HierarchicalFlightRow` object that contains the child elements.

2. You use an `if-let` to check if the row contains a flight. If the `flight` property is not `null`, you display the row for that flight. Otherwise, you show the `label` text as the row's contents.

Run the app to see your results. Note that to expand a date, you must tap the disclose arrow at the right of each row.

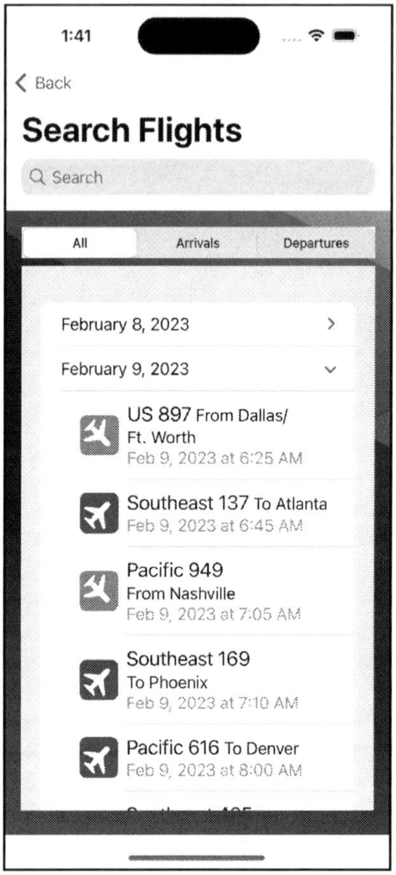

Hierarchical flight list

Note that this structure means it would be easy to add more layers to the hierarchy. For instance, adding the city under the date layer with the flights matching both the city and date as children.

While hierarchical data works well for some types, there's another way to organize data in a list. In the next section, you'll break the list into sections by date.

Grouping List Items

A long list of data can be challenging for the user to read. Fortunately, the `List` view supports breaking a list into sections. Combining dynamic data and sections moves into some more complex aspects of displaying data in SwiftUI. In this section, you'll separate flights into sections by date and add a header and footer to each section.

The good news is that you've done most of the needed work in the previous section. Open **SearchFlights.swift** and delete the `HierarchicalFlightRow` struct, along with `hierarchicalFlightRowFromFlight(_:)` and `hierarchicalFlights`.

Now change the List to the following:

```
// 1
List {
  // 2
  ForEach(flightDates, id: \.hashValue) { date in
    // 3
    Section(
      // 4
      header: Text(longDateFormatter.string(from: date)),
      // 5
      footer:
        Text(
          "Matching flights " + "\(flightsForDay(date:
date).count)"
        )
        .frame(maxWidth: .infinity, alignment: .trailing)
    ) {
      // 6
      ForEach(flightsForDay(date: date)) { flight in
        SearchResultRow(flight: flight)
      }
    }
  }
}
// 7
.listStyle(InsetGroupedListStyle())
```

This view is more complicated than the layouts you've used to this point. Here's what the code does:

1. You're declaring a list, but not passing data in for it to iterate. For a more complex and dynamic layout such as this, you'll often combine multiple `List` and `ForEach` elements.
2. You first will display sections for each date that has flights. You pass the list of unique dates using `flightDates` that you created in the previous section. Since `Date` doesn't implement the `Identifiable` protocol, you must also inform SwiftUI to use the `hashValue` property of the date as the unique identifier.
3. For each date, you start with a `Section`. This struct tells SwiftUI how to organize the data. It can contain optional headers and footer views for each section.
4. The header will display text showing the date for flights in this section. You can find the date formatter in **DateFormatters.swift**.
5. The footer displays the number of matching flights in the section. You apply the `frame(minWidth:idealWidth:maxWidth:minHeight:idealHeight:maxHeight:alignment:)` modifier to have the text fill the footer and align to the trailing side.
6. Inside each section, you use another `ForEach` and the `flightsForDay(date:)` method to loop through only the flights on this section's date.
7. You apply a style to the list that fits the grouped data you're displaying.

Run the app, and you'll see the flights now cleanly grouped by date. Type in part of a city name, and you'll see the view update to reflect the change while still grouping the flights.

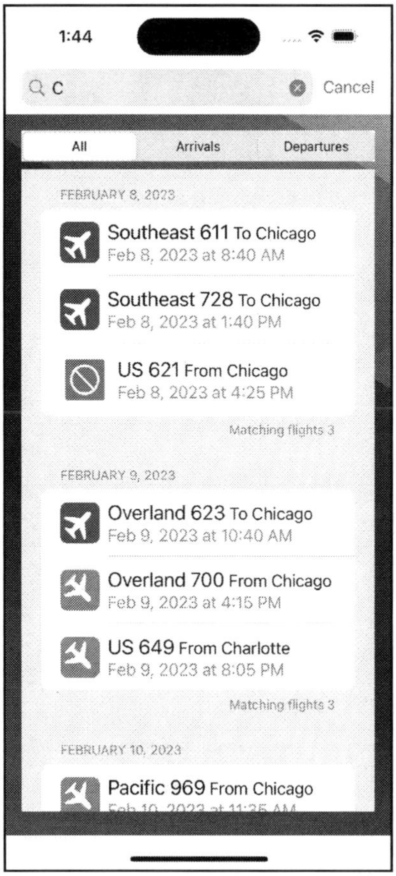

Grouped

Key Points

- A `ScrollView` wraps a view within a scrollable region that doesn't affect the rest of the view.
- The `ScrollViewProxy` lets you change the current position of a list from code.
- SwiftUI provides two ways to iterate over data. The `ForEach` option loops through the data allowing you to render a view for each element.
- A `List` uses the platform's list control to display the elements in the data.
- Data used with `ForEach` and `List` must provide a way to identify each element uniquely. You can do this by specifying an attribute that implements the `Hashable` protocol, have the object implement `Hasbable` and pass it to the `id` parameter or have your data implement the `Identifiable` protocol.
- Building a hierarchical view requires a hierarchical data structure to describe how the view should appear.
- You can split a `List` in `Sections` to organize the data and help the user understand what they see.
- You can combine `ForEach` and `List` to create more complex data layouts. This method works well when you want to group data into sections.

Where to Go From Here?

For more on integrating navigation and views, look at **SwiftUI Tutorial: Navigation** at https://www.kodeco.com/5824937-swiftui-tutorial-navigation.

The **WWDC 2019 SwiftUI Essentials** video provides an overview of Apple's guidelines on how views, navigation and lists fit together:

- https://apple.co/3LhAEvf

To learn more about the changes in the second version, such as hierarchical lists, watch **SwiftUI view Stacks, Grids, and Outlines** in SwiftUI from WWDC 2020:

- https://apple.co/3LhAFPP

Chapter 15: Advanced Lists

By Bill Morefield

The previous chapter introduced the common task of iterating over a set of data and displaying it to the user using the `ForEach` and `List` views. This chapter will build on that chapter and give you more ways to work with lists and improve the user's experience working with lists in your apps.

Adding Swipe Actions

Perhaps the most glaring omission related to lists in the initial versions of SwiftUI came in the lack of native swipe action support. A swipe action provides the user quick access to a few commonly used tasks. **SwiftUI 3.0** addresses this omission with new modifiers that simplify adding swipe actions to your lists. In this section, you'll add a swipe action to the Flight Status Board that will let the user highlight a flight, making it stand out on the long list. You'll use two types of actions, one that produces a small menu of options and a second that can perform a single action on the swipe.

Open the starter project for this chapter. You'll see it continues the app from the end of **Chapter 14: "Lists"**. You should be familiar with lists and the content introduced in the previous chapter before continuing this chapter. Open **FlightStatusBoard.swift** and add the following code after the `selectedTab` property.

```
@State var highlightedIds: [Int] = []
```

This property will store an array with the `id` of each flight the user highlights. You place the property in this view to reference it on the tabs the view contains. You will pass a binding to this array into the `FlightList` view on each tab. Find the three calls to `FlightList` in the view. Add a comma after the existing `flightToShow` parameter. On the following line, add a new second parameter to the calls to `FlightList`:

```
highlightedIds: $highlightedIds
```

For example, the first call will now look like this:

```
FlightList(
  flights: shownFlights.filter { $0.direction == .arrival },
  highlightedIds: $highlightedIds
)
```

Note you do not need to add the `flightToShow` parameter since it will remain `nil` for the first and last tabs. Once you've updated all three views, open **FlightList.swift** and add the following property after the `flightId` property:

```
@Binding var highlightedIds: [Int]
```

You use a binding to modify the contents of the array from within the `FlightList` view. Adding the property also means you need to update the preview to contain this new property. Update the `FlightList` view in the preview to:

```
FlightList(
  flights: FlightData.generateTestFlights(date: Date()),
  highlightedIds: .constant([15])
)
```

Now add the following method to the view, just before the body declaration:

```
func rowHighlighted(_ flightId: Int) -> Bool {
  return highlightedIds.contains { $0 == flightId }
}
```

This new method searches the array for the passed integer and returns `true` if the array contains it. You will use this new modifier to determine which list rows to highlight. Add the following code after the closing brace of the `NavigationLink` that forms the body of the list:

```
.listRowBackground(
  rowHighlighted(flight.id) ? Color.yellow.opacity(0.6) :
Color.clear
)
```

Here, you use the `listRowBackground(_:)` modifier to set a background color for each row in the list. If the user chose to highlight the row, you set the background color to yellow with reduced opacity so the highlight doesn't overwhelm the row's content. Otherwise, you leave the background clear, leaving no visual effect.

With the code to manage and highlight rows in place, you can implement the swipe action that lets the user toggle highlighting for each row. To make the view management easier, you'll create a new view that encapsulates the view and actions contained in the swipe action. Create a new SwiftUI view in the **FlightStatusBoard** group named **HighlightActionView**. At the top of the `HighlightActionView` struct, add the following two properties:

```
var flightId: Int
@Binding var highlightedIds: [Int]
```

These properties hold the flight id for the current row along with a binding to the array. Replace the contents of the preview to provide values for these properties:

```
HighlightActionView(
  flightId: 1,
```

```
  highlightedIds: .constant([1])
)
```

Next, add the following method after the properties for the view:

```
func toggleHighlight() {
  // 1
  let flightIdx = highlightedIds.firstIndex { $0 == flightId
  }
  // 2
  if let index = flightIdx {
    // 3
    highlightedIds.remove(at: index)
  } else {
    // 4
    highlightedIds.append(flightId)
  }
}
```

This method will toggle the current highlight state for the row by adding or removing the flight identifier to or from the `highlightedIds` array. Here's how it works:

1. This code gets the index in the array to the first element that matches the `flightId` passed into the view. If the array contains the flight id, then `flightIdx` will now have the index of that element. If the array does not include the id, then it will be `nil`.
2. You attempt to unwrap `flightIdx`.
3. If that succeeds, then `index` contains the index in the array of the id. You then remove that element of the array and therefore remove the flight id from the array.
4. If the unwrapping of `flightIdx` failed, you add the `flightId` to the array.

Now change the body of the view to:

```
Button {
  toggleHighlight()
} label: {
  Image(systemName: "highlighter")
}
.tint(Color.yellow)
```

You create a button showing the highlighter symbol. The button's action calls the `toggleHighlight` method to add or remove the flight id from the array as appropriate. You apply the `tint(_:)` modifier to change the button away from the default swipe action gray color.

With the new view complete, return to **FlightList.swift**. Add the following code after the `listRowBackground(_:)` modifier on the `List`.

```
// 1
.swipeActions(edge: .leading) {
  // 2
  HighlightActionView(flightId: flight.id, highlightedIds:
$highlightedIds)
}
```

The `.swipeActions(edge:allowsFullSwipe:content:)` modifier tells SwiftUI to attach a swipe action to the row.

1. The edge parameter tells SwiftUI where to place the swipe actions. You can specify separate additional actions for the other edge by adding multiple modifiers or multiple views within one modifier limited only by the available space in the row. Here you attach to the leading edge.

2. The closure provides the view to display when the user performs the swipe action. You use the new view you created earlier in this section.

Run the app and navigate to the **Flight Status** view. Now drag your finger across a row, starting at the leading edge and continuing across the row. You'll see the action triggers. This action occurs because the `allowsFullSwipe` property we didn't specify defaults to `true`. When true, this property states the first action will be triggered when the user does a full swipe. The user can also swipe to reveal the actions and then tap it. Also, note the swipe action does not interfere with the navigation link if you tap on the row.

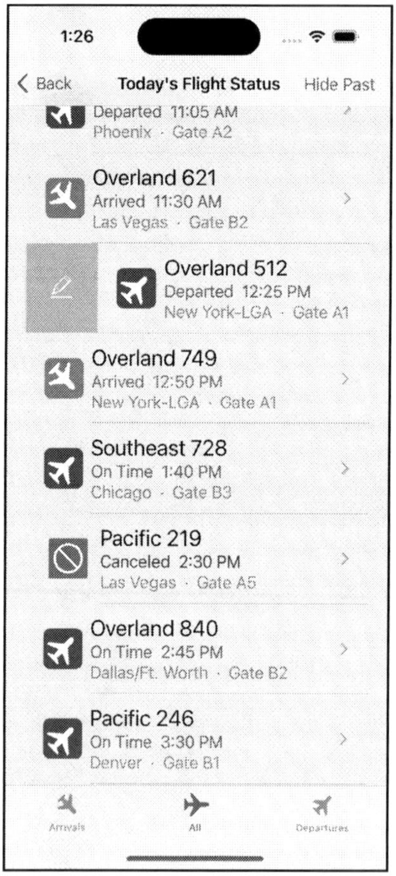

Showing swipe action on a list row

Swipe actions provide a way to give the user faster access to a few common or essential actions related to items in the list. Next, you'll let the user request a manual refresh of the items in the list.

Pull to Refresh

You've probably noticed the static nature of this app. When the user displays a view, the contents never change. Some of that comes from using static test data in the app instead of a web service that would provide updates and changes as flight conditions change. Even when updates are automatic, it's common to provide a way for the user to request a data refresh in an app. The most common of these methods comes to SwiftUI 3.0 with the `refreshable(action:)` view modifier. In this section, you'll add refresh support to the app.

Open **FlightStatusBoard.swift**. First, you'll add an indicator to let the user know when SwiftUI last updated the list. Add the following code before the body of the view:

```
func lastUpdateString(_ date: Date) -> String {
  let dateF = DateFormatter()
  dateF.timeStyle = .short
  dateF.dateFormat = .none
  return "Last updated: \(dateF.string(from: Date()))"
}
```

This method formats a string with a short description of the time from the passed date. Now you'll use it to show the user the last update time for the list. Embed the current `TabView` inside a new `VStack`. Now add the following code to the top of the `VStack`:

```
Text(lastUpdateString(Date()))
  .font(.footnote)
```

This new Text view shows the date of the last update of the view above the tabs. Now run the app and go to the **Flight Status** view. You'll see the new last updated time above the lists.

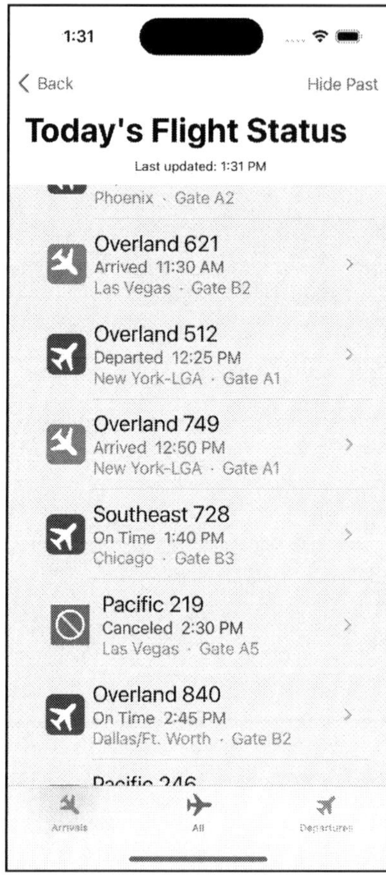

Adding last update time to Flight Status

To reinforce the new update more clearly, you'll also update each flight shown with the difference between the current time and when the flight lands or departs. Open **FlightRow.swift** and add a new property after the existing `timeFormatter` property:

```
var relativeTimeFormatter: RelativeDateTimeFormatter {
  let rdf = RelativeDateTimeFormatter()
  rdf.unitsStyle = .abbreviated
  return rdf
}
```

Now change the first `HStack` that shows the flight status and time to read:

```
Text(flight.flightStatus)
Text(flight.localTime, formatter: timeFormatter)
Text("(") +
Text(flight.localTime, formatter: relativeTimeFormatter) +
Text(")")
```

You added three new lines of code to show the relative time inside parenthesis.

Run the app. Each row shows the relative time between now and the landing or departure of the flight. It automatically uses the correct language for future and past events.

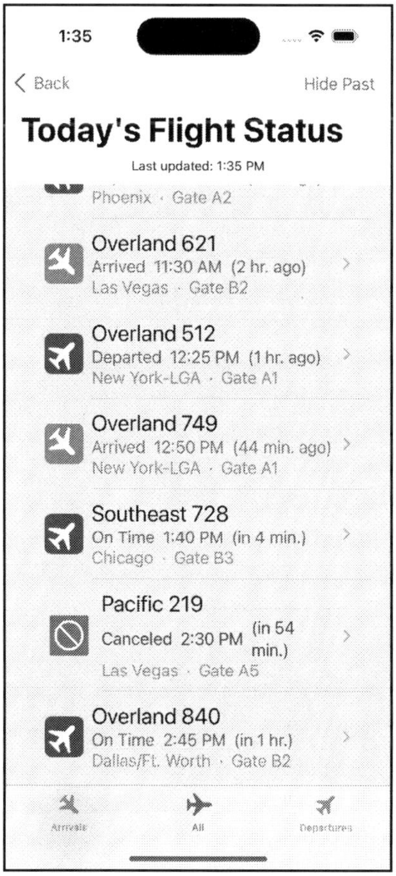

Relative time

Go back to **FlightStatusBoard.swift** and add the `@State` modifier to the `flights` property so it reads:

```
@State var flights: [FlightInformation]
```

This change tells SwiftUI the `flights` property within the view can change so that SwiftUI knows to update the view when it changes. Now you can use the `refreshable(action:)` to do that. Before the `navigationTitle(_:)` modifier, add the following code:

```
// 1
.refreshable {
  // 2
  await flights = FlightData.refreshFlights()
}
```

That's all that you need to do. Here's what each line does in more detail:

1. Adding the `refreshable(action:)` modifier to a view marks it as refreshable for SwiftUI. The modified control will provide the UI for a user-requested refresh. In this case, you've added the standard pull-down action for lists, and the list will display a progress indicator during the refresh. When the user requests a refresh, SwiftUI executes the action provided in the closure.

2. Note the `await` keyword. FlightData.refreshFlights() simulates an API call that takes time (in this case, three seconds) to complete. Using the new async/await support in Swift 5.5 lets this take place without freezing your app. SwiftUI shows the progress indicator during the duration of the awaited action. In this case, the information about the flights will not change since it's still test data, but it will refresh the views you changed `flights` to a `@State` property.

Run the app and navigate to the **Flight Status** view. Note the current time and wait until the time changes to a minute. Go to the top of the list and then pull down and release. You'll see the progress indicator appear for three seconds, and then the view updates to reflect the new time you requested a refresh.

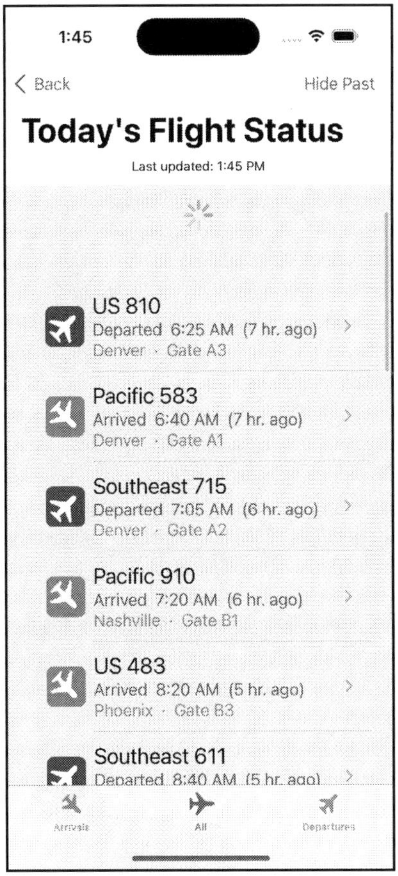

Refreshing a view

While manually updating views is helpful, there are times you want to refresh a view automatically. Previously SwiftUI provided updates based on data changes, but there's a new view that lets you update a view on a time-based schedule. You'll explore it in the next section.

Updating Views for Time

SwiftUI views usually update in response to changes in state. That state change can be driven by user action, such as tapping a button, or through external changes powered buy notifications, Combine or async events. In most cases, you don't need to change a view unless the underlying data changes. Sometimes you'll want to update a view due to the passage of time to provide a better user experience.

In the last section, you added a relative time to each flight. As the clock moves forward, these times should change, but right now, that does not happen unless the user requests a refresh. It would be better to have a way to tell a SwiftUI view to update on a regular schedule. SwiftUI 3.0 added the new `TimelineView` that will update according to a schedule that you provide. In this section, you'll use the `TimelineView` to ensure you always show up-to-date information.

To begin, wrap the `VStack` inside a new `TimelineView`. Use the following definition for the view:

```
TimelineView(.periodic(from: .now, by: 60.0)) { context in
```

You've now wrapped the existing `VStack` inside a `TimelineView`.

You provide a type that implements the `TimelineSchedule` protocol to the `TimelineView` to tell SwiftUI when to update the view. This one uses the `periodic(from:by:)` static type that begins at a specified time and repeats after a given number of seconds. Here, you start now and repeat every sixty seconds. SwiftUI passes a `TimelineView.Context` property to the closure that contains a `date` property with the date from the schedule that triggered the update. It also contains a `cadence` property that provides guidelines on how often the view updates occur.

Update the text showing the last update to:

```
Text(lastUpdateString(context.date))
```

The app now shows the `date` property of the `context` as the last update. In this case, that's the same as the current date when the view updates, meaning you would still get the correct results without this change. Run the app and navigate to the **Flight Status** view. Wait one minute, and you'll see the times update automatically when the minute changes.

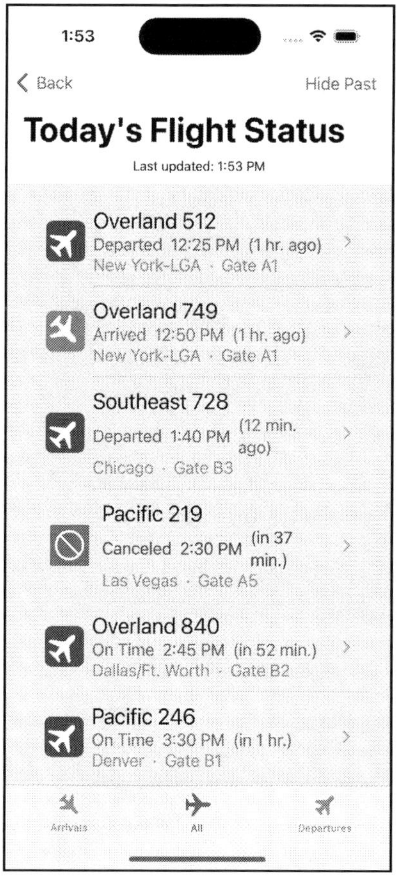

Updating view with TimelineView

Notice that if you run the app just before the minute changes, it will be inaccurate until that sixty seconds pass. You could adjust your start time to the zero-second point of the next minute, but since the need to change at the start of each minute is so common, SwiftUI provides another static type just for it. Change the `TimelineView` to:

```
TimelineView(.everyMinute) { context in
```

Run the app, and you'll see the view updates as soon as the minute changes instead of waiting for sixty seconds to pass. The app will continue to update at the start of each minute.

There's also an `explicit(_:)` type to specify exact times to update the view. In this app, you could pass a list of the times for each flight if you did not want to show the relative time for each arrival and departure to update after a flight arrives or departs. You can use `.animation` to update the view at a specified frequency. As the name implies, this type will be helpful for animations. It also allows easy pause of updates. For more complex scenarios, you can implement a custom type that implements the `TimelineSchedule` protocol.

A `TimelineView` adds the ability to update a view based on the current state. If the state changes, then the view will still update to reflect the change.

Now that you've looked at time-based updates, you'll examine what you may find the most helpful new feature of lists in SwiftUI 3.0 — better search support.

Searchable Lists

In **Chapter 14: "Lists"**, you briefly used the new search abilities added in SwiftUI 3.0 to add a search field when creating the Search Flights view. In this section, you'll explore the search abilities in greater depth.

In the previous section, you saw that adding search uses a new `searchable(text:placement:prompt:)` modifier. Open **SearchFlights.swift**, and you'll see the line of code `.searchable(text: $city)` near the end of the view. This code binds the `city` property of the view to the search text box SwiftUI shows at the top. The `matchingFlights` computed property used for the list contents filters the list of cities whenever the `city` property is not empty.

Currently, you need to know the cities that are options and spell out the city when searching. Using the more advanced SwiftUI search features, you can provide suggestions for search terms. You'll use the `citiesContaining(_:)` static method on the `FlightData` class that provides an alphabetized list of all the cities. If you pass an empty string to the method, you will get a list of all cities. If you provide text, the list will only show cities that include the passed text in the city name. Replace the current `searchable(text:placement:prompt:)` modifier with the following:

```
// 1
.searchable(text: $city) {
  // 2
  ForEach(FlightData.citiesContaining(city), id: \.self) { city
in
    // 3
    Text(city).searchCompletion(city)
  }
}
```

You provide search suggestions in the closure to the `searchable(text:placement:prompt:)` modifier. Defining the search suggestions requires two steps.

1. You use the `citiesContaining(_:)` method on `FlightData` to get an array of cities that contain the current text of the `city` property. You iterate through the results using a `ForEach` loop.

2. The contents of the closure of the `ForEach` loop provide two things. First, you state the text to show the user. In this case, you show only the city name, but you could provide more text to help the user better understand the suggestion. You add the `searchCompletion(_:)` modifier to the `Text` to indicate the search text when the user chooses this suggestion.

Run the app. As soon as you tap in the search field, you'll see an alphabetical list of all cities appear. If you tap one, then it will immediately fill the search field with that city. If you type a few letters, then the list of suggestions reduces to only the cities containing the text. Again tapping a suggestion fills the search field with the complete text.

Added search suggestions

Search suggestions mainly help the user when there are many options, such as in a real airport app with hundreds of possible destinations. It can also reduce frustration due to misspellings or not knowing the complete name for search terms. Suggestions can also help the situations where your search relies on an external API or data source. In the next section, you will look at more ways to deal with searches outside the phone.

Submitting Searches

For searches that have a high cost — whether in terms of time, fees, or limitations — you may only want to search when the user finishes entering their search parameter. SwiftUI supports this process using the `onSubmit(of:_:)` method. You'll make changes to the search view that better works with an API call. First, change the definition of the `flightData` property in the view to:

```
@State var flightData: [FlightInformation]
```

Adding the `@State` property wrapper makes this value changeable within the view. You still can pass in an initial value, but now can change the property when simulating API calls. Now change the `matchingFlights` computed property to:

```
var matchingFlights: [FlightInformation] {
  var matchingFlights = flightData

  if directionFilter != .none {
    matchingFlights = matchingFlights.filter {
      $0.direction == directionFilter
    }
  }
  return matchingFlights
}
```

This change removes the search filter this view previously provided. You'll replace this by calling a simulated API call when the user submits the search. Add the following code after the `searchable(text:placement:prompt:)` method:

```
// 1
.onSubmit(of: .search) {
  // 2
  Task {
    // 3
    await flightData = FlightData.searchFlightsForCity(city)
  }
}
```

Here's how this code implements submission for the search field:

1. The `onSubmit(of:_:)` modifier tells SwiftUI you want to do something after the user submits a view inside the view it modifies. Passing the `.search` identifier to the `of` parameter tells SwiftUI to respond only when the user submits a search field.

2. The closure for the `onSubmit(of:_:)` modifier is not asynchronous. In most cases, you'll use an async call for search when going to an external source since you will wait for a reply and have no control over how long the response may take. To use an async method from a synchronous method, you wrap the async inside a `Task` structure.

3. The `searchFlightsForCity(_:)` method simulates calling an external API and will take three seconds to complete.

Run the app. You'll see the suggestions still appear, but the search doesn't execute until you tap a search suggestion or tap enter on the keyboard.

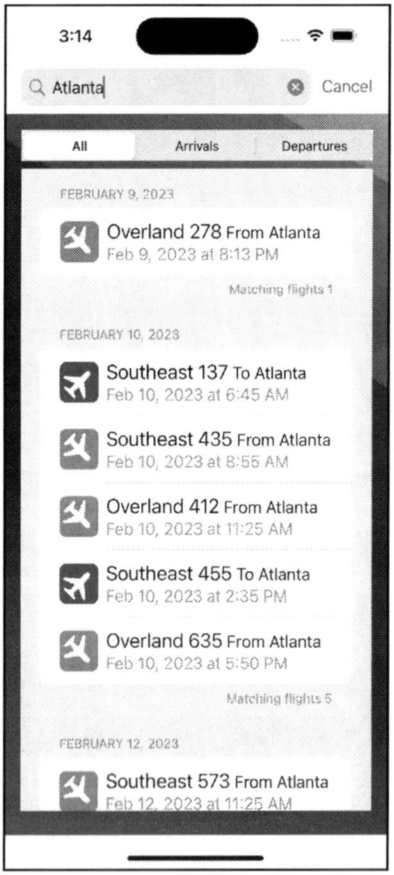

Asynchronous search

You'll notice there's no indication that the search takes place. You'll add an indicator that shows while the search runs to let the user know something is going on.

Add a new boolean property at the end of the existing properties:

```
@State private var runningSearch = false
```

Now update the `onSubmit(of:_:)` method to:

```
.onSubmit(of: .search) {
  Task {
    runningSearch = true
    await flightData = FlightData.searchFlightsForCity(city)
    runningSearch = false
  }
}
```

You've added code to set the `runningSearch` property to true before starting the search and then to false when the search completes. Now you'll add a progress indicator when `runningSearch` is true. Add the following code to the end of the list (before the `listStyle(_:)` modifier):

```
.overlay(
  Group {
    if runningSearch {
      VStack {
        Text("Searching...")
        ProgressView()
          .progressViewStyle(CircularProgressViewStyle())
          .tint(.black)
      }
      .frame(maxWidth: .infinity, maxHeight: .infinity)
      .background(.gray)
      .opacity(0.8)
    }
  }
)
```

Rerun the app, and you'll now see the overlay shows during the search, letting the user know the app is working.

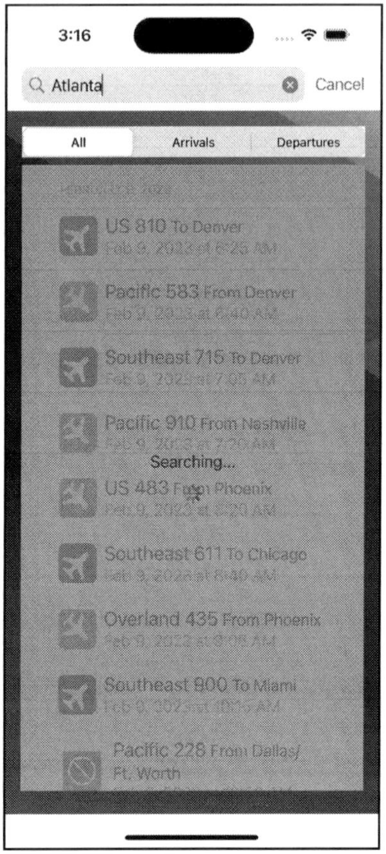

Search in progress overlay

Adding Final Search Touches

You've probably noticed when you dismiss the search that the results still reflect the last completed search. There's no current method you can use to know when the search cancels, but you can get the same effect by monitoring the `city` property that holds the search text. Add the following code after the `onSubmit(of:_:)` modifier:

```
.onChange(of: city) { newText in
  if newText.isEmpty {
    Task {
      runningSearch = true
      await flightData = FlightData.searchFlightsForCity(city)
      runningSearch = false
```

```
      }
    }
  }
```

This code tells SwiftUI you want to execute a code block when the `city` property changes. The new value of `city` will be passed into the block. You check this value, and if empty, you execute the search passing the empty string, which returns all flights from the API.

You've also been using the generic prompt that just reads **Search**. You can provide an optional prompt that tells the user more about the search. Change the `searchable(text:placement:prompt:suggestions:)` modifier to:

```
.searchable(text: $city, prompt: "City Name") {
```

Run the app, and you'll now see the new prompt text.

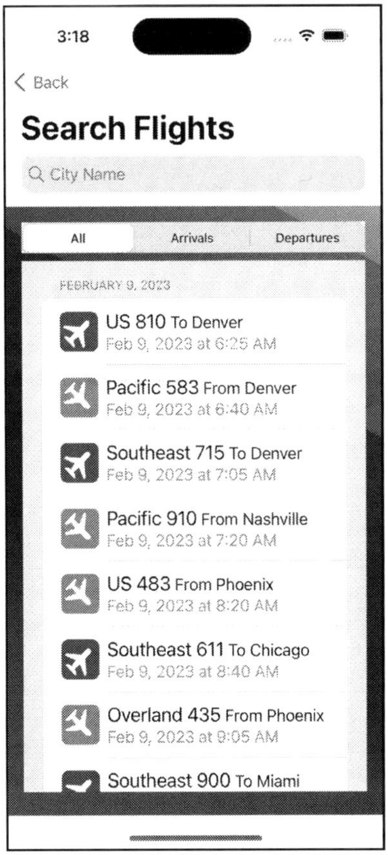

New search prompt

Key Points

- Swipe actions allow the user quick access to a few common or important actions on items in a list. You can place them at either the leading or trailing edge or both.
- The `refreshable(action:)` modifier provides a way to support user initialed data refreshes. It uses the Swift 5.5 async/await framework.
- A `TimelineView` provides a way to update a few on a defined schedule.
- The `searchable(text:placement:prompt:)` modifier provides a framework to support search.
- You can provide suggestions for search terms in the closure of the `searchable(text:placement:prompt:)`.
- You can either update search results immediately or update them when submitted using the `onSubmit(of:_:)` modifier.
- The `onChange(of:)` modifier lets you act when the value of a property changes. Here you used it to refresh the list to the full results when the search term cleared.

Where to Go From Here?

- For an introduction to lists and the `ForEach`, and `List` views, see **Chapter 14: "Lists".
- For more about `async/await`, see the WWDC 2021 video Meet async/await in Swift (https://developer.apple.com/videos/play/wwdc2021/10132/) and async/await in SwiftUI (https://www.kodeco.com/25013447-async-await-in-swiftui).
- For more about allowing the user to modify and change lists and implementing drag and drop, see Drag and Drop Editable Lists: Tutorial for SwiftUI (https://www.kodeco.com/22408716-drag-and-drop-editable-lists-tutorial-for-swiftui).
- To learn more about the new SwiftUI 3.0 features, view the WWDC 2021 video What's new in SwiftUI (https://developer.apple.com/videos/play/wwdc2021/10018/).

Chapter 16: Grids

By Bill Morefield

Stacks and lists provide a one-dimensional arrangement of views. Many data types better fit a two-dimensional grid. A significant weakness of the initial release of SwiftUI was the lack of a native collection view. This view is so helpful that the first two editions of this book included a chapter that walked through creating a reusable grid view. SwiftUI 2.0 added a native grid view. In this chapter, you'll examine and work with grid layouts in SwiftUI.

Building Grids the Original Way

The containers in the original SwiftUI version that let you organize other views shared one thing in common; they work in one dimension. Stacks create horizontal or vertical layouts. Lists create vertical layouts.

You can think of a grid as a set of stacks in one direction wrapped within a stack of the other direction. Because of this, you can create more complex layouts, even with these limitations. You just had to do the work yourself.

Open the starter project and run the app. Earlier editions of this book changed the buttons on the welcome screen to a grid, but that no longer fits the new split navigation design (see **Chapter 13: Navigation**). Instead, you'll explore grids using the new awards view added to the starter project. Tap the **Your Awards** button to look at the initial view.

Initial Awards View

This view displays the user's current awards and those the user hasn't received yet. Currently, the list shows as a vertical stack using a `LazyVStack`. Open **AwardsView.swift** under the **AwardsView** group and change the closure of the `ScrollView` to:

```
// 1
VStack {
  // 2
  HStack {
    NavigationLink(value: awardArray[0]) {
      AwardCardView(award: awardArray[0])
        .foregroundColor(.black)
        .frame(width: 150, height: 220)
    }
    Spacer()
    NavigationLink(value: awardArray[1]) {
      AwardCardView(award: awardArray[1])
        .foregroundColor(.black)
        .frame(width: 150, height: 220)
    }
  }
  // 3
  HStack {
    AwardCardView(award: awardArray[2])
      .foregroundColor(.black)
      .frame(width: 150, height: 220)
    Spacer()
    AwardCardView(award: awardArray[3])
      .foregroundColor(.black)
      .frame(width: 150, height: 220)
  }
  Spacer()
}
.font(.title)
.foregroundColor(.white)
.padding()
```

That's a lot of code but focus on the layout views. You'll see that you're building a grid by nesting two `HStacks` inside a `VStack` to show the first four awards.

1. Using an initial `VStack` creates the overall vertical layout of the grid.
2. This `HStack` builds the first row of the grid. It contains two of the button views separated by a `Spacer`. Note that you manually reference the elements of the `awardArray` array.
3. This `HStack` makes the second row of the grid.

Run the app, and you'll see the grid.

Manual Grid

Before the `Grid` view, this technique was the only way to build a grid. You can see how complex it becomes as you add more items to the grid. This book's first edition included a chapter on creating a generic reusable grid that you can consult if you want to see more of this technique. With the second release of SwiftUI, there's now a native and more flexible way to build a grid. You'll change the app to use that in the next section.

Creating a Fixed Column Grid

The native SwiftUI grid view builds on the existing `LazyHStack` and `LazyVStack` views. As with stacks, there are two grids, one that grows horizontally and one that grows vertically. Change the contents of the `ScrollView` in **AwardsView.swift** to:

```
// 1
LazyVGrid(
  // 2
  columns:
    [
      // 3
      GridItem(.fixed(160)),
      GridItem(.fixed(160))
    ],
  // 4
  spacing: 15
) {
  // 5
  ForEach(awardArray) { award in
    // 6
    NavigationLink(value: award) {
      AwardCardView(award: award)
        .foregroundColor(.black)
        // 7
        .frame(width: 150, height: 220)
    }
  }
}
.navigationDestination(for: AwardInformation.self) { award in
  AwardDetails(award: award)
}
.font(.title)
.foregroundColor(.white)
.padding()
```

Notice this doesn't look that different from the initial `LazyVStack`. That's the beauty of SwiftUI's approach to a grid building off these one-dimensional views. To change the stack to a grid:

1. The `LazyVGrid` builds a set of rows that extend vertically. The corresponding `LazyHGrid` creates a list of rows that extends horizontally.
2. The new parameter for a vertical grid is `columns`. You pass it an array of `GridItem` elements that describes the columns.
3. The array consists of a set of `GridItem`s to describe the grid. Here you use the simplest type of `GridItem`, a fixed column you set 160 points wide.
4. You also pass the optional `spacing` parameter. This parameter sets the space between the rows of the grid. It does not affect the distance between the columns of the grid.
5. Thanks to the grid, you can use `ForEach` to iterate over the `awardArray` array as it separates the elements of the grid in the closure to the `LazyVGrid` from the layout defined using the `columns` parameter to the `LazyVGrid`.
6. Each item in the grid will be a `NavigationLink`, which sets the value to the `award` passed to the closure. It displays the `AwardCardView` for the award as the view.
7. You set the width of the award car to 150 points wide. This width leaves a ten-point margin compared to the 160 points column width you set in step two.

You'll see no need to manually layout each row as you did when building a grid with nested view stacks. You also no longer need to worry about keeping the grid lined up. SwiftUI takes care of those concerns for you.

> **Note**: The code for this chapter uses a vertical grid where you define columns. Everything you'll do also works in a horizontal grid, except you would pass `rows` and pass in descriptions of the grid's rows. The `GridItem` works for both.

Run the app, tap **. You'll see the grid looks similar to that from the last section, but with smaller columns since you set them to 160 points.

Awards Shown in a Grid

Now that's you've seen the basics of grids, you'll look at more flexible layouts in the next section.

Building Flexible Grids

You often want more flexibility when creating columns (or rows) in your grid. A **flexible** element in a grid lets you specify a range of sizes to constrain a grid while setting the number of rows or columns in the grid. Placing the column information inside the view clutters its view, especially when your grid becomes more complicated. Instead, you will specify the column structure using a property. Add the following code after the `awardArray` property:

```
var awardColumns: [GridItem] {
  [
    GridItem(.flexible(minimum: 150)),
    GridItem(.flexible(minimum: 150))
  ]
}
```

This property returns an array of two `GridItem` elements. Since the array contains two elements, SwiftUI will create a grid of two columns.

A `flexible` grid item lets you specify the minimum or maximum width for each column or both. Here you only define the minimum at 150 points. Since you don't specify a maximum width, the column can grow as large as needed to handle the content.

Now change the `LazyVGrid` to:

```
LazyVGrid(columns: awardColumns, spacing: 15) {
  ForEach(awardArray) { award in
    NavigationLink(value: award) {
      AwardCardView(award: award)
        .foregroundColor(.black)
        .frame(width: 150, height: 220)
    }
  }
}
```

Make sure not to lose any of the modifiers attached to the `LazyVGrid`. You replaced the inline columns with the `awardColumns` property you previously added to define the grid columns. Run the app and tap **Your Awards**. The awards still show in a two-column grid but are no longer bound to a fixed size.

Flexible grid screen

In the next section, you'll learn how this more flexible layout works with different sized views.

Interacting Between Views and Columns

It's worth exploring how the container view's size interacts with the settings for columns in the grid. Change the frame for the award card to:

```
.frame(width: 190, height: 220)
```

What effect do you think this will have on the grid? When you have an answer, run the app and go to the awards grid to see if you're correct:

Flexible grid with larger cards

Since you specified a flexible column with only a minimum size constraint, the column expands to accommodate the larger card width. On many phones, such as the one in the screenshot, this larger size will not accommodate the full width of two cards. The cards will overlap as SwiftUI tries to fit the views.

What happens if you specify a maximum column width that's smaller than this new card width?

Change the `awardColumns` property to:

```
var awardColumns: [GridItem] {
  [
    GridItem(.flexible(minimum: 100, maximum: 150)),
    GridItem(.flexible(minimum: 100, maximum: 150))
  ]
}
```

Change the frame for the award card to:

```
.frame(width: 160, height: 240)
```

> **Note**: The preview canvas will not always notice when you change a property. If you see no change, then hide and restore the canvas to force it to refresh.

You specified a maximum width of the column of 150 points and changed the card to a width of 160 points. Run the app and view the awards to see the effect.

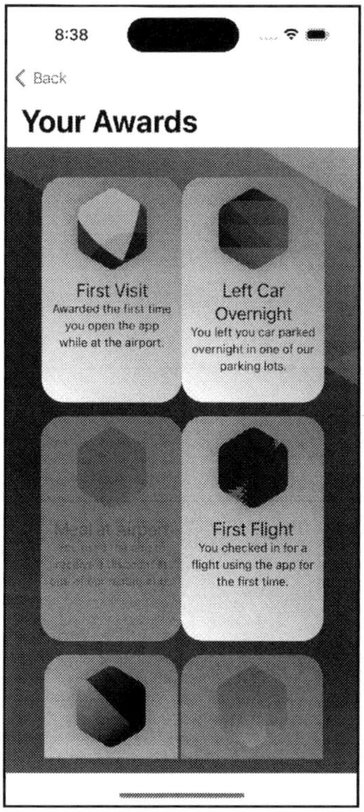

Award grid still clipped

As you might expect, your grid remains a bit cramped. The key to notice is that column does not clip or constrain its containing view to the column. Here, both columns take the full 160 points width despite the column having a maximum width of 150 points.

How do you size views to a grid without running into these concerns? Since you're specifying a size for the grid columns, you might ask whether you need to specify a frame for the card at all. The answer is no, and not doing so lets SwiftUI adjust the size to fit the containing view better.

Removing the subview's frame modifier creates a side effect that you no longer control the dimensions. You can use a different modifier to keep the shape of the view. Change the `awardColumns` property to:

```
var awardColumns: [GridItem] {
  [
    GridItem(.flexible(minimum: 100, maximum: 160)),
    GridItem(.flexible(minimum: 100, maximum: 160))
  ]
}
```

Now change the award card view to:

```
AwardCardView(award: award)
  .foregroundColor(.black)
  .aspectRatio(0.67, contentMode: .fit)
```

You now have a much more flexible view that can adjust to different widths while maintaining its overall shape. You use `aspectRatio(_:contentMode:)` to set the desired ratio of the view's width to its height — in this case, a view three points tall for every 2 points wide — and tell SwiftUI to fit the view to this aspect ratio.

Award grid screen with size by aspect ratio

A limitation on a flexible grid item can be a boon or a problem depending on your app. Run the app and go to the award view. Now rotate the device or simulator, and you'll see that the grid still only shows two columns with lots of space on both sides. You would see the same result when viewing the grid on a larger device such as an iPad.

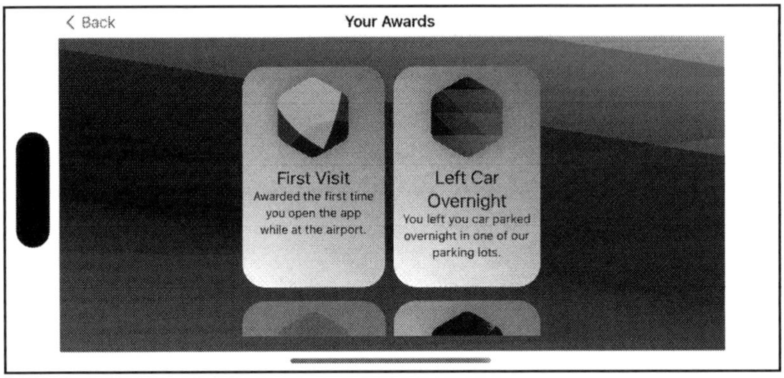

Award grid in horizontal mode with 2 columns

Specifying the number of columns for a grid means you're stuck with that number of columns, even when you have space for more. You could increase the number of columns, which would crowd the views on a smaller display or require you to create different arrays for different devices.

To fill this need, SwiftUI provides a third type of `GridItem`, the adaptive column.

Building Adaptive Grids

The adaptive grid provides you the most flexible option. Using one tells SwiftUI to fill the space with as many columns or rows as fit in the grid. Change the `awardColumns` property to:

```
var awardColumns: [GridItem] {
  [GridItem(.adaptive(minimum: 150, maximum: 170))]
}
```

Run the app, and you'll see the view looks much the same as your flexible grid. Even though you specified only a single column, the adaptive grid elements fill the phone width with two columns.

Adaptive award grid in vertical

The new behavior becomes more noticeable when you rotate the phone device. Rotate the device or simulator, and you'll see the columns fill the display's width instead of limiting it to two columns. SwiftUI chooses a size that allows equal-width columns to maximize the number of columns for the enclosing view. For most current iPhones, that's four columns.

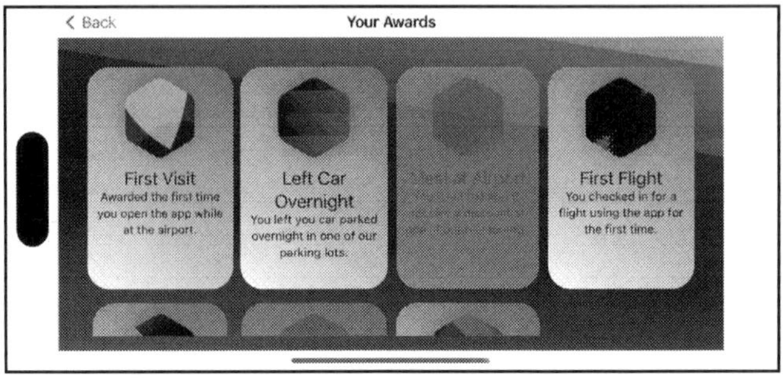

Adaptive award grid in horizontal

Change your device to the 11 inch iPad simulator. Run the app, and you'll see the grid again adapts to use the extra space and shows four columns for the grid.

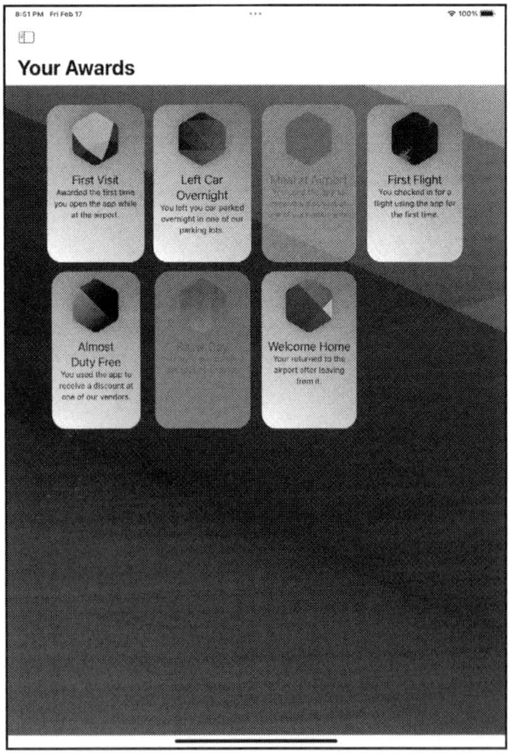

Award grid iPad

The three types of columns each meet a different use case. The `fixed` and `flexible` types allow you to specify a column you want to appear, either limited to a specific size or range of sizes. The adaptive column fills the available space with as many items as will fit in the view. When you need more flexibility, you can mix and combine the different column types in any way necessary for your app.

You'll need to choose the layout depending the data you're showing. For this app, you want to show all the awards in a compact space and will use the adaptive type.

In **Chapter 14: Lists**, you saw that you group data into sections to help users understand what they're viewing. Grids offer this same ability and you'll add that in the next section.

Using Sections in Grids

To help the user understand what award they have yet to receive, you'll divide the awarded and not-awarded items into separate sections. Add two new computed properties below the `awardArray` property:

```
var activeAwards: [AwardInformation] {
  awardArray.filter { $0.awarded }
}

var inactiveAwards: [AwardInformation] {
  awardArray.filter { !$0.awarded }
}
```

These filter the array of all awards to awarded awards and not awarded awards, respectively. Since each section will display the same information, you'll extract the grid into a separate view. At the top of the file after `import SwiftUI`, add the following code:

```
struct AwardGrid: View {
  // 1
  var title: String
  var awards: [AwardInformation]

  var body: some View {
    // 2
    Section(
      // 3
      header: Text(title)
        .frame(maxWidth: .infinity)
        .font(.title)
        .foregroundColor(.white)
```

```
        .background(
          .ultraThinMaterial,
          in: RoundedRectangle(cornerRadius: 10)
        )
    ) {
      // 4
      ForEach(awards) { award in
        NavigationLink(value: award) {
          AwardCardView(award: award)
            .foregroundColor(.black)
            .aspectRatio(0.67, contentMode: .fit)
        }
      }
    }
  }
}
```

You've extracted the view from the grid. Here are the changes you've made:

1. These properties contain the section's title and an array of awards to show in this grid.
2. The `Section` view creates a group within the grid whose contents will be the closure of the view.
3. You pass a view as the `header` property. SwiftUI displays this view at the top of the grid. You could also specify a `footer` view in the same way. In this case, you show the title passed to the view.
4. The closure consists of the loop to show the passed awards you've used throughout this chapter. This closure is the same as the view you had at the end of the previous section.

Now you can use the extracted view in the grid. Change the `LazyVGrid` to:

```
LazyVGrid(columns: awardColumns) {
  AwardGrid(
    title: "Awarded",
    awards: activeAwards
  )
  AwardGrid(
    title: "Not Awarded",
    awards: inactiveAwards
  )
}
```

You'll see you now have two sections, the first showing awards the user has received and the second those the user has not yet received.

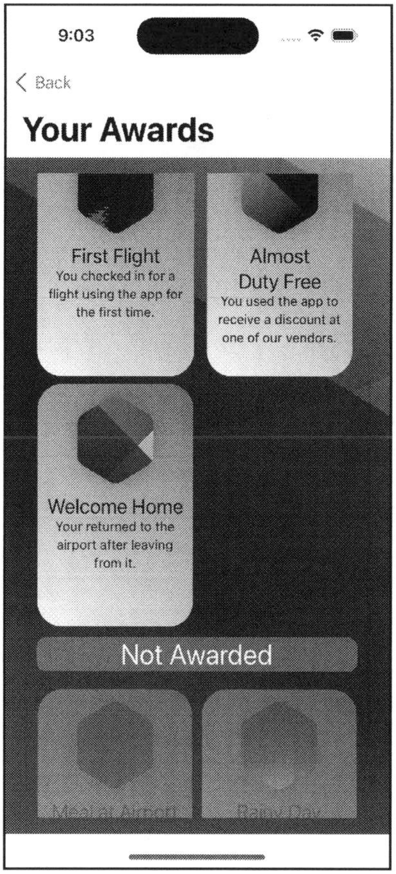

Award grid with sections

Key Points

- SwiftUI provides two types of lazy loaded grids: `LazyVGrid`, which grows vertically and `LazyHGrid`, which grows horizontally.
- You define columns for a `LazyVGrid` and rows for a `LazyHGrid`. A `GridItem` describes the layout for both types of grids.
- A `fixed` grid item lets you specify an exact size for a column or row.
- A `flexible` grid item lets you specify a range of sizes while still defining the number of columns.
- An `adaptive` grid item can adapt to fill the available space in a view using provided size limits.
- You can mix different types of grid items in the same row or column.

Where to Go From Here?

To see more about what creating grids required in the initial release of SwiftUI, see **Chapter 20: Complex Interfaces** in the **second edition** of this book.

These Apple's 2020 WWDC videos offer Apple's introduction to grids in SwiftUI:

- **Stacks, Grids, and Outlines in SwiftUI**, https://apple.co/3LgFNE9
- **What's new in SwiftUI**, https://apple.co/3mQ6VQI

To look beyond linear displays, check out:

- **Creating a Mind-Map UI in SwiftUI** tutorial, https://www.kodeco.com/7705231-creating-a-mind-map-ui-in-swiftui.

Chapter 17: Sheets & Alert Views

By Bill Morefield

In a previous chapter, you learned how to use standard navigation to switch between views in your app. However, sometimes you need to display a view to the user only under certain conditions. You'll often use these views when showing important messages that interrupt the user's current context and need direct feedback or response before continuing.

Presenting a view outside the navigation stack lets the user's focus remain on the task they initiated. It also provides a way for your app to provide critical information or request essential feedback.

Starting in SwiftUI 3.0, Apple appears to be shifting the approach to these views. The initial versions of SwiftUI focused on the type of view to display. The changes to APIs and new modifiers in SwiftUI 3.0 indicate a shift to the view's purpose instead of the kind of view. In this chapter, you'll expand the app to use different conditional views in SwiftUI. Along the way, you'll explore the new SwiftUI 3.0 APIs to prepare your app for the future.

Displaying a Modal Sheet

In **Chapter 14: "Lists"**, you built a view allowing users to search for a flight. One element deferred then was the ability to view details or interact with those results. You're going to add that ability in this chapter. Modal sheets help focus the user's attention on the current view without building through the overall navigation hierarchy. The modal sheet slides a new view over the current view.

SwiftUI provides two ways to display a modal, both based on a `@State` variable in the view. The first method uses a `Bool` variable that you set to `true` when the sheet should display. The second uses an optional state variable that shows the modal when the variable becomes non-nil. You'll use the `Bool` method for this modal.

All modals provide these two options; you'll see an example using an optional variable later in this chapter.

Open the starter project for this chapter; you'll find the project from the end of the last chapter. Go to **SearchResultRow.swift**. Notice the view for each row now resides in a separate view. That will make the code changes for this chapter a little cleaner. Add the following new variable after `flight`:

```
@State private var isPresented = false
```

This line defines a `@State` variable that indicates when to show the modal sheet. Change the view to:

```
// 1
Button(
  action: {
    isPresented.toggle()
  }, label: {
    FlightSearchSummary(flight: flight)
})
// 2
.sheet(
  // 3
  isPresented: $isPresented,
  // 4
  onDismiss: {
    print("Modal dismissed. State now: \(isPresented)")
  },
  // 5
  content: {
    FlightSearchDetails(flight: flight)
  }
)
```

Here's what the elements of the modal sheet do:

1. You wrap the row inside a button. The action of the button toggles the state variable.
2. To tell SwiftUI you want to display a modal, you call `sheet(isPresented:onDismiss:content:)`. This call must attach to an element of the view.
3. Here, you pass the `isPresented` state variable you added earlier, which tells SwiftUI to show the modal when the variable becomes `true`. When the user dismisses the modal, SwiftUI sets the state back to `false`.
4. The optional `onDismiss:` is a closure you can use to execute code after the user dismisses the modal. In an app, this would be the place to react to user actions in the modal. You print a message to the console and show that the state variable's value is now `false`.
5. You provide the view to show on the modal sheet as the closure for `sheet(isPresented:onDismiss:content:)`. For the moment, you'll use the existing `FlightSearchDetails(flight:)` view.

Build and run, navigate to **Search Flights** and tap any row to see the modal appear. Swipe down on the modal to dismiss it. In the debug console, you'll see the state variable become `false` after you dismiss the modal:

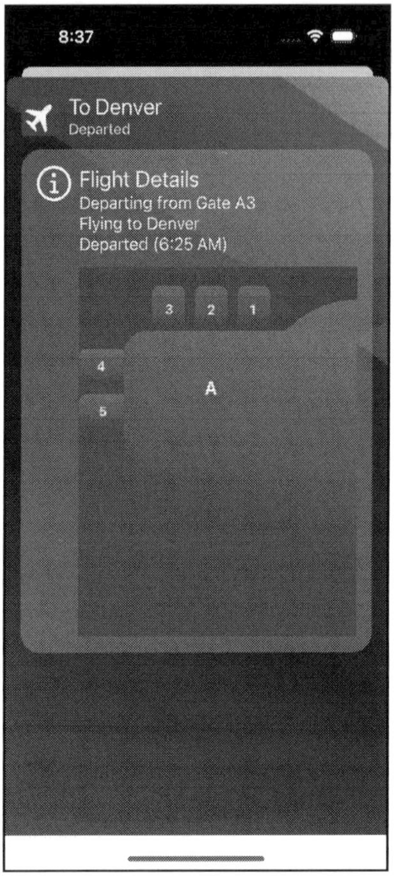

Initial Modal view

Programmatically Dismissing a Modal

You probably noticed that the navigation view disappears in the modal sheet. That's because a modal sheet takes over the whole screen and no longer wraps the view in any existing navigation view. You can even create a new navigation stack on the modal.

You should also add a button to dismiss the modal, primarily since some platforms, such as Catalyst apps, don't support the swipe gesture.

Open **FlightSearchDetails.swift**. First, you'll need a variable to store a `@Binding` to the passed display flag from `FlightRow`. So add the following code after `flight`:

```
@Binding var showModal: Bool
```

You'll add the button next to the header at the top of the modal. Replace `FlightDetailHeader` with this:

```
HStack {
  FlightDetailHeader(flight: flight)
  Spacer()
  Button("Close") {
    showModal = false
  }
}
```

You are adding a **Button** with an action to set the binding to false. Assigning `false` to the `Binding` programmatically from the button tells SwiftUI to close the modal.

Since the view now expects the caller to pass in the state, you need to update the preview to do so. Change the preview to read:

```
FlightSearchDetails(
  flight: FlightData.generateTestFlight(date: Date()),
  showModal: .constant(true)
)
.environmentObject(AppEnvironment())
```

Using `.constant(true)` provides a pseudo-state that lets the preview behave correctly.

Now, go back to **SearchResultRow.swift** and change the call to `FlightSearchDetails` in the closure to `sheet(isPresented:onDismiss:content:)` to pass in the state:

```
FlightSearchDetails(
  flight: flight,
  showModal: $isPresented
)
```

Run the app and tapping on a row to bring up the modal with a **Close** button in the navigation bar. Tapping the button dismisses the modal, just as swiping down does.

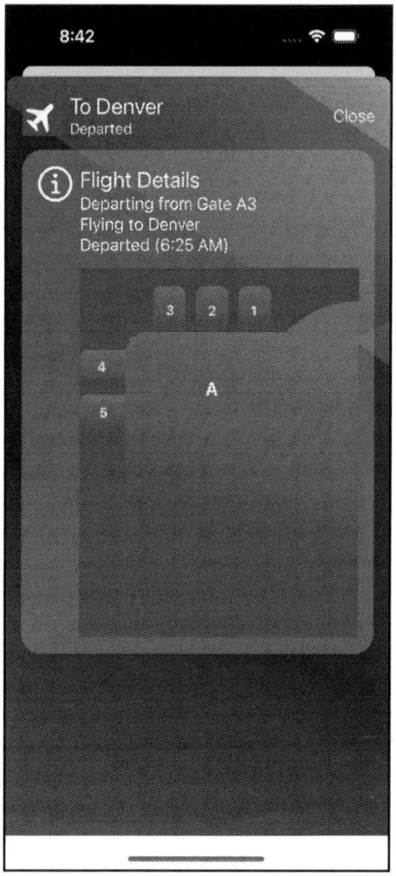

Modal done

SwiftUI allows you to prevent the swipe action from dismissing a view. Go back to **FlightSearchDetails.swift**. Add the following code to the end of the `ZStack` view (after the `onAppear(perform:)` modifier):

```
.interactiveDismissDisabled()
```

Note that you're applying this to the view being shown in the sheet and not to the sheet modifier in **SearchResultRow.swift**. Run the app, and you'll see swiping down no longer dismisses the view. The view does dip, but it returns to the displayed state when you stop your gesture. You now have to use the **Close** button to dismiss the modal.

A modal is an excellent choice when your view needs the user's full attention. Used correctly, they help your user focus on relevant information and improve the app experience. However, modal views interrupt the app experience, so you should use them sparingly. SwiftUI provides three more specialized modal views to help you capture the user's attention: alerts, action sheets and popovers. You'll learn how to use each of those now.

Showing Partial Sheets

The sheets that you've created all take up the entire view. Starting with SwiftUI 4.0, you can create sheets occupying only part of the view. Open **FlightDetails.swift** and add the following state variable after `flight`:

```
@State private var showTerminalInfo = false
```

As in the previous sections, you'll use this state variable to show a sheet when the user taps the view. Add the following code to the end of the `ZStack` before the `onAppear(perform:)` modifier:

```
.onTapGesture {
  showTerminalInfo.toggle()
}
```

This code toggles the `showTerminalInfo` when the user taps the `ZStack`. Now add the following modifier after the `onTapGesture(count:perform:)` you just added:

```
.sheet(isPresented: $showTerminalInfo) {
  Group {
    if flight.gate.hasPrefix("A") {
      TerminalAView()
    } else {
      TerminalBView()
    }
  }
  .presentationDetents([.medium, .large])
}
```

The `presentationDetents(_:)` modifier allows you to provide a set of sizes you want to support for the sheet. Run the app, tap on **Flight Status** and select any flight. Now tap on the terminal map, and the new sheet appears, but it only covers half of the view.

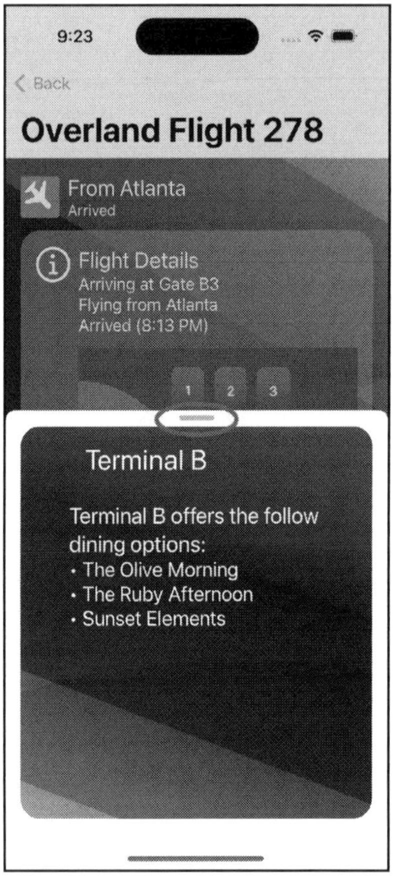

Medium sized sheet covering half of the view with grab bar circled

Notice the grab bar circled in the screenshot. You can drag this to change between the sizes or tap it to cycle through the possible sizes. SwiftUI will always start with the smallest provided option and cycle through them in increasing amounts of the screen covered. The `large` option allows the sheet to fill the entire view. Besides swiping the view to dismiss it, you can tap anywhere outside a view smaller than `large`. You can also specify values as a fraction of the view size using the `.fraction(_:)` modifier. You can use the `height(_:)` modifier to specify a sheet height in points.

Large sheet covers the full view

Change the orientation to landscape. Now the sheet fills the entire view and will be challenging to swipe away. In some situations, a smaller sheet can still fill the whole view, such as an iPhone in landscape orientation. You should ensure the user can dismiss the view even if swiping down and tapping outside the sheet aren't options.

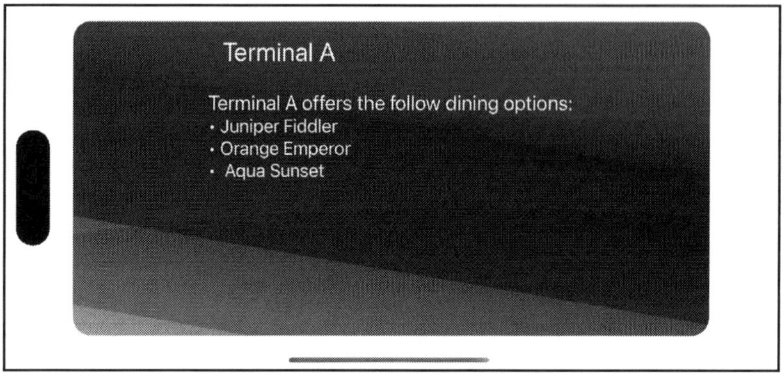

Medium sheet in landscape view

Open **TerminalAView.swift** and add the following presentation property above the body of the view:

```
@Environment(\.dismiss) var dismiss
```

The `@Environment(\.dismiss)` value provides access to the `DismissAction` for the current view. Calling this method will pop the current view from a `NavigationStack` or programmatically dismiss a modal view like a sheet.

Add the following method to the end of the `ZStack`:

```
.onTapGesture {
  dismiss()
}
```

When the user taps the view, you call the `dismiss()` instance to dismiss the sheet. Note that you do this in the view you want to dismiss, in this case the `TerminalAView` view shown in the sheet. Make the same modification to **TerminalBView.swift**.

Run the app, tap on **Flight Status** and select any flight. Now tap on the terminal map, and the sheet appears. Change the orientation to landscape. Tap on the sheet itself, and the `dismiss()` method clears it.

Sometimes you have information you need the user to pay close attention to. In the next section, you'll see how to create views for that purpose.

Creating an Alert

Alerts bring something important to the user's attention, such as a warning about a problem or a request to confirm an action that could have severe consequences.

You're going to add a button to help the user rebook a canceled flight. It won't do anything yet — you're waiting on the back-end team to finish that API. Instead, you'll display an alert telling the user to contact the airline much as you would in the event of an error.

Open **FlightSearchDetails.swift**. You can set alerts, like modals, to display based on a state variable. Add the following state after the `showModal` Binding:

```
@State private var rebookAlert = false
```

Add the following after the `FlightDetailHeader` `HStack` and before `FlightInfoPanel`:

```
// 1
if flight.status == .canceled {
  // 2
  Button("Rebook Flight") {
    rebookAlert = true
  }
  // 3
  .alert(isPresented: $rebookAlert) {
    // 4
    Alert(
      title: Text("Contact Your Airline"),
      message:
        Text("We cannot rebook this flight. Please contact") +
        Text(" the airline to reschedule this flight.")
      )
    )
  }
}
```

Here's what you're doing with this code:

1. The view only displays when the flight status is `.canceled`.
2. The button sets `rebookAlert` to `true` when tapped.

3. You call `alert(isPresented:content:)` on the `Button` to create the alert. You also pass in the state variable telling SwiftUI to show the alert when `rebookAlert` becomes `true`.

4. In the closure, `Alert` defines the alert message to show the user. You don't provide any additional buttons, so the user's only option is to tap the **OK** button to dismiss the alert.

Build and run. Tap **Search Flights**, then tap any **Canceled** flight (look for Pacific 228 From Dallas/Ft. Worth). Tap on the **Rebook Flight** button, and the alert appears.

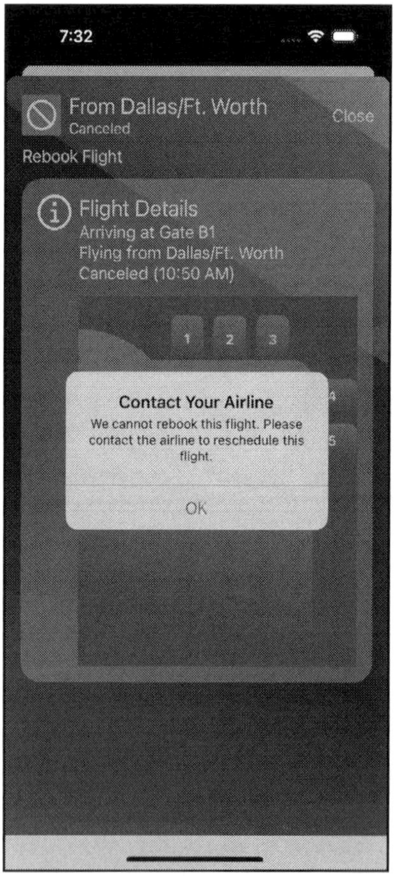

Alert Dialog

Starting with SwiftUI 4.0, you can add `TextField` and `SecureText` views in addition to `Buttons`. In the case of re-booking a flight, you might want to allow the user to enter a contact phone number. Add two new state properties after `rebookFlight`:

```
// 1
.alert("Contact Your Airline", isPresented: $rebookAlert) {
  // 2
  Button("OK", role: .cancel) {
  }
  // 3
} message: {
  Text("We cannot rebook this flight. Please contact") +
  Text(" the airline to reschedule this flight.")
}
```

This code should all look familiar since you're doing the same task with different formatting.

1. The alert now includes the title inside the `alert(_:isPresented:actions:message:)` modifier. You still use the same `rebookAlert` boolean to trigger the alert when it becomes `true`.

2. Instead of an `Alert` struct, you provide a button for the options you want to show in the alert. Note the use of the `.cancel` role on the button. You tell SwiftUI this button cancels the alert, and therefore SwiftUI will automatically set `rebookAlert` to `false`. If you do not include a cancel button, then SwiftUI will add one for you.

3. You now pass the message for the alert as an additional parameter of the `alert(_:isPresented:actions:message:)` modifier.

Run the app, and you'll see this works as the previous version did. Unless you need backward compatibility, you should use this new format for alerts.

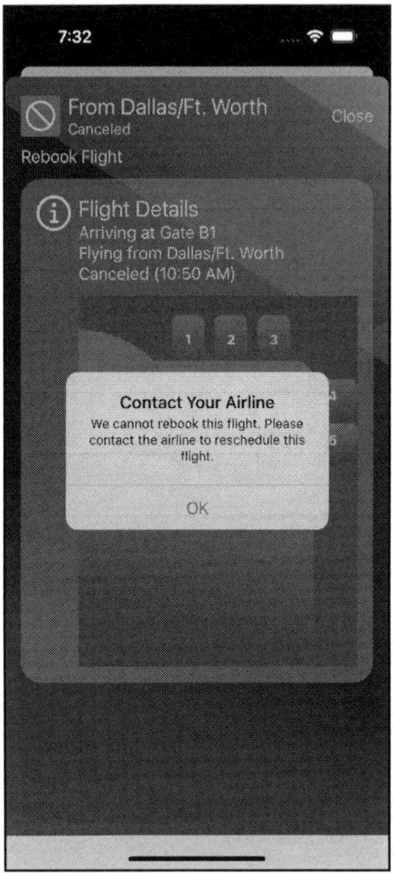

Alert Dialog

Notice in this new API, you add a `Button` to the view. Starting with SwiftUI 4.0, you can also add `TextField` and `SecureText` views. In the case of re-booking a flight you might want to allow the user to enter a contact phone number. Add two new state properties after `rebookFlight`:

```
@State private var phone = ""
@State private var password = ""
```

Now replace the current `.alert` modifier with:

```
.alert("Contact Your Airline", isPresented: $rebookAlert) {
  TextField("Phone", text: $phone)
  SecureField("Password", text: $password)
```

```
    Button("Call Me") {
    }
    Button("Cancel", role: .cancel) {
    }
} message: {
    Text("We cannot rebook this flight.") +
    Text("Please enter your phone number and confirm your
password.")
}
```

You add the `TextField` and `SecureField` to allow users to enter values into the state variables you added. The `SecureField` view doesn't show the user's text and is useful when the user needs to enter sensitive information. Notice you also have two buttons, one to confirm and one to cancel the action. The closure of both remains empty but could contain any code and use the values from the `TextField` and `SecureField`.

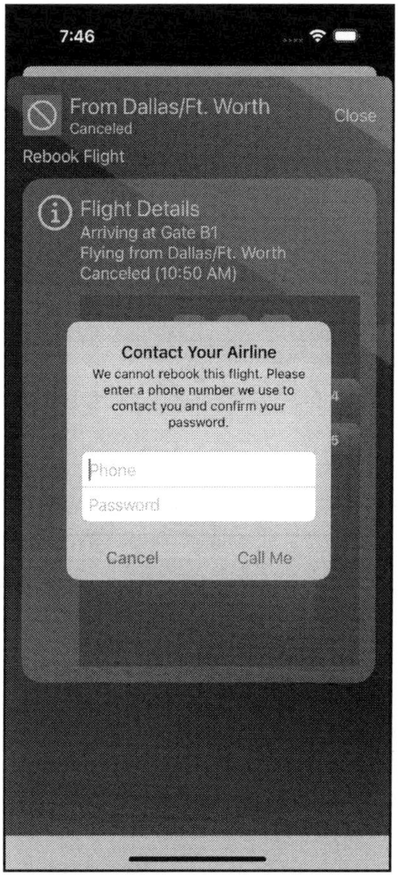

Alert with TextField and SecureField

You can also trigger the alert with a modal sheet by binding it to an optional variable. In the next section, you'll use this method and implement an action sheet.

Adding an Action Sheet

An action sheet should appear in response to a user action, and the user should expect it to appear. For example, you might want to use an action sheet to confirm an action or let the user select between multiple options.

In this section, you'll add a button to let the user check in for a flight and display an action sheet to confirm the request.

Instead of the `Bool` state variable you used for the modal sheet and alert, you'll use an optional variable. You can use either of these methods with any of the modal views in this chapter.

There are a couple of reasons you would use this method over the `Bool` variable. First, none of the views discussed in this chapter can be used more than once for a view. If you try to attach two alert views, for example, only the last one will work. You can attach an alert, modal, or action sheet to sibling views in a view hierarchy, but you can't attach more than one to the same view (or to a child and parent). Using an optional enum, you can use just one, but specify which content you need to display based on the enum.

The second reason to use the optional variable over the `Bool` is to access the variable's data inside the closure. The variable must implement the `Identifiable` protocol discussed in the previous chapter.

You'll create a simple struct that implements `Identifiable` for this action sheet for your next step. Create a new Swift file named **CheckInInfo.swift** under the **Models** group. Change the contents of the file to read:

```
import SwiftUI

struct CheckInInfo: Identifiable {
  let id = UUID()
  let airline: String
  let flight: String
}
```

Here, you define a new `CheckInInfo` struct that implements `Identifiable`. To meet the protocol requirements, you include an `id` member of type `UUID`.

By definition, a `UUID` provides a unique value and implements the `Hashable` protocol, making it a perfect unique identifier when you don't care about anything other than it is unique. You then add `airline` and `flight` strings, which you'll provide when creating the message.

Now, inside `FlightSearchDetails`, add the following state variable to hold `CheckInInfo` after the `password` property:

```
@State private var checkInFlight: CheckInInfo?
```

Next, add the following code after the `if flight.status == .canceled {` condition that wraps the alert you added in the last section and before the `FlightInfoPanel` view:

```
// 1
if flight.isCheckInAvailable {
  Button("Check In for Flight") {
    // 2
    checkInFlight =
      CheckInInfo(
        airline: flight.airline,
        flight: flight.number
      )
  }
  // 3
  .actionSheet(item: $checkInFlight) { checkIn in
    // 4
    ActionSheet(
      title: Text("Check In"),
      message: Text("Check in for \(checkIn.airline)" +
        "Flight \(checkIn.flight)"),
      // 5
      buttons: [
        // 6
        .cancel(Text("Not Now")),
        // 7
        .destructive(Text("Reschedule")) {
          print("Reschedule flight.")
        },
        // 8
        .default(Text("Check In")) {
          print(
            "Check-in for \(checkIn.airline) \(checkIn.flight)."
          )
        }
      ]
    )
  }
}
```

This code looks similar to the code you used to create the modal sheet and the alert, except that the action sheet uses the optional variable in place of a `Bool`. It also needs information about the buttons to display.

Here's how the new elements in this code work:

1. You only show this button for a flight that has check-in available
2. The button's action sets `checkInFlight` to a new instance of `CheckInInfo` that stores the airline and number of the flight.
3. As you did with the alert, you add the action sheet to the button. Here, you use `actionSheet(item:content:)` and not `actionSheet(isPresented:content:)`. You pass the optional variable as the `item:` parameter. When the variable becomes non-nil, as it will when the button's action executes, SwiftUI displays the action sheet. When `checkInFlight` becomes non-nil, it triggers the same way the alert's Boolean binding told SwiftUI to display the alert. You also provide a parameter inside the closure. When SwiftUI shows the sheet, this parameter contains the contents of the bindable value that triggered it.
4. You create an action sheet using the passed-in variable's contents to display the name of the flight to the user on the action sheet.
5. An alert provides a limited ability to gather feedback. You have many more options with an action sheet, though all must be buttons. Here, you pass an array of `ActionSheet.Button` items to the `buttons:` parameter for those you wish to use in this action sheet.
6. The first defined button is the **Cancel** button. Providing a cancel button gives the user a clear back-out option. When the user selects this option, you do nothing, so you don't need any parameter other than text for this button.
7. You use the `.destructive` type method for actions that have destructive or dangerous results. SwiftUI displays the text in red to highlight this action's seriousness. `action:` provides code that SwiftUI executes when the user selects this option. Here, you display a message to the debug console.
8. The default button for the action sheet uses `action:` to display a message to the debug console.

Build and run. Select **Search Flights** and then tap any outgoing flight that's not yet departed. Next, tap the **Check In for Flight** button, and the action sheet will appear.

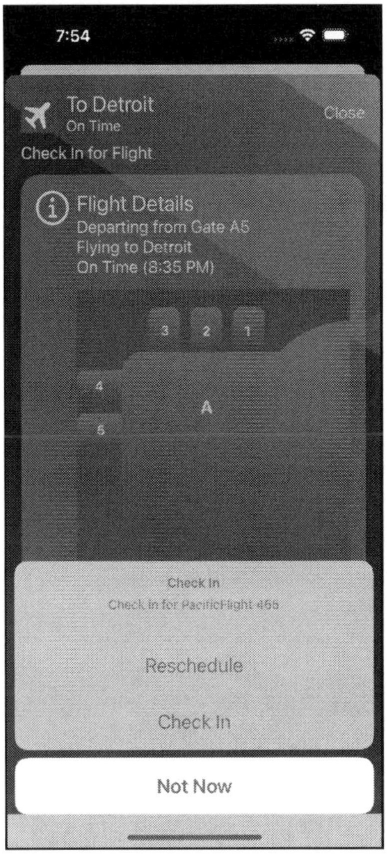

Action Sheet

If you tap the **Not Now** button, nothing happens since you provided no `action` parameter. Tap either the **Check In** or **Reschedule** button, and the appropriate message appears in the console window in the debug area of Xcode.

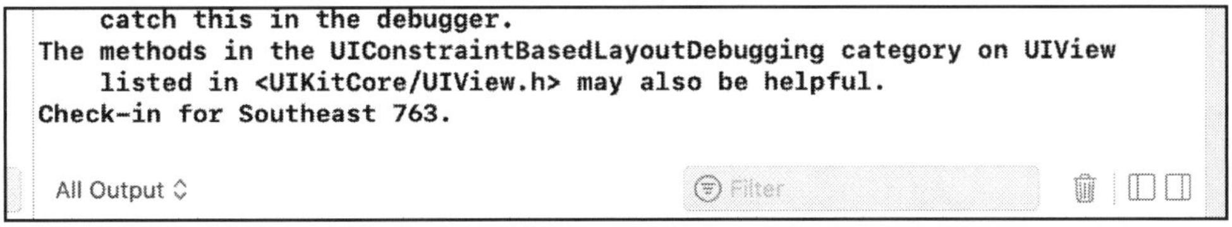

Action sheet console

In the next section, you'll explore how the new SwiftUI 3.0 alert can work in place on an action sheet.

Using Alerts as Action Sheets

The new SwiftUI alert format allows it to work very similarly to an action sheet. In this section, you'll implement the action sheet from the last section using the new alert.

Add the following state to the top of the view after `checkInFlight`:

```
@State private var showCheckIn = false
```

The new alert API doesn't work with an optional parameter. Instead, you must use a boolean to indicate when SwiftUI should show the alert. Replace the current button labeled **Check In for Flight** with:

```
Button("Check In for Flight") {
  checkInFlight =
    CheckInInfo(
      airline: flight.airline,
      flight: flight.number
    )
  showCheckIn = true
}
```

The only change is that you set the `showCheckIn` true and set the `checkInFlight` property with information on the flight. Last, replace the current `.actionSheet` modifier (starting at comment three in the earlier code) with:

```
// 1
.alert(
  "Check In",
  isPresented: $showCheckIn,
  presenting: checkInFlight
) { checkIn in
  // 2
  Button("Check In") {
    print(
      "Check-in for \(checkIn.airline) \(checkIn.flight)."
    )
  }
  // 3
  Button("Reschedule", role: .destructive) {
    print("Reschedule flight.")
  }
  // 4
  Button("Not Now", role: .cancel) { }
  // 5
} message: { checkIn in
  Text("Check in for \(checkIn.airline)" +
```

```
    "Flight \(checkIn.flight)")
}
```

You're replacing the action sheet with the impressive length `alert(_:isPresented:presenting:actions:message:)` modifier. As when you changed the alert to this new API earlier, you'll see a lot of the same code. Here's what's changed:

1. The title moves to a parameter to the `alert(_:isPresented:presenting:actions:message:)` modifier. You pass the new boolean to the `isPresented` parameter to indicate when SwiftUI should show the view. The new `presenting` parameter provides the function that binding to a nullable object previously did. You pass in the `checkInFlight` property here to make it available inside the alert as `flight`.

2. You provide each option for the alert as a standard SwiftUI button view. You can use `flight` to access the object passed in through the `presenting` parameter.

3. You mark this button as `destructive`, letting SwiftUI format it appropriately.

4. As earlier, if you do not provide a button with the `cancel` role, SwiftUI will add one for you. Notice that you do not need to set `showCheckIn` to `false` as the framework assumes this from the button role.

5. The message for the action sheet before now becomes another parameter. The object passed to the `presenting` parameter is available inside the closure as with the alert.

Run the app, and you'll see the new alert doing the same role as the action sheet, though with a different user interface. Which to use will likely depend on the purpose of the view in your app. Notice that adding a third button causes this new button layout. You can combine `TextField` and `SecureField` views with multiple buttons.

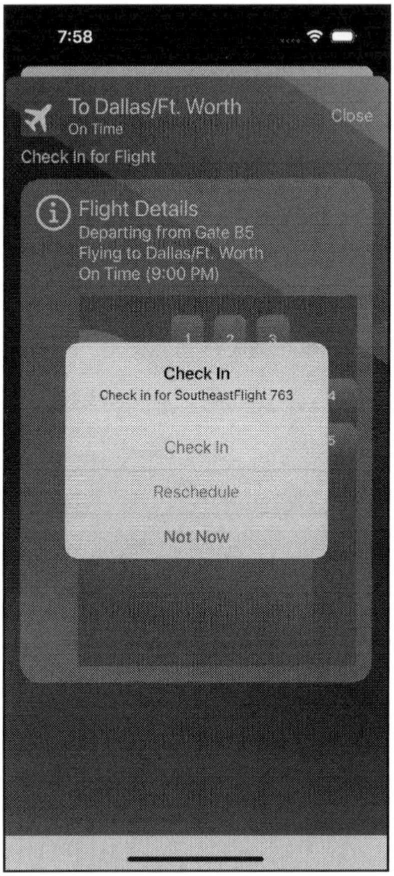

Action Sheet using Alert

As of SwiftUI 3.0, SwiftUI has not deprecated the `actionSheet` modifier as with the older `Alert` struct, but as you can see, the new alert API can handle both roles. In keeping with the new focus on purpose, SwiftUI 3.0 also added another new modifier named `confirmationDialog`. It works almost exactly like the alert dialog you just implemented. You can replace `alert` with `confirmationDialog` in the code you did in this section, and it will work with no other changes.

Replace the `alert` modifier with `confirmationDialog` and run the app.

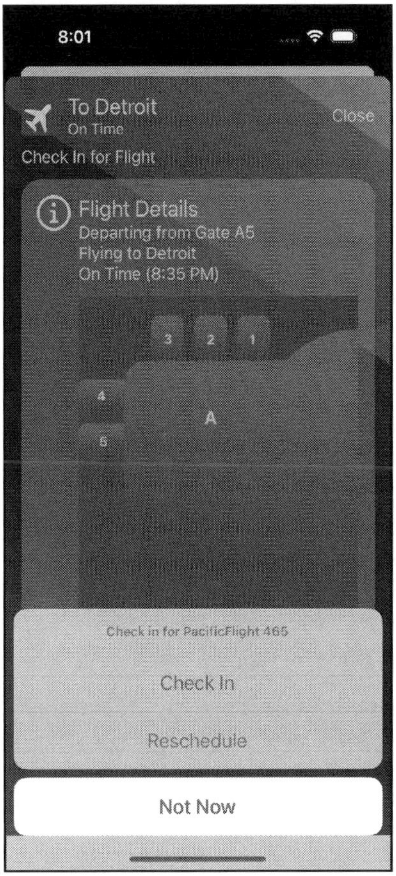

Confirmation Dialog

You'll notice the result looks much like the original action sheet. The `confirmationDialog` displays as an action sheet on smaller devices and a popover on larger devices. You can also specify a popover directly in SwiftUI. In the next section, you'll add a popover to the app.

Showing a Popover

Like the action sheet, you usually display a popover in response to a user action. Popovers work best on larger-screen devices, such as iPads and Macs. On devices with smaller screens, a full-screen view, such as a modal sheet, better serves your needs. If the screen is too tiny, SwiftUI renders the popover as a modal sheet instead.

Your popover should save state changes immediately when it displays because the user can dismiss it at any time.

Creating and using a popover works much like an alert and action sheet. You can use a Boolean or optional type as with the other modal views. You'll use a `Bool` state variable for this example, as you did with the alert.

You'll add a button that shows a popover with a new `FlightTimeHistory` view that shows the flight's recent history in a list.

Start by opening **FlightSearchDetails.swift** and adding the code for a new state variable after the existing ones:

```
@State private var showFlightHistory = false
```

Now, add the following code after the conditional wrapping the alert you added in the last section and before the `FlightInfoPanel` view:

```
Button("On-Time History") {
  showFlightHistory.toggle()
}
.popover(
  isPresented: $showFlightHistory,
  arrowEdge: .top) {
  FlightTimeHistory(flight: flight)
}
```

Again the code resembles that used to add an alert to the view earlier. Alerts, action sheets and popovers all perform the same task — providing a temporary view to inform the user and, optionally, gather a response. As a result, they operate in similar ways. `popover(isPresented:attachmentAnchor:arrowEdge:content:)` watches the `showFlightHistory` state variable to see if it should show the pop-up.

Popovers traditionally show an arrow pointing back to the control that initiated the popover. `arrowEdge` defines the arrow's direction. Here, `.top` instructs the popover sheet to display an arrow at its top, pointing to the control. That means the popover shows below the control.

Otherwise, this code should look familiar. The button toggles `showFlightHistory` to `true`, causing the popover to appear.

If you're using an iPhone device or simulator, you'll see that the popover renders as a modal due to the screen size. Also, note how the new modal nicely stacks on top of your existing modal. You can dismiss it by swiping down, as you would with a modal view.

Popover phone

Now, build and run with an iPad target and follow the same steps to display the on-time history. You'll now see the view render as a pop-up that includes a small arrow back to the button you tapped to display the view. You can dismiss it by tapping anywhere outside the view. Note that it also is stacked nicely on top of the existing modal view.

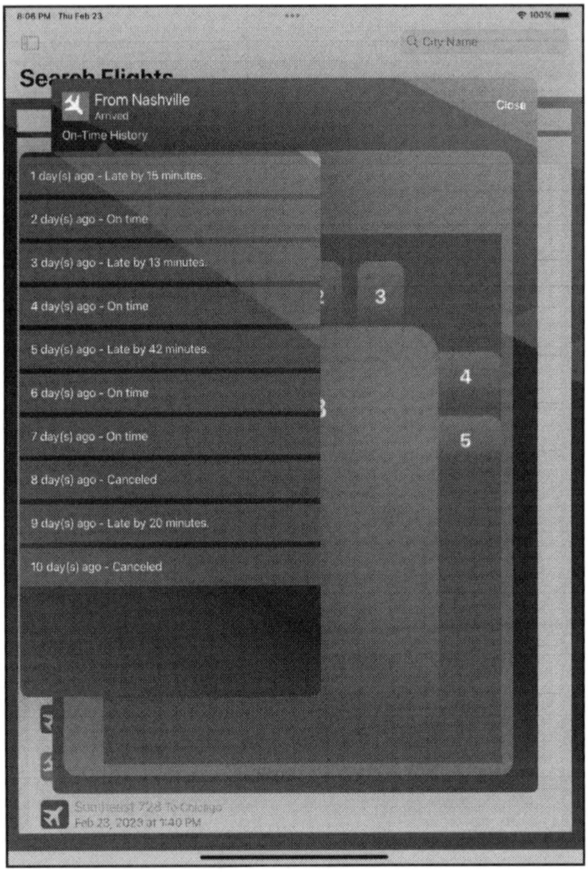

Popover display

> **Note**: The beta for iOS 16.4 introduced a new `.presentationCompactAdaptation(_:)` modifier which tells SwiftUI to show a popover on iPhone as well. As with most SwiftUI model views, you apply it to the view being shown.

As you can see, Apple provides you with different options to grab the users' attention. Try using the best choice for each situation and scenario.

Key Points

- Modal sheets display on top of the view. You can use either a `Bool` state variable or an optional state variable that implements the `Identifiable` protocol to tell SwiftUI to display them.
- The alert, action sheet and popover views provide a standard way to display information to the user and collect feedback.
- Alerts generally display information about unexpected situations or confirm actions that have severe consequences.
- Action sheets and popovers display in response to a user action. You use action sheets for smaller screen devices and popovers on larger screens.
- SwiftUI 3.0 introduced a new API for alerts that provides more flexibility and an easier to understand implementation.
- SwiftUI 4.0 introduced the ability to set and constrain the size of sheets other than full screen.
- SwiftUI 4.0 allows you to prompt the user for text input when showing an alert.

Where to Go From Here?

As mentioned in a previous chapter, the first stop for information on user interfaces on Apple platforms should be the Human Interface Guidelines on Modality for the appropriate SwiftUI operating systems:

- iOS: https://developer.apple.com/design/human-interface-guidelines/ios/app-architecture/modality/
- macOS: https://developer.apple.com/design/human-interface-guidelines/macos/app-architecture/modality/
- watchOS: https://developer.apple.com/design/human-interface-guidelines/watchos/app-architecture/modal-sheets/

The **WWDC 2019 SwiftUI Essentials** video also provides an overview of Apple's guidelines on how views, navigation and lists fit together:

- https://developer.apple.com/videos/play/wwdc2019/216/

Section V: UI Extensions

Push forward your SwiftUI knowledge with complex interfaces implementing animations and custom graphics.

Chapter 18: Drawing & Custom Graphics

By Bill Morefield

As you develop more complex apps, you'll need more flexibility or flash than the built-in controls SwiftUI offers. Fortunately, SwiftUI provides a rich library to assist in creating graphics within your app.

Graphics convey information to the user efficiently and understandably; for instance, you can augment text that takes time to read and understand with graphics that summarize the same information.

In this chapter, you'll add graphics to a view and create a chart to display the history of how well a flight has been on time in the past. In doing this, you'll explore the graphics SwiftUI has to offer.

Using Shapes

To start, open the starter project for this chapter. Run the project, and you'll see the in-progress app for a small airport continued from **Chapter 17: Sheets & Alert Views**.

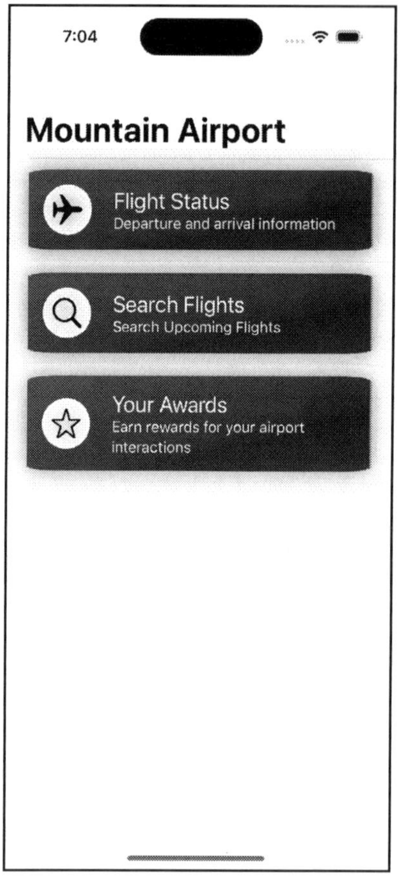

Starter project

Tap **Flight Status**, then tap the name of any flight. You'll see information on the flight, including a map of the terminal where the flight arrives or departs. In the previous chapter, you added information about the restaurants in each terminal that appears when you tap the terminal map. In this section, you'll explore shapes in SwiftUI by adding `Shape` views to represent restaurants and shops in each terminal.

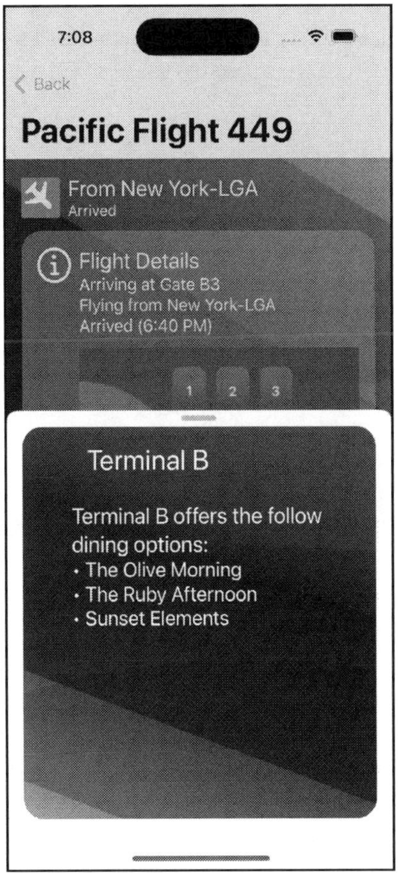

Sheet showing restaurants

Open **TerminalMapView.swift** under the **FlightDetails** group. The view contains a conditional statement to show the correct terminal map. You wrap the conditional inside a `Group` to apply modifiers to the result of the conditional statement.

Add the following code after the `Group`:

```
.overlay {
  Rectangle()
}
```

The views inside the closure to an `overlay(alignment:content:)` modifier will appear on top of the modified view. In this case, the `Rectangle` view is a `Shape` that shows a rectangle that SwiftUI will overlay on top of the image. Using an overlay aligns the view's axes. A `ZStack` also does this, but the `overlay` matches the size of the overlaid view to the original view.

Run the app, tap **Flight Status** and then any flight. Now, you'll see the terminal map covered in black.

The terminal map now covered in black

A Shape is a type of view, but it's still a view and shares many defaults of other views. It will fill the available space, hence why the Rectangle fills the entire view and covers the terminal map. Change the Rectangle to:

```
Rectangle()
  .frame(width: 100, height: 100)
  .foregroundColor(.red)
```

Since the shape is a view, you can apply the same modifiers you would to any other view to change and adapt the shape to your needs. The frame(width:height:alignment:) sets the width and height for the Rectangle. You then set the foregroundColor(_:) to red.

Run the app, tap **Flight Status** and then any flight. You'll now see a red rectangle in the middle of the terminal.

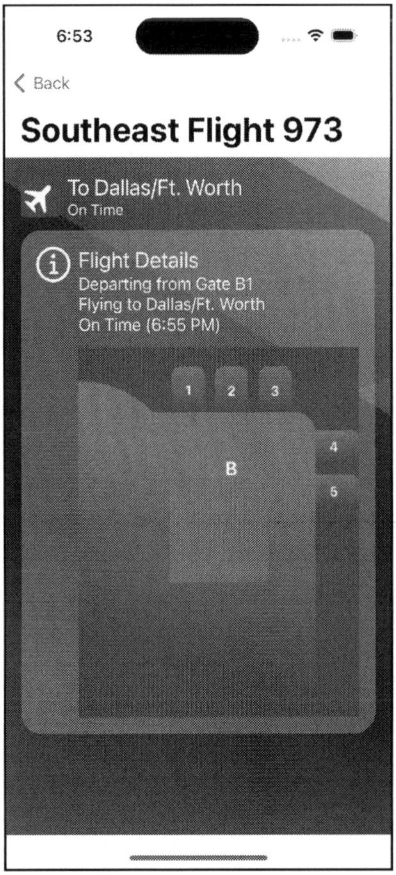

A red rectangle in the middle of the terminal map

SwiftUI provides several of the most common Shapes. The other SwiftUI shapes are:

- **Capsule**: A capsule shape is a rounded rectangle with a corner radius half the length of the rectangle's smallest edge.
- **Circle**: The circle's radius will be half the length of the framing rectangle's smallest edge.
- **Ellipse**: The ellipse will align inside the frame of the view containing it.
- **Rounded Rectangle**: A rectangle with rounded corners instead of sharp corners. It renders so the shape appears within the containing frame.

Ensure you're viewing the next section on an **iPhone 14 Pro** simulator or device, or you may see slightly different results.

The app includes a list of stores in each terminal in the TerminalStore struct. Each store contains information about the store and an indication of how busy it currently is. You'll use this information to show the stores for each terminal.

Add the following new view above the current TerminalMapView struct:

```
struct TerminalStoresView: View {
  var flight: FlightInformation

  var body: some View {
    Text("Hello World")
  }
}
```

You'll create your shapes in this new view to reduce clutter in your code. Now, add a new computed property to the TerminalStoresView view:

```
var stores: [TerminalStore] {
  if flight.terminal == "A" {
    return TerminalStore.terminalStoresA
  } else {
    return TerminalStore.terminalStoresB
  }
}
```

This property will return a list of stores using the static terminalStoresA or terminalStoresB properties of the TerminalStore struct based on the flight passed into the view. Now, change the body of the view to the following:

```
// 1
let firstStoreOffset = flight.terminal == "A" ? 140.0 : -140
let direction = flight.terminal == "A" ? -1.0 : 1.0
```

```
// 2
ForEach(stores.indices, id: \.self) { index in
  // 3
  let store = stores[index]
  // 4
  let xOffset = Double(index) * 85.0 * direction +
firstStoreOffset
  // 5
  RoundedRectangle(cornerRadius: 5.0)
    // 6
    .foregroundColor(
      Color(
        hue: 0.3333,
        saturation: 1.0 - store.howBusy,
        brightness: 1.0 - store.howBusy
      )
    )
    // 7
    .overlay(
      Text(store.shortName)
        .font(.footnote)
        .foregroundColor(.white)
        .shadow(radius: 5)
    )
    // 8
    .frame(width: 70, height: 40)
    .offset(x: xOffset, y: -30)
}
```

Coordinates within a view originate at the view's center. Points then run negatively toward the top and left of the view and positively downward and to the right. To draw shapes for the stores in a terminal:

1. First, you compute a few values to display the stores in the correct place on both terminal maps. In both cases, you want the stores to display starting at the edge of the terminal nearest gate one. Stores in Terminal A will then flow toward the left, and those in Terminal B will flow to the right. You set `firstStoreOffset` to 140.0 for the right side of the image and -140 for the left side of the image. You also set `direction` to negative one for Terminal A and one for Terminal B. You'll see how you use this in step four.

2. You loop through the `indices` of the `stores` computed property. You use the indices instead of accessing the objects directly because you'll use the `index` later.

3. You get the store object at position `index`. Note that if you didn't need the index, you could iterate over `stores` and pass `store` as the parameter to the closure.

4. You specify the location of shapes relative to the top-leading corner. To calculate each store's horizontal position, convert the `index` to a double and multiply it by the `direction` above. When `direction` is one (Terminal B,) this calculation will give you a sequence of **0, 1, 2, etc.** as the index increases, and **0, -1, -2, etc.** when `direction` is negative one (Terminal A). You multiply this by `85.0` to offset each successive store an additional 85 points in steadily decreasing (Terminal A) or increasing (Terminal B) values. You then add `firstStoreOffset` to place the first store in the desired location.

5. The `RoundedRectangle` shape produces a rectangle with rounded corners. Here you provide a `cornerRadius` parameter to tell SwiftUI the radius of the curve in each corner.

6. The `howBusy` property of the `store` object contains a value between zero and one, representing how busy the store is relative to the busiest it usually gets. You create a shade of green using the `Color` initializer that takes a hue, saturation, and brightness instead of the more common red, blue, and green components. A `hue` value of **120** represents green. You then set the `saturation` and `brightness` to one minus the `howBusy` property to produce a lower value as the store becomes busy. Using it for both elements makes a darker shade of green as the store gets busier.

7. You use an `overlay(_:alignment:)` modifier to add a view on top of the `RoundedRectangle`. Here, you add a Text view showing the `shortName` of the store in `white` in the `footnote` font. The `shadow(color:radius:x:y:)` modifier adds dark color around the text to help it stand out against lighter backgrounds.

8. To set the shape and location for the view, you use the `frame(width:height:alignment:)` modifier to apply the width and height of the rounded rectangle, and you use the `offset(x:y:)` modifier to place the rounded rectangle in the desired position of the view.

Replace your current `Rectangle` shape and its modifiers inside the overlay with:

```
TerminalStoresView(flight: flight)
```

This change uses your new view as the overlay for the terminal map. If you look at the preview for either terminal, the stores appear from the side of the first gate and move toward higher gate numbers.

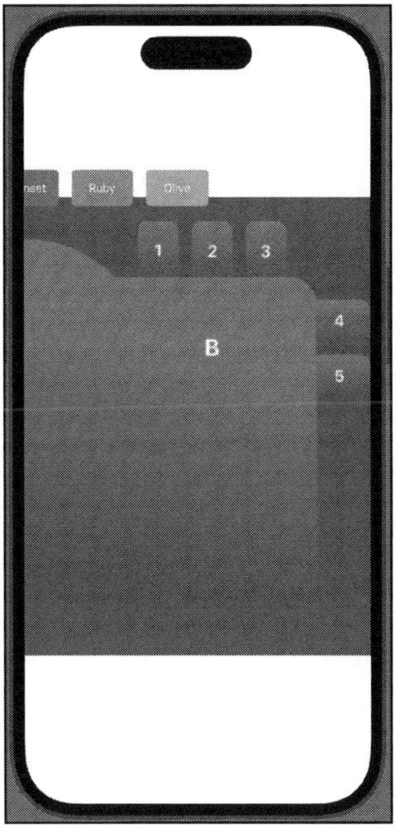

Stores for terminal A in preview

The magic numbers in step six should cause concern. This looks perfect on a view that takes up the full-screen iPhone 14 Pro but will break in most other cases.

Run the app, tap **Flight Status**, then tap any flight in terminal A. The results don't quite look right:

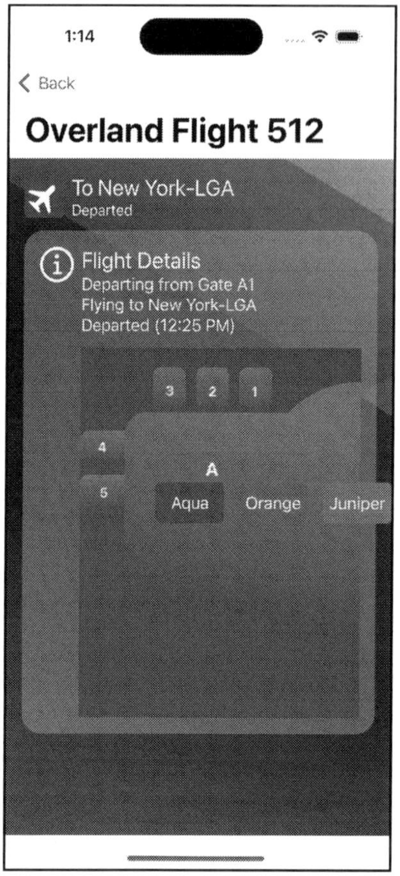

Same view in the app with stores misaligned

Using specified numbers with `Shape` views sometimes works, but when mixing with other views, you make implicit assumptions about the view's size. When those assumptions are wrong, the layout falls apart. When you tap a row on the **Flight Status** page, the `FlightDetails` view shows the terminal map as part of a larger view, and the `TerminalMapView` no longer fills the full view. Even when it does, the same issue occurs when viewed on smaller or larger devices.

So, how do you fix the problem? Well, you need to know the actual size when the view renders on the device. SwiftUI provides a way to access this information, and you'll learn how to do that in the next section.

Using GeometryReader

The `GeometryReader` container provides a way to get the size and shape of a view from within it. This information lets you create drawing code that adapts to the view's size. It also allows you to match your graphics to the available space.

First, wrap the entire body of the `TerminalStoresView` with:

```
GeometryReader { proxy in
  // Current body of the view
}
```

This code places the entire body of the view in a `GeometryReader`. Wrapping a view within a `GeometryReader` causes two immediately noticeable effects. The view now takes up the entire available space within the container view and shifts the origin from the center to the top-leading point of the view. This shift of the origin changes the locations of the shapes, as you can see in the preview.

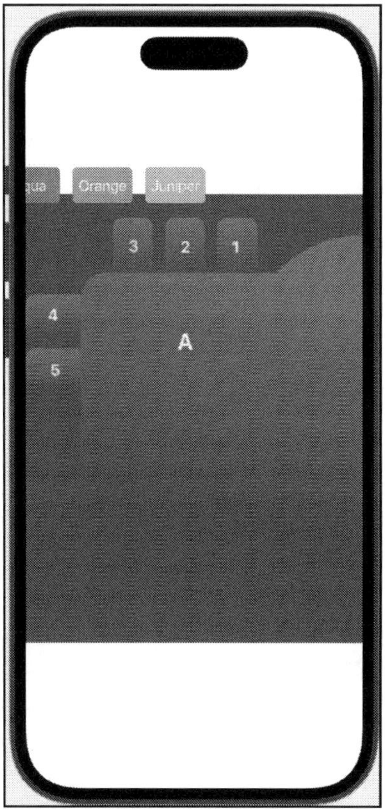

Adding a GeometryReader changes the layout of the view

The parameter to the closure of the `GeometryReader` named `proxy` is of type `GeometryProxy` and provides access to the view's size. The proxy gives you access to the view size, and you can use it to adapt your shapes to the view size. Add the following after comment one and before the existing two variables:

```
let width = proxy.size.width
let height = proxy.size.height
let storeWidth = width / 6
let storeHeight = storeWidth / 1.75
let storeSpacing = width / 5
```

This code stores the `width` and `height` of the view from the `size` property of the `GeometryProxy`. You use these values to calculate `storeWidth`, a width for each store that's one-sixth the width of the view. You determine a `storeHeight` to match the previous 70/40 width-to-height ratio. Finally, you calculate a `storeSpacing` at one-fifth of the view width to represent the separation between adjacent stores.

Now update `firstStoreOffset` to:

```
let firstStoreOffset = flight.terminal == "A" ?
width - storeSpacing :
storeSpacing - storeWidth
```

To calculate `firstStoreOffset`, you have separate cases for each terminal. For Terminal A, you want the store to appear at the left of the image, so you set it to the full width of the view and subtract `storeSpacing` so it will appear on the view's right side. For Terminal B, you want to offset the view by the difference between `storeWidth` and `storeSpacing` between stores.

Notice that you made no change to the `direction` variable because it's not reliant on the view's size. Next, change the `xOffset` under comment four to:

```
let xOffset = Double(index) * storeSpacing * direction +
firstStoreOffset
```

This change replaces the **85.0** with `storeSpacing` calculated above. Now replace the modifiers under comment eight to:

```
.frame(width: storeWidth, height: storeHeight)
.offset(x: xOffset, y: height * 0.4)
```

These values now adapt the size and location of each shape to fit the view. Run the app, Tap **Slight Status**, and tap any flight in Terminal A. The results now look appropriate here as they did in the preview because your code adjusts for the view size.

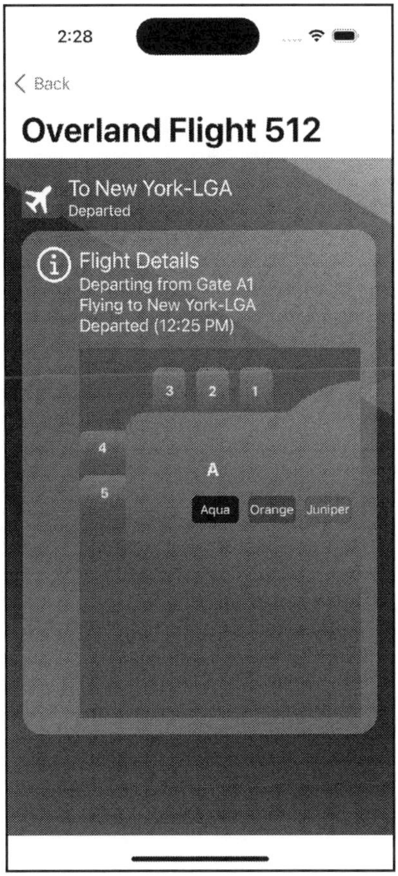

Shapes adjusting to size of the view in Terminal A

Run the app on an iPad, and the shapes adjust to match the larger view.

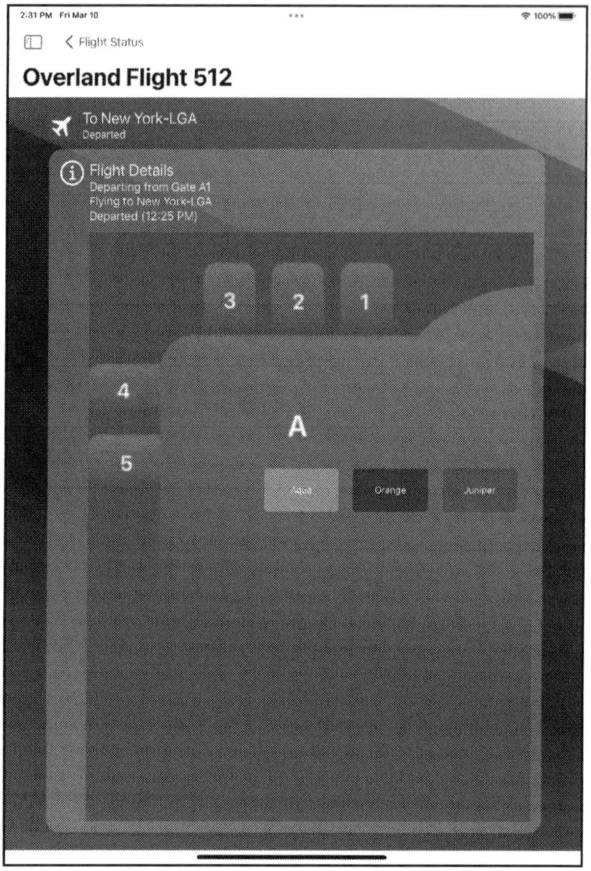

Stores adjusting for an iPad

In this section, you learned to adapt your shapes to work on any view using a `GeometryReader`. While shapes work well, sometimes you need more flexibility than shapes can provide. For those drawings, you can use **Paths**. In the next section, you'll look at implementing a pie chart using **Paths**.

Using Paths

Sometimes you want to define your shape, not use the built-in ones. You use **Paths** for this, which allows you to create shapes by combining individual segments. These segments make up the outline of a two-dimensional shape.

Earlier editions of this book demonstrated drawing by building charts. Along with SwiftUI 4.0, Apple introduced a Swift Charts API that handles many of these cases, and you'll use it in **Chapter 20: View Transitions & Charts** to implement most of the same charts. However, it does not include support for pie charts, and in this section, you'll use `Paths` to add a pie chart that shows the breakdown of flight delays into broad categories. The categories you'll use are:

- On-time: Flights that are on time or early.
- Short delay: A delay of 15 minutes or less.
- Significant delay: A delay of 15 minutes or more.
- Canceled: Canceled flights.

Preparing for the Chart

To start, create a new SwiftUI view under the **SearchFlights** group named **HistoryPieChart**. Add the following to the top of the view:

```
var flightHistory: [FlightHistory]
```

Also, update the preview to provide sample data:

```
HistoryPieChart(
  flightHistory: FlightData.generateTestFlightHistory(
    date: Date()
  ).history
)
```

First, you need a struct to define the information for each pie chart segment. Above the definition for the `HistoryPieChart` struct, add the following code:

```
struct PieSegment: Identifiable {
  var id = UUID()
  var fraction: Double
  var name: String
  var color: Color
}
```

This struct stores information about each pie segment. You've implemented `Identifiable` and set the `id` property to a unique identifier using a new **UUID** for each element to allow you to iterate over `PieSegments`.

Now, add the following computed properties after the `flightHistory` property:

```
var onTimeCount: Int {
  flightHistory.filter { $0.timeDifference <= 0 }.count
}

var shortDelayCount: Int {
  flightHistory.filter {
    $0.timeDifference > 0 && $0.timeDifference <= 15
  }.count
}

var longDelayCount: Int {
  flightHistory.filter {
    $0.timeDifference > 15 && $0.actualTime != nil
  }.count
}

var canceledCount: Int {
  flightHistory.filter { $0.status == .canceled }.count
}
```

These four properties filter the array to return the appropriate number of flights. The categories for each match those used to define the `delayColor` property in **FlightHistory.swift**.

With these counts, you can now determine the size of the pie segments you'll display. Add the following computed property after `canceledCount`:

```
var pieElements: [PieSegment] {
  // 1
  let historyCount = Double(flightHistory.count)
  // 2
  let onTimeFrac = Double(onTimeCount) / historyCount
  let shortFrac = Double(shortDelayCount) / historyCount
  let longFrac = Double(longDelayCount) / historyCount
  let cancelFrac = Double(canceledCount) / historyCount

  // 3
  let darkRed = Color(red: 0.5, green: 0, blue: 0)
  let segments = [
    PieSegment(fraction: onTimeFrac, name: "On-Time", color:
Color.green),
    PieSegment(fraction: shortFrac, name: "Short Delay", color:
Color.yellow),
    PieSegment(fraction: longFrac, name: "Long Delay", color:
Color.red),
    PieSegment(fraction: cancelFrac, name: "Canceled", color:
darkRed)
  ]
```

```
    // 4
    return segments.filter { $0.fraction > 0 }
  }
```

Here's what this code is doing to define the segments:

1. You start by getting the number of **FlightHistory** elements in the array.
2. You use the previously created methods to count the flights matching each category. You divide that number by the array's total number of elements to get a fraction of the flights that meet the criteria.
3. You create an array where each element represents the indicated portion of flights matching the criteria.
4. You return the array after filtering out any segments with no matching values.

Building the Pie Chart

With all that preparation done, creating the pie chart takes less code. Change the view body to:

```
GeometryReader { proxy in
  // 1
  let radius = min(proxy.size.width, proxy.size.height) / 2.0
  // 2
  let center = CGPoint(x: proxy.size.width / 2.0, y:
proxy.size.height / 2.0)
  // 3
  var startAngle = 360.0
  // 4
  ForEach(pieElements) { segment in
    // 5
    let endAngle = startAngle - segment.fraction * 360.0
    // 6
    Path { pieChart in
      // 7
      pieChart.move(to: center)
      // 8
      pieChart.addArc(
        center: center,
        radius: radius,
        startAngle: .degrees(startAngle),
        endAngle: .degrees(endAngle),
        clockwise: true
      )
      // 9
```

```
        pieChart.closeSubpath()
        // 10
        startAngle = endAngle
      }
      // 11
      .foregroundColor(segment.color)
    }
  }
```

There's a lot here. This view loops through the segments of the pie and draws each. You draw each segment after the previous segment ends. A complication arises in that, angles inside a path used with an arc increase counterclockwise. You want to draw segments in a clockwise direction. To do so, you can take advantage of the fact that angles wrap around. An angle of 360 degrees will correspond to the same direction at zero degrees. You start at 360 degrees, then subtract angles to move clockwise around the circle of the pie.

Here's how the individual lines work:

1. You need to determine the size of the pie chart using the `GeometryProxy`. You start by finding the smaller measurement of the height and width of the view. You divide that value by two to calculate the radius of a circle. This radius will produce a pie that fills the smaller dimension of the view.
2. You divide the width and height of the view by two to determine the center point for each dimension and then create a point indicating this location.
3. You can define variables inside a `GeometryReader`. Here, you create a `startAngle` variable that will remain in scope for the rest of the view. The default angle of zero is along the direction the **x** value increases in the view. As mentioned above, you start at 360, so you can subtract angles, making the segments flow clockwise.
4. You loop through the segments taking advantage of `PieSegment` implementing the `Identifiable` protocol.

5. An arc needs starting and ending angles. You already have the starting angle of the arc in `startAngle`. Now you'll calculate the angle of the endpoint. You multiply 360 degrees by the fraction of the full circle this arc will take to get the arc's size in degrees. You subtract this size from the arc's starting point to get the arc's ending position angle, so the segments sweep counterclockwise.
6. The drawing begins. Declaring `Path` creates an enclosure you use to build the path.
7. The `move(to:)` method on the path sets the starting location for the path, which, here, is the center of the view; a `move(to:)` call moves the current position but doesn't add anything to the path.
8. You add the arc to the path. An arc takes the center and radius that defines the circle. Then you specify both the starting and ending angles for the arc. The `clockwise` parameter tells SwiftUI the arc begins at the `startAngle` and moves clockwise to the `endAngle`. Note that you can use degrees or radians by using the corresponding initializer.
9. You close the path, which adds a line from the current back to the path's starting position.
10. Inside the path, you can update and set variables. The following pie segment should appear at the end of this one, so you update the `startAngle` variable to match this segment's ending angle.
11. Lastly, you close the path and then use the `fill()` method to fill the path with the segment's color.

Now you have a pie chart, but you need to add it to the history view. Open **FlightTimeHistory.swift** and add the following code to the end of the `VStack` after the `ScrollView`:

```
HistoryPieChart(flightHistory: flight.history)
  .frame(width: 250, height: 250)
  .padding(5)
```

Run the app and view the on-time history for a flight. You'll see the pie chart at the bottom of the history chart:

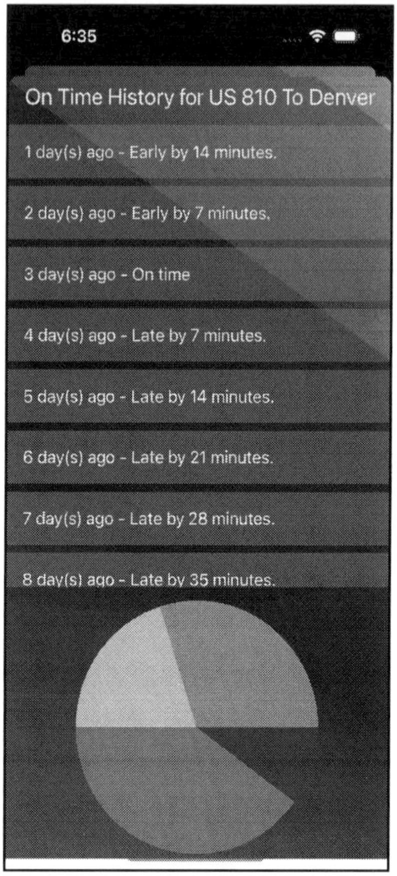

Pie chart

You have a clear pie chart, but it's unclear at a glance what the color of the segments represents. In the next section, you'll add a legend to the chart.

Adding a Legend

You have one more touch to add. The chart looks good, but it needs some indication of each color's meaning. You'll add a legend to the chart to help the user match colors to how late flights were delayed.

Open **HistoryPieChart.swift**. Wrap the `GeometryReader` that makes up the view inside an `HStack`. Now, add the following code at the end of the `HStack`:

```
VStack(alignment: .leading) {
  ForEach(pieElements) { segment in
    HStack {
      Rectangle()
        .frame(width: 20, height: 20)
        .foregroundColor(segment.color)
      Text(segment.name)
    }
  }
}
```

You loop through the segments. For each, you show a small square using the `Rectangle` shape you worked with earlier in this chapter, coloring the square the color of the associated segment. You then show the name for that segment using the `footnote` font.

Run the app, and you'll see the legend makes it clear what each color represents:

Pie chart with legend

The default font is a bit large, so you'll change that. Go back to **FlightTimeHistory.swift** and add the following modifier after the call to `HistoryPieChart()` and before the `frame(width:height:alignment:)` modifier:

```
.font(.footnote)
```

Run the app and view the on-time history for a flight. You'll now see a clear legend next to the pie chart:

Resized pie chart legend

Your pie chart looks clear now, but it would look a bit more traditional if the chart started with the first segment vertically. You could change the angles of the arc, but a more straightforward way is to rotate the finished path. Add the following modifier after the `.foregroundColor(segment.color)` call after comment 11:

```
.rotationEffect(.degrees(-90))
```

Run the app, and you'll see the chart rotated one-quarter rotation counterclockwise. Yes, the direction of the angle when rotating in the view is the opposite of those used when drawing arcs.

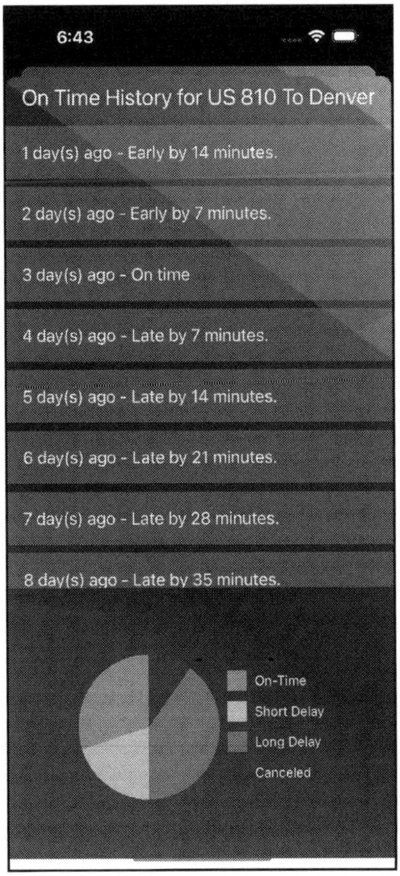

Rotated pie chart

Having created a pair of complex views using shapes and paths to create graphics, you'll now look at performance when drawing in SwiftUI.

Fixing Performance Problems

By default, SwiftUI renders graphics and animations using CoreGraphics. SwiftUI draws each view individually on the screen when needed. Modern Apple device processors and graphics hardware are powerful and can handle many views without seeing a slowdown. However, you can overload the system and see performance drop off to the point a user notices, and your app will seem sluggish.

If this occurs, you can use the `drawingGroup()` modifier on your view. This modifier tells SwiftUI to combine the view's contents into an offscreen image before the final display.

This offscreen composition uses Metal, Apple's high-performance graphics framework, resulting in an impressive speedup in rendering complex views. Note that offscreen composition adds overheard, resulting in slower performance for simple graphics. Using many gradients, shadows, and other effects will most likely result in performance problems.

Wait until you have a performance problem before turning to `drawingGroup()`. Remember that the `drawingGroup()` modifier only works for graphics — shapes, images, text, etc.

Drawing High-Performance Graphics

SwiftUI 3.0 added a new `Canvas` view meant to provide high-performance graphics in SwiftUI. The other graphics views you've seen in this chapter work within the SwiftUI view builder. A `Canvas` view provides immediate mode drawing operations that resemble the traditional Core Graphics-based drawing system. The `Canvas` includes a `withCGContext(content:)` method whose closure provides access to a Core Graphics context compatible with existing Core Graphics code.

You draw using the `GraphicsContext` passed into the closure. The closure to the view also receives a `CGSize` parameter describing the dimensions of the `Canvas`.

While view builder based views aren't directly supported, SwiftUI provides a mechanism to reference and use SwiftUI views within a Canvas. In this section, you'll build a simple `Canvas` view on the **Awards page** that uses a passed in SwiftUI view.

Create a new SwiftUI view named **AwardStars.swift** inside the **AwardsView** group. The view will have one property for the number of stars to display.

Add the following property to the top of the view:

```
var stars: Int = 3
```

This parameter will provide the number of stars to draw. Now change the view body to:

```
// 1
Canvas { gContext, size in
  // 2
} symbols: {
  // 3
  Image(systemName: "star.fill")
    .resizable()
    .frame(width: 15, height: 15)
    // 4
    .tag(0)
}
```

You define a `Canvas` view that uses the `symbols` parameter of the initializer to pass a SwiftUI view into the Canvas:

1. The closure receives a `GraphicsContext` you use to draw along with a `CGSize` parameter with the dimensions of the `Canvas`.
2. The closure of the `Canvas` isn't a view builder, but the closure to the `symbols` parameter is. You pass SwiftUI views into the closure to reference them from inside the `Canvas` drawing commands.
3. You define a SwiftUI `Image` of the **star.fill** symbol resized to 15 points square.
4. To access a SwiftUI view from within the `Canvas` closure, you must use the `tag(_:)` modifier to assign each view a unique identifier.

Now you can begin to fill in the closure of the `Canvas`. Replace comment two with the following code:

```
guard let starSymbol = gContext.resolveSymbol(id: 0) else {
  return
}
```

You use the `resolveSymbol(id:)` method on the `GraphicsContext` to look for a symbol with the **0** tag. The `guard` means the method returns if no matching symbol exists. You can just return because the inside of the `Canvas` closure executes in immediate mode instead of creating a view builder, meaning all parts of the Swift language are available.

Next, add the following code to the Canvas closure:

```
// 1
let centerOffset = (size.width - (20 * Double(stars))) / 2.0
// 2
gContext.translateBy(x: centerOffset, y: size.height / 2.0)
```

These adjust the canvas to center the stars that you'll draw.

1. The `width` property on the `size` parameter contains the width of the canvas. You subtract from the width the number of stars multiplied by 20 as each star will take 20 points of space, including padding. The result will give you the remaining space left in the view outside the stars. Dividing this by two splits the space in half, giving you the position to place the first star to center them horizontally.
2. The `translateBy(x:y:)` shifts the origin of the canvas by the provides points in each direction. The default origin lies in the top right of the `Canvas`. You move the horizontal position by the number of points calculated in step one horizontally and half the height of the canvas vertically.

With the drawing position shifted you can now loop and draw the stars. Add the following code to the end of closure:

```
// 1
for star in 0..<stars {
  // 2
  let starXPosition = Double(star) * 20.0
  // 3
  let point = CGPoint(x: starXPosition + 8, y: 0)
  // 4
  gContext.draw(starSymbol, at: point, anchor: .leading)
}
```

Here are the steps to draw the stars:

1. Since you're not in a view builder, you use a standard `for-in` Swift loop instead of a `ForEach` view.
2. You'll offset each view by 20 points. Remember you sized the symbol to 15 points, so this gives five points of space between stars.
3. In a `Canvas`, you'll use Core Graphics drawing data types and structures. You create a `CGPoint` with the `x` position from step two and zero for the `y` position. With the translated offset from earlier, these values are relative to the new origin.

4. The `draw(_:at:anchor:)` method takes the resolved symbol to draw, the point you want to draw the symbol and how that point relates to the symbol's origin. Using `leading` means the point you pass acts as the leading point of the drawn symbol or at the vertical center of the leading edge. By default, SwiftUI would draw the symbol with the point as the center.

With the view completed, you can now add it to the Awards. Open **AwardCardView.swift**. Before the final spacer, add the following view:

```
AwardStars(stars: award.stars)
  .foregroundColor(.yellow)
  .shadow(color: .black, radius: 5)
  .offset(x: -5.0)
```

You'll set all awards to three stars. You set the foreground color of the view to yellow and add a small black shadow under the view to help the stars stand out. You apply a horizontal offset to account for the padding used on the view. Now run the app and navigate to the **Your Awards** page to view the results:

Awards showing stars

Key Points

- Shapes provide a quick way to draw simple controls. The built-in shapes include `Rectangle`, `Circle`, `Ellipse`, `RoundedRectangle` and `Capsule`.
- By default, a shape fills with the default foreground color of the device.
- `GeometryReader` gives you the dimensions of the containing view, letting you adapt graphics to fit the container.
- `Paths` gives you the tools to produce more complex drawings than basic shapes adding curves and arcs.
- You can modify the appearance of paths in the same manner as shapes.
- Using `drawingGroup()` can improve the performance of graphics-heavy views, but should only be added when performance problems appear as it can slow the rendering of simple graphics.
- A `Canvas` view provides a view focused on high-performance graphics. You can pass SwiftUI views to use in a `Canvas`, but it does not use the view builder approach used in most of SwiftUI.

Where to Go From Here?

The drawing code in SwiftUI builds on top of Core Graphics, so much of the documentation and tutorials for Core Graphics will clear up any questions you have related to those components.

The SwiftUI Drawing and Animation documentation at https://developer.apple.com/documentation/swiftui/drawing_and_animation documents changes in SwiftUI compared to Apple's graphics libraries.

The WWDC 2019 session *Building Custom Views with SwiftUI* at https://developer.apple.com/videos/play/wwdc2019/237/ provides more examples of layout and graphics. It also shows an example of using the `drawingGroup()` modifier.

You can find more examples of drawing charts in SwiftUI in the SwiftUI Tutorial for iOS: Creating Charts at https://www.kodeco.com/6398124-swiftui-tutorial-for-ios-creating-charts.

Chapter 19: Animations

By Bill Morefield

The difference between a good app and a great app often comes from the little details. Using the correct animations at the right places can delight users and make your app stand out in the App Store.

Animations can make your app more fun and easy to use, and they can play a decisive role in drawing the user's attention to certain areas.

Animation in SwiftUI is much simpler than animation in AppKit or UIKit. SwiftUI animations are higher-level abstractions that handle all the tedious work for you. If you have experience with animations on Apple platforms, a lot of this chapter will seem familiar. You'll find it a lot less effort to produce animations in your app. You can combine or overlap animations and interrupt them without care. Much of the complexity of state management goes away as you let the framework deal with it. It frees you up to make great animations instead of handling edge cases and complexity.

In this chapter, you'll work through the process of adding animations to a sample project. Time to get the screen moving!

Animating State Changes

First, open the starter project for this chapter. Build and run the project for this chapter. You'll see an app that shows flight information for an airport. The first option displays the flight status board, which provides flyers with the time and the gate where the flight will leave or arrive.

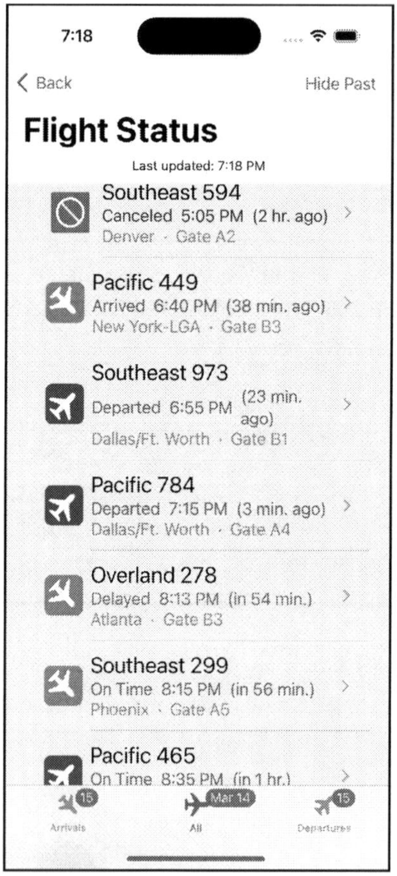

Flight board

Note: Unfortunately, showing animations with static images in a book is challenging. Sometimes, you will see pictures with arrows reflecting the expected motion. You will need to work through this chapter using the preview, the simulator or a device for the best idea of how the animations work. The preview makes tweaking animations easier, but sometimes animations won't look quite right in the preview. Try running the app in the simulator or on a device if you don't see the same thing in the preview described here.

Adding Animation

To start, open **FlightInfoPanel.swift** in the **FlightDetails** group and look for the following code:

```
if showTerminal {
  FlightTerminalMap(flight: flight)
}
```

This code toggles showing the terminal map based on a state variable, `showTerminal`. The following code just before the conditional creates a button toggling the variable:

```
Button {
  showTerminal.toggle()
} label: {
  HStack {
    Text(showTerminal ? "Hide Terminal Map" : "Show Terminal
Map")
    Image(systemName: "airplane.circle")
      .imageScale(.large)
      .padding(10)
      .rotationEffect(.degrees(showTerminal ? 90 : -90))
  }
}
```

This section of code also uses the state change to define the look of the button. The text changes to reflect the action the next tap will cause. You also change the `rotationEffect` angle between two values based on the state of the `showTerminal` variable.

Run the app, and you'll see the rotation flips between the two states.

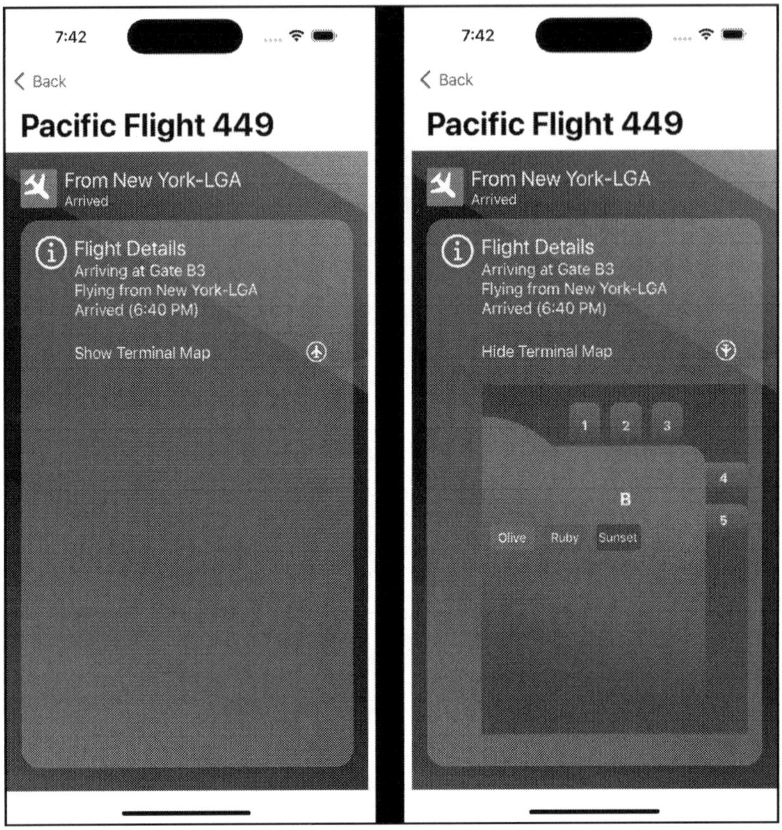

The two states of the terminal map

> **Note**: If you have trouble seeing animations or the differences between animation, you can turn on **Debug ▸ Slow Animations** to reduce the animation speed significantly. Be sure to turn it off when you have finished.

You'll first add an animation to this rotation. In SwiftUI, you simply provide the type of animation and let SwiftUI handle the interpolation for you. After the `.rotationEffect(_:anchor:)` modifier add the following code:

```
.animation(.linear(duration: 1.0), value: showTerminal)
```

In addition to the type of animation, you specify the value whose change triggers the animation. In earlier versions of SwiftUI, you didn't need to provide this parameter as SwiftUI would determine it. That made it very easy to apply animation effects accidentally. The previous call still works but became deprecated in SwiftUI 3.0, meaning support will go away in a future release. New code should provide this value, and you should update any older code to include it. Be sure to test your app afterward, as you may have relied on the previous behavior.

Run the app, tap the **Flight Status** button, and tap any flight on the list. You'll see the terminal map hidden by default. Tap on the text or airplane icon to show the map. You will see the icon slowly rotates between the up and down positions as you toggle the view instead of the nearly instant change from before.

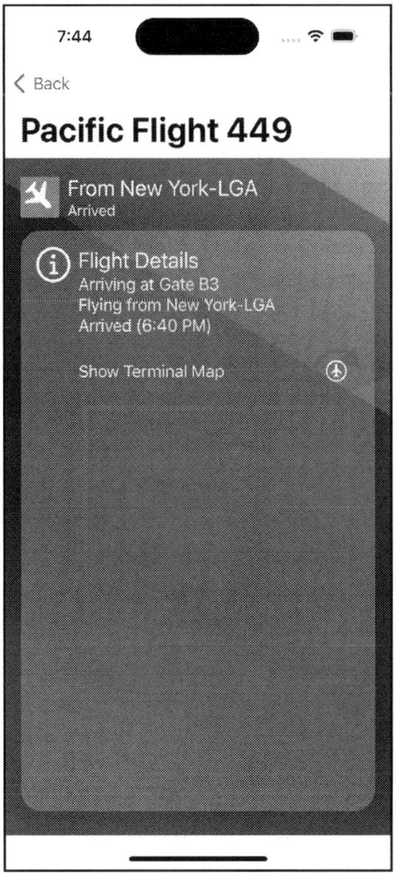

Animation on the image rotation

The rotation from -90 to 90 degrees acts as a state change, and you've told SwiftUI to animate this state change by adding the `.animation(_:value:)` modifier. The animation only applies to the **Image** element's rotation and no other views on the page and only activates when `showTerminal` changes.

Because SwiftUI iterates between the values when animating, the angles matter when you create an animation. You could specify the second angle as 270 degrees since both provide a half rotation from 90 degrees. Change the second angle of the rotation from `-90` to `270`. Now preview and tap the button.

You will see chevron rotates in the opposite direction from before. Positive angle changes rotate clockwise around the origin, while negative changes rotate counterclockwise. Earlier, the chevron turned *clockwise* when moving from upward to pointing downward. Now it rotates *counterclockwise* from 270 to 90 degrees.

You're not limited to the angle of rotations of the 0 - 360 degrees range of a single rotation. Change the `270` to `630` (270 plus a 360 full rotation). Try the app now, and you'll see that it rotates a full time and half before stopping. Notice that the rotation lasts for the same amount of time and speeds up to compensate.

> **Exercise**: Try other angles for both the starting and ending angle to observe how different angles affect the animation and positions.

Before continuing, change the rotation to:

```
.rotationEffect(.degrees(showTerminal ? 90 : 270))
```

Animation Types

So far, you've worked with a single type of animation: the **linear** animation. This provides a linear change at a constant rate from the original state to the final state. If you graphed the change vertically against time horizontally, the transition would look like this:

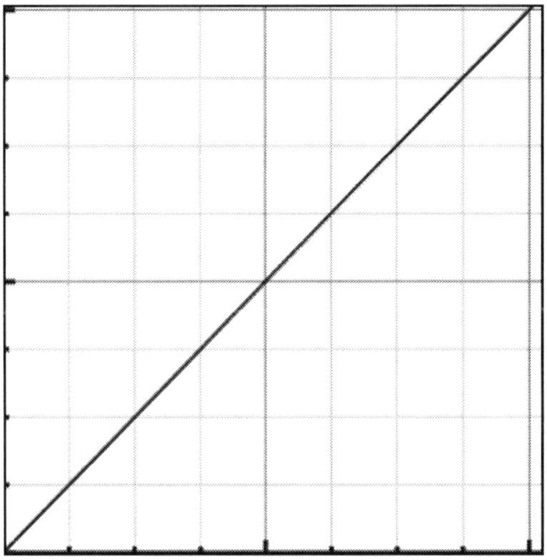

Linear animation

SwiftUI provides several more animation types. The differences can be subtle and hard to see, which is why you stretched the animation out to a second. Not all animation types accept a parameter for the length directly, but you'll learn other ways to adjust it.

You'll add some code to help you see the differences in animations. Between the start of the `HStack` and the `Text` view inside the button, add the following code:

```
Image(systemName: "airplane.circle")
  .imageScale(.large)
  .padding(10)
  .rotationEffect(.degrees(showTerminal ? 90 : 270))
  .animation(.linear(duration: 1.0), value: showTerminal)
Spacer()
```

This change adds a second icon with the text centered between them. This addition, taking half the previous animation time, will help you compare animations in the rest of this section.

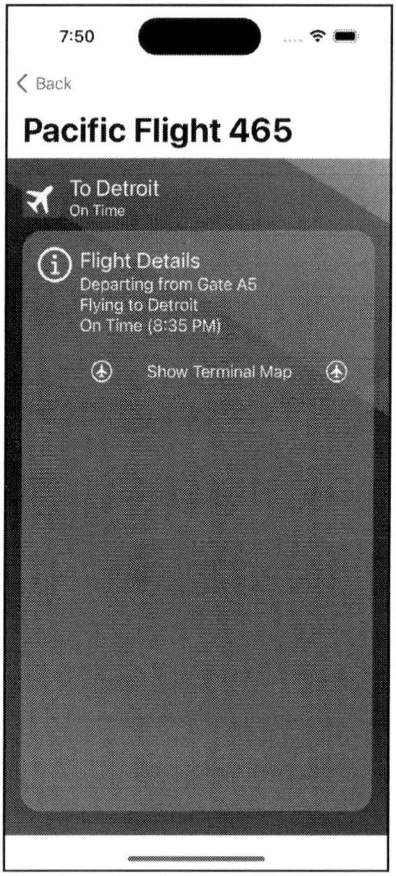

New icons added

For the second icon, change the `animation` modifier to:

```
.animation(.default.speed(0.33), value: showTerminal)
```

You'll notice the addition of the `speed(_:)` method. This method is one of several that you can apply to any animation. It adjusts the animation's speed, in this case slowing it down since the value is less than one. If you use a value greater than one, the animation speed will increase.

Run the app and go to the details for a flight. While not identical, you'll see the animations run at similar speeds. Without changing the speed, the rotation on the right plane would complete three times as quickly.

The **default** animation is a type of eased animation referred to as `easeInOut`. This animation looks good in almost all cases, so it's a good choice if you have no other strong preference. You'll examine the different eased animations in the next section.

Eased Animations

Eased animations might be the most common in apps. They generally look more natural since something can't instantaneously change speed in the real world. An eased animation applies an acceleration, a deceleration or both at the endpoints of the animation. The animation reflects the acceleration or deceleration of real-world movement.

The default animation you just used is the equivalent of the `easeInOut` type. This animation applies acceleration at the beginning and deceleration at the end of the animation.

If you graphed the movement in this animation against time, this animation looks like this:

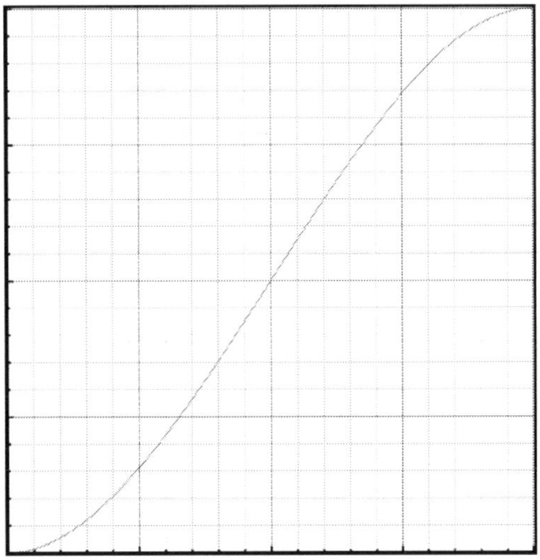

Ease in out

You can get more control using it directly. Change the animation on the second icon to:

```
.animation(.easeInOut(duration: 1.0), value: showTerminal)
```

Eased animations have a short default time of 0.35 seconds. You can specify a different length with the `duration:` parameter. You've used that to set the duration the same as the linear animation of the other icon.

Run the app, and you'll see the two buttons take the same time to animate. The non-linear movement of the second should also be noticeable.

Now change the animation for the second icon to:

```
.animation(.easeOut(duration: 1.0), value: showTerminal)
```

Run the app and toggle the terminal map. You'll see the rotation starts quickly and slows down shortly before coming to a stop.

Graphing the movement in this animation against time would look like this:

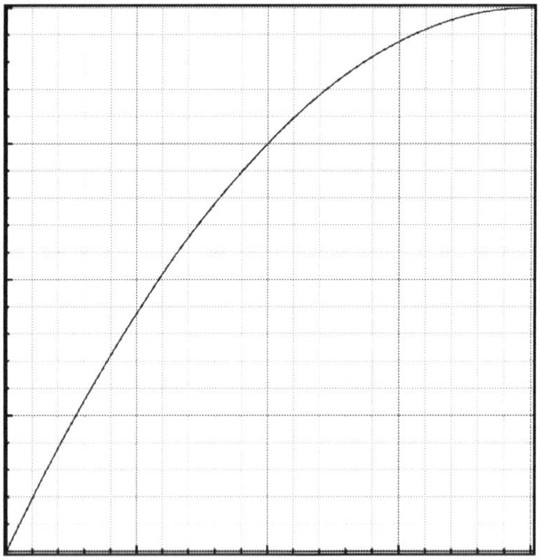

Ease out

In addition to `easeOut`, you can also specify `easeIn`, which starts slowly at the start of the animation then accelerates.

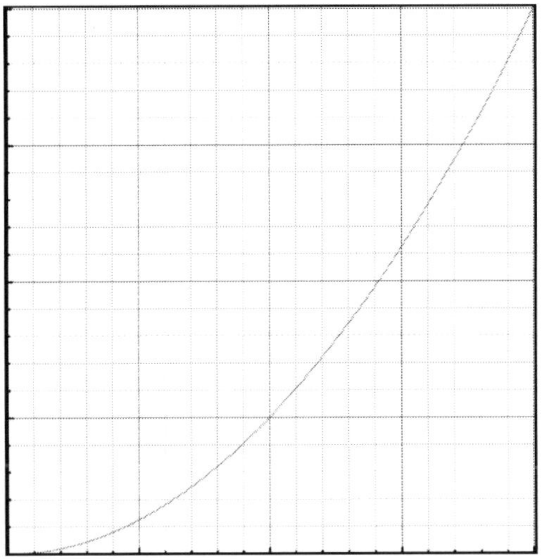

Ease in

If you need fine control over the animation curve's shape, you can use the `timingCurve(_:_:_:_)` method. SwiftUI uses a bézier curve for easing animations. This method will let you define the control points for that curve in a range of 0...1. The shape of the curve will reflect the specified control points.

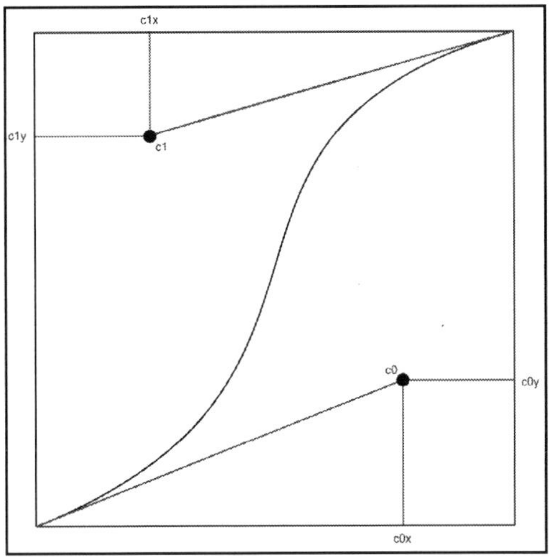

timingCurve

Exercise: Try the various eased animations and observe the results. In particular, see what different control points do in the `timingCurve(_:_:_:_)` animation type.

Spring Animations

Eased animations always transition between the start and end states in a single direction. They also never pass either end state. The other SwiftUI animations category lets you add a bit of bounce at the end of the state change. The physical model for this type of animation gives it the name: a spring.

Why a Spring Makes a Proper Animation

Springs resist stretching and compression — the greater the spring's stretch or compression, the more resistance the spring presents. Imagine a weight attached at one end of a spring. Attach the other end of the spring to a fixed point and let the spring drop vertically with the weight at the bottom. It will bounce several times before coming to a stop.

In the real world, friction and other outside forces ensure that the system loses energy each time through the cycle. This reduction makes the system **damped**. These accumulated losses add up, and eventually, the weight will stop motionless at the equilibrium point.

The graph of this movement looks more like this:

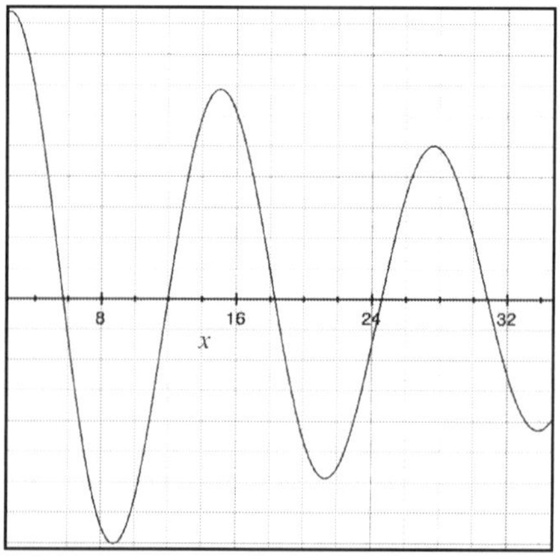

Dampened simple harmonic motion

Creating Spring Animations

Change the animation for the second icon to:

```
.animation(
  .interpolatingSpring(
    mass: 1,
    stiffness: 100,
    damping: 10,
    initialVelocity: 0
  ),
  value: showTerminal
)
```

Run the app, and you'll see the icon now bounces a bit at the end, going past the end and back a few times before stopping at the final position. You'll see the icon continues a bit past the destination, slides back and then bounces around the final position a bit before stopping.

The parameters you pass are the same mentioned above:

- `mass`: Controls how long the system "bounces".
- `stiffness`: Controls the speed of the initial movement.
- `damping`: Controls how fast the system slows down and stops.
- `initialVelocity`: Gives an extra initial motion.

> **Exercise**: Before continuing, see if you can determine how changes to the parameters affect the animation.
>
> ***Hint**: Experiment with one element at a time. First, double a value and then halve it from the original value. Use the first icon to compare two animations with a single changed parameter.*

Increasing the `mass` causes the animation to last longer and bounce further on each side of the endpoint. A smaller mass stops faster and moves less past the endpoints on each bounce. Increasing the `stiffness` causes each bounce to move further past the endpoints, but less affects the animation's length. Increasing the `damping` smoothes and ends it faster. Increasing the `initialVelocity` causes the animation to bounce further. A negative `initialVelocity` can move the animation in the opposite direction until it overcomes the initial velocity.

Unless you're a physicist, the animation's physical model doesn't intuitively map to the results. SwiftUI introduces a more intuitive way to define a spring animation. The underlying model doesn't change, but you can specify parameters to the model better related to how you want the animation to appear in your app. Change your animation to:

```
.animation(
  .spring(
    response: 0.55,
    dampingFraction: 0.45,
    blendDuration: 0
  ),
  value: showTerminal
)
```

The `dampingFraction` controls how fast the "springiness" stops. A value of zero will never stop (try it and see). A value of one or greater will cause the system to stop without oscillation. This **overdamped** state will look similar to the eased animations of the previous section.

You usually use a value between zero and one, which will result in some oscillation before the animation ends. Greater values slow down faster.

The `response` parameter defines the system's time to complete a single oscillation with the `dampingFraction` set to zero. It allows you to tune the length of time of the animation.

The `blendDuration` parameter provides a control for blending the length of the transition among different animations. It only comes into use if you change the parameters during animation or combine multiple spring animations. A zero value turns off blending.

Again, try varying these parameters and compare the animations produced.

Removing and Combining Animations

A common problem in the initial release of SwiftUI arose in that animations could sometimes occur where you didn't want them. Adding the `value` parameter to the `animation(_:value:)` addresses much of this problem. There still may be times that you may want to apply no animation. You do this by passing a `nil` animation type to the `animation(_:value:)` method.

Still in **FlightInfoPanel.swift** add the following extra modifier after the `.rotationEffect` modifier:

```
.scaleEffect(showTerminal ? 1.5 : 1.0)
```

This change adds a scaling of 1.5 times the icon's original size when showing the terminal map. If you view the animation, you will see that the button grows in sync with the rotation. An animation affects all state changes that occur on the element where you apply the animation.

Image scaling and rotating

Next, add the following code between the `rotationEffect()` and `scaleEffect()` methods:

```
.animation(nil, value: showTerminal)
```

Trigger the animation again. You should again see the almost instant fade-out/fade-in effect on the rotation on the icon, but the size change still shows a spring animation. You should think of an `animation` affecting all state changes attached to it.

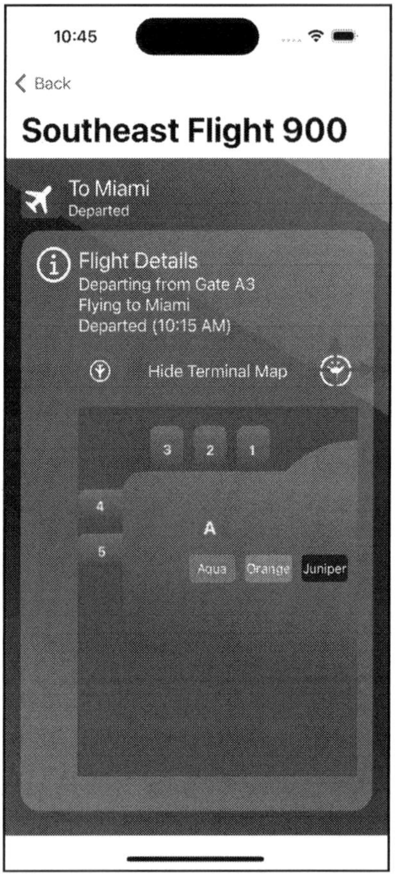

Animation on only one state change

You can combine different animations by using `.animation(_:value:)` multiple times. Change the animation on the `rotationEffect()` from `nil` to:

```
.animation(.linear(duration: 1), value: showTerminal)
```

Run the app, and you'll see the two animations take place simultaneously, but each affects a different state change. The linear animation affects the rotation, while the spring affects the scaling of the icon. Also, note that SwiftUI handles the animations' different lengths cleanly.

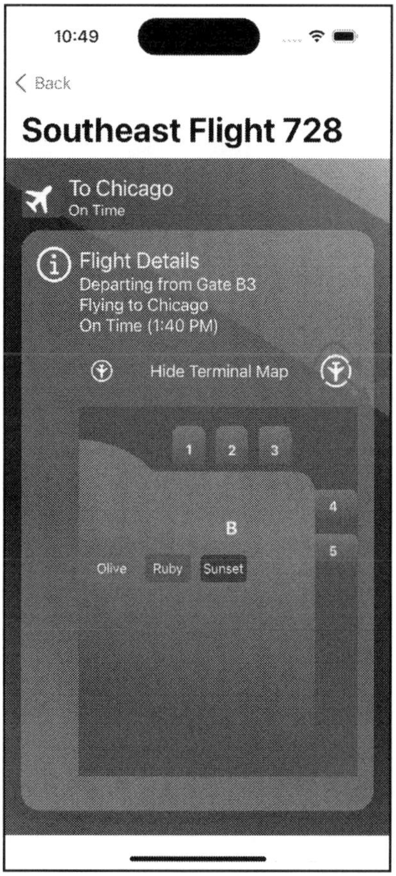

Simultaneously animations

Animating From State Changes

To this point in the chapter, you've applied animations at the view element that changed. You can also apply the animation where the state change occurs. When doing so, the animation applies to all changes that occur because of the state change.

Remove all `.animation(_:value:)` modifiers from the two images. Change the action of the button that toggles showing the terminal map to:

```
withAnimation(
  .spring(
    response: 0.55,
    dampingFraction: 0.45,
    blendDuration: 0
  )
) {
  showTerminal.toggle()
}
```

You wrap the state change to `showTerminal` inside a `withAnimation(_:_:)` method. This call uses a spring animation, but you could pass any animation to this function. Run the app, and you'll see the two images run the same animation in sync.

Using `withAnimation(_:_:)` applies the animation to every visual change that results from the state change in the closure. This method simplifies the code when you wish to use a single animation to multiple changes resulting from a state change. Be careful as SwiftUI applied the animation for **all** state changes, including implicit ones caused by the change. In this example, if another property relied on `showTerminal` value, the animation would also apply to that property.

Now that you understand the basics of animation in SwiftUI, you'll apply animation to other parts of the app.

Animating Shapes

Open **TerminalStoresView.swift** in the **FlightDetails** group. This view displays the stores in a terminal that you created in **Chapter 18: "Drawing & Custom Graphics"**. In this section, you'll add some animation to these shapes when they appear. First, add a state variable to the struct below the `flight` property.

```
@State private var showStores = 0.0
```

Now find the declaration of `xOffset` inside the `ForEach` loop and change it to:

```
let xOffset =
  Double(index) * storeSpacing * direction * showStores +
firstStoreOffset
```

You added a multiplication by the `showStores` state property. Recall from the previous chapter that the rest of this calculation determines the horizontal position of the store. By setting `showStores` to zero, the stores will all appear at the `firstStoreOffset`. By setting `showStores` to one, you get the previous location. Changing the value of a variable like this creates a state change you can animate.

Now add the following code after the `offset(x:y:)` modifier within the `ForEach` loop:

```
.animation(.easeOut, value: showStores)
```

You apply a default ease-out animation when `showStores` changes. You need to trigger the state change to start the animation. Here you'll activate it when the view appears. At the end of the `GeometryReader` add the following code:

```
.onAppear {
  showStores = 1.0
}
```

Code inside `onAppear(perform:)` executes when the attached view appears on the device. Here you change the value of `showStores` to 1.0, which will change the offset.

Run the app, tap **Search Flights** and choose any flight and tap **Show Terminal Map**. You'll see the map appear and the store shapes slide into place.

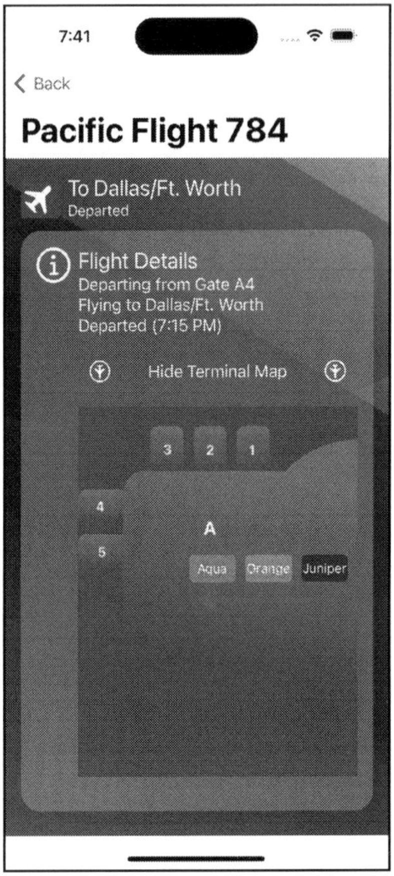

The stores sliding into place

If you hide and show the terminal map several times, you'll notice the animation does not repeat. That's because it takes a short period before SwiftUI destroys a removed view. If you show the view before SwiftUI destroys it, SwiftUI will reuse the existing view and not call `onAppear(perform:)` again.

In the next section, you'll look at you'll explore the `delay()` method in animations.

Cascading Animations

The `delay()` method allows you to specify a time in seconds to pause before the animation occurs. You can also use it to allow animations to chain together and provide a sense of progress or motion.

Open **TerminalStoresView.swift** and change `showStores` to:

```
@State private var showStores = false
```

You change `showBars` to a boolean. Change the definition of `xOffset` inside the `ForEach` loop back to:

```
let xOffset = Double(index) * storeSpacing * direction +
firstStoreOffset
```

This code removes the state change from the calculation. Instead, you'll change the state directly within the `offset(x:y:)` modifier. Change the `offset(x:y:)` modifier to:

Now change the `RoundedRectangle` `offset` to:

```
.offset(
  x: showStores ?
    xOffset :
    firstStoreOffset - direction * width,
  y: height * 0.4
)
```

You also need to change the code inside `onAppear(perform:)` so it reads:

```
.onAppear {
  showStores = true
}
```

Now you can add the delay to the animation. Change the animation after the offset on the `Rectangle` to:

```
.animation(.easeOut.delay(Double(index) * 0.3), value:
showStores)
```

You apply a different animation to each iteration through the `ForEach` loop. This code now uses the same `index` property used to set the position of the store. For each greater index, you delay the animation by 0.3 seconds.

Now run the app. You'll see the result of the delayed animations as the stores snap into place one at a time.

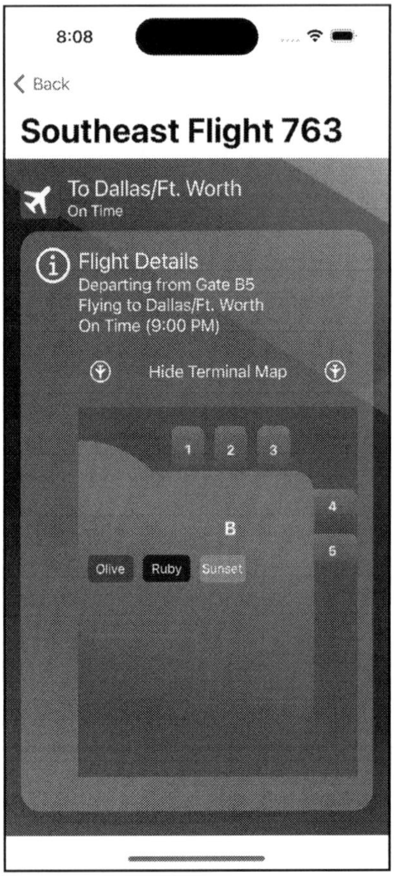

Animation causing stores to appear one at a time

Extracting Animations From the View

To this point, you've defined animations directly within the view. For exploring and learning, that works well. Maintaining code in real apps is easier when you keep different sections of your code separate. In **TerminalStoresView.swift**, add the following code above the `body` structure:

```
func storeAnimation(_ storeNumber: Int) -> Animation {
  return .easeInOut.delay(Double(storeNumber) * 0.3)
}
```

You define a custom animation method to return an `Animation` structure. This one contains the same animation as before. Now replace the `animation(_:value:)` in the view with:

```
.animation(storeAnimation(index), value: showStores)
```

Run the app and confirm the animation did not change. You could reuse this animation elsewhere in the view and only change it in one place. For more complex animations, extracting the animation also improves the readability of your code.

Next, you'll implement a more complex animation adding a visual indicator to the terminal map.

Animating Paths

Open **GatePathView.swift** in the **FlightDetails** group, and you'll see a view that draws a line determined using a set of fixed points scaled to the view's size. The code below draws the path:

```
Path { path in
  // 1
  let walkingPath = gatePath(proxy)
  // 2
  guard walkingPath.count > 1 else { return }
  // 3
  path.addLines(walkingPath)
}
.stroke(lineWidth: 3.0)
```

If you need a review of `Path` and `GeometryReader`, see **Chapter 18: "Drawing & Custom Graphics"**. Here's what this code does:

1. The `gatePath(_:)` method returns an array of `CGPoints` scaled to the current view using the `GeometryProxy`.
2. This check ensures there are at least two points in the array — the minimum for a line — and if not, it returns an empty path.
3. The `addLines(_:)` method expects an array of points. It moves the path to the first point in the array and then adds lines connecting the remaining points.

This view will provide a line to the gate when drawn on top of the terminal map. Go to **TerminalMapView.swift** and add the following code after `TerminalStoresView`:

```
GatePathView(flight: flight)
  .foregroundColor(.white)
```

Run the app, tap **Flight Status** and then tap any flight to see the new path to the gate drawn in white over the map.

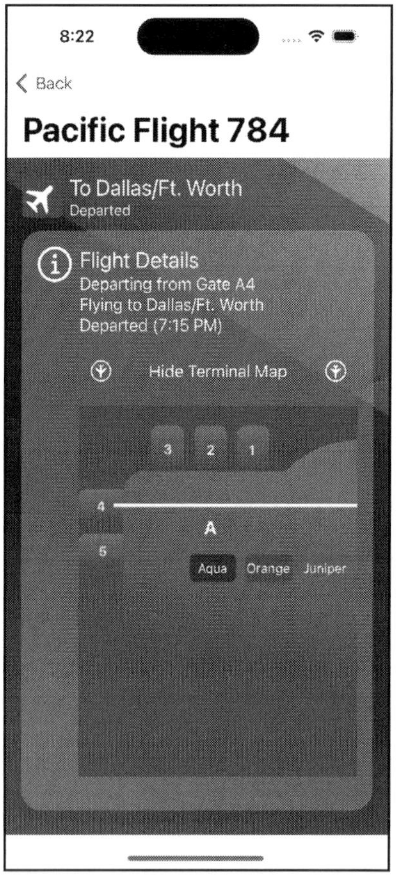

The gate path drawn over the terminal map

In the next section, you'll animate this path.

Making a Path State Change

To animate this path, you need a state change on a property SwiftUI knows how to animate. A SwiftUI `Shape` has a method `trim(from:to:)` that trims a shape to a fractional portion based on its representation as a path. For a shape implemented as a path, the method provides a quick way to draw only a portion of the path.

First, go to **GatePathView.swift** and add the following code after the current `GatePathView` struct:

```
struct WalkPath: Shape {
  var points: [CGPoint]

  func path(in rect: CGRect) -> Path {
    return Path { path in
      guard points.count > 1 else { return }
      path.addLines(points)
    }
  }
}
```

This struct implements a custom `Shape` view that implements the same code as the view. You pass in the array of points and create the path as before. Now add a new state variable after the `flight` parameter at the top of the struct:

```
@State private var showPath = false
```

Then add a new animation property after the `showPath` property:

```
var walkingAnimation: Animation {
  .linear(duration: 3.0)
  .repeatForever(autoreverses: false)
}
```

This code creates a linear animation three seconds long. The `repeatForever(autoreverses:)` method sets the animation to repeat when it finishes. Setting `autoreverses` to `false`, means the animation restarts each time instead of rewinding backward before restarting.

Change the closure for the `GeometryReader` to use the new shape instead of drawing the path directly:

```
WalkPath(points: gatePath(proxy))
  .trim(to: showPath ? 1.0 : 0.0)
  .stroke(lineWidth: 3.0)
  .animation(walkingAnimation, value: showPath)
```

The added `trim(from:to:)` method contains the state change. You also attach the animation to the view telling SwiftUI to animate the state change.

Finally, add the following code at the end of the view after the `GeometryReader`:

```
.onAppear {
  showPath = true
}
```

As earlier, you use the `onAppear(perform:)` modifier to start the animation when the view appears.

Run the app, and show any terminal map. You'll see the line trace out the path to the gate and repeat every three seconds.

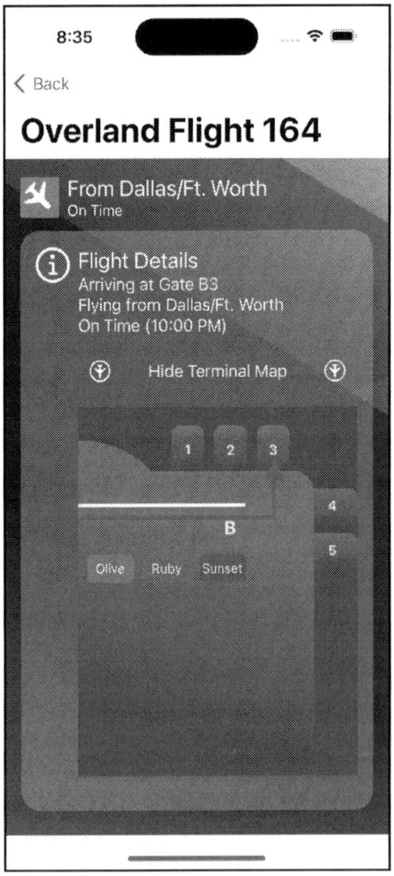

Animated path to terminal

Making Canvas Animations

In **Chapter 18: "Drawing & Custom Graphics"**, you learned about the `Canvas` view meant to provide better performance for a complex drawing, mainly when it uses dynamic data. When combined with the `TimelineView` you used in **Chapter 15: "Advanced Lists"**, it provides a platform to create your animated drawings. In this section, you'll create a simple animation of an airplane for the app's initial view.

Create a new SwiftUI view named **WelcomeAnimation**. At the top of the new view, add the following two properties:

```
private var startTime = Date()
private let animationLength = 5.0
```

The `startTime` property will hold the time the view appears and will be used to determine how long the animation runs. The `animationLength` property will determine how long it takes for the animation to complete.

Next, replace the current body of the view with a `TimelineView`:

```
TimelineView(.animation) { timelineContext in
}
```

You specify the `.animation` schedule asking SwiftUI to update as fast as possible. Inside the `TimelineView` closure, add the following code:

```
Canvas { graphicContext, size in
  // 1
  let timePosition =
(timelineContext.date.timeIntervalSince(startTime))
    .truncatingRemainder(dividingBy: animationLength)
  // 2
  let xPosition = timePosition / animationLength * size.width
  // 3
  graphicContext.draw(
    Text("*"),
    at: .init(x: xPosition, y: size.height / 2.0)
  )
} // Extension Point
```

The `Canvas` view expands to fill its parent view. You use the `graphicContext` for drawing, and the `size` parameter gives you the dimensions of the drawing space. Then you'll do some calculations to perform the animation.

1. You first get the difference in seconds between the date from the `timelineContext` parameter to the closure and the time when the view loaded in the `startTime` property. You use the `truncatingRemainder(dividingBy:)` method on the resulting Double to constrain this value of the range from zero to the `animationLength` property for the view. When the value reaches `animationLength`, it will wrap around to zero.
2. You divide the value from step one by the `animationLength` property to get the fraction of the entire animation length the time represents. You multiply this fraction by the width of the canvas giving the horizontal position for this animation frame.
3. For now, you'll just write an asterisk at the horizontal position from step two and the vertical position centered in the canvas.

To see what you've done to this point, go back to **WelcomeView.swift**. Add the following code inside the `NavigationSplitView` before the start of the `List`:

```
WelcomeAnimation()
  .frame(height: 40)
  .padding()
```

Run the app, and you'll see your animation works as a small asterisk that slides across the view above the navigation buttons.

The animation looks nice, but now we need to add the airplane. It seems a waste to create an airplane when SF Symbols provides a perfectly usable airplane image. Fortunately, SwiftUI allows you to bring external SwiftUI views into a canvas for use.

Go back to **WelcomeAnimation.swift**. Extend the current `Canvas` view with the following additional closure in place of the `// Extension Point` comment so the `symbols` label appears on the same line.

```
symbols: {
  Image(systemName: "airplane")
    .resizable()
    .aspectRatio(1.0, contentMode: .fit)
    .frame(height: 40)
    .tag(0)
}
```

Make sure to begin the new code immediately after the closing brace of the closure, so the `symbols` parameter appears on the same line. The `symbols` parameter for the `Canvas` creates a ViewBuilder to supply SwiftUI views to the canvas. Here you provide an image view with modifiers to produce a 40 point square image. You must give each view inside the `symbols` closure a unique value using the `tag(_:)` modifier.

You can now use this passed SwiftUI view inside the `Canvas`. At the top of the `Canvas` closure, add the following line:

```
guard let planeSymbol = graphicContext.resolveSymbol(id: 0) else
{
  return
}
```

You use the `resolveSymbol(id:)` on the graphics context to access the SwiftUI views. The `id` here should match the id provided in the view's `tag(_:)` modifier. If the symbol doesn't exist, you return since there's nothing to draw, resulting in an empty canvas. Now change the existing `GraphicsContext.draw(_:at:anchor:)` method (after comment three) to:

```
graphicContext.draw(
  planeSymbol,
  at: .init(x: xPosition, y: size.height / 2.0)
)
```

Instead of text, you now draw the SwiftUI view using the same `draw(_:at:anchor:)` method passing in the `planeSymbol` you obtained using `resolveSymbol(id:)`. Run the app to see the finished animation.

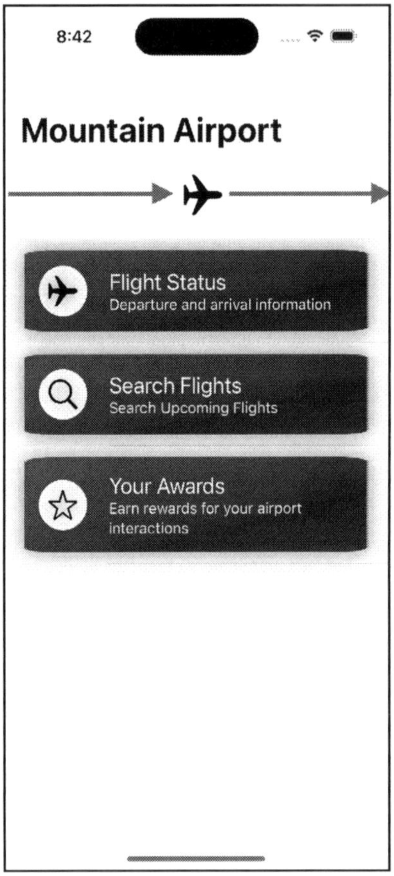

Animated airplane canvas

Key Points

- Don't use animations only for the sake of doing so. Have a purpose for each animation.
- Keep animations between 0.25 and 1.0 seconds in length. Shorter animations are often not noticeable. Longer animations risk annoying your user wanting to get something done.
- Keep animations consistent within an app and with platform usage.
- Animations should be optional. Respect accessibility settings to reduce or eliminate application animations.
- Make sure animations are smooth and flow from one state to another.
- Animations can make a huge difference in an app if used wisely.
- You can create high-performance animations by combining `TimelineView` and `Canvas`.

Where to Go From Here?

If you want to dive deep into creating and using animation in SwiftUI, the book *SwiftUI Animations by Tutorials* at https://www.kodeco.com/books/swiftui-animations-by-tutorials is dedicated to the topic.

This chapter focused on creating animations and transitions, but not why and when to use them. A good starting point for UI-related questions on Apple platforms is the Human Interface Guidelines, here: https://developer.apple.com/design/human-interface-guidelines/.

The WWDC 2018 session, Designing Fluid Interfaces, also details gestures and motion in apps. You can view it at https://developer.apple.com/videos/play/wwdc2018/803.

Chapter 20: View Transitions & Charts

By Bill Morefield

In **Chapter 19: "Animations"**, you explored adding animation to your app. You probably noticed one distinct element you did not animate — views. Open this chapter's starter project, tap **Flight Status**, and then tap any flight. When you tap the **Show Terminal Map** button, the view appears, and the animations of the airplane shapes occur.

The display of the view doesn't show any animation. In SwiftUI, views use a subset of animation called view transitions. This chapter teaches you to apply animations to your app views.

Animating View Transitions

> **Note**: Transitions sometimes render incorrectly in the preview. If you don't see what you expect, try running the app in the simulator or a device.

The first thing you should understand is the difference between a state change and a view transition. A state change occurs when an element on a view changes. A transition involves changing the visibility or presence of a view.

In the starter project for this chapter, open **FlightInfoPanel.swift** and look for the `Text` view between the icons in the button that shows the terminal map.

Right now, it looks like this:

```
Text(showTerminal ? "Hide Terminal Map" : "Show Terminal Map")
```

This code shows a state change. While the text displayed by the view can change, it remains in the same view. Change the code to the following:

```
if showTerminal {
  Text("Hide Terminal Map")
} else {
  Text("Show Terminal Map")
}
```

Now you have a view transition. One view is replaced by a different one when the `showTerminal` state variable changes.

Transitions are specific animations that occur when showing and hiding views. You can confirm this by running the app, tapping **Flight Status**, then tapping any flight. Tap the button to show and hide the terminal map a few times, and notice how the view disappears and reappears. By default, views transition on and off the screen by fading in and out.

Much of what you've already learned about animations work with transitions. As with animation, the default transition is only a single possible animation.

Change the code that shows the button text to:

```
Group {
  if showTerminal {
    Text("Hide Terminal Map")
  } else {
    Text("Show Terminal Map")
  }
}
.transition(.slide)
```

You use the `Group` View to wrap the view change. You then apply the transition to the group. Run the app, go back to the page, and you'll see ... something odd. The old view slides away but doesn't disappear for a few seconds. Since transitions are a type of animation, you must use the `withAnimation(_:value:)` function around the state change, or SwiftUI won't show the specified transition. You already did this back in **Chapter 19: "Animations"** as the action for the button is:

```
Button {
  withAnimation(
    .spring(
      response: 0.55,
      dampingFraction: 0.45,
      blendDuration: 0
    )
  ) {
    showTerminal.toggle()
  }
} label: {
```

As a result, SwiftUI applies both animation and transition. You'll often run into this type of issue when working with animations and transitions, which makes keeping animations with the UI element to change more manageable. For now, change the button to use the `withAnimation` method without an animation type.

```
Button {
  withAnimation {
    showTerminal.toggle()
  }
} label: {
```

There's no animation specified in the `withAnimation(_:value:)` call. It's not needed since you set it at the individual elements in the view. To keep the animations on the plane icons, add the following code after each `Image` view:

```
.animation(
  .spring(
    response: 0.55,
    dampingFraction: 0.45,
    blendDuration: 0
  ),
  value: showTerminal
)
```

Run the app, and bring up the details for a flight. Now tap to show the terminal map, and you'll see that the view now slides in from the leading edge. When you tap the button again, you'll see the view slide off the trailing edge. These transitions handle cases where the text direction reads right-to-left for you.

The animation occurs when SwiftUI adds the view. The framework creates the view and slides it in from the leading edge. It also animates the view off the trailing edge and removes it to no longer take up resources.

You could create a similar result with animations, but you need to handle these extra steps yourself. The built-in transitions make it much easier to deal with view animations.

View Transition Types

The default transition type changes the opacity of the view when adding or removing it. The view goes from transparent to opaque on insertion and from opaque to transparent on removal. You can create a more customized version using the `.opacity` transition.

You also used a slide transition that inserts a view from the leading edge and removes it off the trailing edge. When added or removed, the `.move(edge:)` transition moves the view from or to a specified edge. To see the view move to and from the bottom, change the transition to:

```
.transition(.move(edge: .bottom))
```

Run the app and tap **Flight Status**. Now tap any flight and then tap **Show Terminal Map**. You'll see the new view slide in from the bottom and the vanishing view slide off toward the bottom.

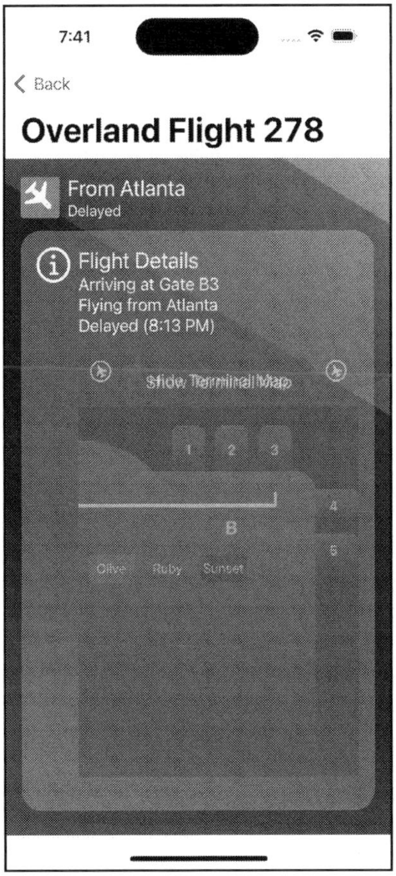

A move transition to the bottom

The other edges are `.top`, `.leading` and `.trailing`.

Beyond moving, transitions can also animate views to appear on the screen. A `.scale()` transition causes the view to expand when inserted from a single point or to collapse when removed to a single point at the center. You can optionally specify a scale factor parameter for the transition. The scale factor defines the ratio of the size of the initial view. A scale of zero provides the default transition to a single point. A value less than one causes the view to expand from that scaled size when inserted or collapse to it when removed. Values greater than one work the same. However, the view at the end of the transition is larger than the final view.

You can also specify an `anchor` parameter for the point on the view where the transition centers. An enumeration provides constants for the view's corners, sides and center. You can also provide a custom offset.

The final transition type allows you to specify an offset either as a **CGSize** or a pair of **Length** values. The view moves from that offset when inserted and toward it when removed.

Exercise: As with animations, the best way to see how transitions work is to try them. Take each transition and use it in place of `.slide` transition in the `FlightTerminalMap`. Toggle the view on and off to see how the animation works as the view appears and leaves.

Extracting Transitions From the View

You can extract your transitions from the view as you did with animations. You don't add it at the **struct** level as with an animation but at the file scope. At the top of **FlightInfoPanel.swift** add the following:

```
extension AnyTransition {
  static var buttonNameTransition: AnyTransition {
    .slide
  }
}
```

This extension declares your transition as a static property of **AnyTransition**. Now use it on the `TerminalMapView`. Change the conditional showing `TerminalMapView` to:

```
if showTerminal {
  TerminalMapView(flight: flight)
    .transition(.buttonNameTransition)
}
```

Run the app and tap **Flight Status**. Now tap any flight and then tap **Show Terminal Map**. You'll see it works as the first transition example did, except it moves in from the leading edge and out to the trailing edge.

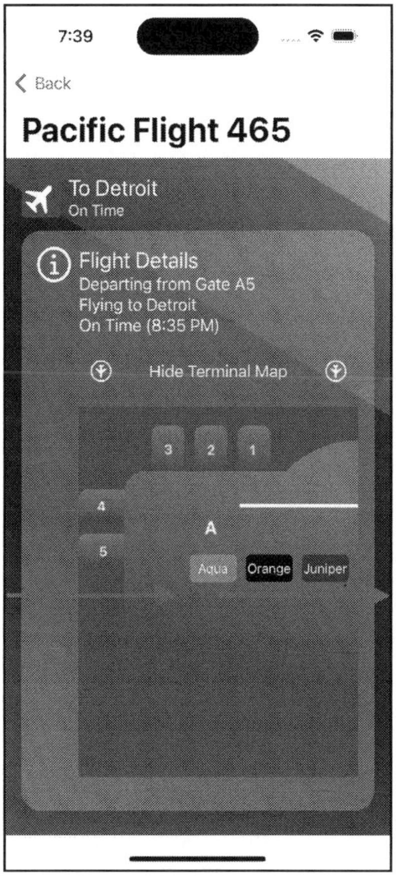

Horizontal slide transition

Async Transitions

SwiftUI lets you specify different transitions when adding and removing a view. Change the static property to:

```
extension AnyTransition {
  static var buttonNameTransition: AnyTransition {
    let insertion = AnyTransition.move(edge: .trailing)
      .combined(with: .opacity)
    let removal = AnyTransition.scale(scale: 0.0)
      .combined(with: .opacity)
    return .asymmetric(insertion: insertion, removal: removal)
  }
}
```

You combine the two transitions with the `combined(with:)` modifier. Preview this new transition.You'll see the view moves in from the trailing edge as it fades in. When SwiftUI removes the view, it will shrink to a point while fading out.

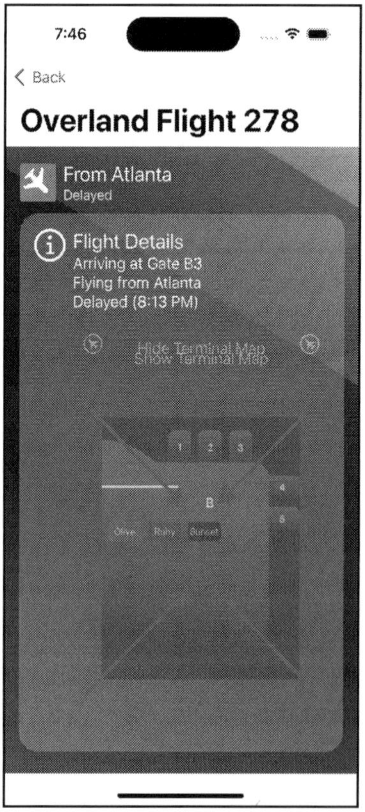

An asymmetric transition

Now that you've learned about animation and transitions, you'll see how to link transitions into more complex animations.

Linking View Transitions

The second release of SwiftUI added many features. You'll use the `matchedGeometryEffect` method in this section. It allows you to synchronize the animations of multiple views. Think of it as a way to tell SwiftUI to connect the animations between two objects.

Open **AwardsView.swift** under the **AwardsView** group. This view displays awards using the grid you developed in **Chapter 16: "Grids"**. When you tap on an award, it transitions to a new view displaying its details. You'll change it to pop-up the award details over the grid.

Add the following code to the top of the view after the `flightNavigation` EnvironmentObject:

```
@State var selectedAward: AwardInformation?
```

When the user taps an award, you'll store it in this optional state variable. Otherwise, the property will be `nil`. Since that tap action takes place in a subview, you'll need to pass this into that subview.

Open **AwardGrid.swift**. Add the following binding after the `awards` property:

```
@Binding var selected: AwardInformation?
```

Using this binding, you'll pass the state from the `AwardsView` to the `AwardGrid`. Change the contents of the `ForEach` loop to:

```
AwardCardView(award: award)
  .foregroundColor(.black)
  .aspectRatio(0.67, contentMode: .fit)
  .onTapGesture {
    selected = award
  }
```

You've removed the navigation link and instead added an `onTapGesture(count:perform:)` modifier to set the binding to the tapped award.

You also need to update the preview to add the new binding parameter. Change it to:

```
AwardGrid(
  title: "Test",
  awards: AppEnvironment().awardList,
  selected: .constant(nil)
)
```

Now, go back to **AwardsView.swift** and change the view to:

```
ZStack {
  // 1
  if let award = selectedAward {
    // 2
    AwardDetails(award: award)
      .background(Color.white)
      .shadow(radius: 5.0)
      .clipShape(RoundedRectangle(cornerRadius: 20.0))
      // 3
      .onTapGesture {
        selectedAward = nil
      }
      // 4
      .navigationTitle(award.title)
  } else {
    ScrollView {
      LazyVGrid(columns: awardColumns) {
        AwardGrid(
          title: "Awarded",
          awards: activeAwards,
          selected: $selectedAward
        )
        AwardGrid(
          title: "Not Awarded",
          awards: inactiveAwards,
          selected: $selectedAward
        )
      }
    }
    .navigationTitle("Your Awards")
  }
}
.background(
  Image("background-view")
    .resizable()
    .frame(maxWidth: .infinity, maxHeight: .infinity)
)
```

You now have a `ZStack` that shows one of two views depending on the `if` statement results. The code inside the else condition didn't change other than passing the binding to the `selectedAward` state variable. There are some changes worth noting:

1. The first change is that you attempt to unwrap the state `selectedAward` state variable. If that fails, you show the grid as before in the `else` part of the statement.

2. If the unwrapping succeeded, you display the `AwardDetails` view that was previously the `NavigationLink` target.

3. When the user taps the view, you set the `selectedAward` state variable back to `nil`. This change removes the `AwardDetails` view and displays the grid.

4. You set the title to the name of the current award.

Run the app. Tap **Your Awards** and then tap any award in the grid. You'll see the view flips to the large details display for the award. Tap `AwardDetails` view, and the grid appears again.

The transition is abrupt. You know you can fix that by adding a view transition. Find the `onTapGesture` modifier in `AwardsView`, under comment three, and change it to:

```
.onTapGesture {
  withAnimation {
    selectedAward = nil
  }
}
```

Hopefully, you remember from earlier in this chapter this tells SwiftUI to animate events caused by the state change in the closure. For the other end of the transition in **AwardGrid.swift**, find the `onTapGesture` modifier in `AwardGrid` and change it to:

```
.onTapGesture {
  withAnimation {
    selected = award
  }
}
```

Run the app, and you'll find the change works better. Now you have a nice fade-out/fade-in effect that smooths the previously harsh transitions between the views. There's still no sense connecting the changes. The two views that you're transitioning between are separate with no connection. That's where `matchedGeometryEffect(id:in:properties:anchor:isSource:)` comes in. It lets you connect the two view transitions.

You must specify the first two parameters. The `id` works much like other `id`s you've encountered in SwiftUI. It uniquely identifies a connection, so giving two items the same `id` links their animations. You pass a `Namespace` to the `in` property. The namespace groups related items and the two together define unique links between views.

Creating a namespace is simple. At the top of `AwardsView`, add the following code after the `selectedAward` state variable.

```
@Namespace var cardNamespace
```

Now you have a unique namespace for the method.

After the `onTapGesture` modifier is attached to `AwardDetails`, add the following:

```
.matchedGeometryEffect(
  id: award.hashValue,
  in: cardNamespace,
  anchor: .topLeading
)
```

You use the existing `hashValue` property as the identifier along with your created namespace. You can use any identifier as long as it's unique within the namespace and consistent. You also specify the `anchor` parameter to specify a location in the view used to produce the shared values. It's not always needed, but in this case, it improves the animation.

Now you have one side set up but need to link the state change in the subview. To do so, you need to pass the namespace into that view. Change the `AwardGrid`s inside the `LazyVGrid` to add it as a parameter:

```
AwardGrid(
  title: "Awarded",
  awards: activeAwards,
  selected: $selectedAward,
  namespace: cardNamespace
)
AwardGrid(
  title: "Not Awarded",
```

```
  awards: inactiveAwards,
  selected: $selectedAward,
  namespace: cardNamespace
)
```

Now open **AwardGrid**. First, you need to add a property to capture the passed namespace. After the `selected` binding, add the following code:

```
var namespace: Namespace.ID
```

When you pass a namespace into a view, it comes in as a `Namespace.ID` type.

You also need to update to preview to pass this new parameter. Add the following to the top of `AwardGrid_Previews` struct:

```
@Namespace static var namespace
```

Update the preview body to:

```
AwardGrid(
  title: "Test",
  awards: AppEnvironment().awardList,
  selected: .constant(nil),
  namespace: namespace
)
```

Now, add the following code after the `onTapGesture(count:perform:)` call:

```
.matchedGeometryEffect(
  id: award.hashValue,
  in: namespace,
  anchor: .topLeading
)
```

Notice this uses the namespace you passed in and therefore is the same namespace as the parent view. Again, you also use the `hashValue` property on the award, the same as used in the parent view. With the two parameters matching, SwiftUI knows to link the transitions.

Run the app now. When you tap an award in the small grid, it shifts and expands while changing to the `AwardDetails` view. Similarly, when you tap `AwardDetails` view, it appears to shrink and move back to the smaller view inside the grid.

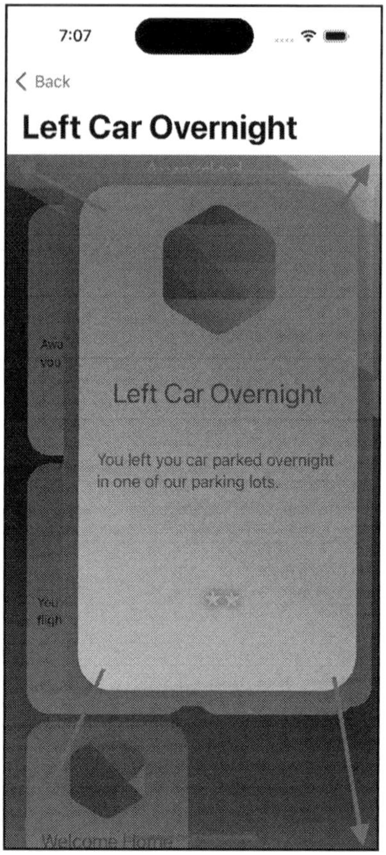

In motion matched geometry effect

Adding `matchedGeometryEffect()` only arranges for the geometry of the views to be linked. The usual transition mechanisms applied to the views still take place during the transition.

Displaying Charts

In **Chapter 18: "Drawing & Custom Graphics"**, you created a pie chart using SwiftUI path components. Earlier editions of this book also walked through creating charts using shapes and paths. SwiftUI provides an easier way to visualize data for your uses — Swift Charts.

Swift Charts allows you to use the declarative syntax of SwiftUI to create charts. Like most SwiftUI components, it supports dynamic font sizes, various screen sizes and accessibility.

Run the app and tap **Search Flights**, then tap the name of any flight. From the flight summary, tap **On-Time History**. You'll see a list showing the recent history of how punctual the flight has been for the last ten days.

> **Note**: The first flight, US 810 to Denver, will provide a suitable range of delays for this section.

Flight delay history

Looking at a few data points can be enlightening, but staring at a long list of numbers isn't the best way to gain insight. A list of numbers isn't the easiest way to display how warm a particular month was or to determine the driest months.

Most people have an easier time grasping information presented graphically. A chart can provide a graphic representation of data designed to inform the viewer. In this section, you'll display this information in a bar chart using Swift Charts.

Creating a Bar Chart

A bar chart provides a bar for each data point. Each bar's length represents the numerical value and can run horizontally or vertically to suit your needs.

Create a new SwiftUI view named **HistoryChartView.swift** under the **SearchFlights** group. First, add a second import to the top of the file:

```
import Charts
```

You must import the Swift Charts module in addition to SwiftUI. Now add a new property to the view:

```
var flightHistory: [FlightHistory]
```

This property will store an array with the flight history you display the chart for. Update the body of the preview to:

```
HistoryChartView(
  flightHistory: FlightData.generateTestFlight(date:
Date()).history
)
```

This code provides sample history data for the preview.

SwiftUI creates charts out of SwiftUI views. As you might expect, you begin with a `Chart` view.

Change the body of the view to:

```
// 1
Chart {
  // 2
  ForEach(flightHistory, id: \.self) { history in
    // 3
    BarMark(
      // 4
      x: .value("Days Ago", history.day),
      y: .value("Minutes", history.timeDifference)
    )
  }
}
```

Since this is your first chart, here's what these parts do:

1. The `Chart` view defines the chart. You'll provide details on the chart within the view's closure.

2. You have a data set to chart in the `flightHistory` array and use a `ForEach` loop to go through it.

3. The `BarkMark` represents data you want to display in a bar chart.

4. You provide the `x` and `y` components of the chart. Here, the `x` parameter indicates how many days ago the current history displays. The `y` parameter shows the delay, which can be a negative number. The `x` component displays horizontally across the chart, while the `y` component displays vertically.

Now go to **FlightTimeHistory.swift** and replace the `ScrollView` and its closure with:

```
HistoryChartView(flightHistory: flight.history)
  .foregroundColor(.black)
  .background {
    Color.white
  }
```

You use the new view you created, passing in the history of the current flight. You apply a black foreground and white background because the default colors don't work well with a darker background like this view has. Don't worry; you'll come back to that late in the chapter.

Run the app, tap **Search Flights** and then tap a flight. You'll see the new bar chart.

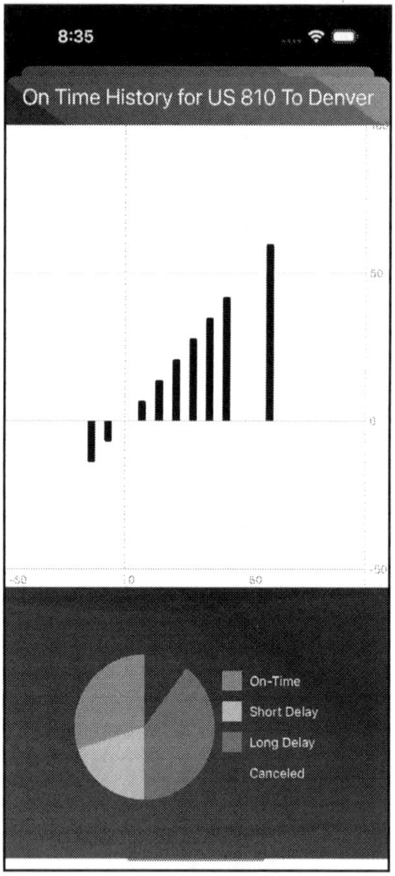

Your first bar chart

You can see the days increasing to the right across the chart with longer delays creating long vertical bars.

Traditional bar charts plot horizontally like this with vertical bars.Because mobile devices limit horizontal space, shifting to a vertical bar chart with the bars drawn horizontally often better uses the available space.

You may think that you can do this by simply swapping the parameters. Try it, change the parameters of BarkMark to:

```
x: .value("Minutes", history.timeDifference),
y: .value("Days Ago", history.day)
```

Now run the app and view the history chart for a flight. You'll see ... something different from what you expected.

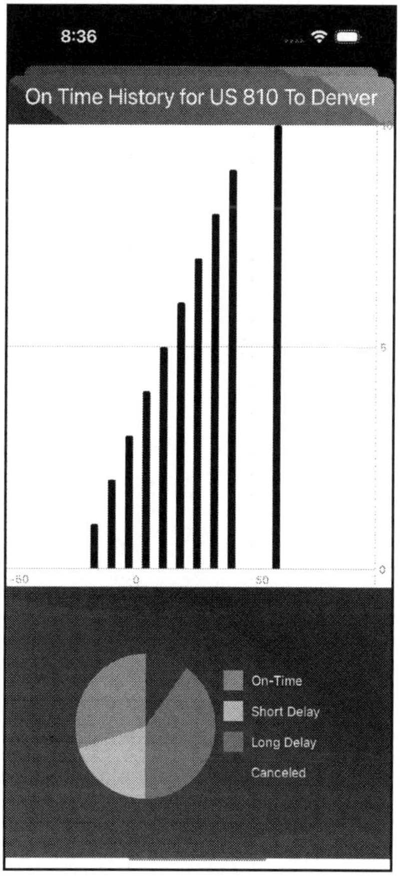

Incorrect vertical bar chart

There are three types of data supported by Swift Charts: quantitative, categorical, and temporal. `Doubles` and `Ints` both fall into the first quantitative category. To get the desired effect, the `y` parameter must be a **categorical** value such as a `String`. Change the `y` property above to:

```
y: .value("Days Ago", "\(history.day) day(s) ago")
```

> **Note: Temporal** values relate to time, but you won't use those in this chapter.

The change produces a `String` that describes the day instead of the `Int`. Run the app, and you'll see what you probably expected earlier.

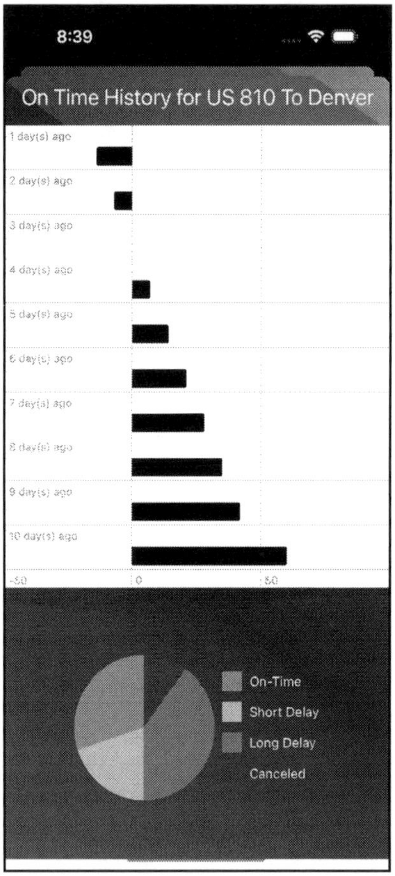

Vertical bar chart

Now that you have a bar chart, you can customize it to provide additional information to the user.

Bar Chart Colors and Annotations

Swift charts will automatically provide colors for the chart unless you specify one. You set the bars to black by applying the `.foregroundColor(.black)` modifier onto the `HistoryChartView` view in **FlightTimeHistory.swift**. Adding color to the bars provides an excellent way to convey additional information. In this section, you'll adjust the bars so the color reflects the length of the delay.

In **HistoryChartView.swift**, add the following modifier to the `BarMark` view:

```
.foregroundStyle(history.delayColor)
```

You set the bar's color to the `delayColor` property from the history. Run the app and view a flight history.

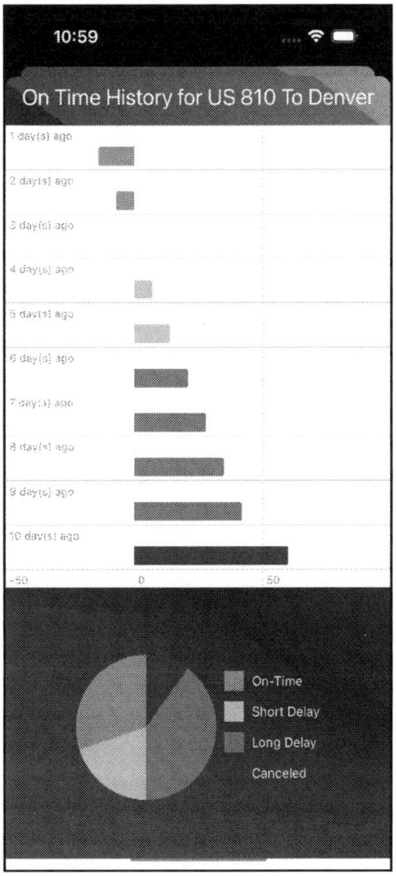

Bar chart with color reflecting the length of the delay

The bars now transition from green, yellow, orange and red as the delays get longer. A solid color fill works well for many cases, but you can apply any SwiftUI style to the bar.

Since the colors have a defined transition, making it a good place to use a gradient. Add the following method after the `flightHistory` property:

```
func barGradientColors(_ history: FlightHistory) -> Gradient {
  if history.status == .canceled {
    return Gradient(
      colors: [
        Color.green,
        Color.yellow,
        Color.red,
        Color(red: 0.5, green: 0, blue: 0)
      ] )
  }
  if history.timeDifference <= 0 {
    return Gradient(colors: [Color.green])
  }
  if history.timeDifference <= 15 {
    return Gradient(colors: [Color.green, Color.yellow])
  }
  return Gradient(
    colors: [Color.green, Color.yellow, Color.red]
  )
}
```

This method returns a gradient consisting of colors from green through the other colors to the color matching the length of the delay. Now you can use the gradient by updating the `foregroundStyle(_:)` modifier on the `BarMark` to:

```
.foregroundStyle(
  // 1
  LinearGradient(
    gradient: barGradientColors(history),
    // 2
    startPoint: .leading,
    endPoint: .trailing
  )
)
```

You use the `barGradientColors(_:)` method to get the colors for the gradient and the following:

1. A linear gradient provides a smooth transition between colors along a straight line through an object, in this case, the rectangle. SwiftUI provides other gradients that change from a central point or sweep around a central point.
2. The values for startPoint and endPoint use a UnitPoint struct. This struct scales a range of values into a zero to one range, making it easier to define a range without worrying about the exact values. UnitPoints origin coordinate is at (0, 0) in the top-left corner of the shape and increases to the right and downward to (1.0, 1.0). The .leading and .trailing static types correspond to points at (0, 0.5) and (1.0, 0.5).

Run the app, and your bars now transition from green to the appropriate color to match the delay. The information is the same, but the gradient makes it feel more dynamic and better conveys the progression of longer delays.

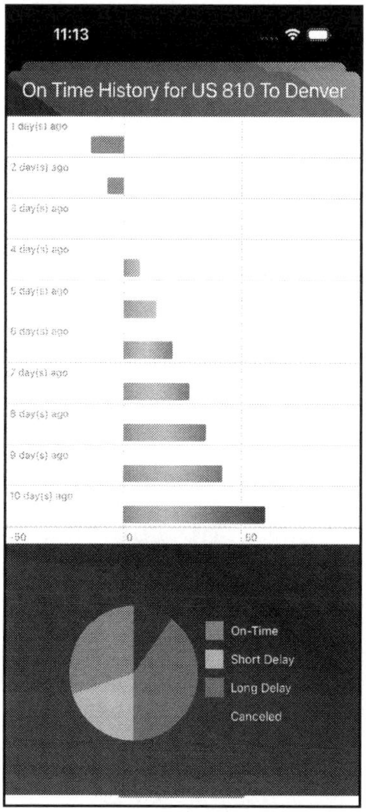

Each bar now has a gradient

With the colors matching the delay length, you'll now add an annotation to each bar of the chart displaying the length of the delay. After the closing parenthesis of the `foregroundStyle(_:)` modifier.

```
.annotation(position: .overlay) {
  Text(history.flightDelayDescription)
    .font(.caption)
}
```

The `annotation(position:alignment:spacing:content:)` modifier allows you to add an annotation to each bar. Here you specify the `overlay` position, showing the annotation on top of the bar. You define the annotation inside the closure. Here that displays the `flightDelayDescription` property for the current bar in the `caption` font.

Run the app, and your new annotations will appear with each bar.

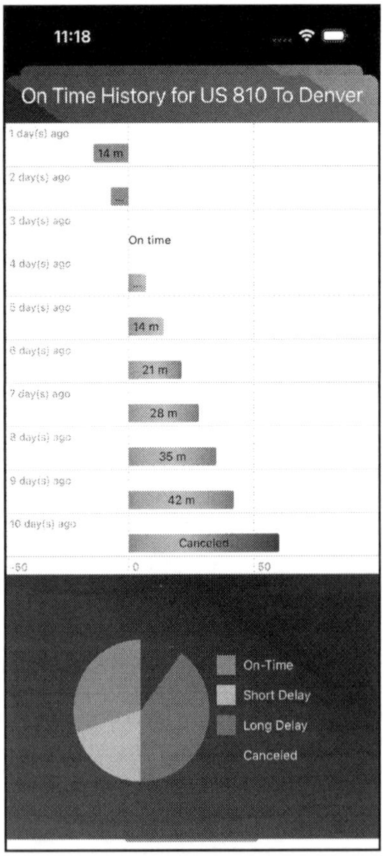

Text annotations added to each bar in the chart

Defining Chart Axes

Swift Charts usually provides a good scale for your chart. In this case, there's a lot of wasted space, especially for negative minute lengths that will never happen. Add the following code after the `Chart` closure to fix this.

```
// 1
.chartXAxis {
  // 2
  AxisMarks(values: [-10, 0, 10, 20, 30, 40, 50, 60]) { value in
    // 3
    AxisGridLine(
      centered: true,
      stroke: StrokeStyle(lineWidth: 1.0, dash: [5.0, 5.0])
    )
  }
}
```

Here's how this code defines the axis:

1. You use the `chartXAxis(content:)` to customize the x-axis of a chart. SwiftUI will no longer provide any default axis, so you must specify all elements for the axis.

2. This `AxisMarks` view tells SwiftUI to draw axis marks. You use the `values` parameter to pass an array of the values where you want to draw a grid line. The closure will be called for each value to show a grid line, in this case, for each value in the `values` array. The `value` parameter will be passed to the closure containing the current axis mark. You'll see how to use this later.

3. The `AxisGridLine` lets you define the characteristics of the grid line. Setting `centered` to true centers the grid line between the two axis values. You specify the attributes for the line drawn to the `stroke` parameter. Here, you draw a one-point wide dashed line alternating between five points long painted and unpainted segments.

Run the app, and you'll see the changes to the chart.

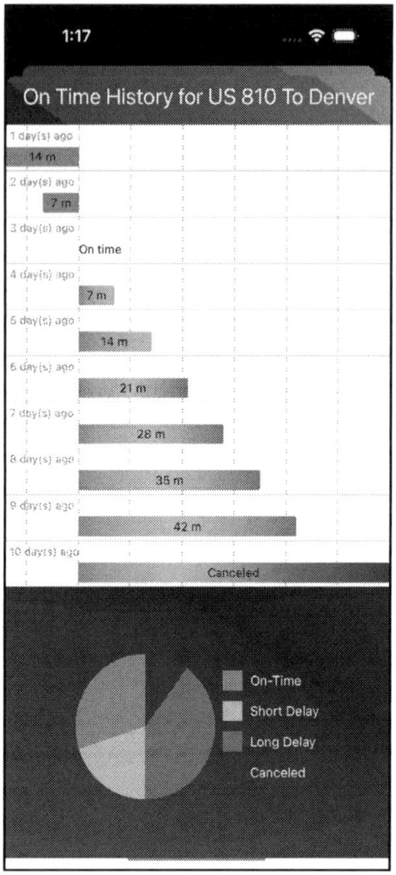

The chart after specifying a custom axis

The chart now tightens on the data with less empty space to help slight differences stand out. Showing more marks helps identify values from the bars without crowding the chart.

Now that you're looking at customization, this makes a good point to address that many default colors don't work well on a dark background. Add the following modifier to `AxisGridLine`:

```
.foregroundStyle(.white.opacity(0.8))
```

This modifier will change the text to white. The `opacity(_:)` modifier mutes the color and helps differentiate between the chart data and the grid line.

Now go to **FlightTimeHistory.swift** and remove the `background(alignment:content:)` and `foregroundColor(_:)` modifiers on `HistoryChartView`. Change the view to:

```
HistoryChartView(flightHistory: flight.history)
  .frame(height: 600)
```

This change sets a fixed height on the chart to space it out. Now wrap the `HistoryChartView` and `HistoryPieChart` inside a `ScrollView` to keep the bar and pie charts visible on smaller devices.

Run the app, and you'll see the new layout. Notice how adding the `foregroundStyle(_:)` modifier lets it appear against the dark background, unlike the defaults.

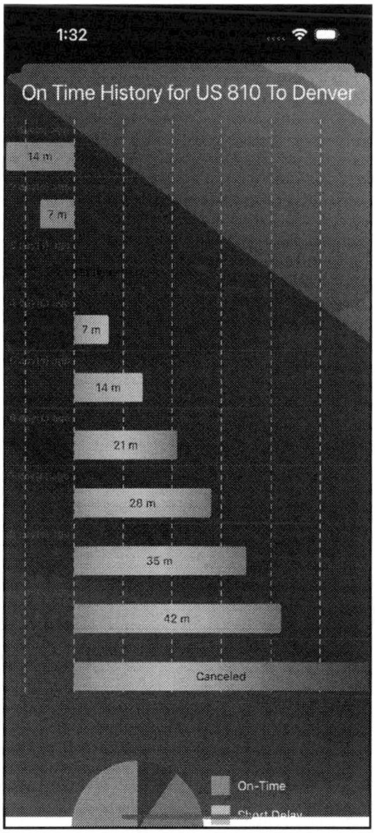

Start of adjust chart to light background

In the next section, you'll finish customizing the chart to show up on this dark background.

Customizing the Chart Colors

You changed the color of the grid lines but not the labels on those grid lines. Add the following code after the `foregroundStyle(_:)` modifier to `AxisGridLine` inside the closure for `AxisMarks`:

```
AxisValueLabel() {
  // 1
  if let value = value.as(Int.self) {
    // 2
    Text(value, format: .number)
      .foregroundColor(Color.white.opacity(0.8))
  }
}
```

This `AxisValueLabel` tells SwiftUI you want to customize the label drawn for the value. Here's how you do that:

1. You attempt to unwrap the current value as an `Int`.
2. If step one succeeds, you create a `Text` view to show the value, and it displays in the same slightly transparent white that you did to the axis line.

Run the app to see the grid labels now appear.

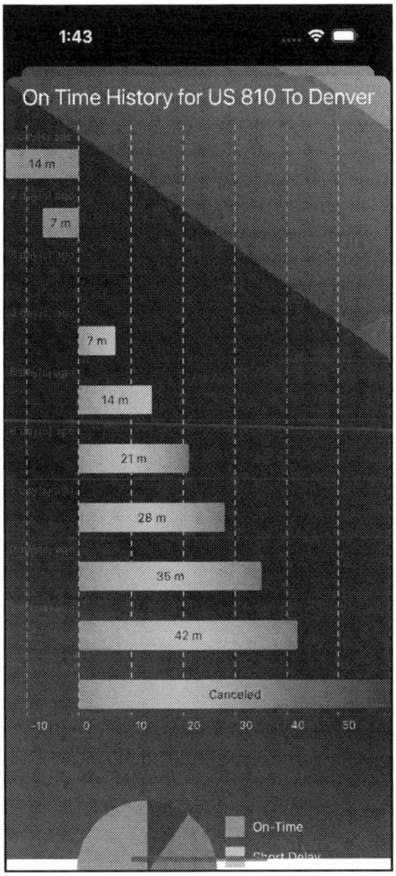

Chart with grid labels

Now, you'll make the changes to the **Y** axis. Add the following code after the `chartXAxis` view:

```
.chartYAxis {
  // 1
  AxisMarks(values: .automatic) { value in
    AxisGridLine(centered: false, stroke: StrokeStyle(lineWidth:
1.0))
      .foregroundStyle(Color.white.opacity(0.8))
    AxisValueLabel() {
      // 2
      if let value = value.as(String.self) {
        Text(value)
          .font(.footnote)
          .foregroundColor(Color.white.opacity(0.8))
      }
    }
  }
}
```

The code is almost identical to what you've already seen. But there are two differences to note:

1. You pass `.automatic` to `values` to let SwiftUI automatically provide axis values, which is the default behavior.
2. You unwrap the `value` as a `String` and use the `footnote` font.

Next, you'll add a label for the **Y** axis. Add the following code after `chartYAxis`:

```
.chartYAxisLabel {
  Text("Delay in Minutes")
    .foregroundColor(.white)
    .font(.callout)
}
```

Using the' callout' font, you create a white label for the **Y** axis. Run the app to see that the chart shows clearly against the dark background.

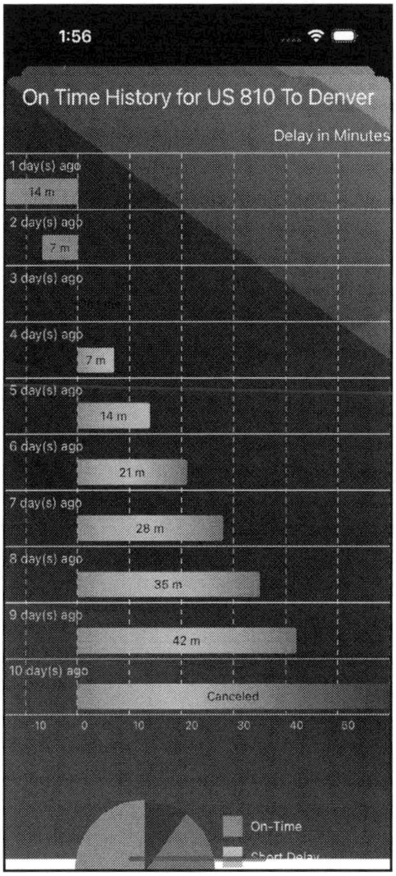

The chart customized to work on a dark background

The chart looks good, but because the axis lines you specified are near the minimum and maximum values, the bars bump right against the chart's edges. To give them some space, add the following code after `chartYAxisLabel`:

```
.chartXScale(domain: -18...63)
```

The `chartXScale(domain:type:)` modifier specifies a scale for the **X** axis. You set a range from three below the minimum and maximum values expected for the chart. If you have data points beyond this range, Swift Charts will cut them off the chart.

> **Note**: As of Xcode 14.2, a bug causes this modifier to break the preview for `HistoryChartView`. It'll show correctly on the `FlightTimeHistory` preview, the simulator, or a device.

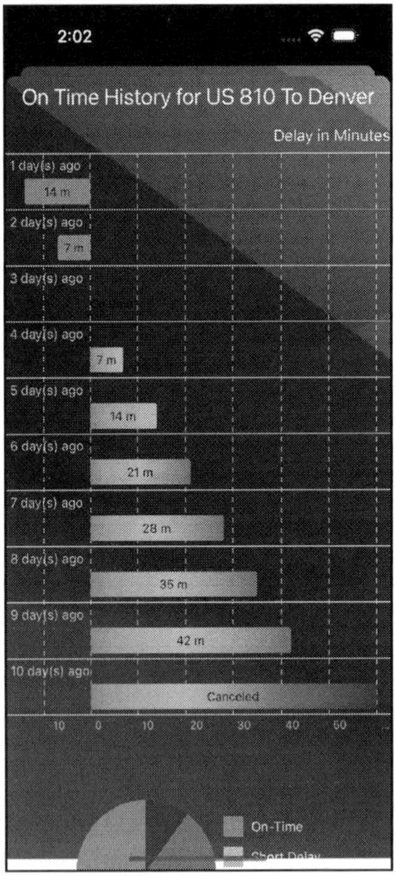

Adding a margin to the sides of the chart using the range

Key Points

- Transitions are a subset of animations applied when SwiftUI shows or hides a view.
- Using `matchedGeometryEffect` lets you link view transitions into a single animation.
- You create charts using the Swift Charts module and the `Chart` view.
- You can customize the axis for a chart using the `chartXAxis` and `chartYAxis` views.
- Within these axis methods, you can use `AxisMarks` to define the grid line values, use `AxisGridLine` to set the properties of the line and use `AxisValueLabel` to control the axis label's appearance.
- You can use `chartXScale` and `chartYScale` to define the range shown on the chart.

Where to Go From Here?

Most references in **Chapter 19: "Animations"** also apply to view transitions.

Chapter 3: "Transitions" of SwiftUI Animations by Tutorials (https://www.kodeco.com/books/swiftui-animations-by-tutorials/) discussed transitions in more detail.

Swift Charts Tutorial: Getting Started (https://www.kodeco.com/36025169-swift-charts-tutorial-getting-started) covers vertical bar charts and line charts.

For examples of drawing charts without Swift Charts, you can view Chapter 18 in earlier editions of this book or SwiftUI Tutorial for the tutorial iOS: Creating Charts (https://www.kodeco.com/6398124-swiftui-tutorial-for-ios-creating-charts).

Chapter 21: Complex Interfaces

By Bill Morefield

SwiftUI represents an exciting new paradigm for UI design. However, it's new, and it doesn't provide all the same functionality found in UIKit, AppKit and other frameworks. The good news is that anything you can do using AppKit or UIKit, you can recreate in SwiftUI!

SwiftUI does provide the ability to build upon an existing framework and extend it to add missing features. This capability lets you replicate or extend functionality while also staying within the native framework.

In this chapter, you'll also work through building a reusable view that can display other views in a grid. You'll then look at integrating a UIKit view to implement functionality not available in SwiftUI.

Building Reusable Views

SwiftUI builds upon the idea of composing views from smaller views. Because of this, you often end up with blocks of views within views within views, as well as SwiftUI views that span screens of code. Splitting components into separate views makes your code cleaner. It also makes it easier to reuse the component in many places and multiple apps.

Open the starter project for this chapter. Build and run the app. Tap on the **Flight Timeline** button to bring up the empty timeline view. Right now, it shows a scrollable list of the flights. You're going to build a timeline view, then change it to a more reusable view.

Simple flight list

It's useful to keep a new solution simple in development instead of trying to do everything at once. You will initially build the timeline specific to your view. First, you'll work on the cards.

Open **FlightCardView.swift** inside the **Timeline** folder and add the following view above `FlightCardView`:

```
struct DepartureTimeView: View {
  var flight: FlightInformation

  var body: some View {
    VStack {
      if flight.direction == .arrival {
        Text(flight.otherAirport)
      }
      Text(
        shortTimeFormatter.string(
          from: flight.departureTime)
      )
    }
  }
}
```

This view displays the departure and arrival times for the flight with the airport's name above the other end's time.

Add the following code after the just added view:

```
struct ArrivalTimeView: View {
  var flight: FlightInformation

  var body: some View {
    VStack {
      if flight.direction == .departure {
        Text(flight.otherAirport)
      }
      Text(
        shortTimeFormatter.string(
          from: flight.arrivalTime
        )
      )
    }
  }
}
```

Now to use those new views. Inside `FlightCardView`, add the following code at the end of the `VStack`:

```
HStack(alignment: .bottom) {
```

```
    DepartureTimeView(flight: flight)
    Spacer()
    ArrivalTimeView(flight: flight)
  }
```

Run the app, view the Flight Timeline and you'll see your changes.

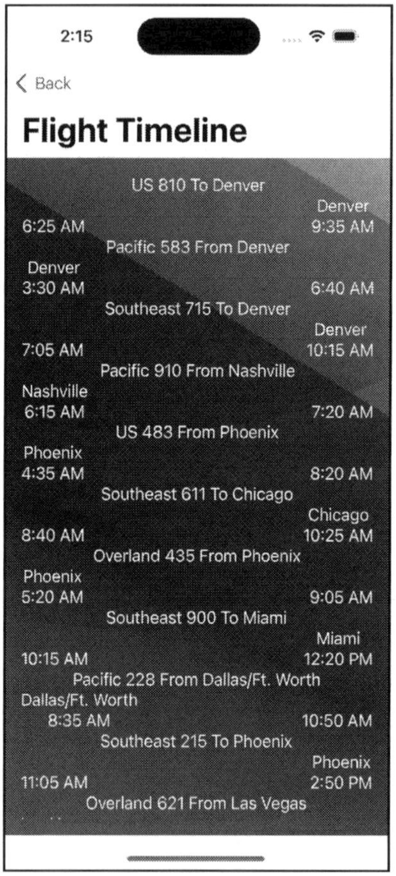

Simple flight cards

Showing Flight Progress

Next, you'll add an indicator of the progress of a flight to the card. The status of a flight will usually be either before departure or after landing. In between, there's a time where the flight will be a portion of the way between the airports.

Add the following code to the **FlightCardView** view after the `flight` parameter:

```
func minutesBetween(_ start: Date, and end: Date) -> Int {
  // 1
  let diff = Calendar.current.dateComponents(
    [.minute], from: start, to: end
  )
  // 2
  guard let minute = diff.minute else {
    return 0
  }
  // 3
  return abs(minute)
}
```

This method takes two `Date` objects and returns the number of minutes between them.

1. The `dateComponents(_:from:to:)` method returns the differences between two dates in the requested units, in this case, minutes.
2. If something went wrong and the `minute` property doesn't exist, then return zero minutes.
3. Return the absolute value of the number of minutes. The absolute value returns only the magnitude ignoring the sign, always resulting in a positive value.

Now you case use this method to get the progress of the flight as floating point value. Add the following code after the `minutesBetween(_:and:)` method:

```
func flightTimeFraction(flight: FlightInformation) -> CGFloat {
  // 1
  let now = Date()
  // 2
  if flight.direction == .departure {
    // 3
    if flight.localTime > now {
      return 0.0
    // 4
    } else if flight.otherEndTime < now {
      return 1.0
    } else {
      // 5
      let timeInFlight = minutesBetween(
        flight.localTime, and: now
      )
      // 6
      let fraction =
        Double(timeInFlight) / Double(flight.flightTime)
      // 7
```

```
      return CGFloat(fraction)
    }
  } else {
    if flight.otherEndTime > now {
      return 0.0
    } else if flight.localTime < now {
      return 1.0
    } else {
      let timeInFlight = minutesBetween(
        flight.otherEndTime, and: now
      )
      let fraction =
        Double(timeInFlight) / Double(flight.flightTime)
      return CGFloat(fraction)
    }
  }
}
```

There's a lot here, and it's somewhat repetitive:

1. You put the current `Date` into a variable as you'll refer to it often in this method.
2. The first case covers departing flights. The case for arriving flights works the same, but with the local and other times swapped.
3. If the `localTime` for the departing flight is after now, then it's not departed yet, meaning the fraction is zero.
4. If the `otherEndTime` parameter for the departing flight is before now, then the flight arrived, meaning the fraction is one.
5. If neither is true, then the flight is somewhere in the air. This code uses the `minutesBetween(_:and:)` method to get the minutes between now and the flight's departure time in minutes.
6. The `flightTime` parameter gives the total length of the flight. You calculate the fraction as the value calculated in the last step, divided by the flight's length.
7. You return the value as a **CGFloat** to make it easier to work with drawings. For more on this, look in **Chapter 18: "Drawing & Custom Graphics"**.

The case for arriving flights works much the same as described except the roles of the local and remote times swapped.

With a method to calculate the flight location, you'll now add a graphical representation in the next section.

Adding Inline Drawings

In this section you'll add a view to show the flight progress. Add the following view after the `ArrivalTimeView` view struct:

```
struct FlightProgressView: View {
  var flight: FlightInformation
  var progress: CGFloat

  var body: some View {
    // 1
    GeometryReader { proxy in
      Image(systemName: "airplane")
        .resizable()
        // 2
        .offset(x: proxy.size.width * progress)
        .frame(width: 25, height: 25)
        .foregroundColor(flight.statusColor)
      // 3
    }.padding([.trailing], 20)
  }
}
```

If you need a refresher on drawing, see **Chapter 18: Drawing & Custom Graphics**. The specifics for this view:

1. The `GeometryReader` causes the view to fill the space. It also provides a `GeometryProxy` you will use to get the width of the view.
2. You get the view's width using the `size` property on the `GeometryProxy`. Multiplying this value by the fraction of the flight gives an offset to reflect the flight's progress.
3. The `offset` in step two ignores that the offset controls the left side of the image. Setting the offset to the far edge pushes the image outside the view. You add a 20 point padding to the view's trailing edge, providing a space for the image.

Now use the new view. In the `HStack` within `FlightCardView` replace the `Spacer` between `DepartureTimeView` and `FlightProgressView` with a call to the function:

```
FlightProgressView(
  flight: flight,
  progress: flightTimeFraction(
    flight: flight
  )
)
```

Build and run the app, and you'll see the progress indicator added to each flight.

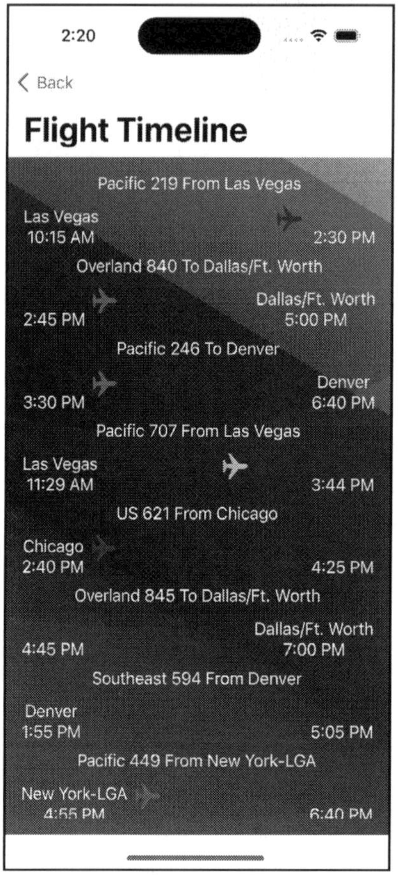

Showing flight progress

Now that you have the underlying grid in place, you'll let the caller specify the view inside the grid.

Using a ViewBuilder

The timeline you've created always shows the same view. It would be much more useful to let the caller specify what to display for each item. That's where the SwiftUI **ViewBuilder** comes in.

Recall the initial code for this list below:

```
ForEach(flights) { flight in
  FlightCardView(flight: flight)
}
```

You passed `FlightCardView` to the closure of the `ForEach` loop. `ForEach` uses a `ViewBuilder` to create a parameter for the view-producing closure. You'll now move the timeline to a separate view and update it to take a passed view through the closure instead of hard—coding it.

Create a new SwiftUI view named **GenericTimeline** in the **Timeline** group. First, update the struct definition to the following:

```
struct GenericTimeline<Content>: View where Content: View {
```

This change allows `GenericTimeline` to accept `View` values as dependencies. With that, update the contents of `GenericTimeline` to the following:

```
// 1
let flights: [FlightInformation]
let content: (FlightInformation) -> Content

// 2
init(
  flights: [FlightInformation],
  @ViewBuilder content: @escaping (FlightInformation) -> Content
) {
  self.flights = flights
  self.content = content
}

// 3
var body: some View {
  ScrollView {
    VStack {
      ForEach(flights) { flight in
        // 4
        content(flight)
      }
    }
  }
}
```

Here's what you've added:

1. This new `GenericTimeline` view will take a list of `FlightInformation` values and a closure that instructs how this view should use `FlightInformation` to display a view.
2. In order to make use of `content`, you need to use the `@ViewBuilder` function builder. You'll create a custom initializer that applies the function builder. The initializer sets the internal properties to the values passed into the initializer.
3. Your new `body` property displays a list of generic views that are constructed using the `content` view builder.
4. The view passed in to the `ViewBuilder` will appear where you use the `content` method.

Next, update the preview to include the new changes you've made:

```
GenericTimeline(
  flights: FlightData.generateTestFlights(
    date: Date()
  )
) { flight in
  FlightCardView(flight: flight)
}
```

Now that `GenericTimeline` is set up, navigate to **FlightTimelineView.swift**. Find the following block of code that creates the list of views:

```
ScrollView {
  VStack {
    ForEach(flights) { flight in
      FlightCardView(flight: flight)
    }
  }
}
```

Replace the above code with the following:

```
GenericTimeline(flights: flights) { flight in
  FlightCardView(flight: flight)
}
```

Take a moment to appreciate what you've created here. Instead of hard coding the list-view behavior in `FlightTimelineView`, you're now using a generic view that does this for you.

Run the app and verify the timeline looks as before. While there's no change in appearance, you've gained a more flexible way to choose the view to show for each flight.

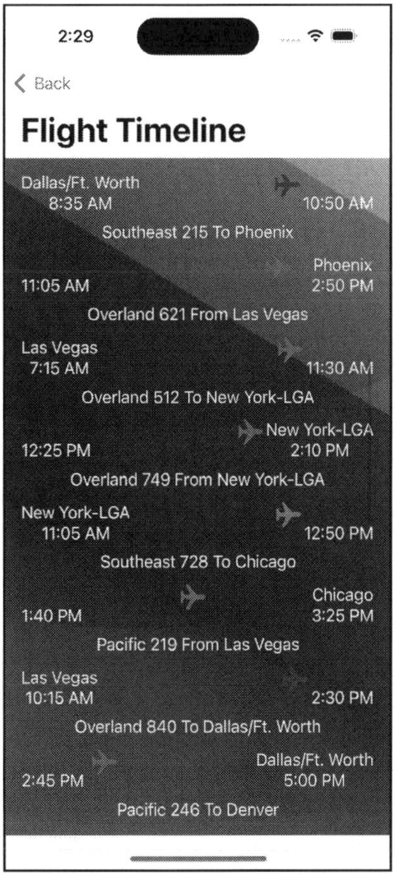

Timeline with enclosed view

While this change makes it easier to specify different views, it still relies on the `FlightInformation` structure preventing reuse in other projects. In the next section, you'll address that limitation.

Making the Timeline Generic

Generics allow you to write code without being specific about the type of data you're using. You can write a function once and use it on any data type.

First, change the declaration of the view to:

```
struct GenericTimeline<Content, T>: View where Content: View {
```

You're saying here that you want to use a generic type in the struct. Instead of specifying `Int`, `FlightInformation` or another type, you can now specify `T`. You can now change the other references to `FlightInformation` into the generic type `T` instead. Change the declaration of the `flights` property to:

```
var events: [T]
```

You're also changing the name to reflect this value no longer ties only to flights but also works with any event. You also need to change the type for the parameter passed into the closure. Change the definition of the `Content` property to:

```
let content: (T) -> Content
```

You'll also need to change the custom initializer to use `T` instead of the `FlightInformation` type. You also need to change the `flights` property to `events`. Change the `init()` method to:

```
init(
  events: [T],
  @ViewBuilder content: @escaping (T) -> Content
) {
  self.events = events
  self.content = content
}
```

Now you need to change references in the view to `flights` to `events`. First change the preview to use the new parameter name:

```
GenericTimeline(
  events: FlightData.generateTestFlights(
    date: Date()
  )
) { flight in
  FlightCardView(flight: flight)
}
```

There's a hidden problem lurking in the view that results from using a generic. Change the view to:

```
ScrollView {
  VStack {
    ForEach(events) { flight in
      content(flight)
    }
  }
}
```

You'll see an error:**Referencing initializer 'init(_:content:)' on 'ForEach' requires that 'T' conform to 'Identifiable'**.Generics add flexibility, but this is the cost of that flexibility. There's no way for SwiftUI to know that the type you later specify will implement the `Identifiable` protocol required by `ForEach`. To work around this, change the code to:

```
ScrollView {
  VStack {
    ForEach(events.indices, id: \.self) { index in
      content(events[index])
    }
  }
}
```

Instead of iterating over the collection items, you iterate over the collection's indices, which `ForEach` happily accepts. You reference the individual elements of the collection using the index.

Now back in **FlightTimelineView.swift** change the parameter on `GenericTimeline` from `flights` to `events`:

```
GenericTimeline(events: flights) { flight in
```

You're done. Generics let you pivot from a specific reference to the generic represented by `T` in this case. Swift handles the rest.

Run the app to see that your timeline still works.

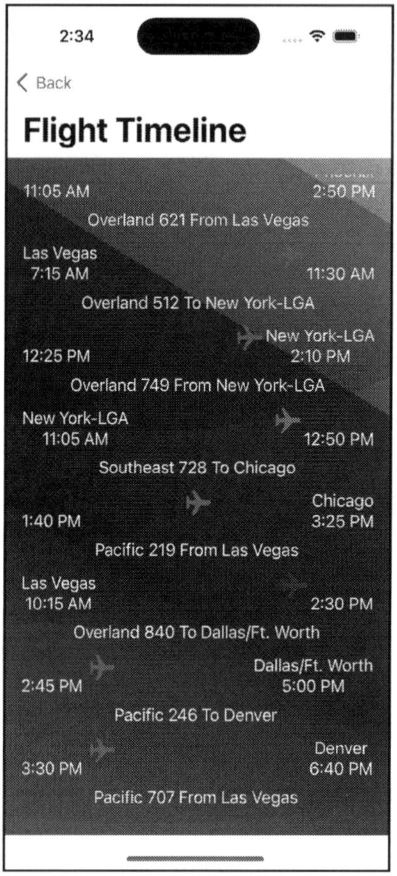

Generic timeline

Right now, your timeline isn't that much of a timeline. Let's change that. You'll also learn about another feature of Swift used in SwiftUI — **KeyPaths**.

Using Keypaths

A `KeyPath` lets you refer to a property on an object. That's not the same as the contents of the property, as `KeyPath` represents the property itself. You use them quite often in SwiftUI. In fact, you're already using them. In the last section you used a KeyPath in the following code:

```
ForEach(events.indices, id: \.self) { index in
```

When using `ForEach` with a collection of objects that don't implement `Identifiable`, you pass in a KeyPath to the `id` parameter. The KeyPath provides SwiftUI with a property that identifies each element uniquely. Here `\.self` is a KeyPath telling SwiftUI that the object uniquely identifies itself.

Since your timeline takes a generic type, meaning you could pass in any object, you need a way to let the view know the property on the object that contains the time information. That's the perfect use for a KeyPath.

First in **GenericTimeline.swift** add the following property after `content`:

```
let timeProperty: KeyPath<T, Date>
```

Declaring a KeyPath takes two parameters. The first is the type of object for it. In this case, you use the same `T` generic type you added in the previous section. The second parameter tells Swift that the parameter the KeyPath points to will be of type `Date`.

You also need to update the `init` method to add the new property:

```
init(
  events: [T],
  timeProperty: KeyPath<T, Date>,
  @ViewBuilder content: @escaping (T) -> Content
) {
  self.events = events
  self.content = content
  self.timeProperty = timeProperty
}
```

Next, update the preview to pass in the new parameter:

```
GenericTimeline(
  events: FlightData.generateTestFlights(
    date: Date()
  ),
  timeProperty: \.localTime
) { flight in
  FlightCardView(flight: flight)
}
```

This KeyPath tells SwiftUI to use the `localTime` property of the `FlightInformation` objects to determine each object's time. Now that you can specify a KeyPath, you can use it.

Now that you can indicate the time property, you can change the view to look bit more like a timeline. Add the following code after the `init` method:

```
var earliestHour: Int {
  let flightsAscending = events.sorted {
    // 1
    $0[keyPath: timeProperty] < $1[keyPath: timeProperty]
  }

  // 2
  guard let firstFlight = flightsAscending.first else {
    return 0
  }
  // 3
  let hour = Calendar.current.component(
    .hour,
    from: firstFlight[keyPath: timeProperty]
  )
  return hour
}
```

This method takes the events and sorts them in ascending by the property specified using the KeyPath:

1. The method first sorts the objects using the KeyPath. The $0 syntax within the `sorted` method's closure indicates one of the objects under evaluation. To access a property of it defined using a KeyPath, you use the `[keyPath: timeProperty]` syntax.
2. The first element should be the earliest. If there is no first element — the array is empty — then return the earliest possible hour.
3. You then get the hour component of the first element and returns it. You use a similar syntax as in step one to get the time property using `firstFlight[keyPath: timeProperty]`.

Now add a similar method after this one to get the latest hour in the events:

```
var latestHour: Int {
  let flightsAscending = events.sorted {
    $0[keyPath: timeProperty] > $1[keyPath: timeProperty]
  }

  guard let firstFlight = flightsAscending.first else {
    return 24
  }
  let hour = Calendar.current.component(
    .hour,
    from: firstFlight[keyPath: timeProperty]
```

```
    )
    return hour + 1
  }
```

This method does the same thing, except it sorts from latest to earliest, so the first element will be the hour of the latest event. You add an hour since you will use an open range in the loop. For no events, it returns the latest possible hour.

Next add a method to get the events within a specified hour:

```
  func eventsInHour(_ hour: Int) -> [T] {
    return events
      .filter {
        let flightHour =
          Calendar.current.component(
            .hour,
            from: $0[keyPath: timeProperty]
          )
        return flightHour == hour
      }
  }
```

Like the other two methods, this one uses the KeyPath to filter only flights where the hour component of the time matches that passed into the method.

Add one more method:

```
  func hourString(_ hour: Int) -> String {
    let tcmp = DateComponents(hour: hour)
    if let time = Calendar.current.date(from: tcmp) {
      return shortTimeFormatter.string(from: time)
    }
    return "Unknown"
  }
```

This one takes a passed hour and creates a string displaying the time at that hour.

Now you'll update the view using these new methods. Change the `body` for the `GenericTimeline` to:

```
  ScrollView {
    VStack(alignment: .leading) {
      // 1
      ForEach(earliestHour..<latestHour, id: \.self) { hour in
        // 2
        let hourFlights = eventsInHour(hour)
        // 3
        Text(hourString(hour))
          .font(.title2)
```

```
        // 4
        ForEach(hourFlights.indices, id: \.self) { index in
          content(hourFlights[index])
        }
      }
    }
  }
```

You've added a few more features to the timeline. Here are the new items:

1. You now loop through the hours of events using the `earliestHour` and `earliestHour` properties.
2. For each hour, you use the `eventsInHour(_:)` method to get only the events taking place in that hour.
3. Each hour shows a header with the time using the `hourString` method.
4. You now only loop through the `hourFlights` indices since you're splitting the overall events into hours.

With a generic timeline done, you can now use it in your view.

Using the Timeline

First let's give a nicer appearance to the cards. Open **FlightCardView.swift** and add the following at the end of the `VStack`:

```
.padding()
.background(
  Color.gray.opacity(0.3)
)
.clipShape(
  RoundedRectangle(cornerRadius: 20)
)
.overlay(
  RoundedRectangle(cornerRadius: 20)
    .stroke()
)
```

Back in **FlightTimelineView.swift**, update the `GenericTimeline` to:

```
GenericTimeline(
  events: flights,
  timeProperty: \.localTime) { flight in
    FlightCardView(flight: flight)
}
```

Run the app to see your improved timeline.

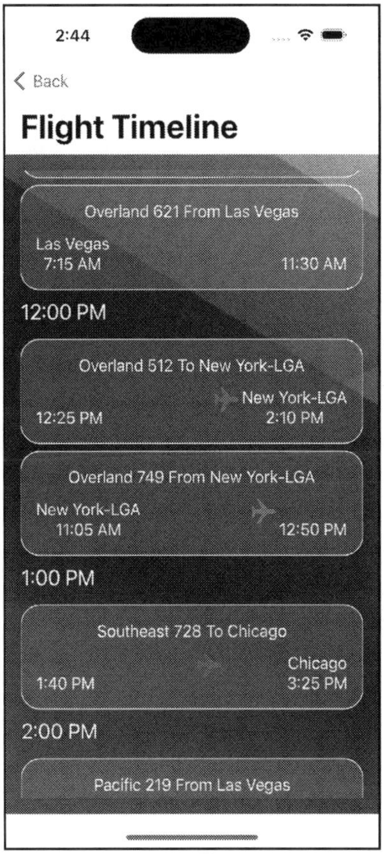

Completed timeline

That's the power of SwiftUI, Swift, KeyPaths and generics. In this section, you've built a timeline and encapsulated it so you can pass any object and display the results. Great work!

Integrating With Other Frameworks

SwiftUI continues to add new features, but it can't do everything possible in UIKit or AppKit. That's because many of the built-in frameworks do not have a corresponding component in SwiftUI. Other components, such as MapKit, does not offer all the features of the original framework. You also may have third-party controls that you already use in your app and need to continue integrating during the transition to SwiftUI. In this section, you'll look at using your generic timeline with MapKit.

To work with UIViews and UIViewControllers in SwiftUI, you must create types that conform to the UIViewRepresentable and UIViewControllerRepresentable protocols. SwiftUI will manage these views' life cycle, so you only need to create and configure the views. The underlying frameworks will take care of the rest.

Create a new Swift file — *not* SwiftUI view — named **FlightMapView.swift** in the **Timeline** group.

Replace the contents of **FlightMapView.swift** with:

```
import SwiftUI
import MapKit

struct FlightMapView: UIViewRepresentable {
  var startCoordinate: CLLocationCoordinate2D
  var endCoordinate: CLLocationCoordinate2D
  var progress: CGFloat
}
```

This code imports the MapKit UIKit for this file. You next create the type that will wrap the MKMapView. SwiftUI includes several protocols that allow integration to views, view controllers and other app framework components. You pass in a starting coordinate and ending coordinate to display on the map along with a progress fraction. This fraction indicates how much of the path to draw.

There are two methods in the UIViewControllerRepresentable protocol you will need to implement: makeUIViewController(context:), and updateUIViewController(_:context:). You'll create those now.

Add the following code to the struct below the progress parameter:

```
func makeUIView(context: Context) -> MKMapView {
  MKMapView(frame: .zero)
}
```

SwiftUI will call makeUIViewController(context:) once when it is ready to display the view. Here, you create a MKMapView programmatically and return it using the Swift feature that treats a single-line method as an implicit return. Any UIKit ViewController would work here; there are similar protocols for AppKit, WatchKit and other views and view controllers on the appropriate platform.

Now add this code to the end of the struct to implement the second method:

```
func updateUIView(_ view: MKMapView, context: Context) {
  // 1
  let startPoint = MKMapPoint(startCoordinate)
```

```
    let endPoint = MKMapPoint(endCoordinate)

    // 2
    let minXPoint = min(startPoint.x, endPoint.x)
    let minYPoint = min(startPoint.y, endPoint.y)
    let maxXPoint = max(startPoint.x, endPoint.x)
    let maxYPoint = max(startPoint.y, endPoint.y)

    // 3
    let mapRect = MKMapRect(
      x: minXPoint,
      y: minYPoint,
      width: maxXPoint - minXPoint,
      height: maxYPoint - minYPoint
    )
    // 4
    let padding = UIEdgeInsets(
      top: 10.0,
      left: 10.0,
      bottom: 10.0,
      right: 10.0
    )
    // 5
    view.setVisibleMapRect(
      mapRect,
      edgePadding: padding,
      animated: true
    )
    // 6
    view.mapType = .mutedStandard
    view.isScrollEnabled = false
  }
```

SwiftUI calls `updateUIViewController(_:context:)` when it wants you to update the presented view controller's configuration. Much of the setup you would typically do in `viewDidLoad()` in a UIKit view will go into this method. For the moment, you define the map to show.

1. When you project the curved surface of the Earth onto a flat surface, such as a device screen, some distortion occurs. You convert the start and end coordinates on the globe to `MKMapPoint` values in the flattened map. Using MKMapPoints dramatically simplifies the calculations to follow.

2. Next, you determine the minimum and maximum `x` and `y` values among these points.

3. You create a `MKMapRect` from those minimum and maximum values. The resulting rectangle covers the space between the two points along the rectangle's edge.

4. Next, you create a `UIEdgeInsets` struct with all sides set to an inset of ten points.

5. You use the `setVisibleMapRect(_:edgePadding:animated:)` method to set the map's viewable area. This method uses the rectangle calculated in step three as the area to show. The `edgePadding` adds the padding that you set up in step four, so the airports' locations are not directly at the edge of the view and, therefore, easier to see.

6. You set the type of map and do not allow the user to scroll the map.

Since you created a Swift file and not a SwiftUI view, you didn't get a preview by default. To fix that, at the bottom of the file after the `FlightMapView` struct, add the following code:

```
struct MapView_Previews: PreviewProvider {
  static var previews: some View {
    FlightMapView(
      startCoordinate: CLLocationCoordinate2D(
        latitude: 35.655, longitude: -83.4411
      ),
      endCoordinate: CLLocationCoordinate2D(
        latitude: 36.0840, longitude: -115.1537
      ),
      progress: 0.67
    )
    .frame(width: 300, height: 300)
  }
}
```

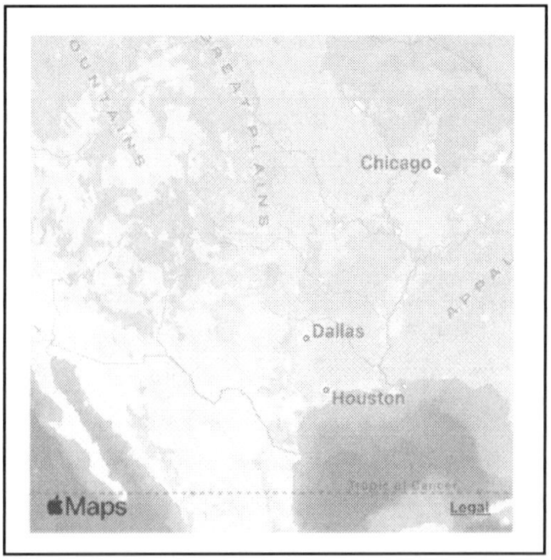

Wrapped mapview

Now that you have a map, you'll add an overlay to it to show each airport along with the progress for active flights. In the next section, you'll learn how to handle delegates when wrapping non-SwiftUI components.

Connecting Delegates, Data Sources and More

If you're familiar with MKMap in iOS, you might wonder how you provide the delegate to add overlays to this `MKMapView`. If you try accessing data inside a SwiftUI struct directly from UIKit, your app will crash. Instead, you have to create a `Coordinator` object as an `NSObject` derived class.

This class acts as a transition or bridge between the data inside SwiftUI and the external framework. You can see `context` passed in as the second parameter in the `updateUIViewController(_:context:)` method. Add the following code for the new class at the top of `FlightMapView.swift`, before the `FlightMapView` struct:

```
class MapCoordinator: NSObject {
  var mapView: FlightMapView
  var fraction: CGFloat

  init(
    _ mapView: FlightMapView,
    progress: CGFloat = 0.0
  ) {
    self.mapView = mapView
    self.fraction = progress
  }
}
```

You're creating the class and a custom initializer to pass in the flight information to the class. This `Coordinator` will allow you to connect the delegate. It's also where you could connect a data source for something like a `UITableView` along with a place to deal with user events.

You need to tell SwiftUI about the `Coordinator` class. Add the following code to the `FlightMapView` struct after `makeUIView(context:)`:

```
func makeCoordinator() -> MapCoordinator {
  MapCoordinator(self, progress: progress)
}
```

This method creates the coordinator and returns it to the SwiftUI framework to pass in where necessary. SwiftUI will call `makeCoordinator()` before `makeUIViewController(context:)` so it's available during the creation and configuration of your non-SwiftUI components.

You can now implement the overlays that need a delegate. In `updateUIView(_:context:)` add the following code to the top of the method:

```
let startOverlay = MKCircle(
  center: startCoordinate,
  radius: 10000.0
)
let endOverlay = MKCircle(
  center: endCoordinate,
  radius: 10000.0
)
let flightPath = MKGeodesicPolyline(
  coordinates: [startCoordinate, endCoordinate],
  count: 2
)
view.addOverlays([startOverlay, endOverlay, flightPath])
```

You create three overlays. The first and second are circles located at the start and end coordinates. You next create a `MKGeodesicPolyline` connecting the start and end coordinates. An `MKGeodesicPolyline` creates a shape that follows the contours of the Earth along the shortest path between points. As mentioned earlier, the movement from the Earth's curved surface to the flat map distorts shapes. An `MKGeodesicPolyline` reflects the shortest path over the Earth. It often appears curved when shown on a flat map. It also provides a good representation of the route a plane would take flying between two points.

If you're familiar with `MKMapView`, then you know you need implement the delegate for the overlays to show. Add the following class extension after the current `MapCoordinator` class definition:

```
extension MapCoordinator: MKMapViewDelegate {
  func mapView(
    _ mapView: MKMapView,
    rendererFor overlay: MKOverlay
  ) -> MKOverlayRenderer {
    if overlay is MKCircle {
      let renderer = MKCircleRenderer(overlay: overlay)
      renderer.fillColor = UIColor.black
      renderer.strokeColor = UIColor.black
      return renderer
    }

    if overlay is MKGeodesicPolyline {
      let renderer = MKPolylineRenderer(overlay: overlay)
      renderer.strokeColor = UIColor(
        red: 0.0,
        green: 0.0,
        blue: 1.0,
        alpha: 0.3
```

```
      )
      renderer.lineWidth = 3.0
      renderer.strokeStart = 0.0
      renderer.strokeEnd = fraction
      return renderer
    }

    return MKOverlayRenderer()
  }
}
```

This extension handles the overlays. For the `MKCircle`, it merely colors the circles black. For the `MKGeodesicPolyline`, it strokes the line with a mostly transparent blue color. It sets the `strokeEnd` property on the renderer using the `fraction` property passed into the `MapCoordinator` class. This ending location lets it reflect the partial distance of flights that are in progress. Note that this class and control know nothing about SwiftUI. The code you've used here works as it does in UIKit.

Now that you've implemented a `MKMapViewDelegate`, you can set it for the `MKMapView`. Update `makeUIView(context:)` to:

```
func makeUIView(context: Context) -> MKMapView {
  let view = MKMapView(frame: .zero)
  view.delegate = context.coordinator
  return view
}
```

Now you can add the new view to the app. Open **FlightCardView.swift** and add the following code at the end of the `VStack`:

```
FlightMapView(
  startCoordinate: flight.startingAirportLocation,
  endCoordinate: flight.endingAirportLocation,
  progress: flightTimeFraction(
    flight: flight
  )
)
.frame(width: 300, height: 300)
```

Build and run the app. Tap on the **Flight Timeline** button, and you'll see the new timeline in action:

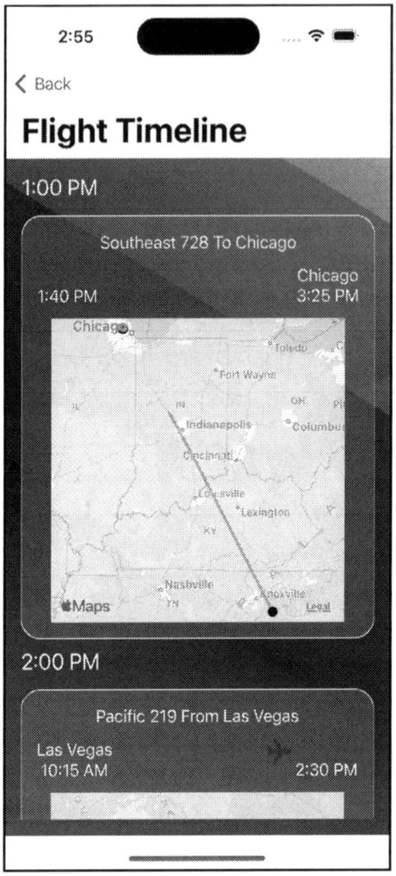

Timeline with map

It doesn't take a lot of work to integrate pre-existing Apple frameworks into your SwiftUI app. Over time, you'll likely move more of your app's functionality to SwiftUI when possible. The ability to integrate SwiftUI in your legacy apps gives you a neat way to begin using SwiftUI, without having to start from scratch.

Key Points

- You build views using `Representable` — derived protocols to integrate SwiftUI with other Apple frameworks.
- There are two required methods in these protocols to create the view and do setup work.
- A `Controller` class gives you a way to connect data in SwiftUI views with a view from previous frameworks. You can use this to manage delegates and related patterns.
- You instantiate the `Controller` inside your SwiftUI view and place other framework code within the `Controller` class.
- You can use a `ViewBuilder` to pass views into another view when doing iterations.
- Generics let your views work without hard-coding specific types.
- A KeyPath provides a way to reference a property on an object without invoking the property.

Where to Go From Here?

- For more on using UIKit within SwiftUI see Interfacing with UIKit (https://developer.apple.com/tutorials/swiftui/interfacing-with-uikit).
- For more on KeyPaths, see the **Key-Path Expression** section of the Expressions (https://docs.swift.org/swift-book/ReferenceManual/Expressions.html) chapter of the Swift Programming Language Manual.
- For more about generics in Swift see Swift Generics Tutorial: Getting Started (https://www.kodeco.com/3535703-swift-generics-tutorial-getting-started).

Section VI: SwiftUI for macOS

Learn how to implement all you know of SwiftUI in macOS desktop applications.

Chapter 22: Building a Mac App

By Sarah Reichelt

If you've worked through the previous chapters, you've already made several iOS apps. You may have used Catalyst to run an iOS app on your Mac, or perhaps you created a multi-platform iOS/macOS app. But in this chapter, you'll write a purely **Mac app**. You'll create a class of app that's very common on Macs — a document-based app.

Many Mac apps are document-based. Think of apps like TextEdit, Pages, Numbers or Photoshop. Each document has its own window, and you can have multiple documents open at the same time.

In this chapter, you'll build a **Markdown** editor. Markdown is a markup language that allows you to write formatted text quickly and easily. It can be converted into HTML for display but it's much more convenient to write, read and edit.

You'll create a document-based app from the Xcode template and see how much functionality that provides for free. Then you'll go on to customize the file type for saving and opening as well as adding HTML preview, menus and a toolbar.

The Default Document App

Open Xcode and create a new project. Select **macOS** and choose **Document App**. Make sure the interface is **SwiftUI** and the language is **Swift**. Call the app **MacMarkDown**.

Once you've saved the project, build and run the app. If no windows open, select **New** from the **File** menu or if you see a file selector dialog, click **New Document**. You'll see a single window showing some default text. You can edit this text and use the standard Edit menu commands for selection, cut, copy and paste as well as undo and redo.

Select **Save** from the **File** menu:

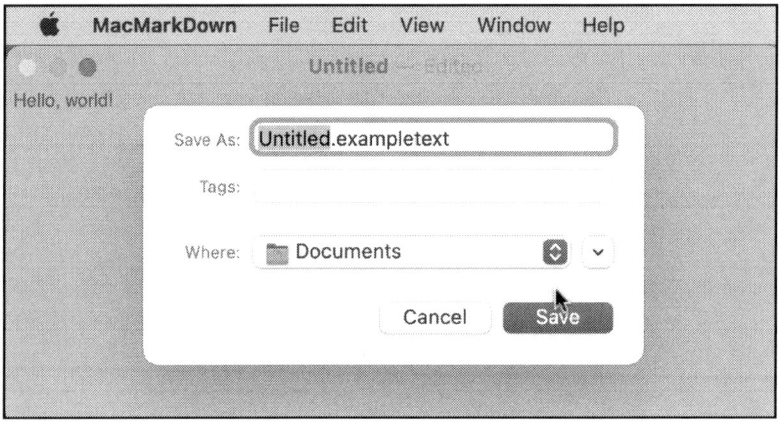

Saving the default document

> **Note**: If you don't see the file extension in the save dialog, go to **Finder ▸ Settings ▸ Advanced** and turn on **Show all filename extensions.** This'll make it easier to follow the next part of this chapter.

The default app uses a file extension of **.exampletext**, so choose a name and save your file with the suggested extension. Close the window and create a new window using **Command-N**. Now try opening your saved document by choosing **Open...** from the **File** menu.

And all this is without writing a single line of code!

Close the app, go back to Xcode and look at **MacMarkDownApp.swift**. Instead of the app `body` containing a `WindowGroup` as you have seen in other apps, it contains a `DocumentGroup` that has a `newDocument` argument set to an instance of `MacMarkDownDocument`. The `ContentView` gets a reference to this `document`.

Looking in **ContentView.swift**, you'll see the only view inside the `body` is a `TextEditor`. This view allows editing long chunks of text. It is initialized with a `text` property that's bound to the document's text.

Open **MacMarkDownDocument.swift** to see where the file saving and opening happens. The first thing to note is the `UTType` extension. **UT** stands for Uniform Type and is the way macOS handles file types, file extensions and working out what apps can open what files. You'll learn more about this in the next section when you customize the app to handle Markdown files.

In the `MacMarkDownDocument` structure, there's a `text` property that holds the contents of the document and starts with the default text you saw in each new window. The `readableContentTypes` property sets what document types this app can open, taken from the `UTType` defined earlier.

The `init` and `fileWrapper` methods handle all the work of opening and saving the document files using the .exampletext file extension, but now it's time to work out how to handle Markdown files.

Configuring for Markdown

When you double-click a document file on your Mac, Finder opens it with the default application: TextEdit for .txt files, Preview for .png files and so on. Right-click any document file and look at the **Open With** menu — you'll see a list of the applications on your Mac that can open that type of file. Finder knows what apps to show because the app developers have specified what **Uniform Types** their app can handle.

To set up a document-based app to open a particular file type, you'll need three pieces of data:

- The Uniform Type Identifier or UTI.
- What standard file type this conforms to.
- The file extension or extensions.

Apple provides a list of system-declared uniform type identifiers (https://apple.co/3iSjUwz), which can often be useful when working out file types for an app, but in this case it doesn't help as Markdown isn't on the list.

However searching for "markdown uniform type identifier" gets you to Daring Fireball (https://bit.ly/3vob8vK), where John Gruber, the inventor of Markdown, says that the Uniform Type Identifier is "net.daringfireball.markdown" and that this conforms to "public.plain-text".

Search for "markdown" at FileInfo.com, and you'll see that the most popular file extensions for Markdown are ".md" and ".markdown".

Armed with this information, you're ready to switch your app from working with plain text with the extension .exampletext, to working with Markdown text with the extensions of .md or .markdown.

Setting Document Types

Go to the project settings by selecting the project. That's the item with the blue icon at the top of the Project navigator. Select the **MacMarkDown** target and choose the **Info** tab from the selection across the top.

Expand the **Document Types** section and change the Identifier to "net.daringfireball.markdown":

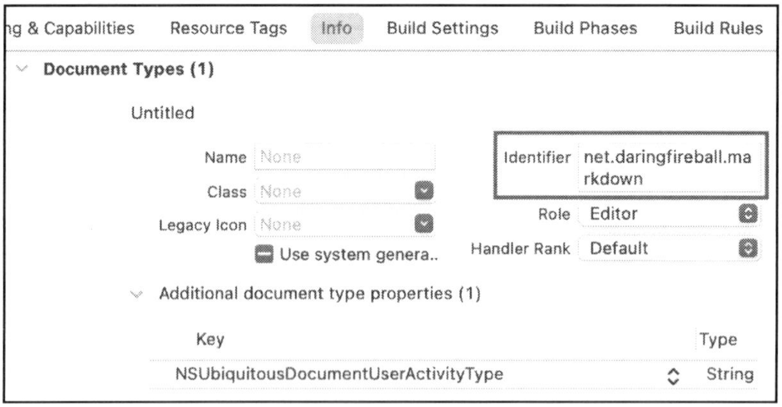

Document type

Next, expand the **Imported Type Identifiers** section and make the following changes:

Description: Markdown Text

Extensions: md, markdown

Identifier: net.daringfireball.markdown

All the other settings can stay the same as the **Conforms To** field already contains "public.plain-text".

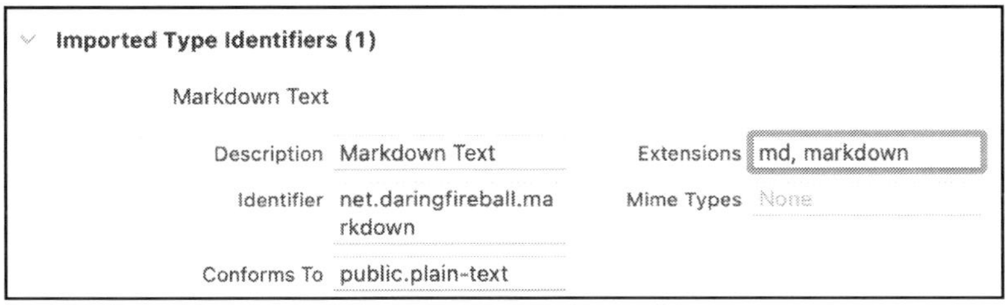

Imported type

There's only one more place to make changes before your app can save and open Markdown files. Go back to **MacMarkDownDocument.swift** and replace the `UTType` extension with this:

```
extension UTType {
  static var markdownText: UTType {
    UTType(importedAs: "net.daringfireball.markdown")
  }
}
```

This creates a new `UTType` called `markdownText` that uses the Uniform Type Identifier you just entered.

Inside the struct, change `readableContentTypes` to use this new type:

```
static var readableContentTypes: [UTType] { [.markdownText] }
```

And just for fun, change the default text in `init` to "# Hello, MacMarkDown!", which is the Markdown format for a level 1 header.

Testing the New Settings

Build and run the app. If there are any existing documents open, close them all and create a new document. Check that the default text is "# Hello MacMarkDown!". Now, save the document and confirm that the suggested file name uses the .md file extension:

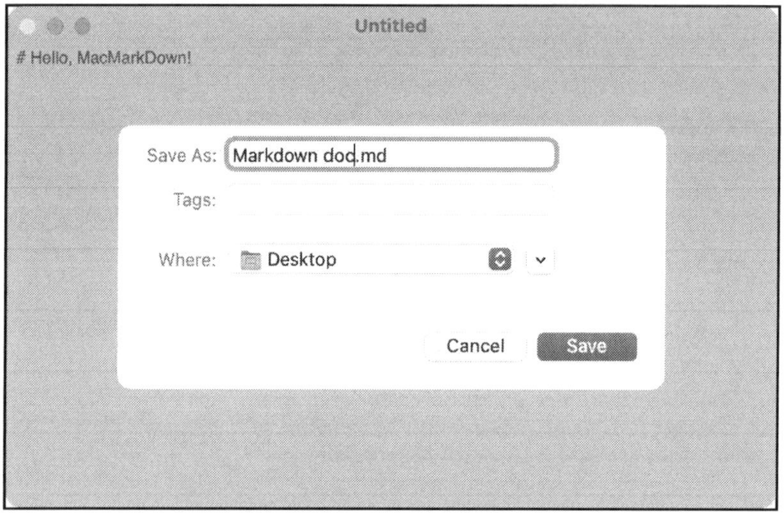

Saving with the Markdown extension

Save and close the document window, and then find the file in Finder and right-click it to show its **Open With** menu. You'll see **MacMarkDown** listed there because your settings told Finder that your app could open Markdown files. If you have any Markdown files created by another app, you'll be able to open them in MacMarkDown too.

Phew! That was a dense section with a lot of detail, but now you have a document-based app that saves and opens Markdown files. In the next sections, you'll learn more about Markdown and add a preview ability to your app.

Markdown and HTML

Markdown is a markup language that uses shortcuts to format plain text in a way that converts easily to HTML. As an example, look at the following HTML:

```
<h1>Important Header</h1>
<h2>Less Important Header</h2>

<a href="https://www.kodeco.com">Kodeco</a>

<ul>
  <li>List Item 1</li>
  <li>List Item 2</li>
  <li>List Item 3</li>
</ul>
```

To write the same in Markdown, you can use:

```
# Important Header
## Less Important Header

[Kodeco](https://www.kodeco.com)

- List Item 1
- List Item 2
- List Item 3
```

I think you'll agree that the Markdown version is easier to write and more likely to be accurate.

You can find out more about Markdown from this helpful cheatsheet (https://bit.ly/3FWagmM).

In MacMarkDown, you write text using Markdown. The app will convert it to HTML and display that in a web view.

Swift doesn't have a built-in Markdown converter, so the first thing is to import a Swift Package to do this. The one you'll use is Swift MarkdownKit (https://bit.ly/3Cbowao).

Converting Markdown to HTML

Back in Xcode, select the project in the Project navigator and this time, click the MacMarkDown project instead of the target. Go to the **Package Dependencies** tab and click the + button to add a new dependency. Enter this URL into the search field at the top right:

```
https://github.com/objecthub/swift-markdownkit
```

When Xcode has found the package, make sure it's selected and click **Add Package**. Xcode starts downloading it for you:

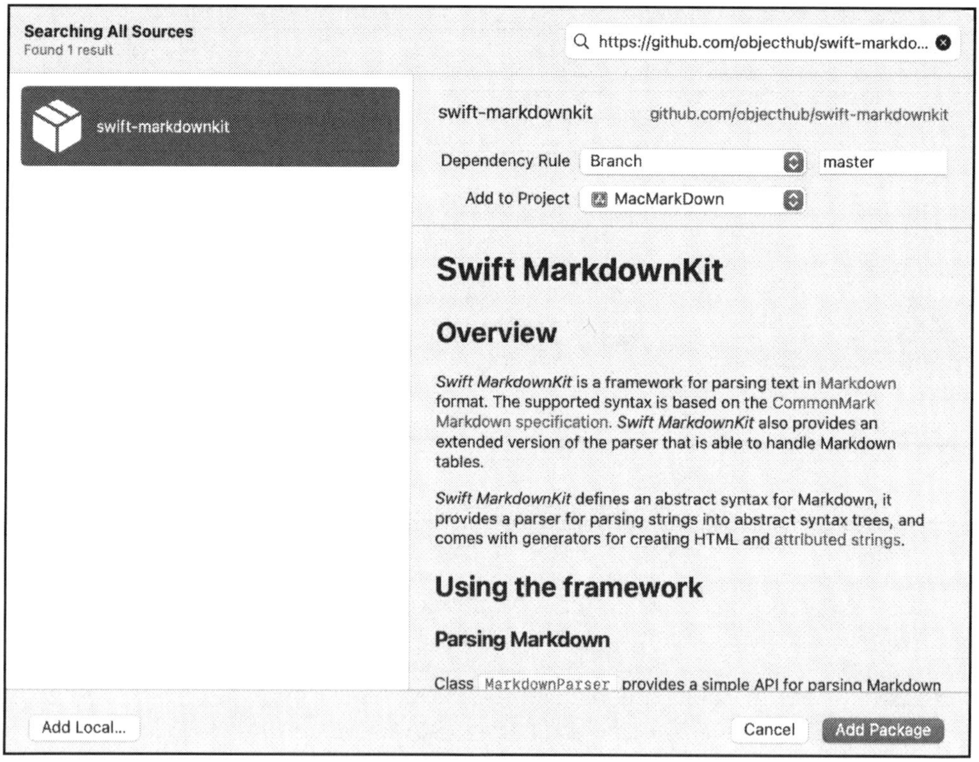

Find the package

Once the download is complete, you'll see a new dialog asking you what parts of the package you want to use. Check the MarkdownKit Library and click **Add Package** to insert it into your project:

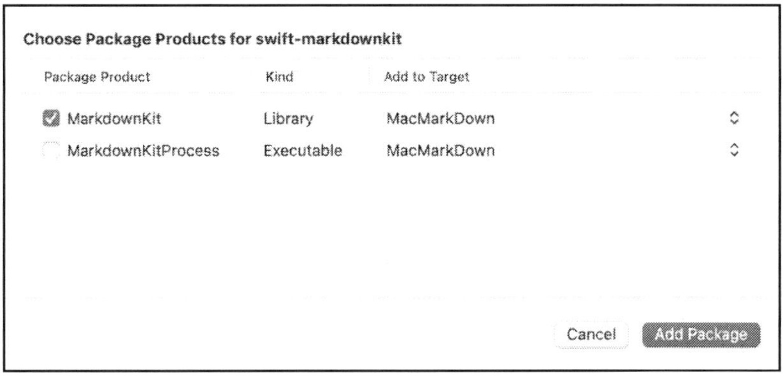

Import the package

The next step is to edit **MacMarkDownDocument.swift** so it can create an HTML version of the document. To use the new package, add `import MarkdownKit` at the top of the file:

```
import MarkdownKit
```

Under the `text` property, define an `html` property:

```
var html: String {
  let markdown = MarkdownParser.standard.parse(text)
  return HtmlGenerator.standard.generate(doc: markdown)
}
```

This code creates a computed property using MarkdownKit's `MarkdownParser` to parse the text and its `HtmlGenerator` to convert it to HTML.

Your document now has two properties. One is the text that's saved in each document file. The other is the HTML version of that text that MarkdownKit creates.

Adding the HTML Preview

The app needs a web view to display the HTML but SwiftUI doesn't have a web view yet. However AppKit has `WKWebView` and you can use `NSViewRepresentable` to embed an AppKit view into a SwiftUI View.

Create a new Swift file called **WebView.swift** and replace its contents with this code:

```
// 1
import SwiftUI
import WebKit

// 2
struct WebView: NSViewRepresentable {
  // 3
  var html: String

  // 4
  func makeNSView(context: Context) -> WKWebView {
    WKWebView()
  }

  // 5
  func updateNSView(_ nsView: WKWebView, context: Context) {
    nsView.loadHTMLString(
      html,
      baseURL: Bundle.main.resourceURL)
  }
}
```

Stepping through this:

1. `NSViewRepresentable` is part of the `SwiftUI` library, and `WKWebView` is in the `WebKit` library.
2. `WebView` is the name of your custom SwiftUI view that this structure defines. It conforms to the `NSViewRepresentable` protocol, which provides a bridge between AppKit's views and SwiftUI.
3. This `struct` only needs one property: a `String` to store the HTML text.
4. `NSViewRepresentable` has two required methods: `makeNSView` creates and returns the `NSView`, in this case a `WKWebView`.
5. The second required method is `updateNSView`. SwiftUI calls this whenever there's a change to the properties that requires a view update. In this case, every time `html` changes, the web view reloads the HTML text.

Now it's time to display this web view, so head over to **ContentView.swift**, which must be feeling rather abandoned. Usually it gets a lot more attention in a SwiftUI app!

Displaying the HTML

To display the two views side-by-side in resizable panes, you're going to embed the `TextEditor` and a `WebView` in an `HSplitView`. This is a macOS-specific SwiftUI view for exactly this purpose.

Replace the contents of `body` with this:

```
HSplitView {
  TextEditor(text: $document.text)
  WebView(html: document.html)
}
```

`TextEditor` has a binding to `document.text` as indicated by the `$`. This means that it can make changes to `document.text` that flow back to the document. `WebView` doesn't makes changes, it only displays, so it doesn't need a binding.

Don't run yet, there's one more setting you need to change. Mac apps run in a sandbox by default. You can turn this off, but if you plan to put your app on the Mac App Store, sandboxing is essential, and it's generally a good idea as a protection for your app and your Mac. But the standard settings block web views from loading anything, even local data.

Go to the project settings and select the **MacMarkDown** target. Click the **Signing & Capabilities** tab.

Now you can check **Outgoing Connections (Client)**, which allows your `WebView` to load content:

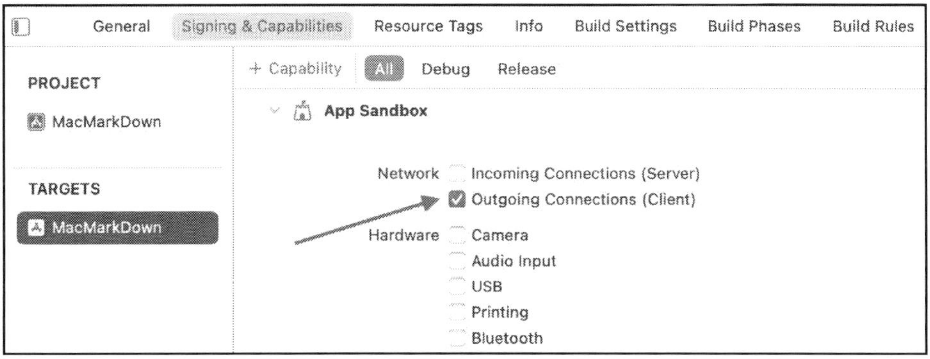

Sandbox setting

Build and run the app:

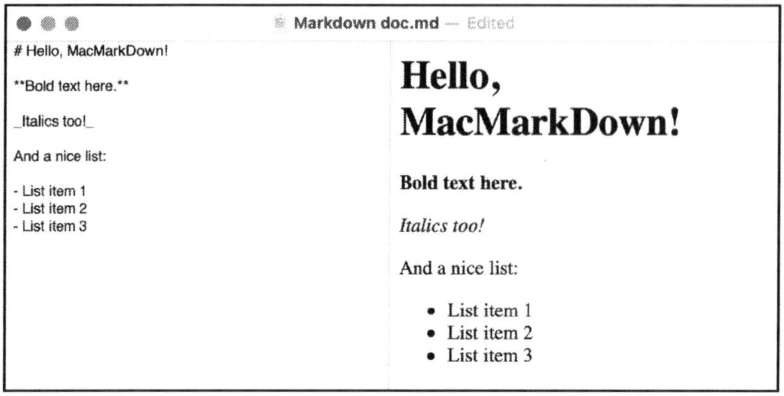

Web preview

Type in some Markdown and see the HTML appear in the side panel. Try dragging the divider bar left or right and test resizing the window. It looks like some size restrictions would be a good idea.

Framing the Window

When an app runs on an iPhone, it works out the available screen size and expands to fill it. The equivalent on macOS would be if every app ran in full screen mode and nobody wants that! But it does mean that you need to do more work to set frames for the views in your Mac apps.

In this case, you want the `TextEditor` filling the left side of the window and the `WebView` filling the right side. They should both resize as the user resizes the window and as the user drags the divider between them. But the divider should never allow either view to disappear and the window should have a minimum size.

Back in **ContentView.swift**, add this `frame` modifier to both the `TextEditor` and the `WebView`, which makes sure they can never get narrower than 200:

```
.frame(minWidth: 200)
```

And add this `frame` modifier to the `HSplitView`:

```
.frame(minWidth: 400, minHeight: 300)
```

This sets the minimum size for the window but allows users to expand it as much as they want. The minimum width is big enough for both panes at their minimum widths.

Build and run again and try resizing each pane and the window. That's better. :]

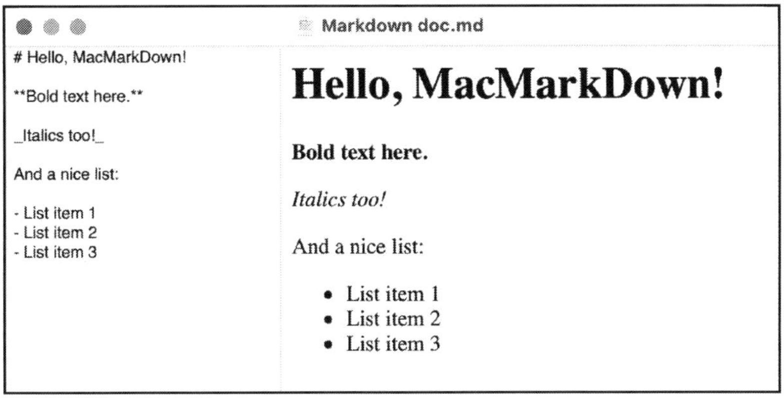

Resizing the window

Adding a Settings Window

Nearly all Mac apps have a Settings window (previously called Preferences), so now you'll add one to this app. Make a new **SwiftUI View** file and call it **SettingsView.swift**. Update `body` to look like this:

```
var body: some View {
  Text("Settings")
    .padding()
}
```

This changes the default "Hello, world" text to say "Settings" and adds a `padding()` modifier, so when you run the app, you can confirm that the correct view appears.

Now it's time to configure the app to show this view as the Settings window.

Open **MacMarkDownApp.swift**. Inside the `body` after `DocumentGroup` add these lines:

```
Settings {
  SettingsView()
}
```

It's always important to explain complex chunks of code, so here's what this does:

- Create a **Settings...** menu item in the app's File menu.
- Add the standard keyboard shortcut: **Command-,**.

- Set up a settings window titled "MacMarkDown Settings".
- Configure the settings window to display `SettingsView`.
- Establish window controls so only one copy of this window is ever created. Trying to open Settings again if the window is already open just brings it to the front.

Not bad for what could be a single line of code. :]

Build and run the app, then select **Settings...** from the File menu or type **Command-,** and your Settings view appears. It's tiny — only large enough to hold the text "Settings" — but it's there, and now you can modify it:

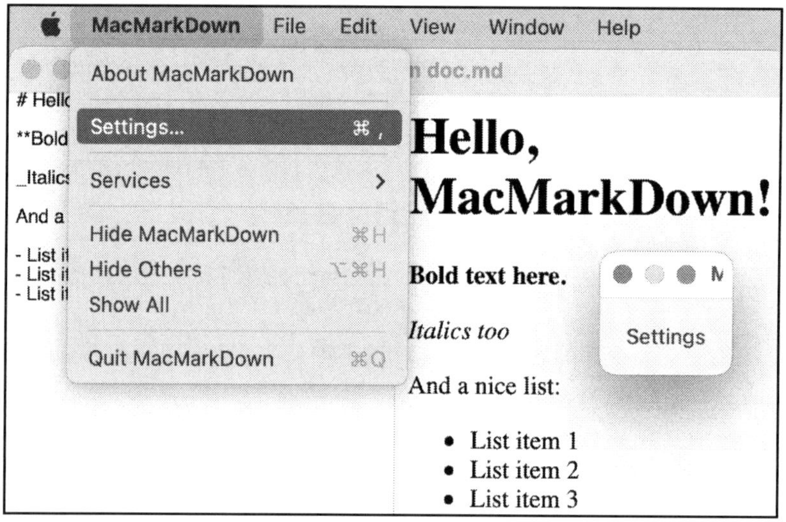

Settings

Using AppStorage

SwiftUI uses property wrappers extensively to let us assign extra functionality to our properties, structures and classes. One of these property wrappers is for saving settings. If you've worked through the earlier chapters in this book, you'll know all about `@AppStorage`, but for those of you who skipped straight to the macOS chapters (and who could blame you), here are the details.

Previously, you may have used `UserDefaults`, which works well for storing small chunks of user data, but you have to keep them in sync manually. If a UI element changes a setting, you have to write to `UserDefaults`. If you're displaying the UI, maybe you need to read from `UserDefaults` to set the state of a checkbox or to implement the choices made. And what if a setting changes after the app has drawn the display?

The`@AppStorage` property wrapper makes all this so much easier. Under the hood, it's still using `UserDefaults` but it handles all these details.

Choosing a Font Size

You'll add the ability to change the editor font size. In **SettingsView.swift** insert the following code inside the `SettingsView` structure but before `body`:

```
@AppStorage("editorFontSize") var editorFontSize: Int = 14
```

This is only one line, but it packs in a lot of functionality:

- `@AppStorage` sets up this property to use the `AppStorage` property wrapper.
- The text in brackets assigns the name of the `UserDefaults` setting.
- Then define the property as usual, with a type and a default value. It's neater if you use the same name for the `UserDefaults` name and the property name, but this isn't strictly necessary.

Now for some UI to change this setting. Replace the default `body` contents with:

```
Stepper(value: $editorFontSize, in: 10 ... 30) {
  Text("Font size: \(editorFontSize)")
}
.frame(width: 260, height: 80)
```

To apply this setting, go back to **ContentView.swift** and add the same `@AppStorage` line to the top of the struct. This allows `ContentView` to access this setting even if the user has never opened the Settings window.

Add a `font` modifier to the `TextEditor`:

```
.font(.system(size: CGFloat(editorFontSize)))
```

Now build and run the app again. Make sure there's some text in the editor, so you can see it change. Open the Settings window and use the arrows to change the font size. The editor font size automatically changes as you change the setting:

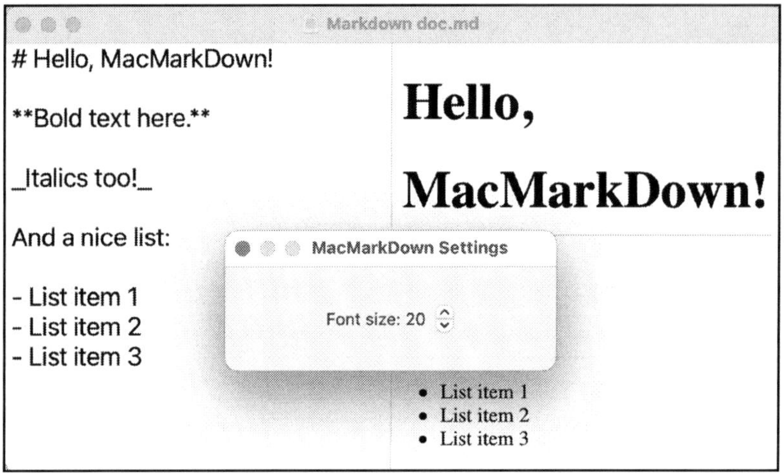

Font size

Make a new window, so you have more than one open at the same time. Confirm the font changes size in both windows. And if you quit and restart the app, your new font size setting is still there.

Changing and Creating Menus

All Mac apps have a menu bar. Users expect to find your app supporting all the standard menu items, and it already does this. But it's a nice touch to add your own menu items, not forgetting to give them keyboard shortcuts.

SwiftUI provides two ways to add new menu items. You can use a `CommandMenu` to insert a completely new menu. Or you can use a `CommandGroup` to add menu items to an existing menu. You apply both of these by adding a `commands` modifier to the `DocumentGroup`.

You can include the contents of the `commands` modifier directly in **MacMarkDownApp.swift** but since menu definitions can get quite extensive, it makes your project easier to read if you separate them into their own file. Create a new Swift file called **MenuCommands.swift** and replace the contents with this:

```
import SwiftUI
```

```
// 1
struct MenuCommands: Commands {
  var body: some Commands {
    // 2
    CommandGroup(before: .help) {
      // 3
      Button("Markdown Cheatsheet") {
        showCheatSheet()
      }
      // 4
      .keyboardShortcut("/", modifiers: .command)

      Divider()
    }

    // more menu items go here
  }

  // 5
  func showCheatSheet() {
    let cheatSheetAddress =
      "https://github.com/adam-p/markdown-here/wiki/Markdown-
Cheatsheet"
    guard let url = URL(string: cheatSheetAddress) else {
      // 6
      fatalError("Invalid cheatsheet URL")
    }
    NSWorkspace.shared.open(url)
  }
}
```

So what's happening here?

1. Menu content and its `body` must conform to the `Commands` protocol so you can use this structure to set up menus for your app.
2. You position a `CommandGroup` either before, after or in place of existing menu items. Delete `help` and press **Escape** to see the autocomplete menu of items you can use. Reset to `help` when you've finished looking.
3. Here you're adding a `Button` as a menu item with a `Divider` below it to make the menu look better.
4. The button has a keyboard shortcut of Command-/.
5. The menu item button calls a method to open a URL in the default browser.
6. If you typed a web address incorrectly, it's better to catch it in development with a fatal error instead of hiding the mistake in a guard statement.

To make this new menu item appear, go to **MacMarkDownApp.swift** and add this modifier to `DocumentGroup`:

```
.commands {
  MenuCommands()
}
```

Build and run the app, then look at the Help menu. Select the new menu item or type **Command**-/ to open the cheatsheet in your browser:

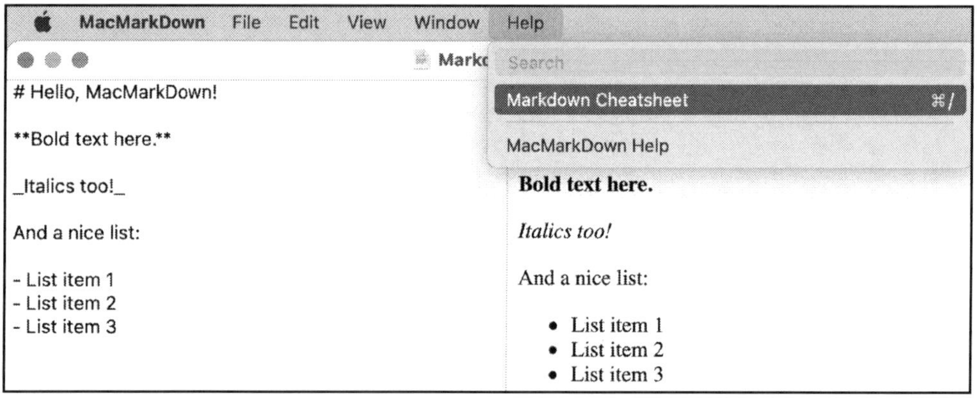

Help menu

Adding a New Menu

Now it's time to create your own menu. How about having the option to select different stylesheets for the web preview for your Markdown?

Open the **assets** folder in the downloads for this chapter and find the **StyleSheets** folder. Drag this folder into your Project navigator, checking **Copy items if needed**, selecting **Create groups** and confirming that the folder will be added to the target. This folder contains a small collection of CSS files plus a Swift file containing an `enum` listing these styles.

To display these in a menu, go back to **MenuCommands.swift** and add this property:

```
@AppStorage("styleSheet") var styleSheet: StyleSheet = .github
```

This creates a new `@AppStorage` property for a `StyleSheet` and sets it to use the GitHub style as the default.

Replace the `// more menu items go here` comment with:

```
// 1
CommandMenu("Stylesheet") {
  // 2
  ForEach(StyleSheet.allCases, id: \.self) { style in
    // 3
    Button(style.rawValue) {
      styleSheet = style
    }
    // 4
    .keyboardShortcut(style.shortcutKey, modifiers: .command)
  }
}
```

Here's what this code does:

1. To create an entirely new menu, use `CommandMenu` giving it the title of the new menu.
2. Loop through all the cases in the `StyleSheet` enum.
3. Each style has a menu item button with the title set to the `rawValue` string for the case. These buttons change the `styleSheet` property.
4. Set a keyboard shortcut for each one using a key equivalent set up in the `enum`.

Displaying the Styles

To make the web view use these styles, head over to **WebView.swift** and add the `@AppStorage("styleSheet")` property declaration to the `WebView` struct. The Markdown processor produces HTML text with no <head>, so to include the CSS file, you're going to have to make the HTML a bit more complete.

Add this computed property to `WebView`:

```
var formattedHtml: String {
  return """
      <html>
      <head>
         <link href="\(styleSheet).css" rel="stylesheet">
      </head>
      <body>
         \(html)
      </body>
      </html>
      """
}
```

This uses multi-line string syntax to wrap the `html` and `styleSheet` properties into an HTML document. Because you set the app's `Bundle.main.resourceURL` as the web view's `baseURL`, you can use a direct link to the CSS files inside the app.

Replace `updateNSView(_:context)` with.

```
func updateNSView(_ nsView: WKWebView, context: Context) {
  nsView.loadHTMLString(
    formattedHtml,                    // Changed line
    baseURL: Bundle.main.resourceURL)
}
```

Build and run the app. Use your new menu to change to a different stylesheet:

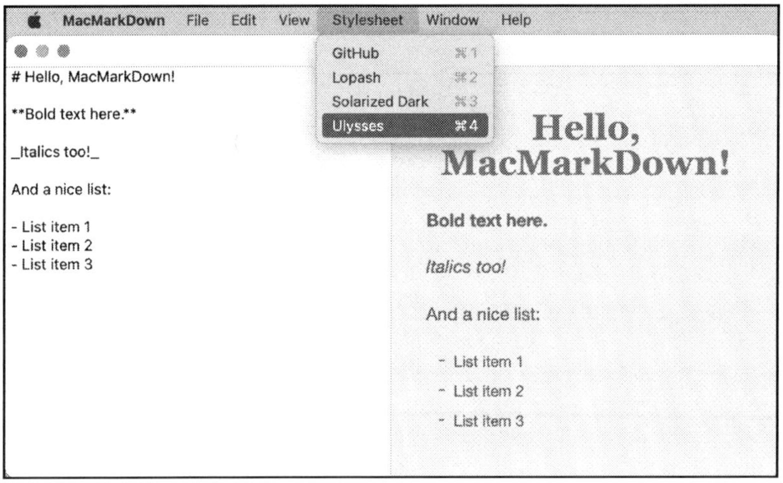

Stylesheet

Creating a Toolbar

Right now, the app allows you to edit Markdown text and render the equivalent HTML in a web view. But it would be useful sometimes to see the actual HTML code. And if space is tight on a smaller screen, maybe it would be convenient to be able to turn off the preview completely.

So now you're going to add another UI element that's very common in Mac apps — the toolbar. In the toolbar, you'll add controls to switch between three preview modes: web, HTML and off.

You add a toolbar as a modifier to a view, in this case `ContentView`. It can be in the same file, but as you did with the menu contents, you're going to put this in its own file. Create a new Swift file and name it **ToolbarCommands.swift**. Open the new file and change the import line to `import SwiftUI`.

You're adding the ability to switch between three states, so this seems like a good use case for an `enum`. In **ToolbarCommands.swift** insert this:

```
enum PreviewState {
  case hidden
  case html
  case web
}
```

Next, add this structure:

```
// 1
struct PreviewToolBarItem: ToolbarContent {
  // 2
  @Binding var previewState: PreviewState

  // 3
  var body: some ToolbarContent {
    // 4
    ToolbarItem {
      // 5
      Picker("", selection: $previewState) {
        // 6
        Image(systemName: "eye.slash")
            .tag(PreviewState.hidden)
        Image(systemName: "doc.plaintext")
            .tag(PreviewState.html)
        Image(systemName: "doc.richtext")
            .tag(PreviewState.web)
      }
      .pickerStyle(.segmented)
      // 7
      .help("Hide preview, show HTML or web view")
    }
  }
}
```

This looks like a lot, but take it one step at a time.

1. So that you can set this structure as the content of a Toolbar, mark it as conforming to the `ToolbarContent` protocol.
2. A binding variable receives the selected preview state from the parent view and passes any changes back to it.
3. The `body` also needs to conform to the `ToolbarContent` protocol.
4. `ToolbarContent` views are either `ToolbarItem` or `ToolbarItemGroup`. As this only shows a single view, a `ToolbarItem` is the right one to use.
5. Since this switches between three possibilities, a segmented picker is a good UI choice.
6. Each segment displays an SF Symbol image and has a tag set to the corresponding `PreviewState` case. Apple's SF Symbols app or Xcode's Library shows all these icons, so you can search for appropriate ones.
7. The `help` modifier provides a tooltip and accessibility text.

Using the Toolbar

Now to attach the toolbar to **ContentView**. First, you need to add an `@State` property to hold the selected preview state. This is set to `web` by default:

```
@State private var previewState = PreviewState.web
```

Next, add a `toolbar` modifier to the `HSplitView` after the `frame` modifier:

```
.toolbar {
  PreviewToolBarItem(previewState: $previewState)
}
```

This creates a toolbar and sets its content to the `PreviewToolbarItem` you just created, passing in a binding to the `previewState` property, so that changes flow back.

Build and run the app to see a toolbar with these three options at the far right. You can click each one and see the visual differences that indicate the currently selected option. Notice how this changes the look of the document's title:

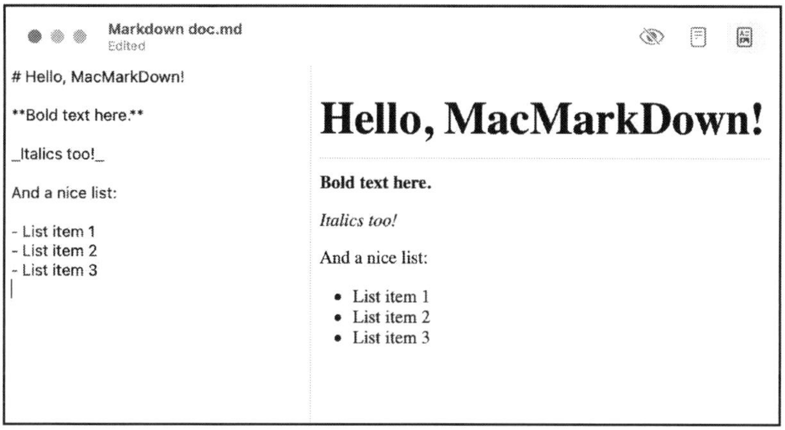

Toolbar

But so far, this does nothing to change the display, so head back to **ContentView.swift**.

In the `HSplitView` you have the `TextEditor` and the `WebView`. Now there are three possible combinations:

- `TextEditor` alone.
- `TextEditor` plus `WebView`.
- `TextEditor` plus something else to display the raw HTML.

To handle the first two options, wrap the `WebView` in an `if` like this:

```
if previewState == .web {
  WebView(html: document.html)
    .frame(minWidth: 200)
}
```

The `body` ends up looking like this:

```
var body: some View {
  HSplitView {
    TextEditor(text: $document.text)
      .frame(minWidth: 200)
      .font(.system(size: CGFloat(editorFontSize)))

    if previewState == .web {
```

```
        WebView(html: document.html)
          .frame(minWidth: 200)
      }
    }
    .frame(minWidth: 400, minHeight: 300)
    .toolbar {
      PreviewToolBarItem(previewState: $previewState)
    }
  }
```

Build and run the app again. The web version of the Markdown text disappears when you select either of the first two buttons and appears again when you select the third button:

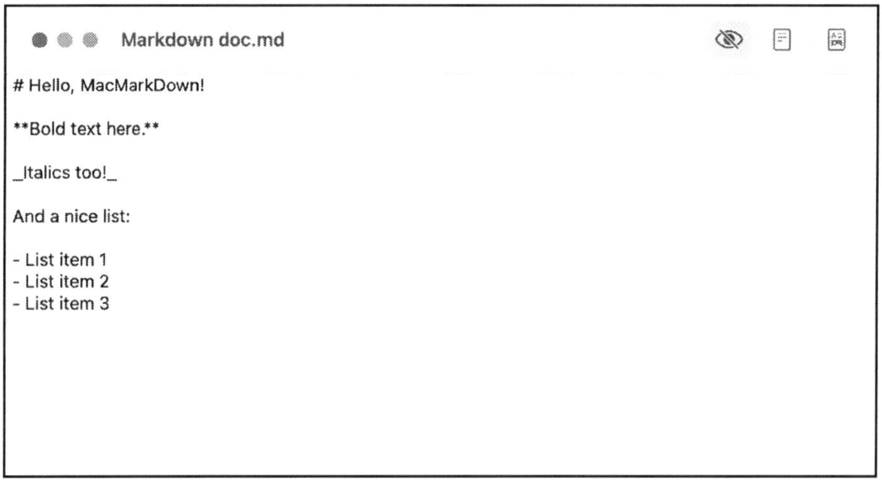

No preview

Adding the HTML Text Preview

For the raw HTML display, add this after the previous `if` block:

```
else if previewState == .html {
  // 1
  ScrollView {
    // 2
    Text(document.html)
      .frame(minWidth: 200)
      .frame(
        maxWidth: .infinity,
        maxHeight: .infinity,
        alignment: .topLeading)
      .padding()
      // 3
```

```
            .font(.system(size: CGFloat(editorFontSize)))
            // 4
            .textSelection(.enabled)
    }
  }
```

Here's what's going on:

1. After checking to see if this view should be visible, the new view starts with a `ScrollView`, so that the text can scroll if it's longer than the height of the window.
2. Use a `Text` view to show the HTML text. Set the view to fill all the available space with some padding around the edges and with the same minimum width as the web view.
3. It seems appropriate to use the selected editor font size for this display too.
4. Make the text inside `Text` views selectable, so users can copy it.

Build and run the app now and you'll be able to toggle between the three preview states. Use the Settings window to change the font size and confirm that the HTML view font size changes too:

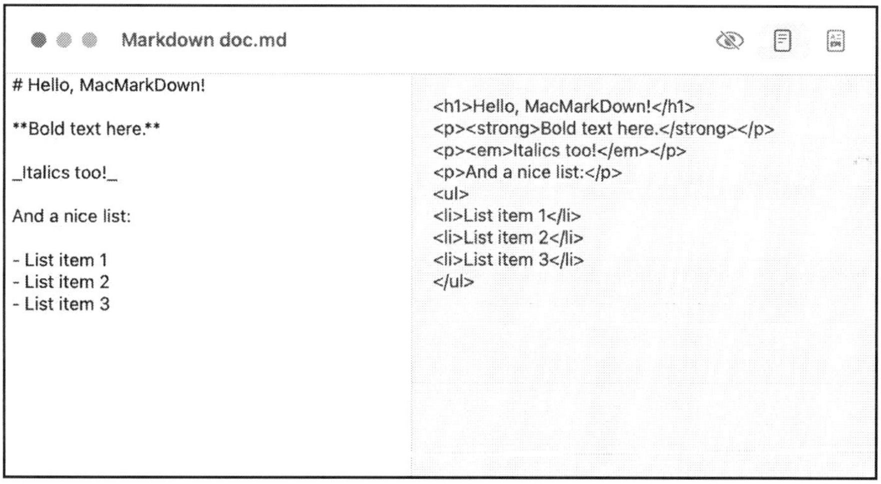

HTML preview

Markdown in AttributedStrings

SwiftUI has an **AttributedString** that can format Markdown. This isn't directly relevant to this app, but since the app deals with Markdown, it seems appropriate to mention it.

Convert the raw HTML preview to use an `AttributedString` temporarily by adding this computed property to `ContentView`.

```
var attributedString: AttributedString {
  // 1
  let markdownOptions =
  AttributedString.MarkdownParsingOptions(
    interpretedSyntax: .inlineOnly)
  // 2
  let attribString = try? AttributedString(
    markdown: document.text,
    options: markdownOptions)
  // 3
  return attribString ??
  AttributedString("There was an error parsing the Markdown.")
}
```

What's happening here?

1. Set up the parsing options. These are optional but the defaults don't preserve linefeeds or tabs.

2. Try to parse the document's Markdown text using these options.

3. Return the parsed `AttributedString` or an error message.

To display this, change the `Text` inside the `ScrollView` to:

```
Text(attributedString)
```

Build and run the app, switch to the raw HTML preview mode and you'll see something like this. Notice how the font modifier is still applied, but not all the Markdown tags are supported.

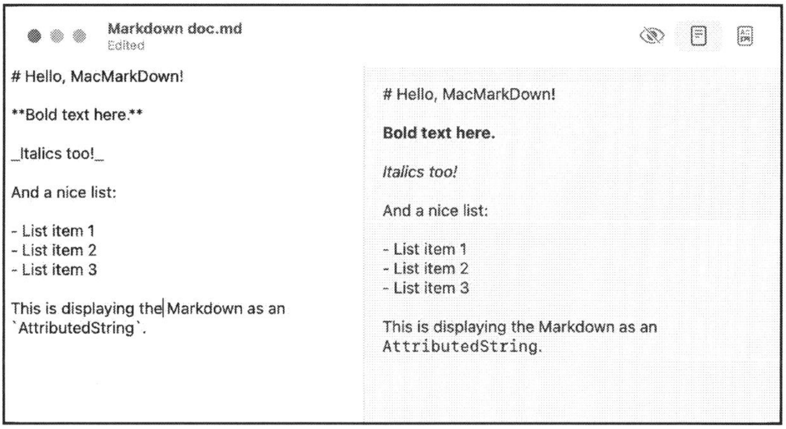

AttributedString from Markdown

This technique could be useful for formatting display text in SwiftUI apps, but for this app, switch the `Text` back to `Text(document.html)` and delete the computed property.

Installing the App

With an iOS App, when you build and run an app on your device, Xcode installs it on your iPhone or iPad and you can use it there, even after closing Xcode. For a Mac app, this isn't quite as simple. Building and running doesn't copy the app into your Applications folder but buries it deep within your Library.

To install your app so you can use it easily, make sure the app is running. Right-click the app icon in the Dock and select **Options ▸ Show in Finder**. Now you can drag **MacMarkDown.app** into your Applications folder.

Challenge: Add Another File Extension

When you set up the file types, you allowed the app to use either ".md" or ".markdown" for the file extensions. But some people use ".mdown" for Markdown files. Edit the project so that ".mdown" is a valid extension. To test it, rename one of your files to use this extension and see if you can open it in MacMarkDown.

Have a go at implementing this yourself, but check out the **challenge** folder if you need some help.

Key Points

- Apple provides a starting template for document-based Mac apps that can get you going quickly, but now you know how to customize this template to suit your own file types.
- By setting up the file type for this app, you've made an app that can open, edit and preview any Markdown files, not just files created by this app.
- Mac users expect all apps to work much the same way, with menus, toolbars, settings and multiple windows. Now you have the tools to make an app that does all these things.
- And you have a Markdown editor you can use! The completed project is in the **final** folder for this chapter.

Where to Go From Here?

Well done! You made it through this chapter. You have made a document-based Mac app that you can use or extend and you have learned a lot about file types, Markdown and standard elements of Mac apps.

Chapter 23: Converting an iOS App to macOS

By Sarah Reichelt

If you've worked through the early chapters of this book, you've built several iOS apps. In the previous chapter, you've also made a document-based Mac app. But in this chapter, you'll make a macOS app from an iOS app. You'll use the code, views and assets from an iOS project to make it.

Most Swift and SwiftUI tutorials, and examples on the internet, are for iOS, primarily specifically for iPhones. So knowing how to re-use the code in an iOS project to create a real Mac app is a valuable skill.

Getting Started

Open the **starter** project from the downloaded materials for this chapter, which is the iOS app you'll convert. You may have already built this app in earlier chapters, but please use this **starter** project even if you have.

Build and run the app in an iPhone simulator and click through all the options to see how it works.

iOS app screens

The iOS version uses a common navigational pattern where the initial screen offers a selection of choices. A `NavigationSplitView` shows the options, displaying other views. These secondary views sometimes have even more options, including full views, sheets or dialogs.

For the Mac version, where you can assume much wider screens, you'll have the navigation in a sidebar on the left. The main portion of the window on the right will display different views depending on the navigation selections.

As you work through this chapter, there'll be a lot of editing, which can be difficult to explain and follow, but if you get lost, open the **final** project and check out the code there.

Setting Up the Mac App

In Xcode, create a new project using the **macOS App** template and by selecting **SwiftUI** for the Interface and **Swift** for the Language. Call the app **MountainAirportMac** and save it.

Importing Code Files

To start, switch to Finder and open the **MountainAirport** folder inside the **starter** project folder.

Then select the following folders and files, and drag them into the Project navigator for your new Mac project.

Be sure to select **Copy items if needed** and **Create groups** for each one. Confirm that the **MountainAirportMac** target is checked.

1. All the **.swift** files in the **MountainAirport** folder.
2. **AwardsView** folder.
3. **FlightDetails** folder.
4. **FlightStatusBoard** folder.
5. **Misc** folder.
6. **Models** folder.
7. **SearchFlights** folder.

After you move the files, delete **MountainAirport.swift** from your project. This is an iOS-specific file that you don't need for your new Mac app.

By the end of that process, your Project navigator should look like this:

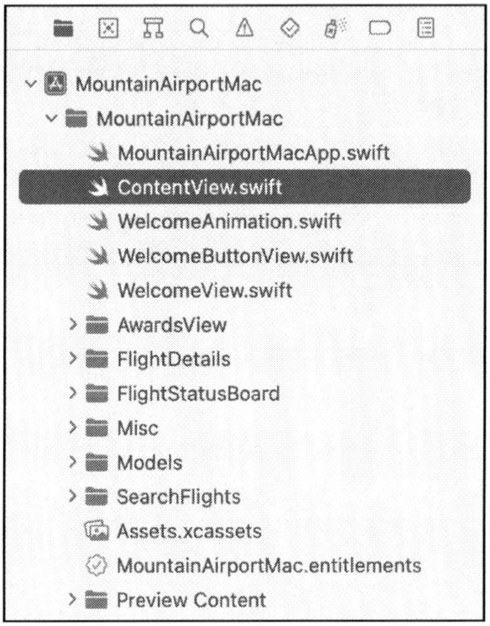

Project navigator after imports

You've now got a lot of code from the iOS app in your macOS app. You can assume that the model classes and structures mostly work as expected and don't need you to change anything. Your main task is to change the SwiftUI code to make the user interface work on a Mac. But you've already saved yourself a lot of time and trouble by importing all this code. Next, you'll import assets.

Importing Assets

As well as the **.swift** files, you can import the assets the iOS app uses, primarily the app icon and any images used in the app's UI.

First, go to **Assets.xcassets** in your Xcode Project navigator and then open the **Assets.xcassets** folder in the iOS project's Finder window. If you're not showing file extensions, these may appear as **Assets** without the **.xcassets** extension. Now, drag every folder inside this folder into your list of assets.

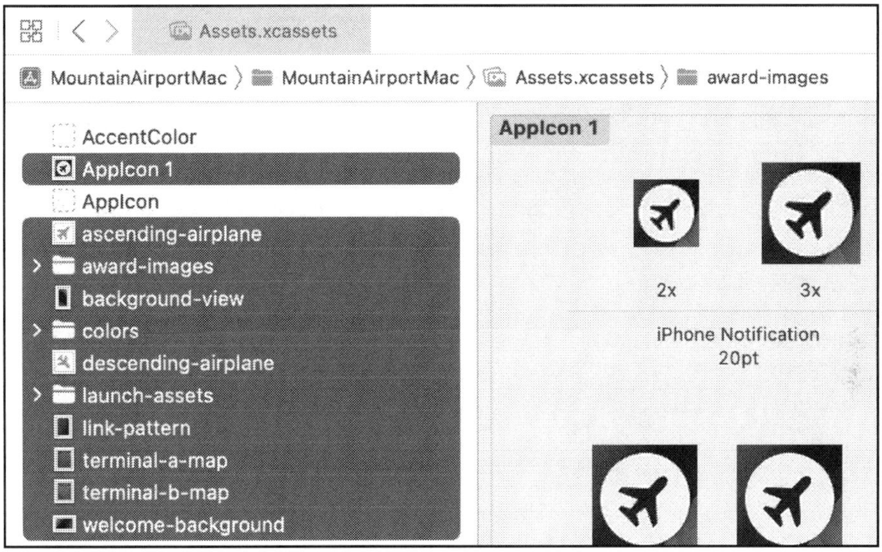

Imported assets

This adds all the assets, but an iOS project configures its assets differently from a macOS project, so now you've got some housekeeping to do, starting with the app icon.

In the assets list, there's **AppIcon**, part of the app template, and **AppIcon 1**, which you imported. Unfortunately, iOS and macOS have different image size requirements for their app icons. The best solution is to take the largest of the images from **AppIcon 1** and use an icon creator utility to make all the correct image sizes, but for now, you'll need to cheat and take the easy way out.

- In **AppIcon 1**, select the icon at the bottom: **App Store iOS 1024pt** and press **Command-C** to copy it.
- Go to **AppIcon**, select **App Store - 2x** and press **Command-V** to paste in the copied image.
- Now you can delete **AppIcon 1**, and your Mac app will use the imported icon.

> **Note**: For an iOS app, you supply square icons, and iOS rounds the corners for you. Mac app icons have rounded corners with transparent padding, which you have to apply. If you're releasing a Mac version of an iOS app, you'd need to re-design the icon, but the square icon will do for now.

Select the **ascending-airplane** asset, click on the image, and ensure you can see the Attributes inspector on the right.

In the Devices section, **Universal** is checked, meaning this image works on any Apple device. But the image is in the 3x box for the high-resolution iPhones and iPads, and 3x images don't work in a Mac app. Drag the image from the 3x box to the 2x box to make it Mac-compatible.

Repeat this process for all the 3x images, not forgetting the ones in the **award-images** folder.

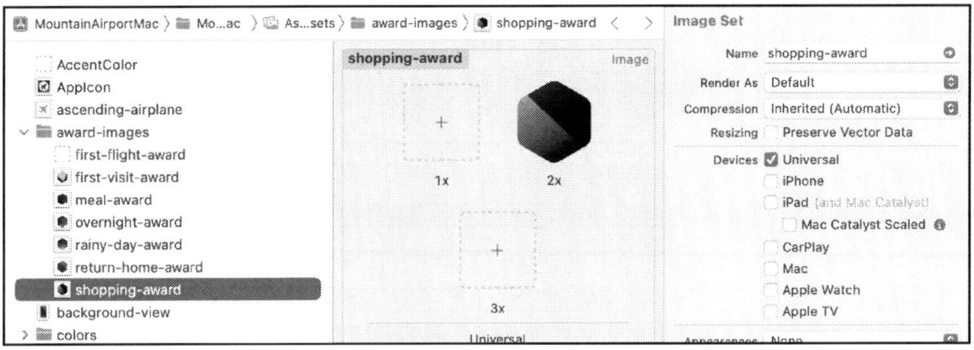

Image assets

Now it's time to build!

Fixing the Build Errors

You've imported all the code files, imported the assets, set up your app's icon and configured the other images for the Mac. The big task now is to get the app to build.

Press **Command-B** to build the app, but don't panic when it doesn't work. You have to expect this when you import code that was written for a different platform.

Open the **Issue navigator** to see the first set of problems. There's a report of an invalid redeclaration of `ContentView_Previews`. The iOS app uses `WelcomeView` as the initial view, but the preview provider in **WelcomeView.swift** is still called `ContentView_Previews`.

To set the Mac app to open with `WelcomeView`, open **MountainAirportMacApp.swift** and replace `ContentView()` with `WelcomeView()`. Now you can delete **ContentView.swift** and try again. Press **Shift-Command-K** to clean the build folder and then **Command-B** to build. Doing a clean build after fixing errors is always a good idea, especially if you deleted any files.

The next error is "Cannot find type `UIColor` in scope" which is in **FlightInformation.swift**. Click the error in the Issue navigator to jump to the file and the location of the error.

`UIColor` is a UIKit color object. The equivalent in AppKit is `NSColor`, but the Mac version doesn't use this property, so delete the `timelineColor` computed property to eliminate the error.

Subsequent builds give these errors in either order:

- `InsetGroupedListStyle` is unavailable in macOS — **SearchFlights.swift**:

Search the Developer Documentation for the `ListStyle` protocol and check the available list styles. You can click through each and check the availability for macOS. Once you've looked at the options, replace the error line with:

```
.listStyle(.inset(alternatesRowBackgrounds: true))
```

This styles the list and makes the rows easy to distinguish.

- `navigationBarItems(trailing:)` is unavailable in macOS — **FlightStatusBoard.swift**:

Instead of a navigation bar item for this `Toggle`, you'll use the Mac toolbar. Replace the `navigationBarItems` modifier and its contents with this:

```
.toolbar {
  Toggle("Hide Past", isOn: $hidePast)
}
```

This uses the same `Toggle` control but wrapped in a `toolbar` instead of in `navigationBar`.

Press **Command-B** again, and the app builds with no errors this time.

Well done! You now have a Mac app project populated with a lot of code and assets from an iOS app and with no build issues!

Now, press **Command-R** to run the Mac app.

Expand the window and the sidebar to see the three navigation buttons and the animated plane. Click **Your Awards** to see the awards display. It isn't pretty, but it works! **Search Flights** is similar — it works, but the display is messy. In the next sections, you'll make it look much better.

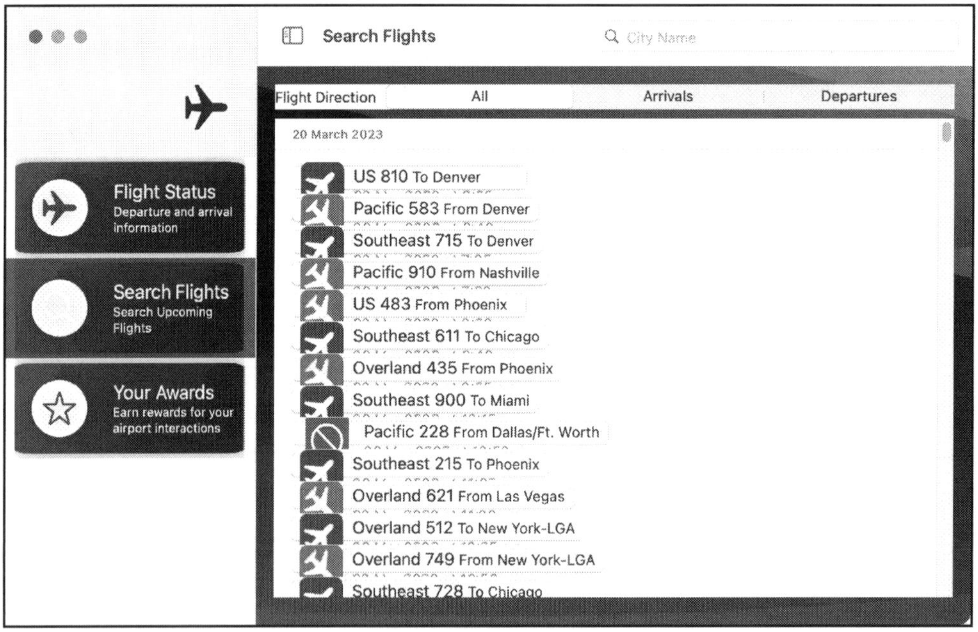

First run

Now click **Flight Status**. Not so good. This is a crasher. It needs fixing before anything else.

Diagnosing the Crash

Don't worry — this sort of thing happens, and learning how to track down crashes is a useful skill, especially as Xcode isn't always very helpful. In this case, the crash report points to `@main` in **MountainAirportMacApp.swift**, which tells you nothing useful. Time for some detective work.

Open **WelcomeView.swift** and check out what happens when you click **Flight Status**. The `ViewButton` has an `id` of `FlightViewId.showFlightStatus`, and clicking the button sets `selectedView` to this. The `NavigationSplitView` then shows `FlightStatusBoard` in its detail.

Following the clues, open **FlightStatusBoard ▸ FlightStatusBoard.swift**. The main view here is a `TabView` with three tabs. Each tab shows a `FlightList` with a different set of flights. A good way to track down display bugs is to replace suspicious views with placeholder `Text` views. If the Text view works, you've found the culprit.

In **FlightStatusBoard.swift**, you'll replace each use of `FlightList` with `Text` and see what happens. Double-click the opening parenthesis after the first `FlightList` to select the view and its parameters. Press **Command**-/ to comment it out, and on the line above, insert `Text("Arrivals List")`. Place the cursor before `.tabItem` on the last commented line and press **Return** to re-enable that modifier.

Repeat this with the other two `FlightList`s, inserting `Text("Complete List")` and `Text("Departures List")` and re-enabling the `tabItem` for each.

Build and run the app again. This time clicking **Flight Status** works, and the three tabs show their `Text` views:

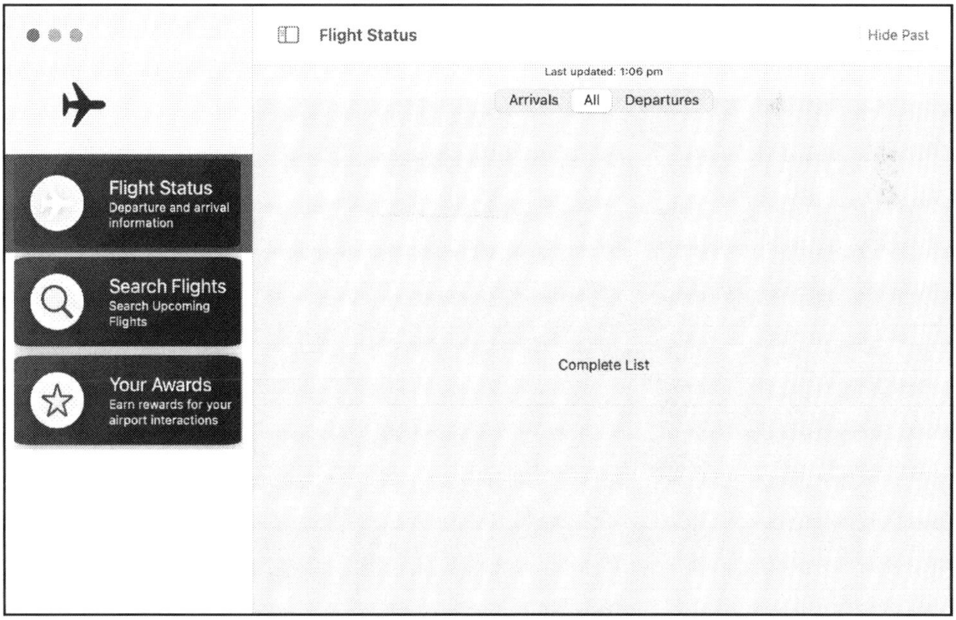

Using Text placeholders

Now you know the problem is in `FlightList`. Good detecting, Sherlock!

> **Note**: You may see more errors appearing in the Issues navigator now, but you can ignore them. They don't stop the app from running, and they'll disappear as you work through the rest of this chapter.

Open **FlightStatusBoard ▸ FlightList.swift** and look at `body`. It uses a `NavigationStack` to display a `ScrollViewReader` and then a `List` — maybe this is a problem on macOS.

To test this out, comment out the `NavigationStack` line. Then comment out its closing brace on the line above `onAppear`.

Back in **FlightStatusBoard.swift**, press **Command-Z** repeatedly until you've re-enabled the three `FlightList` views.

Build and run to see what happens:

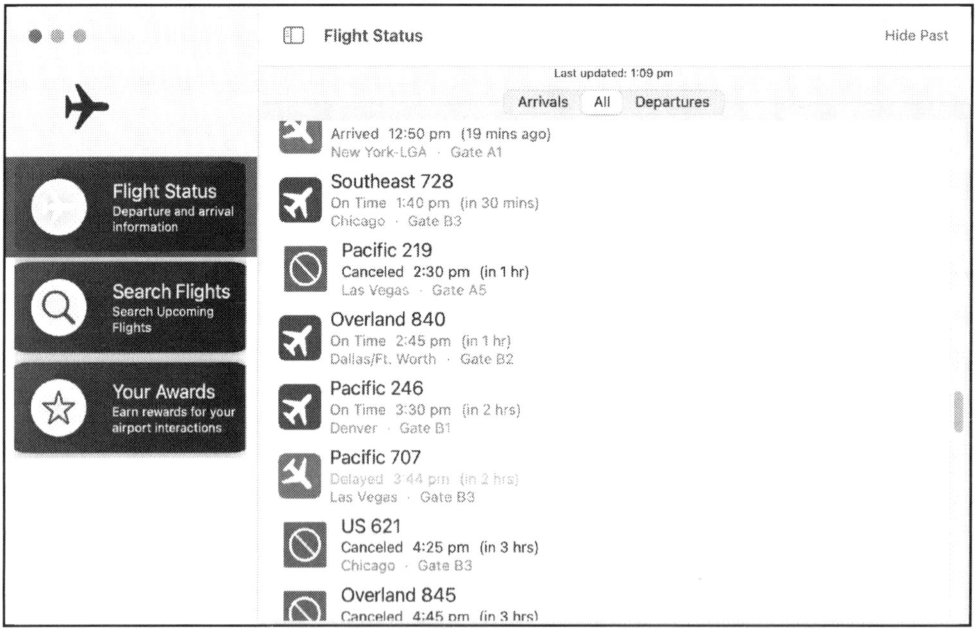

Without the NavigationStack.

The list appears, the tabs show the correct data and the Hide Past toggle does what it should. Great work! You've found the exact cause of the crash, and now you can fix it.

Navigation in macOS

A `NavigationLink` inside a `NavigationStack` slides the current view out and a new one in, while providing a way to go back. This works great in an iPhone app, but this isn't always the best way in a macOS app with more available space.

Here, it would be better to divide the display, showing the list of flights on the left and the selected flight on the right. The crash is due to a bug in SwiftUI for Mac, but avoiding it gives a better result for a Mac app.

To make this happen, open **WelcomeView.swift**. This uses `FlightStatusBoard` in two places, once for the flight status and again for the last viewed flight, if there is one.

But before you change this, you need to add properties to store the selected flight and the last viewed flight.

Inside `WelcomeView`, before `body`, insert this:

```
// 1
@SceneStorage("selectedFlightID") var selectedFlightID: Int?
@SceneStorage("lastViewedFlightID") var lastViewedFlightID: Int?

// 2
var lastViewedFlight: FlightInformation? {
  if let id = lastViewedFlightID {
    return flightInfo.getFlightById(id)
  }
  return nil
}

var selectedFlight: FlightInformation? {
  if let id = selectedFlightID {
    return flightInfo.getFlightById(id)
  }
  return nil
}
```

What's happening here?

1. In earlier chapters, you read about `@AppStorage` that provides a property wrapper for `UserDefaults`. `@SceneStorage` is similar to `@AppStorage` but stores settings for each window and not for the entire app. Since users may want multiple windows open showing different flights, it makes sense to use `@SceneStorage` here. `selectedFlightID` stores the `id` of the flight selected in `FlightStatusBoard`. `lastViewedFlightID` stores the `id` of the flight that you looked at last. Both are optional `Int`s.

2. `@SceneStorage` and `@AppStorage` can only contain primitive types like `String`, `Int`, `Double`, `Bool`, or enums that conform to these types. So you're using these computed properties to get optional `FlightInformation` objects from the `id`s.

When `FlightList` used a `NavigationStack`, it was able to show the selected flight using a `NavigationLink`. Without that, you need to record the selected flight and display it manually if it exists.

Modifying the Flight List

Next, open **FlightList.swift** and replace body with:

```
// 1
@SceneStorage("selectedFlightID") var selectedFlightID: Int?

var body: some View {
  ScrollViewReader { scrollProxy in
    // 2
    List(flights, selection: $selectedFlightID) { flight in
      FlightRow(flight: flight)
        // 3
        .tag(flight.id)
    }
    .onAppear {
      // 4
      scrollProxy.scrollTo(nextFlightId, anchor: .top)
    }
  }
}
```

This adds some code and removes some:

1. Give `FlightList` access to the `@SceneStorage` property that holds the `id` of the selected flight.

2. Bind this as the selection parameter for the list.

3. Assign a tag to each line on the list. When the user clicks a list item, you use this to set `selectedFlightID`.

4. This `scrollTo` was there before, but a `top` anchor works better on macOS.

So now, `FlightList` can set `selectedFlightID` and `WelcomeView` can detect this. The next step is to display the selected flight.

Showing the Selected Flight

Open **FlightDetails ▸ FlightDetails.swift**. This is the view that displays the details of a flight, either directly from the flight list or as the last viewed flight. Right now, it always expects a valid `FlightInformation` object, but this may be `nil` in the new arrangement.

Start at the top of `FlightDetails` and add a question mark to make `flight` an optional:

```
var flight: FlightInformation?
```

This causes errors down below. **Command-click** on `VStack` and select **Make Conditional** from the popup menu:

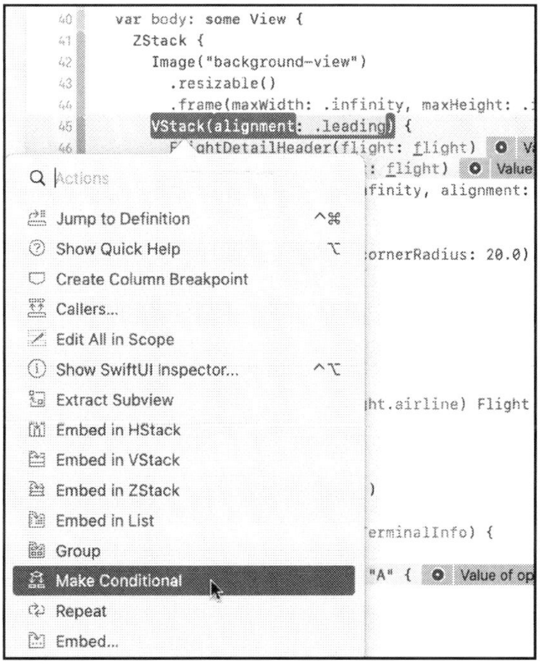

Make Conditional

Replace the `true` placeholder with `let flight`.

In the `else` block, replace `EmptyView()` with:

```
Text("Select a flight…")
  .foregroundColor(.white)
```

To solve the next error, replace the line with:

```
if flight?.terminal == "A" {
```

This uses optional chaining to check the value of `terminal` only when there's a valid `flight`.

The final error requires two steps. First, add this property declaration to `FlightDetails`:

```
@SceneStorage("lastViewedFlightID") var lastViewedFlightID: Int?
```

This gives it access to the `@SceneStorage` property that records the last viewed flight in this window.

Then replace the `onAppear` block with:

```
.onChange(of: flight) { _ in
  lastViewedFlightID = flight?.id
}
```

Whenever you view a new flight in `FlightDetails`, this detects it and sets `lastViewedFlightID` to match.

This has been a lot of work, but you're nearly there. The data is in place, and `FlightList` and `FlightDetails` are ready. Now back to **WelcomeView.swift** to use them.

Replace the `showFlightStatus` case in the `NavigationSplitViews` `detail` with:

```
case .showFlightStatus:
  // 1
  HSplitView {
    // 2
    FlightStatusBoard(flights:
flightInfo.getDaysFlights(Date()))
    // 3
    FlightDetails(flight: selectedFlight)
  }
```

This is what's changed.

1. The displayed view is now an `HSplitView`, which divides the view into two parts arranged side-by-side.
2. The first part is the same as before.
3. The second half shows `FlightDetails`, connected to the `selectedFlight` computed property. When the user clicks a flight in `FlightList`, the list selection changes `selectedFlightID`. This updates `selectedFlight` and SwiftUI displays the new data inside `FlightDetails`.

Build and run the app now. Click **Flight Status** in the sidebar and then select different flights:

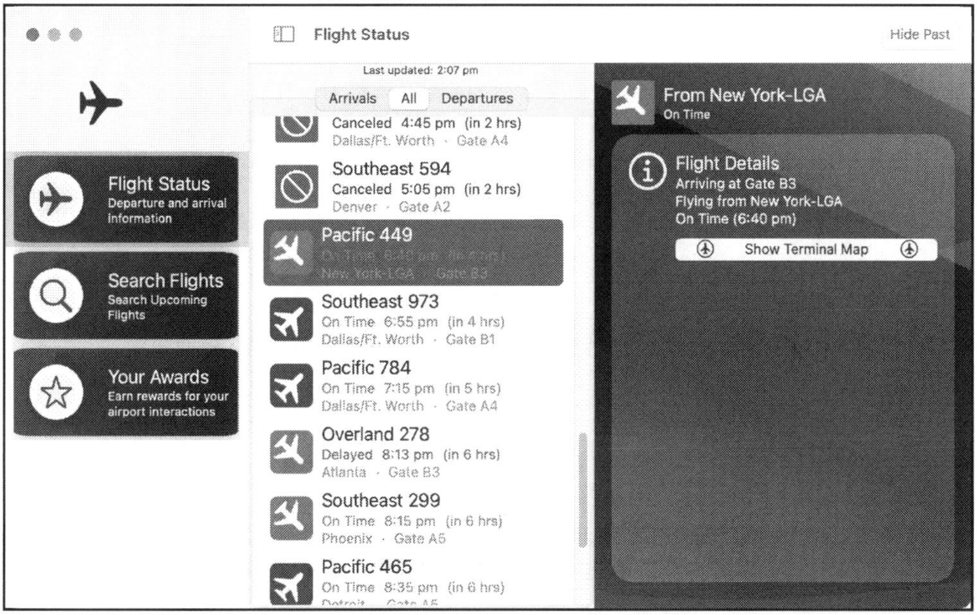

Selected flight

Hooray! No crash *and* you can see flight details. But there are some things to fix in the details display.

Styling the Flight Details

You'll first notice the **Show Terminal Map** button. It shows the map and all the animations work perfectly, but the button looks wrong. A macOS button is styled differently from an iOS button by default, but you can fix this.

Open **FlightDetails ▸ FlightInfoPanel.swift** and look for `Button`. After the `label`, on the line before `if showTerminal {`, add this line:

```
.buttonStyle(.plain)
```

That makes the button look better.

But there's another problem.

Setting Frames

With iOS apps, the available space is pre-defined. An iPhone app fills the entire screen, and most iPad apps do the same. With Mac apps, a screen can be huge, so as an app developer, it's your responsibility to set sizes for components in your app.

Run the app again, select a flight and click anywhere in the flight details display outside the button:

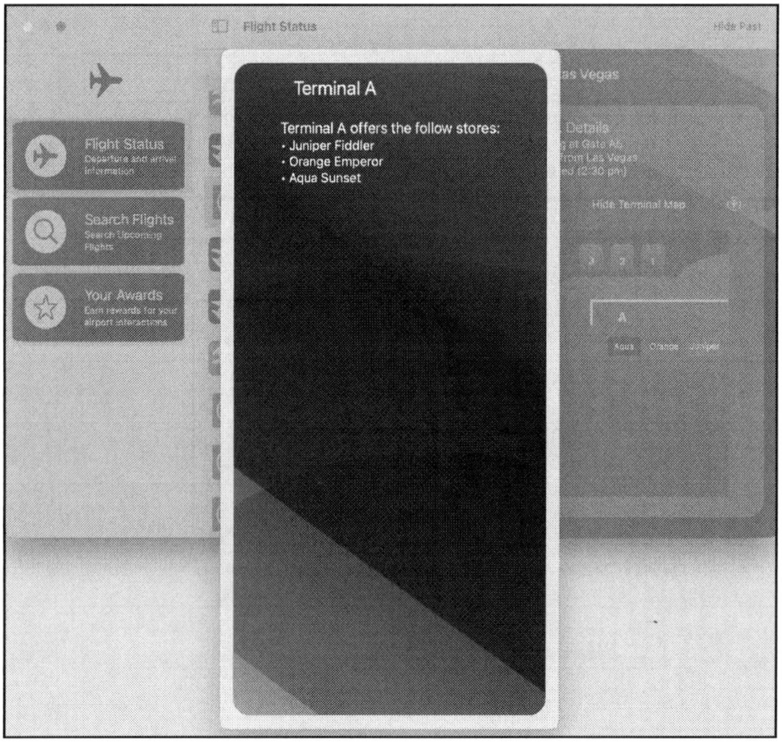

Terminal details

A sheet with information about the terminal pops up, but it's much too tall. Click anywhere in the sheet to dismiss it. These sheets are in **FlightStatusBoard ▸ TerminalAView.swift** and **FlightStatusBoard ▸ TerminalBView.swift**. The height is set by the background image, which is sized to fill a tall iPhone screen.

The `Image` in each of these files has a `frame` modifier. Replace this in both files with the following:

```
.frame(height: 300)
```

This fixes the height to a setting tall enough to show all the information without wasting space.

You need to set limits for the main window as well. Try moving the various parts around. Shrink and expand the window, resize the sidebar and adjust the slider in the middle of the `HSplitView`. Each of those parts needs a frame modifier.

Start in **FlightDetails ▸ FlightDetails.swift**. Find the `.contentShape(Rectangle())` line and insert this before it:

```
.frame(minWidth: 400, minHeight: 400)
```

That makes sure the details can never get too small in either dimension.

Next, open **FlightStatusBoard ▸ FlightStatusBoard.swift**. Double-click the curly brace on the `TimelineView` line to select the entire block and locate the closing curly brace. After the closing brace, add this:

```
.frame(minWidth: 300, minHeight: 400)
```

Finally, the sidebar. Open **WelcomeView.swift** and insert this line after `.listStyle(.plain)`:

```
.frame(minWidth: 250, minHeight: 400)
```

Run the app again, select a flight and re-arrange the components. Then try shrinking the entire window. Despite setting minimum limits for each component, the overall width can still need to be bigger. The height is good, but not the width:

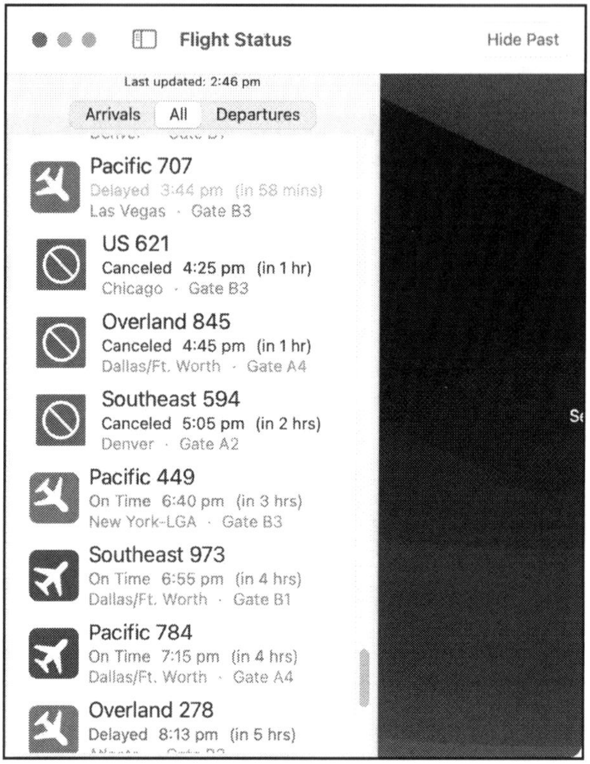

Narrow window

The final step is to open **MountainAirportMacApp.swift** and add this modifier to `WelcomeView()`:

```
.frame(minWidth: 700)
```

This is small enough to let the sidebar collapse but keeps the `HSplitView` intact.

Searching for Flights

The app's first section is complete, so click the **Search Flights** button in the sidebar to look at the next section.

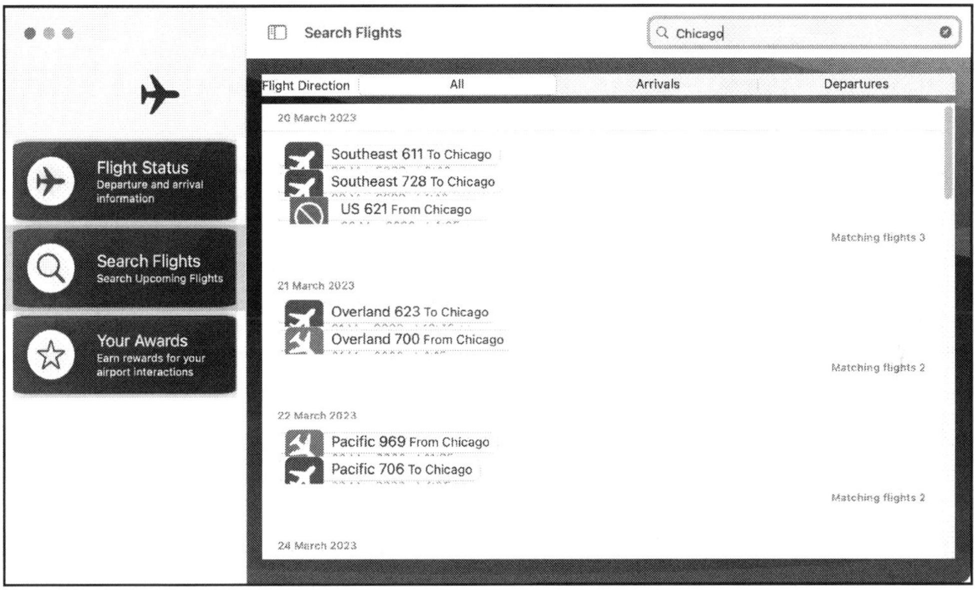

Search

The data is all there, the segmented picker at the top works, and the search field in the toolbar allows you to select from a list of cities. But the display needs work, and clicking on a flight shows another tall sheet.

Fixing the display is the first step. Expand the **SearchFlights** group, and open **SearchResultRow.swift**. This uses a `Button` to contain the data view, and as before, you need to set the style of this button.

Underneath the `Button` and before the `.sheet` line, add this modifier:

```
.buttonStyle(.plain)
```

Build and run the app again to see an immediate improvement. However, you have to click some text or the icon to show the flight information. It would be good to be able to click anywhere in the row.

Open **SearchFlights ▸ FlightSearchSummary.swift**. Find the closing brace at the end of the `HStack` block. On the line before this, insert:

```
Spacer()
```

And on the line after the brace, add:

```
.contentShape(Rectangle())
```

The `Spacer` makes the `HStack` fill the row, and setting the `contentShape` makes the entire rectangle clickable.

Build and run the app again, search the flights and click any row:

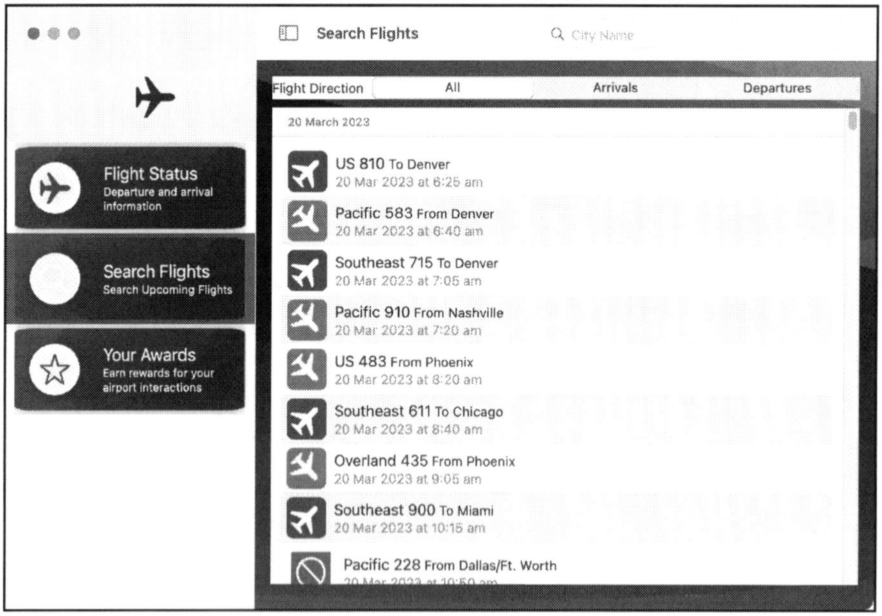

Search result

Like before, the background image makes the sheet too long.

Open **SearchFlights ▸ FlightSearchDetails.swift** and scroll down to near the end. Before `.interactiveDismissDisabled()`, add this line:

```
.frame(width: 400, height: 600)
```

This locks the size of this popup sheet, which is often a good thing to do in a Mac app. It stops people from resizing an element that doesn't need resizing.

Build and run the app and click **Search Flights**. Select a flight and click **On-Time History**:

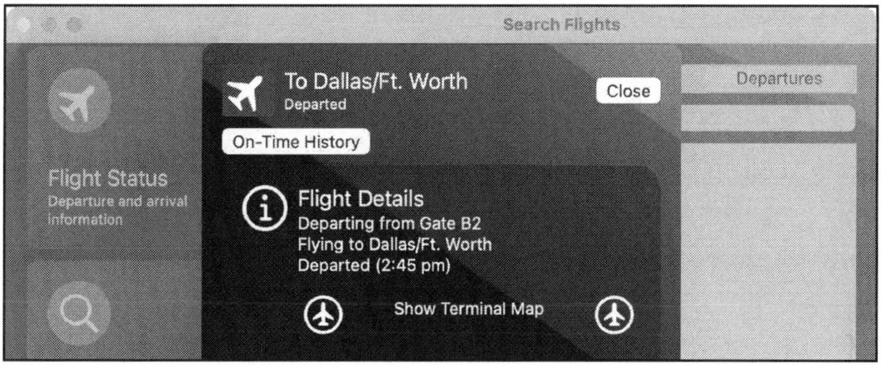

Search details

This view uses some custom drawing code to make a pie chart, and it all just works, even though that's iOS code!

Showing the Flight History

But now that `FlightTimeHistory` shows the on-time history, you've got a problem. How do you get rid of it? On iOS, you'd swipe down, but that doesn't work on macOS, so you need to find another solution. For starters, return to Xcode and click the **Stop** button to quit the app.

In **FlightSearchDetails.swift**, find the **On-Time History** button. This button toggles a Boolean called `showFlightHistory` and that property controls the display of `FlightTimeHistory` in a `sheet`.

Change this `Button` to show a popover like this:

```
Button("On-Time History") {
  showFlightHistory.toggle()
}
.popover(isPresented: $showFlightHistory) {
  FlightTimeHistory(flight: flight)
}
```

Now try again, and you'll be able to click anywhere outside the view to dismiss it:

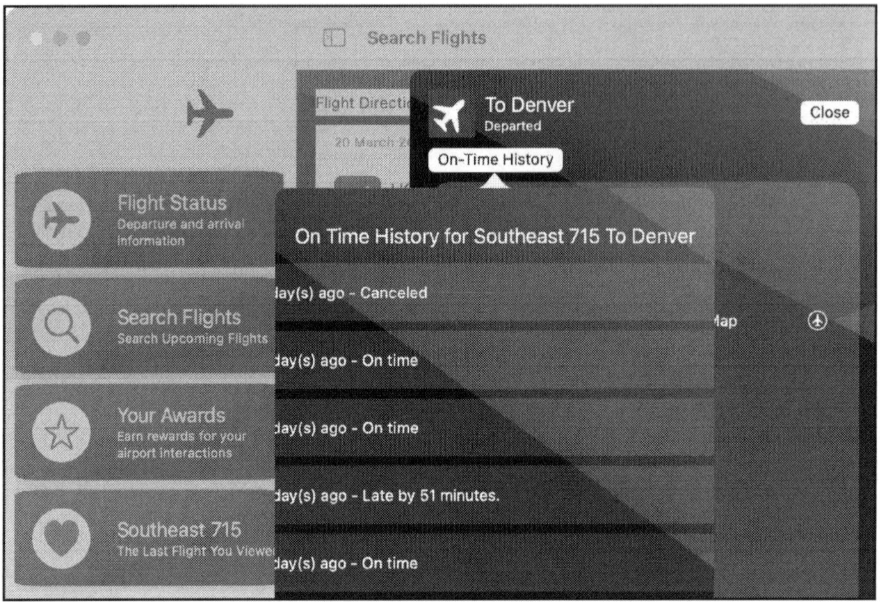

On-time popover

But the display isn't right. You can't see the beginning of each line of text. Again, the culprit is the background image.

Open **SearchFlights ▸ FlightTimeHistory.swift** and find the `Image` containing background-view. This has an `aspectRatio` modifier that expands the image past the popover's edges. This means that the start of the text is outside the view, where you can't see it.

Delete the `.aspectRatio(contentMode: .fill)` line to solve this one.

Display Dialog Boxes

View a canceled flight and click **Rebook Flight**. This shows an `alert` with two entry fields — one of them a secure field for passwords. There are two problems here. Try typing something in the fields. They use white text, which is almost invisible. This is because the parent view has set the `.foregroundColor` to white.

In **SearchFlights ▸ FlightSearchDetails.swift**, look for the **Rebook Flight** button. It has its contents and its `message`. After `message`, insert this line:

```
.foregroundColor(.primary)
```

This sets the `foregroundColor` for the alert to the system's primary color: black for light mode and white for dark mode. The rest of the view still has the required white foreground color.

Run the app again, search for a canceled flight and try entering some information. And now you can see the second problem:

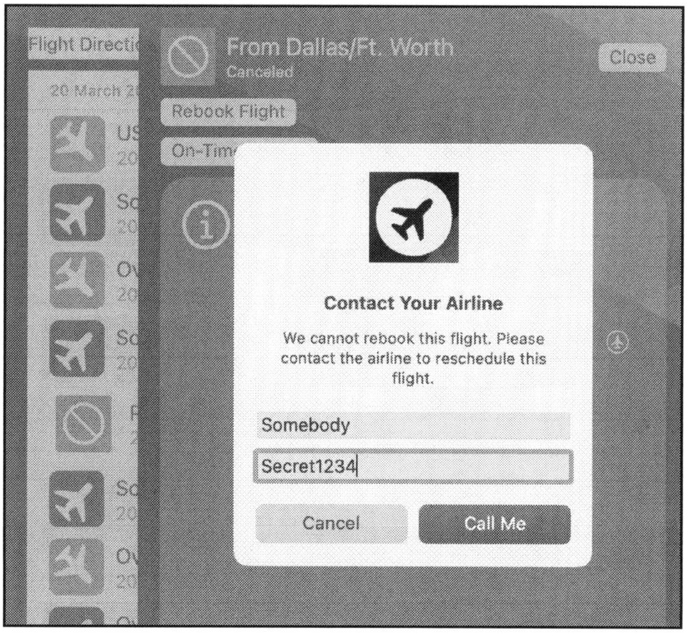

Password entry

My super secret password isn't as secret as I'd hoped!

This is another macOS bug. The workaround is to use a `sheet` here instead of an `alert`, but I'll leave that as a challenge for you.

Search for a departing flight that hasn't left yet. This shows a **Check In for Flight** button that uses a `confirmationDialog`. This works without any modifications, and now this view is totally functional.

On to the next...

Awards View

When you click **Your Awards**, you see a mess:

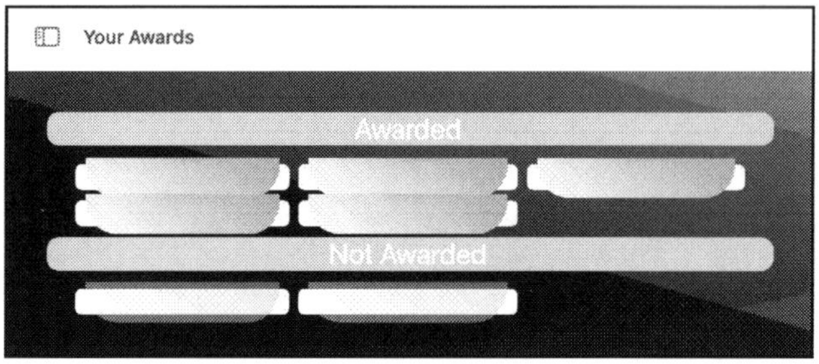

Awards in a mess

Open **AwardsView ▸ AwardsView.swift** to see the `AwardGrid` struct, which lays out each section of the view. Each `AwardCardView` is inside a `NavigationLink`. The thing is that a `NavigationLink` is basically a button, and these links use the standard macOS button appearance.

Find the closing brace at the end of the `NavigationLink` and after that, insert:

```
.buttonStyle(.plain)
```

Build and run now, and it looks a *lot* better:

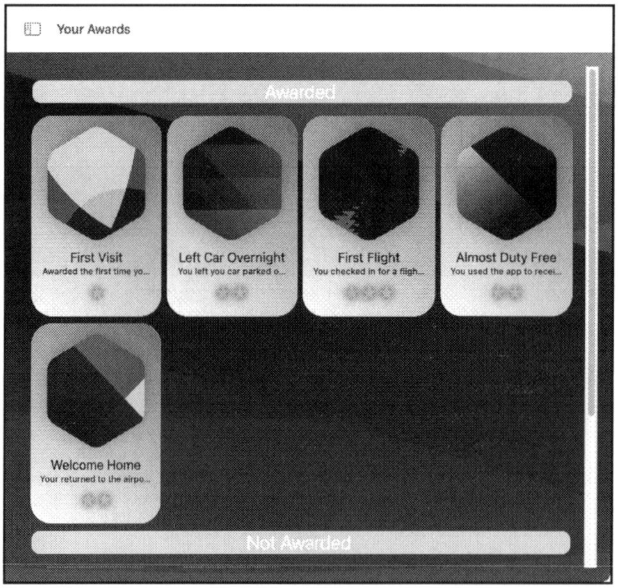

Awards

Click any award card to show the award in a new view with a back button in the toolbar.

> **Note**: If you don't see all the images, drag them all from the 3x box to the 2x box in **Assets ▸ award-images**.

Another problem is that the section headers use white text on a grey background. Delete the `.background` modifier from the `Section` header. The white text shows up nicely on the background image.

The scroll bar is rather ugly and set in from the edge of the window, which looks strange. One solution is to hide it.

Find `ScrollView` in `AwardsView ▸ body`and replace that line with:

```
ScrollView(showsIndicators: false) {
```

Run the app again to check out the improved look:

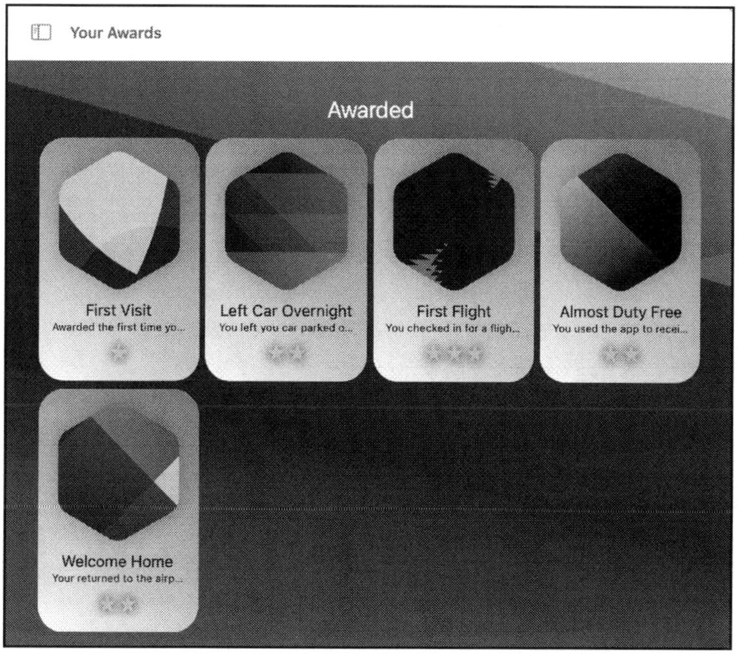

Awards

You've completed another part of the app!

The Last Viewed Flight

The **Last Viewed Flight** button appears in the sidebar after you select a flight in the **Search Flights** section. Clicking it shows the list of flights but no details about the flight.

Open **SearchFlights ▸ FlightSearchDetails.swift** and scroll down to the `onAppear` modifier. This sets a published property in an `@EnvironmentObject`. For the Mac app, where the user can have multiple windows open, you want to use the `@SceneStorage` property you set up earlier.

Back up at the top of `FlightSearchDetails`, add the property:

```
@SceneStorage("lastViewedFlightID") var lastViewedFlightID: Int?
```

Scroll down to `onAppear` again, and replace the contents with:

```
lastViewedFlightID = flight.id
```

So now, whenever the user shows the details for a searched flight, this property is set to the `id` of that flight.

Next, open **WelcomeView.swift**. The first step is to display the button if there's a last-viewed flight. At the top of `WelcomeView`, there's a computed property called `sidebarButtons` that supplies an array of buttons to display. The last entry checks for a last-viewed flight.

Replace the last button entry with:

```
// 1
if let flight = lastViewedFlight {
  // 2
  buttons.append(
    ViewButton(
      id: .showLastFlight,
      title: "\(flight.flightName)",
      subtitle: "The Last Flight You Viewed",
      imageName: "suit.heart.fill"
    )
  )
}
```

In this code, you:

1. Use the `lastViewedFlight` computed property to check if there's a value in `lastViewedFlightID` that points to a flight.
2. If there is, construct the `ViewButton` as before.

To handle what happens when you click this button, scroll down to the `switch` that controls the detail part of the `NavigationSplitView`.

Replace the `showLastFlight` case with:

```
case .showLastFlight:
  // 1
  if let lastFlight = lastViewedFlight {
    // 2
    HSplitView {
      // 3
      FlightStatusBoard(flights:
flightInfo.getDaysFlights(Date()))
      // 4
      FlightDetails(flight: lastFlight)
    }
  }
```

How does this show the flight?

1. As with the button, check that there's a flight to show.
2. Display an `HSplitView`, like for the flight status display.
3. Show the `FlightStatusBoard` listing all of today's flights.
4. Add a `FlightDetails` view, passing in the last viewed flight.

Build and run the app. Search for a flight and view its details to see it appear in the sidebar. Then close the details display, and click the last button in the sidebar to jump to the flight list and details:

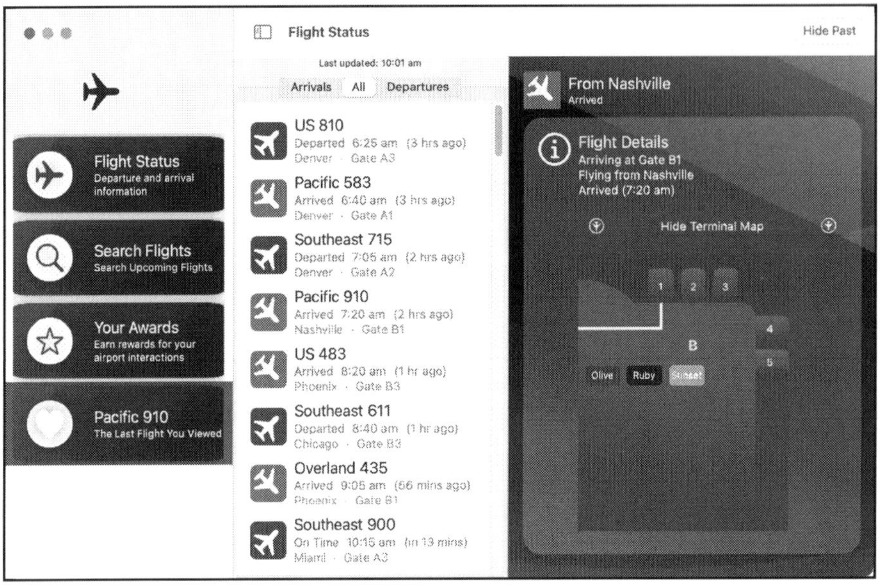

Last viewed flight

Open a second window from the **File** menu. It lets you select different flights in the flight status board and have a different last viewed flight. Because you used `@SceneStorage`, the app remembers your last viewed flight when you quit and restart.

There's one oddity remaining. With two windows open, display Flight Status in both. Now change the tab, switching between **Arrivals**, **All** and **Departures**. Both windows change to show the same tab.

Open **FlightStatusBoard ▸ FlightStatusBoard.swift** and check the properties at the top. The `selectedTab` property is marked with the `@AppStorage` wrapper. Change this to `@SceneStorage` to make the windows independent.

And that's it! You've done it. The app now has nearly all the features of its iOS counterpart.

Challenge

In **SearchFlights ▸ FlightSearchDetails.swift**, swap the alert that displays the password for a sheet that hides it correctly.

Hint: Create a new view for the sheet's contents and display it instead of the alert when `rebookAlert` is `true`.

Try this yourself, but check out the project in the **challenge** folder if you get stuck. All the changes are in **FlightSearchDetails.swift**.

Key Points

- There's a lot of iOS code around, and you can use a great deal of it in your macOS apps with little or no changes.
- macOS apps can have multiple windows open at once, so you need to make sure that your settings apply correctly. Do they need to be app-wide or per window?
- iOS apps have fixed-sized views, but on the Mac, you must be aware of different possible window sizes.
- When faced with a conversion task, take it bit by bit. Get the app building without error first, even if this means commenting out some functionality. Then go through the interface one section at a time to see what works and what you have to change.
- You imported **37 Swift files** into your app. **23** of them required no editing, and only **3** of the 14 changed files had significant numbers of changes! That has saved an enormous amount of time and effort, but you still ended up with a native Mac app.

Where to Go From Here?

Congratulations! You made it. You started with an iOS app, and you re-used code and assets to make a Mac app. You've learned how to fix the bugs caused by importing iOS code and how to adjust the user interface to suit a Mac.

There are lots of ways you can make the app more Mac-like:

- Add menus and menu items to perform some of the commands.
- Style elements to suit the Mac better — don't forget to test in dark and light modes.
- Apply more frames to make the windows behave more consistently.

Then, select another interesting iOS project, maybe one of your own, one of the other Kodeco apps or perhaps something open-source. See if you can use these techniques to convert it to a Mac app.

24 Conclusion

We hope you're as excited about SwiftUI as we are! This new approach to building user interfaces might seem a bit strange at the start. But we're sure that if you've worked through the chapters in this book, you now have a much better understanding of declarative programming and the infinite possibilities of SwiftUI. Remember, SwiftUI is a new, modern approach, so it keeps improving; it still has a lot to learn and a lot of growing ahead. And you've also just made your own first steps in working with this wonderful new framework.

The possibility of using SwiftUI for all Apple devices opens up the playing field for a greater number of developers on all Apple platforms, which will hopefully turn into many more amazing apps adapted for the iPhone, Mac, iPad, Apple Watch, Apple TV... and even new devices to come!

We encourage you to try to put the book concepts in practice. Combine SwiftUI with UIKit & AppKit and see how well they get along together. Try Stacks, navigation, testing, and all the cool concepts explained throughout the book. Keep learning, and share your projects with us!

If you have any questions or comments as you work through this book, please stop by our forums at https://forums.kodeco.com and look for the particular forum category for this book.

Thank you again for purchasing this book. Your continued support is what makes the books, tutorials, videos and other things we do at Kodeco possible. We truly appreciate it!

– The *SwiftUI by Tutorials* team

```
struct ThankYouView: View {
    var body: some View {
        Text("Thank you very much")
    }
}
```

Made in United States
Orlando, FL
10 November 2026

90498887R00411